THE
FRANKLIN
REPORT®

Et Veritas Liberabit Vos

www.franklinreport.com

CONNECTICUT &
WESTCHESTER COUNTY

Allgood Press
New York

AN ALLGOOD PRESS PUBLICATION

EDITOR IN CHIEF
Elizabeth Franklin

EDITORIAL MANAGEMENT
Jason Carpenter, Chase Palmer

MAIN CONTRIBUTORS
Emily Max Bodine, Liza Bulos, Deborah Horn

GRAPHICS/TECHNOLOGY DIRECTOR
Sarah Heffez

TECHNOLOGY TEAM
Michael Brennan, Charles "Skip" Schloss

COVER CONCEPT & ILLUSTRATION
J.C. Suares, Chesley McLaren

HOUSE ON COVER DESIGNED BY
Shope Reno Wharton Architecture

PROJECT EDITORS
Carolyn Anderson-Feighner, Amy Chozick

SPECIAL THANKS TO
Pete Mueller, Jeffrey Sechrest

ISBN 0-9705780-5-9

Printed in the United States of America

First Edition

1 2 3 4 5 6 7 8 9 10

For information about permission to reproduce
selections from this book, write to Permissions at
permissions@allgoodcompany.com

To purchase books directly from The Franklin Report,
call our toll free number, 1-866-990-9100

Library of Congress Cataloging-in-Publication Data
Please check directly with the Library of Congress for
The Franklin Report cataloging data, which was
not available at the time of initial publication.

Please forward any corrections to editor@franklinreport.com

Allgood Press
New York

Table of Contents

THE
FRANKLIN
REPORT ®

INTRODUCTION

Welcome to the new first edition of *The Franklin Report* (*Connecticut & Westchester County*), the regional edition of a national series of guides. *The Franklin Report* has created a comprehensive survey, based on client reviews, of the area's top home service providers. Some of these companies and individuals have been profiled in national magazines, and others are well-kept secrets or rising stars, but all reportedly excel in their fields.

In this guide, you will find factual information and opinions about service providers from architects and interior designers to electricians and millworkers. We invite you to use this guide and participate in our project. To submit reports on providers you have used, please visit our website at www.franklinreport.com or use the reference forms provided at the end of this book. We are committed to keeping all reviews absolutely anonymous.

Our mission is to simplify the task of choosing a home service provider by codifying the "word-of-mouth" approach. We do the homework for you with detailed fact checking, research and extensive interviews of both service providers and clients. We then give you and the community a chance to contribute to this ongoing dialogue. We hope you will join us.

The evaluations and reports on the service providers in *The Franklin Report* are based on factual information from the providers themselves, publicly available information, industry experts and thousands of in-depth customer interviews and surveys submitted through our website and by email, fax, telephone and in person. The Summary, Specific Comments and Ratings that make up each entry are based on these sources and do not reflect the opinion of The Franklin Report. You can always visit our website www.franklinreport.com for the latest information on these service providers.

We have gone to great lengths to ensure that our information originates from verifiable and reliable sources and conducted follow-up interviews when any questions arose. In addition, it is our policy to disregard any unsubstantiated information or surveys that differ markedly from the consensus view.

Each service category opens with a brief, informative introduction to the specific home service industry. These summaries provide facts and valuable insights on how to choose a service provider, including realistic expectations and cost considerations. Armed with this information, you'll be well prepared to speak to service providers listed in *The Franklin Report* and make your best choice. In addition, the following section, *What You Should Know About Hiring a Service Provider*, covers general issues that apply to all the home service categories, from interior design to air-conditioning.

Each listing contains the following components:

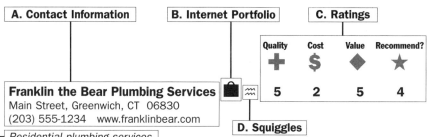

| A. Contact Information | B. Internet Portfolio | C. Ratings |

	Quality	Cost	Value	Recommend?
	✚	$	◆	★
Franklin the Bear Plumbing Services 🛍 〰	5	2	5	4

Main Street, Greenwich, CT 06830
(203) 555-1234   www.franklinbear.com

D. Squiggles

Residential plumbing services

References roar with praise for Franklin the Bear. We hear that principal Franklin and his band of service "cubs" ably attend to the plumbing needs at some of Connecticut and Westchester County's fanciest tree houses. Available 24 hours for emergencies, clients tell us that Franklin and his crew actually work better at night, especially in the summer months. One note of caution, however—getting service in the dead of winter seems to be quite difficult, and clients note that Franklin's cheerfulness fades a bit as the days grow shorter.

Franklin the Bear has been a family-owned and -operated business for generations. The firm undertakes full plumbing renovations as well as maintenance work.

"Frankly, my dear, the Bear is the best!" "Great service. Just try to avoid January."

| E. Services and Specialties | F. Summary and Specific Comments |

A. Contact Information: Service providers are listed alphabetically by the first word in the name of the company (Alexander Zed Designs comes before Zach Anderson Designs). Some vendors provide multiple home services and are listed in more than one category.

B. Internet Portfolio: Visit The Franklin Report website at www.franklinreport.com to see a portfolio of online images of this company's work and a description of their recent projects and working philosophy.

C. Ratings: Providers are rated in four columns—Quality, Cost, Value and Recommend?—on a 5-point scale, with 5 as the highest rating. Keep in mind that because we only include the firms that received the most positive reviews, a 3 in Quality is still an excellent score: the ratings differentiate the top providers.

Quality is a factor of customer service, challenge of design, level of materials used and the overall finished product. Note also that while a high rating is generally better, a higher Cost rating means that company is more expensive. Reading the introductory section of each home service category will help you understand the specific pricing structure in each profession. Value is determined by the relationship between Quality and Cost. Recommend? indicates whether the customer would use the provider again or recommend the firm to a friend, which we believe is the most important rating category.

Quality
5–Highest Imaginable
4–Outstanding
3–High-end
2–Good
1–Adequate
0–Poor

Value
5–Worth Every Penny
4–Good Value
3–Fair Deal
2–Not Great
1–Poor Value
0–Unconscionable

Cost
5–Over the Top
4–Very Expensive
3–High-end
2–Moderate
1–Inexpensive
0–Bargain

Recommend?
5–My First and Only Choice
4–On My Short List, Would Recommend
3–Very Satisfied, Might Hire Again
2–Have Reservations
1–Not Pleased, Would Not Hire Again
0–Will Never Talk to Again

 Open folders indicate that while we did not feel we had enough information to issue a rating, we've heard good things about this firm. If you have worked with any of the firms with open folders, please fill out reference reports on these providers on our website or on the forms provided in this book.

D. Squiggles: The graphic of two squiggly lines indicates a significant number of mixed reviews about a provider.

E. Services and Specialties: This describes the main services the company provides.

F. Summary and Specific Comments: The Franklin Report editors distilled information from all sources to write a summary profiling each service provider that reflects the consensus view. In select categories, where appropriate, we use several abbreviations to indicate certain special recognitions the firm has received:

KB 2000: featured in a Kips Bay Showhouse in that year
AD 100, 2000: listed in Architectural Digest's top 100 in that year
HB Top Designers, 2000: listed in House Beautiful's annual compendium
ID Hall of Fame: Interior Design's Hall of Fame Award

A number of schools are mentioned throughout this section, with the indicated abbreviations: Fashion Institute of Technology (FIT), New York School of Interior Design (NYSID), Parsons School of Design (Parsons), and Rhode Island School of Design (RISD).

In Specific Comments, clients describe the process of working with the service provider—and the end results—from their perspective.

What You Should Know About Hiring a Service Provider

Hiring a service provider to work in your home is not a task to be undertaken lightly. In addition to issues of quality, cost and scheduling, keep in mind that these professionals and their team may become an integral, albeit temporary, part of your life. The following eight-step process will help you make the best choice.

1. Determine Your Needs

First, you need to think about the nature and scope of your project. The service provider that may be perfect for a full-scale renovation may be unresponsive and unnecessarily costly for repair or maintenance work. Are you looking for simple built-in bookcases or an integrated, elaborate library? Next, weigh your priorities. Is it crucial that the project is done by the holidays? Or is it more important to get a particular style? Is budget a driving factor? Evaluating your requirements will make it easier to decide upon a vendor, because you will know where you can compromise and where you can't. Your requirements may evolve as you learn more about what is in the marketplace, but it's a good idea not to stray too far from your original intent.

2. Identify Possible Candidates

To find the best professional for the job, start by asking for recommendations from friends, colleagues, neighbors, or related service providers you trust. *The Franklin Report* will help you evaluate those candidates and identify others by offering insight into their competitive strengths and weaknesses.

3. Check Public Records

To make most efficient use of your time, first do quick background checks of the candidates to eliminate those with questionable records. For each specific category, city or state licenses may be required or professional associations may offer additional information (check *The Franklin Report* overviews for specifics on each category). If you are investigating *The Franklin Report* service providers, you will be informed of past client satisfaction in this book and on our regularly updated website, www.franklinreport.com.

4. Interview Service Providers

While it may not be necessary to conduct a face-to-face interview with a provider who is going to do a one- or two-day project, phone interviews are recommended before they show up. For larger projects, it is wise to meet with the potential providers to learn all you possibly can about process, expectations, quality and price and to judge your potential compatibility. Don't be shy. Personality and style "fit" are extremely important for longer-term projects that will involve design decisions or complicated ongoing dialogues, but are less critical when seeking a professional steam cleaner.

The following are general interview questions that will help you make the most of discussions with potential vendors. More specific questions that apply to each specific profession may be found in the category overviews.

- ❖ How long have you been in the business?
- ❖ What are your areas of expertise?
- ❖ Have you recently completed similar jobs? Can I speak with these clients for a reference?
- ❖ Who will be my primary day-to-day contact? What percentage of time will they spend on-site?
- ❖ What sections of the job will be done by your employees and what sections will be subcontracted?
- ❖ Are you licensed, registered and insured? What about the subcontractors? (It is crucial to verify that all workers are covered by workman's compensation—otherwise, you may be liable for any job-site injuries.)
- ❖ How long will the project take to complete? Any concerns or qualifications?
- ❖ Do you offer warranties? Do you provide written contracts? Will the contract have an arbitration clause?
- ❖ Are you a member of any national or local professional associations? (While not essential, this can show dedication to the profession.)
- ❖ How will we communicate with each other? Will we have regular meetings?

Other things to consider:

- ❖ How long it took them to return your initial phone call.
- ❖ Whether or not the firm's principal attended the initial meeting.
- ❖ How receptive they were to your ideas.
- ❖ How thoughtful and flexible they were in pricing, budgeting and scheduling.
- ❖ Personality/fit and how interested they were in your project.

Licenses, registrations, insurance, bonding and permits are key parts of the equation, but are category dependent (again, check the overviews). Any suspicious activity on this front, like a contractor who asks you to get the permits yourself or can't seem to find his proof of insurance, is a red-flag event. Similarly, anyone who refuses to give you references, asks for all the money up front or who tells you what a great deal you can have if you sign today should be eliminated from your list.

5. SPEAK WITH PAST CLIENTS

In discussions with references provided by the potential candidates, be aware that these clients should be their greatest fans. For a more balanced view, review their Franklin Report write-up.

Suggested questions for client references:

- ❖ What was the scope of your project?
- ❖ Were you happy with both the process and quality of the result?
- ❖ How involved were you in the process?
- ❖ Were they responsive to your concerns?
- ❖ Were work crews timely and courteous, and did they leave the job site clean?
- ❖ Did they stick to schedule and budget?
- ❖ Were they worth the cost?
- ❖ Were they communicative and professional about any issues or changes?
- ❖ Were they available for any necessary follow-up?
- ❖ Would you use this firm again?

6. ASK ABOUT COST

Each service category works differently in terms of pricing structure. Projects may be priced on a flat fee, estimated or actual time, a percentage over materials, a percent of the total job (if other contractors are involved) and a host of other variations. What appears difficult and costly to some providers may be routine for others. Many providers will be responsive to working with you on price (and it is always worth a try). However, under strong economic conditions, the service provider may only be pushed so far—they may actually be interviewing you during your call. For more specific details and recommendations, see the pricing discussions in each of *The Franklin Report* category overviews.

7. EVALUATE THE BIDS AND MAKE YOUR CHOICE

Narrow your list and ask for at least three bids for substantial jobs. Describe your project clearly and thoroughly, including any timing constraints. Once received, do your best to compare the bids on an "apples to apples" basis. Ask each provider to break down their bids so you can see whether some include more services or higher quality specifications (processes and materials) than others. Don't be afraid to keep asking questions until you fully understand the differences between the bids.

Cheaper is not always better, as a bid might be lower because the workers are less skilled or the materials are of lower quality. Compare samples where possible. If speed is important, you may be willing to pay more for the person who can start next week instead of six months from now and who checked out to be more reliable on timing.

8. NEGOTIATE A CONTRACT

Just as with pricing, you will need to understand what the acceptable business practices are within each industry and negotiate a contract, if appropriate. Most service professionals have standard contracts that they prefer.

SMALLER JOBS: For one-time-only situations that you will be supervising (rug cleaning, window washing, etc.), a full-blown contract approved by your lawyer hardly seems necessary. Just ask for a written estimate after you thoroughly discuss the job with the provider.

LARGER JOBS: For larger projects, like a general contracting job that will cost multiple thousands of dollars and will involve many people and lots of materials, a detailed contract is essential. Don't be afraid to ask about anything that is unclear to you. This is all part of the communication process, and you don't want to be working with a service provider who intimidates you into accepting anything that you don't understand.

The contract should clearly spell out, in plain English, the following:

✧ The scope of the project in specific, sequential stages.
✧ A detailed list of all required building materials, including quality specifications. They should meet minimum code standards, unless otherwise specified.
✧ Completion schedule. Don't be too harsh here, since much may be contingent upon building conditions or supply deliveries. Some, but very few, providers are open to a bonus/penalty system in meeting specific timing deadlines.
✧ A payment schedule.
✧ Permit issues and responsibilities if applicable.
✧ A description of how any scope changes ("change orders") will be processed and priced.
✧ The specific tasks and accountability of the service provider, noting exactly what they will and will not do.

Once the contract is written, you may want an attorney to review and identify any potential issues. While most homeowners do not take this step, it could save you from costly and frustrating complications further down the road.

9. Overseeing the Job

No matter how professional your team of service providers may be, they need your input and direction to satisfactorily complete the job. Be specific as to who will supervise on-site and who will be the overall project manager (responsible for the interaction between service providers and, ultimately, the dreaded punch lists). This task will fall to you unless you assign it away.

On larger projects, generally the architect (usually within their standard fee contract) or the interior designer (usually for an additional fee) will fulfill the project manager role. You should be available and encourage periodic meetings to ensure that there are no surprises in design, timing or budget. Whether or not you have a project manager, stay on top of the process (but do not get in the way), as this will be your home long after the dust settles and these professionals move on to the next project.

The Franklin Report website—a virtual companion to this reference book—is updated regularly with new vendor commentaries and other helpful material about home repairs, maintenance and renovations, at www.franklinreport.com. With expert, accessible information guiding you through the process and dedicated professionals on the job, every stage of your home project will move smoothly toward completion. Knowledge is power, regardless of whether you're engaging a plumber for a contained upgrade or a general contractor for a new custom home. *The Franklin Report* is your companion in this process, with current, insightful home service information.

Hiring an Air-Conditioning & Heating Service Provider

Known in the trades as Heating, Ventilation and Air-Conditioning (HVAC), this home service industry keeps your climate controlled and your family comfortable. It is also often responsible for custom sheet-metal work, such as kitchen hoods and copper window dressing. An HVAC system means central air, central heat and central convenience, and when it's expertly installed and maintained, that means you can keep pretending global warming doesn't exist.

An HVAC Primer

All air-conditioning (AC) systems operate on the same principle: a fan sucks in your home's warm air, sends it across coils that contain a refrigerant (freon), and the cooled air is then blown into the room. Central AC operates with two principle components: a condensing unit and an evaporator coil. The condenser pressurizes the refrigerant to cool it. Heat is released in the process, so the condenser must be located outside the home or with an opening to the outside. The cooled refrigerant is then pushed to the evaporator coil, where it cools and dehumidifies the warm air collected from your plenum (the dead space above the ceiling). Finally, this cool air is directed via ductwork back into the rooms. And you thought an air conditioner just contained a fan and a block of dry ice!

Heating is supplied in one of three ways: forced air, hydronic or steam. In the forced-air system, air is heated by your furnace or a heat pump, and a blower pushes it through the heat source, then into your home. While a furnace heats the air by burning natural gas, oil, wood or coal, a heat pump functions like an air conditioner with the refrigerant cycle reversed. Chill is captured by the condenser and warm air is produced with the evaporator coil. The air is further heated through electric heating coils at the blower. In the hydronic system, water is heated via gas or electricity in a boiler and distributed to radiators. The steam system works similarly to the hydronic with steam, rather than water, distributed directly to radiators.

How Much Do You Need?

Believe it or not, it's not the air that makes your room a delightful temperature. It's math. By understanding the following, your eyes will not glaze over when your HVAC man starts spouting acronyms such as BTU, SEER and CFM. All of this has to do with the efficiency of your system. Heating is measured in BTUs (British Thermal Units). Cooling is measured in tons. The capacities of furnaces, boilers, heat pumps and air conditioners are determined by how many tons or BTUs they carry. One ton equals 12,000 BTUs. The standard for an 800-square-foot area is about 30,000 BTUs of heat and two tons of air-conditioning. Obviously, the bigger the space, the more capacity you will need.

The SEER, or Seasonal Energy Efficiency Rating, measures the relationship between space and the energy needed to properly condition its climate. The minimum SEER in New York is ten. Equipment with a higher SEER will properly condition more space with less capacity. The higher the SEER, the higher the quality (and cost) of the equipment and the lower your energy bills. Ducts are a significant aspect of HVAC system efficiency. Obviously, you want to have as direct a path as possible between the heat/cool source and the space it's meant to condition. If the ductwork is too small, the distance from the source too far, or if there are too many bends and jogs, the airflow will suffer. Designers specify the amount of CFMs (Cubic Feet per Minute—the measurement of the airflow through your ductwork) necessary to properly condition a space. If this isn't met, the efficiency of your system is compromised because your equipment has to work harder than it should for a given space.

On Cost and Contracts

As in any other trade, you'll be charged for labor, materials, and a ten to twenty percent markup for overhead, profit and tax. Demand a flat fee for equipment and installation of new systems. Make sure the estimate specifies any other associated work—electrical, plumbing, plaster—that may be necessary for the installation. All makes and models of equipment should be spelled out on the bid proposal. It's okay to sign off on the bid proposal to execute the work, but it should refer to drawings (best generated by an engineer as opposed to a sketch on the back of a napkin) and they should be attached. Clean up, transportation, commencement and completion dates, payment schedule, change-order procedure, licensing and insurance information should all be included in the contract if not on the bid proposal. The technician should be responsible for the cost and time of obtaining permits. If your HVAC professional is fishing for a service agreement to cover the gaps in the warranty, see if you can get him to discount his price.

On Service

There are a lot of variables in HVAC, so warranties count. One year for parts and labor is typical. You should get your mechanical contractor to do a checkup once a year. Many offer early-bird spring maintenance specials before the busy AC season of summer begins, when pinning down a date with a technician is just impossible. Travel or truck fees are often charged with the diagnostic, with average rates in the 'burbs running from $85 an hour for a single technician to $125 for a team.

Treat HVAC like oral hygiene—you wouldn't neglect to brush your teeth between check-ups, and you shouldn't neglect your filters between visits from the HVAC guy. Change them once a month in the summer—dirty filters will degrade the system's efficiency. It's easy to do—just get a lesson before the installer leaves. Also know where the gauges and valves are and learn how to read them. And try to maintain a good relationship with your mechanical man after the job. You don't want to have to pay someone else to become familiar with your custom-designed, intricate home system.

What Should I Look For in an HVAC Professional?

Your HVAC service provider is essentially putting the lungs into your house, and you don't pick your surgeon based on a nudge and a wink. Talk to general contractors and ask who they recommend. Know that HVAC invariably involves plumbing and electrical work. You want to know whether the person you hire can handle the work necessary to make the system function, or if you'll have to bring in other trades to assist. If there is going to be work in and around your existing space, find out how clean and careful he is.

Choose the service provider and system best suited to your project. For renovations in tight spaces like condos or historic farmhouses, where ceiling height is precious, high-pressure air-conditioning systems that utilize small-diameter ducts permit retrofitting with little disruption to the surrounding structure. Large residences often demand computerized multiple-zoning systems, which allow for regulating different temperatures in different parts of the house. When renovating around steam, many HVAC professionals will recommend switching to hydronic. For the green-minded, ozone-friendly refrigerant, while a little more expensive, should be an option given by every high-end mechanical pro. Your research into a good HVAC person will be more effective if you learn a few things about how these systems work. There's more to HVAC than thermostats. Learn the language, so that when the installer asks if he can cut ducts in your apartment, you won't immediately report him to People for the Ethical Treatment of Animals.

CREDENTIALS, PLEASE

HVAC is a complicated field. With all the inter-trade coordination, mechanical-speak and math involved, your mechanical contractor should be backed up with the required licensing and insurance. This includes coverage for general liability, workman's comp and property damage. Manufacturers and distributors are a great source for recommending mechanical contractors, and often distinguish the best with awards. The EPA requires anyone working with refrigerant to be licensed. For more information, check out the Air-Conditioning Contractors of America website at www.acca.org.

QUESTIONS YOUR HVAC CONTRACTOR WILL ASK

✧ Where is the interior unit going to go? Large utility room? A closet?
✧ Do you have permission to place a condenser outside?
✧ Is there enough ceiling height to add ductwork?
✧ Where do you want the controls? How many zones?

Quality	Cost	Value	Recommend?

AIR-CONDITIONING & HEATING

ABM Air Conditioning & Heating Inc. 3.5 3.5 4 4
11 West Cross Street, Hawthorne, NY 10532
(914) 747 - 0910   www.abmhvac.com

Heating, cooling and air quality

Sources say ABM, founded in 1969, shows the latitude, ability, resources and creativity required to meet the mutual goals of both clients and associates in the most professional and personalized way possible. ABM provides heating, ventilating, air-conditioning and related services with reliability and quality workmanship to commercial, industrial and residential customers. The firm also takes on building controls and indoor air quality. Sources report that ABM's service and pricing have attracted major corporations as well as residential and small business customers in the Tri-State area.

Air Systems 4 4 4 4.5
140 Selleck Street, Stamford, CT 06902
(203) 348 - 5511   www.airsys.net

HVAC and electrical installation and service

"A breath of fresh air" is more than just the cute company jingle—it's also the customer's experience. Since 1976, Air Systems has cared for the year-round indoor comfort needs of families and businesses throughout Fairfield and Westchester counties. We're told the firm dispatches the area's largest team of qualified service professionals. In addition to design and installation of heating, air-conditioning and duct cleaning (indoor air quality) systems, the company also provides routine maintenance and repairs for even the most complex systems.

Sources say the firm offers comprehensive annual service agreements to help keep your heating and cooling systems in top working order. Air Systems also sidelines in electrical work, wiring computers and audio-video rooms, installing generators and making all kinds of electrical repairs.

Alliance Heating & Air 4 4 4 4
25 Brookfield Avenue, Bridgeport, CT 06610
(203) 335 - 9464

Air-conditioning and heating systems

Top builders tip their hats to this HVAC pro for "good quality and decent pricing." Alliance Heating & Air installs and maintains systems for an affluent Fairfield County clientele.

AMHAC 4.5 3.5 5 5
365 White Plains Road, Eastchester, NY 10709
(914) 337 - 5555   www.amhac.com

HVAC design, installation and service

All Makes Heating and Air-Conditioning (AMHAC) specializes in challenging high-end retrofits and serves as a full-service HVAC contractor that clients call "thoughtful and reliable." With more than 40 years in the business, we're told this well-equipped firm serves more than 15,000 residential and commercial customers in Manhattan, the Bronx and Fairfield and Westchester counties. Clients are impressed by the company's "professional" and "polite" staff of 70 which includes design engineers, licensed electricians and field technicians. We hear this team tackles the most complex installations and the most mundane maintenance items with equal dedication.

Still, it's the intimidating projects, like multi-zone hot-water heating systems and radiant-floor heating, that have the region's most discriminating general contractors turning to AMHAC. The firm, one of only two Carrier Distinguished Dealers in the area, also specializes in Alerton Systems and, as the name implies, can work with pretty much any and all makes.

Their 30,000-square-foot Eastchester facility showroom displays different types of heating and air-conditioning units as well as zoning controls, lighting controls and more. AMHAC's deep resources, which include a fleet of service vehicles, enable it to offer 24-hour heating and 48-hour AC response times. Response can be even quicker if you have an ongoing maintenance contract. AMHAC also offers Saturday office hours and 24/7 phone service. Cost is often at the high end of the scale, but customers insist that it's worth it.

"A unique company. AMHAC cares." "They excel in customer service." "Would recommend with flying colors." "A job well done and worth paying more for." "Their proposal was the most professional and they actually follow up." "The only contractor we felt was reliable, honest and full service."

Blackstone HVAC   4.5   3.5   4.5   4

14 Chauncey Avenue, New Rochelle, NY 10801
(914) 235 - 0809
High-end HVAC installation and service

References say this small company, led by owner James Black, is a rock-solid choice for heating and cooling installation and service. Established five years ago, the majority of Blackstone's work is in Manhattan and Westchester County. He can take on most mechanical systems, including air balancing, but tends to stick with high-end gear like geothermal systems. We're told Blackstone excels in design, conjuring innovative and conscientious solutions.

Clients say the work and site Blackstone personnel leave behind are immaculate, noting they make sure installations run quietly and have fail-safe measures. If something does go wrong, however, clients are serviced on a 24-hour emergency basis. Blackstone isn't the lowest-cost company out there, but the higher rates are reflected in the extra effort put into each project. It's this reputation for excellence that can get Blackstone overbooked.

"Fabulous at solving problems and making things fit." "Don't wait until summer to reach him!"

Connecticut Air Systems   3.5   3   4   4.5

270 Rowe Avenue, Milford, CT 06460
(800) 322 - 4070   www.ctairsys.com
Complete HVAC service and installation

We hear Milford-based Connecticut Air is a tremendous resource for heating, air-conditioning, sheet metal, air purification and humidification systems for both homes and businesses. The company installs and services systems from a variety of manufacturers, all of which are fully warrantied.

President Tony LaLuna partnered with Bob Kobryn (who has since retired) over twenty years ago to lay the foundation of this firm. LaLuna, who started as a young skilled technician working for a local heating and air-conditioning contractor, now oversees his own dedicated staff of licensed, thoroughly trained HVAC professionals.

	Quality	Cost $	Value ◆	Recommend? ★

Cottam Heating & Air

| | 4 | 3 | 5 | 4.5 |

492 City Island Avenue, City Island, NY 10464
(718) 885 - 3328 www.cottamhvac.com

High-end HVAC system installation and service

Clients say this friendly, skillful company "renewed my faith in HVAC people." Cottam Heating and Air services and installs high-end HVAC systems in residential and commercial properties in Manhattan, Westchester County and Greenwich. Among the company's areas of expertise are high-efficiency and environmentally minded systems and retrofit applications. Sources say the firm is "interested in 100 percent satisfaction" of its customers and selectively chooses installations to maximize comfort.

Owner Gary Cottam opened the doors to his heating and cooling company in 1984. These days twelve service personnel and lab installation crews round out the Cottam team. The firm designs projects and operates a full sheet metal shop. We're told Cottam and company are very professional throughout and stay on top of issues in follow-up. The firm offers 24-hour emergency assistance on gas and central AC systems.

"There is no comparison. Cottam is the best and most honest!" "They answered all my questions, were always available to discuss my concerns." "They were clean and concentrated on their work." "I was shocked when they said they would be there the same day." "Everyone was extremely helpful—from sales to installation and finally maintaining the new system."

Custom Air Systems

| | 4.5 | 3.5 | 4.5 | 4.5 |

765 Housatonic Avenue, Bridgeport, CT 06604
(203) 333 - 1906

High-end air-conditioning and heating installation and service

Discerning designers tell us they "don't talk to anyone else" for their heating and air-conditioning needs. Insiders say this big company delivers a dynamite product with "totally reliable" service for its Fairfield County clientele. Head honcho John Senior, an ex-Marine, gets especially flattering reviews for his rigorous competence and good nature.

"John's macho, but a pussycat at the same time." "I totally trust the firm. When there's a problem, John's the first one out here."

CVN Heating & Air Conditioning

| | 3 | 3 | 4 | 4 |

136 Sagamore Road, Tuckahoe, NY 10707
(917) 664 - 2900

High-end HVAC installation

The curriculum vitae on CVN Heating & Air Conditioning shows a firm dedicated to high-end heating and cooling installation. Some of Westchester County's better general contracting professionals highly recommend the firm. Sources say owner Charles Van Nees is "excellent" to work with and his workers are "very neat," reserving a special recommendation for Kenny to do the work.

	Quality ✚	Cost $	Value ◆	Recommend? ★

Donald Creadore HVAC Inc.

	4	3.5	4.5	5

1777 Harrison Avenue, Harrison, NY 10528
(914) 835 - 0747

HVAC design and installation

This "totally capable" family-operated HVAC heavyweight comes with nothing but kudos from the area's finest general contractors. Established by Donald Creadore, whose clients describe him as a "true gentleman engineer," the firm offers design and installation for high-end central heating and air-conditioning systems. A second generation of Creadores join top-flight technicians to care for a Fairfield/Westchester clientele.

Edgerton Inc.

	4	4	4	4.5

786 Main Street, Monroe, CT 06468
(203) 268 - 6279

Service and installation of heating and cooling systems

Interior designers and their clients highly recommend this venerable and "extremely capable" company. Edgerton Inc. services and installs heating and cooling systems for residential, commercial and industrial applications. Established in 1956 by Charles Edgerton, the firm fields a staff of 50 and offers 24-hour emergency service.

ENCON Inc.

	5	4.5	4.5	5

80 Hathaway Drive, Stratford, CT 06615
(203) 375 - 5228

High-end HVAC installation and service

Widely heralded as "the best HVAC" contractor money can buy in Fairfield County, an impressive roster of celebrated architects, heavyweight contractors and A-list clients call on ENCON. Established in 1969, this large company specializes in the design, installation and service of heating and cooling systems for commercial and custom residential projects.

Clients tell us Encon achieves excellence in the field of customer service and demonstrates a strong commitment to providing the highest quality workmanship. Clients who insist on the best won't be disappointed—just don't be surprised when this firm insists on charging top dollar for the experience.

"Tops in Fairfield." "Nothing is ever a problem." "Highest bidder, but worth it in the long run, all clients agree." "Great service."

GC Reliable Service Inc.

	3.5	3.5	4	4

80 Grove Avenue, New Rochelle, NY 10801
(914) 633 - 3535

Air-conditioning and heating installation and service

Hanington Engineering Consultants

	4.5	4	4.5	4

501 Fifth Avenue, New York, NY 10017
(212) 338 - 9801

Residential HVAC consultants

The region's premier residential HVAC consultant, Hanington engineers the climate control of *Architectural Digest*-worthy homes in New York City and the suburbs. Leading architects, contractors and private clients rely on this firm to create the most efficient, attractive heating, cooling and indoor air quality systems in town.

	Quality	Cost	Value	Recommend?
	+	$	◆	★

Joseph J. Ginter Heating
& Air Conditioning

30 Skunk Lane, Wilton, CT 06905
(203) 329 - 0211
HVAC service and installation

Clients call Ginter a "very competent HVAC guy" who services residences and small businesses. The firm also installs heating and cooling systems.

New England Air Systems

3.5   3   4   4

PO Box 2327, Danbury, CT 06813
(203) 798 - 7111
HVAC design, service and installation

This "energetic and youthful" firm splits its efforts between new installations and renovations of HVAC systems for a Fairfield County clientele. We're told New England Air Systems designs all of its own systems and will maintain anyone's existing system through the company's service division.

Robert Buzzco, who has twenty years of mechanical experience, started this small shop in 1997. He oversees a staff of ten industry-educated mechanics. We're told the firm stays on top of progressive technology and shows concern for acoustical issues, energy conservation and environmentally sound applications.

Pack-Timco

4.5   4   4   4.5

2 Ruby Street, Norwalk, CT 06850
(203) 847 - 8781
Full-service heating and cooling

A unanimous recommendation by industry insiders for "good quality" and "good service" at a "good price," Pack-Timco provides design, installation and planned maintenance of all things HVAC. Its expertise includes air-conditioning, heat pumps, boilers, furnaces and indoor pool systems. For more than 30 years the firm has been helping folks throughout the Fairfield and Westchester area enjoy total indoor air comfort in their homes and businesses.

We hear Pack-Timco's professional staff receives the most up-to-date training available. A roster of repeat clients attests to the firm's "awesome approach." Estimates are free and 24-hour emergency service is available.

Putnam Plumbing & Heating Inc.

5   4.5   4.5   5

77 North Water Street, Greenwich, CT 06830
(203) 661 - 6806
High-end plumbing and heating systems

See Putnam Plumbing & Heating Inc.'s full report under the heading Plumbers

Tucker Associates

4.5   4   5   5

36 Grassy Plain Street, Bethel, CT 06801
(203) 748 - 6224   www.tucker-associates.com
Air conditioning and heating consulting and engineering

Clients turn to this HVAC expert for rigorous coordination between mechanical systems and architectural styles. The firm has serviced Fairfield County architects, contractors and homeowners from its Bethel location for 25 years. It provides design and consulting on custom residential heating and cooling systems, as well as for commercial properties. Established in 1977 as a specialist in solar power and energy conservation, the firm remains dedicated to alternative energy resources. Tucker Associates satisfies clients' needs on any size project, from a garage to a $25 million mansion. We're told that unlike its commercial-minded counterparts, this company stays in tune with the specific sound, comfort, control, zoning and humidity requirements of residences.

Quality	Cost	Value	Recommend?
✚	$	◆	★

Owner Glenn Tucker, who hails from a carpentry and construction background, steers each job with the assistance of a small team of project engineers and draftsmen. The firm charges a lump sum design fee or an hourly rate, increasing from $65 for a draftsman to $150 for the principal.

"Mr. Tucker is very nice to work with." "Very responsive to our needs and dependable." "Strengths—alternative energy sources engineering, mechanical engineering, electrical engineering, 'debugging' existing systems, control interface technology."

Turner & Harrison Inc.   4   4   4   4
135 Lafayette Avenue, White Plains, NY 10603
(914) 949 - 5010

HVAC systems installation and maintenance

Winds Mechanical   4   3.5   4.5   4
1401 Blondell Avenue, Bronx, NY 10461
(718) 824 - 6700   windshvac@aol.com

HVAC design and installation

Winds Mechanical is a small, family-run company with a big reputation for reliability and ability. From design and installation of custom, top-of-the-line central AC systems to setting window AC units, and brand-new construction to retrofitting existing buildings, we hear this firm can handle the call. Its sister-service firm, Winds Service covers all repair and maintenance contract work. While the majority of its work is in Manhattan, more significant projects take Winds up to Westchester County. The City's most established general contractors and the industry's leading manufacturers, like SpacePak, trust Winds.

A trade vet with more than 28 years of experience, principal Charles Babish is dedicated to providing the maximum amount of comfort at a minimum amount of operation and maintenance costs. Clients concur, saying these trade winds always blow in the right direction.

Hiring an Architect

Creating a home will be one of the largest investments in your lifetime. An excellent architect can make your dreams come true and, just as important, help you avoid construction nightmares. He is the protector of your investment, and your ally in ensuring that the subcontractors deliver exactly what you have envisioned. Famous architects have made history with their brilliant work as well as their eccentricities: Frank Lloyd Wright demanded control over every inch of a house's design, right down to the table settings; Stanford White brought as much drama to his life (and death) as he did to the stunning spaces he created. But don't get your heart set on achieving fame through an architect who brings celebrity to your address. The best matches are usually made with talented, hardworking and experienced professionals who are able to commit themselves fully to your project. An architect's work lives on indefinitely, leaving an indelible mark on people's lives and on the community.

The architect is your guide through the entire building process—from refining your vision and defining your needs to documenting them in plans and specifications; from suggesting contractors to counseling on budget; from monitoring the progress and quality of construction to certifying payment to the contractor and from answering questions to settling disputes. He is the point man working on behalf of your interests. The clarity and thoroughness of his drawings and the extensiveness of his involvement in the design and building process are keystones to a successful project. If the architect forgets a beam, the whole job could come crashing down—and more likely, you'll have to pay a little extra to get that beam retrofitted.

Where Do I Start?

Choosing an architect isn't easy. Each professional has his or her own design philosophy, style and way of doing business. Talk to friends, realtors and contractors. You should interview three to five firms to get a sense of what you're looking for. Make sure to meet with the individual who will be designing the project, not just a principal selling you on the firm. If you and the architect don't click, move on. The most important thing to look for is stylistic understanding and good chemistry. You're going to be working closely for a long time, bouncing ideas and problems off each other with a lot at stake. You want somebody with whom you'll enjoy the ride. Not surprisingly, architects consider the same thing when choosing which clients to take on.

Get a sense of the quality of the architect's past designs. Ask to see not only his portfolio, but the blueprints of those past jobs. The architect's clarity and thoroughness will be evident in the detailing and the notes. Not all blueprints are created equal, and the same goes for the people who draft them. Another important step is to get feedback from past clients. You want to know if a prospect was accessible and collaborative, if he was expedient in turning drawings around, responsive to questions and revisions and if he visited the site and met with the contractor regularly.

If an architect makes his living doing leading-edge homes and you have a French Tudor house, it's clear that this collaboration isn't going to work. Go with somebody who is well-versed in the style you're looking for. Also keep in mind that the specific structure to be designed is as important as the style. An architect who has never designed a pool house in Greenwich is bound to be ignorant of certain details and codes that will inevitably become major factors in the job. This may also be the case if you are renovating a farmhouse in New Canaan and are subject to historic preservation restrictions. Your architect should relate to your personality, preferences, vision, logistical constraints and lifestyle.

SPECIFIC CONSIDERATIONS

It's very important to have a realistic sense of the constraints and possibilities regarding budget and building codes. It's the architect's job to define these things for you. Identify how familiar a candidate is with the local codes, and whether he is sensitive to cost. He needs to be able to help you navigate the permitting and inspection process and massage the budget by substituting materials and methods or modifying the design. Also, you should be vocal about any special stylistic interests and timing specifications you have from the outset. If using a particular contractor or building an environmentally considerate and efficient home is important to you, speak up. Remember, certain architects only dip their toes in certain ponds.

ON COST AND CONTRACTS

If you think you've found a partner, it's time to start thinking about the fee. There are no set fees for architectural services. The scope of the job, the level of quality and detail, the pace and length of schedule and the amount of other clients the firm has already taken on all factor into how an architect calculates his service. An architect will typically charge either an hourly rate or a percentage of construction, but some do a combination of the two. For example, some architects may charge hourly through the schematics stage and then charge a percentage of construction cost for the remainder of the project. Alternatively, there may be a fixed fee based on hourly rates, or an hourly rate that is not to exceed a certain percentage of construction. Regardless of the method of calculation, standard fees for Connecticut and Westchester County will typically range from twelve to fifteen percent of the total construction cost. Larger projects generally have smaller fee percentages. At some of the more established and high-profile firms, the percentage might be elevated, based on the architect's status and reputation in the industry.

The fee, the responsibilities associated with it (revisions through permitting, frequency of on-site visits, payment certifications and punch list review) and the compensation procedure for any extra work should be spelled out in a contract. This can be an Architect's Letter of Agreement or a standard contract issued by the American Institute of Architects (AIA).

LICENSES AND PERMITS

To earn his title, an architect must have a state license. He does not have to be a member of the AIA (Frank Lloyd Wright never joined). The typical qualifications for licensing are: 1) a degree from an accredited school of architecture, requiring three or more years of study, 2) three years of apprenticeship under the supervision of a licensed architect and 3) passage of a five-day exam. Exact requirements vary from state to state. Cities require that drawings submitted for permit review be certified by a state-licensed professional.

It is also essential that your architect be very familiar with local building code requirements and regulations. Local codes vary widely, and a small misunderstanding can lead to a big inflation of budget and schedule after everyone's committed to a particular plan. In New York State, as in most places, any alteration that does not fit the building code's definition of a minor repair requires an architect's application and certification of plans for approval and issuance of a building permit. The city building department also requires the architect to certify completion of the construction before anyone can occupy the space. If you live in a landmark building, you will also have to consider the approval of your local landmark or historical district authority. Your architect should be responsible for filing all the appropriate paperwork and addressing any code concerns during the permitting process.

THE ARCHITECTURAL DESIGN PROCESS

Whether you're courting your architect or have already made the plunge, communication is critical. You're choosing someone to translate an epic fantasy that only you have imagined into a three-dimensional reality. For an architect to develop an idea, you need to be able to convey in detail what it is you are looking for. Bring sketches, pictures, notes, clippings, Rorshach tests—anything that will tune him in to the same frequency. And take your turn to listen. Your architect will invariably come up with design ideas, offering inventive solutions and innovative alternatives to your rough-hewn proposal. Also, you want an architect who can deliver options.

Once you've made your architect the designer of record, your first big discussion should involve fleshing out your nebulous dreams into cold hard details. The number of rooms, how and when you will use them and the flow of space are questions he will need answered in order to come up with a first round of schematic designs. Don't panic if these are incomplete. These rough sketches and drawings will be revised and refined as you review them until you are satisfied. The architect may produce a model to help you visualize the layout of your future residence.

HOW LONG WILL IT TAKE TO DRAW UP A PLAN?

The easy answer is as long as you keep changing your mind. But even when you are finally satisfied, you'd be astounded by the number of people who get to throw in their two cents before construction begins.

After you and your architect have agreed on the drawings, they may pass through the hands of various historical, design or landmark review boards; planning and zoning boards; structural, mechanical, electrical and plumbing engineers; fire life/safety and Americans with Disabilities Act (ADA) reviewers; and your kids. After the experience, you'll know how a writer feels when he tries to get his screenplay through the Hollywood system unscathed. Depending on the complexity of the job and profile of the location, expect the process to take from two to six months.

Once the basic layout is approved, the architect can move forward and prepare more detailed drawings to define the scale and scope of the project. It's never more true than in construction that the devil is in the details. You must communicate absolutely everything your heart desires. Finishes, brands, models, installation methods, notations on code, fixture selection, materials to be used—all need to be documented in plans and specs by the architect. At this point, the estimate for cost gets a whole lot clearer.

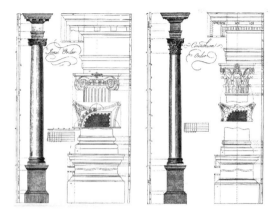

THE ARCHITECT THROUGH THE PROCESS

Most people approach contracting candidates with thorough and clear documents in hand. However, it is recommended that you include a contractor at the outset of the design process in order to get a realistic assessment of construction costs or else you may be disappointed by budget-busting bids. Your architect will manage (or assist you in) the process of hiring a contractor to coordinate construction. Your architect should be able to recommend several candidates from a stable of reliable and friendly contractors. Or, you may have your own ideas. It is typical for several contractors to bid a job. Your architect can help you sift through the proposals to make sure that everything necessary is included and that you are comparing apples to apples. Ultimately, however, the decision to hire the contractor is yours.

Throughout construction, the architect is responsible for making frequent appearances on-site to monitor job progress, troubleshoot, answer questions and verify that all details and code requirements are being met per his plans and specs. It is becoming increasingly common for banks to require the architect of record to certify pay applications in order to release funding to the contractor. Again, this requires the architect to visit the site to assess whether or not the work completed is commensurate with the request for payment. As construction draws to a close, the architect must lead the "punch list process" of those missing, incomplete, unpolished and mishandled loose ends.

Working with an architect who matches your personality, ideas and particular project will make this one of the most memorable adventures of your life. You may enjoy building your house so much that, like Thomas Jefferson, you'll immediately make a habit of it. "Architecture is my delight," wrote Jefferson, "and putting up and pulling down one of my favorite amusements."

DRAWING IS JUST THE BEGINNING. YOU HIRE AN ARCHITECT TO:

- ✧ Interpret code
- ✧ Estimate budget and schedule
- ✧ Offer options for materials and methods
- ✧ Recommend contractors and review bids
- ✧ Document contractual obligations
- ✧ Sign and seal plans for permitting
- ✧ Review and certify pay applications
- ✧ Monitor progress and quality

ARCHITECTS

Alan Wanzenberg Architect, PC   4.5   4   4.5   5
211 West 61st Street, New York, NY 10023
(212) 489 - 7840   alan@awapc.com
Understated, rich custom residential architecture

With a well-known gift for creating "wonderfully understated" detailing driven by the client's taste and the context of the project, Alan Wanzenberg is admired by his clients and his peers. With an understanding of the history of his craft, Wanzenberg's style has classical underpinnings that reveal his innate appreciation for proportion and scale. The architect is also receptive to more modern projects, which clients say he has done with great success. Wanzenberg is known to have a high-level of involvement and "a personal connection" and is driven by "intellectual pursuits in design." Insiders say Wanzenberg takes great interest in the detailing of libraries, kitchens and bathrooms, where his design skill truly shines.

Wanzenberg, who holds a Master of Architecture from Harvard, is the sole principal of this 22-person staff, which he founded in 1981. The firm's commissions tend to be large-scale projects, for which budgets average $1.5 million to $3 million—but Wanzenberg has been known to do much smaller jobs for repeat clients. The firm concentrates solely on residential architecture and works mainly in New York City, Westchester County and Connecticut, but has also completed projects in Colorado, Australia and Switzerland. The firm takes on equal numbers of New York City apartment interior architecture endeavors, historically significant renovations and new single-family homes.

Sources tell us Wanzenberg is a man of integrity, up front about costs and budgets so that money doesn't become an issue in the design process. Described as a "big time client advocate," Wanzenberg has been known to meet with a potential client four times before taking on a job in order to fully understand their needs. The firm charges standard fees based on an hourly rate with a percentage cap.

Alexander Gorlin   5   5   5   5
137 Varick Street, 5th Floor, New York, NY 10013
(212) 229 - 1199   www.gorlinarchitects.com
Contemporary high-end architecture

Sources praise Alexander Gorlin for his deft creation of "modern, sensual spaces" that maximize the use of space and natural light. Both industry insiders and clients alike laud Gorlin for his ability to blend the spaces he creates seamlessly within the surrounding environment. Described as highly intellectual and extremely talented, Gorlin has earned respect from the industry and clients alike since establishing this firm of nine in 1987. He takes on seven to ten residential projects each year, consisting of large new-home construction or gut renovations.

Gorlin holds degrees from Cooper Union and Yale and trained with I.M. Pei. He also taught at the Yale School of Architecture and has long been sought by clients in the media and fashion industries. His portfolio is diverse and includes designs for household items, furniture, apartments, houses, office buildings, synagogues, museums and city parks. Clients say that Gorlin is committed to creating a work of art, though some caution that he can be a bit rigid in his thinking about style. Regardless, Gorlin draws praise for his "impeccable taste" and design sense. To that end, Rizzoli has published a monograph of his work featuring 28 projects.

Although much of his work takes place in New York City, Gorlin has completed numerous homes across Westchester and Fairfield counties, and has projects underway from Nova Scotia to California. The firm charges a higher percentage of construction costs. AD 100, 2000, 2002.

"He has a great sense of design, style and integrity." "Not only do you get an amazing home, you get a thorough education in the craft and process of architecture." "I love the simple elegance of the design." "We never even talked to another architect, we picked him straight away." "The plans are very detailed. In fact, the contractor said they are the most complete and explicit plans he's ever seen." "He was very quick to pick up on exactly what we wanted and I love his tremendous artistic expertise."

Allan Greenberg, Architect, LLC   5   4.5   5   5
45 East Putnam Avenue, Greenwich, CT 06830
(203) 661 - 0447   www.allangreenberg.com
Classical New England-inspired custom residential architecture

Sources tell us Allan Greenberg's name alone "instantly recalls images of classic New England architecture." The firm's eight annual residential projects are evenly split between large-scale renovations and new-home construction. In addition to sprawling classical estates, Greenberg designs working traditional farms, stables, greenhouses and barns. Working strictly within a classical context, Greenberg and his staff will take on projects with budgets ranging from $500,000 to $20 million. We're told, however, that the firm prefers to take on quaint (richly detailed) homes.

Greenberg established this firm of 25 in 1960 and remains the sole principal. His forty-plus years in the business puts discriminating clients at ease because "he has a very rational and thorough process that's as tight as a drum." The firm charges a higher fee based on hourly costs or a percentage of overall construction costs.

"When you talk about fine architecture in and around southern Connecticut, you would be remiss to leave out Allan's name."

Austin Patterson Disston Architects, LLC   5   4.5   4.5   5
376 Pequot Avenue, Southport, CT 06490
(203) 255 - 4031   www.apdarchitects.com
Highly detailed, versatile custom residential architecture

Well known for innovative designs for difficult sites—waterfront in particular, the architects of Austin Patterson Disston are well versed in the historical roots of Revival and Shingle styles and the streamlined simplicity of contemporary homes, while maintaining a sensitivity to scale and detail no matter what the language. Insiders say the "quirky and really clever" David Austin is a wealth of knowledge with a refreshing sense of humor. And forget about trying to find one of the partners relaxing in a posh corner office. Sources tell us they are in the "design trenches" with the rest of this 30-person staff, constantly exchanging ideas in a fluid environment. It is this kind of genuine enthusiasm and collaborative approach that clients say makes this one of the most sought-after firms in the area.

After training with Philip Johnson, Austin started the firm in 1963 and later partnered with McKee Patterson in 1982 and Stuart Disston in 1994. Organized as a three-prong structure, each partner of Austin Patterson Disston is heavily involved in the design process while overseeing one third of the projects. Clients say the firm's impeccable attention to detail is second only to its superior client relations. "You don't buy a product with them," we're told, "what you buy is a solution to a unique design challenge."

In 2000, the firm opened a second office in Quogue, serving the Hamptons. Handling about 30 projects of budgets ranging from $400,000 to $10 million at any given time, Austin Patterson Disston designs mostly large residential projects in southern Connecticut. The firm bills on standard hourly, fixed or percentage-based fees.

"In about an hour and a half, McKee came up with some drawings and four weeks later, they were perfect and we never changed a single thing." "They're definitely creative, but they don't put you into something that's too far out." "A great outfit to deal with, and no attitudes either, thank God." "They could have built some dopey ranch for me, but they came up with a beautiful carriage house." "It was expensive, but we knew that going in and there were no surprises."

Baker Batchelder Architects   4.5   4   5   5
27 Unquowa Road, Fairfield, CT 06430
(203) 255 - 6847   baker.batchelder@earthlink.net
Thoroughly-planned residential architecture sensitive to zoning restrictions

Baker Batchelder's style is "undoubtedly traditional, with experience in every kind of American architecture" with a recent push for "Nantucket-looking houses." The vast majority of the firm's work is in Fairfield County, although it has completed homes in Washington, DC, Florida and Nantucket. Sources tell us the architects prefer to do "nice, small, special homes" over massive endeavors, but won't turn down a project simply because of the size of its budget. However, if you want the services of this firm, you may very well have to take a number—they aren't always available immediately. The firm's principals are known to be "control freaks in a good way," handling all aspects of the project, right down to the drafting. Insiders say the architects are sensitive to the zoning and wetland regulations of the area's coastal communities and the stringent rules of its historical districts.

Ben Baker, who holds a Bachelor's degree from Harvard and a Master of Architecture from Yale, started this small firm of four in 1983. Partner Linda Batchelder holds an architecture degree from Penn State. Clients praise Baker Batchelder for painstakingly selecting materials that "are durable, reasonably priced and look good." The firm has a reputation for working well with contractors, and it's a good thing, because Ben Baker is said to "spend an awful lot of time on the site during construction." Baker Batchelder typically has about eight active projects at any given time, ranging from one-room renovations to massive homes—but budgets generally come in between $300,000 and $1.5 million. The firm charges standard fees based exclusively on an hourly basis.

"The home is such a retreat for us—when we walk in the door, our blood pressure immediately drops." "They're very well versed in historic architecture, but they add distinguished contemporary ideas to their design." "An amazing sense of detail—It's not fussy architecture, but you can bet all the detail is right there." "We bought a piece of property partially because we wanted to work with them again." "We had to wait for them to get to us, but when they're available, they're fully available."

Beinfield Architecture PC   4.5   4   4.5   5
1 Marshall Street, Suite 202, Norwalk, CT 06854
(203) 838 - 5789   www.beinfieldarchitecture.com
Cerebral selective residential architecture with verve

Bruce Beinfield is widely viewed as a "real thinking architect" who can interpret the "romantic notions that clients have" about what their dream house should be.

This interpretation often becomes a unique amalgamation of classic New England Colonial architecture with modern forms and lifestyle functionality. We're told he excels in tricky waterfront site design. Beinfield is a master of materials. That's what sources in the industry as well as past clients say about this architect, who "has a gift for taking otherwise cold materials such as steel and concrete, and using them in a way that transforms the common feel and perception of the materials." He does this by integrating other carefully chosen materials that "have a richness, patina of age and texture to them without running up the budget."

Beinfield, who holds an Master of Architecture from Colorado, is the sole principal of this firm of eight, which he established in 1987, formerly known as Beinfield Wagner. Insiders say Beinfield delivers creative architectural solutions with utmost respect for the client as a homeowner and purveyor of fine architecture. The vast majority of the firm's work is in Fairfield County, around Darien and Westport, but Beinfield has been known to travel for intriguing design challenges in places like Maine, Wyoming and the Bahamas.

Of the firm's roughly 30 annual projects, about two thirds are residential, ranging from $500,000 renovations to $3.5 million ground-up homes. A typical Beinfield project carries a $1.5 million budget. The firm recently completed an 8,000-square-foot cottage on a waterfront site in Darien that included a heightened sensitivity to environmental and coding issues. The firm charges a standard percentage of construction costs.

"He's a true artist. I feel he has a wonderful aesthetic sensibility." "It was a real give and take, but he was always available." "The house ended up being a reflection of us, although his aesthetic is also in there, which makes it even better." "We've lived in a lot of houses and we've always had something we wanted to change about them. I don't feel that way about this house. I just love it."

BKSK Architects 4 4 4 5

28 West 25th Street, New York, NY 10010
(212) 807 - 9600   www.bksarch.com
Modern and traditional residential architecture

Often working on projects that have a historic component, BKSK has attracted clients whose projects include new home construction, historic preservations and multi-story apartment buildings. The firm generally takes on substantially sized projects that range up to $30 million. We hear the firm is not committed to a particular style and takes pride in its versatility, creating designs from modern to traditional. We have heard BKSK is adept at creating modern, livable spaces and effectively merges its clients' tastes and needs into the dictates of a project's setting. We have heard, however, that junior architects at the firm may take on more of the workload than clients expected.

Principals of the firm are Stephen F. Byrns, Harry Kendall, George Schieferdecker and Joan Krevlin. The firm had been in business since 1985 as BKS, but added another "K" when the firm combined forces with Krevlin in 1992. Of the firm's annual commissions, about 70 percent is dedicated to residential projects. Roughly half of the company's projects occur in Manhattan, but BKSK also takes on projects in the Hamptons as well as Westchester.

Recent projects include a fifteen-story loft-style apartment building in the historic district of TriBeCa, a new 15,000-square-foot visitor's center for Queens Botanical Garden, and a 25,000-square-foot townhouse development in the Bronx. BKSK charges an hourly fee with a maximum not to exceed a standard percentage of total construction costs.

"Devised innovative designs." "The house is spectacular, the product is great." "His follow-up was excellent and he really knew the coding issues well." "They get the highest rating in regard to articulating our ideas into the plan." "Always available to meet, and really went the extra mile." "He's a man of integrity—he's doing everything he said he'd do." "We think of him as a friend—how often does that happen with an architect after a multimillion dollar project?"

Boris Baranovich Architects   4.5   4   4   5
153 Waverly Place, Suite 1200, New York, NY 10014
(212) 627 - 1150
Traditional residential French, English and American architecture

Clients and peers recognize Boris Baranovich mostly for his traditional, classical style of architectural design with an emphasis on French, English and American Shingle styles. Baranovich is also known for being a "finisher"—always tying up loose ends. While some say his style can be a bit heavy, all appreciate his attention to detail and high-quality work. Clients also praise Baranovich for his accommodating nature and ability to execute their wishes. They describe him as thoughtful, polite, honest and a strong communicator.

Baranovich holds a degree from Pratt and is the sole principal of this eighteen-person firm, which has been in business since 1984. The firm takes on six to eight new projects each year. Large projects start under $1 million and go up to the tens of millions. His work can be seen from Greenwich to the Hamptons. The firm charges an hourly rate that is translated into a standard percentage of total construction costs.

"His extensive knowledge of traditional architecture is beyond what we expected." "He's good and he knows it, but Boris is worth every penny." "He is always ready to make a trip out to the site within minutes." "Delivers what he claims—and then some."

Carol J.W. Kurth, AIA Architect, PC   3.5   3   4.5   4.5
The Arcade Building, Bedford, NY 10506
(914) 234 - 2595   www.carolkurtharchitects.com
Traditionally inspired residential architecture and interior design

Known best for her "ability to give buildings character that otherwise would have none" and a high level of customer service, Carol J.Weissman Kurth has carved out a successful niche in the Bedford area. Kurth's office has recently seen an influx of traditional renovations with classic New England detailing of Shingle style, neoclassical and Tudor homes. She's also noted for her keen ability to sprout homes from "the steepest, craziest sites." The talented, fourteen-person firm is noted for its sensitive detailing of interior finishes, cabinetry and other built-ins.

Kurth earned a Bachelor of Architecture from City College of New York, where she also spent five years on staff teaching architecture. The firm, which was established in 1995, takes on about ten to fifteen custom residential projects and "renovation transformations" each year in addition to collaborating with developers on high-end residential communities. Her custom projects range from $250,000 renovations to $6 million new single-family homes.

While most of the firm's work takes place in Westchester, Kurth has completed projects across New England and is about to embark on work in the Virgin Islands. Kurth herself has a deep understanding of the construction industry through her collaborations with developers and brings her affinity for site meetings and job inspections to her clients. The firm charges a standard percentage of overall construction costs.

"She's amazing, professional, and brings a lot of composure to the whole process." "Nothing is a tragedy, nothing is overly dramatic when something goes awry. She's just very cool." "Has an amazing perspective on life—she's very down to earth." "As efficient as can be, and has an extremely organized office and practice." "Easy to warm up to." "She's got a very keen aesthetic...she's constantly changing and is influenced by everything going on around her, as well as her client's design sensibility."

	Quality	Cost	Value	Recommend?
	+	$	◆	★

Centerbrook Architects and Planners, LLC   5   4   5   5

PO Box 955, 67 Main Street, Centerbrook, CT 06409
(860) 767 - 0175 www.centerbrook.com

Residential architecture and planning

This large, national firm has earned praise from clients, peers, the media and some of the world's finest educational institutions for designing a wide range of spaces—from those that house families to those that encompass law schools and art collections. With an approach that is distinctly American, sources tell us Centerbrook has extended itself not only to participate but to excel in numerous architectural styles—from modern to traditional, based on the needs of the client. Sources express enthusiasm for the firm's meticulous attention to detail, noting that it has an uncanny ability to work out all the details while keeping clients' visions at the forefront. Others commend Centerbrook for the ability to deliver within estimated timetables and its overall design quality.

Centerbrook was established in 1975 and is located in a renovated factory on the Falls River in Centerbrook. This firm of seventy architects takes on dozens of projects each year, of which about fifteen percent are residential. Partners of the firm are William H. Grover, Jefferson B. Riley, Mark Simon, Chad Floyd and James C. Childress. James A. Coan and Charles G. Mueller serve as principals.

Insiders say the firm's innovative work and stylistic versatility has won them many awards as well as many happy return clients. Residential projects include new construction, renovation and additions and range from $500,000 to $15 million. This prominent firm has received national recognition for its work, including the AIA Firm Award. The firm charges a standard percentage of over-all construction costs.

"The architects designed a work of art that is also a wonderfully comfortable home to live in."

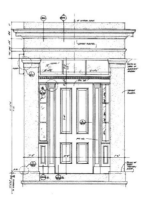

Charles W. Reppenhagen Architect   3.5   2.5   5   5

137 Route 37S, Sherman, CT 06784
(860) 354 - 2500

Traditional New England-inspired renovations

Sources say Charlie Reppenhagen is a true New England architect of times gone by. He works on his own, using outside consultants only when necessary, and prefers to handle each project from design through construction. With more than 40 years experience, Reppenhagen is said to find great joy in "designing spectacular rooms one at a time." The majority of Reppenhagen's work ranges from one-room remodels to million-dollar guts. He also handles the occasional ground-up home, but we're told the architect prides himself on designing additions "that look like they've been there forever." Reppenhagen favors using materials that have "a natural patina or proud age" to them.

In addition to his efforts to effectively preserve vintage architecture, insiders say Reppenhagen is a big supporter of practicality and functionality. He's a local architect who works exclusively in Westchester and Fairfield (mostly in Sherman, Woodbury and Newtown). Reppenhagen created the firm in 1965 with a recently retired partner and only takes on about eight projects a year. In addition to his residential work, Reppenhagen, a graduate of RPI, has also done a number of church renovations. Insiders say he "absolutely loves creating beautiful spaces," which may explain why he has some of the most reasonable hourly rates of any architect in the area.

"We basically took a chainsaw and knocked down half the house and he built it back up into a gorgeous living space." "Reppenhagen listens, which is the most important quality about him and he translates our ideas into magnificent drawings." "He spends enough time with you to work out every last detail—from where to put the power outlets to the type of molding to go around the windows."

Colangelo Associates Architects   4   4   4   5
66 Broad St, Stamford, CT 06901
(203) 967 - 4747   www.colangeloassociates.com
Collaborative, service-driven high-end architecture

Many clients trust Vincent Colangelo's sense of style so openly that they simply tell the architect what they don't want and give him creative control from there. Sources agree this kind of trust isn't given, it's earned—and Colangelo's 30 years of experience is the clincher. His styles are wide-ranging, as clients say he's just as capable of the historically sensitive renovation of an Elizabethan-style home as he is designing a contemporary house from scratch. We're told he "builds homes that are intimate with the site."

Colangelo, an architecture graduate of Kent State, started the four-person firm in 1979 after training at New York City firms for several years. Colangelo takes on twice as many ground-up designs as renovation projects, but sources say he is void of any pretense and will take on smaller renovation projects of $125,000 all the way up to massive homes that carry construction budgets of $7 million. And as for detail, it's not uncommon for Colangelo to "burrow in" for a year or two on a large scale project "to get the details just right." And that means everything right down to the hardware.

Clients say "he always watches out for you, especially with the contractor" and is very mindful of budgets. The bulk of his work comes from "cocktail party chats" yet he remains very grounded and accessible—we're told he returns phone calls in a matter of minutes. We hear he'll even follow up with a client years later just to see how the home is holding up. The firm charges a slightly lower than standard percentage of construction costs.

"I had a very normal Colonial house and he transformed it into a spectacular house." "He listened to what I wanted and just took it to another level." "I'd challenge you to find a better kitchen—even in a $5 million house." "The details, moldings were magnificent." "I would only work with him. He's my architect for life. I love him."

Crozier Gedney Architects   📁   📁   📁   📁
41 Elm Place, Rye, NY 10580
(914) 967 - 6060   cgapc@aol.com
Residential architecture

Daniel L. Colbert Architect   4   3.5   4.5   4
309 Greenwich Ave, Greenwich, CT 06830
(203) 661 - 1739
High-end residential architecture with a personal touch

We're told that when Daniel Colbert draws something "it can really be built that way." The architect purportedly has no ego and creates simple, yet elegant designs that call for good materials rather than "flashy buildings that are made of junk."

Colbert leans toward rich wood floors for his interiors and rugged materials such as cedar shingles, stone facades and slate roofs for the exterior. While Colbert enjoys contemporary design, most clients come to him for his traditional work, which ranges from Colonial to Shingle style to log homes.

Colbert, a practicing architect for 30 years, holds two architecture degrees from Columbia and trained with the inimitable Robert A.M. Stern in New York. While many architecture firms grow at breakneck clips, Colbert has actually shrunken the size of his firm with the belief that "it's better to keep each job in one brain rather than parcel it out." He's now a one-man show and clients say he "doesn't rush his decisions," so that he can "deliver a carefully crafted product."

Colbert generally takes on one major gut renovation each year, in addition to three to four smaller projects. On occasion, he is asked to design a home from the ground up. A typical Colbert project carries an $800,000 construction budget. The Architect tends to work with a well-established empty-nest kind of clientele. He charges a slightly lower fee based on an hourly rate.

"He's become a good friend of ours and that's a sure sign that it worked out very very well." "I interviewed quite a few architects, and the combination of his person- ality, drawings and style just fit with us." "He listens very carefully and although he's strong in his opinion, we simply worked very well together." "Our home is wonderfully unusual." "His attention to detail is like nothing I've ever seen." "I don't think you could get my husband out of here, except for feet first—against his will or dead."

David Bergman Architect　　　　4　　4　　4　　4.5
241 Eldridge Street, Suite 3R, New York, NY   10002
(212) 475 - 3106　www.cyberg.com

Modern-edged residential and commercial architecture

Praised as much for his trustworthy nature as his excellent architecture skills, David Bergman has earned the respect of his loyal clientele. These clients tell us they refer Bergman to friends and family for projects that range from one-room ren- ovations to sprawling single-family homes. We hear Bergman's style is fairly contemporary—warm modern—with distinct touches reflecting his clients' ideas. Working in a close collaborative environment with Bergman, clients say the archi- tect takes their ideas very seriously. Bergman's designs are said to be flawless and his execution seamless.

We are told Bergman is quick to solve problems that may arise throughout the course of a project and is a meticulous manager of any endeavor he undertakes. The firm works in Manhattan, the Hamptons and Westchester and Fairfield coun- ties. Clients say they trust Bergman to the point of leaving large projects in his hands, unsupervised for long periods of time, with the confidence that he will deliver on time and on budget.

Bergman received an Master of Architecture from Princeton and currently teaches at Parsons. Clients and colleagues alike have lauded him for his technical and aes- thetic skills. The architect also designs his own line of "Fire & Water" lighting and furniture. The firm charges an hourly rate not to exceed a percentage of construc- tion, which can slightly exceed standard percentages on smaller projects.

"A talented architect but also a good person." "He's almost too easy to work with." "His teaching skills clearly came through in my experience as I asked him many ques- tions that probably drove him crazy." "Has a tremendous amount of patience."

David Christopher Dumas Architect　　4.5　　4　　4.5　　4.5
& Cheryl Dixon Interiors
1616 Post Road, Suite 7739, Fairfield, CT   06824
(203) 336 - 9326　cdixoninteriors@aol.com

Refined, engaging, thoughtful interior design

See David Christopher Dumas Architect & Cheryl Dixon Interiors's full report under the heading Interior Decorators & Designers

	Quality ✚	Cost $	Value ◆	Recommend? ★

David D. Harlan Architects, LLC
938 Chapel Street, New Haven, CT 06510
(203) 495 - 8032   www.ddharchitects.com
Client-driven, personalized custom residential architecture

📁	📁	📁	📁

David Graham Architects
175 Main Street, Ossining, NY 10562
(914) 941 - 3889   dgarchitects@netzero.net
Residential architecture

📁	📁	📁	📁

DCA Architects Planners
158 Danbury Road, Ridgefield, CT 06877
(203) 431 - 6001   www.dcaarchitects.com
Personalized custom residential architecture

3.5   3   5   4.5

Sources say DCA stands out from the crowd because of its ability to drastically change the style of old drab buildings into stunning homes with traditional undertones and modern livability. Principals Peter Coffin and John Doyle are also said to practice "masterful site planning" of heavily wooded and hilly lots. Client relations are held in the highest regard, with an emphasis on staying in touch with former customers—whether it's in the form of a Christmas card or a surprise visit to the home years later. DCA tends to work with younger families in the area—some of whom are second-generation clients.

Coffin himself is second-generation—his father started this firm of ten in 1973. Peter Coffin holds degrees from Penn and Miami of Ohio and partner John Doyle has architecture degrees from Maryland and Texas. The two met while working at the much vaunted firm, Centerbrook Architects. Sources say the elder Coffin passed along his innate ability to listen to clients and to "manage expectations." Most of the firm's projects are residential endeavors in and around Wilton, Fairfield, Ridgefield and Westport, although DCA has completed some notable church renovations as well.

Described as "just incredibly nice easygoing guys," Coffin and Doyle usually take on projects with budgets upward of $500,000—although the firm "doesn't hold it against people if they don't have a lot of money" as long as there is an interesting design challenge. The firm charges a slightly lower percentage of overall construction costs.

"I gave him a mind map, which was flexible on style and fairly loose in concept, yet Peter and I always seemed to be in sync." "I knew what I wanted, but I didn't know what I didn't know I wanted—and Peter helped me figure it out." "I always felt like part of the team and never felt caught in between the architect and the contractor." "It's the little details they included in the home that I enjoy every day."

Deborah Berke & Partners Architects LLP
211 West 19th Street, 2nd Floor, New York, NY 10011
(212) 229 - 9211   www.dberke.com
Residential, commercial and institutional architecture

4.5   3.5   4.5   4.5

Deborah Berke, an associate professor of architecture at Yale University, has gained an international following for her simple spaces designed in a distinctive, minimalist style. Berke and her "exceptional staff" have been described as "very talented" and "totally professional," producing beautiful, elegant and functional designs. A co-editor of the 1997 book, *Architecture of the Everyday*, Berke recognizes and emphasizes the allure of simple, serviceable materials in her designs. Clients who have retained Berke for residential work commend her as "an artist" and praise her work for its "ease of living."

Her work's "easy elegance" has earned her a number of distinguished jobs, including homes and stores in the planned community of Seaside, Florida, as well as CK Calvin Klein boutiques and the new Yale University School of Art. Berke works extensively in Westchester, Fairfield and Litchfield counties. ID Hall of Fame.

"On a scale of one to five for quality, I give her a ten!" "The only problem with the project is that it is going to end soon."

DiBiase Filkoff Architects   4   4   4   5

Empire Building Village Green, Box 187, Bedford, NY 10506
(914) 234 - 7014   www.dibiasefilkoffarchitects.com
Historically sensitive, understated traditional architecture

Sources tell us the architects at DiBiase Filkoff have solved the riddle of making things look as if they have been there for 100 years, while making them timeless and functional. They say the firm is "big on custom windows and understated elegance." A skill for highly detailed design, a commitment to high-quality materials and an eagle's eye for scale and proportion are characteristics sources use to describe the firm. While trained as modernists, the architects are highly respected for their sensitivity to the vernacular, "not imposing their style on anyone" and for virtually being design "chameleons."

Cynthia Filkoff and Armband DiBiase, both Syracuse graduates in architecture, head the firm. Created in 1992, the firm currently employs seven. The practice handles only six or seven projects at any given time in order to maintain high levels of personalized client services and to devote the necessary amount of time to the design process. Clients say Filkoff, who worked for several years with the prestigious firm of Shope Reno Wharton Associates, is "an honest and fair person who is always looking out for the client."

The majority of the firm's work is in significant renovations and new home design that can top $3 million in construction costs. However, the firm happily does much smaller projects, particularly for return clients. The firm charges a standard percentage of overall construction costs.

"Cynthia responds very well to those little surprises you get when you open up the walls in an old house. Our insulation turned out to be hay and manure, so she obviously had to fix that little problem." "She is always on time—and that's saying something because she was pregnant and had a baby during our project, but she was there for every meeting." "I later had to put the house on the market and it sold in one day—and I regret having to leave it."

Donald M. Rattner Architects   4.5   4.5   4   4.5

462 Broadway 3rd floor, New York, NY 10013
(212) 625 - 3336   www.thecivilstudio.com
Large-scale classical residential architecture

Insiders say Donald Rattner's extensive experience as an architect and teacher, combined with a commitment to classical and traditional design, makes this newly created firm one of the highest integrity. We're told Rattner holds the belief that "context suggests the style" of each project, and he possesses an affinity for regional vernacular "under the umbrella of traditional design." The majority of his projects are residential in nature, focusing on large-scale gut renovations and ground-up homes up and down the eastern seaboard.

Rattner, who has an undergraduate degree from Columbia and a Master of Architecture from Princeton, created the firm after a successful partnership in the firm Ferguson Shamamian & Rattner. He now partners with Andrew Friedman, who holds a degree from Cooper Union. Insiders say Rattner established this firm in order to devote more time and attention to each project that comes across his desk. Most are located in Westchester and Fairfield counties as well as Manhattan with the remainder in Martha's Vineyard, West Virginia and Georgia.

While the larger part of the residential work carries significant budgets ranging from $500,000 to $3.5 million, Rattner is known to take on smaller projects such as a kitchen or bathroom renovation for select clients. In addition to residential commissions, the firm is also active in working with developers to create resorts and golf facilities. Standard fees are based on a combination of hourly rates and/or a percentage of overall construction costs.

"He has a reputation and a body of work that speaks for itself." "Clearly has a carefully honed understanding for fine design and the classical elements that make it so." "Don has a great collaborative approach balanced with a natural ability to lead and teach."

Elizabeth Jahn Architecture

| | | 4 | 3.5 | 5 | 5 |

34 East Putnam Avenue, Greenwich, CT 06830
(203) 863 - 0040
High-end residential architecture with personalized service

Insiders say it would be difficult to find a one-architect firm with the talent, personality and pedigreed experience to rival Liz Jahn. Her traditional designs are said to reflect a "tasteful human scale" and proportion to the site and surrounding community. Jahn is noted for being talented at contemporary design, but you're more likely to see her Shingle and Federal style homes and barn renovations. Sources say she is a genuine "people person" who enjoys dealing with a wide variety of clients, from empty nesters to young families.

Jahn has trained with some of the most notable names in the business—like Allan Greenberg, Robert A.M. Stern and Shope Reno Wharton. A graduate of Miami and Virginia, Jahn started her firm in 2000. Her work is dominated by high-end renovations—although they range from small one-room makeovers to large-scale guts with budgets of $1.5 million. Sources say the firm would probably be overextending itself if approached with a large-scale ground-up home simply because of the lack of manpower. Much of Jahn's work takes place in Greenwich, Wilton and Rye, but she has also worked in North Carolina and Colorado.

Although she will use outside consultants for bigger jobs, Jahn handles all aspects of each project. She is known to closely monitor the construction process and works in close coordination with builders. Jahn puts a lot of stock in selecting high-quality materials with an affinity for windows and doors, calling them "the best investment you can make." The firm charges a slightly lower fee based on a percentage of overall construction costs.

"Her greatest strength is her ability to work classical design without overdoing it or spoiling it." "She brought an eclectic twist to our previously classic look and we love it." "We sold it in three days for our asking price—what more can I say?" "She didn't cave in to the builder and always had our best interests in mind." "Excellent with dealing with those little surprises that pop up during a renovation."

ERG Architect

| | | 4.5 | 4.5 | 4 | 5 |

25 Lewis Street, Suite 306, Greenwich, CT 06830
(203) 661 - 7472   ergarchitect@earthlink.net
Traditional, classical residential architecture

For highly customized, classical design of major renovations, sprawling single-family homes and estates, clients say ERG is second to none. Clients extol the firm's disciplined and methodical approach to creating luxurious and elegant residential spaces. Based in Greenwich, insiders tell us ERG Architect is a small three-person firm with big clients. Edward Ronald Gushue (known simply as Ron) is the sole proprietor, and has built up a clientele of those who work in New York City but live in exclusive neighborhoods outside the metro area—in addition to a number of city dwellers. Insiders tell us it would be wise for potential clients to study this high-end firm's work before inquiring about services, particularly for projects with modest budgets.

Founded by Gushue in 1984, the firm takes on about twelve large projects each year with construction costs that often eclipse seven and eight figures. The vast majority of ERG's work is residential, although Gushue, who earned a Bachelor of Architecture from the University of Idaho, has completed several high-profile commercial projects. The firm generally focuses on major projects but will do smaller renovations or additions for repeat clients, which we hear make up nearly all of ERG's business. ERG is flexible in its fee structure and can charge an hourly rate, fixed price or a standard percentage of total construction costs.

"Ron has a very good sense of balance and proportion and is able to effectively translate his ideas." "He's very well-regarded and has a very easygoing personality." "His greatest asset is that he has an unparalleled knowledge of the materials that make up these high-end types of projects." "I trust him to work on almost anything. We love our house and we're going to have him do a carriage house for us."

Faesy and Sanders Architects PC   4   4   4.5   5
523 Danbury Road, Wilton, CT 06897
(203) 834 - 2724   rsanders@faesy-sanders.com
Historically sensitive custom architecture—renovations

Clients tell us the ivy-league educated tandem of Rob Sanders and Robert Faesy "is as an intelligent and well-spoken duo as you'll find." With their "sympathetic additions" and "trend-bucking" design philosophy, Faesy and Sanders are in high demand. The firm is lauded for its honest response to traditional, regional and historical context—"they don't do imitation old buildings," we're told. The firm's interpretations of the Federal- and Shingle- style homes are well received by clients and insiders alike. Faesy and Sanders is best known for its renovation, alteration and addition designs, with many taking place in the historical districts of Ridgefield, Wilton, Greenwich and Darien.

Faesy, a graduate of Yale, and Sanders, who holds a degree from Cornell, created this firm of eight in 1985. While the bulk of the firm's commissions carry budgets of $750,000 to $1.75 million, the firm will handle much smaller (and larger) projects. The firm tends to work with younger families, who view their homes "as precious assets" and we're told the architects "treat them as such." Sources say the firm revels in the renovation of turn-of-the-century wood and timber frame homes, creating homes that "lean toward the rustic side of traditional." The firm charges a standard percentage of overall construction costs.

Ferguson & Shamamian   5   4.5   4.5   5
270 Lafayette Street, Suite 300, New York, NY 10012
(212) 941 - 8088
Classical, large-scale residential, institutional and commercial architecture

This renowned firm is best known by clients (and peers alike) for its traditional styles of design, especially those borne of classical roots. Insiders tell us the firm is extremely efficient in its design process and pays close attention to providing personal service—with a principal involved in every project. Clients say the designs are unique, detailed and highly customized within a traditional setting. We are told the firm uses an extremely broad range of materials and vocabularies, working seamlessly with the area's finest interior decorators. Ferguson & Shamamian has achieved iconic stature in architecture circles for the firm's intellectual approach and view of classicism as the purest form of design. We understand the partners strongly prefer to work with clients who share their architectural philosophy. Clients say a combination of talent, quality and attention to detail makes this a much-sought-after firm, especially by those seeking the very best.

This large firm, created in 1988 by former employees of Parish-Hadley Associates, currently employs 65 in one office in New York, although it takes on somewhere between twelve and twenty projects each year from coast to coast. The partners of the firm are Mark Ferguson, who holds an Master of Architecture from Princeton, and Oscar Shamamian, who holds an Master of Architecture from Columbia. More than half of the firm's current commissions consist of single-family new-home construction, the remainder being gut renovations, alterations and additions of apartments, townhouses and freestanding homes. Ferguson & Shamamian also offers master planning and design of resort communities. An hourly rate is charged, which is higher than the standard percentage of total construction costs.

"To say the house is wonderful is an understatement." "Their design sensibility is unparalleled." "The spirit of their work is like the craftsman of generations past." "They cater ultimately to the client despite being a big, influential firm."

FZAD Architecture + Design   4   4   4   4
77 Sunset Drive, Briarcliff Manor, NY 10510
(914) 923 - 1000   www.fzad.com
Adaptive residential architecture

With his own brand of "modern classic," Frederic Zonsius has fostered a loyal clientele from California to Westchester. Frederic and his wife Pamela head this firm of five, which they founded in 1986. FZAD is best known for its sensitivity to existing structures and has earned a reputation as a superb renovation firm. Frederic holds a bachelor's degree in architecture from Cornell and Pamela graduated from FIT in New York City. The firm takes on about nine projects each year that range from $100,000 renovations to $4.5 million ground-up homes. The average architecture project is in the $500,000 to $1 million range and the company also does interiors starting at $30,000.

George Penniman Architects LLC   4.5   4   4.5   4.5
2 South Main Street, Essex, CT 06426
(860) 767 - 2822   www.pennimanarchitects.com
High-end traditional residential architecture with a twist

With a "traditionally based vernacular" as sources put it, Penniman's renovations from Shingle style to Tudor and Colonial homes "are not slaves to tradition." This, however, should not lead potential clients to think the architect's work is contemporary. It is not. From Greenwich to coastal locales in Rhode Island and the Hamptons, sources tell us Penniman excels in combining "green" architectural elements in tasteful and appropriate ways. He encourages the use of geothermal and solar energy sources like solar paneling and materials from recycled or eco-friendly products. His handling of ocean views and complicated waterfront sites is said to be "exemplary."

Penniman, who holds a Master of Architecture from Virginia, founded this firm of four in 1994. His impressive resume includes a stint at the esteemed firm, Centerbrook Architects. We're told Penniman has no ego to keep in check and often "helps people out even on non-glamorous projects." He even turns away work rather than expand his practice, simply because he wants to retain design control and attend site meetings, which he truly believes "is the most fun part of the job; watching the house get built." Nearly all of the firm's work is residential in nature and dominated by large-scale alterations, but the firm does an occasional ground-up residence or commercial office space.

At any given time, Penniman and his staff have four major projects (budgets of $750K or better) and five to seven smaller commissions. Penniman tends to work with an older clientele, many of whom are converting vacation homes into half-year homes. The firm charges slightly lower fees based on a combination of a percentage of construction costs, fixed fee and hourly rate.

Gleicher Design Group   4   3   4.5   4.5

135 Fifth Avenue, 2nd Floor, New York, NY 10010
(212) 462 - 2789   www.gleicherdesign.com
Comprehensive high-end residential architecture

A "keen knowledge of zoning regulations and permitting issues" coupled with the "versatility to design both handsome modern and elegant traditional spaces," is what clients say is the key to Gleicher Design Group's success. They tell us the firm excels in gut renovations of apartments and townhouses on the Upper East and Upper West sides, but it also does new homes and additions in Westchester and Connecticut. We are told Paul Gleicher's honest, thoughtful and involved approach to design is just one of many reasons clients have returned for other projects. Apart from his design sense, sources speak of Gleicher's soothing personality and how he is able to take the stress out of any situation with his positive outlook.

This firm of six was created in 1989 by sole principal Paul Gleicher after spending time at Davis Brody & Associates and Haverson-Rockwell Architects. He holds a Master of Architecture from Columbia. Gleicher and his associates average about fifteen new projects each year, several of which are in Westchester County. Gleicher Design Group has worked with numerous celebrity clients and also does interior decorating upon request. The firm charges a slightly lower percentage of overall construction costs.

"Moving from Manhattan to Westchester was daunting, but they understood what we wanted even when we couldn't articulate it." "He's just got an extraordinary gift for a brand of modern design that is warm and rich without being austere." "His judgment and taste are terrific, and his integrity is of the highest order." "It gives you a sense of ease when you know you're working with someone who's incredibly talented, professional and trustworthy."

Gray Organschi Architecture

35 Crown Street, New Haven, CT 06510
(203) 777 - 7794
Environmentally sensitive, context-driven architecture

With a heightened sensitivity to a home's site and regional environment, this firm has won accolades from clients, architects and advocates of "green" architecture. Gray Organschi is said to "work wonders" with difficult topography, siting homes so that they make "the least possible impact" on the site. Additionally, the firm uses existing natural elements to enhance the living experience of its clients while upholding its minimally invasive approach.

Gullans & Brooks Architects   4.5   4.5   4   5

87 Main Street, New Canaan, CT 06840
(203) 966 - 8440   www.gullansandbrooks.com
Elegant residential architecture and highly detailed documentation

Gullans & Brooks draws consistent praise for its "roundtable design approach," sensitivity to the vernacular and the seamless integration of new additions to old homes. But design is only one reason for the firm's success; insiders say they deliver "great documentation" and a knowledge of the permit process that is "second to none." Sources say the design is firmly rooted in traditional design and has completed numerous Colonial, Georgian, Shingle- and Craftsman-influenced homes and barn conversions. It's no secret that the firm goes to great lengths to work collaboratively with contractors and decorators from the beginning.

Louise Brooks and Vincent Falotico, AIA, stand at the helm of this firm which currently has a team of twenty. Brooks established the firm in 1986 and holds a BFA from Drexel and studied architecture at Notre Dame and Drexel. Falotico is a graduate of Syracuse University School of Architecture. Sources say both partners are very accessible and are always part of the project. The firm makes liberal use of steel and fieldstone and doesn't hesitate to use cedar shingles whenever appropriate. Clients are quick to praise the firm for its personal touch and excellent client relations.

Gullans & Brooks signs about 40 new project contracts each year, which vary in size from $200,000 renovations to $10 million ground-up homes. While Fairfield County is the site for much of its local work, Gullans & Brooks has extended itself to Vail, Nantucket, Cape Cod, Montana and Georgia. The firm charges a higher percentage of overall construction costs.

"Superb technical skills and the uncanny ability to show earnest sensitivity to the existing architecture, yet satisfy our needs." "They adapted materials so well that I still can't tell what's old and what's new." "They have a massive pool of knowledge and it goes well beyond the design of space." "The process is very clear and articulated with plenty of room for creativity." "They have a tremendous vision in the end product."

Gwathmey Siegel & Associates Architects   5   5   5   5
475 Tenth Avenue, 3rd Floor, New York, NY 10018
(212) 947 - 1240   www.gwathmey-siegel.com
Modern, dramatic institutional, commercial and residential architecture

Praised by clients, acknowledged by the press and admired by industry professionals, the award-winning Gwathmey Siegel & Associates is one of country's most prestigious firms. Clients hail this firm for its intricate detail, completely original designs and passion for creating spaces of the highest quality and stylistic integrity. We are told the firm is evenhanded in its selection of natural materials and clients say the firm leaves its indelible signature on every project without being repetitive— all while being sympathetic to the client's needs and tastes. Geometric and precise, and with great clarity of design, the firm's projects have won Charles Gwathmey and Robert Siegel a devoted following and more than 100 awards.

This firm of 80 has been commended for displaying a sculptor's sensitivity to shape and light in projects that put forth an unquestionable modernism. Observers describe the firm's work as "luxurious and sleek." We are told these architects believe that complete architectural solutions should integrate the details of interior design. Gwathmey Siegel only accepts projects with broad budgets—each topping more than $5 million and any residential projects tend to be large single-family homes or large full-scale renovations.

Gwathmey, a Fulbright scholar, graduated in 1962 from Yale with a master's degree in architecture and became a Fellow of the AIA in 1981. Siegel is a graduate of Pratt and Harvard, became a Fellow in 1991 and remains active in the Pratt community. This partnership was founded in 1967 and both architects have taught at some of the country's most prestigious universities. The firm charges a higher percentage of total construction costs plus the fees for any necessary consultants or engineers. AD 100, 2000, 2002. ID Hall of Fame.

"We were able to get an architectural masterpiece without sacrificing practical living comfort." "It's been exhilarating, exciting and an education in the modern aesthetic." "The most amazing part about it was watching Charlie's ideas come to fruition. I would do it all again." "The execution right down to the last detail was absolutely flawless." "It was a perfect collaboration of our ideas and enlightenment by them."

Halper Owens Associates Architects LLC   4.5   4.5   4   4.5

225 Mill Street, Greenwich, CT 06830
(203) 531 - 5341   www.halperowens.com

Understated, tasteful, versatile residential architecture

Jon Halper and Reese Owens are said to bring a "quiet tastefulness" to their work, whether it's the ground-up design of a modern home clad in glass walls or the renovation of an Italianate Victorian home. We're told the firm painstakingly matches, clones and authentically details its renovations and additions to preserve the integrity of the original structure and the intent of the original architect. Both Halper and Owens are said to have "very strong design principals" and are deeply involved in each project, working collaboratively with the client to incorporate their design ideas.

Principals of the firm are Jon Halper, who holds degrees from Harvard and University of Illinois, and Reese Owens, who graduated from Yale and the University of Virginia. The partnership started in 1987, but the two have managed separate locations since 1996 with a total of eight employees. Owens oversees the Washington Depot office and Halper manages the Greenwich location. Sources say the architects favor the use of natural materials that "are as true to the spirit of the architecture to elevate the art of it."

The firm generally handles projects in the $1.5 million to $3 million range, but will take on projects with budgets starting at $350,000. The majority of Halper Owens commissions are residential projects, but the firm sometimes does retail and corporate interiors or educational facilities. The firm charges a slightly higher percentage of construction costs.

"Jon is one talented dude." "The design and drawing actually make sense when it comes time to be built." "Drew a picture on a piece of sheetrock and we built it right there." "It felt like an evolution, bouncing ideas back and forth until they came to fruition." "The house is unbelievable. It's so solid, beautifully designed and extraordinarily detailed." "I just called him recently to tell him again how gorgeous the house is." "Jon is always willing to listen to the other professionals involved."

Hamady Architects   4.5   4   4.5   5

1 Village Green Circle, Suite 201, Charlottesville, VA 22903
(434) 977 - 5592

Site-inspired residential architecture and landscape design

Working with Hamady architects is a "labor of love—and time," according to insiders. Principal Kahlil Hamady is also a trained landscape designer who "won't even design the house until he sees the site in all four seasons." With that kind of planning and thought going into the design of a home, it's no wonder clients in Connecticut and Westchester are willing to work with Hamady, even though his office is located in Virginia. The firm is said to be "proficient in all architectural languages," but most often designs under the umbrella of traditional regional design, including Arts & Crafts, Shaker and Colonial homes.

Working on mostly large properties in New England and Virginia, Hamady and his staff of eight has about ten projects in varying degrees of completion at any given time. Hamady founded the firm in 1997 after graduating with a Master of Architecture from University of Virginia and working for respected New York architect Jacquelin T. Robertson. Projects range from $500,000 renovations to $5 million custom new construction. Nearly all of the firm's work is residential.

We're told the firm is highly involved from concept design to construction and Hamady is hailed for his "availability and accessibility." This availability may be compromised by his Virginia location, but clients say "he'll be on a plane that day if you really need him." Because of his immersion in each project, Hamady "truly understands the context and culture" of each project he designs. The firm charges a slightly lower fee based on an hourly rate with a cap.

"This guy is brilliant, doesn't have an ego, and has a great true-to-form classical approach to architecture." "He just has a great eye for proportions, materials, siting and a distinguished sympathy for existing structures." "His renderings are among the best I've ever seen, and I've worked with the best architects from New York." "There is a real Jeffersonian feeling to this guy and what he brings to the design." "The planning department of Greenwich, which is notorious for being a pain in the neck, said they've never seen such a detailed plan in their tenure."

Haverson Architecture and Design   4   3.5   4.5   4.5
63 Church Street, Greenwich, CT 06830
(203) 629 - 8300   www.haversonarchitecture.com
Traditionally based residential architecture with a contemporary flair

Working with Haverson means you'll get "heavy principal involvement from initial design through construction administration"—an attribute hailed by clients. We're told the design process is highly interactive between architect and client, with Jay Haverson himself actively encouraging a collaborative environment. Most of the firm's fifteen annual projects are highly customized traditional designs with a slight contemporary flair in terms of color, lighting and materials. Clients say the staff is always accessible with a simple phone call.

Jay Haverson, a graduate of Columbia and Syracuse, started the firm in 1993 after ten years as a principal in a New York City firm. He and wife Carolyn, a graduate of Syracuse and Parsons, are principals. Carolyn Haverson leads the firm's graphic design services, which is offered both in collaboration with the architecture or completely independently. Interior design is billed out hourly with no markup on product. Clients say they appreciate the emphasis placed on the seamless integration of exterior and interior design. For those who are building a home as an investment to eventually be sold, Haverson is a good match—we're told the firm designs with the foresight of resale value and aesthetic beauty.

Haverson Architecture and Design takes on projects starting with $200,000 construction budgets and averaging $1 million to $2 million. The firm works mainly in the Greenwich/New Canaan and Northern Westchester areas and also in the Hamptons. Haverson charges a slightly lower fee based on a fixed fee or a percentage of construction costs.

"Jay is just an excellent, calming, confident, positive and encouraging person." "Just the right combination of personality and talent." "He's always negotiating on our behalf—and was very sensitive to my budget." "They're quite the dynamic duo. He's an astounding architect and she's a powerhouse designer and artist." "He saved us from a complete nervous breakdown." "It was a real mutt of a house and he turned it into something that is just beautiful without being grandiose." "Jay watched over our nightmare-of-a-contractor like a hawk."

Hilton-VanderHorn Architects
31 East Elm Street, Greenwich, CT 06830
(203) 862 - 9011   www.hilton-vanderhorn.com
Traditionally rooted residential architecture

With a solid reputation across southern Connecticut and Westchester County, Hilton VanderHorn Architects is known to be skilled in traditionally based residential design. While the firm is able to create "distinguished and well-crafted" residences, insiders say Hilton-VanderHorn isn't interested in leaving its fingerprint on the home. Instead, we're told the firm is concerned with creating a home that

Quality	Cost	Value	Recommend?
✚	$	◆	★

accommodates the client and fits "appropriately" into the structure's surroundings. The firm is best known for being sensitive to the architectural ideals of generations past, while creating designs that are suitable for modern living. The firm also works in New York, New Jersey and Rhode Island.

J.P. Franzen Associates Architects   4.5   3.5   5   4.5
95 Harbor Road, Southport, CT 06890
(203) 259 - 0529

Adaptive, high-end custom residential, commercial, and institutional architecture

Citing that "people treasure the unique flavor every little town in New England has," Jack Franzen has made it a point to be a student of those subtle changes from place to place. Clients say he "gets it right" and "gives you something that feels wonderful." With a landscape architect on staff, J.P. Franzen Associates designs gardens, pools and hardscape. Most clients look to Franzen's staff for its traditional work, although the firm is said to be just as coherent in a contemporary design language. Sources say Franzen has "fantastic sources" and is said to be a master at choosing rich natural woods. Sources tell us Franzen has become a magnet for clients with difficult sites—particularly those with waterfront property or those with tricky zoning rules.

Franzen created the firm in 1986 and stands at ten strong—with no plans on growing any bigger. He holds two architecture degrees from Cornell and is a Fellow of the AIA. We're told Franzen works mostly locally, preferring to "draw instead of drive too far" and is personally involved in each project. Insiders say Franzen has a knack for turning those difficult sites into beautiful homes that fit into the landscape and take advantage of views. The firm's commissions carry budgets of $250,000 to $8 million.

The firm charges a slightly lower fee based on a percentage of overall construction costs. Of the company's fifteen annual residential projects, about five are ground-up projects. The rest are large-scale renovations, with many taking place in historic districts, which Franzen knows all too well as a member of the historic district commission in Fairfield.

"I couldn't be more delighted with Jack. He's just a pleasure to work with." "As long as you keep the lines of communication open, everything will go smoothly." "No hidden fees or change-order costs."

James Schettino Architect   4   4   4   4
1031 Oenoke Ridge, New Canaan, CT 06840
(203) 966 - 5552

Residential architecture specializing in waterfront and rural projects

Sources say James Schettino has an "affinity and exemplary talent" for designing equestrian-related projects on rural farm-like sites. Schettino, whose style has definite classical overtones, has a reputation as a "master of making new things look old." But when he's not on the farm, we're told Schettino employs a sophisticated handling of rugged waterfront sites. When it comes to materials, clients say Schettino is shingle crazy: He uses shingles for facades, roofs and just about anywhere else he can put a shingle—as long as it adds to the design. Clients most often approach the architect with projects having classical roots—including variations of Shingle style, period homes and Colonial Revival.

Schettino, a graduate of Clemson, started this small firm of five in 1972. He and his staff take on about 25 projects each year, half of which are major endeavors with construction budgets ranging from $1.5 million to $5 million. Most of these projects are large high-end custom gut renovations to single-family homes. However, for repeat clients, the firm will do much smaller projects. Schettino stays close to home, working mainly in Greenwich and New Canaan in order to maintain his frequent site visits, but has worked in the Hamptons and South Carolina. The firm charges a lower fee based on a percentage of overall construction costs.

Jeff Wilkinson, R.A.   4   3.5   4.5   4
178 Main Street, Beacon, NY 12508
(845) 838 - 9763   www.jwra.com
Traditionally inspired residential architecture for modern living

Described as "hands on" and "always on site," Jeff Wilkinson is a dedicated architect who "isn't afraid to get his boots dirty." We're told his designs are traditionally inspired, with a wide range of influence ranging from classical to Craftsman. Clients appreciate Wilkinson's accommodating approach to design, with modern living being a major factor—"he implements modern design solutions for modern living, yet maintains the integrity of traditional design." Wilkinson is deeply involved in each project and is known to sketch during meetings, which has become a big hit with clients and contractors alike.

Wilkinson founded this firm of three in 1994, after working with the likes of Robert A.M. Stern and serving as the editor of *Old House Journal.* He holds an architecture degree from RISD. Wilkinson also builds furniture for select clients and designs interiors (with the exception of fabrics). The architect favors using stone, heavy timbers and salvaged products in his buildings. We're also told he is big on energy-efficiency practices but puts design as the highest priority.

The firm takes on about ten projects annually, with two thirds being renovations. Budgets start around $300,000 go and up to $2 million. The bulk of the firm's work is done in Westchester County, although Wilkinson has done work across New England and Michigan. The firm charges a lower fee based on an hourly rate not to exceed a certain percentage of overall construction costs.

Jeffrie Lane Architect   4   4   4   4
62 Burd Street, Nyack, NY 10960
(845) 353 - 8007
Historically sensitive residential architecture

Jeffrie Lane keeps a small firm that enables him to be intimately involved in each project and to interact with clients from start to finish. He's known to handle much of the drawing himself and carry the bulk of the load of each project to maintain his high standards of design. While sources say Lane is "acutely sensitive" to historical styles of architecture such as Victorian, Colonial and French Normandy, he is not committed to a particular style. Some say Lane can come off "cool" at first, but quickly warms up to clients who share his design vision.

Lane, who attended Syracuse University, started this three-person firm in 2003 after a partnership with another architect and five years working with David Easton. All of Lane's commissions are residential, and he takes on a limited number of projects each year. Most are substantial renovations, which tend to carry budgets in the $1 million to $2 million range. He also takes on new home designs that can command eight-digit price tags. Lane works exclusively in Westchester, Rockland and Fairfield counties.

We're told Lane is a highly collaborative architect who works seamlessly with big name decorators and landscape architects. He also favors rich millwork and collaborates with the finest craftsmen. The firm charges a slightly higher fee based on a combination of hourly rates and a percentage of overall construction costs.

	Quality +	Cost $	Value ◆	Recommend? ★

John B. Murray Architect, LLC

4.5 4.5 4 4.5

36 West 25th Street, 9th Floor, New York, NY 10010
(212) 242 - 8600   www.jbmarchitect.com

High-end residential architecture

Clients consider this firm extremely traditionalist, with projects ranging from classical and formal to a relaxed vernacular. Sources praise Murray for his exceptional architectural sense and dedication to traditional design and form. Many say they approach him for his depth of experience and amiable personality. We have heard that Murray is extremely busy but makes himself accessible at all times, and his follow-up is said to be thorough.

Principal John Murray, a founding partner of Ferguson, Murray and Shamamian before starting his own firm in 1998, generally embarks on large-scale gut renovations. Still, we hear the firm will take on smaller projects with an interesting twist or that pose an intriguing challenge. While some say Murray's taste for the highest form of design occasionally leads him to suggest more changes than are perhaps necessary, he is known to be receptive to clients' suggestions and sympathetic to their design and budgetary needs. Murray is a graduate of Carnegie Mellon.

Most of Murray's work can be seen from Connecticut to New York City, although he takes on projects across the country. Sources say that while his fine work still suits high-end tastes, he is considerably more affordable now that he is on his own. The firm generally charges a slightly higher percentage of overall construction costs but will occasionally work on an hourly rate.

"The weekly meeting minutes he provides are invaluable to ensure that the project remains on track." "He isn't a bargain, but he's a great value." "Not only is John courteous, but he is eager to teach and discuss ideas." "I have gone from a nervous client to an eager, excited and happy client." "His follow-up is absolutely incredible." "A magnificent sense of classical design." "He upholds the very top standards of quality, at all times."

John Mastera & Associates

4.5 4 4.5 5

102 Forest Street, New Canaan, CT 06840
(203) 966 - 6696   www.masteraarchitects.com

Historically sensitive architecture with a specialty in renovations

Sources tell us John Mastera's goal is "to get inside the mind of the original architect" to create a renovation that is "true to the structure." Sources say it's impossible to label Mastera with a particular style of design, however, he is often approached with renovations of Victorian, Shingle style and other traditionally inspired designs. Insiders say if Mastera "had his druthers, he'd be using traditional materials to create more contemporary spaces." Sources tell us Mastera is particularly talented at choosing materials that are straightforward and easy to build with while being easy on the eye—white cedars, rich woods, metal, glass and concrete are staples.

Originally from Colorado, Mastera created the firm in 1987 three years after graduating from Nebraska with a Bachelor of Architecture. After graduation Mastera apprenticed with Frank Lloyd Wright's granddaughter, Elizabeth Wright Ingraham. Mastera has reportedly kept his practice small—he currently has a staff of five—in order to maintain a "quality response to the client's needs." The firm takes on about twenty residential projects each year, with an emphasis on renovations—some of which are one-hundred-year-old historical homes. Mastera takes on projects that start with modest budgets of $100,000 on the low end, but his larger, new home designs have reached as high as $6 million.

Mastera engrosses himself in each project, putting countless hours into the design process. The vast majority of the firm's endeavors take place in Fairfield County, although the firm has finished projects in Florida, Massachusetts, Nebraska and New York City. The firm charges a standard percentage of overall construction costs.

	Quality	Cost	Value	Recommend?
		$	◆	★

Jones Footer Margeotes & Partners
245 Mill Street, Greenwich, CT 06830
(203) 531 - 1588 www.jfmp.com

Classic, bold, clean high-end interior design

| | 5 | 5 | 4 | 5 |

When Jones founded the firm in 1980, she was known to strap on a toolbelt herself because "that's what it took to get the job done." As the firm expanded, we're told she assembled a team of highly talented partners who strive for the same functional, well proportioned and highly detailed design. Historic authenticity and materials that blend into the environment take precedent over "making an architectural statement." This "hands-on, service-oriented" firm, generally handles commissions dealing with Tudor, Georgian and Shingle style homes.

Lori Jones and Jim Margeotes play major roles in directing the architectural direction of the firm and its projects. While the two will never admit to having a particular style, insiders tell us the firm does mostly traditionally based design with a heightened sensitivity to scale and comfort. Maureen Wilson Footer joined Jones & Associates in August of 2002, taking the helm of the firm's interior design department of five. Footer's distinct flair featuring dramatic backgrounds, fine art and antique textiles is now softened by the calming golden shades favored in Connecticut. Clients report that the community has welcomed her strong communication skills, efficient approach and can-do spirit.

This full-service firm works across Westchester and Fairfield counties and tends to stick to that geographic area. The firm takes on about fifteen new projects each year, the majority of which are large-scale residential renovations, with budgets starting at $1 million and averaging $3 million to $5 million. We're told no detail goes ignored and no stone unturned—the firm assembles all consultants necessary to get the project finished and diligently researches the permitting process and local codes. With this kind of coordination, plus interior design services, it's no wonder this firm is one of the most expensive in the area—but we're told the price is worth the peace of mind. ASID. KB 2002.

"Lori responded to my eclectic, 'out there' kind of personality and had fun with the project." "I love the warmth, the feeling about the house that gives it a marvelous character." "She even redesigned the new part of the house so we could fit in the twelve-foot Christmas tree." "I love that they were able to maintain the character of the house, yet still be logical about how it flowed." "Maureen is extremely service oriented and wonderfully focused, yet easy." "In interior design, they were able to suggest a range of high quality alternatives to keep the budget in line." "Maureen has real abilities to create quiet drama. It is amazing what she can do with a can of paint and a few pictures."

Joseph Matto Architects

37 Geneva Road, Norwalk, CT 06850
(203) 866 - 5777

High-end residential architecture

	Quality ✚	Cost $	Value ◆	Recommend? ★

Kaehler/Moore Architects

	4.5	4	4.5	5

80 Greenwich Avenue, Greenwich, CT 06830
(203) 629 - 2212

Timeless high-end exterior and interior design

Clients return to this "very versatile" architect for well-detailed and well-executed construction. Kaehler/Moore's pragmatist style adroitly integrates interiors and exteriors that are responsive to site conditions, social context and the client/project-team collaboration. Sources tell us the firm integrates old furniture and fixtures into new construction with fabulous results, and clients rave about the firm's architectural interiors. While schools and libraries count among this firm's institutional work, the tide of its efforts flows mostly to residential new construction in the regional area.

Although the firm works across the US, Kaehler Moore is known as one of the most respected and sought-after firms in the Westchester/Fairfield area. Principals Joeb Moore and Laura Kaehler are known to take time and pride in servicing clients who tell us the partners "don't make you feel stupid or silly for your ideas." Each partner oversees their own architecture and interior projects working with a team of the company's thirteen on-hand architects and two assistants. Kaehler and Moore have increasingly turned their attention to the interior development of their work, offering full interior and landscape design services in addition to architectural design. In fact, Moore is currently working on two projects for which he plays the role of interior designer and architect.

Moore received his Bachelor of Arts and an Master of Architecture from Clemson University. He laster attended Yale's MED program in architectural theory. He is now Assistant Director and Adjunct Professor of architecture at Columbia University. Kaehler holds a Bachelor of Architecture from RPI. The firm offers its services for either a percentage of construction sliding on the upper end of the scale, especially for renovations, or at an hourly rate that is often the choice for clients with no cap of fees.

"Personable people." "Just to sit down with Joeb and talk about architecture in general is a joy in and of itself." "So active and well respected within the design community." "Sets the bar for high standards." "Listens to the client. Gives the client what they want." "Constantly working on the project. Constantly there."

Kaufman Harvey Architect PC

	4	3	4.5	4.5

96 Main Street, New Canaan, CT 06840
(203) 966 - 7880

Classically-inspired residential architecture with a contemporary twist

With more than 40 years experience, Harvey Kaufman is said to make each design "a unique response to the client," with design worked from the inside out. We're told Kaufman favors symmetrical designs, which are contemporary in feel, but have an intrinsic classical undertone. These spaces tend to have large windows, open floor plans, and simple, yet elegant decoration and lines. Kaufman is noted for his detailed custom built-ins, cabinetry and fixtures. We're told he is adept at dealing with a wide range of site conditions—from waterfront to cliffside locations.

Kaufman, who holds a Bachelor of Architecture from Cornell, created this firm of four in 1980. The firm once had 25 employees, but Kaufman slowly reduced the size of the firm in order to get more personally involved in each project. We're told this move has made his practice "efficient," creating homes that are "artfully done." The firm generally handles four to five residential projects each year that carry significant budgets starting at $500K and topping out at $6 million.

The majority of Kaufman's work takes place in Fairfield County, but he also does work in Rhode Island, New Jersey, New York, Pennsylvania and Florida. The firm charges a lower percentage of overall construction costs.

	Quality	Cost	Value	Recommend?

Kenneth R. Nadler Consulting, LLC 4.5 3.5 5 5
103 South Bedford Road, Mount Kisco, NY 10549
(914) 241 - 3620   www.nadlerarchitects.com
High-end custom residential architecture with a light and airy feel

A "real stickler for detail," Nadler designs every last light fixture, molding, tile and floor pattern.   And don't forget site planning, permit approvals and zone requirement interpretation. Sources tell us Nadler and his staff are students of historical architecture, proper proportion and "just the right patinas on the materials to make them look weathered but not abused."   We're told Nadler can deftly design in a range of styles, from stark modern to formal classical. Most clients, however, come to him with traditional projects such as Tudor, English Country, Federal, Georgian and New England farmhouses.

Nadler founded the firm in 1975 and currently has a staff of twelve. He holds a Bachelor of Architecture from Pratt. Clients often approach Nadler with properties "that seem impossible to build on" and he will find a way for the structure to work as a seamless part of the natural landscape. Sources applaud Nadler for his careful incorporation of sunlight, foliage, vistas and views into the overall living experience. Nadler is so intent on getting the perfect design for the site and client that he will "draw it over and over again until he gets it right."

The firm has about a dozen residential projects in various stages of completion at any given time. Most are in the Westchester/Fairfield area, but select projects are around the US. Nadler takes on large-scale gut renovations that start at about $1 million and designs large new homes that top out at $15 million. The firm charges a standard to slightly lower percentage of construction costs.

Kroeger Woods Associates, Architects 5 4 5 5
255 King Street, Chappaqua, NY 10514
(914) 238 - 5391   kwaarch@aol.com
Highly intuitive, intelligent residential architecture

There is no doubt that the firm's clientele leans toward traditional design, but insiders say Kroeger Woods enthusiastically welcomes highly modern projects. We're told the architects are drawn to older, traditional materials used in traditional ways—such as masonry and stonework done in the old-world manner. These self-described "contextualists" create site-specific and client-specific designs that fit into the landscape and take full advantage of the unique aspects of the locations. Each home is said to be "nonimposing and uniquely different." For those whose lifestyle hinges on the incorporation of outdoor living with the indoor aspect, Kroeger Woods is said to be "incredibly talented at creating courtyards that move through the site and slowly develop an implied understanding of time and place."

Kroeger Woods currently has six employees, led by Keith Kroeger, who holds degrees from Princeton and Yale, and Leonard Woods, who has degrees from Washington and Yale. This duo has worked together since 1981 and began a partnership 1990. The firm takes on about 20 projects each year, with renovations starting at $150,000 budgets and new homes that start at around $1 million. However, despite the cache that comes with working with this firm, we're told the principals will work "with anyone who's interested in fine design and realistic about what it will cost."

This "anti-ego, laid-back" group of architects is said to hold their client relationships on high, looking for a working chemistry, collaborative relationship and an approachable aura. The firm has completed projects from Aspen to Maine, but the bulk of its commissions come from Fairfield and Westchester counties. Kroeger Woods charges a standard fee based on a combination of percentage of overall construction costs and hourly rates.

"The whole thing was drawn and laid out in such a way that it was a very logical and personal process—it's wonderful." "I admired their attitude that restrictions sometimes bring unique results and I believe we really achieved that due to the design challenges we put forth." "It's an intelligent, logical approach." "They really

had a willingness to work with us and they made the extra effort to understand what we wanted—and it ended up being quite unique." "Very accommodating and easy to work with." "We're absolutely thrilled, the house is just fabulous."

Laurent T. DuPont, Architect   4   4   4   4.5
191 Main Street, New Canaan, CT 06840
(203) 966 - 5185

Complete architectural and interior design services

Widely recognized for his "sensitive and tasteful handling" of waterfront sites, this firm truly provides "soup to nuts" services, doing everything from the architecture to interior design right down to the tile, hardware and fixtures. "There's always someone on-site from the firm," clients say, which contributes to the secure environment DuPont and his staff create. Rink, as he is known to his clients, is said to be most comfortable working on projects dealing with a bent on historical architecture—ranging from New England Shingle style to Adirondack and Georgian. DuPont himself handles all preliminary design and pores over renderings that detail the interior, exterior, furniture and overall feel of the house he is designing.

DuPont started this firm, which currently employs seven, in 1973. He is a graduate of Columbia and RISD. Sources tell us DuPont maintains a steady stream of projects, but will turn away work if he is unable to devote the necessary time to the project—he'll even recommend another architect. It is this kind of loyalty and integrity that has generated a clientele that produces, through references, 95 percent of the firm's work.

A good number of the firm's projects originate in the Greenwich and New Canaan areas, although DuPont has been known to travel across New England when the "right design challenge presents itself." The firm takes on projects with budgets starting at $500,000, but typically range in the $1-million to $4-million range. The firm charges a standard fee based on a percentage of overall construction costs.

Lawrence Gordon Architects   4   2.5   5   4.5
17 North Chatsworth Avenue, Larchmont, NY 10538
(914) 834 - 1641   gordonarchitects@aol.com

Residential architecture inspired by indoor/outdoor living

Known for a "balanced aesthetic appeal," Gordon is said to take cues from the existing structure and the community and "interpret it with a vocabulary established in a modern idiom." We are told Gordon and his staff excel in the creative use of the land and views of small plots of land—many less than one acre. The firm stresses the use of natural light by implementing larger expanses of glass in homes they design to create balanced relationships between indoor and outdoor spaces. This harmonious and often seamless relationship between outdoors and indoors is a client-valued characteristic of a Lawrence Gordon home.

Gordon, a graduate of Cooper Union with an Master of Architecture from MIT, is a design professional committed to excellence. He started the firm in 1977. Today, he leads a cohesive team that includes national award winning architects with extensive and varied experience. Turnover of employees is said to be extremely low, which allows for a steadfast team that is afforded long-term relationships with its clients, both on and off site.

The majority of the firm's annual residential projects are ground-up home designs with budgets up to $4 million. The firm will take on renovations as small as a single room, but the average budget is around $200,000.

Leigh Douglas Overland, Architect   4   3   5   4.5

225 Main Street; The Galleria Suite 104, Danbury, CT 06710
(203) 794 - 9001   www.ldoverland.com

Eclectic residential architect geared toward contemporary living

When you sign on with Overland, "you get more of an experience versus a style," which is an esoteric description of the architect's otherwise eclectic aesthetic. In a bit of an architectural dichotomy, Overland's designs are said to "have the warmth of traditional architecture with the excitement of contemporary living." With a highly detailed plan that includes the number of hinges and recommended lightbulbs, Overland and his staff "leave no question unanswered." And when it comes to zoning and building permits, we're told Overland "hunts down answers like a detective." While Overland spends a lot of time with clients to learn their lifestyles and spends a lot of time on-site, some say there's a distinct "business approach" to the project, that could be intimidating to those who haven't worked with an architect before.

Overland, a graduate of the New York Institute of Technology, started this firm of five in 1980. He and his staff take on about twenty to twenty five projects each year, half of which are residential in nature. These are generally medium-sized renovations with budgets starting at $100,000—however, the firm has designed new homes of up to $2.5 million. Sources tell us Overland doesn't choose projects based on the size of their budgets—"he'll do a finished basement if it's creative enough." Overland has also designed religious buildings, office spaces and restaurants.

The architect practices mostly in Fairfield County, but he's also worked in the Hamptons, Massachusetts and New Jersey. Sources tell us the efficiency of the firm allows it to finish projects at very reasonable prices—especially since Overland draws bids on construction. The firm charges a lower fee based on a percentage of overall construction costs or hourly fees.

Lichten Craig Architects, LLP   4   3   5   5

6 West 18th Street, 9th Floor, New York, NY 10011
(212) 229 - 0200   www.lichtencraig.com

High-end residential architecture and interior design

Classic style, strong standards and a personable approach are the qualities most often used to describe Lichten Craig Architects. Headed by Kevin Lichten and Joan Craig, the firm creates designs known for sophisticated detail and regularly handles Park Avenue apartments, townhouses and suburban and country homes. Many clients also use Joan Craig for interior design. Lichten Craig is highly recommended by clients for clear design vision that combines comfort and function. References describe the team as very willing and able to accommodate clients' interests and style preferences.

The principals previously practiced separately for over a decade, joining forces in 1995. Lichten holds a Bachelor of Arts degree from Brown and a Master of Architecture from Yale, and he practiced with both Edward Larrabee Barnes and Fox & Fowle. Craig holds a Bachelor of Arts from Wesleyan and a Master of Architecture from Princeton. She practiced with Skidmore, Owings & Merrill as well as Buttrick, White & Burtis. Most clients are located in and around the Tri-State area with other recent projects in New Mexico, Brazil and New England. The firm is opening a Chicago office in 2004.

Lichten Craig's projects usually entail substantial renovations and new construction, but the firm is also willing to undertake smaller projects. References say that the principals are readily available and that the support staff is helpful. The firm also receives high marks for understanding family living and working well with contractors. The practice charges standard architectural percentage rates or a fixed fee. Interior design is done on a standard design fee plus markup.

"They are professional and really want to please the client." "They were more disciplined on budget than we were." "Their coordination was terrific—the furniture and window treatments were installed immediately after construction finished." "Joan carefully listened to my ideas, then came up with creative solutions beyond my initial thoughts." "They stayed with me when the contractor said it was impossible to build a straight staircase between the three floors of my apartment. And they made it work just perfectly." "When the construction is finished, I will be sad to not see them regularly."

Lisa M. Mockler Architects, LLC
32 Greenwich Avenue, Greenwich, CT 06830
(203) 622 - 4276   lisa.mta@verizon.net
Detailed custom residential architecture

Louis Mackall, Architect   4.5   3.5   5   5
135 Leetes Island Road, Guilford, CT 06437
(203) 415 - 6988   louismac@pantheon.yale.edu
Collaborative architecture, millwork specialist

Clients rave about Louis Mackall, who is said to be brilliant, kind and keenly attuned to the client's needs. With fans from the Dakota in Manhattan to Connecticut, Westchester and Long Island, this "consistently creative" architect and "Renaissance man" is lauded for his willingness to both lead and follow new design paths. Clients say he "constantly outdoes himself, making each rendition more exciting" and developing the maximum impact for reasonable fees. A graduate of Yale and Yale Architecture School, Mackall has been practicing architecture since 1968 and also co-helms Breakfast Woodworks, one of the region's best millwork outfits.

Clients tell us they are impressed with Mackall's guidance during the project, saying that he turns around drawings and ideas swiftly, keeping the project on track. He is known to be gentle with clients and tough with subs in the same calm, measured manner that both respect. Clients tell us he "saves money on the spot," and that he is almost "too fair" when it comes to pricing, which he does typically on an hourly basis. We hear he takes on only a few jobs at a time and is completely dedicated to making each one a success.

"His always calm manner and a well-timed sense of humor combined with his skill and flexibility made it easy and fun to work with him." "He gave this neophyte good guidance throughout the project." "Louis took a napkin sketch and turned it into a collective dream, adding value in the details, conceptualization and execution where we didn't know it existed." "A no-brainer-type of recommendation." "I had two ratty apartments. He turned it all into a $5-million spread." "We had a roof leak and he came down and stood there to make sure every nail was pounded in."

Macintyre Associates Architects
157 Heather Drive, New Canaan, CT 06840
(203) 966 - 2203
Residential architecture

Mark P. Finlay Architects, AIA
1300 Post Road, Fairfield, CT 06824
(203) 254 - 2388   www.markfinlay.com
Traditionally-inspired architecture suited for modern living

Mark Finlay has earned a reputation from clients and peers alike for his respect for traditional architecture while implementing his strong sense of contemporary living. He is also noted for highly detailed and thorough site plans. The firm takes on a substantial number of high-end residential endeavors, but also designs multi-family homes as well as historical renovations and commercial commissions. With homes that fit seamlessly into their environments, Finlay is said to "make the complicated dreams of his clients become reality."

Finlay, who holds a Bachelor of Architecture from Kentucky, is the principal of this firm he established in 1984. Finlay currently has a staff of twenty strong, with seven registered architects. While the firm takes on numerous projects in Connecticut, it is also registered in Arkansas, Colorado, Florida, Georgia, Massachusetts, New Jersey, New York, North Carolina, South Carolina, Rhode Island Vermont and Wisconsin.

Melanie Taylor Architecture & Gardens   4   4   4   5
688 Orange Street, New Haven, CT 06511
(203) 498 - 0820
Lively classical residential architecture

From initial client meetings through the end of construction, clients applaud Melanie Taylor for her accessibility and "selfless dedication" to each project. Taylor is known for her "spirited and vivacious interpretations of classical design" including renovations to vernacular American architecture peppered with Caribbean and Southern influences. Her traditionally styled shells are often filled out with traditional interiors, but with an eye to contemporary functionality. These open floor plans are said to be "warm, friendly and inviting."

This six-person practice was established in 1990 after an eight-year partnership in another firm, and training with the highly respected Allan Greenberg. Taylor keeps her workload manageable, taking on only five or six projects each year, ranging from $300,000 renovations to $3 million ground-up homes. Most of the firm's work takes place in Fairfield and Middlesex counties, but Taylor has traveled to the Bahamas, Colorado and Rhode Island for clients.

She has established relationships with a particular contractor but is said to work freely and collaboratively with contractors chosen by the client. Handling all aspects of the design, Taylor is said to be gifted at dealing with shoreline and waterfront sites—a clear influence of her upbringing in the Bahamas. The firm charges a standard fee based on a price per square foot or hourly rate.

Murphy Burnham & Buttrick Architects   4.5   4.5   5   4.5
48 West 37th Street, 14th Floor, New York, NY 10018
(212) 768 - 7676   www.mbbarch.com
Residential and institutional architecture and interior design

This highly regarded firm is said to work within the context of the site or existing structure with talent and ease. Clients appreciate the manner in which the firm builds and maintains relationships, creating a loyalty that keeps the vast majority of clients coming back for multiple projects. The firm generally accepts single-family, new-home construction projects ranging from around 1,200 square feet to upwards of 8,000 square feet and major gut renovations. The majority of the firm's projects have substantial budgets that reach multimillion dollar proportions, but they will also do smaller projects with modest budgets for repeat clients. The firm does institutional, commercial and residential works that, we are told, bridge modern and traditional idioms.

Partners Harry Buttrick, Mary Burnham and Jeffrey Murphy each bring extensive knowledge gained from working on projects for some of New York's most treasured institutions. Most of the firm's work is done in New York, Connecticut and Florida, although it has also completed projects throughout the US, Europe and Africa. The twenty-person firm takes on twenty five to thirty new projects each year and offers a complete range of architectural, planning and interior design services. Buttrick has worked as an architect in New York for 40 years—he previously founded Buttrick, White & Burtis. He holds multiple degrees from Harvard. Burnham (Buttrick's daughter) was principal of her own firm for six years and holds degrees from Penn and Yale. Murphy practiced as principal of his own firm for seven years after working with I.M. Pei and Gwathmey Siegel & Associates. He received a bachelor's degree from the University of Virginia and an Master of Architecture from Harvard.

The firm charges a higher hourly rate or percentage of total construction costs and structures proposals to meet the needs of its clients. Clients strongly recommend them as one of the only firms in New York to bring an "institutional memory" and distinct awareness of historically based traditions and "upscale nomenclature" to a project with classical proportions.

"We just love working with this team. They are thoughtful, kind, considerate and masters of their craft." "They understand what is 'correct' and aim for the highest standards." "They renovated our historically based apartment, and it is as fresh and thoughtfully conceived as the original design was 80 years ago." "They can do traditional or contemporary, whatever is appropriate." "Harry's strength of character is reflected in his architectural work and in his client base."

Naiztat and Ham Architects   4.5   3   5   5

45 Perry Street, New York, NY 10014
(212) 675 - 2932   www.naiztatandham.com

Residential architecture

Clients find this experienced husband-and-wife team "truly a gem," while peers tell us they "keep getting better with each job as well." Not bad for a firm many already consider one of the most professional and talented architecture outfits in New York City. Naiztat and Ham is equally comfortable designing in modernist or traditional styles, creating interiors that are "at once innovative and classic." The two met while studying at Cornell. Their thirteen-year-old firm commands a high volume of work, both residential and commercial, mostly within New York City. A gut renovation or sub renovation is the norm, running from $200,000 to $15 million. For new clients it needs to be a full project, but for old clients we're told the firm will do anything that is interesting. It has undertaken work in Westchester and Connecticut.

References describe the small shop as creative and reliable and its partners as very approachable and amazingly responsive, noting the team was "always on the spot during unexpected problems, devising solutions with care, compassion and efficiency." Clients add that Naiztat is "one of the most visionary designers they have had the opportunity to work with" and that she is thorough, meticulous and full of "great ideas with color and space." The firm is commended for its ability to listen to ideas while remaining honest to the integrity of the structure. Sources agree that "they know their business well and are fun and easy to work with" and say they will return for future projects. Naiztat and Ham charge a flat fee for a scope of work and hourly for anything above and beyond that established scope.

"Get them while you can. Or at least get on their waiting list." "They have a knack for maximizing design within the constraints of a real budget." "I especially enjoyed the dynamic between Diane and Alexander, and they're both extremely creative in their own way." "The professionalism and attention to detail that Diane

Naiztat and Alexander Ham bring to each project is unsurpassed." "They take ownership of the project, delivering quality customized service." "The duo was absolutely tenacious, working through the problems inherent with the existing structure until they created something that far exceeded our wildest dreams." "Having worked with dozens of architects, they are the best I have seen and currently the only architects I will use on the 100 or so projects I will be doing."

Neil Hauck Architects

859 Post Road, Darien, CT 06820
(203) 655 - 9340
High-end residential architecture

Oliver Cope Architect

151 West 26th Street, 8th Floor, New York, NY 10001
(212) 727 - 1225   www.olivercope.com
Distinguished, classically-inspired residential architecture

Specializing in a variety of "historic styles," Oliver Cope is praised by insiders for his "comprehensive and thorough" approach to the design of truly American homes. Cope encourages clients to be highly involved and an integral part of the design team. We're told the firm works closely with the best contractors to ensure a "seamless product" with the highest detail and custom craftsmanship. Sources say the firm is careful to respect the ideals of traditional design while implementing the most modern amenities. Cope has completed numerous distinguished homes in and around his New York City location—and beyond.

With a team of fifteen, Cope leads this relatively small firm and is personally involved in each project. Cope and Co. collaborate on everything from conceptual design, interior design, millwork and construction administration. Cope holds two degrees from Harvard, including a Master of Architecture. With his "tasteful, elegant" designs, he is an architect with a loyal client base who comes highly recommended from industry insiders. Fees are said to be in line with other upper-echelon architects in the area.

Opacic Architects

	4	2.5	5	4.5

24 North Astor, Irvington, NY 10533
(914) 591 - 4306   opacicarchitects@aol.com
Residential architecture

References are "completely blown away" by this architect's imaginative designs and incredibly detailed drawings. Opacic focuses on larger, extensive residential renovations, splitting its work between New York City and Westchester. Clients tell us Opacic's specialty (besides the meticulous thought he gives to all of the details of a design) is that each project is marked by direct and continuous involvement by the principal of the firm. They say he guides them through the design process from inception to completion, and while he "has definite ideas," he "always listens well." Rad Opacic is described as conscientious, considerate, and enjoyable to work with. Schedules and budgets were easy to discuss with Opacic, we hear, with any changes along the way to the original plan "worked out well as to not delay the project." After such a "great experience" many have rehired the firm and recommend Opacic to friends, who are also extremely pleased.

"Wonderful work, wonderful people. Very fair, considerate, good listeners." "At the start of the project I gave each of the people at the firm Swatch watches to remind everyone that time was important. It must have worked because everything ran on schedule." "Beautiful moldings, lovely woodwork, plans to die for, so detailed and well drawn." "Really nice. Overall, you are working with someone who is conscientious and extremely pleasant, so little things and slight delays do not matter." "Has great ideas. They do very detailed work and respond to my wishes."

	Quality	Cost	Value	Recommend?
	✚	$	◆	★

Patrick Gerard Carmody
4	3	5	4.5

523 Hudson Street, Suite 2FS, New York, NY 10014
(212) 206 - 3620
Traditional residential architecture

Carmody's classical approach to architecture extends beyond style to execution. He tends to work in a traditional vein with a light touch. Clients say Carmody has particular gifts with space design and the relationship of functional elements. In his methodical management of details and patient attention to client preferences throughout many rounds of revisions, this young architect has come to produce "the best work by a sole practitioner I have ever seen," says one contractor.

Before starting his own firm four years ago, Patrick Carmody studied architecture at Rice University and then worked at Saunders and Walsh. He now does mainly high-end residential projects in New York City, many of them 3,000- to 4,000-square-foot gut renovations on Park and Fifth avenues. Projects outside Manhattan have included a Shingle style house in Westchester and a clean-lined Art Deco style home in Miami's South Beach.

Carmody is described as "highly professional, efficient and a perfectionist" by both clients and contractors. He is known to always have the client's best interests at heart. In turn, they find him a "lovely man" and tell us he is "very good at managing the small and large details of the project, which made me feel that nothing was getting lost between the cracks." Carmody's work is described as "top-notch" and well worth the comparatively modest fee based upon cost of construction.

"What continues to impress us is the outstanding quality of his work and his high standards of excellence." "I could not imagine a better architect—I just wish he'd consider becoming a contractor." "His quick mind and lively imagination mix winningly with his quaint Louisiana charm." "We quickly learned to read his silences." "His design was graceful, simple and precise, deceptively so."

Paul Benowitz Architects
📁	📁	📁	📁

55 Locust Avenue, Rye, NY 10580
(914) 967 - 0557
High-end residential architecture

Paul F. Hopper Associates
📁	📁	📁	📁

20 Bruce Park Avenue, Greenwich, CT 06830
(203) 869 - 2422   archopper@aol.com
Custom residential architecture

Peter Cadoux Architects PC
4	3.5	4	4

35 Post Road West, Westport, CT 06880
(203) 227 - 4304   www.cadouxaia.com
Traditionally rooted, site-sensitive residential architecture

Sources say the charismatic Peter Cadoux takes on projects "of significant detail and creative design" that are predicated more on the unique architectural challenge than the size of the home—or its budget. From formal Federal and Georgian homes to more laid-back Nantucket Shingle style residences, Cadoux most often designs in a traditional language. Each project is said to be "site-intuitive" with extensive study of prevailing winds, topography and other site conditions. Cadoux and his staff are said to "creatively bring the feel and theme of the exterior into the interior" by designing right down to the hardware, fixtures and appliances.

The firm handles numerous waterfront projects, and clients say Cadoux knows all the nuances, intricacies and code requirements of coastal construction. From single professionals who work in the city to empty-nesters expanding family estates, Cadoux has a diverse client base, nearly all of whom live in Fairfield County. With a busy and successful firm with an exclusive clientele, sources say, "don't be surprised if there's a waiting list" for Cadoux's services.

Cadoux, a graduate of Rhode Island School of Design, established this firm of eight in 1992. He and his staff take on about six new homes and ten renovation projects each year, carrying budgets of $500,000 to $10 million, although "he'll do an interesting kitchen if it's up to his standards." The firm charges a slightly lower than standard percentage of overall construction costs.

Peter Talbot Architects

10 Titus Road, Washington, CT 06794
(860) 868 - 9408   talbotarch@msn.com

Custom residential architecture

Philip D. Goiran, AIA

861 Post Road, Darien, CT 06820
(203) 656 - 3003   pgoiran@snet.net

Custom renovations centered on family living

3.5   2.5   4.5   4.5

The thrust of Goiran's work revolves around a "socio-centric point of view" that is broken into four parts: private and public spaces; adult-chid relationships; and diurnal/nocturnal and seasonal patterns. It is this highly cerebral family-oriented approach that attracts couples who are looking to create the perfect living environment to raise children and "grow old with the home." By creating a dialogue between the original structure and its renovation work, Goiran is able to seamlessly integrate the new with the old while "amplifying the vocabulary of generations of architecture." Goiran concentrates primarily on renovations in which his eclectic design works effortlessly with a broad spectrum of styles from colonial to modern.

Goiran is a sole practitioner who began designing on his own in 1982. He holds a Master of Architecture from Penn and an undergraduate degree from Brown. The architect works locally, with most of his projects taking place in and around Greenwich. He doesn't have a website or e-mail address—so reaching him by phone is your only option. Goiran generally takes on about ten projects each year, ranging from small $200,000 jobs to $1 million gut renovations. The firm charges a lower fee that is based on a combination of a fixed fee through schematics, a percentage of the construction budget and an hourly rate.

Richard Henry Behr Architect

2 Weaver Street, Scarsdale, NY 10583
(914) 722 - 9020   www.rhbpc.com

High-end custom residential, commercial and institutional architecture

From quaint guest homes in and around New York City to lavish oceanfront homes in Florida, Richard Henry Behr is known to have a discriminating clientele that "appreciates fine design." We hear Behr is particularly adept at maximizing views, assessing sites and placing the home to blend appropriately into the surrounding community and natural environment. The firm is reputed to work "effortlessly" in a traditionally inspired environment, but is adaptable to many styles of design depending on the context of the area and the client's tastes. The firm works extensively throughout Westchester County, with a fair share of work in southern Connecticut and Vermont.

Behr, who holds an MBA from NYU and a Bachelor of Architecture from Minnesota, established the firm more than 25 years ago. The firm has two studios—one in Scarsdale and the other in Burlington, VT. Handling dozens of projects each year, Behr and his staff design everything from highly customized single family homes to large commercial institutional endeavors. He's even designed the Muppets' New York City studios. Behr's select residential projects are often substantial in size—and in budget.

Richard King Architects   3.5   3   4.5   4.5

12 Old Boston Post Road, Saybrook, CT 06475
(860) 388 - 9395

Traditional New England architecture with a twist

Known as a "regionalist" architect, Richard King is known to put a contemporary spin on traditional New England designs. He is said to bring a refreshing interpretation of the classic Shingle style homes, particularly on the waterfront. However, it is King's ability to sense a home's "proper setting" with regard to the client's needs and the neighborhood's legacy that has clients and industry insiders recommending this respected architect.

King, a sole practitioner, started his firm in 1998. He holds two architecture degrees from Clemson University. King works with a wide range of clients, from first homes for young couples to retirement residences for retirees. About 25 percent of King's work is residential, and most of that is dominated by renovations. Most of the architect's work is institutional, dealing with colleges, universities and religious institutions.

Preferring to work alone to "think and draw at the same time," King is a local architect who works mainly in Middlesex and New London Counties. Projects range from $100,000 renovations to new homes of $1 million. The firm charges a lower hourly rate.

Richard Meier & Partners, Architects   5   4.5   5   5

475 Tenth Avenue, 6th Floor, New York, NY 10018
(212) 967 - 6060   www.richardmeier.com

Modern, forward-thinking institutional and residential architecture

An architectural deity himself, it's fitting that Richard Meier's clients include the Vatican. While museums, high-tech and medical facilities, commercial buildings and major civic commissions distinguish Meier's work, he still blesses residential clients with his renowned talent. We hear the Cornell-educated Meier selects serious projects with serious budgets. Recognized worldwide for his emphasis on light, geometric precision and extensive use of glass, Richard Meier's modern work exemplifies the architect's own definition of his profession: "Architecture is the thoughtful making of space."

Meier's work shows the influence of Le Corbusier in the balance, mathematical rhythm and cubic forms it employs, but focuses on creating volumes of space within a building. Meier's predominantly white palette highlights vertical and horizontal elements and shifting grids, and porcelain panels often lend luminosity to otherwise monochromatic surfaces. A winner of the prestigious Pritzker Award in 1984, Meier's arguably most acclaimed work is the Getty Center in Los Angeles. AD 100, 2000, 2002. ID Hall of Fame.

"As good as it gets." "The Itzhak Perlman of architecture." "The most serious architect working today."

	Quality	Cost	Value	Recommend?
	✚	$	◆	★

Robert Dean Architects   5   4.5   4.5   5

111 Cherry Street, New Canaan, CT 06840
(203) 966 - 8333   rdean@robertdeanarchitects.com

Distinctly planned, historically sensitive residential architecture

Sources tell us Dean's greatest attribute is his "sensitivity of time and space and the historical aspect of architecture," with a particular knack for renovations of landmark buildings. Possessing a "scholarly take on style," Principal Robert Dean's aesthetic is firmly rooted in the traditional vein with an interest in preserving the design ethic of the original structure. Dean is known to have an eagle's eye for rich woods and the rugged beauty of fieldstone, selecting materials that are appropriate for the site, client's lifestyle and budget. Sources say Dean makes an effort to "enhance the historical environment rather than disrupt it."

At any one given time, Dean will have about twelve active residential projects, mostly renovations or additions with a few ground-up homes. While his commissions generally command significant budgets ranging from $1 million to $5 million, insiders tell us Dean is extremely accommodating for repeat clients, doing much smaller projects in the name of sustaining the relationship. On top of that, Dean is said to "flat out be one of the nicest guys you'll meet."

Dean, who holds architecture degrees from Penn and Columbia started the firm of eight in 1986 after working with some of architecture's most notable firms, including Robert A.M. Stern and Philip Johnson. The firm charges a standard percentage of overall construction costs.

"Rob is just so easy to work with—he doesn't lock into a certain plan and say that's how it's going to be." "You'll have a conversation with him about the design and he'll come back in minutes with drawings." "Such wonderful detail and craftsmanship." "He keeps the integrity of the structure and it's simply stunning." "Rob knows how to use clever and creative ways to get the most out of the space he's working in."

Robert Orr & Associates   4   4.5   4   4.5

441 Chapel Street, New Haven, CT 06511
(203) 777 - 3387   www.robertorr.com

Traditional custom residential architecture with grace

Robert Orr and his staff are known for a unique design approach that incorporates sociological elements with the "dignity, grace and charm of traditional architecture." Orr, who is known as a highly intelligent and abstract thinker, has no style of record but creates homes that are "appropriate"—whether it's a humble farmhouse in a field or an imposingly elegant estate on the waterfront. Sources say Orr has such a strong grasp on old-time architecture that his designs effectively "resurrect the craftsmanship of generations long gone by."

Orr started his firm, which currently employs fifteen, in 1982 after working with legendary architects Philip Johnson and Allan Greenberg. Orr holds a Master of Architecture degree from Yale. The firm takes on about fifteen residential projects each year, with renovations starting at $200,000 and new homes carrying budgets of up to $10 million and beyond. Clients say Orr has an affinity for rich natural materials but also uses "warm man-made materials" that can save on costs without compromising the design.

	Quality	Cost	Value	Recommend?
	✚	$	◆	★

The firm works nationally and is said to excel in challenging site configurations including sandy lots in Florida, the Colorado mountain terrain and the coastal Connecticut wetlands. The firm charges a slightly higher fee based on fixed fees, hourly fees or a percentage of construction costs.

Robert Stewart Burton Architect

65 Pondfield Road, Bronxville, NY 10708
(914) 779 - 2171

Residential architecture

Roger Bartels Architects, LLC   4.5   4   4.5   5

27 Elizabeth Street, Norwalk, CT 06584
(203) 838 - 5517   www.rogerbartelsarchitects.com

Exquisitely-detailed waterfront residential architecture

For custom waterfront residences, clients say Roger Bartels Architects is "simply one of the best." In creating masses of light, space and maximizing views, the firm doesn't commit to a particular style, but one insider described it as "a modern interpretation of Shingle style." With an attention to detail and understanding of the historical context versus the modern lifestyle, it's no wonder clients repeatedly seek the Roger Bartels' services. The firm is praised for its ability to "capture and seize the true opportunities" presented with each site while "maximizing the human experience of the project."

Roger Bartels started the firm of seven in 1974. Principals of the firm are Roger Bartels, a Columbia graduate with a Master of Architecture and Chirs Pagliaro, who earned an architecture degree from Catholic University. Nearly all of the firm's work is residential, and is full-service—designing all cabinets, hardware and lighting. The firm also employs a licensed interior designer and conducts construction administration for the client.

The firm takes on 30 new projects each year, which carry budgets ranging from $500,000 to $7 million, with an average of about $1.5 million. Renovations are typically large-scale guts that alter the entire home. The majority of Roger Bartel Architects' work takes place in Fairfield County, but the company also works in Westchester, New York City, New Mexico, New Zealand, Rhode Island and beyond. The firm charges a standard percentage of construction costs.

"The creativity and attention to detail reflected in the plans prepared by Roger Bartels Architects is superior." "Roger was a zealous advocate of ours prior to and during the entire construction project." "Their designs are world class—creative, unique, proportioned and dramatic." "Their commitment to the client is unsurpassed." "Having experienced their work, we would never consider another architect!"

Roger Ferris + Partners   5   5   4.5   5

90 Post Road East, Westport, CT 06880
(203) 222 - 4848   www.ferrisarch.com

Intelligent, highly detailed custom residential and commercial architecture

According to sources this large architecture firm works and "feels" like a small one. First, this fifty-person office is divided into two studios—residential and commercial. The residential studio has twenty employees, yet takes on only six to eight projects each year, devoting the time and attention needed to uphold a lofty standard of detail and design diligence. Insiders say regardless of the style, Roger Ferris and his able staff "really dot all the 'Is and cross all the 'Ts.'" From its stark minimalist to Shingle style to "green" creations, the firm is recognized not for a style, but for excellence in design—and has seventeen AIA awards to prove it. Ferris is widely know for producing some of the best construction documents in the industry.

Residential work is split evenly between new-home design and large-scale renovations—however, the firm is selective about commissions it takes on. Those with very small projects should probably shop elsewhere, as Roger Ferris + Partners takes on projects starting at $1 million and topping out at $20 million. The firm works mainly in Westchester, Fairfield and New York City, but has completed projects as far away as L.A. and the Bahamas.

Principals of the firm are Roger Ferris who has a Master of Architecture from Harvard, David Beem who has a degree from RPI and Robert Marx who has a Master of Architecture from Texas. The firm also has a 30-person commercial design studio, handling high-end retail and office spaces as well as country clubs. The firm charges a slightly higher than standard percentage of overall construction costs.

"He really wants his work to matter." "Is not interested in leaving his fingerprint on the project, yet definitely leads the way with regard to design." "Roger is very exacting, definitive and upfront." "You couldn't get me to move out of this house for all the tea in China." "The columns seem to be floating right out of the yard." "His design is bold without being overpowering. Subtle and sophisticated at the same time." "I wouldn't even talk to another architect."

Saniee Architects   4   3.5   4.5   4.5
36 West Putnam Avenue, Greenwich, CT 06830
(203) 625 - 9308   www.sanieearchitects.com
Clean traditional residential architecture

Sources tell us the talented Mahdad Saniee displays a calm demeanor, subtle color palette and quiet confidence that "won't slap you in the face," but his tasteful and timeless design "will definitely wow you." With traditional detailing and an inventive view the architect pointedly address the needs of his clients, a Saniee home is said to exude a cross between modern and traditional design, using the ideals of classical architecture "as a springboard." His homes incorporate careful ornamentation with subtle traditional elements—and he is known to favor stone construction when it appeals to the client.

Saniee holds two degrees, including a Master of Architecture from the University of Edinburgh in Scotland. He also studied architecture at the British School in Rome. He started the firm of four in 1995 after working for nine years at the esteemed firm, Centerbrook Architects. The firm accepts five projects each year, and most are residential endeavors, although Saniee is known also for his educational and religious institutional work. Of the residential commissions, many are renovations starting at $400,000, and a few ground-up homes that start at about $1.5 million.

Saniee Architects works mainly in southern Westchester County and across Fairfield County, but has gone as far north as Maine and as far south as Maryland for projects. We're told Saniee is an excellent listener, and respects his clients' limitations, whether they are budgetary or site-related. The firm charges a slightly lower fee based on a combination of hourly rates and percentage of overall construction costs.

Shelton, Mindel & Associates   5   4.5   4.5   5
216 West 18th Street, PH, New York, NY 10011
(212) 243 - 3939
Residential, corporate and retail architecture and interior design

Tailors of "very handsome," "cutting-edge" design, Peter Shelton and Lee Mindel, FAIA, are known to "examine a polarity between modernism and traditional architecture" in their work. References laud the pair's ability to seamlessly integrate clients' romance with classical American icons and a contemporary clarity to create refined, controlled spaces that are minimal yet rich in detail. While not characterized by a signature style, after two decades in business the firm is generally recognized as conservative modernists. It is intimately involved in the interior design of its spaces, often creating custom furniture and lighting schemes that are said to be "brushstrokes of the larger plan."

	Quality	Cost	Value	Recommend?
	✚	$	◆	★

Clients report partners Shelton and Mindel are "smart, likeable, forward-thinking" architects who "exhibit zero attitude." The firm is also highly respected throughout the building and design professions. While we hear the rigor with which the firm pursues the realization of its design vision sometimes leaves less regard for creature comforts, clients say there's no question they feel at home in Shelton and Mindel's highly original, deft architecture. Both began their studies at the University of Pennsylvania. Shelton graduated from Pratt in 1975 and then joined Edward Durell Stone and later Emery Roth & Sons. Mindel graduated from Harvard in 1976 and worked for Skidmore, Owings & Merill and then Rogers, Butler, Burgun.

The firm currently employs about fifteen people and has received many tributes, including sixteen AIA awards and a place in the Interior Design Hall of Fame. The firm also designs products for Waterworks, Nessen Lighting and V'Soske. The firm charges a flat percentage of the overall construction to cover both their architecture and design fees. AD 100, 2000, 2002. HB Top Designers, 1999. ID Hall of Fame.

"Lovely people. Chic." "I highly recommend them for their high standards, impeccable designs and strong professionalism." "Absolutely highest quality, and high cost. Clients love them." "They can also do traditional, but not the chintz thing." "You must do it their way." "Very, very successful. Good designers. Very professional."

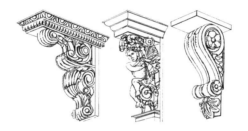

Shope Reno Wharton Architecture   5   5   5   5
18 West Putnam Avenue, Greenwich, CT 06830
(203) 869 - 7250   www.shoperenowharton.com

Cerebral, detailed, elegant, traditionally inspired custom residential architecture

Clients say this architectural team "harkens back to historical architecture with traditional shapes and details," yet creates homes that are "perfectly suitable for modern living." With open floor plans, liberal inclusion of glass and an emphasis on indoor/outdoor living, clients claim a Shope Reno Wharton design "is the best of both worlds." While sources tell us "the client dictates the style of the house," it is safe to say Shope Reno Wharton is best known for its fluency in traditional vocabulary and distinct interpretations of American Shingle style. Clients laud the architects of this firm for being able to "capture the spirit of the land and translate that into the spirit of the house." The firm's principals see the design and construction process as a "a symphony between the architect, builder and client." Despite their industry acclaim for being some of the finest architects in the country, clients tell us "you still get the partners and you get the team—there's no individualism."

Principals of this firm, which was founded in 1981, are Allan P. Shope, Bernard M. Wharton, Arthur Hanlon and Jerry Hupy. The firm generally accepts about a dozen new residential projects each year. All of these are ground-up residences that carry major budgets of up to $20 million—and averaging $2.5 million to $5 million. The firm has left its mark on waterfront homes and is said to approach such sites "with vigor and creative solutions." We're told a Shope Reno Wharton home has "a sense of permanence" with regard to fitting into and aging with its surroundings. Shope Reno Wharton also designs golf clubhouses, academic buildings and museum spaces.

Potential clients are strongly advised to be familiar with the firm's work and realize that Shop Reno Wharton is highly selective of its projects, regardless of budget. In fact, sources say the "perfect client" for the firm is one who "is highly involved, curious and full of ideas." While half of the firm's commissions take place in and around Greenwich, Darien and Scarsdale, this national firm has worked in 40 states from Florida to Wyoming. The firm charges a standard percentage of construction costs, however, it must be noted that its projects carry much larger budgets than a typical home. AD 100, 2000, 2002.

Stephen L. Lloyd
42 Liberty Street, Chester, CT 06412
(860) 526 - 5094
Custom residential architecture

Stephen Tilly   4   4   4.5   4.5
22 Elm Street, Dobbs Ferry, NY 10522
(914) 693 - 8898   www.stillyarchitect.com
Timeless 21st-century residential architecture

Stephen Tilly "does really good design work that lasts," sources tell us. It is this long-lasting and timeless design that has clients clamoring for Tilly's services. With an attentive approach to client input and a habit of hanging around construction sites monitoring contractors, Tilly is known to see each project through to the end. The architect's style is difficult to finger, but is said to be "21st-century personified." We're told he is "traditionally sympathetic" to existing structures during renovation but is well-versed in the technology of everyday living. His designs are described as "warm, but clean and spare."

Tilly employs environmentally friendly technologies in his homes that are known to be "closely related to the landscape and beautifully planned." Sources say that while Tilly may at first come across as soft spoken and reserved, the architect "loves talking about design and is intuitive and extremely thoughtful." Tilly and his staff are said to handle the difficult rocky and hilly sites across the Hudson Valley with ease. Tilly established the firm, which currently employs 21, in 1985.

The firm takes on about six substantial projects each year, and most are large-scale renovations. Construction budgets range from $400,000 to $5 million, with an average budget of about $1 million. Tilly earned a Master of Architecture degree from MIT. The firm charges a slightly higher than standard percentage of overall construction costs.

Studio DiBerardino, LLC   4   3   5   4.5
59 Grove Street Suite 1A, New Canaan, CT 06840
(203) 972 - 8704   studiod@discovernet.net
Historically sensitive residential architecture

Louis DiBerardino is best known for creating "simple, yet elegant" additions and "sensitive" renovations to older, historically significant homes across southern Connecticut. The firm works in many styles ranging from Colonial and Greek Revival to New England farmhouses and even Cape and Ranch style homes from the 50s and 60s. Insiders say DiBerardino simply knows how to create spaces "that make the most impact" given the restrictive homes and properties he works with. The firm tends to work with families who are seeking to expand their primary residences to accommodate their evolving lifestyles.

Concentrating on residential architecture almost exclusively, DiBerardino is a sole practitioner who started the firm in 1993. While the vast majority of his projects are renovation and additions with budgets starting at about $250,000, this architect also takes on an occasional ground-up residence whose budget can eclipse $2 million. For these larger projects, DiBerardino employs the services of a stable of outside consultants. DiBerardino, who holds an architecture degree from the RPI, keeps his practice small to work very closely with each client and to "control the outcome as directly as possible." The firm charges a moderate fee based on a combination of hourly rates and a flat fee.

Studio Dumitru   4   3.5   4   4

49 Richmondville Avenue, Suite 106, Westport, CT 06880
(203) 226 - 5156   www.studiodumitru.com

Traditionally inspired regional residential architecture

George Dumitru is praised by insiders for his meticulous documentation—whether it's keeping track of budgets, meeting deadlines, sourcing materials or overseeing the construction process. Sources tell us the firm is "happily busy," yet not in a big hurry to expand its staff of three. We're told Dumitru's clients are mainly those who seek renovations to homes of traditional design—particularly Colonial, Victorian, Shingle and/or Georgian influence. A big draw for many of Dimutru's clients is the personal attention he gives them—even if it means putting in hours on the weekends. His sensitive inclusion of large windows and use of lead-coated copper when possible is the architect's subtle trademark.

Dumitru was trained in his native Romania, where he earned a college degree and then earned a second at Pratt Institute. Dumitru earned his stripes with some of the area's most respected firms including Shope Reno Wharton and Kaehler Moore. He is the lead artist and principal of this small studio he founded in 1999. At any given time, the firm has three to five residential projects in various levels of completion. We're told Dumitru "takes all projects very seriously—even small renovations." However, his projects carry construction budgets anywhere from $200,000 to $1.5 million.

The vast majority of Dumitru's work comes from Fairfield County, although he has worked in Westchester and Rhode Island. The firm charges a slightly lower fee based on a percentage of overall construction costs or a fixed fee.

Taft Architects   🗁   🗁   🗁   🗁

5 Boutonville Road East, Bedford, NY 10590
(914) 763 - 6488

Highly-detailed custom residential architecture

Wadia Associates, LLC   5   4.5   4.5   5

112 Main Street, New Canaan, CT 06840
(203) 966 - 0048   www.wadiaassociates.com

Highly detailed elegant large-scale traditional architecture

Wadia Associates is noted for its broad range of expertise in all languages of traditional design—from American to English to French vernaculars. Clients frequently call on Dinyar Wadia and his team to create Victorian, Georgian, Tudor and Provincial styles of architecture. Wadia is personally, involved in each project, from conceptual design to "the last nail hammered." Clients say Wadia has unmatched sources here and abroad, and a keen ability to select materials that are full and rich, yet cost effective through the sources. We are told when you ink a contract with Wadia Associates, you truly get "soup to nuts" services, including interior design and building services upon request. Wadia Associates will even draw all custom tiles, moldings, cabinetry and libraries.

Dinyar Wadia received his architectural education in his native India and also earned a Master of Architecture from Columbia. He established the firm in 1975. Wadia keeps a staff of just seven in order to retain the "name on the door" philosophy, with personalized client relations. He attends just about every meeting personally and sees the project through construction. The firm works with an established clientele, who seek to turn their homes into homesteads for future generations—accepting two or three projects each year with budgets averaging from $5 million to $7 million.

All of the firm's work is residential and takes place in locales such as New Canaan, Greenwich, Darien, Norwalk and New Castle. Interior design services are also available independent of its architecture work. The firm charges a higher fee based on a percentage of overall construction costs, but we're told this includes all necessary outside engineers and much of the interior design.

William Green & Associates   **4   3.5   4   4**
6 West 18th Street, 7th Floor, New York NY   10011
(212) 924 - 2828   www.wgaarchitects.net
Residential and commercial architecture and interiors

This "boutique operation" achieves what we hear is an elevated level of service as a result of principal William Green's full-tilt management style. Sources say Green is adept at creating classically-oriented designs that are timeless and have a distinct respect for proportion and scale. He also approaches the actual drawing in a classic way, with everything being done by hand, right down to the tiniest molding or hardware detail. The architect is also known to design in a modern context with equal skill. He has continued to follow his vision of building homes that project "a sense of place" in the community, as well as creating designs that are sensitive to budgetary constraints without compromising the quality.

Green heads a team of four and projects are typically gut renovations, split between residential and commercial clients. However, the firm continues to take on more and more new-home construction outside the City, taking it to places like Greenwich, Upstate New York, the Hamptons and as far as Japan and France. The firm takes on approximately fifteen residential projects each year of varying scopes. Green is known to control all aspects of a project, be it design of architecture, landscape, interiors, or furniture, and we hear he pursues his vision through to the end.

Green is a very gentle, dedicated man, we hear, who tries to bring a serious artistic component to every project. Green is also known to be committed to ecological issues. He received his BFA from Tufts and a Master of Architecture from University of Colorado. Before starting the firm in 1986, Green worked with design giants Skidmore Owings and Merril and Davis Brody. The firm charges a standard fee based on hourly or a percentage of construction costs.

"Bill has such a calming demeanor, nothing rattles him and that quality tends to create a really pleasant atmosphere." "He truly believes in what he is doing and his ideals are rock solid." "Have had a ten-year relationship with Bill working on both small and multimillion-dollar projects and I've never been disappointed." "Does beautiful work and has great taste." "A clear and meticulous thinker." "Offers visionary, competent and perfect service."

Hiring an Audio/Visual or Telecommunications Service Provider

These days, one doesn't have to crave global domination to enjoy a room that can, at the push of a button, transform itself into a ground-control headquarters that rivals any James Bond movie scene. Home theaters, multi-zone entertainment systems, home-automation and lighting controls, online capability—if you can dream it, they can hook it up. Just make sure you ask for the remote, or you may never be able to use what you paid for.

Audio/Visual (A/V) home service providers can seamlessly integrate almost anything—media walls, touch-screen panels, speakers, structured cabling—into your existing components or the architectural integrity of any room. And if they can't, they will build new cabinets to accommodate the equipment. Custom installation is the name of the game.

What to Expect From an A/V Specialist

A/V providers can be contracted through general contractors, designers or directly by you. Whomever they bill, communication with the homeowner is essential. When courting your A/V guru, remember that they may specialize in only a few of the following areas: audio, video, telephone, Internet, security, lighting and climate control. Many A/V designers and installers in Connecticut and Westchester County are also experts in telephone network installations, so keep this in mind when you are planning out the various communications and A/V systems for your home.

You should also keep in mind the following regarding telephone systems:

- ◇ Local telephone companies now offer a wide array of services: voice mail, call forwarding, three-way calling and caller ID (with or without ID block). A good telecom service provider will be able to customize a system that integrates multiple phone lines, intercoms and door buzzers to a networked and net-savvy home office.
- ◇ If you're putting in a home office, know how many lines you will need, where the fax and printers are going to be located, which computers will be networked and online and where you're going to sit.
- ◇ Most telephone system service providers have licensing agreements with certain system manufacturers and will deal only with them. If you're keen on a particular system, it's a good idea to contact the manufacturer for preferred service providers in your area. On the whole, all systems perform the same functions (automated directories, voicemail boxes, multiple lines/extensions, on-hold music, interoffice paging, caller ID) and offer the same accessories (headsets, holsters). It's the brand of the system, sophistication, complexity of integration with other systems and convenience of use that affect the cost. Systems can be purchased outright, leased or financed.
- ◇ Don't forget that a service provider who excels in home theater installation and telecommunications systems may not be as well versed in, or even deal with, security. You should also know whether the service provider can perform all the functions of integration. Determine your needs, get references, ask questions. Will the A/V specialist both design and engineer your project, or will he or she be coordinating with other trades?

✧ Even when working through a designer, a good A/V contractor will want to meet with you one-on-one to assess your needs. Make the time. You don't want your system to outreach your ability or desire to operate it. Don't get swept up in your tech-happy A/V provider's enthusiasm for all the bells and whistles available to you. Stand fast. Are you really looking for a movie palace complete with stadium seating, and does it really need to be tied into the landscape lighting and the air conditioner in the kitchen? Remember, the latest may not be the greatest if the newest innovation hasn't been around long enough to be tested. Some A/V contractors prefer a lag time of six months after the introduction of a product so they can follow its performance before recommending it to their customers. If you're the first one in on a new gizmo, know that you may be the first one to discover its flaws.

✧ The means of customization and the materials used differ widely from shop to shop. Some contractors only work in certain brands. Others will install anything you want. Request an itemized bid proposal and a sketch if you want the finished product to perfectly match your dreams.

Who Will Install My New System?

Although you'll talk first with either a principal or a representative of the A/V firm, traditionally a crew of field technicians will be dispatched to perform the installation and service. Don't fret—this crew is likely to be as well-informed and passionate about its business as any front man, so you should feel you're in good hands. But it's invaluable to be able to speak to the same person from the beginning to the end of the project.

Miscommunication commonly surrounds the role of the electrician in an A/V installation. Some A/V providers want your electrician to pull the low-voltage cable if he's already on site and holds a permit, eliminating a coordination headache. Many prefer to do it themselves, knowing that some electricians treat delicate cables with the care of baggage handlers at JFK or Bradley. Check that someone's on it before the walls close up. Also, know that A/V contractors won't usually install or relocate electrical outlets that will power up your system and provide the jolt for the sub-woofers.

Pricing and Service Warranties

The cost of your A/V project will be a reflection of the design work involved, the degree of customization, the type and number of devices and pieces of equipment to be installed, the length of cable to be pulled and the anticipated man hours, plus overhead and profit. Many jobs require a deposit of up to 50 percent, with progress payments to be made when materials and equipment arrive on site, and a final payment upon job completion. The warranty should appear on the bid proposal. A year of free service is standard.

LICENSE CONSIDERATIONS

Because this is a new field, there is currently no licensing requirement for A/V services in Westchester County or Connecticut. Fortunately, this also means that no permit is required. Check your municipality, however, because some areas require that these service providers be licensed and insured. If you're still confused, the Custom Electronic Design and Installation Association (CEDIA, at www.cedia.org) is an excellent resource.

NEW TRENDS

When it comes to home theater, digital video disc (DVD) players have become the staple of a good A/V system, offering much higher sound and visual quality than videos or laser discs. A movie on a DVD comes through with 500 lines of resolution, double the clarity of a 250-line videocassette. DVD players also offer lush Dolby Digital Surround Sound (DDSS). The quality of television output has advanced, too, with the advent of High Definition Television (HDTV) and Plasma TVs (those sleek, thin TVs, only four inches in depth that can be hung on the wall). Cutting-edge, multi-zone entertainment systems allow you to play CDs jukebox-style or listen to the radio or TV in any room of the house. For example, programming the system to air your favorite classical radio station through the bathroom speakers while you relax in the jacuzzi can be simply a matter of pressing a touch screen.

Some A/V companies also provide a full line of home automation services, including wireless lighting controls that you can operate from your phone (to turn the lights on if you'll be working late) or from a pad clipped onto your car's sun visor. Home automation also applies to climate control, with wireless systems that let you turn on the heat, air conditioning or lawn sprinklers from any room in the house—or from virtually anywhere, via telephone. Thanks to the latest user-friendly A/V programming systems, the days of not being able to program your VCR are over.

HOW TO GET THE MOST OUT OF YOUR SYSTEM

- ✧ Sit down with the installer to discuss your wants and needs in detail.
- ✧ Don't rush for the newest technology.
- ✧ Only install gear you'll actually use.
- ✧ Don't fall asleep during the technician's instructions on how to program each device.

AUDIO/VISUAL & TELECOMMUNICATIONS DESIGN & INSTALLATION

Aaron's Media Inc.   3.5   2   4.5   4.5

107 Harper Terrace, Cedar Grove, NJ 07009
(973) 477 - 3544   aaronsmedia@msn.com

Audio/visual and home theater installation and service

Customers roundly praise Aaron's Media and its principal, Aaron Brown, as effective, attentive and up-to-date on the latest technology. We're told that this small, three-person company works closely with clients, architects and designers to build and install the system that best suits the customer's needs.

Working across Westchester, Fairfield and the rest of the Tri-State region, Aaron's Media mainly focuses on larger projects that include whole-home audio and video and home integration systems. However, sources say the company is just as diligent about smaller-scale projects. References also note that they found Aaron's reliable and trustworthy, so much so that several have felt safe leaving their keys with Brown for installations.

"Service is his middle name." "No surprises." "Focuses on making sure the customer is happy." "Aaron even made my mother happy, which is not easy to do."

Ambiance Systems   3.5   3.5   4   4

1650 Route 9, Clifton Park, NY 12065
(800) 694 - 0770   www.ambiancesystems.com

Audio/visual home theater, lighting and multimedia installation and integration

Many high-profile clients in Westchester and Fairfield counties say they have relied on Ambiance since its founding days in 1986. Ambiance has grown from a local company working with clients in upstate New York to ranking among the top 50 dealers nationwide, according to *CE Pro* magazine. Although the company's specialty is in high-end systems, we're told the firm will also take on moderately sized home A/V projects. Ambiance will work with clients directly or through their architect, contractor or designer to provide a range of technological solutions, including home theater, lighting control, home automation, data/communications and closed-circuit TV surveillance.

We're told every job is assigned to a project manager who is quick to answer questions and concerns. Clients also appreciate the on-call 24/7-availability service. The systems designed are described as fully integrated, highly customized and easy to use, and clients are given a thorough training lesson to get to know their system.

"The technician spent a long time with me, making sure I understood how to use the system. Very thorough instructions, and I felt comfortable using it from the start."

Audio Command Systems   5   4.5   4.5   4.5

694 Main Street, Westbury, NY 11590
(516) 997 - 5800   www.audiocommand.com

Audio/visual design, installation and integration and home automation

Rated by *CE Pro* magazine as the highest-revenue-producing firm in the United States in 2000, Audio Command Systems (ACS) is recognized by clients and peers alike as one of the best in the business. We're told the ACS staff members have the latest training and knowledge in emerging technologies and provide superb service. Founded in 1976, ACS handles audio, video, home theater systems, home automation and telephone systems. In addition, the company coordinates the electronic management of automated lighting, home ventilation and air-conditioning, security and other "smart house" system components.

With four facilities in New York, California, FLorida and Georgia, a staff of more than one-hundred and over thirty installers in New York, sources tell us ACS is in great demand and generally works on large, high-end projects. Typical projects run at $75,000 and up, so this may not be the company for a small project. ACS works all over Westchester and Fairfield counties as well as New York City. The company boasts a 13,000-square-foot Westbury facility where technicians build, assemble and test systems as well as perform demonstrations for potential clients. Insiders say the one- to two- year service warranty is exceptional—as are the high-end products such as Crestron, Runco, B&W, Fujitsu, Sony and JBL.

"Big staff with big ideas." "The best technology available, and you can tell the staff is passionate about it." "Extremely professional and timely—a very well-oiled machine." "Recommending these guys is the best favor I could do for any audiophile."

Audio Video Crafts   4.5   3.5   4.5   4
9-09 44th Avenue, Long Island City, NY 11101
(212) 996 - 8300   pa@avcrafts.com
Audio/visual home theater, intercom and lighting design, installation and integration

Audio Video Crafts' reputation for high-end, quality custom systems is backed by a client list with many high-profile celebrities. Rated by trade magazine *CE Pro* as one of the top 50 dealers nationwide, this firm designs and installs custom home theaters, audio/video systems, lighting and intercoms. Principal Paul Austi established the company in 1987 and quickly earned a reputation with New York's more recognizable figures. Audio Video Crafts focuses solely on residential projects, with an average budget of $100,000 or more.

If the job is a big one (and we hear many of its projects are), the design, which is computer-aided, is free, as the firm charges retail for the components and installation services. Audio Video Crafts currently has a staff of twenty-two, with twelve installers, and the company is said to charge a lower service fee. Sources tell us the company has greatly improved its service on smaller projects and offers a full two-year warranty on all of its work. The firm has a showroom available by appointment only and has been featured on the cover of *CE Pro* and *Sound and Sight* magazines.

"They no doubt have an A-List clientele." "Initial installation and response was great." "They actually get great joy out of designing and demonstrating high-end systems to potential clients." "These guys are serious professionals. I respect their love of the business and desire to design to the highest quality standards."

Audio Video Systems Inc.   5   4   5   5
40 West Elm Street, Greenwich, CT 06830
(203) 861 - 0707   www.audiovideosystems.com
Audio/visual design, installation and integration and home automation

In business for over 25 years, Audio Video Systems designs and installs high-end home entertainment and integration systems for a variety of residential and commercial customers across Westchester and Fairfield counties. Acclaimed by manufacturers and industry publications alike, this 30-person firm delivers top-quality service to the greater New York area with its talented and accessible technicians and Greenwich showroom.

Locally, the firm has completed many large-scale projects including screening rooms complete with popcorn makers, plush theater seating, hidden projectors and motorized screens. Designers and contractors recommend the firm for its eye for detail and ability to coordinate, while clients are repeatedly impressed by follow-through and willingness to please after the job is finished. Audio Video Systems has established itself as one of the "best and brightest" in the industry, rated by *CE Pro* magazine as one of the five top-selling firms in the country.

"Went beyond the call of duty and exceeded all my expectations. Their technicians were courteous and professional, and their response time was quick and efficient." "Head and shoulders above the rest." "These are my guys—I wouldn't go with anyone else." "They make things idiot-proof." "Came back to teach my child about the system after he wasn't initially around to learn it." "They treated my project with the utmost respect and didn't make me feel like my job was too small for them. Customer service was great, too—very friendly and informative."

Audio/Video Excellence, LLC   3   3   4   3.5
343 Manville Road, Pleasantville, NY 10570
(914) 747 - 1411
Audio/visual and home automation

For the simple to the most advanced custom home entertainment systems, from Sherman to Mamaroneck, Audio/Video Excellence delivers. For more than seventeen years, this firm has specialized in whole-house audio and video distribution, custom media rooms and home theater designs. Insiders note the company's exceptional service team does on-site service and repair which is a major draw for its clients. Audio/Video Excellence also has a large home theater showroom.

Additionally, the company handles home automation by linking lighting, heating, ventilation, security and telephone systems to operate in total harmony. Sources are generally pleased using Audio/Video Excellence to refine their lifestyle by bringing 21st-century technology to their home, including laying down the wiring for local area home computer networks and installing closed-circuit television surveillance systems.

Audiodesign   4   4   4   4
1955 Black Rock Turnpike, Fairfield, CT 06432
(203) 336 - 4401   www.audiodesign.com
Custom home theater design and retail sales

Clients say Audiodesign's one- and two-year warranties are a huge reason for the firm's dedicated clientele and busy schedule. The firm has been in business since 1983 and was bought by current owner Ira Fagan in 1999, and serves all of Westchester and Fairfield counties as well as New York City and beyond. With a growing business designing dedicated media rooms, residential cinemas and multiroom A/V systems, Audiodesign handles upwards of 150 projects each year that range from small $5,000 retail jobs to massive $500,000 custom systems.

Nearly all of the firm's work is residential (with the occasional boardroom or restaurant project), with labor rates ranging from $75 to $130 per hour. Audiodesign has a staff of eleven, five of whom are installers. The company also installs telephone, lighting and climate-control systems—but not computer networking or wiring. Although the firm does sell products at retail, we're told it is highly service-oriented and really helps the end user feel comfortable with the system.

"Hey, with a two-year warranty that includes service and in-home maintenance, I certainly wouldn't roll the dice and go somewhere else." "Good work, good workers."

	Quality +	Cost $	Value ◆	Recommend? ★

Cabling Technologies, LLC   4   4   4   4.5
78 Spring Hill Avenue, Norwalk, CT 06850
(203) 831 - 8230   www.ctcable.com

Home integration and technology

See Cabling Technologies, LLC's full report under the heading Computer Installation & Maintenance

Cerami & Associates Inc.   4   4   4   5
404 Fifth Avenue, New York, NY 10018
(212) 370 - 1776   www.ceramiassociates.com

Audio/visual system design, acoustical engineering, telecom and soundproofing

While Cerami & Associates won't come to your home and install A/V systems, we're told the firm's acoustical engineers are adept at consulting and designing high-end systems. Most of the company's projects are large-scale commercial and institutional jobs. Cerami & Associates does about twenty custom residential projects each year. The company works on projects around the country, but focuses its attention on suburban and metropolitan New York.

With a staff of 35, this company has been consulting on acoustical issues since 1965 and working on large home theaters, home automation, telephone systems, computer networks and video conferencing since 1995. Cerami's rates are on the higher end of the spectrum, but clients say it's a small price to pay for peace of mind. While there is no written warranty, we're told Cerami & Associates will always fix any glitches with their design.

"This is a serious company for serious systems when it comes to residential work." "The only game in town for high-quality acoustical engineering." "They preserved my neighbors' sanity and our relationship due to the sound of my gym over their bedroom."

Davco Custom Sound & Video Contractors   4   3   5   4
50 Commerce Street, Norwalk, CT 06820
(203) 662 - 0040   www.davcoinc.com

Wide-ranging residential audio/visual and automation systems

Sources say John Davis knows high-end residential sound and video. With all of his work being in the residential arena, Davco is known to be a highly competent company with very reasonable rates. In business since 1980, Davis is experienced in designing home theater, A/V, home automation, telephone and lighting-control systems from Manhattan to Cape Cod. The company has a one-year warranty on its workmanship and a 1,500-square-foot showroom that features manufacturers Elan, Lutron, Crestron, Bose and Sony, among others.

Davis and his partner, Greg DellaCort, work directly with clients on most projects, although the company enjoys a steady stream of projects from architects, designers and contractors. The company currently has ten employees, five of whom are installers. About half of Davco's 50 annual projects are big ones with budgets of more than $100,000, although we're told the company does a number of smaller projects ranging from $5,000 to $75,000.

"Their installation and service costs are hard to beat." "Can do just about anything and do it well." "Doesn't make you feel silly when you ask questions. He knows not everyone understands technobabble."

Design Installations   4   4   4   4
4 New Canaan Avenue, Norwalk, CT 06851
(203) 847 - 2777   dean@designinstallations.com

Complete low-voltage services

With nearly all of the company's projects focusing on high-end residential audio/visual and home automation systems, Design Installations has earned a stellar reputation from clients and the competition alike. The company serves all of Westchester and Fairfield counties as well as New York City and select projects in Vermont, Martha's Vineyard and the Hamptons. Typical projects, which can include high-end large-scale home theater systems, telephone systems, computer networking and lighting controls range from $30,000 to $40,000 and can be upwards of $200,000. Labor rates range from $75 to $125 per hour.

More than half of the company's projects come directly from client referrals, but Design Installations also works very closely with architects, designers and contractors. In business since 1984, this firm of eight (six of whom are installers) is headed by partners Dean Smith, Rick Samuels and Dave Church. With a 2,000-square-foot showroom featuring Crestron, Lutron, Runco, AMX, Marantz and Yamaha products (among others), Design Installations is said to provide excellent service and up-to-the-minute knowledge at good prices.

"Rick and the rest of staff are serious about what they do and know the ins and outs better than most." "It's really great that these guys can do it all and I don't have to call seven different companies."

Electronic Interiors Inc.   4.5   4   4.5   4.5
40 West Elm Street, Greenwich, CT 06830
(203) 629 - 5622   JillKent@aol.com
Highly customized high-end audio/visual systems and home theaters

With more than twenty years' experience designing cutting-edge home theater systems, Jill Kent of Electronic Interiors has built an A-list clientele that includes some of Hollywood's most recognizable names as well as sports figures and corporate tycoons. Kent takes on about twenty projects each year with substantial budgets starting at $50,000. Most of her referrals come from the trade, but she does a fair amount of work directly with homeowners. Using Crestron integration systems and Lutron lighting systems exclusively, insiders say Kent creates highly customized systems based on the client's needs.

Kent's services also include home automation systems, lighting controls and 35mm screening rooms upon request. Kent has a Greenwich showroom and offers a one-year parts and labor warranty and honors all manufacturers' warranties. She is a founding member and current board member of the CEDIA trade association. Having been featured in *Architectural Digest*, *Fortune* and *New York* magazines, Electronic Interiors Inc.'s services do not come cheap, but we understand the quality is of the highest caliber.

"Terrific client presentation." "You can tell she knows her stuff after about 30 seconds talking with her." "She's got great sources that are well-priced." "I'm kinda tech challenged—I can't even program my VCR, but this stuff is fun to play with and she taught me well." "A delight to work with."

Electronics Design Group Inc.   4.5   4   4   4
60 Ethel Road West, Suite 4, Piscataway, NJ 08854
(732) 650 - 9800   www.edgusa.com
Audio/visual, home theater, lighting, telephone/intercom systems integration

This New Jersey-based firm has been at work for more than fifteen years, providing state-of-the-art electronic technology for residents and corporations across the Tri-State area. Recognized as one of the country's top 50 dealers by trade magazine *CE Pro*, Electronics Design Group specializes in the integration and installation of sophisticated home theater, multi-room audio, lighting, home automation and telephone/intercom systems.

Clients comment on the smooth interaction between Electronics Design Group and architects, builders and interior designers, although the firm also works directly with homeowners. While the quality of the firm is hardly questioned, some report that getting a response from the company, at least in the beginning, is a bit of a challenge.

"An A+ rating from me." "After an initial phone call, I didn't hear back for quite some time." "These guys proved to be the most efficient, reliable and overall best A/V company that I have had the pleasure of working with."

Harvey Electronics   3   3   4   3.5

2 West 45th Street, New York, NY 10036
(212) 575 - 5000 www.harveyonline.com

Audio/visual and home theater installation and service

With six locations throughout New York, New Jersey and Connecticut and roots dating back to 1927, Harvey Electronics has practically become a household name. Customers tell us the staff at Harvey has intimate industry know-how and delivers an excellent product—but some warn that this company has grown to a point where customers may feel lost in the shuffle. Local sources tell us Harvey is a good solid shop, but personable client interaction is not a strong suit.

The company's specialty is installation and design of home theaters and audio systems, including consultation on design or collaboration with clients' architects or interior designers. Though clients note that working with Harvey involves paying retail, they report the company offers the added benefit of accepting trade-ins on old components. Customers report being pleased with the technicians' work.

"A good dose of the new technologies here." "Offers tons of alternatives, and the client service was better than I expected."

Innerspace Electronics Inc.   4.5   4   4.5   5

179 Summerfield Street, Scarsdale, NY 10583
(914) 725 - 4614

Home integration systems

Since 1988, the husband-and-wife team of Andrea and Barry Reiner has been designing and installing home theater, audio/video, lighting control, home automation, acoustical design, soundproofing intercom systems and boardrooms for high-end clients locally and nationally. With a staff of twenty-six that includes ten installers and five engineers, Innerspace Electronics is said to have reasonable service rates and the ability to handle projects ranging from $12,000 to $750,000 (with a typical project of $80,000 to $150,000).

Clients praise the "sophisticated, yet simple to use" systems, and references say Innerspace is the place to go for those interested in home management systems. Sources say the staff comes with a wealth of knowledge and the company receives high marks for remaining available to clients long after the project is finished. With high-end products such as Runco, Sonance, Audio Request and Crestron combined with a good one-year parts and service warranty, clients say the company is worth its higher-end price tag.

"Will stay late and often until the job is done right." "Responded right away when I messed things up." "Not only really good at what they do, but Barry and Andrea are just genuinely nice people." "We're thinking of flying them to California to wire our home out there, because we can't find anyone else as good."

	Quality	Cost $	Value ◆	Recommend? ★

Lyric Hi-Fi Inc.   4   4   4   4.5

146 East Post Road, White Plains, NY 10601
(914) 949 - 7500   www.lyricusa.com
Audio/visual and home theater installation and service

Since launching the business more than twenty years ago, we're told Lyric remains on the cutting edge by identifying trends before they reach the market. The White Plains office is an extension of the New York City operation, and has a total of five employees (three installers) and covers all of Westchester and Fairfield counties as well as Bergen County, New Jersey and points north. The company's work can be seen and heard in homes around the world including the Bahamas, India, Brazil, the south of France and Italy.

The company handles a wide range of projects, from smaller home A/V systems of $10,000 up to $500,000 home automation and cinema systems. Lyric is roundly applauded for its excellent follow-up, remaining available to clients long after the job is complete. Labor rates are on the expensive side, but Lyric offers a one-year warranty on all parts and labor for manufacturers such as B&W, Marc Levinson, Magnepan, Loewe, Runco and others.

"Company is well trained and experienced." "Although the office isn't as big as the New York one, it's just as capable." "Work was well thought out and included extra capacity wiring to allow for future capabilities." "Responded immediately whenever renovation contractor was ready for his work or had a question."

Metro A.V.   3.5   3   4.5   4.5

128 Musgnug Avenue, Mineola, NY 11501
(516) 294 - 2949
Audio/visual systems and integration

For more than fourteen years, partners Tom Dolciotto and Chris Washburn have grown this small firm from the seeds of exemplary customer service, installing home theaters, audio systems, home integration and CCTV. We hear their attention and responsiveness have been welcomed from Westchester and Fairfield to Manhattan and Long Island. Metro is known to work in concert with the client's architect and designer to get exactly what is needed both visually and technologically. Clients describe this firm as professional, honest, dependable and personable.

"Well worth the money because they provide a value-added service that you can't get elsewhere." "Wiring up all the rooms of my penthouse was a challenge, but Tom Dolciotta and his staff did an excellent job."

OPUS   4.5   4   4.5   4.5

85 Willow Street, New Haven, CT 06511
(203) 498 - 0407   www.opusavc.com
Custom audio/visual design and installation, lighting control and home theater

Clients love the service, personal attention and "technophile know-how" of the entire Opus staff. With one of the best warranties in the business (two years parts and labor), superior products and a real sensitivity to deadlines, Opus has earned itself a loyal following that includes entertainment celebrity-types and corporate big-wigs. Founded in 1990, the original partners, Eric Borgstrom and Mark Nimrod have recently expanded to include David Barson. The company is said to excel in the highest-end custom A/V systems. OPUS handles about fifteen major projects each year, with budgets starting at $100,000 and topping out at a whopping $1 million.

Opus has eight employees, four of whom are certified installers. Most of Opus' work is residential and comes from architects and contractors, with projects from Boston to the Hamptons. Customers can visit a 2,000-square-foot showroom at the company's New Haven office. Sources say the firm has fostered a loyal clientele through "establishing long-term relationships through personalized services and being good listeners." Opus' services don't come cheap, although clients in the high-end say they expect to shell out a little extra for a top-tier product.

	Quality	Cost	Value	Recommend?
	➕	💲	◆	★

Performance Imaging · 4.5 · 4 · 4 · 4.5

115 East Putnam Avenue, Greenwich, CT 06830
(203) 862 - 9600   www.performanceimaging.net

Audio/visual, integration and home theater installation

In its six years in business, Performance Imaging has established itself as an industry leader and is recognized by *CE Pro* to be among the top 50 dealers nationwide. Even the company's competitors acknowledge the company's good track record and ability to handle large, cutting-edge home automation and A/V projects. Located in Greenwich, Performance Imaging receives enthusiastic applause from clients for their designs and installations of residential and commercial audio and video distribution, lighting, home automation and security systems.

Architects and designers praise Performance Imaging for creating systems that are invisible until activated. Homeowners agree and say their attention to detail and willingness to explain technical details is worth noting. While the company's services don't come cheap, sources say excellent maintenance services and diligent follow-ups make it all worthwhile.

"*No doubt, they're one of the big dogs in town. They handle some serious projects.*" "*Accommodating, resourceful and sensitive to my budget concerns.*" "*They were able to use my old equipment to keep costs down.*" "*Dependable.*" "*I am a lifelong audiophile, and I couldn't be happier or more impressed with the system they designed.*"

Scott Trusty · 4 · 2.5 · 5 · 5

127 Joffre Avenue, Stamford, CT 06905
(917) 459 - 8901   bok22@optonline.net

Audio/visual, home theater installation and repair

Clients trust Scott Trusty. Trusty's services include complete design, installation and repair of custom audio, video and home theater systems, with a particular interest in home automation and control systems. Trusty has been working in Westchester and Fairfield counties for more than 30 years and works almost exclusively on residential systems. While he has earned a reputation for installing and repairing high-end systems, Trusty has recently stepped up his consulting services, walking clients through the "maze of conflicting information" about home audio and video.

One reference, a professional in a related field, tells us that Trusty "knows everything about sound." We hear he is just as attentive on small jobs as he is on larger projects and that he doesn't miss the details, right down to working with the contractor on the appropriate type of plasterboard to be used for the ultimate acoustics or doing research on the perfect TV for a client's specific space and budget needs. Trusty generally takes on projects of less than $50,000 and clients appreciate his personalized attention on each one.

"*He's a straight-shooter—you won't get any BS from him.*" "*He's been around long enough to tell the difference between a gadget and a meaningful piece of equipment.*" "*Passionate about what he does, great with people and he delivers.*" "*Absolutely fantastic.*" "*He's the only contractor my wife feels comfortable leaving alone in the house.*"

	Quality	Cost	Value	Recommend?
	+	$	◆	★

Sound Ideas

28 Kaysal Court, Armonk, NY 10504
(914) 273 - 2510

Audio/visual, integration

For more than five years, principal Tommy Alleva and his congenial staff of twenty have been fitting Westchester and southern Connecticut with custom home theaters, multi-room audio, home automation and central control systems. Sound Ideas also specializes in structured cabling and design layout. This service-oriented company generates almost all its business by satisfied customer buzz.

Video Installations Plus Inc.   4   3   4.5   5

45 East Hartsdale Avenue, Hartsdale, NY 10530
(914) 328 - 1771   www.avtelecom.com

Audio/visual design and installation

Insiders tell us principal Alan Poltrack's philosophy that "people need help on all levels and budgets" makes this company popular with its customers. Whether a client wants a $200,000 home automation and cinema or a $15,000 Hi-Fi audio system, we're told the staff at Video Installations Plus listens intently to questions and provides excellent service. The company is best known for integrating audio, video, satellite, telephone and lighting systems for clients from Westchester to Connecticut to Long Island—and will even outfit your boat.

The vast majority of the company's 30 annual projects are residential and come from client referrals—however, Video Installations Plus is known to work very closely with architects and contractors. A small company of six, Video Installations Plus earns glowing comments from customers for designing systems that are user-friendly with a solid one-year warranty covering parts and labor on all its craftsmanship.

"A small company that really takes the time to work with you individually." "Very willing to explain and teach how to use the equipment." "Has more than twenty years experience in the business and it shows." "Consistently does excellent work."

Hiring a Computer Installation & Maintenance Service Provider

Maybe you'd like to connect the computer in your home office to the one in your teenager's room in order to share Internet access. You're worried, however, that if you do it yourself, your "network" will turn on the ceiling fans and trip the security system. Fortunately, there are plenty of computer service providers who install networks and software, set up new computer systems and do other tasks that would take up much of your precious time. Today's world requires a new approach to home computer needs, and computer technicians have up-to-the-minute knowledge. Though home networks aren't that common quite yet, they are fast becoming essential in a high-speed world of connectivity. Your computer setup needs to be as custom fit as a tailored suit for you to get the full benefit. While common sense dictates that you should leave the nitty-gritty details to a skilled technician, knowing what to expect will streamline the process.

Do I Need a Computer Network?

What is a network, exactly? A cable modem? DSL? A wireless network? A firewall? And, most important, are any of these relevant to your needs or current system?

The most basic network is two computers connected to each other so they can share files, Internet access and printers. If you have to save something to a disk, then put that disk into another computer to open a file on the second machine, you are not on a network. Network size is almost limitless, and the largest corporations and government offices have a mind-boggling number of computers exchanging information. A common home network consists of three computers: the home office machine, the kids' computer and maybe a laptop. In a network, computers are linked to an Ethernet hub, which is then linked to a printer and a modem. This usually requires running wire throughout the house and coordinating phone/cable jacks.

Why should you consider a home network? Quite simply, convenience. With a home network files can be transferred easily, printers, scanners and Internet access shared and phone lines freed up for that important incoming call from your mother-in-law. While this may seem like a sophisticated setup for a home, times are changing. Many kids now do their homework on the computer, more people work from home and everyone wants to be on the Internet—all at the same time. Home networks can save money because they avoid the added expense of multiple printers and Internet hookups. You'll need to buy a hub, the connection point for all elements of a network, which starts at about $50. Though most new computers already have network software installed, you may need to buy network cards, which cost from $15 to $50.

High-Speed Internet Connections

Internet access through a conventional phone line severely limits your online speed and efficiency. Both a Digital Subscriber Line (DSL) and a cable modem are as much as 100 times faster than a standard analog (telephone) hook-up. A DSL line uses the same cabling as regular telephone lines, but it operates on a higher, idle frequency, allowing the user to be on the Internet and the telephone at the same time. Also, DSL service is always connected, so the user never has to dial up and wait for a connection. Cable is a broadband connection, which means that lots of information can travel simultaneously (that's how all those cable channels can be available at the same time). A cable modem is also always "on," but it runs on TV cable lines. The speed is comparable to DSL, with one difference: Cable modems use a shared bandwidth. This means that speed depends on how many users are using that cable service: The more users, the more traffic, and the slower the connection. Because DSL runs on single telephone lines, this isn't an issue. In both cases, find out whether the telephone lines and cable connections in your area are equipped with this service. There are various providers, and promotions offering free installation are common. Computer technician companies will install the DSL connection, but generally are not providers themselves. Monthly service for your connection will cost between $35 and $60. The monthly charge for broadband connections (usually for businesses) can be as high as $300.

Most broadband service packages and home network packages come with a firewall installed. This indispensable part of any Internet-ready computer protects the system from hackers and includes options such as a parental control feature, which allows parents to block inappropriate sites.

THE WIRELESS ALTERNATIVE

Wireless networking is newly available and can be a practical choice in some cases. It saves having to drill holes through your walls and makes the layout of a home office or computer network more flexible. If the network needs to be expanded, wireless networking makes the change easy and inexpensive. A wireless network consists of an Ethernet hub and PC cards inserted into the computers. These cards extend slightly from the machine and each has a small antenna that sends and receives information. Wireless networks can operate as quickly as a standard network. The hub can cost anywhere from $200 to $600, and the PC cards range up to $150. Have a computer technician advise you on whether or not a wireless system is best for you.

BUYING A NEW COMPUTER: WHERE DO I START?

If your experience lies specifically with PCs (IBM compatible) or Macintoshes, you may want to stick with the type of computer already familiar to you. (Some technicians focus on one type or the other, which can narrow your search for a good techie, too.) If there are children in the house, consider what machines their schools use. One computer technician suggests starting with an issue of *PC* magazine or *Macworld* to see what's available and use it as a reference when you speak to someone about models, memory sizes and accessories. This way you can get a clear idea of what appeals to you and have a more productive conversation with your computer consultant.

ON COST

Computer technicians generally charge an hourly service fee, which can range from $65 to almost $200 per hour. In *The Franklin Report,* standard costs fall in the range of $100 to $125 per hour. However, please remember there are other factors that may affect the final cost. Before you hire a technician, ask whether the fee is calculated only in hourly increments. If you go fifteen minutes into the next hour, are you charged for a full additional hour? You will be charged extra for whatever hardware or software you purchase. Discuss exactly what will be installed to avoid hidden costs.

The key to any home service is the quality of the time spent, not the quantity. A good service provider will not squander the hours for which they are billing you but will arrive prepared to solve your problem as quickly as possible. Ask whether the technician charges for advice on the phone after he's made a house call. Often he won't if you just need clarification on the service he recently provided. Once you're a customer, some technicians will even respond to a new question if it doesn't take too long, but others will want the clock to start running again. Find out your techie's policy and how flexible he is. Some consultants offer a package containing a given number of help hours, which can be a combination of an initial house call, follow-up visits at home and time on the phone. This might be a good option for someone just starting out.

INSURANCE AND CONTRACTS

Most computer maintenance technicians carry some sort of business insurance protects them from the repercussions of damaging your computer or network. This insurance is for everyone's benefit, and any service that handles office networks as well will carry it. If you chose a smaller operation, find out if and how they are covered. Computer service providers may have contracts with business accounts, but it is rare with home service. Ask your technician about the firm's policy.

WHAT TO EXPECT FROM A TECHIE

Depending on the scope of the service, the principal of the company may perform the work personally or send out technicians. The key is finding someone who responds quickly and whose service is reliable. Also, since the computer industry moves at such a fast pace, it's infinitely helpful to work with someone who knows where it is going and shares that knowledge.

Steer clear of computer service professionals who act as if everyone should have been born with a computer gene. In truth, a lot of people just nod when they are told they need an updated USB port in order to handle the increased amount of EDI coming in over the DSL lines. You want someone who will listen to you, set up exactly what you need and ensure that you fully understand it. Quickly try to get a sense of whether the techie helping you only speaks in techno-babble. Believe it or not, there are technicians out there who can make computers understandable—even to you—and you shouldn't have to put up with someone who does not patiently explain things in plain English.

Keep in mind that chimps in university labs can learn how to play computer games. If Cheeta can do it, so can you.

Internet Jargon
(At least you can sound like you know what you're talking about.)

✧ **bandwidth:** Measured in bits per second (bps), bandwidth is the amount of data that can be both sent and received through a connection.

✧ **bozo filter:** An email feature that allows the user to block messages from specific individuals. Can help reduce spam by creating a list of unwanted addresses affectionately named a "bozo list."

✧ **cookie:** A message a web server sends to your browser when certain web pages are visited. The cookie is stored and a message is sent back every time the user requests that page. This allows the page to be customized. For example, after you purchase something on Amazon.com, your user name will appear to welcome you every time you log on from the same computer.

✧ **cyberspace:** The interconnected, nonphysical space created by the Internet and the World Wide Web, where information is transferred and people communicate electronically through computer networks.

✧ **DSL (Digital Subscriber Line):** A method for sending data over regular phone lines. A DSL circuit is much faster than a regular phone connection. It uses the same wires already in place for regular phone service, but since it uses an unused frequency you can talk on the phone while connected to the Internet with only one line.

✧ **ISP (Internet Service Provider):** A company that provides access to the Internet, usually for a monthly fee. Most homes use an ISP such as AOL or CompuServe to connect to the Internet.

✧ **LAN (Local Area Network):** A computer network limited to the immediate area, for example, a private residence. Ethernet is the most common type of connection used for LANs.

✧ **modem:** A communication device that allows a computer to talk to other computers. Modems vary in speed from slower telephone modems to significantly faster DSL and cable modems.

✧ **netiquette:** The accepted rules of conduct that define polite behavior in cyberspace. If you breach the rules of netiquette, you can be sure your fellow users will let you know.

✧ **network:** Any two or more computers connected together to share resources such as files, a printer or Internet access.

✧ **newbie:** Term for someone who is new to computers or the Internet. It is not an insult, just a description. If you are reading this, you could be a newbie.

✧ **snail mail:** Regular paper mail delivered by the US Postal Service. Why use the Postal Service when you can shoot a letter over in seconds via email?

✧ **spam:** Junk mail over your email, which wastes your time and the network's bandwidth. Ways of combating spam include filters or private service providers such as AOL.

✧ **T-1:** A wide bandwidth Internet connection that can carry data at 1.544 megabits per second.

✧ **URL (Uniform Resource Locator):** Represents the address used to locate a certain file, directory or page on the World Wide Web.

✧ **web browser:** Software such as Netscape Navigator or Internet Explorer that allows the user to access the World Wide Web by translating the language used to build web pages. Short term: "browser."

Computer Installation & Maintenance Service Providers

Cabling Technologies, LLC   4   4   4   4.5
78 Spring Hill Avenue, Norwalk, CT 06850
(203) 831 - 8230   www.ctcable.com
Home integration and technology

Brian Jaworski is known as a "no-nonsense professional" who "stays on top of all types of technology." While our sources specifically praise this company of four for its home computer and networking services, Cabling Technologies is also a reputed firm for all types of home integration—from lighting control and HVAC systems to design and installation of customized high-end A/V home theaters. For its computer services, the firm handles installation, network setup, consultation on products and on-site training mostly for PCs. They have a close relationship with Dell computers, which keeps prices down.

The firm's coverage area includes all of Fairfield and parts of Westchester counties—and there is no charge for travel time. When it comes to a service call for the computer end of the business, we're told Cabling Technologies's free phone support for existing clients can take care of most problems. However, for all its services, the company offers a 24-hour emergency service line to resolve issues over the phone. But if a service call is needed, be prepared to pay $175 per hour after hours and a reasonable $110 per hour during business hours.

Clue Enterprises   📁   📁   📁   📁
101 Cassilis Avenue, Bronxville, NY 10708
(914) 961 - 2175
Computer networking and servicing

Computer Guru of New York   4   2.5   5   5
31 Union Square West, Suite 15E, New York, NY 10003
(212) 243 - 0532   david@silberman.org
Computer training and troubleshooting

The Computer Guru, aka David Silberman, is a dedicated technician who is available seven days a week, and offers training and troubleshooting for both Macs and PCs. Insiders tell us he also provides installation, networking and consulting services to businesses and individuals, and backs it all up with phone support. Silberman does not sell hardware or software—nor does he do repairs. But he does offer consultation for clients looking to purchase systems, and can recommend a repair specialist. Silberman has clients across the New York City area and handles projects in Westchester and Fairfield counties—but you'll have to pay his traveling costs. Given that his rates are some of the best in the business, it just might be worth summoning him from the city. Clients report that Silberman is generous with his time, and they are happy to recommend this fair and friendly company.

"Top-notch in every regard—and a bargain." "I always recommend him to friends." "I consider it a plus that he calls to alert me if he'll be late." "He's an extremely honorable guy."

	Quality	Cost	Value	Recommend?

Computer SuperCenter   4   4   4   4

103 Mason Street, Greenwich, CT 06830
(203) 869 - 0910   jonathan@computersupercenter.com
Service-oriented home technology

Sources tell us Jonathan Gould and his staff of fifteen "really go out of their way to establish long-term relationships" with their clients. It is because of this highly personalized approach that Computer SuperCenter relies on mostly repeat clients to keep the business prospering. The SuperCenter handles both Macs and PCs, including installation, fully authorized repair, network installation and consultation on systems carried at the company's retail location/service center.

Computer SuperCenter charges a reasonable fee of $119 per hour, but doesn't offer 24-hour service (or any service on Sundays). The firm does charge for travel time, billed on its hourly rate. Existing clients get free phone support for minor glitches. The firm has been in business since 1982 and serves most of Fairfield County and parts of Westchester.

"Their technicians really know their stuff."

CTSI Consulting/Computer Tutor   3.5   3   4.5   4

118 West 79th Street, New York, NY 10024
(212) 787 - 6636   CTSI@nyc.rr.com
Computer consulting and training

Bruce Stark and CTSI Consulting/Computer Tutor has offered consulting and training services for all types of computers for nearly twenty years. CTSI can help you research and purchase a system as well as provide training and support for small networks, wireless networks, DSL and cable installations. The firm has four technicians, and sources tell us the trustworthy staff is competent and reliable. While CTSI has a devoted client base in Manhattan, the company has also gained a following in Westchester—but customers will pay for travel costs. Phone service is also available for existing clients.

"Quick, responsible, honest, fair. Only good things to say about Bruce—he's our computer guy." "He's extremely trustworthy—I give him the keys to my house. I love this guy." "He's technically competent and personable to boot." "They're there when we need them."

DGH Technologies Inc.   4.5   4   4   4.5

648 Central Park Avenue, Suite 455, Scarsdale, NY 10583
(914) 779 - 7409   www.dghtechnologies.com
Home and small business technology services

Clients say David Hoch is the go-to man in Westchester County for all your home (PC-based) technology needs. Hoch will "walk you through the process" from identifying what kind of computers you need to what kind of network you'll require. He's only got a staff of two, so make sure you give him a little lead-time—but because of the small operation, clients say they get sensible advice and "soup to nuts" service. Hoch is happy to answer quick questions over the phone to existing clients and doesn't bill for travel unless it's one hours' drive from his office.

Hoch has more than fifteen years in the information technology business, and sources say "he is a good guy with great service." Typical projects include a small home network with three desktops and a laptop connected wirelessly to the Internet. However, Hoch has a few corporate clients and can handle systems of up to 75 computers. He offers 24-hour service—but before you call him with an e-mail problem at 2:00 AM, remember that he bills at 1.5 times his steep $140 hourly rate.

"He has offered us the highest level of service, support and consultation I have experienced." "David has always been extremely professional in every aspect of the job." "He executed on what was proposed and did it in the time frame promised."

	Quality	Cost	Value	Recommend?
	✚	$	◆	★

EastEndTech   4   3   4.5   4.5

PO Box 1593, New York, NY   10028
(212) 772 - 1758   www.eastendtech.net

Computer installation and consulting

Don Klein brings more than 40 of years experience to EastEndTech, offering comprehensive computer services whether it's for a single PC in the home or consulting for a large company.   This includes installation, designing a system, service and most networking or Internet needs. Servicing everything the company sells (and much they don't sell), EastEndTech has earned a superior reputation for prompt and courteous service calls.

While the firm is knowledgeable of all things PC, EastEnd doesn't service or install Macs. The firm serves Westchester, southern Connecticut and other suburban New York locales in addition to Manhattan and Long Island. EastEnd only carries enough inventory to honor its service contracts, so if you're looking to purchase a large system, don't expect it on the spot. However, once you're an established customer, hardware is supplied at cost.

"Always responded in a most timely manner and most of the time solved the problem." "Not only has he always been extremely reliable and available to solve any problems that arise, but he has helped our production by suggesting new products, networking and interesting ideas."

Family Computer Services   4   2   5   5

196 Danbury Road, Wilton, CT   06897
(203) 761 - 7915   www.ez13.com

PC-based home technology installation and service

For everything from PC tuneups to software phone support, sources tell us Family Computer Services "has got it all covered." Working exclusively with Windows-based computers, George Hill and his four-person crew handle installation, repair, networking, consulting and on-site training. Family Computer Services sells software and parts (with a markup) but doesn't sell complete systems. The firm currently has more than 50 clients in the lower Fairfield area and some of Westchester County. Most of these are home-based businesses with a smattering of commercial projects.

Family Computer Services is said to be very good at handling typical technology issues such as viruses, installing wireless networks, installing new hardware and fixing hard drive mishaps. The firm charges a low hourly rate of $75 and guarantees its results. If your problem isn't fixed, you don't pay. On evenings (only 'till 10:00 PM) and on weekends, you'll pay an extra ten bucks on the hourly rate. On long-haul projects, Hill charges by the mile, and if a hotel stay is necessary, it's on your dime.

MacTechnologies Consulting   3.5   3.5   4   4

545 Eighth Avenue, Suite 401, New York, NY   10018
(212) 201 - 1465   www.mactechnologies.com

Computer consulting, networking and training

As this company's name implies, MacTechnologies Consulting has offered Macintosh consulting services for the past ten years. In addition to consulting, Kem Tekinay and his staff provide custom programming, networking, troubleshooting, maintenance and on-site training, including e-mail, Internet and software support. MacTechnologies handles clients in Westchester County and New York City (a one-hour minimum is required), although technicians will travel farther afield—but there is a a two-hour minimum charge. Clients tell us that MacTechnologies does not sell Macs but can comply with most other customer requests.

	Quality	Cost	Value	Recommend?
	+	$	◆	★

Merritt Technology Group, LLC

544 Old Post Road, Suite 3, Greenwich, CT 06830
(203) 661 - 0357   www.merritttech.com

Residential and commercial technology consulting

NuLogic Inc.   4.5   4   4.5   4.5

360 East 88th Street, Suite 21C, New York, NY 10128
(212) 427 - 7408   www.nulinc.com

Comprehensive commercial and residential computer consulting

Whether building networks or firewalls, NuLogic gets clients' computer systems up and keeps them running. NuLogic specializes in Internet technologies and security, but the company also offers installation, upgrades, maintenance and consultation on all types of computers and platforms. Lars Larsen comes highly recommended by his clients, who concur that he is a master of his trade, and is extremely responsible and pleasant. Larsen doesn't sell hardware or software, but clients tell us he can help sort out the good from the bad and recommend a system for you. Though NuLogic works with businesses of all sizes, we hear that many individuals also call on the company for help with their home or home office needs. Larsen and his staff of consultants also do work in Westchester County, Connecticut, New Jersey and across New York City.

"Lars has never ever let us down. He is always there, fixing our problems and keeping our business running smoothly." "Lars is reliable, dependable, brilliant—he can solve any problem, no matter how difficult." "Timely, responsive and, above all, a nice guy. I couldn't wish for a better computer guy." "Lars is exceptional at what he does, as well as extremely pleasant and very responsible. He is a valuable, irreplaceable part of my work life."

Reality Works Consulting   4   3   4   5

49 Hopbrook Road, Brookfield CT 06804
(203) 740 - 7082   tristerk@aol.com

Computer networking and high-speed connections

Reality Works Consulting provides large, corporate-level information technologies to small businesses and individuals in Westchester County, southern Connecticut and New York City. Chris Doherty, the company's principal, is particularly skilled at addressing connectivity solutions for high-speed Internet access.

Additionally, Reality Works offers installation, troubleshooting, repair, networking and consultation services for both Macintosh and PC systems. References tell us that Doherty is patient and efficient, and they appreciate his down-to-earth approach of explaining complicated problems in terms they can easily understand.

"He has become a part of my life. We would be lost without Chris. You could not find a nicer guy and he is always there in an emergency."

Quality	Cost	Value	Recommend?
✚	$	◆	★

The Mac Doctor

5	3	5	5

50 Church Street, 1st Floor, Greenwich, CT 06830
(203) 869 - 1787   austinp615@aol.com

Mac-centric computer care

If your Macintosh is acting erratically or is feeling under the cyber-weather, it's probably time to call The Mac Doctor, otherwise known as Austin Pryor. This doctor makes housecalls and only operates on Macs—but Pryor is also into preventative maintenance. He'll come and give your healthy computer a checkup from time to time and set you up with the latest virus remedies (although Macs don't get viruses very often). He's also the Mac stork, as he will bring new additions to your Mac family after working closely with you to decide what kind of system works best for you.

And if you're a regular customer who doesn't really know how to take care of your new Mac, don't worry, just call Pryor's "Mac 911" and you'll get step-by-step emergency care over the phone. Just remember, this doctor doesn't work 'round the clock and calling him after 9:00 PM isn't advised. Pryor has been caring tenderly for Macs young and old from Norwalk to Rye for the past five years. Return patients all agree that Pryor's computer care even comes at a good price—$80 per hour.

"Austin provides the most efficient, timely service possible, plus he is an absolute pleasure to have around." "Austin has tackled every Mac problem we have ever had from the sublime to the complicated with humor and grace without sparing me a joke or two." "Austin helped me to accomplish all of my computer goals with clarity and with flair."

Hiring a Contractor or Builder

Understanding a big repair or renovation can be intimidating, especially the thought of selecting the top person in charge, the commander-in-chief—the contractor. That's why an excellent contractor is vital to any major household work. This professional, like a general, takes in the big picture as well as the details, is seasoned through experience, knows his troops and the system, gets the job done well and on time and wins your admiration in the process. Here's a field guide to enlisting a five-star contractor:

Job Description

A traditional general contractor (GC) bids and builds from an architect's or designer's plans and specifications (the contract documents). The GC's duties are to interpret the drawings, execute the contracts, secure the permits, supervise the trades, manage the budget, make the schedule, deliver the quality and call it a day. There are design/build contracting firms that will draw up the contract documents, eliminating the need for an architect. Be aware, however, many firms which call themselves design/build really only offer conceptual assistance. They do not have practicing architects in-house, and must farm out design services to certified professionals.

Some comment this one-stop shop approach more often than not results in uninspired design and cookie-cutter "McMansions," while others believe that nobody is more qualified to see a set of plans realized than its designer. It really depends on the aesthetic acumen of your builder. While the design/build route often appears less costly than hiring an outside architect, the architect serves as a critical check and balance to the GC.

Construction management offers an alternative to hiring the traditional GC. Clients themselves contract with individual trades and the construction manager handles all payments and project administration for a fee based on total job cost. Some clients laud this "open book" approach, while others say it lacks an incentive to save and adds another layer of costs.

We've often found the best GCs want to be involved early in the project and work closely with the architect or designer, even at the conceptual stage. It is at this point they can lend their experience to head off potential problems with the execution of certain designs, and help formulate a more precise picture of the project budget. Often homeowners will have the architect design the apartment or townhouse of their dreams, and then keel over when the bids come in 30 percent over budget. Using a GC in preconstruction gives the homeowner the ability to tailor their dreams to their budget without losing sleep.

What to Look for in a Contractor

Picking the right general contractor is all about communication. A homeowner needs to know as much about the GC's capabilities as the GC needs to know about a homeowner's expectations. With stakes this high—mortgages, reputations, living another day at your in-laws—it's time for everyone to feel completely secure in the leadership on the job and the direction of the project. You should feel comfortable stating your wishes to the contractor and have confidence in his ability to listen, explain, cooperate and delegate. Is this someone you can work with?

If you take the traditional bid and build route, make sure your contract documents are clear and thorough before you approach any GC. If you choose to go design/build, look for a firm sympathetic and attuned to your sense of style, and make sure the company does indeed produce quality detailed drawings. Signing up for preconstruction services gives you an opportunity to vet your GC without committing to the whole job. Your candidate should be experienced in jobs of a similar type: restoration, renovation or new construction. Do you want a versatile GC or one that specializes? The GC should be well versed on the architectural features, building applications, specialty installations, customization and level of quality you expect. Consider the scale of the GC's past jobs, including cost and total square-footage. You don't want to be the job stuck below the radar screen of a commercial-minded contractor, or hook your wagon to a little guy who can't muster the horsepower.

You want the GC to be fluent in the code requirements and logistical considerations of your locale. Negotiating the wetlands restrictions in New Canaan is very different from building on the shore in Greenwich or rehabbing a landmark home in Bronxville. The city and state permitting and inspection processes, guard-gate community boards, and building management companies are notorious instruments of delay. Also, nail down your GC's availability. If he can't commit to a target start date, you cannot depend on his ability to stick to a completion date, and chances are you'll be living in a construction battle zone for an indefinite time.

Finally, you wouldn't let a stranger in your door, so before you invite a platoon of workers brandishing power tools and sack lunches, get references. The GC's listed in this section are certainly among the most reputable we've found, but talk to clients and inspect jobs in progress yourself to get a feel for a GC's abilities and current slate of jobs. Also talk to those clients with jobs completed to get a reading on how a GC maintains his word and work.

On Cost

Typically, three bids should suffice for a clear and fair comparison of estimates of project cost. But in a hot market it still may mean approaching twice that number just to get a telephone call returned. The more established GC's may bid only for architects with whom they have a relationship, or referrals, or on particularly plum projects. The most sought after work on a negotiated fee, and are hired not for the bottom line, but for the fact a client feels 110 percent secure with his choice.

Cost is a reflection of material and labor (as provided directly or through subcontractors), bonding and insurance, the general conditions (overhead to keep the job running) and the fee. General conditions and the fee are calculated as percentages of the total hard-construction costs, approximately 12 to 25 percent in Connecticut and Westchester these days (20 percent is the norm), though the percentage will vary depending on the cost, size, complexity and location of the job. Bonding offers insurance against a GC's failure to perform or pay subcontractors. It's a protection against negligence and liens—claims of debt that can be attached to the title of your property and prevent it from being sold until all liens are settled. Insurance covers full liability and Workman's Compensation. Any and all associated permit fees (calculated by the city as a percentage of total job cost), deposits or taxes also figure into the cost.

For the most part bids should fall within several thousand dollars, and the degree to which prices vary depends on the quality and cost of their subcontractors, internal resources and overhead, their ability to interpret plans accurately and honestly, their ability to meet the schedule, how conservative they wish to estimate, and of course, you. At the end of the day your choice of materials and methods of construction, as well as change orders, determine where the chips are likely to fall.

In *The Franklin Report* a 3 Cost reflects a contractor typically charging twenty percent profit and overhead on $10,000 to $500,000 projects that involve standard high-end technical or decorative work.

NEGOTIATING THE BIDS

Jumping on the low bid may be tempting, but don't take the bait. If a bid is enticingly low, it almost assuredly signals that the GC doesn't fully grasp the scope or has value-engineered without your consent. If a major cost discrepancy in the bidding process does arise, chances are someone either caught an unnoticed problem and accounted for it (in which case hire them), did not thoroughly read the plans (in which case don't hire them), or the architectural documents themselves are too vague (in which case get on your architect.)

A good GC doesn't lowball, he negotiates. Don't be shy about requesting a thorough cost breakdown. If the GC's numbers come from subcontractors, you may ask for the subs' bid sheets. Remember, the more subcontractors are employed, the more overhead and fee markups will inflate the bottom line. In-house carpenters, for example, are a plus, giving the GC direct control over a trade many consider the engine that drives the job. Any top GC draws from a small, consistent stable of subcontractors. These prices tend to be higher due to lack of competition and constant demand for the subs' service. While loyalty speaks for standards of quality, it's always your prerogative to ask the GC for an alternative sub. Just don't be surprised if he refuses.

COMMISSIONING YOUR GENERAL

Cost is always a factor, but at the end of the day personality is at least as important. Again, can you work together? Don't settle for anything less than a principal of a contracting firm who expresses interest in the status of your job both at the outset and throughout. The tone is set from the top. You should feel like you can trust not only your GC with the keys to your house, but also enjoy having him around. Goodness knows he'll be spending enough time there.

Once the job begins, he should dispatch an on-site supervisor and assign a project manager. In some cases a working foreman will super on-site, in others it may be the company owner. In any case, these on-site managers will be the ones coordinating with your architect or designer. Weekly site meetings are a must. As with picking the right GC, running a smooth and successful job is all about communication.

GET IT IN WRITING

Every detail should be recorded on paper. The plans and specs furnished by your designer provide the fundamental outline of the job. This means noting every raw material and product—including brand, model number, color and installation method. Be meticulous. If it's not on the drawings, it's not going to show up in your home, unless of course you're willing to sign the change order.

The change order, you ask? If you make a request that deviates from the project's scope as defined by the contract documents, expect to pay. Some changes may be inevitable, if you are unfortunate enough not to have x-ray vision or if you fall prey to your own whimsical inclinations halfway through the job. But be sure that any charges passed under your nose weren't already in the original contract. Ask your architect or construction manager to investigate each submission to make sure everything's on the level, otherwise its up to you. Spell out in the contract how change orders will be handled. A smart idea is to fix the unit costs for labor and material that were established with the original contract so there are no surprises about price of extras.

Be warned, a GC's obligation to meet code does not shield you from a city's permitting and inspection schizophrenia. Your contract documents must refer to the applicable codes. Because many are open to interpretation, a city official on a bad day can be a major source of change orders. The rub: if it's not on the drawings, the GC will not claim responsibility. Remember, however, that the GC should be absolutely responsible for obtaining the necessary permits for the job. This includes filing your plans and specs with the city for review and approval.

DECIDE UPON A PAYMENT SCHEDULE

If your partnership with a GC is a waltz, and contract documents the choreography, then payment provides the music. Your contract should specify the schedule of payment. Nothing will undermine a job more than misunderstandings about money. If payment is expected on a certain date, don't expect workers to show up if you miss it. Commit to what you can do. The most desirable arrangement is progressive payment on a phase-completion basis. Use benchmarks, like pouring the foundation or rocking up the walls, to close the end of a phase. Agree on the amount of each payment beforehand. It's a great incentive to push the GC through each phase.

Monthly payments are an alternative, but this setup commands more attention to accounting and is less of an incentive. A request for bi-weekly payments does not bode well—it may indicate that the GC doesn't have the capital to run the job properly. In any case, if you don't want to be dropped, keep the music going. Be sure to hold on to retention—ten percent of the money owed on the job—until all punch list items have been completed and all warranties, manuals, etc. have been handed over.

With many mortgage agreements mandating higher interest charges during construction, penalties charged for not making move-in deadlines and the cost of renting space elsewhere, you might find a bust schedule more painful than a bust budget. Use incentives to motivate the GC to keep costs low and to make schedule. Bonuses go over much better than "damages clauses" that threaten penalties for blowing a deadline. Most GCs won't go for them, and anyway, they're almost impossible to enforce.

TIE UP LOOSE ENDS

Punch-list items are loose ends such as missing fixtures, polishing finishes and fine-tuning systems. Left hanging, the punch list and warranties are things that will keep your GC in your life much longer than either of you care for. Spell out the procedure and schedule for generating, attacking and revisiting punch list issues. A good GC doesn't need to be handheld through the process, but it should be clear from the outset who's doing what. And give him a break if everything is not perfect at first. Be patient.

Most of the warranties passed on by the GC are from the subs and manufacturers. Many GCs will offer an umbrella warranty. Ideally you want to have one contact person if things go wrong. Some firms have a computerized database for tracking customer warranties. Warranties can range from one year on parts and labor for equipment to ten years on workmanship items. Any decent GC will be attentive to past clients long into the future. No warranty should kick in until the day the certificate of occupation or completion is issued by the city or municipality.

COVER YOUR BACK

Remember, success is as much about being thorough in your research and preparation as it is about personal chemistry and communication. All this can be wrapped up in a tidy little standard AIA (American Institute of Architects) contract with the usual qualifications attached: plans and specs, the GC's bid proposal, terms and conditions, gated community regulations and anything else you want to include.

TIPS FOR A PAINLESS JOB

✧ Make contract documents as detailed, clear and complete as possible.
✧ Establish good chemistry and communication between yourself, the GC and the architect.
✧ Have GC hold weekly site meetings with subcontractors.
✧ Make payments on schedule.
✧ Trust the contractor and keep a sense of humor.

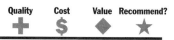
CONTRACTORS & BUILDERS

AJ Duggan Contracting Inc. 3.5 3 4 4
140 East Lewis Avenue, Pearl River, NY 10965
(845) 735 - 5651
Interior remodels and custom millwork

Clients say AJ Contracting is A-OK for interior remodeling work, minor renovations and deck construction in Westchester and Manhattan. The firm works closely with clients to realize their ideas from concept to completion, custom creating every piece of project millwork. Clients enjoy an excellent experience with AJ and are eager to call the firm back for repeat projects.

Principal Andrew Duggan went through an apprenticeship as a cabinetmaker in his native Ireland and plied his trade in London before bringing his skills stateside. He established AJ in 1992 and works with a crew of two. We're told the firm makes every effort to be available if anything needs tightening up after the project is over.

Allen J. Reyen Inc. 4.5 4.5 4.5 5
PO Box 16759, Stamford, CT 06905
(203) 357 - 0218 reyben@aol.com
High-end custom homes and gut renovations

Both industry insiders and homeowners laud this very selective firm for its ability to execute hyper-detailed new residences or seamless additions to historical homes. Allen J. Reyen Inc. only takes on two projects simultaneously, nearly all in Greenwich and in the million-plus range. We're told principal Reyen is intensely involved in every aspect of a project, collaborating closely with architects and clients at the conceptual phase to develop budgets. While this general contractor is often called upon to realize the most challenging designs, he is also available to past clients for maintenance and repair.

Recognized in both local and international competitions for his carpentry skills, Reyen founded his firm in 1976 after a four-year apprenticeship. He fields two project managers who have been with him for twenty-five and twenty years respectively, and maintains long-established relationships with a stable of talented tradesmen. Word is Reyen leaves jobs extremely complete, with no punch list and few callbacks.

"Allen Reyen is the most meticulous individual I have encountered in sixteen years as a Greenwich architect." "Allen and his people are totally trustworthy and highly competent." "His limited number of accepted projects means that his clients each get his personal attention. Really!" "He has become a family friend. He stands behind his projects and is available 24/7."

Anthony DeVito, LLC 4 3.5 4.5 5
54 Orchard Hill Road, Katonah, NY 10536
(914) 767 - 0403 www.devitobuilders.com
Residential maintenance, remodels and gut renovations

A fourth-generation builder with "strong integrity" who "really listens," Anthony DeVito shields his clients from any possibility of a bad experience. From bathroom remodels to projects over $1 million, the firm offers contracting, construction management and design/build service in Fairfield and Westchester. DeVito also provides estate maintenance (limited to the Bedford, Katona, Greenwich, New Canaan areas) for those nagging little jobs and seasonal chores. Whether it's walking customers through cost-efficiency scenarios at the design stage or flying Nordic timber in from Finland to match the old-growth grain in a restoration, we're told this firm always goes the extra mile.

Principal Anthony DeVito's engineering degree complements his legacy in construction. When he's not face-to-face with clients, he oversees a custom millwork shop (see Richard Anthony Millwork), a crew of painters and a staff of project managers. Clients praise the firm's "superb" workmanship, "versatile" management and "reliable" service, saying, "we certainly got our money's worth."

"Unusually good quality work, delivered in a well-organized manner, with excellent controls." "Anthony has never let me down."

Artisans Inc.   4.5   4.5   4.5   4.5

143 Rowayton Avenue, 1st Floor, Norwalk, CT 06853
(203) 831 - 9716   www.artisansbuilders.com

General contracting, construction management, high-end renovations and custom homes

Combining a craftsman's pride with corporate panache, Artisans Inc. performs construction management and general contracting of million-dollar-plus renovations and new construction on five-figure-square-foot homes. We hear the firm achieves a level of detail few can match. An in-house woodworking shop fashions each project's specialty pieces such as exterior railings, curved crown and oak door saddles. Covering Westchester and Fairfield, the firm has also been dispatched to Nantucket and Moscow.

Artisan Inc.'s reproachless reputation dates back forty years, with partners Bill Marshall and Christopher Philips at the helm for the last fifteen. Civil engineers by education and each a holder of an MBA, one of the two partners acts as project manager for each job. Laptop-issued, office-networked supers direct the day-to-day work on-site with the professionalism, documentation and efficiency of a commercial builder. We're told the firm offers an option of a fixed-price shell package and cost-plus finish package for those clients who want to hunt and peck for the right product for their buck with flexibility.

"Highest standard of integrity. Total attention to detail. Utmost competence." "Delightful workers." "Highly ethical, very reliable, always returns calls within hours." "Tradesmen all top-notch and very pleasant to work with."

Bashford Construction Co. Inc.   4.5   4   4.5   5

4 Bashford Street, Yonkers, NY 10701
(914) 963 - 7177

High-end renovation and new construction

This "superb organization" inspires fierce loyalty not only from clients and design professionals but from everyone who works for it as well. We hear Bashford Construction creates a family-like atmosphere while creating "meticulous and beautiful" work. The firm focuses on high-end renovation and some new construction in Westchester County, but is open to projects of all sizes, schedule permitting. Sources say Bashford takes a thoughtful approach to the design process, and is available to shape a budget early on or to assess potential home purchases. Word is the firm meets tight time lines without missing a beat.

Schooled in carpentry by his father and uncles, owner Tom Gallego studied architecture and received a degree in construction technology. He worked as a manager for a commercial contractor before opening his business in 1977. We're told he goes "the extra mile" to make sure everything is completed "on time and with the highest standard." Gallego heads a staff of six carpenter-foremen with a combined total of 64 years with the firm. Clients find Bashford's crew "fast, honest, thorough, detail oriented, intelligent and helpful" and its prices nothing to be bashful about.

"Before I asked a question Tom already had the answer. The best!" "We were so appreciative of Tom and his crew that we hosted a catered Christmas and Easter luncheon at the job site as a thank you for their incredible work." "I wish I could afford to do another renovation just to have him and his crew back." "I recommend him to my friends and they are not disappointed."

	Quality	Cost	Value	Recommend?
	+	$	◆	★

BD Remodeling & Restoration   5   4.5   4.5   4.5
79 East Putnam Avenue, Greenwich, CT 06830
(203) 983 - 6083   www.bdrrusa.com
High-end construction with a historic flare

This full-service, residential construction company focuses on high-end restorations and new construction. BD Remodeling & Restoration has great skills in adaptive reuse of old materials and in the integration of historic structures (post and beam barns) into new spaces. The firm has completed new construction projects, major renovations, and smaller master suite and custom kitchen projects. The firm has two primary offices in Greenwich, CT and Fishers Island, NY. The firm works with its sister architecture firm, BD Design Inc., as well as other nationally known architecture firms. The firm has its own full-time carpenters on staff at both its locations and has developed strong ties with a list of superior subcontractors. The firm's Fishers Island office also has a full-service maintenance capability and directly employs a full staff of electricians, painters and plumbers year-round.

Principal David Beckwith spearheads the design work of the company's architecture firm and oversees the work of BD Remodeling & Restoration's project manager. Clients find the firm's open and honest channels of communication keep them comfortable and confident throughout the process.

Berkshire Construction & Management   4   4   4   4
126 Old Ridgefield Road, Wilton, CT 06897
(203) 761 - 9943   www.berkshireconstruction.com
High-end custom homes

Bernsohn & Fetner   5   5   4   5
625 West 51st Street, New York, NY 10019
(212) 315 - 4330   www.bfbuilding.com
Residential and commercial general contracting, construction management

When time is of the essence, industry insiders "look no further" than Bernsohn & Fetner to deliver the finest quality. The bulk of the company's work is large, very high-end, custom residential projects for an A-list roster of clients in New York City, Westchester and Fairfield. B&F also performs swank corporate and retail build-outs and ongoing maintenance at Manhattan's most distinguished addresses.

References report B&F heads projects with "go-get-em efficient supervision," and that the firm's affable, easygoing principals offer hands-on assistance in all undertakings. We hear the B&F team sees all projects through to the end, leaving no detail outstanding. This "very team-oriented" management outfit subs out its trades. The result, clients say, is "amazing," while "the pricing is very competitive" considering they are "the absolute best."

"Honest and professional. Beyond any expectation." "This is the very best at top, top prices." "They deliver museum quality." "We can give them the work and not have to worry about them getting it done, and done right." "Very nice. Randy is low-key." "They have to do good work. Their clients demand it." "Very blunt about cost."

	Quality ✚	Cost $	Value ◆	Recommend? ★

Blansfield Builders Inc.

| | 4 | 3.5 | 4 | 5 |

2 High Fields Drive, Danbury, CT 06811
(203) 797 - 9174 www.blansfieldbuilders.com

Residential general contracting

This "very creative" client-handholding contractor handles anything from $250,000 gut remodels to $4 million new homes. In addition to pleasing clients, Blansfield Builders has received numerous awards from its peers. The firm invests itself early in the design process to nail down a budget and can play matchmaker between the homeowner and architect. The company climbs aboard a limited number of jobs at any given time so president Jim Blansfield stays intimately involved.

His background as a physician's assistant and teacher at Emory University accounts for his polished way of dealing with clients. We hear Blansfield possesses "excellent taste and ideas" and will even accompany a client shopping for the right finish item. Supporters say everyone in the Blansfield organization contributes to the smooth process. The firm's fee for oversight during drawing development will count towards the overall construction budget if the client decides to hand the reins over to Blansfield to build.

"Extremely nice, honest contractor with great expertise in all areas of home building." "Very quick to follow up on all issues." "This is our fifth project with Blansfield over the past twelve years and every experience has exceeded our expectations."

Bourke & Matthews

| | 5 | 4.5 | 4.5 | 5 |

779 North Street, Greenwich, CT 06831
(203) 622 - 0100 www.bourkeandmatthews.com

High-end custom estate construction and renovation

A builder of Connecticut and Westchester's finest estates for over 25 years, this firm's "reputation is unassailable." Discriminating clientele from Maine to Nantucket commission Bourke & Matthews for teardowns, custom homes, gut renovations and large-scale additions priced anywhere from $3.5 million to $35 million. The company's diverse portfolio boasts squash courts, basketball courts, movie theaters, indoor pools and photography labs. It also fields a small-jobs crew to care for existing clients' odds and ends.

A graduate of Columbia with an MBA, owner Matt Matthews got his start with a real estate developer whose guesthouse he happened to be renting right out of school. Matthews established Bourke & Matthews 25 years ago and still personally walks the client down the critical path, from design development to punch list. Clients appreciate this active role as well as his accessibility, and say he demonstrates "exceptionally good taste and judgment" on all matters. A staff of twenty project managers, supervisors and office staff aids in the process. While certainly expensive, the firm works with clients and architects in choosing trades and is known to fight for the owner's money.

"It takes an outstanding builder to build in his own neighborhood." "A very attentive company with a fine reputation, I would be hard pressed to consider anyone else should I build another home." "Mr. Matthews pays close attention to detail and is highly accessible, which is very important." "We're planning to do it again. Matt is the best!" "Building was a new and daunting adventure and Matt made it a true pleasure for my husband and me." "With every challenge, he had a solution."

Brindisi & Yaroscak

| | 🗀 | 🗀 | 🗀 | 🗀 |

39 Leroy Avenue, 2nd Floor, Darien, CT 06820
(203) 656 - 1948

Custom home builder

Quality	Cost	Value	Recommend?
✚	$	◆	★

Cayley Barrett Associates

| 4 | 3.5 | 4.5 | 4.5 |

238 East Grand Street, Fleetwood, NY 10552
(914) 667 - 4527   cba1993@aol.com

General contracting and project management

This "hardworking," thoughtful construction management firm specializes in interior renovation, architectural restoration, kitchens and baths. Cayley teams with architects or works in a design/build capacity on projects ballparking between $65,000 and $600,000-plus in Westchester, Fairfield and Manhattan. There are no true minimums, but if the budget is unrealistic for Cayley quality, principal Joy Licht will tell you.

Clients find Licht a "pleasure" to work with, and "marvelous" at coming up with practical solutions. We hear she is always cheerfully available, whether it's the weekend or a call before bed to put a client's mind at ease. Her crews of in-house carpenters and decorative finishers are determined to make each project a success. We're also told that for a fair-minded price, Cayley Barret produces quality that is "true to the bone."

"Joy is one person I cannot live without." "It was a pleasure working with Joy Licht and company. Reliable, professional and highly qualified." "If Joy gave you a price it was all encompassing." "Whatever it took, she did it." "Really vets the issues beforehand. Made good suggestions." "Absolutely would use again."

Chartwell Builders

| 4 | 4 | 4 | 4.5 |

119 Villa Avenue, Mamaroneck, NY 10543
(914) 698 - 6114

High-end residential renovation

Chilmark Builders Inc.

| 4.5 | 4 | 5 | 5 |

1 Vanderbilt Avenue, Pleasantville, NY 10570
(914) 769 - 3416   jg@chilmarkbuilders.com

High-end residential, institutional and commercial general contracting

Praised as a "finisher" by clients, Chilmark has garnered accolades as a high-end residential general contractor of large-scale renovations and new construction in Westchester County, New York City and Greenwich, CT. With its specialty millwork shop, the firm demonstrates skillful replication and old-world craftsmanship. Chilmark also offers construction management and consulting services.

The industry stamps principal John Ginsbern "a stand-up guy" while clients come away impressed by his intelligent, reliable and efficient management team. We're told the firm's recommendations improve the quality of the job both before and during the process. A preferred builder for many prominent Gotham architects, Chilmark promises an experience that is nothing less than "absolutely fantastic."

"Extremely professional. Chilmark goes the extra mile." "Top of the line." "Got the sense that no matter what the cost, I was getting big quality." "Contributed a lot of ideas that enhanced the value of my house and the look I was going for."

Colonial Housewrights, LLC

| 3 | 3 | 4 | 4 |

371 Hammertown Road, Monroe, CT 06468
(203) 452 - 9119   colhousewright@aol.com

Interior build-out and renovations

This small shop strives to produce work that in ten years time, still looks like it was finished yesterday. Colonial Housewrights concentrates on interior renovations, in which a change in floor plan, new kitchen, bathroom remodel or window replacement drives the project. Clients say the respectful and tidy firm works well around their existing space and life. Colonial's mill shop handles the task of fabricating the more intricate woodworking items, and will take on jobs directly from homeowners as well.

Quality	Cost	Value	Recommend?
✚	$	◆	★

Owner John Martinsky earned his stripes with a Swedish builder renovating historical homes, and has been doing it on his own for more than a decade. We're told he is patient and flexible as the point person on each project. Supporters also say Martinsky researches old-world design elements and methods of construction he is not familiar with to best reproduce the effect.

Cornerstone Contracting Group   5   4.5   4.5   5
23 Benedict Place, 2nd Floor, Greenwich, CT 06830
(203) 861 - 4200   www.cornerstone-builders.com

High-end custom residential construction and landscaping

Clients tell us Cornerstone manages projects with "a high degree of professionalism and style," putting them "right up there" among the elite builders in Westchester/Fairfield. The firm splits its skills between ultra high-end residential renovations and new construction, typically of a larger scale going from $3.5 million to $20 million multi-phase, multi-year projects. Grand landscaping is often part of the effort, and we hear the firm has created everything from ski slopes to lakes on its clients' estates. Cornerstone will take on million-dollar range renovations with exceptionally unique design intent and property location when schedule permits. It also facilitates one design/build job a year.

Experienced contractors Robert Kolton and George Pusser joined forces in 1993. Kolton, who holds a master's in architecture, manages the office, while Pusser oversees operations in the field. Cornerstone's corps of 70 employees includes carpenters, painters, cabinetmakers and project managers, all of whom contribute to the "superb finish quality." The company also operates a small mill shop in Norwalk to care for extreme specialty work, such as grilles and furniture. Most contracts are negotiated with the firm working on a weekly fee tabulated by the complexity of the job rather than a percentage of the cost of construction. Pre-construction assistance is based on an hourly fee.

"Highly organized and methodical." "They staff projects well and provide excellent in-house craftsmen." "We adored their work ethic from start to finish." "We plan to use them again and again." "Each project manager was a pleasure to deal with. My client was thrilled with the results." "Immediately responsive. Very service oriented. Whatever we need." "Extremely businesslike and professional throughout—right down to the punch list."

Davenport Contracting Inc.   4   4   4   4
78 Harvard Street, Stamford, CT 06902
(203) 324 - 6308   bmacdonald@davenportcontracting.com

High-end residential general contracting

Clients enjoy an "extremely positive relationship" with this well-regarded general contractor. Davenport Contracting takes on teardowns, showpiece restorations and high-end apartment renovations in Manhattan and the surrounding Connecticut and Westchester County suburbs, with budgets from $700,000 up to eight figures. The firm's satellite mill shop, DCI, contributes casework and cabinets with efficiency and expediency while its property management company keeps everything buttoned up for past clients.

Principals Brian MacDonald and Richard J. Koch have been building for over two decades. We hear Davenport professionals are "open and constructive in dealing with changes and issues" as they pop up, and keep everyone well informed. The firm dispatches its own seasoned carpenters, and we hear MacDonald and Koch stay visible throughout the process.

"Not withstanding the magnitude and complexity of the job, they performed admirably and in a friendly, spirited way." "They are very fair, reasonable people to deal with and very organized in terms of paperwork and process." "They provided real value in getting appropriate specialists involved." "We have recommended them to others who we understand were impressed as well."

David Anspach   4   3   5   5
225 Ridgefield Road, Wilton, CT 06897
(203) 834 - 2565
General contracting—renovations and teardowns

This small firm, guided by owner David Anspach, performs mostly renovations and teardowns in Westchester and Fairfield counties. These jobs range from small maintenance and repair work to new construction that reaches the multi-millions. Anspach's company also fabricates and installs most of its own cabinets and will do so for outside customers. Insiders tell us Anspach excels at reproducing old-world workmanship, seamlessly blending the old and the new. In addition, the firm works fast, often outpacing the paperwork. It is available to give preliminary budgets for design/build services on smaller projects.

Anspach began his career as a painter and there isn't much in construction he hasn't done with his own two hands. He started building over twenty years ago and continues to manage each project personally, assisted by his small crew and trusted subs. We're told clients "appreciate his assuring, hands-on approach," which results in a high-caliber finish for a price you won't recoil from.

"David is true problem solver, and I am always 100 percent confident utilizing his services for our projects of the greatest complexity." "Excellent eye, has tremendous respect for historical buildings." "Dave Anspach and his various contractors are all exceptional. Each of them is highly professional and skilled."

DHI Construction Services Inc.   3.5   3   4   4
37-47 57th Street, Woodside, NY 11377
(718) 639 - 3200   dhi@nyc.rr.com
Residential and commercial construction

References praise this "accommodating" and "diligent" contractor for "commercial timing" and "residential sensitivity." DHI does corporate interiors, residential renovations and new construction in the Tri-State area, with projects ranging from $50,000 to $10 million. We hear the firm is often called upon to meet tight schedules, and that it has completed a litany of work for the area's most discriminating country clubs, including Union Club, Yale Club and Piping Rock.

With inside experience at an architecture firm, principal Howard Dym possesses an appreciation for and knowledge of both sides of the construction coin. As such, he has fashioned his firm as a collaborative builder staffed with "good clear communicators." Five project managers, all with over seven years of experience, run an "honest" and "responsible" group of subs. While the firm can be trusted with large projects, it will tend to small items as well. Contracts are often negotiated and in order to keep a lid on the budget, the firm gets involved very early in the design phase.

"Howard and the guys at DHI are kind and practical. Decent human beings trying to make a decent living." "I had a zillion change orders that were all me and every time they always charged fairly." "Subs get the job done." "They might not initiate the aesthetic, but they will implement." "Good about their promise on time frame. The architect didn't notice how an AC vent interrupted the molding, and they reconfigured it with no muss and fuss with their own guys at minimal cost."

	Quality	Cost	Value	Recommend?
	✚	$	◆	★

Drew Construction
3.5   3.5   4   4.5

888 Eighth Avenue, Suite 20P, New York, NY 10019
(212) 489 - 1715

Small to midsize renovations

Clients applaud this "extremely professional" and "trustworthy" firm. Drew Construction performs small to mid-size projects throughout the Tri-State area, from full apartment renovations, kitchens and showrooms in Manhattan to additions in Westchester. The firm even takes on maintenance and repair jobs, sustaining an elevated level of service whether it's a one-day job or an eight-month project. Clients who remain in the house during renovation find this firm adept at tiptoeing (albeit with power tools) around their lives.

Principal Andrew Ferris has been working in the high-end residential building field since he was fourteen. Today Ferris leads his young company by working alongside his crew and listening to his clients. They say he's "articulate and patient" and is "really good at explaining things to befuddled clients." The firm's "good clear billing" establishes a comfort level for its customers, who tell us Ferris handles changes and add-ons well.

"I have done three renovations with different contractors. Andrew and Drew Construction are definitely the best." "Good crew, good work, excellent client communication." "As long as Andrew's in business, I won't bother calling any other contractor." "This man is knowledgeable, honest and utterly reliable. I would recommend him to anyone without hesitation or reservation." "Very helpful, reliable, honest, got the job done quickly. Overall very satisfied with them."

Egan Construction Inc.
3.5   3   4.5   5

40 Devoe Avenue, Yonkers, NY 10705
(914) 377 - 9100   Odhren@aol.com

General contracting and renovations

Customers applaud this friendly and dependable family-run business, which "doesn't take the scope of work lightly." Working in Manhattan and Westchester, the firm does a wide variety of general contracting and renovation work, from painting and plasterwork to whole house guts. Sources count on Egan's prompt, neat service to meet not only their specifications but the client's expectations.

References trust principal Pat Egan's good word, which they say is backed up with the help of an "incredibly talented" group of craftsmen. Millwork is an often-cited specialty. The firm offers free on-site estimates and delivers "attentive" service at a "fair price" with "no surprises."

"Pat and his crew were perfectionists." "They showed up when they said, kept a crew on the job every day and finished with pride and quality workmanship. I have already recommended Pat to family and friends." "When we knocked out a wall in our apartment they searched our building and found an apartment that was putting in a new floor. They got the pieces of the old flooring to fit in where we knocked out the wall. It matched up beautifully."

Fabry Contracting Corporation
3.5   3   5   5

169 Jennifer Lane, Yonkers, NY 10710
(914) 337 - 4591

Residential renovations, restorations and additions

It's no surprise this firm's "perfect communication" results in old-world quality and a schedule delivered "as promised." Fabry Contracting Corporation specializes in renovation, restoration and additions. From kitchens and bathrooms to gutting an entire residence, the firm's pride in matching the old with the new is evident in its work and in the fact that it is usually booked a year in advance. Based in Bronxville, the firm serves all of Westchester County, limiting its slate so it can remain available to respond to past customers' needs.

A retired Bronxville policeman, Fabry moonlighted as a renovation specialist for several years until he took up building full time in 1991. Today, Fabry, with his son, Chris, and partner Paul Atkinson, acts as figurehead of the organization and manages each job personally. We hear they "choose only the best subs" and field a long-standing in-house crew of carpenters. Clients rave that the "men who do the work are delightful and seemed like a part of the family" and tell us this proud GC can out-punch list the customer.

"We own a 100-year-old Tudor home, and Fabry Contracting helped us improve and maintain its comfort and beauty." "This is the third time in seven years that we have used Fabry Contracting." "The whole family became very close with Chris and all his workers." "He showed me what was being done each step of the way and all the work was perfectly done—even better than it had to be." "No problems, no complaints, no 'negative' anything."

Form Ltd.   3.5   4.5   3.5   4

32 West Putnam Avenue, Greenwich, CT 06830
(203) 869 - 6880 www.formlimited.com
Kitchen and bath design and installation

See Form Ltd.'s full report under the heading Kitchen & Bath Designers

Fort Hill Construction   5   5   4   5

200 Riverside Drive, Suite 1C, New York, NY 10025
(212) 665 - 1583 www.forthill.com
High-end residential general contracting

From East Coast architects to Hollywood studio back lots, Fort Hill is the contractor of choice. The firm helms tent-pole projects from custom new homes to historic restoration that range from minimalist to mammoth. Fort Hill takes on a select number of projects each year, pairing with a creative clientele and acclaimed design professionals who provide challenging, inspired opportunities. The A-list is awed by the museum-quality work and ceaseless attention to detail delivered by this 30-year-old construction management and general contracting firm. Fort Hill also maintains a drafting/minor design division to accommodate smaller projects and a service unit to care for existing customers. Headquartered in L.A., Fort Hill is also firmly entrenched in Boston and New York and can rotate its considerable manpower between cities when necessary.

George Peper, Jim Kweskin and the other original partners have cultivated a family business into a "factory" of "perfectionism." The Fort Hill family extends to the ranks of craftsmen, supervisors and managers that run generations deep. Clients report that the firm's famously unflappable staff does very well to get even the biggest egos through a home's front door.

Undoubtedly the place to go for superior service, Fort Hill's cache comes with "take it or leave it bids." However, clients who sign on to the program love every minute.

"If you had a separate ranking for honesty these guys would be the highest of all the contractors." "Top-top notch. Among top four in NY history." "They would make great recommendations." "We liked Fort Hill so much that we are doing phase two of our project with them." "Has been around a long time. Does extremely good work."

	Quality	Cost	Value	Recommend?
	+	$	◆	★

Gerhard Isop Inc.   4.5   4   4.5   4.5
2 Close Hill Road, Croton Falls, NY 10519
(914) 277 - 4933

General contracting—renovations, additions and teardowns

Clients line up for the chance to work with this "awesome but hard to get" family-operated contracting company. Founded in 1974 by Gerhard Isop Sr., who was classically trained as an apprentice carpenter in his native Germany, the firm takes on new constructions, renovations and additions as well as teardowns. Isop Inc. builds exclusively in Westchester on projects budgeted anywhere from $50,000 to $2 million and specializes in custom built-ins, floors, vanities and libraries. Most of the millwork is done in-house.

A holder of a bachelor's degree in engineering, Gerhard Jr. took the reins ten years ago from his father, who can still be found in the field. Gerhard Jr.'s brother and mother also contribute to the company. We hear the firm interfaces well with clients and architects, generally working with the same designer again and again. Isop Inc. performs all its own framing, trim, siding, roofing, layout and excavation work and enjoys second-generation relationships with its subs. Contracts are AIA cost-plus or fixed price.

"He's fantastic. A small operation." "A lot of people will just wait for him. I had a client who waited seven months to get him."

Godwin Inc.   4.5   3.5   5   5
215 East 58th Street, Suite 503, New York, NY 10022
(212) 308 - 0558   www.godwin-inc.com

Residential general contracting, kitchen and bath design, gut renovations

Supporters describe Godwin Inc. with "awe and pleasure." At the conclusion of projects, we hear neighbors often end up bearing thankful gifts to this residential construction company's well-heeled clients for making the street or building more beautiful. Specializing in kitchens, baths and gut renovations, Godwin Inc. is known to be capable and skillful in a wide variety of areas and has served clients from Connecticut to Aspen to the UN Plaza. The firm partners with McIver-Morgan Interior Design to offer interior decorating services.

Customers are pleased with the intelligence, insight and initiative owner Steve Godwin brings to a job. They tell us his suggestions lead to a better overall product, and his explanations invite them into the process. We're also told the solid, on-site project management brings cost in "exactly as projected."

"Steve gives constant attention to detail, and has enough vision to make his perfectionism cost-effective." "The results made me realize that other work I had experienced was inferior." "The job he did altered the course of my life. Wouldn't have embarked on the home if it weren't for the success of the apartment project. I have to say I would never think of doing anything with anyone else." "The quality difference is so outstanding that friends who came to visit after the renovation thought I had moved."

Graphic Builders Inc.   3.5   3.5   4   5
45 West Fort Lee Road, Bogota, NJ 07603
(201) 488 - 8638   graphicbuilders@earthlink.net

General contracting, custom cabinetry

"A real find passed among friends," this boutique general contractor "thrills" clients with its dedication and attentiveness. We hear the firm is as comfortable and diligent at taking care of the odds and ends of jobs as well as overseeing major renovations, showing superior skill in woodworking. Projects average $800,000, with a $250,000 as a minimum, and are located in New York City, Westchester and Fairfield counties.

Clients are consistently impressed by the way owners, Martin and Mary McElroy "don't just listen, but hear" their wishes. From the back office to the painters, references report everyone is friendly and eager to help. We hear "they keep good track of everything" and "are excellent on the final punch list." Graphic works hard to make its pricing agreeable, work that we hear really pays off for the client.

"They deliver service one would usually get with larger and more expensive firms." "They are fair, honest and good." "Fixed things out of the contract just because he knew they should be done." "Graphic is one of the most thorough firms we have ever had the pleasure of working with."

Grunow Builders

5 Quintard Avenue, Old Greenwich, CT 06870
(203) 637 - 1123
High-end residential construction

Gundersen Brothers Realty Corp.   4.5   4   5   5

3 Palmer Place, Armonk, NY 10504
(914) 273 - 9268
High-end custom home construction and renovation

While the jury's still out on whether Leif Eriksson discovered the New World, there's no doubt this Norwegian import builds the most "amazing work" in Westchester. Reider Gundersen and his brother put down the stakes of the firm in 1964. It excels in constructing high-end new homes, with the occasional $200,000 to $500,000 renovation and addition if it can be fit into the schedule. While the Vikings needed a boat, area architects, city building inspectors and corporate mogul clients all tell us this firm "walks on water."

Today Reider works alongside his two sons, Galenn and Dan. The Gundersens provide more than complete hands-on supervision—they actually perform the rough framing and interior carpentry themselves. The result is a greater attention to detail, expert trim work and intricate custom built-ins ranging from custom media centers to kitchen cabinets. Those clients lucky to get the Gundersens get a superior product with the signature of a true craftsmen.

"A pleasure to work with, also worked well with our architect and designer. Has come back years later for small repairs." "Most people report unhappy experiences when building. We had the opposite happen to us, twice, ten years apart! We loved having the Gundersens build our homes. It was a pleasure working with them in every respect of both projects. People who visit us rave about the workmanship and detail of our house. They are the best in Westchester County."

Hampton Court Estate Builders Inc.

65 Hedgebrook Lane, Stamford, CT 06903
(203) 968 - 6030
Residential general contracting

Hobbs, Inc.   5   5   4.5   5

27 Grove Street, New Canaan, CT 06840
(203) 966 - 0726   www.hobbsinc.com
High-end custom construction and renovation

This third-generation builder is widely considered the "best of the best" of Connecticut and Westchester residential builders. With a project management corps loaded with top-brass talent who could be running their own first-class contracting companies and a brutally honest estimating department, Hobbs Inc. is wholly equipped to tackle its average $5 million jobs. At the project's completion, the firm can dispatch an estate maintenance group to clean gutters, change screens and perform general change of season chores for a monthly fee. It also fields a small jobs division.

Brothers Ian and Scott Hobbs now helm the company, established in 1954 by their grandfather. Lifelong New Canaanites, Ian and Scott first attended Johns Hopkins and Duke, respectively. They then received their MBAs from Columbia and assumed the mantle of the venerable family enterprise from their father, Michael, in 1998. The duo coordinates a staff of 70, including a full-time safety official and crews of trade professionals for all the finish surfaces and hard-scapes. While Hobbs Inc. may appear to cost more up front, area architects insist it "will save money in the long run" on big-ticket projects.

"You pay for the firm's identity. But it's better at estimating than anyone." "Professional, thorough, comprehensive and helpful. All Hobbs project managers are good." "Strong management and administrative support for all projects. Principals actively involved. Depth of stable subcontractors."

Innovative Concepts 　　　　 3.5　 3　 4.5　 5
Studio #1 Old Field Lane, Weston, CT 06883
(203) 222 - 1319

Residential remodels and custom construction

This meticulous construction manager and general contractor provides clients with "peace of mind" and workmanship "that speaks for itself." Innovative Concepts remodels bathrooms, restores antique homes and builds additions as well as one ground-up residence a year. Projects cost anywhere from $10,000 to $1 million, with $150,000 to $300,000 the norm. The firm manufactures uniquely detailed cabinetry out of its Redding, CT shop and employs its own stable of painters and masons. Catering primarily to a Connecticut and Westchester clientele, Innovative Concepts has also worked from Manhattan to Rockland County.

A former research scientist in bio-medical engineering, principal Diane Slovak has applied her detail-oriented approach to the homebuilding industry for over twenty years. Sources say Slovak's technical and aesthetic suggestions "never lead you down the wrong road." A member of ASID, she can lead a client through design/build or be heavily interactive with an architect. Homeowners find Slovak maintains a presence as the main project facilitator, while aided by a full-time on-site super.

"Diane always knows what to do to tackle any problem. Her subs are all first rate. I wouldn't take a project without her." "A superb professional." "A very detailed and thorough contractor. No details are overlooked." "Our cottage looks magnificent—and was a major selling point when our house went on the market." "Diane was highly professional. Her work was done on time and she demanded quality workmanship."

Integkral Design & Construction, LLC 　　 3　 3　 4　 4.5
24 Sodom Lane, Derby, CT 06418
(203) 732 - 2992   www.integkral.com

Residential general contracting and design/build services

Careful planning, strong management and exacting standards prove Integkral to this small firm's success. An interior renovation specialist, this firm's projects encompass bathroom remodels, monster guts and apartment renovations in Connecticut, Westchester and Manhattan. Principal George Kral holds a master's degree in architecture and can facilitate design/build services.

Quality   Cost   Value   Recommend?

We hear clients often implement the agreeable and knowledgeable Kral's creative suggestions throughout the job. They tell us the firm is dependable and highly responsive, and that someone responds to Kral's calls instantaneously. The staff is described as professional and pleasant, and the firm is known to be as accommodating to its clients as it is to its neighbors.

"Nice beyond description—I loved working with George." "Very reliable." "Start to finish, I had a purely pleasant experience" "We have found Integkral to be very responsive, on time and accurate in estimating costs." "Very careful planners. Super quality." "It's George's attentiveness that keeps things on track."

JN Contracting Inc.   4   4   4   5

774 White Plains Road, Suite 210, Scarsdale, NY 10583
(914) 725 - 5328
High-end residential renovations and additions

When replicating and matching the integrity of the original craftsmanship in renovations and additions is as critical as beating the schedule, clients recommend JN Contracting. The firm performs mostly gut renovations in the $300,000 to $1.5 million range as well as smaller remodel projects. JN breaks down budgets for architects in the conceptual stage and works directly with homeowners, who tell us "all phases of the project were completed to complete satisfaction." Principal Joseph Nannariello opened the doors of JN in 1990 after years of experience as a union carpenter. He remains the point man for all projects, while wife Lauren assists in the office. Nannariello staffs seven "personable and totally trustworthy" superintendents and foremen, and we hear his subs "have been with him for years and hold him in the highest regard." Clients confirm JN Contracting "addresses any concern on a very timely basis" and "continues to check in even after a job."

"Joe is a man of integrity! He is straightforward and always in communication." "JN Contracting has done six different jobs for us. Their work was very high quality and, in all cases, done ahead of schedule." "The inevitable short list is truly a short list and addressed right away." "A measure of his quality is evident by those who work for him—they think, and readily say, he's the best." "We missed the men when we were finished." "Change orders smooth and fairly priced."

John Desmond Builders Inc.   4.5   4   5   5

2315 Post Road, Fairfield, CT 06824
(203) 259 - 7323
High-end custom construction, remodels

The second-generation is now at the helm of this four-decade-strong contractor. George and Sean Desmond join their father in executing high-end custom construction for residential clients in Fairfield and selected Westchester enclaves like Pound Ridge and Chappaqua. Projects range from $10,000 to $6 million and up. The work includes maintenance and remodels in which "the mixture of preservation and upgrade mesh perfectly" as well as brand new estates. The firm can execute for the most demanding and distinguished architectural masters or help flesh out the details for more conceptual designers. Clients "couldn't be happier with both the work, the people and the two-year follow-up to insure all is well."

One family member is on the job site every day, assisted by a crew of twenty that includes full-time carpenters, foreman and laborers. Clients say they are made to feel like one of the family, with Desmond and crew having gone so far as bringing in the groceries. The firm endeavors to deliver the best project for the best value, and clients agree, "they cut no corners, made no substitutions for specified items unless agreed upon." Contracts are negotiated cost-plus.

"I worry about people who don't use Desmond." "The Desmonds allowed me, an opinionated artist, to determine plans of visual elements and details and then they enhanced or corrected as advised." "John and his team are professional, knowledgeable, responsive and provide just outstanding workmanship. This historical house is extremely visible in the community and all who see/view it are clearly impressed and inspired by the work that was done." "Their answers to the problems caused by dealing with a 100-plus-year-old structure were considered and correct."

	Quality ✚	Cost $	Value ◆	Recommend? ★
Kais Custom Builders, LLC	4	4	4	4.5

114 East Avenue, Norwalk, CT 06851
(203) 857 - 4795   nsbilia@kaisllc.com
High-end custom residential construction

	Quality	Cost	Value	Recommend?
Kenneth F. Bacco Inc.	4.5	4	4	4

27 Pine Street, New Canaan, CT 06840
(203) 972 - 7641   www.kennethfbacco.com
High-end custom residential construction

Industry insiders can't stop recommending builder Ken Bacco. Squarely in the "upper echelon" of quality, the firm takes on residential contracting duties in Westchester and Fairfield counties. Architects appreciate principal Ken Bacco's "fanatical attention to detail" and "very businesslike" approach, while clients find Bacco a kick to work with.

"Part nut, but fantastic at what he does. Great management skills."

	Quality	Cost	Value	Recommend?
Kettleridge Construction	5	4	5	5

170 Teakettle Spout Road, Mahopac, NY 10541
(845) 628 - 0380
High-end renovations, alterations and historic renovation

Clients insist that "if you are lucky enough to interview the Zen Master" Tim Shilling of Kettleridge, "hire him ASAP!" Shilling's the secret, a "thorough, responsible and, above all, honest" contracting professional who "makes you feel wonderful all the time." With over twenty years experience retrofitting 100-year old homes, Shilling's expertise rests primarily in renovations, with a typical job starting at $500,000. He occasionally does new construction, often associated with additions. Shilling works closely with the client to maintain the spirit of the original home while pushing the boundaries of its potential. The firm works with architects from the get-go and wouldn't take a job without one.

A third-generation carpenter, Shilling worked in the union for ten years. He then helped build spec homes on St. Andrews golf course until he established the firm in 1988. Architects call Shilling a calm "little Buddha" who anticipates everything, while homeowners "never feel anything but happiness when talking to him." Shilling's small staff, which includes a working foreman, carpenters and subs "is overwhelmingly polite and considerate throughout the process" and "quickly responded (and continue to do so) to any questions or needs." All Kettleridge contracts are cost-plus.

"Tim must have the hugest ulcers, because he absorbs all the issues and never lets the clients know everything is anything but perfect—which he makes perfect." "Professionally, I work with many contractors and Kettleridge was the best I could have hoped for on my personal project." "Not many homeowners actually enjoy renovation, but with Tim and his outstanding foreman, Bob, we found it almost painless. They are incredibly organized, careful about costs with a can-do attitude and amazingly clean during demolition and construction." "There is no one like this man on earth."

	Quality	Cost	Value	Recommend?
Lico Contracting Inc.	5	4	5	4.5

29-10 20th Avenue, Astoria, NY 11105
(718) 932 - 8300
High-end residential general contracting

In its fifth decade of building, this family-owned firm's reputation is nearly as "impeccable" as its museum-quality work. Lico performs mainly large gut renovation projects in Manhattan, Long Island, Westchester and Connecticut for a roster of blue-chip clients in a diplomatic and timely manner. A "very helpful" staff of upwards of 85 performs carpentry and millwork services in-house and produces what we hear are beautiful shop drawings. Industry sources say Lico has entrenched relationships with the best subcontractors in NYC.

Clients say principal Rich Bruno and his professional on-site managers orchestrate a fine experience. Lico's workers take care with details and communicate well about all aspects of a project. Like any elite player in the field, expertise comes at a premium.

"An older company with great experience." *"Mindful of everything that involves the clients and their home comfort."* *"Bruno is the Daniel Boulud of contractors."* *"Strives for strong customer service."* *"We have had them work on two of our apartments, and they have always been extremely professional, conscientious, fair and, most important, very proud of what they do."*

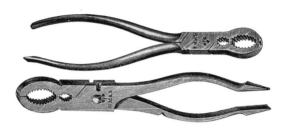

LoPiccolo Construction Corp.   4.5   3.5   5   5
81 Union Valley Road, Mahopac, NY 10541
(845) 656 - 2245

Residential general contracting—historical renovations, rehabs and expansions

Clients cite this "spectacularly responsible" general contractor as displaying a unique "care for the craft" that makes it "sympathetic to an old house." They tell us LoPiccolo Construction excels in expansions, small remodels and historical rehabs in Manhattan and the outlying counties of Westchester, Putnam and Fairfield. Jobs, which typically last three months to one year, are taken one at a time. Booked well in advance for its "110 percent" personal service, the small firm is reputed to treat clients like kings, homes like precious artifacts and schedules like holy decrees.

The son of an excavator/builder, owner Peter LoPiccolo has logged 34 years behind the wheel of his own firm. Clients describe LoPiccolo as "the perfect guy" who "enjoys the puzzle" of renovations. He is joined by his three sons among his staff of six, and calls upon the same cadre of subs he's worked with since the 1970s. We're told the firm is meticulous, caring and "priced-well."

"Fits into that mold of best of the best." *"Did homework on the old house. Studied the original Yankee gutters and learned how to replicate them perfectly."* *"Conscientious and careful about money."* *"A+."* *"Honorable guy."* *"Understands drawings."* *"Straightforward. Direct."* *"Choose people who do it right. Everyone is working at Peter's level of consciousness."* *"Didn't slavishly try to restore it. He was really sensitive."*

Mead & Mikell Inc.   4   4   4   4
150 West 80th Street, Suite 8A, New York, NY 10024
(212) 874 - 3300 www.meadandmikell.com

High-end renovation and restoration

This interior renovation and restoration guru "does everything just right." Whether combining a duplex in Manhattan or adding to a historic Greek Revival in Westchester, Mead & Mikell achieves brilliant results for the most complicated of projects. The firm's decision makers inspire such confidence in homeowners that they have faith in the firm even in their absence during the process. After a project is completed, clients still call on him to manage any subsequent issues.

President Pinkney Mikell spearheads every project. We're told Mikell "couldn't be nicer" and that his accommodating company attracts a dedicated group of top-tier subcontractors and architects. Clients couldn't recommend Mead & Mikell more highly, particularly for "rich friends with lots of time."

"Just the right person for a highly demanding client who loves the renovation process." "Pinkney takes care of people." "After six to eight months you still like him. There's a lot to be said about that." "Fewer problems than I would have expected given the scale of the renovation."

Miller and Raved

2 Hamilton Avenue, New Rochelle, NY 10801
(914) 632 - 3555

High-end general contracting

4	4	4	4

Celebrated names in the design world turn to Miller and Raved for "meticulously detailed projects and exceptional quality." Active primarily in Manhattan, this "extremely reliable" 40-year-old firm takes on everything from $500,000 whole-house renovations in Westchester to megabuck international hotel developments.

Clients tell us partners Charles Miller, who tends to the details, and Roy Raved, who manages the clients, exhibit intense dedication to each project. We also hear they weave knowledge, staunch professionalism and planning expertise into a tapestry of overall outstanding project management. The firm is more expensive than most.

"Very loyal to their clients." "If 100 is the highest quality, then they are 101!" "Really exceptional." "High-end, great guys. Very reliable." "Their timing is terrific." "They are smart and know exactly what to do and how to put it together."

Montanari Construction

61 Peaceable Hill, Ridgefield, CT 06877
(203) 438 - 9826

Residential general contracting

3.5	3.5	4	5

MZM Construction Corp.

3 Elyse Drive, New City, NY 10956
(845) 638 - 2694

Residential, institutional and commercial construction

4	3	5	4.5

Whether outfitting slick corporate HQs or remodeling cozy country kitchens, this straight-arrow general contractor strikes a bull's-eye. Established in 1992, MZM works in New York City, Westchester and Fairfield on a diverse slate of jobs budgeted between $200,000 and $2 million. We're told the firm does well to commit fully to every client, taking on only about four projects at a time. Notably, MZM's broad background affirms its ability to execute technically challenging projects that might require special forms, shoring and structural elements with no room for error.

Principal Mike Hirsch's 25-plus years in the construction industry has taken him from project engineer on the French and Japanese Pavilions at EPCOT Center, in Orlando, Florida to rehabbing a seven-story TriBeCa residence. His partner, Robert Winnicki, brings 25 years' experience of his own in running the firm's field operations. From superintendents and carpenters, MZM's staff is reported to be "easier to get in touch with and more reliable" than the competition. The firm's commercial connections make it an exceedingly good value as well.

"Mike is a calming influence, very rational." "They've come in to fix the little tiny things after the job." "He has a great supervisor on site, but I can always call Mike." "Attention to detail, they hand filed all the cornices to make them fit perfectly."

New Horizon Builders

948 Valley Road, New Canaan, CT 06840
(203) 966 - 9879

Custom residential construction

📁	📁	📁	📁

Nordic Custom Builders Inc.

	Quality	Cost	Value	Recommend?
	4	3.5	4.5	5

125 Greenwich Avenue, 3rd floor, Greenwich, CT 06830
(203) 629 - 0430

High-end general contracting and construction management

Nordic receives a flurry of compliments. Clients and professionals alike "can't say enough good things" about this "first-class operation with first-class people." A general contractor and construction manager specializing in custom residential construction in Manhattan, Fairfield and Westchester, Nordic is known for "well-organized, accurate scheduling" and a "commitment to the work that is equal to that of the designer and architect." "A talented woodworking resource," Nordic's 15,000-square-foot millwork facility is located in Mount Vernon, New York.

Principals Thor Magnus and Eamonn Ryan have been working together since 1992. We hear one of the partners stays involved with each job on a day-to-day basis. Clients tell us Magnus and Ryan "adopt the client's perspective" and show "outstanding judgment" throughout the process. Nordic runs an "honest and incredibly hardworking" crew, including in-house carpenters. They rave that the firm's "attention to detail is unsurpassed" and paperwork is "impeccable," all at a "cost below that of comparable builders."

"Nordic is my first choice for every project in Manhattan and Fairfield. Among the best I've worked with anywhere in the country." "They did everything right, were fast, professional and accurate." "A consummate professional, always a source of inspiration and exceptionally honest." "A building experience we would definitely repeat." "They are responsive, insist on the highest quality work and are also flexible." "I would hire Nordic in a flash."

Pine Creek Builders

80 Century Drive, Stratford, CT 06615
(203) 380 - 8277

High-end custom homes

Pinecrest Builders Inc.

PO Box 71, Riverside, CT 06870
(203) 637 - 9711

High-end custom homes and renovations

Profile Renovation Inc.

	Quality	Cost	Value	Recommend?
	4	3.5	4.5	4

433 West 260th Street, Riverdale, NY 10471
(718) 796 - 5770

Residential general contracting, interior renovations

We hear the star of this "eager to please" general contracting firm is "on the up and up." In its eighth year, Profile tackles both small and large jobs, focusing on interior renovation of up to $1 million. Many repeat Manhattan and Westchester County homeowners tell us the company's "young and reassuring" principals make them feel their job is the only one, while those in the trade consider Profile a steal.

"Great guys to work with—very responsible, responsive and always pleasant." "They work really hard and have rewarded us time and time again."

Prutting & Co. Custom Builders, LLC

	Quality	Cost	Value	Recommend?
	4	3.5	5	4.5

70 Pine Street, New Canaan, CT 06840
(203) 972 - 1028   www.prutting.com

Residential general contracting and construction management

For "good advice and attentive service," the proof is in the Prutting. This mom-and-pop shop "goes the extra mile" to "get the right result" with special touches and an "exceptional" level of craft, steering both major and minor residential construction jobs. Clients from Scarsdale to Wilton comment on the firm's "top-tier woodwork" and say they were "happily surprised" with the "interesting" experience.

Starting as a carpenter in Cape Cod, principal Dave Prutting has notched more than 30 years in the trades. We're told he and his wife, Deborah, have assembled a tight-knit staff that sources describe as "extremely prompt, neat, friendly and professional." The firm both negotiates and bids jobs, and is considered an excellent value.

"Dave is detail-oriented, meticulous and thorough in his approach and work. He is also very fair on pricing." "He's honest and sincerely cares and takes pride in the quality of his work." "Integrity second to none. Really suggests excellent ideas." "Carpentry and millwork is their greatest strength. Good paperwork and billing." "The results were fabulous. Our home has been photographed and included in trade magazines."

RC Metell Construction Inc.   4.5   4   5   5
198 West Haviland Lane, Stamford, CT 06903
(203) 968 - 1777   roncminc@optonline.net
High-end residential general contracting

Clients roundly compliment RC Metell's "consummate dedication to details and quality." The firm takes on very high-end residential interiors and new construction in Fairfield County and New York City, with the average project falling between two and four million. Considered a committed team player, RC Metell works well with designers and can navigate a client's restrictive schedule.

We hear that Ron Metell is a personable man with a great sense of humor, but serious about the quality of his work and the integrity of his business. Clients who have worked with Metell on multiple projects (including one whose project he rescued after another contractor dropped it) appreciate his dedication to their interests. They also appreciate his "accurate and timely billing."

"Ron is extremely personable and proactive." "No corners are cut, but they will offer alternatives to the architectural details if they seem unreasonable." "Extremely high-attention to detail and follow-up." "Works well with our interior design firm." "Ron was very considerate of summer hours and got the job done before school started."

Round Hill Properties Inc.
35 Mason Street, Greenwich, CT 06830
(203) 869 - 6267
Custom new home construction and renovation

Seakco Construction Company   3   3   4   4
114 North Stamford Road, Stamford, CT 06903
(203) 329 - 8839   seakcoconstr@aol.com
General contracting

This "cooperative," "budget-conscious" contractor is well suited to homeowners interested in having a greater hand in the design of their construction projects.

Seakco seeks rehab and new construction assignments with budgets going from $100,000 to over a million dollars. Principal Bob Evans, who studied at the University of Kentucky Architectural School and worked for a construction management firm in Atlanta, started Seakco in 1982.

Evans both collaborates with architects and realizes clients' design ideas himself. He leads a crew of eight, made up of site superintendents and framing/finish carpenters. Insider sources say Evans is "competent, nice to work with" and "not overly expensive for what he does."

"I have worked with this company for seventeen years in one form or another. Every project has finished on time or early; I have referred them often." *"A very reliable contractor. Strong front-end capabilities."*

Shaw Builders, LLC   4   3.5   5   5
154 New Milford Turnpike, New Preston, CT 06777
(866) 968 - 1040   www.shawbuilder.com
Residential new construction and restoration

Clients tell us this "team of artisans" works with uncommon "skill, precision and pride of craftsmanship." Shaw Builder's reverence for old-world detail shows as much in the firm's restorations as its new construction. Budgets range from $1 million to $5 million for customers in Westchester, Fairfield and Lichtfield counties. New York City clients can monitor the progress of their county homes via Shaw's website, where the firm constantly posts correspondence and progress photos on a password protected page.

Founded by Thomas Shaw in 1949, son Marc now runs the show. His siblings, Dave and Eric, are subcontractors with the company. We hear Marc Shaw welcomes ideas in the design phase and gets personally involved during construction. The firm employs 45, including CAD draftsmen and expert masons and cabinetmakers. Shaw charges hourly for design and a percentage of the total budget for construction.

"We are normal people who appreciate the detail of quality work but work with a tight budget. Marc and his team treated us with the same respect reserved for his celebrity clientele."

Stasio Inc.   4.5   3.5   5   5
PO Box 1035, 57 Golf Lane, Ridgefield, CT 06877
(203) 431 - 3946
Residential historic renovations and custom homes

When the winds of change are ready to sweep through your home, working with this contractor is a breeze. This small boutique operation takes on a diverse selection of residential projects and is "characterized by dependability, integrity and follow through." Historic remodels are a specialty, with a recent commission by the Preservation Trust in Ridgefield to dismantle and rebuild a 1713 home. The firm works in lower Fairfield and Westchester counties on projects starting at $250,000 upward of a couple million. Clients tell us Stasio Inc. shuns volume and embraces building as a very intimate, social process.

Coming from carpentry, Dan Stasio founded the company in 1983. Sources say he is "a true gentleman" and a "very fair person" who collaborates extremely effectively with clients, designers and tradespeople. A management staff helps to ensure that projects go "without a hiccup," while Stasio's custom cabinet shop can reproduce original details. The firm works on a fee to develop a budget that is rolled into the construction contract if it's hired for the main event.

"Effortless to work with, anticipates everything." *"Great follow-through, decisionmaking and communication."* *"Worked on many projects and never had a hiccup."* *"Dan Stasio, his job foreman, his office staff and the subcontractors he uses have all been very professional, flexible and accommodating as they efficiently did their jobs while trying to minimally inconvenience us."* *"I recommend them a lot and our friends are very pleased too."* *"Exceptionally patient to work out problems which arose."*

	Quality	Cost	Value	Recommend?
	+	$	◆	★

Sullivan Construction Company, LLC   4   3.5   5   4.5

860 Canal Street, Stamford, CT 06902
(203) 975 - 0000   stephan@sullivanconstruction.biz
Alterations, additions and new construction

This family-owned business brings "a lot of pride" and an "immaculate reputation" to Fairfield County (and occasionally Westchester) addition and alteration projects. Clients tell us they are "very pleased" with Sullivan Construction, whose projects range from $300,000 up into the millions. In addition to high-end residential work, the firm also takes on commercial interiors. We hear the "attentive" and "tidy" team of Sullivan especially excels during live-in renovations, where single-room remodels often snowball into substantially larger commissions.

Brothers Ken and Steve Sullivan partnered up three decades ago. Today, their sibling Frank joins them in the office. Every client gets a Sullivan as a point person. Word is they are as responsive during pre-construction as they are with follow-up. The firm also personally does the framing and finish work for all its projects. The touchiest of clients trust Sullivan's crew to work in the house unsupervised and have even given Steve keys to watch their house. At the end of the day, we hear this "very talented builder makes you feel comfortable in your own home."

"There were never any surprises regarding cost as everything was well laid out before bills were received." "Wonderful with detail. Superb workmanship. Reliable, honest and dependable." "Every person in the firm is outstanding and wonderful to work with. We recommend them highly." "They simply are the best. We wouldn't let any other team do our projects."

Taconic Builders Inc.   5   4.5   5   5

125 Spencer Place, Mamaroneck, NY 10543
(914) 698 - 7456   www.taconicbuilders.com
High-end residential general contracting

This class-act contractor has established a reputation over its fifteen-plus years for being "first rate in every way." Architects, decorators and homeowners all praise both the quality of the work and the ease of teaming with Taconic, which keeps its job sites plugged in with Internet-ready field terminals. The firm splits its efforts between Westchester and Fairfield enclaves and New York City on jobs squarely at the $2 million to $3 million-dollar mark, with $250,000 the minimum for new clients.

Supporters say co-owners Gerry Holbrook and James Hanley "hire the most competent people for the job and demand perfection," and that Taconic's professional staff "addressed issues with prompt attention and efficiency." The outfit works equally well with clients who want to keep plugged into the minutiae of their project as it does with those who are away in Paris for the duration. We also hear Taconic's service staff keeps projects fine-tuned long after completion.

"A very professional organization from the top to the on-site management." "Everything they did for us was fabulous." "We were delighted and surprised that our relationship with a New York contractor could be so positive." "The job has been a pleasure from beginning to the end. Excellent suggestions and advice throughout the job." "I give Taconic my unconditional recommendation."

Tallman Building   5   4.5   5   5

1853 Post Road East, Westport, CT 06880
(203) 254 - 3055
High-end residential builder

This even-handed firm stands tall among Fairfield County's elite general contractors. The go-to guy for upper-echelon architects and designers, Tallman Builders takes on anything from the $300,000 renovation of an outbuilding to new construction on a 24-acre estate. While Tallman's client list reads like a who's who of Wall Street, "his team of seasoned professionals are always excited to tackle anything of great challenge." We hear the firm "loves to work with antique-distressed materials and embraces the opportunities to work with master carvers and old-world artisans."

Clients "love" the fact that after 30 years in business, principal Paul Tallman is still "passionate about his work." He stays selective about the number of jobs to maintain a personal touch. He'll join a client to shop for fixtures and encourages an open and on-going conversation about budgetary options and design issues. An in-house carpentry corps keeps the schedule clipping along and is always available for follow-up. Those that work with Tallman Builders on a regular basis say they never come away disappointed.

"Always the contractor of choice—handles 90 percent of high-end jobs in town." "Paul Tallman is a very honest contractor who delivers on everything he promises." "Paul has earned the highest level of integrity in our building market." "I was truly impressed with how quickly the job was completed and quite amazed that the project was completed within the parameters we had set for a budget." "Our project was managed very well, the job was done with minimal mess and his employees were very professional."

The I. Grace Company Inc.   4.5   4.5   4.5   4.5
1065 North Street, Greenwich, CT 06831
(203) 422 - 5550   www.igrace.com
Commissioned private residences

This large, nationally renowned residential construction company possesses both finesse and firepower. I. Grace offers end-to-end building and renovation services for spaces ranging from New England country estates to New York City lofts. In addition to the large-scale museum quality projects for which the company is best known, I. Grace maintains ongoing relationships with clients by completing small projects through a service arm. Its impressive roster of clients includes Wall Street execs, celebrities and other power players.

Founded over sixteen years ago by Douglas Cohen, I. Grace engages the construction management process with six divisions and a hundred-plus employees. We hear the firm "demonstrates a responsiveness to client needs, concerns and ambitions consistently from the CEO to the project manager." For those who can afford it, I. Grace promises white-glove treatment with white-collar acumen.

"As a construction manager, they showed professionalism, social coping skills and an interest in being a creative partner with architects in solving problems." "Fabulous. Did whatever they had to do to get the job done." "The firm respects the budget and schedule of the client and is straightforward and complete in advancing quality work, clearly delineating trade-offs without creating straw-man comparisons."

Watters Construction Inc.   3   2.5   5   5
127 Pennsylvania Avenue, Tuckahoe, NY 10707
(646) 302 - 0984
Residential general contracting

In the rough seas of residential renovations, we hear this firm keeps a client's head above water. Watters Construction performs smaller and mid-sized high-end residential contracting jobs in Manhattan and Westchester. It works closely with renowned architects and produces its own millwork, even designing cabinets on its own accord.

	Quality	Cost	Value	Recommend?
	+	$	◆	★

Clients adore principal Martin Watters, who they find friendly and flexible. The company's smallish size means Watters wades knee-deep in every project. We're told he is quite the professional, laying everything out in advance and sharing cost-saving tips with his clients.

"Not only did the contractor respond to our phone calls and keep appointments, we found that there were no hidden costs whatsoever." "He fixed another contractor's mess and did an excellent job." "He is an excellent communicator and is always there when you need him." "A door fell off a cabinet two days before Christmas and Martin came right over to fix it." "We highly recommend Watters. He is worth every single penny."

White Birch Builders, LLC   3.5   3   4   4
18 Beech Street, Greenwich, CT 06830
(203) 531 - 0300   www.whitebirchbuilders.com
Remodels, renovations and additions

Insiders glowingly recommend White Birch Builders for medium-sized and large-scale renovations as well as new additions. Working mostly in Greenwich and the surrounding areas, the firm often outfits homes in the high-tech style. While White Birch always teams with an architect, its own designer is available to create kitchen and millwork shops and adjusts details on the fly. Clients say the firm's proactive and communicative stance minimizes surprise.

Experienced contracting pros Kevin Erenson and Chris Wuest joined forces in 1994. They command an in-house corps of carpenters and cabinetmakers and coordinate a faithful constellation of subs, all of whom we hear religiously adhere to schedule and show overwhelming precision in their execution. Clients also say White Birch Builders proves quite price-competitive at the high-end level.

Woodstone Contracting Inc.   3.5   3   4.5   4.5
51 Compo Beach Road, Westport, CT 06881
(203) 227 - 9245
Building & interior renovations

Clients agree Woodstone's craftsmen "hold themselves to exacting standards," all while maintaining the standard of living for homeowners hunkered down through the renovation. The firm takes on high-end residential jobs in Manhattan, Westchester and Fairfield going from $50,000 into the multimillions. It teams closely with the architect or designer, and we hear "anticipated problems that might have occurred due to minor errors in the plans."

A second-generation builder, boss John Caputo founded Woodstone in 1976. In addition to the Westport location, Woodstone also has a Scarsdale office. Clients remark that Caputo "intuitively knew when and what changes needed to be made to make the space the way we envisioned." The firm furnishes its own carpentry and masonry personnel and signs subs dubbed "top caliber from painters to tile-men." References report there "wasn't a day that passed that the premises were left nothing short of immaculate."

"Attention to detail is over the top." "Even with those items where we had a change of mind or where there may have been some confusion, they handled the matters in a prompt and courteous manner." "On top of the project every step of the way." "John has outstanding taste and his first priority is top quality." "After each day the space was left broom clean."

Wright Brothers Builders, Inc.   3.5   3.5   4   4.5
325 Post Road West, Westport, CT 06880
(203) 227 - 8215   www.wrightbuild.com
Residential builder and remodeler

This solid Westport-based builder has enjoyed longevity and a strong reputation for quality, timeliness and cost effectiveness. Wright Brother Builders takes on

new construction and renovation for both residential and commercial properties. Named one of *Remodeling* magazine's top 50 contractors, the firm's good work ethic and trustworthiness doesn't go unnoticed by clients either.

President Kelly Wright teams with his brother Chris and a seasoned staff of career craftsmen to offer active, ongoing supervision of each project. We hear the completion of a job is just the beginning of the Wrights' relationship with a client. The firm provides fixed-price contracts, cost-plus, or other mutually agreed upon arrangements and is deemed a good value by insiders.

"Problem solvers with a team approach." "Their concern for meeting our needs and working closely with us to create the exact look that we wanted to achieve was top-notch. And they did so within the budget that we set forth."

Xhema Remodeling Co.   4.5   4.5   4   4
Oak & Division Street W, Greenwich, CT 06831
(203) 531 - 6070

High-end residential general contracting and design/build

The area's most discerning clientele turn to Xhema Remodeling for flawless interpretation of architectural design, rigorous project management, superb attention to every detail and unsurpassed excellence in residential building. The firm takes a full-service, integrated approach to custom construction, from ground-up French chateaus to renovations on Park Avenue duplexes. We're told Xhema's offices in Rye, Greenwich and Manhattan are literally staffed seven days a week to care for clients.

Owner Jim Xhema, who comes from a background in painting, founded the firm over 30 years ago. He dispatches a team of highly skilled craftsmen and supervisors to guide and advise the homeowner and architect through every step of the building process. Sources say the firm regularly searches worldwide for unique building materials that make all the difference—historically accurate stone, exotic wood, or aged tile already worn smooth. While these richly polished surfaces are of the highest quality, some say Xhema produces an aesthetic that can be "over the top."

"Wants the work to look like a classic design that never changes."

York & Company Decorating   3.5   3.5   4   4.5
Contractors Inc.
1076 East Putnam Avenue, 1st Floor, Greenwich, CT 06870
(203) 698 - 3460   nick@yorkinc.net

Designer-oriented interior renovations

We hear this interior build-out-focused firm is a decorator's best friend. York & Company Decorating Contractors is a perfect fit for those projects where a full-blown general contractor is overkill. Jobs for the trade range from a $5,000 quick cosmetic fix to $800,000 gut renovation of a whole house. York also does masonry and exterior work, and will work directly with design-savvy homeowners who know what they want. Working most often in Fairfield county, the firm's work can be found from Wilton to Manhattan.

In just its second year, York is the product of a partnership between Nick Barile and Brian Conners, the principals of two respected area firms. Barile's electrical company and Conners' decorative painting outfit form the backbone of York & Company. Each principal acts as project manager, coordinating trades and implementing design intent. Clients call them "nice guys" who hit problems head on. They're noted for bringing in competent personnel who are "never sloppy" and always cognizant of the client's space.

"A divine contractor."

HIRING AN ELECTRICIAN OR
LIGHTING DESIGNER

Birds of a different feather, these two professions still flock together, both peddling a little Thomas Edison magic. An electrican's main concerns are about practicing safety and delivering convenience. A lighting designer's interest is in conjuring atmospheres that at once massage a client's mood, amplify architectural elements and provide late-night safety. While the true measure of a successful lighting design job is its inspiration to the eye, a good electrician's work is invisible.

HOW TO CHOOSE AN EXCELLENT ELECTRICIAN

Dealing with electricity and wiring is intimidating, and for good reason—you are placing your family and home at risk if it is not handled properly. This is not the area for cutting costs by doing it yourself, or by choosing the lowest-priced service provider. Think of Chevy Chase putting his Christmas light cords into one giant, sagging cluster of adapters in *National Lampoon's Christmas Vacation*. Hilarious, but maybe a little too close to home.

The first thing you should consider about an electrical contractor is the firm's commitment to safety. This is not a trade that should cut corners. Companies that will not take the time to meticulously lay out projects, that perform hit-and-run installations or pass off cheap product should be avoided. Talk to contractor and homeowner references to get the inside scoop on what firms do inside the walls.

You'll also need to identify the right electrician for your scope of work. Some do only large installations while others concentrate on service and repairs. A company that specializes exclusively on "designer" electrical work, such as the lighting of artwork and retrofitting museum-quality finishes, may not be geared for a large gut renovation. In addition to providing the high-voltage infrastructure that supports the myriad outlets, switches, fixtures and appliances in your home, many electricians also install the low-voltage cabling that supports audio/visual, telecommunications, computer and lighting systems. For these low-voltage systems, they will typically not install the hardware nor do the programming, but should coordinate with the specialists who do.

HOW TO CHOOSE AN EXCELLENT LIGHTING DESIGNER

When considering a lighting designer, listen to your gut. With the exception of its role in nighttime security, lighting design is an aesthetic enterprise. Be it bathing interiors in a soothing glow, dramatically highlighting the architectural features of your home's facade, illuminating artwork or bringing a magical feel to landscapes, a lighting designer tries to capture a mood. These professionals work as consultants, sitting down with the client and walking through the space in order to come up with a lighting scheme that best reflects one's lifestyle. As such, expect them to ask a lot of questions in order to pinpoint what presses your buttons. And speaking of buttons, don't be pressured into buying lighting schemes, fixtures or systems just because they're deemed the best technology out there. What's best for you is what counts.

A lighting design professional works with industrial and custom-created fixtures interfaced with the high-tech lighting control systems by Lutron, Vantage and LightTouch to achieve their vision. In some instances, especially when only low-voltage wiring is involved, they can install their own work without the help of an outside electrician. For the most part, these designers will produce lighting layouts, and the electrician will perform the installation and interface with the control systems. Whoever is responsible for programming these systems should walk the homeowner through the control operations.

IMPORTANT PRE- AND POST-PROJECT CONSIDERATIONS

Electrical and lighting work often requires cutting into a wall to gain access to wires. There are two issues to think about here—cleanup and repair. Sheetrock debris and plaster dust are very difficult to clean up, so the electrician should either inform you of this at the time or put up protective plastic sheeting to keep dust from infiltrating your entire house. Some will repair the wall with plaster, but it is unlikely that they will sand and repaint it. Be sure to discuss this beforehand, clearly identifying the extent of the electrician's responsibility—and get it in writing.

When doing renovation or installation work, your electrician may suggest additional wiring for future use. This may sound like he's just trying to charge you more, but it's actually a very good idea. It is easier to add wiring and setups in the beginning for that dreamed-of central air-conditioning system, six-line phone system or computer network you envision in your future. This avoids the headache of having to tear up walls and floors several years down the road and saves a great deal of money, too.

Also, before your electrician or lighting consultant leaves, make sure you know what switch controls do what and that all circuit breakers are labeled properly. Do not let him disappear without doing this, because he is the only one who knows. Wandering around in the dark in search of a phantom blown fuse or being tormented nightly by landscape lights that snap on at 3:00 AM because you don't know how to reprogram, can be quite annoying.

ON COST

For smaller jobs and service calls, which include repair and maintenance, most companies will charge an hourly rate, anywhere from $50 to $100, with $65 corresponding to a 3 cost rating in *The Franklin Report*. Some companies charge a set fee for a visit, or a higher rate the first hour, then have flat-rate charges for each task performed, such as per outlet relocated or fixture installed. Others insist on doing a consultation to provide you with an estimate before any work is started.

On large scale new electrical installations and renovations, the electrical contractor will submit a total bid for the work. The price should be broken down by each task performed so you can compare apples to apples with other bids. A company's standards in relation to product and safety, the depth of its resources and the demand it is in can all affect cost. Fees for contract renovation work are typically higher per hour and per square foot than those for new construction.

A lighting designer may also charge an hourly rate—anywhere from $100 to $150 an hour—for design and oversight of installation. For larger projects they may charge a fee based upon the total budget or square footage of the project.

With a little preparation, you will be able to save money by saving the service providers time. Often an electrician will need to cut into walls to gain access to wires or to replace fixtures. This is something you should think about before the workmen arrive. You may want to move or cover up that priceless antique sideboard near where the sconces are being installed rather than leaving it to the electrical crew. By taking care of little things in advance, you allow your electrical professional to get right to work, you will not have to worry about the safety of various objects and your billable time will be less.

In the end, consider the company with the best reputation for quality and service, not just the low bidder.

LICENSING, INSURANCE AND PERMITS

You should only consider a full-time licensed professional for your electrical needs. A license from the Department of Labor is required for any electrical work, and all work must be filed with the city. This includes any installation related to light, heat and power. Lighting designers require no licensing; however, those that program lighting control systems should be certified by the manufacturers to do so. As always, ask for the contractor's license number, proof of workman's compensation and liability insurance. Your electrical contractor should always be responsible for obtaining all permits necessary for your job.

GUARANTEES AND SERVICE AGREEMENTS

Your service provider should always stand behind all of his work. Be sure to ask about service agreements. Many electrical professionals provide regular "checkups" and inspections. It may seem like wasted money at first, but over time these measures can prevent an emergency. Lighting designers may offer focusing sessions to readjust and fine-tune your lighting scheme according to season.

Electricians & Lighting Designers

	Quality	Cost	Value	Recommend?
Air Systems	4	4	4	4.5

140 Selleck Street, Stamford, CT 06902
(203) 348 - 5511   www.airsys.net
HVAC and electrical installation and service

See Air Systems's full report under the heading Air Conditioning & Heating

	Quality	Cost	Value	Recommend?
Carraige Light	3.5	3	4	4

561 South Pine Creek Road, Fairfield, CT 06468
(203) 254 - 2644   carlignorth@aol.com
Electrical service and remodeling

	Quality	Cost	Value	Recommend?
Chestnut Electric	5	4	4.5	5

26 Cricket Lane, Wilton, CT 06897
(203) 834 - 1130
High-end electrical service and installation

Customers tell us this is one chestnut you want in your stocking. Donald Winters and Tony Dorn established the firm in 1979, and bring a combined 52 years of electrical experience to each project. Chestnut Electric provides full service residential installation and repair, from hanging a fixture to outfitting a $10 million estate. Winters and Dorn field a crew of 26 veteran employees, including six full-time service professionals, all of whom are described as "exceptionally courteous and efficient."

Sources say lighting designers, white glove contractors and movie stars all use Chestnut. Project schedules are strictly respected and cost, like the service, is high end.

"Chestnut Electric works hand-in-hand with us to delight our customers and they share our commitment to work on time and with schedule in mind." "Best electrician for quality and service." "Ability to keep up with new, state-of-the-art technology." "Friendly, becomes like family."

	Quality	Cost	Value	Recommend?
D. Sal Electrical Contractors Inc.	4	3.5	4	4.5

201 Little Hill Drive, Stamford, CT 06905
(203) 322 - 8963
Electrical installation and repair

President Frank Macchio and his recently retired partner opened D. Sal in 1964 and the company has sparked electrical jobs ever since. The firm works primarily as a sub for high-end contractors but is willing to take minor repair and installation jobs for homeowners. D. Sal's commercial experience compliments its knowledge of the complex mechanical and lighting control systems prevalent in today's high-end residential home. Its men are schooled installers and programmers for Lutron HomeWorks and RadioRA wireless systems.

Macchio oversees seven electricians, with someone always on staff in the office to answer phones and questions. Sources say D. Sal cares for its high-end clients by creating custom brackets to hang antique fixtures or specialty adaptors on boxes to take European fixtures. Satisfied customers report that Macchio has built an abundantly qualified crew.

"Excellent staff. Quick turnaround time. Very knowledgeable workers. Fine ethics."

	Quality	Cost	Value	Recommend?
	✚	$	◆	★

Davenport Electric Company, Inc.   4.5   3.5   5   4.5
1 Fawn Meadow Lane, Weston, CT 06883
(203) 454 - 9995

Designer-oriented lighting system installation and service

This electrical contracting firm's ability to cater to the intent of design professionals and the needs of demanding clients is what sets it apart. Michael O'Conner, who has over 25 years experience in the trade, established Davenport Electric in 1988 as a one-stop destination for high-end residential electrical systems.   Davenport divides its efforts between new construction projects, renovations and service for established customers. The firm's fifteen electricians work in Westchester, Fairfield and lower Putnam County.

As picky as an interior designer and with an understanding of the level of quality and taste expected by his well-heeled clientele, O'Conner is fully sensitive to his work within the context of the overall product. He brings ideas and solutions to the table in regard to design, and considers framing issues before hammering the first nail. Service calls are billed for time and material.

DCM Electric Inc.   4   4   4   5
541 North State Road, Briarcliff Manor, NY 10510
(914) 941 - 3433 dcmelec@aol.com

Layout, installation and service of complete electrical systems

DCM's venerable service on high-end residential and commercial properties has developed life-long devotees. Distinguished management agencies call on the company to care for their buildings while city building officials in Briarcliff Manor deem this the only electrical contractor they would absolutely recommend. The firm offers service and repair tip to tip in Westchester County, as well as layout and installation of complete electrical systems, including lighting and dimming controls.

DCM founder, Darin Christopher Mattina, has worked as an electrician since he was fourteen. He gained union experience after high school and established his own firm in 1989. Today Mattina supervises a crew of five and can be found in the field himself, something clients appreciate. They tell us his firm shows particular expertise in snaking walls in renovations, sparing finishes and keeping everything spic n' span. Mattina takes a design fee for lighting design and charges a competitive hourly rate for service calls.

Focal Point Outdoors, LLC   4   4   4.5   4.5
151 Sound Beach Avenue, Old Greenwich, CT 06870
(203) 698 - 3260

Outdoor and landscape lighting design and installation

See Focal Point Outdoors, LLC's full report under the heading Landscape Architects/Designers

Genovese Electric Co. Inc.   3.5   3.5   4   4.5
10 Tally Drive, Norwalk, CT 06851
(203) 855 - 9521

Electrical renovations, repair and service

This firm, established in 1984 by Stephan A. Genovese, takes service seriously. An ordained deacon in the Roman Catholic Church, Genovese preaches the gospel of fine workmanship to his six electricians. The firm's forte is high-end renovations, snaking walls and hanging fixtures without damaging finishes and aggravating homeowners. Genovese electricians move furniture out of harm's way and man a bottle of Windex to clean up any smudges left behind. In addition, this CAT-5-certified firm helps homeowners computerize their homes.

	Quality	Cost	Value	Recommend?
	✚	$	◆	★

Clients trust the Genovese team, which runs in three crews of two. Every charge is itemized, and while the company's service isn't cheap, it leaves customers singing hallelujah!

"Nice, good, dependable." "They installed all our incredible chandeliers. We are very happy. Will use time and again." "Because they are so good, they can be very busy. Nonetheless, I always wait as I know the job will be done correctly."

GT Electric   4   3.5   4   4
20 Brookfield Street, Norwalk, CT 06851
(203) 849 - 1316
Electrical and lighting system installation and service

Homeowner's Electrical Co. Inc.   3   3   4   4
67 Lincoln Avenue, Pelham, NY 10803
(914) 738 - 2807
Electrical installation and repair

JC Beach Electricians   4   4   4   4
66 Babbitt Road, Bedford Hills, NY 10507
(914) 666 - 3484
Electrical and lighting system installation and service

Mancuso Electric   3.5   3.5   4   4
PO Box 75, Cos Cob, CT 06807
(203) 975 - 0523
Electrical installation and repair

Mark Ballard, Electrical Contractor   4   4   4   4.5
211 Wolfpit Avenue, Norwalk, CT 06851
(203) 847 - 8007
Electrical installation and repair

Mecca Electrical   3.5   3   4.5   4.5
19 Purchase Street, Rye, NY 10580
(914) 967 - 8051
Electrical and lighting system installation and service

Be it changing out a fixture or rewiring an estate, clients worship at the doors of Mecca. Licensed in both Fairfield and Westchester, the firm services and installs lighting and electrical systems in homes and businesses, new and old. Owner Anthony Nostro has over a dozen years in the trade and we hear his staff is as competent as they are respectful. Service calls are reasonably priced and emergencies responded to within the hour.

Millennium Electric   4   4   4   4
850 Route 22, Brewster, NY 10509
(845) 897 - 9670
Electrical renovation, installation and service

	Quality	Cost	Value	Recommend?
	✚	$	◆	★

Mordente Electric Inc.
4.5   3.5   5   5

21 East Brown Street, West Haven, CT 06516
(203) 932 - 6253

Electrical installation, remodels and repair

This "quiet and thoughtful" father-and-son tandem comforts clients and impresses architects with its personalized, detailed approach. Lifelong electrician Rick Mordente opened the business in 1985. The firm handles Fairfield County clients and works on small bathroom remodels and head-to-toe installations in new homes. Areas of expertise include emergency generators, home automation and lighting control systems.

The family takes on only one or two jobs at a time, limiting service to existing customers so they can be immediately helped. Clients tell us they welcome Mordente's nifty suggestions regarding switching, traffic flow and timers.

"Can do really difficult and creative work."

Neilson Electric
3   3   4   4

18 Cassidy Park, Greenwich, CT 06830
(203) 552 - 9829

Electrical installation and repair

Nick's Electrical Service Inc.
4   3.5   4.5   4

774 Post Road, Scarsdale, NY 10583
(914) 723 - 1498

Electrical installation, remodels and service

P&M Electric
5   4   4.5   5

1775 Front Street, Yorktown, NY 10598
(914) 962 - 3581

High-end electrical service and installation

Pete and Mike, the eponymous P&M of this well-regarded electrical business, have been friends and colleagues for 33 years. Two generations of contractors, architects and homeowners in Westchester and Putnam counties have counted on them. The well-rounded and well-connected firm does it all, from minor service work to major-league installations. It even fields a bucket truck to change neighborhood lamppost bulbs.

The firm's twenty-two-person staff reflects this reservoir of experience, with two foremen logging nearly twenty-five years with P&M. We hear the company's consideration for honesty, neatness and safety has established a winning reputation not only with clients but also with city inspectors. Mike even sits on the Yorktown Electrical Board. Prices surge into the high-end, but clients say the results will light up your life.

"Excellent service, comes quickly, does great work. Excellent pleasant workers, always clean up after themselves." "Excellent. On-time, high quality, very professional."

Pioneer Electrical Contractors, LLC
4.5   4   4   4.5

34 Laddin Rock Road, Greenwich, CT 06830
(203) 698 - 2455

Electrical installation, remodels and service

Richard Boshka Electric, LLC
4   3.5   4.5   4.5

27 Northhill Street, Suite 5W, Stamford, CT 06907
(203) 325 - 9511

Electrical renovation, installation and service

We hear this small company will work around the clock to make customers happy. One client was so smitten with the service, that he flew Boshka electricians down for a job in St. Croix. From a plug to a new addition, the firm provides all-encompassing installation and service. With more than fifteen years experience working with high-end clients in the Westchester and Fairfield areas, Richard Boshka knows the ins and outs of wiring smart homes, home theaters, and computer and telephone systems, as well as European fixtures.

Clients appreciate the one-on-one interaction with owner Boshka, who they say is open and responsive. We're also told he is especially serious about showing up and getting the job done when he says it will be done. Rates are decent and the firm's many repeat customers always come first.

Richport Associates Electrical Contractor   4.5   4   4.5   4
1076 East Putnam Avenue, 1st Floor, Greenwich, CT 06870
(203) 698 - 4800
Designer-oriented electrical and lighting system installation and service

Richport Associates has patina-conscious clients seeing the light. Accommodating decorators and homeowners in Westchester, Fairfield and New York City say this firm develops and implements lighting schemes and electrical systems. Richport Associates installs, remodels and services both residential and commercial properties.

Owner Nick Barile brings his certified lighting designer and crew to each job. His firm's expertise can also be tapped through York Decorating Contractors, an interior design-oriented contractor co-owned by Barile and painting master, Brian Conners. (See review in Contractors & Builders)

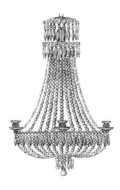

Strathmoor Electric Inc.   4.5   4   4.5   5
1261 Stratford Avenue, Stratford, CT 06497
(203) 377 - 4261
Electrical and lighting system installation and service

The Lamp Doc   3.5   2.5   5   5
311 Arkansas Drive, Brooklyn, NY 11234
(917) 414 - 0426
On-site lamp repair and rewiring

This Doc makes house calls, and clients are "overjoyed" at such "a unique service," which rewires lamps right on the premises. Be it a chandelier, mini-halogen, temperamental three-way, or European fixture converted to US voltage, the Lamp Doc is on call. Making his rounds in Westchester and New York City, he is even available to assess antique finds before purchase. He will take down and put back up most fixtures and if necessary, take them to the shop.

"Doc" Roy Schneit, who works alongside "Nurse" (and wife) Lois, has over 30 years experience in the lighting business and previously owned a lamp shop in the City. Clients call the pair "prompt, professional, knowledgeable and obliging." Prices are always quoted over the phone and range from $55 to several hundred dollars per repair.

"Neat and careful, great with antiques." "His professional competence is matched by his unfailing courtesy and punctuality." "The cost was exactly as he quoted beforehand on the phone." "It would have been such a nuisance to schlep these lamps to a repair shop. And a 'regular' electrician would have charged substantially more." "Roy brought all the necessary equipment and repaired all my lamps, including some antiques I inherited, and I'm in my eighties."

Yankee Electric Construction Co.   4.5   3.5   4.5   4
150 Carter Henry Drive, Fairfield, CT 06430
(203) 259 - 5499

Electrical and lighting system installation and service

Sources say Yankee knocks the ball out of the park every time. The firm is recruited to design, install, troubleshoot and service high-end electrical systems for a commercial and residential clientele in Fairfield County. This includes computer rooms, home offices, and window shade and lighting controls like Lutron and LightTouch systems. A notably user-friendly electrician, Yankee is said to interface well with clients, providing both the documentation and support to keep homeowners comfortable with their systems long after the job is done.

Friends from high school, partners Ray Barry and Gary Kopsco formed Yankee in 1975. Between them, they oversee seventeen electricians and a three-person office. Rates compete with those of other elite electrical contractors.

Hiring a Flooring
Service Provider

The builders and renovators of the sprawling mansions and historic homes in Westchester and Fairfield Counties know that more than any other part of the home, flooring creates the basic ambiance of the room and gets the steadiest use. Be it carpet, vinyl, wood, tile, stone, cork, rubber, bamboo or concrete, flooring must be durable as well as attractive.

What Are My Choices?

There are many options in flooring, each falling into five basic categories: wood, laminate, vinyl, carpet and hard tile (see section introduction to Tile, Marble and Stone). To get ideas, look through home furnishing magazines and pay a visit to a flooring showroom or two. Internet sites that will help you learn more about flooring options and the best way to care for them include Floorfacts, a consumer site filled with links and information (www.floorfacts.com) the Carpet & Rug Institute (www.carpet-rug.com) and the National Wood Flooring Association's site (www.woodfloors.org). After considering the following descriptions of basic floor types, you should be able to choose flooring that best meets your specific demands for beauty and maintenance.

Wood

A real wood floor never goes out of style and probably has the best resale value. It complements every decor, from minimalist to Louis XIV, and generally ages gracefully. The most popular woods used in flooring are oak and maple, which can be stained or color-washed to your exact specifications. Wood flooring can be designed in numerous patterns, limited only by your imagination (and budget). Some of the most popular are parquet, plank, strip and herringbone. When choosing a stain color, have your contractor apply a few samples and look at them in different kinds of light. Think of the ambience you are trying to create in the room—traditional or modern, casual or formal—spacious or cozy. Wood floors can be bleached—for a light and airy look—or painted. Hardwood floors can be customized to satisfy every taste and personality and installed in any room, regardless of what type of flooring—concrete existing boards or particleboard subflooring—is already there.

Aesthetically, a wood floor is stunning. But consider a few issues before you make this your final choice. What kind and how much traffic does the room get every day? Hardwood floors can be dented and scratched, especially from high-heeled shoes, and may not be the best choice for beachfront properties where sand and salt water are traipsed around. Although a variety of urethane finishes provide excellent protection (and shine), they do not completely prevent dents and scratches. These same finishes, however, make wood floors much easier to clean and maintain than those of previous generations. Humidity is another factor to consider. If the humidity in your area varies from season to season, a wood floor will expand and contract with the rise and fall of moisture in the air. Storing the wood on-site for a period of time before installing will allow it to acclimatize to the specific humidity level in the home. The service provider should consider whether the floor is being installed in a particularly humid or dry time of the year, and make his measurements accordingly.

Laminates

If you love the look of real wood but have an active household, laminate flooring may be the perfect choice for you. Laminates are plastic- or wood-based products that look like hardwood. They come in various textures and are durable and easy to maintain. Laminates can also imitate the look of stone, marble or tile, offering a wide variety of creative styles you may not have imagined. A wood-patterned laminate floor has some significant advantages over the real thing—for example, it will not be discolored by sunlight and is very scratch-resistant. Laminate floors wear well and usually come with a guarantee of ten years or more; however, they cannot be refinished like wood.

Cleanups are also a breeze with laminate flooring. Laminates repel liquid and do not allow stains to set in. This point alone saves your floor, your time and your psychological well-being. Design snobs will, however, look down their noses at laminate as an imitation.

Both hardwood floors and laminates, while possessing the great qualities of longevity and beauty, are expensive. If you are looking to invest less money, you may want to explore vinyl or carpet floor coverings.

VINYL/LINOLEUM

The retro chic of vinyl or linoleum is often the least expensive choice and offers more options than any other type of flooring, with an eye-popping palette of colors, marbling, prints and patterns. Linoleum is primarily made from all natural products such as flax, wood powder and resin. The backing is made from a natural grass called jute, while vinyl's backing is made from polyester. Both are durable and easy-to-maintain.

Although it resists moisture, vinyl can stain, so spills need to be handled quickly and carefully according to the manufacturer's directions. The material is vulnerable to scuffing and can also tear—from furniture that may be moved across it or sharp objects that fall to the floor.

CARPETING

A cozy, lush floor covering, carpeting adds warmth, soundproofing, texture, color and insulation to a room. When considering carpeting, think about whether you'll need a light, medium or heavy duty type. Industry experts suggest light duty for occasionally trafficked areas, medium duty for the bedroom or office and heavy duty for hallways, stairs and other high-traffic areas. Carpeting requires extra maintenance, as stains are more difficult to remove and general cleaning is more work. Wool is a whole lot easier to deep-steam clean than nylon, but is more expensive. Also, a protective sealant may be applied to fend off future spills and stains. Lastly, if you or someone in your home is allergy-prone, carpeting is not the best option, because it retains dirt, dust and other particles.

HARD TILE

Ceramic, quarry (stone, including marble) and terra cotta make up this premium category of floor covering. The look and feel of a hard-tiled floor is unlike any other, with grooves and textures that can be felt underfoot. Often used in kitchens and baths, and ideal for indoor/outdoor rooms, tile flooring can give a distinct look and originality to any room in your home. In light colors, these materials do take on stains, so keep this in mind when choosing hard tile for particular rooms. Tile may be one of the most expensive kinds of flooring, but its remarkable beauty and longevity make it a good investment.

SPECIALTY OPTIONS

Cork floors, made from the ground-up bark of an oak tree, are a hot option these days. A natural material, each tile shows variations in shades and tones, and is finished like a hardwood floor. While comparable to wood in price, cork has a more buoyant feel under the feet. Cork's ability to weather spills receives mixed reviews.

A contemporary, cool option is polished or stamped concrete. Installation can be quite involved and comes at a higher price.

ON COST

Some floor installers charge by the square foot and others by the job. Most providers charge by the hour for cleaning and repairing. If your service provider charges by the hour, confirm whether this fee is per person per hour or for the whole team. Will they charge for moving furniture around? Make sure your order includes extra quantities of flooring in your dye lot to replace broken, worn or stained sections in the future. This is especially crucial with hard tile, which can crack if something heavy is dropped on it, and any other material which stains easily.

KNOW YOUR FLOOR

Insist upon receiving written information about the care and maintenance of your new flooring. What cleaning products should you use and what should you definitely avoid? Is there a standard timetable for cleaning your hardwood floor or carpeting? Does your carpet warranty come with a consumer hotline for stain emergencies? Who can you call for advice about stains and/or damage?

SERVICE AND WARRANTIES

Before you sign a work agreement, find out exactly who will be installing your floor: will your contact from the firm be doing the job himself, or bringing in a different crew? Make sure that the firm will supply nails, glue and other installation accessories. Does the company have its own workshop or warehouse? If so, it will have more control over the product than one that purchases its materials from another supplier. Ask the company if it does repairs as well as installation. It's always a good idea to have the installer supply the material, so he can't point fingers at the product manufacturer if there is a problem. Both the flooring company and the flooring material manufacturers should have warranties for your new floor coverings. Remember, whatever material you choose, it's only as good as the installation.

FLOORING COMPARISON CHART

RATINGS: Very Poor *   Poor **   Average ***   Good ****   Excellent *****

BASIC FLOOR TYPES:	VINYL	WOOD	LAMINATE	HARD TILE	CARPET
Ease of Maintenance	****	***	****	****	***
Damage Resistance	**	***	****	*****	***
Moisture Resistance	****	*	***	*****	*
Stain Resistance	***	**	*****	*****	**
Fade Resistance	***	**	*****	*****	***
Scratch Resistance	**	***	****	****	N/A
Ease of Repair	*	***	**	**	*
Softness Under Foot	**	*	*	*	*****
Design/Color Selection	*****	**	**	***	****
◇Price Range (sq. ft.)	$.50 - $4.50	$2.50 - $6.00	$2.50 - $5.00	$2.50 - $8.00	$.50 - $5.00

◇The price range is for material only and is to be used as a general guideline. Prices will vary from supplier to supplier.

Flooring Installation & Repair

800 Rug Wash   4   2   5   5
20 Enterprise Avenue, Secaucus, NJ 07094
(800) 784 - 9274   rugwash@aol.com
Rug and upholstery cleaning and repair, flooring installation and maintenance

See 800 Rug Wash's full report under the heading Rugs–Cleaning, Installation & Repair

All Boro Floor Service   3   2.5 4.5 4
135 East 233rd Street, Bronx, NY 10470
(718) 231 - 6911   allboroflooring@aol.com
Wood flooring installation, refinishing and waxing

Satisfied clients and well-known contractors have used All Boro for years on multiple jobs. All Boro installs hardwood floors and does scraping, refinishing and staining for residential and commercial clients. Its workmen also specialize in custom flooring and paneling. In business for twelve years, this firm works mostly in Manhattan, Westchester, Connecticut and New Jersey. Recent noteworthy projects include Gracie Mansion and The Castle in Greenwich.

"Hardworking, skilled and honest," is how users reference this firm. The company, open all year 'round, gives free estimates, and sources say prices are moderate to upper end." "Proficient. They get the job done under difficult circumstances." "Above what I expected." "Floors are holding up."

Amarko Marble & Granite   3.5 3   4   4
60-14 60th Place, Maspeth, NY 11378
(718) 821 - 0323   amarkomarble@aol.com
Marble flooring installation and maintenance

Amarko installs, cleans, polishes and hones marble floors. Though serving mostly commercial clients, this firm also deals with some residential clients. Additional services include cleaning and refinishing countertops and other marble and granite surfaces. Amarko's success can be measured through its stonework requested by some of the city's top hotels and well-heeled clientele in Manhattan, Westchester and Connecticut. Clients appreciate their efficient service and the moderate prices that go with it.

"A pleasure to deal with." "Quick, efficient." "Great craftsmen. Amazing stonework."

American Custom Wood Flooring   3   3   4   4
3615 Greystone Avenue, Bronx, NY 10463
(718) 548 - 9275
Wood floor installation, cleaning, repair, custom designs and inlays

American Custom Wood Flooring specializes in the installation, repair, cleaning and maintenance of wood floors only. The company also creates custom designs and inlays. The firm generally takes on commercial projects in Manhattan and Westchester, working with contractors and architects, but will occasionally work directly with homeowners. In business for fifteen years, the firm usually charges by the job and works on new construction and existing structures. Licensed, bonded and insured, this five-man company will move furniture if requested, but customers will be charged extra. Clients say that the firm is very professional, prompt, neat and adheres to budget and deadlines.

"Understand their business." "Performed professionally." "Have used them for several years." "Good quality at a fair price."

Architectural Flooring Resource Inc.   4   3   5   4
151 West 28th Street, Suite 2W, New York, NY 10001
(212) 290 - 0200
Flooring installation, refinishing and maintenance

Sources say that Architectural Flooring is an architect's dream resource for flooring needs. The firm supplies, installs, cleans and maintains wood, tile, cork, rubber, vinyl, laminates and wall-to-wall carpets. Sources tell us the majority of the firm's work is commercial. Although most of Architectural Flooring's few residential projects are from architects, designers and contractors, owner Cathy Leidersdorff and her team will work directly with homeowners. Established in 1993, this company serves most of the Tri-State area and has some national accounts as well.

Enthusiastic clients tell us this company has a great work ethic, is extremely responsive and that Leidersdorff can accommodate almost any budget due to the huge amount of resources available to her. We hear that pricing is moderate to upper end and definitely worth the efficient service.

"One of the few I really trust." "Excellent installation team." "Open to ideas and suggestions." "Wide selection of floors." "Good customer service."

Architectural Wood Flooring   3   2.5   4   3
8441 261st Street, Floral Park, NY 11001
(718) 347 - 8306   flooring@prodigy.net
Wood flooring installation, refinishing, maintenance, repair and retail

This firm, which handles mostly residential projects, was established in 1988 and continues to serve Manhattan, the Hamptons, Greenwich and most of upper Westchester. Architectural Wood Flooring specializes in all kinds of wood flooring services. The company sells, installs, repairs, restores, refinishes, sands, stains, cleans and maintains high-quality flooring. We are told that the company believes in proper prepwork for every project and ensures that all subfloors are correctly installed and firmly glued. The company also takes pride in its antique restorations and custom designs and inlays, such as the herringbone, one of their most popular patterns.

"Small company ensures personalized service." "Gets the job done."

Aronson's Floor Covering Inc.   3.5   2.5   4.5   4.5
135 West 17th Street, New York, NY 10011
(212) 243 - 4993   aronsonsfloors.com
Flooring installation and retail

Who says flooring has to be boring? One of the oldest flooring companies in New York doesn't think so. Aronson's believes flooring shouldn't be stodgy and dull, but fun and cool and its showroom certainly reflects this with their "action figures" (Vinyl Vixen, Carpet Cowboy, Tile Temptress, etc) representing each floor type. Licensed, bonded and insured, this firm has been serving clients in Manhattan, the Hamptons, Fairfield county and other areas in the Tri-State area since its founding in 1867 by Samuel Aronson.

The company is now owned and run by Aronson's great-nieces, Laura and Carol Swedlow. This residential and commercial institution sells, installs, creates custom designs and does some repair on wood, cork, rubber, linoleum, area rugs, wall-to-wall carpets and mats. This eighteen-man business works with

	Quality	Cost	Value	Recommend?
	+	$	◆	★

architects, contractors and designers as well as directly with homeowners. Insiders say the firm has a wide selection of flooring products and a trip to their showroom is a treat in itself.

Clients are delighted with this firm's efficient service. They say that Aronson's staff is tidy, punctual and will fix any problems promptly. Cost is figured per square foot and the firm is said to have "very fair prices."

"My one-stop source for flooring needs." "Customer satisfaction is important, and they deliver." "Crews are self-supervising." "Lovely work." "Good quality, reasonable prices and great attitude." "Wonderful customer service."

Atlantic Hardwood Flooring   3.5   2.5   4   4.5
3265 Johnson Avenue, Bronx, NY 10463
(718) 601 - 4082
Wood and laminated flooring installation and repair

Since its establishment in 1980 by Jerry Plunkett, Atlantic Hardwood Flooring has been installing and repairing hardwood and laminated floors for residential interiors. The company serves parts of Westchester County, the Bronx and Manhattan's East Side. Impressed clients tell us that the workers are always on time, neat, courteous and conscientious. Satisfied customers appreciate the capable service Atlantic provides and the reasonable prices that go along with it.

"Work executed professionally from beginning to end."

Bradley Floors Inc.   4   3   4.5   5
1010 Sherman Avenue, Bronx, NY 10456
(718) 538 - 8242   woodman1010@aol.com
Installation, refinishing, repair and restoration of hardwood only

Willie Bradley's jovial demeanor and knowledge of his craft make him an industry favorite. This "good-natured" artisan has been in the flooring business for 35 years. Bradley, who worked with marble before switching to wood, established his company in 1967 and began his quest to learn more about the workings of wood. He journeyed to Africa and Brazil, where he studied exotic woods, particularly African teak and Brazilian mahogany. Bradley Floors installs, refinishes, sands and creates custom designs, inlays, borders and medallions for its floors.

The firm also mills and cuts some of the wood themselves. Bradley's A-list of clients includes senators, decorators, architects and celebrities who often call on the company to do projects all over Westchester and Fairfield counties, New York City, the Hamptons, Chicago, Memphis and Palm Beach. Pricing is usually per square foot and estimates are free, with Bradley doing most of them personally. Sources tell us that Bradley and his team talk to the client intelligently about the workings of wood and what the project would entail, making the client a part of the whole process—and not just a bystander. Bradley's work has been featured in publications like *New York* magazine and *Architectural Digest.*

"Amazing detail." "He really understands how wood works." "Excellent in restoring old wood." "My favorite floor guy." "From strip parquet to cutting-edge black floors—he can do it all." "Very pleasant demeanor and a hands-on businessman."

C&C Flooring   3.5   3   4   4.5
4276 Oneida Avenue, Bronx, NY 10470
(718) 994 - 1496
Wood flooring installation and refinishing

For standard flooring needs at reasonable prices, C&C is your best bet. Founded in 1995, it is managed by brothers Bryan and Keith Chapman. The company does flooring for new construction and existing structures. C&C works mainly in Manhattan with some projects in Westchester, Fairfield and Mamaroneck. C&C serves both residential and commercial clients, including a number of high-end management companies, decorators, architects and Columbia University. With a full-time staff of eight skilled workmen, C&C can handle large projects and is small enough to give personal attention to each client. The firm specializes only in wood floors and will clean, repair, restore, refinish, create custom designs and install.

Insiders say the Chapmans are perfectionists and are on the site "all the time" to ensure that everything goes smoothly. Clients tell us that they are responsive, prompt, polite and courteous.

"Absolutely superb work—and fast." "Will go out of their way to help you out." "Extremely reliable."

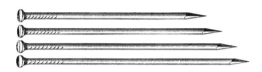

Classical Country Floors
3	3	4	4

7 Windsor Brook Lane, Tappan, NY 10983
(845) 359 - 7413

Installation and repair of clay terra-cotta floors

A specialist in terra-cotta floors, Tony Viglietta established Classical Country Floors 25 years ago. This family business installs, maintains and refurbishes aged floors in this style. The team at Classical Country Floors can also create custom designs and inlays, which they cut and install on the premises. The company serves residential clients in Scarsdale, Bronxville, Greenwich, Stamford, the Hamptons, Sag Harbor and Fire Island.

References tell us the company's terra-cotta floors are "beautiful and unique." We hear that Viglietta and his team are very knowledgeable about terra-cotta and will inform their clients as to the proper care and maintenance of the floors.

"The floors are holding up beautifully." "A bit expensive, but certainly worth it. You get what you pay for."

Cordts Flooring Corp.
3.5	3	4	3.5

111 Route 9 South, Fishkill, NY 12524
(914) 737 - 8201   www.cordtsco.com

Wood, rubber and cork flooring manufacturing

Cordts Flooring manufactures and installs wood, rubber and cork floors. Established in 1986 by Thomas Cordts, this firm serves mostly residential clients across Manhattan, Greenwich, Norwalk, Westport, Stamford and some areas in Long Island. Though the company generally coordinates with architects and decorators, it also works directly with homeowners. Cordts specializes in creating custom designs and inlays, and we are told the company creates authentic-looking antique reproductions.

Whether you prefer a Normandy-style home or an old Parisian look, sources say Cordts can create both with quality and ease. This firm also manufactures floors—both modern and antique reproductions. Clients praise the firm's full-service manufacturing facility. Though Cordts doesn't do installations, the firm will contract installers for the client.

Clients say the company is very accommodating, easy to work with and claim the work is rugged—and of high quality. Pricing is per square foot, estimates are free and floors come with a ten-year warranty on the wood.

"My floors are holding up after several years." "Neat and punctual. They get the job done." "Meets deadlines, cleans up afterwards, sticks to the budget— a dream flooring contractor."

	Quality	Cost	Value	Recommend?
	+	$	◆	★

Elite Floor Service Inc.   3.5   2.5   4.5   4.5

12 Saratoga Avenue, Yonkers, NY 10705
(212) 228 - 1050
Wood flooring installation and refinishing

References are impressed with this ten-year fixture in the flooring business. Many praise the politeness and workmanship of Elite craftsmen, while others told us that the Elite staff is helpful, prompt and efficient. Clients say that this company is conscientious about follow-ups and the prices are reasonable. Some references express minor concerns about neatness, but others say projects were carried out in a tidy manner and most would hire Elite again or recommend the company to friends.

Elite specializes in all types of wood floors. The company installs, refinishes, sands, repairs, creates custom designs and inlays and does a lot of staining and pickling. The firm works generally in Manhattan, New York's outer boroughs, Greenwich, Stamford and parts of Westchester. The company has a large number of clients who need standard floor installation and refinishing service. Aside from standard installations, Elite also does historic restoration such as the George C. Scott Estate (circa 1780) in South Salem. This mostly residential firm works with designers, architects, contractors and directly with homeowners. Pricing is usually by the job and estimates are free.

"Unbelievably polite, considerate. They do a great job." "I was very pleased. There were no surprises." "Could have been more responsive." "Conscientious. They clean up on their own."

Empire Hardwood Floors   4   2.5   4.5   5

120 Saint James Terrace, Yonkers, NY 10704
(914) 776 - 5832   www.empirehardwoodfloors.com
Hardwood floor installation, finishing, repair and custom designs

This small company specializes in finishing, installing, repairing and creating custom designs and inlays for hardwood floors. Michael Barrett is the man at the helm of Empire Hardwood Floors, which he founded in 1983. With twenty years of business experience behind them, the company has accumulated a strong following among respected contractors and builders, as well as distinguished residential clients in Connecticut, Westchester, New Jersey and New York City. Pricing is per square foot and estimates are free. There is a modest minimum for the firm to do a project.

We hear that Barrett and his team are frequently called upon for standard renovations, repairs and installations, although they are said to be just as capable of handling more complicated jobs. The workmen are described as polite and are great at "getting the job done quickly and without fuss."

"Saved me hundreds of dollars by repairing a messed up job by another company." "This small but thriving business may make booking them a bit difficult." "Beautiful color work."

F. Zarra Greenwich Flooring Inc.   4.5   3   4   5

1157 Westover Road, Stamford, CT 06902
(203) 531 - 6509   greenwichfloorz@aol.com
High-end wood floor installation, refinishing and repair, custom designs and inlays

An old-timer in the flooring business, F. Zarra Greenwich Flooring Inc. specializes in wood floor installation, finishing, restoration, repair, specialty finishes and custom designs and inlays. The company was founded by Francesco Zarra in 1969, who at 72 years of age, is still very much a part of this family business. The company is now headed by his son Gary, and the five-man team serves clients in Connecticut, Westchester and New York City.

Pricing for sanding, installations and refinishing is per square foot and repairs and waxing are usually billed by the hour. Typical projects range from a 500-square-foot refinishing job to a 3,000-square-foot installation for a gut renovation.

Though the bulk of the company's customers are residential, it also handles a few commercial projects. References cannot say enough good things about the firm, telling us that the workmen are meticulous, polite and "a pleasure to work with."

"Not the cheapest in town, but high quality work." "Responsive and courteous—they make me feel like I'm their most important customer." "Fixes problems before they become an issue." "I have been getting the same quality since they opened shop."

Farrell Floorcraft   3.5   2.5   4.5   5
67 Noble Street, Stamford, CT 06902
(203) 323 - 7332

Wood floor installation, finishing, repair, custom inlays and borders

Farrell Floorcraft's distinguished patrons sing the company's high praises for doing floors "the old-fashioned way." Established in 1936 by Robert Farrell, the firm works exclusively with wood floors. Farrell Floorcraft installs, finishes, repairs and restores wood floors for residential clients. Now managed by Robert's grandson, Donald Brandy, the company handles projects in Connecticut and Westchester County.

Most of the company's work deals with the restoration and refinishing of old floors. Farrell Floorcraft collaborates with architects, designers, contractors, or directly with homeowners. Free estimates are provided and pricing is usually by the square foot, with intricate repairs priced by the hour or job. References across the board agree the workers are diligent and efficient, with Brandy—who is described as "fussy about his work"—doing most of the work himself to make sure every inch "is nothing short of perfect."

"Donald is meticulous and a real craftsman." "The only ones who can touch my clients' floors." "Very proud of their work. Will stand behind every square foot they install." "Pleasant to work with."

Frank Welles   5   4   5   5
55 Railroad Avenue, Building 8, Garnerville, NY 10923
(845) 429 - 6508   www.frankwelles.com, www.sutherlandwelles.com

High-end installation and restoration of antique and reclaimed wood, specialty finishes

We are told that Frank Welles "puts art back in floors." A fine-arts painter, Welles was born in Mexico City, raised in New York and was educated in France and at Duke University. It was in the late 1960s that Welles "fell in love" with wood and began the self-education process that would establish him as one of the leading authorities in wood flooring and specialty finishes. Being dissatisfied by the finishing products currently available in the market, Welles discovered that tung oil brings out the beautiful "hand-rubbed patina of aging wood." Today, his company markets the Sutherland Welles Ltd. label and restores, installs, finishes and sands hardwood floors.

The company works mostly in Westchester, Greenwich, Easton, Weston and the Hamptons. The Frank Welles client list reads like a who's who—Richard Gere, David Easton, Eric Smith, Hobbs Construction, Linda Douglas, Mimi Horton, along with other prominent residential clients and celebrities. The firm has also done some work for the New York Historical Society and helped restore the Vanderbilt House (circa. 1918). Pricing is usually per square foot and projects usually start at $30,000.

Sources tell us Welles is an artist in every way. Some say that he is a joy to work with and is very knowledgeable, while others describe the experience with the "eccentric" artist as "not the smoothest, yet not the most turbulent." Although a Frank Welles floor does not come cheap, everyone across the board agrees that it is definitely worth every penny.

"Very well qualified at what he does." "The floors just sing to you." "Superb use of color." "Quite difficult to reach at times, as he gets very busy." "The floors look like they've been in the house forever." "Eccentric." "The person to call for authenticating old wood."

	Quality	Cost	Value	Recommend?
	✚	$	◆	★

Geysir Hardwood Floors

	4.5	3.5	5	5

PO Box 216, 510 Fenimore Road, Mamaroneck, NY 10543
(914) 698 - 9040   www.geysirfloors.com

Hardwood floor installation, refinishing, restoration and repair, custom designs and inlays

Like a well-oiled machine, the departments at Geysir run like clockwork to ensure that every client ends up with an ideal floor. Merging old-world crafts-manship with new technology, Geysir was established 30 years ago by John Vogestad who learned all about woodworking in his native Norway. This fifty-man company has two divisions—Geysir Hardwood, is in charge of distribution and con-sultations, has licensed inspectors who can administer moisture tests and such. The other division—Geysir Contracting, deals mainly with builders and architects and handles new installations. The team at Geysir are frequently called upon to conceptualize, design and create custom designs, borders, medallions and inlays.

The firm works all over Connecticut and Westchester, some areas in New Jersey, Manhattan and even California. While known for tackling huge projects, Geysir will not turn its nose up on small projects and there is no set minimum for them to do a job. Not only does the company take pride in its "superb customer service," but also the fact that everyone in the firm—from the refinishers to the bookkeepers—are certified by the National Oak Flooring Manufacturers Association (NOFMA). Although prices are considered by many as "expensive," everyone agrees "you get what you pay for" and that a Geysir floor is worth every penny. The company is an allied member of The American Institute of Architects, a board member of The Home Builders Association in Fairfield, a member of the Westchester Builders Institute, Hudson Valley Builders and The National Wood Flooring Association (NWFA).

"Good billing system." "A contractor's dream." "Can work with any design aes-thetic." "Responsive to phone calls, but hard to get through as they can get really busy." "From standard oak to exotic wood to complicated inlays—name it, they can do it—and beautifully, too."

H&K Hansen Flooring

	4	3	4.5	5

580 Old Stage Road, East Brunswick, NJ 08816
(732) 251 - 0989

Wood flooring refinishing and sanding

A family-run business established thirteen years ago, H&K Hansen specializes in sanding and finishing wood floors. The firm is run by Kurt Hansen (a third-gen-eration Hansen in the flooring industry) and his uncle. H&K serves only residential clients in Manhattan and parts of the Hamptons, Westchester and Connecticut. The firm works with decorators, contractors and directly with homeowners. Pricing is usually per square foot, unless the project is really small, in which case H&K charges by the job.

The majority of sources tell us that H&K's work is excellent—some say the best in the area—and that some amount of "artistic" attitude may go along with get-ting this top-quality work.

"Best finisher!" "Reliable and pleasant." "Extremely knowledgeable. He gives realistic schedules and the quality of work is superb." "Highest integrity." "Very small company, but good."

	Quality ✚	Cost $	Value ◆	Recommend? ★

Harlequin Flooring

PO Box 4072, Greenwich, CT 06830
(203) 531 - 9509

Wood floor installation, finishing and repair

4.5   3   4.5   5

Sources describe Michael di Stephano of Harlequin Flooring as "professional, thorough and definitely a hands-on businessman." The company, which was founded by di Stephano eight years ago, serves commercial and residential clients in Connecticut, Westchester and New York City. The firm is a favorite among contractors and homeowners alike for standard refinishing jobs and installations. Though specializing in wood floors, Harlequin also installs laminates.

References say they appreciate the "boutique feel" of this small company and describe prices as "upper end."

"A great refinisher!" "Very thorough, especially when working with exotics." "Good color work."

Haywood Berk Floor Company Inc.

180 Varick Street, New York, NY 10014
(212) 242 - 0047

Wood flooring installation, refinishing, custom designs and repair

4.5   4.5   4   4

As one of the oldest flooring companies in New York, Haywood Berk is now on its third generation since Otto Berk established the company in 1921. It is now managed by his grandson Roger, who is described by sources as a knowledgeable craftsman—dedicated and very professional. Indeed, references are quick to say good things about this firm and praise its attention to detail and commitment to offering a high-quality service. Though some residential clients feel that the company's responsiveness to inquiries is not its strongest point, most agree that Haywood staff members are efficient and experts in the field. In fact, we are told, many top-tier designers would not consider anyone else for their discriminating clients.

The firm deals only with wood and performs services such as installation, restoration, custom designs, staining, pickling, refinishing and repair. Most of their projects are in Manhattan, the Hamptons, Westchester, Connecticut and Los Angeles. This residential and commercial firm takes on almost 200 jobs per year. Recently, Berk finished projects in Carnegie Hall and the South Street Seaport Museum. They are also a member of the Maple Flooring Manufacturers Association.

"Good job. Do it until they get it right." "Hard to get through to sometimes, but I know that their work quality will always be excellent." "As a decorator, I can schedule their work within two weeks on a consistent basis." "Roger understands his products, but more important he understands his high-end client base."

Hoboken Wood Floors

979 Third Avenue, New York, NY 10022
(212) 759 - 5917   www.hobokenfloors.com

Wood floor distribution, installation, maintenance, custom design and repair

4   3.5   4.5   4.5

Hoboken Wood Floors started out as a small company in New Jersey and is now one of the nation's largest flooring distribution and installation companies. It has nine distribution centers and two design centers. The company's New York offices and showroom are located at the prestigious D&D Building in Manhattan. This business, with 500 full-time employees, serves both high-end residential and commercial clients. Established in 1932 by Joseph Sakosits, the firm is now run by his grandson Brian Sakosits and his partners. Hoboken installs, repairs, restores, sands, finishes, stains, bleaches and creates custom designs and high-quality borders for wood floors.

Hoboken works directly with homeowners in addition to designers, architects and contractors, and will basically go anywhere for a project. The firm does projects mostly in Manhattan, other New York boroughs, Greenwich, Westport, Darien, Stamford, Bedford, Scarsdale and the Hamptons. Pricing is by the job and estimates are free. The firm also has branches in Georgia, Florida, Delaware, Massachusetts and Maine.

	Quality	Cost	Value	Recommend?
	✚	$	◆	★

Customers say they appreciate the company's efficient service and excellent work ethic. Although prices are upper end, clients say it is a good value for the service they provide. Decorators often call on their services, knowing they will do an excellent job at a respectable price.

"Never had a problem with them." "My floors are beautiful." "One of the best." "Very reliable quality without killing you on price." "They are a professional company—not three guys and a truck." "One of the largest wholesalers on the East Coast."

I.J. Peiser's Sons Inc.   3.5   3   4   5

475 Tenth Avenue, New York, NY 10018
(212) 279 - 6900   stephen@ijpeiser.com
Wood flooring installation and refinishing

Known for its hand-scraped and finished floors, I.J. Peiser's is one of New York's oldest flooring companies. Owned and managed by Stephen Estrin, the company was established by his great-grandfather in 1909. The company installs, cleans and repairs all types of wood floors. The firm also takes pride in its custom designs and inlays, which are created in Peiser's own workshop. This company serves most of Manhattan, some areas in the Hamptons, and clients' second homes in Westchester, Connecticut, Palm Beach and Oklahoma. Estrin also has a strong commercial following, some of which includes prestigious hotels like The Palace and The Carlyle and some of the top construction and architectural firms in the area.

Sources describe Estrin as professional, honest, reliable and easy to work with. Delighted customers also say that the firm meets deadlines, adheres to budgets and is willing to fix any problem that arises. Clients say the excellent service and quality of the floors are well worth the high-end prices.

"Excellent." "Extremely cooperative." "One of the finest craftsmen around." "Honest." "Been here a long time." "On schedule. Reliable." "Excellent installers."

Janos P. Spitzer Flooring   4.5   3.5   4.5   4

133 West 24th Street, New York, NY 10010
(212) 627 - 1818   www.janosspitzerflooring.com
High-end wood flooring installation, custom design, repair and restoration

Serving high-end clients and satisfying their discriminating tastes are not easy tasks, but clients say Janos Spitzer does both flawlessly—the same way that he creates his exquisite wood floors. Established in 1962, Spitzer installs, restores, repairs, sands and finishes wood floors for residential and some commercial interiors. Preferred by contemporary architects and decorators, but also used by some traditionalists, this company is known for producing wood floors with low-grain definition—"like shields of glass." The firm serves most of Manhattan, the Hamptons and Westchester and Fairfield counties. Samples of Spitzer's work can be viewed at his 2,400-square-foot showroom, which is regarded by insiders as a "must-see" in the city.

Spitzer's impressive roster of clients include Mark Hampton Inc., The Four Seasons, David Anthony Easton and Philip Johnson, to name a few. Everything is crafted and fabricated in the company's own workshop.

We hear that the Spitzer team is prompt, attentive, accommodating and very professional. References say that Spitzer himself is honorable, honest, a "hands-on dedicated businessman" and generally "just terrific to work with." Although some say that his talent is matched with an artistic temperament, the majority agrees that the firm's extensive knowledge, commitment to excellence, elegant designs and attention to detail are definitely worth the expensive prices.

"No one can quite match his ability for color work." "He really understands how to make the perfect wood floor." "Excellent work ethic." "Very, very good—not the cheapest in the world, but worth every penny." "Great people." "A genius with a temperament." "A wonderful old-world craftsman."

Jensen Flooring Company Inc.   3   2.5   4   4

6 Valley Pond Road, Katonah, NY 10536
(914) 248 - 5504

Hardwood floor installation and refinishing

Jensen Flooring Company installs, sands and finishes all types of hardwood floors. The company was established in 1904 by Maurice Jensen and is now managed by David Bingham, who took over when Jensen retired. Licensed, bonded and insured, this company of five works mostly on residential projects in upper Connecticut and lower Westchester.

"Good for mid-range, standard flooring installations."

Kent Hardwood Floors   4   3   4.5   5

36 Lake Avenue Extension, Danbury, CT 06811
(203) 743 - 5591

Hardwood flooring installation, refinishing, restoration, repair, custom design and inlays

If you're looking for a company to fulfill your standard hardwood flooring needs, we hear that Kent Hardwood Floors fits the bill perfectly. This firm of twenty was founded thirty years ago by Sigmund Nokland, who has been working with hardwood floors since early adulthood when he worked in his native Norway. This firm installs, sands, finishes, restores and repairs hardwood floors. Kent Hardwood works with both domestic and exotic woods and can create custom designs, borders and inlays.

With a mostly residential following, this firm works with many general contractors and architects in areas like Ridgefield and Milford, Westchester, Putnam, Dutchess and Fairfield counties, as well as Dover and Manhattan. Pricing is usually per square foot and estimates are free. Average projects are in the 1,000- to 5,000-square-foot range. The company's 2,500-square-foot headquarters houses its workshop and offices.

"Very helpful." "Good with exotics." "Can meet even the most demanding builders' schedules."

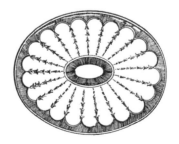

New York Floor King   3   2.5   4   4.5

27-15 41st Avenue, Long Island City, NY 10128
(914) 964 - 8378

Wood flooring refinishing, sanding and waxing

New York Floor King was established in 1984 by David Kaye. It specializes in wood floor refinishing, sanding, repair, buffing and waxing. The firm serves most of Manhattan, Westchester and Bergen County, NJ. Sources say the company rarely does any installations and has mostly residential clients. Pricing is generally per square foot. The business also gives a six-year warranty on their floors.

"They got the job done at a reasonable price." "Easy to work with." "Great for standard sanding and refinishing jobs."

	Quality	Cost	Value	Recommend?
	✚	$	◆	★

Petise Flooring Co. Inc.   4   3   4.5   5
16 Nedley Lane, Greenwich, CT 06830
(203) 531 - 9534

Wood floor installation, repair, finishing, inlays and borders

Clients describe Frank Petise as a "genuine old-world crafstman." A former member of the US army, Petise joined his brother Dom (who established Petise Flooring in 1948) in his flooring business and fell in love with the trade. Frank is now at the helm of this small family company and is training his nephew as the next Petise to carry on the family flooring legacy. The firm serves mostly residential clients in Fairfield, Westchester and New Jersey.

A specialist in wood, Petise installs, finishes, sands, stains, distresses and creates and cuts inlays and borders. Known for its "amazing custom designs and color work," the firm is a favorite choice among contractors, builders and architects for custom floor installations. Clients also frequently call on the firm for floor waxing, saying it is one of the few who "actually know how to wax a floor." Pricing is by the square foot and the workmen are described as competent, prompt and pleasant, with Petise doing a lot of the work himself.

"Beautiful custom work." "The man to call for wide-planked, formal-looking floors." "Pleasant but with an artistic temperament." "A gentleman."

Phoenix Hardwood Flooring   4.5   3   5   5
1 Muller Avenue, Norwalk, CT
(203) 845 - 8094   www.phoenixfloors.com

Hardwood floor installation, finishing, restoration and repair, custom design and inlays

A well-kept secret among high-end builders and contractors, Phoenix Hardwood Flooring has built a solid reputation among its clients for the past thirteen years. Established in 1990 by Ed Myers, Ken Myatt, Stan Hill and Jeff Samoncik, the business that started out with just ten people is now a company with three offices/showrooms (Norwalk, Guilford and Southbury) and 125 employees. Phoenix installs, repairs, restores, sands, finishes and creates custom designs, medallions and inlays for hardwood floors only. The firm does mostly new construction for residential interiors in Connecticut, Westchester County, New York City and beyond.

There is no set method for pricing, but a lump sum is quoted for each job after a personal estimate. Projects can range from a simple $500 refinishing to $350,000 installations. Aside from new installations, Phoenix also boasts of museum-quality and historic restorations including The Bush-Holley Museum in Greenwich and The Lockwood Mansion in Norwalk.

Sources are delighted about the firm's "excellent customer service" and "creative, problem-solving" workers. The company assigns a project manager for each job. Thus the client deals with only one person from start to finish. The firm has two 10,000-square-foot warehouses and three showrooms open to the public.

"Very resourceful. Found us floors in France in order to match what we had." "Can accommodate any design aesthetic." "Easygoing. A pleasure to work with."

William J. Erbe Company Inc.   5   5   4.5   5
560 Barry Street, Bronx, NY 10474
(212) 249 - 6400

High-end wood flooring installation, refinishing, custom design, restoration and repair

Flooring as art? Sources say for the William J. Erbe Company, it certainly is. Erbe is considered by clients, architects, designers and even acknowledged by other high-end flooring companies as being the best and most expensive producer of handmade and hand-scraped wood floors. The company installs, repairs, refinishes, sands, restores and maintains wood floors for residential and commercial interiors and designs some of the most intricate floor patterns. Its workmen are few and in demand, and Erbe himself or one of his sons supervises each project.

Though based around New York, Erbe's projects are mostly out-of-state or outside the country. The firm enjoys an impressive roster of local and international clients such as top designers David Easton and Mark Hampton Inc., the Metropolitan Museum of Art, The White House and The Royal Family in Kuwait, to name a few. Known for his custom designs and antique restorations, Erbe scours France looking for chateau owners parting with their antique parquet floors, imports them and meticulously restores the exquisite pieces for clients. Called by *The New York Times* "the Rolls-Royce of flooring companies," this family business was founded by Erbe's great-grandfather in 1907.

Sources say that this company can reproduce and create any kind of floor, and that they are dedicated, professional and "the most amazing craftsmen around." Indeed, whether it be Erbe's famous parquet de Versailles, antique or modern finish, with inlays or without, flooring at the William J. Erbe Company has been elevated to an art form.

"As an architect, I would not consider risking a client's floors with anyone other than Erbe—no one can compare." "Seriously the best floor company around." "Exquisite craftsman. Exceeds my expectations." "If there was a New York God of Wood Floors, William Erbe would be it." "They only accept a limited number of projects." "Über flooring."

Wood Floors Direct   3.5   3   4   4

1088 Central Park Avenue, Scarsdale, NY 10583
(914) 713 - 2440 www.woodfloorsdirect.com

Hardwood floor installation, refinishing and inlays

Wood Floors Direct focuses primarily on installing hardwood floors. The firm works with both domestic and exotic woods and will also refinish, sand, stain, pickle and repair floors. We hear that Gerry Flynn and his crew are professional and knowledgeable about their craft. Pricing is generally by the square foot and estimates are free. There is, however, an extra charge for prepwork.

The firm is a sister company of East Side Floors of Manhattan (est. 1985) and moved to its present home in Scarsdale in 2002. It serves both residential and commercial clients in areas like Greenwich, Scarsdale, Putnam County, Rockland County and Fishkill. The firm has installed floors in the Foxwoods Casino and the Time-Life Building in Manhattan. Wood Floors Direct is a member of the National Wood Flooring Association and has been featured in *Home* magazine and *Journal News*.

"A lot to offer for a fair price." "Very accommodating." "Very informative—the whole process wasn't a huge mystery to me."

Hiring a Furniture Repair & Refinishing Service Provider

Does your prized baroque chair need restoration? Do you refuse to get rid of your comfortable thrift store couch but admit it needs sprucing up? Will your bedroom finally be complete with the addition of a twin reproduction of your favorite antique nightstand? Or perhaps you have a piece that has survived fire or flood damage, a teething puppy, climate changes or just general wear and tear. Before surrendering your furniture to the hands of a professional, you should know a few things about it and the artisan who will repair, restore or conserve it.

Where Do I Start?

Before hiring a professional to repair your piece, take the time to verify that your thrift shop bargain isn't a priceless antique in disguise and that your heirloom isn't actually an ordinary reproduction. Inappropriate restoration of an antique can greatly compromise its value. Sometimes a seemingly simple repair can actually cause further, irreparable damage. So be sure to have your piece's history and condition closely examined—preferably by several people—before allowing any work to be done.

Most professionals will visit your home to provide a price estimate and a detailed explanation of how your piece should be treated. Some charge fees for on-site verbal and written estimates; others don't. Estimates should include the cost of labor, materials and transportation. You should also discuss how your piece will be insured and whether or not a warranty will be provided for the work and under what conditions.

Knowing the value of your piece is important not only in determining the type of work that it needs and how well it should be insured, but also how much to invest in the work. If your thrift store table simply needs its broken leg replaced, you may not want to pay top dollar for labor fees. However, if you're concerned about transporting your original Louis XIV dining room table, you may opt to keep it at home and pay for a specialized restorer to work on-site.

On Cost

Many professionals base their fees on an hourly or daily rate that is subject to increase, depending on the condition of your piece, the work it needs and where the work takes place. As a general guideline, hourly rates can range from $45 to $150. Other restorers, however, charge by the piece. Costs can vary depending on the condition of the piece and how much work needs to be done. In the case of per-piece fees, request an itemized estimate that clearly explains where each charge came from. Be sure you receive a written contract for the amount of work agreed upon and the cost. If additional work is needed, the professional should notify you before taking action and a new fee should be agreed upon.

Choosing the Right Specialist for You

No licensing bureaus or governing boards regulate furniture restorers, so it is crucial that you take the time to find the right professional for your particular piece. Although furniture restorers tend to be well-versed in all styles and periods, each has a specialty. You wouldn't take a broken toe to an allergist, nor would you want to take your japanned armoire to a caning specialist. Inquire about the professional's area of expertise. For example, if your dining room table needs to be refinished, be wary of a craftsman who wants to use French polish and says you'll be eating from your table within a day or two. French polish is typically saved for show pieces such as game tables and armoires and is not used on surfaces that are prone to spills or burns. If you do want a French polish, know that applying it is a time-consuming process that requires numerous layers of shellac and alcohol to be applied, dried and rubbed before being reapplied. Keep in mind that moisture captured between the layers can cloud the surfaces irrevocably, so humid weather will prolong the process. Be patient because a good professional will not want to rush the job.

Also, be wary of someone who is eager to refinish your Federal bureau, or any of your antiques. Much of the value of any antique derives from its rarity, quality and condition, and an original finish is an important part of this. Be sure to find a professional who is as interested in preserving the unique qualities of your piece as you are.

Questions to Ask a Furniture Professional

Although your main contact will most likely be the firm's principal, most firms have numerous employees, each with a different area of expertise. Ask who is working on your piece and what he will be doing. The person who recreates the leg of your table may not be the person who finishes it.

Don't be afraid to ask about the firm's expertise, including whether individuals have been trained in a particular style or period. Ask where they've worked and with whom. Also, ask to see their portfolios and to speak with numerous references. Make a point of speaking with the references. They know the work and will tell you if actual fees exceeded the estimate, if the work took twice as long as expected or—the best scenario—if the work was beautifully done.

Furniture Care Tips

✧ Protect furniture from direct sunlight, which fades colors, bleaches wood and clouds polished surfaces.

✧ Avoid exposing furniture to excessive heat—do not place it near a radiator or set hot objects upon it, as this damages surface coatings, veneers and underlying adhesives.

✧ Place coasters on surfaces to protect them from liquids, which can stain.

✧ Wipe up water-based spills with a towel, but dab alcohol spills carefully to prevent spreading the spill—alcohol breaks down finishes.

✧ Invest in a humidifier/dehumidifier to minimize large fluctuations in humidity.

✧ Use a buffer when writing on a table top. Pens and pencils can cause unsightly indentations.

✧ When moving furniture, lift by the strongest units or rails—never drag!

FURNITURE REPAIR & REFINISHING

Anglo-Inscape Inc.　　　　4.5　3　5　5
2472 Broadway, Suite 368, New York, NY 10025
(212) 924 - 2883　www.angloinscape.com
Custom furniture and high-end finishes

See Anglo-Inscape Inc.'s full report under the heading Millworkers & Cabinetmakers

Antiquity Preservation Network　　　4.5　2.5　5　5
By appointment only, Oradell, NJ 07649
(201) 261 - 8147
Antiques restoration, refinishing and reproduction

Dennis DeCarlo earns praise from both professionals and private clients for his wealth of knowledge and kind nature. He specializes in 18th- and 19th-century English furniture, but works on continental and Eastern pieces as well. The Merchant House Museum entrusts its collection of American antiques with DeCarlo and even had him teach a seminar on antique restoration. Sources praise DeCarlo's work in structural repair, marquetry, carving, turning, water and oil gilding and French polishing, as well as reproduction and metalwork. Labeled an "expert" with veneers, DeCarlo is said to be completely honest and reliable.

In addition to running Antiquity Preservation Network for the last nine years, DeCarlo also has twenty years of experience that include serving as senior furniture conservator and quality control manager at Sotheby's and working with the Metropolitan Museum of Art.

"*As a museum professional, my goal is to preserve the furniture for future generations. I choose Dennis to do that, which should tell you a lot.*" "*He knows his stuff, and his qualifications and credentials are incredible.*" "*Top-notch, no question about it.*" "*I couldn't recommend anybody any better.*" "*Dennis is the nicest person in the world—he's a lovely man.*"

Artifact Design Group　　　4.5　4　4　5
245 Newtown Turnpike, Weston, CT 06883
(203) 454 - 9697　www.artifactdesigngroup.com
Furniture repair, antiques restoration and brasswork

When it comes to old-world antique finishes and "one-stop furniture restoration and repair," sources say Artifact Design Group sets the standard. The firm offers a vast array of services that include French polishing to custom creation and replacing of broken furniture parts. We're told the firm is careful to uphold the integrity of the original piece and adheres to the notion of "acceptable restoration as opposed to over restoration." Owner Gregory Clark has been restoring furniture since he was a youngster, helping out with his family's antiques restoration business. He started his own firm in 2000 and currently has a staff of seven craftsmen.

Projects generally start with just a few pieces, then "end up being all the furniture in the house," and range from $1,000 to $50,000. Nearly all of the firm's work is done in its workshop, but on very delicate pieces, Clark will make housecalls. Artifact Design Group deals mostly with very high-end American antiques. The company will provide in-home estimates, and will pick up and deliver the furniture, the cost of which is built into the estimate. Working from Boston to Philadelphia and everywhere in between, this firm, known to be a bit pricey, will accept commissions for custom furniture from all over the country, including Hawaii.

"They produce beautiful work and are just a joy to work with." "I can't exaggerate my delight with them." "Extraordinarily creative."

Budd Woodwork Inc.   4   4   4   4
54 Franklin Street, Brooklyn, NY 11222
(718) 389 - 1110
Historic restoration and preservation of millwork

    See Budd Woodwork Inc.'s full report under the heading Millworkers & Cabinetmakers

Carlo Ciardi & Son Furniture Restoration   4.5   4.5   4   4.5
23 Old Dam Road, Fairfield, CT 06824
(203) 259 - 2050
Fine furniture repair and restoration

    The father-and-son team of Carlo and Chris Ciardi, is known for one simple concept: "They will not cut corners." And with that, clients have come to expect great things from this firm, which has been in business for more than 35 years. This duo is known to repair furniture "in any style, from any period," although clients most often bring delicate chairs in for fixing. The Ciardis prefer using French polish or other methods of restoring custom finishes, but they will strip and refinish when necessary. All work is done by hand and no chemicals, power sanders or power tools are used in the process.

    All work is done at the company's workshop, and pickup and delivery is provided at no extra charge. Projects can be as small as a "rickety old rocking chair" to a collection of "fine dining and living room chairs." The firm has worked with a number of celebrity clients, museums, antiques dealers and decorators. The Ciardis provide free estimates at the home, and insiders say they "always stand by their estimates, even if they lose money on the deal." You're going to pay more for this company's services, but sources across the board say it's still low for the product's quality.

Curry & Hovis   4   3.5   4   4.5
254 Westchester Avenue, Pound Ridge, NY 10576
(914) 764 - 1138
Restoration and repair of fine English furniture

    John Curry has been doing woodwork all his life so it's no wonder that he started his own firm along with partner Clinton Howell in 1991. The duo now takes great care in restoring 18th-century English furniture with the belief that it's "some of the only furniture made well enough that's worth repairing." The company also does a fair amount of French polishing, veneer work and gilding. Sources tell us Curry & Hovis generally works with clients "who know their stuff."

    A typical project entails restoring of five to ten pieces. While the firm is "happily busy," Curry & Hovis takes on projects directly from homeowners in addition to designers and dealers. However, be prepared to wait—the average lead time is about eight weeks. The company works across southern Connecticut, Westchester County and New York City. The partners work either in clients' homes or in the workshop, depending on the number and the condition of the pieces.

D. Miller Restorers Inc.   4.5   3   4.5   4.5
166 East 124th Street, New York, NY 10035
(212) 876 - 1861   RMiller236@aol.com
Furniture restoration and sculpture mounting

    D. Miller is a third-generation family business. Loyal clients describe principal Robin Miller as reliable and attentive, and her work as "brilliant and superb." The three-person firm restores European antiques and mounts sculpture for private clients, the trade, dealers and museums. The company's French polish and gilding draw praise, as do the reasonable prices. We hear Miller is extremely accommodating and will tailor the restoration job to the quality of the piece, so no job is too small. Over the years, the firm has done work for some of Manhattan's most famous residents.

"Always on time. Great attention to detail." "Everything they've done for me has been first class. No one else can compare." "I have worked with two generations of Millers and am now on the third. Obviously, I am more than satisfied with their work—in fact, I'm ecstatic!"

London Joiners 5 4 5 5
23 Westchester Avenue, Pound Ridge, NY 10576
(914) 764 - 4216
Antiques restoration with old-world techniques

Willy Godziemba-Maliszewski is a purveyor and restorer of "antiques of virtue." Handling antiques restoration and conservation, Godziemba-Maliszewski generally works on furniture from the 17th to early 19th century and prefers to work with clients "who know exactly what they have." This master cabinetmaker and ebiniste works closely with a number of A-list decorators but also takes inquiries from the public by appointment. His projects range from French polishing of a single dining room table to the restoration of an entire collection. But no matter what kind of project, we're told Godziemba-Maliszewski uses only the "least intrusive methods of restoration" and "respects the integrity of the antique and the intent of its original maker." He's also earned a reputation for making antique reproductions that could fool the most discriminating eyes.

Godziemba-Maliszewski started this company in 1981 and currently has a staff of two. He spent years training across Europe learning from the best ebinistes in England, Ireland, France and Italy. We're told the company "really takes their time" and you should allow them plenty of time to get the job done—and done to perfection. Godziemba-Maliszewski offers free in-home estimates but usually transports the piece to this Pound Ridge workshop. The firm is known to be on the upper-end of the pricing scale.

M&M Antique Restoration 4 3 4.5 4.5
436 East 75th Street, Suite 1RW, New York, NY 10021
(212) 772 - 3857
Antique furniture restoration and veneer work

Michael McPhail might be located in New York City, but a lot of his furniture repair work comes from Fairfield and Westchester counties. McPhail, a second-generation antiques restorer, started his company in 1980 and has since built a dedicated client base that includes Christie's auction house, antiques warehouses, estates and individual homeowners. McPhail and his four-person staff make housecalls across the area, polishing furniture for projects that can take up to a week. While the company doesn't handle lacquer work, M&M does all kinds of touch-up and French polishing. McPhail is known as a master of matching ancient veneers.

M&M handles American, European and Asian furniture and outsources all lacquer and gilding work. McPhail works very closely with designers, although he will take inquiries from the public. The company charges a standard hourly rate for their services.

	Quality	Cost	Value	Recommend?
	+	$	◆	★

Midtown Antiques Inc.   3   2   5   4

310 City Island Avenue, Bronx, NY 10464
(212) 529 - 1880   www.midtownantiquesinc.com

Antiques center—dealership, retail and restoration

In their 62 years of business, Mort and Violet Ellis at Midtown Antiques have been known to be extremely charming, honest and kind. Besides offering retail antiques with an in-house dealer, we hear Midtown loans antiques to publications and movie studios for creating a period looks. Midtown has a restorer on the premises who also makes house calls and reportedly does it all—from refinishing and painting restoration to cabinetry repair, japanning, gilding and gesso. We hear the company specializes in libraries, paneling, railings and doors and that its fine work can be found in elite Westchester and Connecticut residences, in addition to Gracie Mansion and Manhattan's City Hall. This third-generation restorer trained in South America under his father, and sources call his work exquisite.

"A magnificent restoration job." "Such nice people with so much integrity." "They restored our family blackamoor collection that was damaged in an earthquake back to its original state."

Reardon Restoration Inc.   4   4   4.5   5

180 Yonkers Avenue, Yonkers, NY 10701
(914) 965 - 2179   www.reardonrestoration.com

Old-world furniture repair, antique restoration, decorative painting and Venetian plaster

Reardon Restoration offers custom wall and furniture glazing, gilding, faux bois, Venetian plaster, furniture restoration, repair, upholstery and retro-fitting. Owner Steve Reardon is known to make house calls to polish antiques and conduct small repairs and touch-ups to maintain furniture. He oversees every job and personally attends every pickup, delivery and installation to ensure the safety of family heirlooms or priceless antiques. Insiders say Reardon Restoration prides itself in creative problem solving.

The family-operated company traces its beginnings back ten years to Reardon, who, armed with a Bachelor of Fine Arts, trained with some of the area's most respected decorative painters and furniture restorers. In between decorative painting jobs he worked with craftsmen in antique stores, learning old-world restoration, polishing and finishing techniques. Today, Reardon is known to take "a conservator's approach" to valuable antiques, or use creative techniques to bring a designer's vision to life.

The company collaborates extensively with designers, but won't hesitate to work directly with clients. Steve's wife and brother work for the company and when you call Reardon Restoration, you are guaranteed to talk directly to one of the Reardons, who stake their family's name in every project.

"Honestly, finding people who do the kind of work that he does and do it as well as he does, is hard to do." "Steve is very professional, reliable and knows how to treat customers—he's very easy to work with." "Steve can restore anything you give him."

Richard Moller Ltd.   4.5   3   5   5

178 Upper Shad Road, Pound Ridge, NY 10576
(914) 764 - 0121   rrmoller@optonline.net

Antique furniture repair and refinishing

Clients call Richard Moller efficient and conscientious. They appreciate his ability to work on-site, which protects pieces from travel damage and means clients don't have to go without their furniture. Having trained with European craftsmen in New York, Moller specializes in 18th- and 19th-century European pieces. Trade professionals rely on Moller, but we hear he also takes on new private clients. After 30 years in the business, Moller has a loyal following. Sources say many long-term clients' children employ Moller for their collections.

"He is always available and is completely reliable."

	Quality ✚	Cost $	Value ◆	Recommend? ★

Stair Galleries & Restoration Inc.

4.5   3.5   5   5

33 Maple Avenue, Claverack, NY 12513
(518) 851 - 2544   www.stairrestoration.com

Furniture reproduction and restoration and fire and water damage repair

Stair Galleries & Restoration was created in 2001 after Sotheby's Restoration was consolidated to take on only a small number of projects each year. Colin Stair left Sotheby's to create his own firm, which is located in Upstate New York but welcomes inquiries from the city and can be reached at (212) 860-5446. This firm is currently taking on numerous project referrals from Sotheby's.

Clients laud Colin Stair for his professional demeanor, friendly disposition and quality workmanship. His firm handles fire and water damage repair and refinishing for all styles and periods of furniture as well as interior woodwork, paneling, veneering and polishing. According to references, Stair will also make expert furniture reproductions that clients say can't be distinguished from the originals. One customer told us that when her young daughter's favorite doll's bed broke, a call to Stair was all it took. He made a house call, whisked the bed away and within two weeks the bed was delivered "in perfect condition" for a surprisingly small fee.

Stair will assist clients at auctions, providing advice on the worth and restoration potential of pieces. References say Stair performs expert custom work with the highest caliber of integrity and skill—at a price that is considered reasonable.

"When it comes to finishes, he's the best around—and the finish is the most important and difficult task to undertake." "A really nice guy who really is amazing at what he does." "The service is not cheap, but it's not nearly as much as it could be, given the quality."

Timothy G. Riordan Inc.

3.5   3   4   5

50 Webster Avenue, New Rochelle, NY 10801
(212) 360 - 1246

Antique furniture restoration

Timothy Riordan has been restoring, gilding and polishing fine antique furniture for over seventeen years. He has an enviable background, having worked at Sotheby's during the early years of its restoration program. Over the years, American, French and English antiques have become his areas of specialty. He works on an hourly basis and does a considerable amount of work across Southern Connecticut and New York.

Tudor House Furniture Co. Inc.

4   3.5   4.5   4.5

929 Sherman Avenue, Hamden, CT 06514
(203) 288 - 8451   hemargo@aol.com

Trade Only—Custom Upholstery

See Tudor House Furniture Co. Inc.'s full report under the heading Upholstery & Window Treatments

Vitanza Finishing & Upholstery

4   3   5   5

728 East 136th Street, New York, NY 10454
(718) 401 - 1022   www.vitanzafurniture.com

Furniture restoration, particularly Art Deco, upholstery

Founded in 1930, Vitanza is known to be dedicated to the restoration of fine wood furniture using handcrafted, traditional methods. Since then, the firm has been involved with some extremely high-profile jobs, including the chair of Pope John Paul and the Sotheby's auction for the estate of Jacqueline Kennedy Onassis. Principal Michael Maytel has gained a reputation for being one of the premier experts in the restoration of 20th-century modern design, specializing in Art Deco and 1950s furniture.

We hear the firm's craftsmen excel in both contemporary and antique restorations and are adept with lacquer, polyurethane, antique white, French polish, custom color and custom finishes. Clients also praise the line of custom-built furniture. Clients say Vitanza uses only the finest materials to reupholster furniture, from fabrics appropriate to the period to horsehair stuffing and coil springs. Sources call Maytel the "top in the business" and say he works closely with clients, designers, architects and showrooms on both large and small projects.

"Michael is simply the man for the job. I've had nothing but good experience with him." "Michael is fabulous. The best."

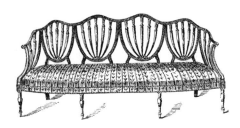

Yorkville Caning   4   2   5   5
31-04 60th Street, Woodside, NY 11377
(212) 432 - 6464   yorkvillecaning@aol.com
Furniture refinishing, caning and wicker repair

New York's top designers, regional designers and the Metropolitan Museum of Art rely upon principal David Feuer for his restoration abilities. A family business, Yorkville Caning has been recaning chairs, repairing wooden and wicker furniture, refinishing and reupholstering for 102 years. We're told Yorkville works with genuine rush—a service fast becoming a lost art. Insiders gush that Yorkville gives life to pieces deemed irreparable by others, using a special glue from NASA. Yorkville's staff of twelve earns praise for wicker repair and restoration and has also found the time to become expert upholsterers and refinishers.

"Everyone loves them." "Yorkville saved my chairs." "Worth lugging the client's fine antiques down from Connecticut. You know it will be done properly."

Hiring an Interior Designer or Decorator

The decoration of homes has captivated people throughout recorded history. In 67 BC, Cicero commented, "What is more agreeable than one's home?" Interior designers put their style, creativity and experience to work to help a home reach its full potential—be it an estate, cottage or a multi-million dollar spread.

Despite recent press clippings questioning the integrity of the profession, *The Franklin Report* has uncovered over 90 design firms that clients adore and revere for their abilities and professionalism. Clients believe that these firms saved them considerable time and money by finding unique objects and avoiding costly errors. Each firm has its own style and personality, which is described on the following pages. For our inaugural Connecticut/Westchester County edition, we have tended to highlight the most prominent designers, which often translates into higher costs and minimums. Additional firms may be found on our website (www.franklinreport.com) which is updated regularly.

Finding a Match

After you fully assess your needs and your budget (see *What You Should Know About Hiring a Service Provider*, page 5), we recommend that you gather photographs from magazines and books to share with potential design candidates to communicate your preferences. Through our research, we have found that the best interior decorator-client bonds are founded on common ideas of style and taste. Even the best designers can falter and lose interest in a project if they are not excited by the end goal. So, as you gather potential names from *The Franklin Report* and from friends, focus on the preferred style of the designer—even if they say they can do anything.

As you narrow down your list and begin the interview process, think about your working relationship with the interior designer, who, for better or for worse, will become a big part of your life. Will you be seeing the principal on a regular basis or the project managers? Are you interested in a collaborative process or looking for strong direction? Will you be offered a wide range of budgetary choices? Finally, the prospect of working with this person should feel positive and enjoyable. Given the amount of time and money you are about to spend, it ought to be fun.

On Cost

Only a client can determine the worth of an interior designer's services. The "great masters" of interior design are considered exceptional artists who may charge whatever the market will bear. No one ever valued a Picasso based on a markup over the cost of materials. That said, the vast majority of designers are not masters, but competent professionals looking for a reasonable profit.

Interestingly, very few designers earn huge sums, due to the inherent unscalability of the process. Since clients generally want to talk to the Name-on-the-Door and not a senior associate, a name designer can only handle so many projects a year, usually about eight. Therefore, even with an average job size of $200,000 and a markup of 33 percent, net annual profits to a designer working with five clients equal only $62,500—a good living but not a fortune (especially compared to their clients).*

---

*Assumes net cost of products of $150,000 with a designer markup of 33 percent, totaling $200,000 of cost to the client and $50,000 of gross revenue to the designer. With a 25 percent profit margin (after all operating costs) net profit to the designer is only $12,500 for a client, or $90,000 for five clients (before tax).

Just a handful of designers have the clout to make serious money. This can be done by charging unusually high markups or hourly fees, employing multiple senior project managers, selling custom products (which carry very high, undisclosed markups) and/or accepting only clients with very expensive purchasing habits. While you should know standard industry pricing practices, many clients are willing to pay more for additional service or amazing talent.

STANDARD INDUSTRY PRICING

There are three fundamental services for which an interior designer may receive fees: 1) up-front design plans, 2) the purchasing of products (new and antique) and 3) the oversight of construction and installation. The pricing indications described below are what you can expected from a very competent, experienced professional—neither a part-time designer nor a grand master.

UP-FRONT DESIGN FEES: Many interior designers will charge an up-front, non-reimbursable design fee or retainer of about $500 (for a cosmetic rehab) up to $1,000 (for an architectural transformation) per major room, or about $5,000 to $10,000 for a major whole-house renovation with well-written plans (known as "Standard" in *The Franklin Report*). The extent of these plans can range considerably, from loose sketches to extensive architectural drawings with coordinating furniture memos, swatches and a detailed electrical plan. Qualify these expectations before you sign on.

Some designers will calculate the design fee as a flat rate and others on an hourly basis (both should fall into the cost range above). Occasionally half, and rarely all, of this fee is reimbursable against future product fees. Many designers will not charge repeat customers a design fee. Certain regional, but not many New York designers, will operate on an hourly consultation basis, with the client doing all the subsequent shopping, purchasing and implementation.

NEW PRODUCT FEES BY PERCENTAGE: Designers earn most of their fees by delivering products such as upholstery, case goods, window treatments, rugs and accessories. The vast majority charges clients a markup over the net (or wholesale) price. Designers who search high and low for the lowest-cost materials might charge a substantial markup, but still offer a very good value to clients.

♦ **Product Markup Over Net:** About half of the designers who work in the region charge a flat 33 to 35 percent markup over net cost on all new products, including workroom costs. This pricing is considered "Reasonable" in *The Franklin Report*'s designer reviews (as it is about 11 percent below the suggested retail price on fabrics). Below 33 percentage markup is delineated as "Low" in the book.

♦ **Classic Retail:** Many established designers charge "Classic retail," or 50 percent above net cost on fabrics, 66 percent on new furniture and 33 percent on new rugs. These percentages are based on the discount the decorators receive off the manufacturer's suggested retail price. For example, if the decorator were charged a net price of $100 per fabric yard, the client's Classic retail price would be $150. Workroom costs are usually marked up 25 to 50 percent at Classic retail (this is a very squishy number that should be clarified). This overall pricing is described as "Classic retail" in *The Franklin Report*'s interior designer reviews.

✧ **Retail Outside New York City:** Fabric and other showrooms ticket the suggested retail price as 100 percent over the net price, 50 miles outside New York City (vs. 50 percent within the area). So be extra sure to discuss what "retail" means with your decorator, especially if you live further than 50 miles from the City. This is described as Historic retail in the book.

✧ **Pricing Structure:** Remarkably, virtually no one charges under any other price structure—it is either Reasonable, Classic or Historic Retail (about one-third up). This is an interesting unifying principle in an industry that contains so many variables.

ANTIQUE PRODUCT FEES: Antiques are much trickier. First, the retail and net prices are usually negotiable with the dealers. Once retail price is established, most dealers offer designers a further discount of 10 to 20 percent. This presents a conundrum. For the designers to make their normal 33 to 50 percent markup, they may have to charge the client substantially above the new retail price (which could be above or below the original retail price). This is further complicated by the fact that most antique dealers are happy to sell directly to the public.

The most satisfactory solution used in many successful client-designer relationships seems to be full disclosure with a sliding scale. These designers charge a markup over the new price, with their usual 33 to 50 percent markup for lower priced items and a much smaller markup for larger items (often a lower percentage for items over $50,000, etc.). Many designers further guarantee that clients will never pay over the original or negotiated retail price. The most prominent designers appear to be able to hold to a set markup and/or not disclose the net prices. For expensive antiques, an independent appraisal may be warranted.

There is an additional point that needs clarification between a client and the designer on antique purchasing. If a client happens to walk into an antique dealer on Madison Avenue or an auction at Sotheby's and finds the perfect sideboard that has been eluding the decorator for months, should the decorator get a fee? Arguments may be made both ways, especially if that piece has been specified in the design plans, the decorator has spent time shopping for that piece (educating the client along the way) or the client seeks approval from the decorator before making the purchase.

Most decorators have a strong enough client bond to withstand these issues, and the client will not balk if, in fact, the designer deserves the fee. But specific contracts help in these times. An elegant solution that some of the more sophisticated designers use is to charge an hourly consultation fee under these circumstances or to take a much larger up-front design fee to cover all antique and auction purchases.

HOURLY PRODUCT FEES: A small but growing minority of designers charge clients on an hourly basis for all product procurement, including antiques, and pass the net prices through to the client. This methodology eliminates confusion and uncertainty on pricing, but introduces debates on how long it can take to order all the trims and fabrics for a sofa (it takes longer than you think). Hourly fees are particularly popular with architecture-trained designers (as that is how architects usually charge). These fees generally range from $75 per hour for a design assistant to $250-plus per hour for a grand master, with $125 to $175 as the "Standard," well-established Name-on-the-Door designer rate.

OVERSIGHT FEES: Some (but not many regional) designers charge a fifteen to twenty percent oversight fee for the management of the subcontractors from whom they are not already making a profit. Usually these are the subcontractors who work with design elements such as bathroom and kitchen design, architectural woodworking, etc. Other designers will ask for fifteen to twenty percent of the general contractor's net product costs to coordinate the artistic direction of the entire project. Or the designer can bill hourly for these consultations. This service may be unnecessary if you are using an architect who takes on the project manager's role. Some designers will also charge for every meeting and "look-see" outside of their immediate responsibilities, so this should be clarified in advance.

FLAT FEES AND OTHER NEGOTIATED TERMS: A limited but increasing number of designers will consider a flat fee for all of the services listed above. This fee would remain stable within a specified expenditure range, and go up or down if the product costs far exceeded or came in significantly lower than the estimates. But the key lesson here is that most interior designers are fairly negotiable on pricing and other terms, within reason.

CONTRACTUAL AGREEMENTS

Given the wide variance of markups and methodologies, it is highly recommended that you and your designer agree upon an explicit price scheme for each type of product and service before embarking upon a renovation. While not normally necessary, it is not unreasonable to ask to see all bills and receipts.

Also, before you sign, it is customary to speak with of one or two past clients (and occasionally, see the projects first-hand). Once the contract is signed, a retainer will be paid, the design plans will be drawn and purchases will be made. Timing expectations should also be addressed in the contract, but in many cases the timing of materials is out of the control of the designer. Therefore, if you have specific deadlines, the designers should be directed to order only in-stock items.

LICENSING OF INTERIOR DESIGNERS

The debate over the potential licensing of interior designers has been spirited. Currently it is not necessary to hold any type of degree or license to legally be an interior decorator in New York State or Connecticut. However, there are title regulations. In Connecticut,.you may not be called an interior designer unless you have seven years of relevant education and experience and pass the NCIDQ. In New York State, you must also have seven years and pass the NCIDQ to be called a Certified Interior Designer (but may be called an Interior Designer with no qualifications, interestingly though, only a miniscule percentage of the New York designers and less than half of the designers in Connecticut have complied). Many designers describe these tests as having more to do with health and safety issues (generally handled by architects) than with design competency. In fact, the tests do include sections on space planning, historical styles, fabric selection and all the necessary algebra, but do not really test creativity.

From a residential consumer viewpoint, there seems to be little correlation in *The Franklin Report* data between the passing of the NCIDQ exam and the satisfaction of the customer. Although, ASID membership or NCIDQ qualification should impress a potential client with the professionalism of the designer, as discussed in *What You Should Know About Hiring a Service Provider*, it is incumbent upon the homeowner to do a thorough investigation of the competency of any potential service professional through extensive interviews, referral information and a competitive analysis.

Final Considerations

As further described on the following pages, an overwhelming majority of the countless clients we talked with had very positive feelings toward their interior designers. While it may be possible to purchase "trade-only" fabrics and furnishings in other ways, truly successful decorating is about creating an intangible upgrade in mood and lifestyle that only an expert can accomplish. Professional designers also have the creative energy and resources to manage projects in a cohesive manner from start to finish, realizing clients' dreams more effectively and efficiently.

What You Should Not Expect From Your Interior Designer or the Design Process

- ✧ That the designer will maintain interest in the project if you cannot make any decisions.
- ✧ That you attend each shopping trip or be shown every possible fabric available.
- ✧ That the designer can read your mind.
- ✧ That there will be no misunderstandings or mistakes along the way.
- ✧ That the designer will bid out every subcontractor. There is a reason that the designer has been working with the same upholsterer and decorative painters for years. On the other hand, if you have a favorite supplier, the designer should be accommodating.
- ✧ That the designer will supervise other's work without an oversight fee. (The designer should be there, however, to oversee the installation of their products at no additional fee.)
- ✧ That the designer becomes your new best friend.

WHAT YOU SHOULD EXPECT FROM YOUR INTERIOR DESIGNER

✦ The sense that your interests and opinions matter.

✦ That some of your existing furnishings will be integrated into the new design, if you wish.

✦ Being shown a full range of options and products—creative ideas well beyond the D&D building. However, you should not feel forced to take whatever they purchased on their last worldwide jaunt (and pricing is really fuzzy here).

✦ Assurance that the designer will stick to a budget (and not tempt you with "the best" unless you insist).

✦ A full understanding of your lifestyle and use of your living space.

✦ The ability to see the net cost of every item, if you desire.

✦ An accessible and proactive effort, taking the initiative to complete the job to your satisfaction.

INTERIOR DESIGNERS & DECORATORS

A. Michael Krieger Inc.   4   4   4.5   5

45-17 21st Street, Long Island City, NY 11101
(718) 706 - 0077   amkriegerinc@aol.com

Updated, amalgam, historically referenced interior design

Almost every designer in America currently describes his or her style as eclectic—but Michael Krieger takes the prize. Creatively charged with a strong desire to please, each project becomes a diorama of the life of the client. Surprises rule the day with exotic and interesting artifacts and memories of a client's favorite voyage often counterbalancing streamlined, more neutral backgrounds. But this is a designer who can do traditional with punch or contemporary with formal antiques. Negotiating this composite can be tricky, but growing up in Westport and attending Weston High, Krieger understands the look and the territory.

With over twenty years experience in design—including associations with Kevin McNamara, Mark Hampton, Melvin Dwork and Donghia—Krieger certainly has breadth. Described as "engaging, smart and knowledgeable," supporters remark that his designs do not have the stamp of a decorator. The owner of an antiques shop in Hudson, NY, it's no surprise he's noted for his excellent use of antiques. Over half of his clientele is in the regional area.

Krieger charges a flat fee within the Standard range, half of which is deductible against future purchases. Classic retail is charged on products. He is happy to start with just a few rooms so long as the budget can support good-quality work. While plans have been known to go over budget, this is compensated with original, budget-minded ideas for art and accents. Clients are very pleased with Krieger's organized and detailed design plans, contracts and back office. Furthermore, he seems to have great patience, whether escorting clients to the D&D or to London. We hear if the client is not satisfied, he will "go back to the drawing board." HB Top Designers, 1999, 2000.

"My husband resisted hiring a decorator but is now begging Michael to review everything, including our landscape plans." "He turned our big vanilla box of a new house into a warm, comfortable home." "I was overwhelmed by our big new house, which had marble everything. He transformed the aesthetic and made it inviting." "He's able to find a beautiful object in what looks like a pile of junk to me." "I purchased some antiques five years ago on Michael's advice. I now realize they were a steal." "We learned so much in the process." "Michael has a Yankee-cost mentality, which we really appreciated. While he will sometimes use the very best, he will often have an excellent secret source." "We totally trust Michael's judgment. "He is a gentleman and a living doll."

Barclay Fryery Ltd.   4.5   4   4   4.5

271 Greenwich Avenue, Greenwich, CT 06830
(203) 862 - 9662   www.askbarclay.com

Gutsy, fresh interpretation of classical interior design

Is Barclay Fryery a designer, a media blitz or a personality? Many argue that this multifaceted whirlwind cannot possibly be all things to all people. But when it comes to decorating, his clients and favorite antiques dealers sing his praises. Taking on just a few large and a few smaller projects a year, Fryery takes a rough sketch of a concept and turns it into a spectacular reality with his "full heart and soul." Just two years ago, his designs were described by *House Beautiful* as "updated American Federal" and last year transformed to "simple, hip and alive." The truth is that Fryery will do whatever pleases the client, as long as it is unabashedly chic with historical reference.

Nothing describes Fryery better than his website, which is a multimedia exhibition of the worlds in which he operates: his favorite music, books, art, recipes, fashion designers, restaurants, furniture, events, travel tips, TV and radio appearances and weekly column for the Greenwich Post are all highlighted with aplomb. He is also featured on A&E's Mansions, Monuments & Masterpieces. Despite this hectic schedule, clients say that Fryery will still come over when needed "at the drop of a hat" and graciously deals with all budget levels (not to say that he does not esteem the best.) He is most appreciated for his design creativity, which is "not what the neighbors have."

Raised in Mississippi, Fryery's interior design career began in college where he would decorate his friends' dorm rooms in exchange for cheeseburgers. Fryery moved to Greenwich in 1991 and formally began his design firm in 1995. A minimal flat fee is paid up front and Classic markups are paid on product. HB Top Designers 2001, 2002.

"Barclay does what it takes. Flowers? Linens? No problem." "He is really a lifestyle guru and proud of it." "Quite the man on the scene in Greenwich. Not your typical local decorator." "The custom upholstery he designed for me was the utmost in quality, including horsehair innards." "Barclay was completely on top of our complicated renovation. After a full evaluation he laid out a course of action with a timeline and stuck to it." "While he may take four cell calls in the course of one conversation with you, he gets it done." "He is wired in more than one sense—Barclay makes a business of knowing the latest but is not an interior design fashion victim. He develops schemes with beautiful classic lines that will last and then wires the home for the future." "He absolutely fills a need and has such a good heart."

Beautiful Country Homes   4   4   4   4
306 Twin Lakes Road, Salisbury, CT 06068
(860) 824 - 1375
Tailored country-inspired interior design

Beverly Ellsley Design Inc.   3.5   3.5   4   4
175 Post Road West, Westport, CT 06880
(203) 454 - 0503   www.beverlyellsley.com
Kitchen design and interior design, custom handmade cabinetry

See Beverly Ellsley Design Inc.'s full report under the heading Kitchen & Bath Designers

	Quality	Cost	Value	Recommend?
	✚	$	◆	★

Bilhuber Inc.   5   4.5   4   5

330 East 59th Street, 6th Floor, New York, NY 10022
(212) 308 - 4888   bilhuber@aol.com

Gutsy, handsome, modernly classical interior design

One of the primary architects of the New American classicism, Jeffrey Bilhuber has clearly influenced the design world. His compositions featuring streamlined neutrals highlighted by touches of eminence simultaneously speak to modern comfort and mid-century elegance. Clients and peers alike regard him as one of the great talents of his generation. Bilhuber has done about a dozen projects in the last few years in the regional area, with an interest in bringing a fresh, modern spirit to family sensibilities. He might place fresh, light chintzes upholstered inside out near antique benches bleached white by years in the sun. While some may say he is a marketing machine with a very distinctive point of view, his work remains respected by all.

The design firm, established fifteen years ago, takes on about ten projects at a time. Clients have included Randolph Duke, Anna Wintour, Elsa Peretti, Peter Jennings, and Iman and David Bowie and the new NYC City Club Hotel—but Bilhuber is also open to doing less prominent projects. He will do a few rooms in the suburbs, if there is a connection with the client. His office is said to be very professional and responsive, even six months after the project's completion. Bilhuber wins accolades for being "completely dedicated to getting things done on time and on budget."

Pre-shopping effectively, Bilhuber is not the kind of guy to spend the day at the D&D with clients on a daily basis. Living rooms can run in the $250,000 neighborhood, but Bilhuber has also won the hearts of those clients with much lower budgets with a mix of "the humble and the high." He is also known to make great suggestions to the architecture during renovations and will ship back anything the client does not like "in the blink of an eye." AD 100, 2002. HB Top Designers, 1999, 2000, 2001, 2002. KB 1991.

"In Connecticut, when we needed Jeffrey we would get him and he attended every design meeting." "He has a very large personality but is always very professional." "The chicest person in Greenwich was amazed at what Jeffrey did. She dragged me away from my guests to see every room." "Gives many newly wealthy clients a distinct design voice making sure they take the edge off." "While our budget was minuscule compared to others, he made us feel like his only client." "He takes your personality and turns it into a design vision. But you have to appreciate his perspective to start." "He listens and then pushes the envelope." "We have done sixteen houses with Jeffrey and would not consider doing it any other way." "His spirit is contagious."

Brian McCarthy Inc.   4.5   4.5   5   4.5

1414 Avenue of the Americas, Suite 404, New York, NY 10019
(212) 308 - 7600   www.bjminc.com

Stylish, strong, articulate, traditional interior design

Whether doing a Greenwich manor home full of 18th-century master paintings or a period-pure 18th-century square-cut log cabin, Brian McCarthy does all things to perfection. Admired for his innate desire to create rooms of unique character and grace, McCarthy finds extraordinary pieces that are coherently placed in classic frameworks. Many recent clients are collectors of fine works of art or furniture. The firm has a full-time employee stationed in Paris to assist these clients. Trained by master designer Albert Hadley, McCarthy displays both Hadley's professionalism and skill in combining the expected and the traditional with elements of more modern or gutsier protocol.

McCarthy's clients are generally very well established, many with stately homes or apartments, looking to create a personal magnum opus. Regionally, McCarthy has done projects in Conyer's Farm, Stonington and North Salem. Supporters say the firm's client service is outstanding—issues disappear and billing is presented clearly. Additionally, McCarthy is hailed for his depth of knowledge, clarity of presentation and warm personality. About eight active projects are pursued at a time, with nine on staff including three experienced project managers.

References consider McCarthy's work quite expensive, but worth it. Living rooms can be in the $250,000 to $400,000 range before fine antiques. On the other hand, he recently did a local Arts and Crafts home on a much more reasonable budget and is said to be quite practical in children's rooms, using washable $15 per yard fabrics. Also, McCarthy is commended for his "amazing sources here and abroad that can duplicate originals for a quarter of the cost." Supporters are protective, considering McCarthy a friend and a fabulous secret source. They cannot wait to embark on another project with this designer.

"Everyone who walks in is blown away by the warmth and details." "Brian is on an intellectual mission to find the beauty in any period." "He strongly encourages you to find your own design viewpoint." "The best part about working with Brian is having a drink with him at the end of a long day. He is such delightful company." "We hired him just to do the public rooms, but fell in love with his work and did the whole house." "While you spend more than you care to think about, you are always investing in pieces of quality." "Brian was in the right place at the right time." "Three years later, Brian is more than gracious about finding just one little lamp." "My curtains rival any of Marie Antoinette's dresses." "We couldn't recommend him more highly."

Brooks & Orrick Inc.   4   4   4   4

63 Pemberwick Road, Greenwich, CT 06831
(203) 532 - 1188
Refined, updated, classical interior design

With Monique Brooks heading interior design and Alicia Orrick on architecture, the firm has built a solid reputation for offering a full range of services. The firm is involved in designing homes from the ground up, with a strong emphasis on an integrated approach. The homes may be planned around the interior objectives from the start and furniture is often purchased as the house is being built or renovated. Most of the spaces are open and clean, tailored and comfortable, fashioned after the client's interests.

Brooks and Orrick joined forces in 1994, after each worked separately for several years in the business. Orrick graduated with a degree in art from Colby College with a BFA and NYSID, then worked in retail and for herself for several years. Brooks graduated from Skidmore College and received a masters in architecture from Yale, then worked for Cesar Pelli, Warren Platner and for herself for several years. Together, they have a staff of nine, including two licensed architects. About three larger and eighteen total projects are undertaken at a time, including sites in Greenwich, Darien, Florida, Nantucket and London, Colorado, Boston, New York City and Vermont.

The pair will take on a few rooms, and have done a number of kitchen/bath renovations that led to significantly larger situations. The firm works on a percentage basis for design work, Classic retail on product and Reasonable markups on workrooms. The two are said to have very good budget tracking systems, enabling them to meet timing and economic targets and tight deadlines.

"Alicia is very much plugged into the Greenwich community and totally understands the genre." "They are totally pleasant to work with." "Every room is livable and geared to family practicalities." "Alicia and Monique understand excellent quality, but are flexible and engaged about spending your money wisely."

Budd & Allardyce Interiors, LLC   3.5   3   4   4.5

84 Keelers Ridge Road, Wilton, CT 06897
(203) 762 - 1235
Convivial, timeless, mostly traditional interior design

With an aim to please her predominantly traditional clientele, Nancy Budd offers a refreshing view on traditional, featuring crisp color, clean lines and a restraint of

	Quality	Cost	Value	Recommend?
	✚	$	◆	★

concept. Budd believes that a few good pieces support a room, and has thus developed a skilled group of artisans to fulfill that vision and an appreciative group of customers who report that Budd understands the bottom line. Whether doing a small rental or a bigger renovation, traditional or contemporary, Budd is credited for working collaboratively and effectively.

After graduating from Loomis Chaffee and Wheaton, Budd received a certificate at NYSID. She worked for a Park Avenue designer for several years and then opened her own shop in 1993 in Wilton. Budd, also a lacrosse coach, is said to "completely comprehend the active Wilton family scene, becoming part of the family." An individual owner, Budd works integrally with the clients who note her focus, accessibility and calm, straightforward nature.

Realistically approaching each project, Budd has a Low hourly fee for design planning and a Low product mark-up. Reportedly, much is salvaged from the client's preexisting inventory and a wide range of economic levels can be implemented.

"Nancy is amazingly adaptable. She first did a spruce-up on our rental, which worked out so well that we are now having her do our new home." "It is so easy with Nancy. I do not feel like I am jumping into the deep end." "The craftsmen at her command are fabulous. I never would have had access to those resources." "Nancy has a really good balance. She keeps the project moving but is never too much." "I consider myself a color connoisseur, and she really impressed me." "Not only good with decoration, Nancy also reviewed the architectural plans and made some really helpful suggestions." "Nancy had no issues at all when I used my old curtain maker." "She respects the budget and makes it happen."

Bunny Williams	4.5	5	4	4.5

306 East 61st Street, Fifth Floor, New York, NY 10021
(212) 207 - 4040   www.bunnywilliams.com

Lovely, exalted, traditional interior design

Awash in charm and elegance, Bunny William's rooms enchant clients with their cohesive medley that unpretentiously speak to a genteel past and a current comfort. Clients report that she can expertly execute a range of styles but gravitates toward a refined, welcoming English sensibility awakened with fresh, modern finishes and unusual pieces of character. An 18th-century English chest might be crowned with a 50s mirror or a French Moderne desk flanked by Regency chairs. Combining this bespoke approach with her extraordinary professionalism, talent and energy, Williams has obtained near cult status in the decorating community.

Raised in Albemarle County, Virginia (home to Nancy Lancaster), Williams carries on the craft of gracious Southern living. Trained at the venerable Parish-Hadley, she opened her own firm in 1988. Her organizational skills and strong back office allow for excellent efficiency and quick project development. The firm has four integrated design teams, each headed by a senior design associate. Williams is said to travel extensively but is the design inspiration behind each creation. With a weekend home in northwest Connecticut, Williams travels through the regional area regularly, easily stopping by Fairfield County, which constitutes about fifteen percent of her client base.

Most projects are quite substantial, ranging from a classic Cape Cod-style compound on the Connecticut side of the Sound to Manhattan penthouses to large homes in California, Palm Beach, Atlanta, Maine, Texas and the south of France. Clients confirm William's "ladylike nature" and her ability to "do it all," saying that she is a woman of her word. Prices are reportedly extraordinarily high but can be brought under control. Williams also has a great passion for gardening. Joining forces with antiques dealer John Rosselli, they own Treillage, a garden furniture shop in Manhattan, and Williams is the author of the book *On Garden Style*. HB Top Designers, 1999, 2000, 2001, 2002. ID Hall of Fame. KB 1990, 1998.

"You tell her how much you want to spend, and she develops a design plan very quickly." "We hired Bunny for a relatively modest project and she totally got it." "Much less chintz than you would expect and Bunny is developing a real fondness for simplicity of line." "There is a complete understanding inside and out. She interweaves the mood and the design integrally." "She treats design like a cottage industry—she has an amazing array of specialists at hand who she can dispense at a moment's notice." "The staff is a bit stretched given the substantial client base, but always wonderful." "She also did my friend's apartment, and I was surprised to see some of the same elements as in mine." "We have meetings every three weeks, and she is always very prepared." "Bunny even showed us how to make the beds in the correct manner." "She is not a prima donna and was very thoughtful in her allocation of our budget." "Her rooms have extraordinary style and grace." "She is dazzling in a quiet kind of way."

Casa Linda Designs Ltd.　　　　4　　3.5　　4.5　　5

2-4 Weaver Street, Scarsdale, NY 10583
(914) 725 - 0700　casalindadesign@earthlink.net
Full-service interior design

Kim Amann and her team at Casa Linda have won the hearts and souls of clients by delivering an excellent product, from top-to-bottom, with no fuss. From the massive gut renovation of the Judy Garland estate in Scarsdale to a modest kitchen in Bronxville to the complete interior outfitting of a large new home in Greenwich, the firm is lauded for its handsome, practical rooms and effective project management skills. Recent other clients include the Winged Foot Golf Club, the Larchmont Shore Club and the Elm Street Oyster House restaurant in Greenwich.

Amann started Casa Linda in 1999, after gaining a degree from NYSID, and several years at a home renovation collaborative in Philly and at Bloomingdale's Shop at Home. Her energy is contagious, with Amann directing all the interior design work and also eliminating much of the need for either a separate contractor or architect. The staff of five is said to be highly capable and knowledgeable. Recently moving to their new location in Scarsdale, the showroom features several lines of custom cabinetry, lighting, tile, countertops and appliances for a one-stop shop.

Given the firm's multiple roles, clients report a very coordinated process and lower overall fees. There are small up-front design fees, Standard hourly design and shopping fees, and product is purchased at 25 percent of list retail. Clients are effusive in their praise of Casa Linda.

"Meeting Kim was the most fortunate thing that happened to us on this project. We went from disorder, confusion and fiscal rape to clarity and order." "I can not come up with words positive enough to describe Kim's contributions to our renovation." "Not only did Kim do her job well but she found and managed all the subs, who were also excellent." "Kim always managed to find a better way, and usually at a lower cost."

	Quality	Cost	Value	Recommend?
	✚	$	◆	★

Charlotte Barnes Interior Design   5   4   4.5   5
32 Evergreen Road, Greenwich, CT 06830
(203) 622 - 6953

Opulently casual, refined interior design

Roundly regarded among the best in her class, Charlotte Barnes creates timeless, thoughtful environments steeped in historical reference. Known for a stylistic melange built with luxurious materials, fine antiques, attention to detail and restraint, Barnes has a loyal following. Each room has at least one extraordinary and memorable feature, be it a pleated arched window dressing, a mahogany tester frame or a chintz-covered dollhouse platform, all streamlined and elegant.

Barnes began her interior design firm in 1993, after returning stateside from a stint in London helping to expand Ralph Lauren in Europe. Once her own home was featured in *British House & Garden*, the calls for her design advice never ceased. Barnes has an excellent office that includes Bettina Routh, who clients also admire. About eight projects are undertaken at one time, all with full budgets. Recent clients include major financiers, the CEO of an auction house and the CEO of a top fashion house.

Product is carefully considered and vendor relationships are assiduously cultivated with the best. Higher quality is encouraged, with auctions frequented or tag sale favored over repro. A Standard design fee is taken along with Reasonable markups. Barnes considers every detail down to the custom lampshades. Clients respond in kind with repeat business as the norm.

"Charlotte is every bit as good as any New York designer, but much more practical." "She absolutely understands antiques, and has such a good eye that you can pay less for more look." "Charlotte is one of the few people we know that can be both incredibly nice and incredibly professional." "Each project projects the hopes and vision of the client." "It is so chic but also stately."

Christman Stuart Interiors   3.5   3   4   4
381 Main Street, Ridgefield, CT 06877
(203) 431 - 4752   thiwilton@aol.com

Traditional, livable, unified interior design

With a strong traditional base that is at once familiar and appreciated by clients, Debbie Christman Stuart offers a "warmer shade of the expected." Making an effort to take customers' clues, all feel that they have achieved something special and individual. European and American reproductions are intermingled with brass accents, botanical prints and ribboned mirrors.

Building on her family trade, Christman Stuart opened the business in 1974. About five projects are taken on at once, mostly with regional supporters looking for a low-key approach. Some have been clients for over twenty years and are on their third project with the firm. Approachable, the firm will take on anything from a sofa to consulting on new construction.

Working with a nominal design fee and good discount to retail, Christman Stuart is very practical in her economics. There is a 3,000-square-foot shop at the address above with reproductions, accessories and rugs. ASID.

"Debbie could not be nicer." "It all made sense, even the lighting." "Even my husband realized the upgrade from Ethan Allen." "Debbie was so good about using what we owned from the old house, even the draperies were reused." "A much improved version of what we could have done." "Debbie would jump through hoops for us."

Christopher Coleman   4   3   5   4.5
70 Washington Street, Suite 1005, Brooklyn, NY 11201
(718) 222 - 8984   ccoleman1005@hotmail.com

Colorful, bold, witty, contemporary interior design

Clients appreciate Christopher Coleman's confident mix of geometric shapes, clean lines, exuberant colors and warm undertones. They also applaud his

	Quality	Cost	Value	Recommend?
	+	$	◆	★

enthusiasm, charm and willingness to take design risks. His usual chromatic style and dashing melange of 20th-century items is finding a new voice in Westchester with an "amazingly practical and uplifting use of each space so that the family uses it on a daily basis."

Following five years with Renny Saltzman, Coleman founded his design practice in 1993. Based in Brooklyn, Coleman recently made his LA debut but continues to do a few projects a year in the region. Past clients include former Harper's Bazaar editor Kate Betts, Helen Henson (Jim's wife), former Time Inc. chairman Don Logan, established professionals and young couples decorating their first homes. Clients credit Coleman for taking time to educate them about the design process—be it on classical historic styles, economic alternatives or timing. Other strengths include a sensitivity to family living, with notable contemporary art next to the jigsaw puzzle collection. Reportedly Coleman will always create a place for all the children's toys and gadgets, often in stylish Lucite or bleached beech wood. He also enjoys bringing the "inside out and the outside in." References say Coleman is very available, highly attentive and lots of fun.

Coleman works with a Low up-front design fee, a Low percentage over net for products and no hourlies. He is known for his ability to make the most of less with some living rooms in the $40,000 range and a willingness to work in phases. Clients note that Coleman is highly professional and straightforward—all bills and the background paperwork are presented on a regular basis. A new line of Coleman's carpets was recently introduced by Doris Leslie Blau. HB Top Designers, 1999, 2000, 2001, 2002.

"Christopher finds the most unique furnishings. Whatever he cannot find at a reasonable price he has made. His upholstery people can do the highest-quality sofas for half the price of what we expected and deliver in half the time." "He is overtly modern without being rehashed-retro." "We so enjoy his creativity. Anything can become an interesting design motif to him—country, ethnic, old maps." "He is the only guy in the business who can do red vinyl successfully." "When I was after a particular, very expensive Italian look, he found a very good match at Crate & Barrel." "We interviewed twenty decorators over the phone and five in person and feel so lucky to have found Christopher." "He has a wicked sense of humor and a hip design sensibility to match."

Connie Beale Inc.   4.5   4   4   4.5

125 East Putnam Avenue, Greenwich, CT 06830
(203) 661 - 6003   www.conniebeale.com

Dashing, luxurious, updated, classical interior design

Connie Beale is known as an assertive decorator with fine taste who settles for nothing but the best in quality materials and products. Beale is described as extremely hands-on, occasionally taking hammer in hand to demonstrate to contractors how something should be done. Beale's design style has been called "casually elegant," featuring a more modern flourish than is often seen in the regional area. With a fresh, radiant approach, upholstered lines are tailored, layouts are pared and a comfortable openness is achieved. References tell us each project is a unique work and hail Beale as extremely collaborative, yet resolute in her overall vision. Many of Beale's products are of her own design, often forming the dramatic focus point in a room (be it a sculptural iron chandelier or artistic palm frond finials on a tester bed).

Beale, a native of Louisiana, holds a degree from Louisiana Tech and established this ten person firm in 1979. One of a handful of firms in the regional area who have attracted national attention, the firm does commercial work in New York, including the interiors of The Regency Hotel on Park Avenue. In Greenwich, there are ten on staff including three excellent project managers and a draftsman.

Beale and senior designer Brian del Toro (with his own client base) oversee all major design decisions. Brian recently joined Beale after working with New York's prestigious Parish-Hadley and David Kleinberg. References are impressed with the clear paperwork and back office management.

The firm discusses budgets up front in great detail, establishing a standard starting budget that can skyrocket given the client's preferences. Supporters who have used Beale for numerous projects say they completely trust her creative (and sometimes unorthodox) ideas, and let her work largely unsupervised through much of the project. The firm charges Standard hourly rates and Classic product markups. There is a hip and evocative, 1,000-square-foot store called Button that features vintage and handcrafted goods next door. ASID. HB Top Designers, 1999, 2000. KB, 2001.

"Connie breathed life into our house, which started as a boring spec house." "While I seriously questioned the eggplant walls, she was right and we now love it." "She spoiled us by introducing us to the best. A favorite expression is 'you can do better' and we did." "It was virtually decorated overnight. In six months, it looked as if we had lived there five years." "The budget quickly went out the window." "Not soft, she is no-nonsense and doesn't play games. Says it like it is with no fluff, but she's not a prima donna or a diva." "I am at a point now where I just give her the keys and tell her to do it." "We have nothing but compliments and raves."

Constantin Gorges Ltd.   4.5   4   4   4.5
26 East 63rd Street, New York, NY 10021
(212) 753 - 3727   gorgesc@aol.com
Adroit, modern-hued, traditional interior design

Constantin Gorges has impressed clients with interiors that are reflective of worldly sophisticated pastiche jauntily poised on the leading edge. Designs may range from clean 20th-century modern to continental traditional luxury, but are typically a mix. This creates an interplay of energy and form, consistently described as exquisite. Gorges favors luxurious materials and fine antiques, used with restraint. Architecture usually sets the tone—English country in Bedford, funky 50s on the West Side, New Age on the 77th floor—but all are said to be gracious. He has completed a number of large-scale projects and also enjoys working with younger clients on smaller projects.

Gorges is sympathetic to budget constraints, expertly integrating clients' existing furnishings into the design plan. While he knows and offers the best, he always seems to have a well-priced alternative "up his sleeve." Because of his excellent and multifarious training—Parsons, Noel Jeffrey, Peter Marino and Parish-Hadley's architecture department—Gorges, according to appreciative clients, often becomes the project manager. While he wins accolades for delivering fantastic architectural details (including lighting schematics) and intelligent design elements, some say he has less interest in selecting the detailed accessories such as books, picture frames, etc.

Gorges is known to be very fair with his fees, waiving charges for things that are redone even if he originally followed a client decision. He charges a Standard design fee and a Reasonable percentage over net. Oversight fees may be charged by the hour or on a percentage basis. Clients highly recommend Gorges for his cohesive vision and outstanding project management skills. KB, 2001.

"He has an amazing work ethic—if the client is not happy then Constantin feels he has not done his job properly." "He will find or make a knock-off if you can't afford the real thing." "He is clear on price and there are never any surprises." "Constantin is a trendsetter, not a trend follower." "The living room can be a Bentley and the kids' rooms attractive VW Bugs." "He pre-shops and doesn't waste your time" "He is the kind of decorator that your husband would also like, but he is not going to take the place of your best girlfriend." "There is a tendency for the more formal that you can tone down." "Constantine is 100 percent dependable and particularly effective at getting suppliers to deliver." "He is always available and has no attitude, and your apartment will have tons of personality."

	Quality	Cost	Value	Recommend?

Country Design   3.5   3   4.5   4
150 Elm Street, New Canaan, CT 06846
(203) 966 - 9131

Chromatic, layered, traditional interior design with spunk

With strong local contacts and a clear sense of the customer's needs, Laura Sigg, her mother-in-law, Fiona Sigg, and the team at Country Design deliver traditional environments with a flair for the exuberant. Checks and tassels meet stripes and needlepoint with floral patterns intermingled. Supporters praise the firm for its "classic but not stuffy designs" and its excellent flexibility.

Country Design was started in 1977 as a large antiques and reproductions store anchoring a New Canaan corner by Dr. Sigg (a dentist by profession). His wife, Fiona Sigg, began the auxiliary interior design business in 1997. There are six designers, most of them part-time, and Laura who joined the firm six years ago and reportedly works more than full-time. An impressive twenty-plus projects are active at one time, with many long-term relationships.

Patrons consistently mention sensitivity to family living with most of the fabrics and furniture budget-minded and kid and dog friendly. While the "layers and babbles do add up," the fees are very low. The firm charges no design fee (but a minimal consultation fee), a Reasonable product markup and no oversight fees. Budgets can start at $250 for a few pillows to $30,000 for a starter home and go up from there. ASID.

"I like my home to be fun and cheerful, and they completely understood." "When they delivered a bed that I had approved but looked more distressed than I would have liked, they came back the next day, took it apart and that was the last I ever heard of it." "This was my first experience decorating a house. Laura talked me into making the dining room more formal and she was completely right—mahogany over pine works." "Laura is busier than she used to be—but that speaks to a job well done." "They transformed the house with new curtains and accessories, keeping an eye on the bottom line."

Cullman & Kravis Inc.   5   5   4   4.5
790 Madison Avenue, New York, NY 10021
(212) 249 - 3874   ellen@cullmankravis.com

Exquisite, stately-yet-accessible, traditional interior design

Cullman & Kravis is roundly credited for its consistently impeccable taste, versatile design skills and a client list to die for. Founded in 1985 by Elissa Cullman and the late Heidi Kravis, the firm is often called upon to design around superb collections of fine art and antiques. Cullman's own Fairfield home is filled with the results of a lifelong devotion to fine Americana, a theme often carried to patron's country homes. Clients are consistently impressed by the firm's "traditional yet creative" textures, project management acumen and extreme attention to detail.

Clients have included the CEOs of Philip Morris, Goldman Sachs, Paramount, Solomon Brothers and Miramax, as well as the estate of John Singer Sargent. While the firm may have as many as 25 projects at any one time (in various stages), a full staff of "super competent" project coordinators helps manage project operations. Cullman's supporters see her as the design inspiration, based on the client's interests. In Connecticut, most clients note that Cullman was fairly available (on her way up and back to her own abode) and were pleased with their strong project managers.

Customers consider pricing top of the market but worth it. The firm charges a Standard design fee, Classic retail on product and workroom, Standard markup on antiques and Standard hourly fees for oversight. While "no expense is spared," the contract reportedly is followed to the line. The firm's outreach to superior craftsmen is described as "unparalleled." Supporters highly recommended the firm for those who appreciate effective oversight of the highest caliber quality. AD 100, 2000, 2002.

"I really respected Ellie's integrity. With our new home she insisted that we first put the money into the proper architecture, saying that the sofas could be purchased anytime." "The firm's incredible organizations skills are very comforting." "If she could not find the perfect antique, she would find a really good substitute." "Even though slipcovers are not Ellie's thing, she did what I asked and made it look great." "Many of the same chintzes and tartans are used, even in the same colorways." "Ellie personally vetted every antique and kept a close eye on the associates assigned to us." "We lucked out and I loved my young project manager, but things did not work out so well with my friend." "I did not want to be involved on a detailed basis, and I certainly did not need to be." "My husband is crazy about Ellie—it amazed me that he got involved at all." "Ellie's knowledge of antiques and rugs is extensive and central to her stately decorating." "The designs are less predictable than you would have thought." "While progressing, I would not say they are on the edge of pizzazz." "She delivers an American original—extraordinarily luscious designs that withstand the test of time. It is classic opulence meets livable comfort." "Expensive, but worth it."

Davenport & Co.   4.5   4   4   4.5

79 East Putnam Avenue, Greenwich, CT 06830
(203) 629 - 9181   davnportco@aol.com

Refined, eloquent, unpretentious traditional interior design

Highly respected by peers and the established Greenwich set, Jane Gleason and Isabelle Vanneck of Davenport are consummate traditionalists, and proud of it. Classical bones and the finest European and American antiques are awakened with strokes of livable, saturated color, often with amusing oriental highlights or trompe l'oeil details. Well-worn Persians complement Adams mantels. In each room there is also a sublime element of surprise, be it a contemporary abstract or a Biedermeier chair, distinguishing the composition.

Forming Davenport together in 1996, Gleason was previously with Katherine Cowden for over eight years and Vanneck with several art and antiques dealers. Currently, the firm has an extremely capable staff of four, and is engaged in about five large and another eight or so small projects at a time. It is usually a team effort, with Gleason more focused on the palette and soft goods and Vanneck guiding the selection of antique case goods and porcelains. One room redos are often expanded to full home renovations, sometimes including the books on the bookshelf.

Clients span several states and report that the firm knows best but is also very practical. Younger clients may start with just a few good pieces and build over time. No upfront fees are taken, with Classic retail on product and Standard hourly fees on non-commission product. Patrons have absolute trust in the designers to get it just right.

"These two represent the epitome of high-end traditional Greenwich design." "Not only are they great in person, but they were able to completely guide me through the process long-distance, via email." "For the most discriminating they can shoot the moon, but were quite practical when they did my daughter's home." "Jane and Isabelle are also terrific advocates when it comes to the contractor." "They are now at the point where they know better than I what will work in my home."

	Quality	Cost	Value	Recommend?
	+	$	◆	★

David Christopher Dumas Architect & Cheryl Dixon Interiors

4.5   4   4.5   4.5

1616 Post Road, Suite 7739, Fairfield, CT 06824
(203) 336 - 9326   cdixoninteriors@aol.com

Refined, engaging, thoughtful interior design

Lauded for their sophisticated designs infused with warmth and character, David Dumas and Cheryl Dixon create homes that inspire and delight their clients. Stretching the bounds of classic traditional, the pair takes the tried and true, twisting it ever so slightly so as to charm and enlighten each room. Balustrades are spiraled, garages are turreted and eyebrow windows wink. Interiors are flooded with light and a calming melange of interesting shapes in harmonious tones. With Dumas on architecture and Dixon on interior design, clients appreciate the integrated, professional approach which "speaks to the heart of the client."

Dumas and Dixon both spent twelve years with Banks Design before establishing their own firm just this year. Dumas, who has wanted to be an architect as long as he can remember, has been registered in Connecticut since 1989, after receiving his Bachelor of Architecture from the University of Arizona. Dixon received her interior design certificate from Sacred Heart University after graduating the University of Bridgeport in painting and art history. There is just one associate who works for the firm full time, so clients get the principals' direct attention. About half the work is done in tandem, and about half independent of each other. On the architecture side, about three-quarters of the commissions are renovations and one-quarter new construction. Most of the projects are in the immediate Connecticut area—Darien, Greenwich, Guilford, New Canaan, Wilton.

Before all projects commence, Dumas & Dixon have lengthy discussions with the client and together develop a "concept statement" which becomes the strategic plan. Thus, the lifestyle vision and the architectural and interior reality converge. The firm will do consultation work and phased design. For larger projects, a very low upfront design fee is charged with Reasonable hourly rates and Low product markups.

"I have worked with many, many designers in the area and David and Cheryl stand out as incredibly professional." "These guys can do anything. "There are no words to describe how David transformed the façade of our boring Dutch Colonial into a home of exquisite taste and charm." "It is so tasteful, but simultaneously a joyful departure from what everyone else has in Darien." "The colors and materials are more modern, but fit right in." "When the contractors could not figure out how to place the patio stair, David came right out and solved the issue." "Cheryl is so accommodating. She makes everything work for you."

David Easton Inc.

5   4.5   5   4.5

72 Spring Street, 7th Floor, New York, NY 10012
(212) 334 - 3820   www.davideastoninc.com

Extraordinary, timeless, elegant interior design

David Anthony Easton is clearly recognized as one of today's great patriarchs of interior design. His striking ability to instantly visualize the perfect solution, acquire masterful product and manage (with a large support system) a comprehensive process with the highest standards sets him apart. While best known for interiors that recapture the elegance of the classic English country manor with a modern sweep, he is equally capable of using other styles. Supporters say he is brilliant, funny and friendly. Earlier this year, Easton and partner Charlotte Moss went separate ways, after a fairly brief time in business together. Easton has "not lost a beat," recently hiring a "COO" to oversee all project management.

And project management is where the firm excels. There are about fifteen to twenty large commissions at a time, and a process for everything—including how to manage the painters. Most of the firm's jobs are exceedingly large and expensive including homes for Patricia Kluge and Carol Petrie. While Easton is quite involved with the upfront design plans which are lovingly drawn much by hand (and working fifteen hours a day, seven days a week), experienced projects mangers take over from there. With a large library of "Easton-approved" materials, much of it created by exclusive European artisans (with exclusive markups), the managers cannot stray too far from the master. About twenty percent of the work is done in the Fairfield/Westchester area. Easton also has recently launched new lines with Lee Jofa, Henredon, Walter's Wicker and Beauvais Carpets.

Easton has a devoted following. While Easton's clients generally acknowledge that costs are over the top (reportedly, living rooms of $600,000 to $1.2 million are the norm), most say the firm's extraordinary results and overall client services are worth every penny. AD 100, 2000, 2002. HB Top Designers, 1999, 2000, 2001, 2002. ID Hall of Fame. KB 2000, 2003.

"I so enjoyed my time with David—he instantly connects with people and I learned so much from him. He has a masterful touch, and his spaces are extraordinary, livable and timeless." "David was amazing about thinking how each family member would use the house." "For Room 101 there is Carpet 101.1, etc. And with their bi-monthly meetings, there are never any surprises." "While we liked our project manager, I only saw David about once a month and he was always about to fly somewhere else. While we were very pleased with the end product, we did not enjoy the process." "The meter is always running." "In Greenwich, I have seen a different, easier sensibility that very much relates to the landscape and a calm, genteel living." "All the antiques are vetted and valued, which gives me tremendous confidence." "After a long wilderness period, there is new energy at the firm." "David's unique products and superior client service are unmatched."

David Scott Interiors Ltd.   4.5   4   4.5   4.5
120 East 57th Street, 2nd Floor, New York, NY 10022
(212) 829 - 0703 www.davidscottinteriors.com
Characteristic, joyful, modern-hued interior design

With youthful verve and a dedicated soul, David Scott creates transitional rooms with a view to the future and a nod to the past. Neutral backgrounds often highlight a thoughtful mixture of vintage, antique and sculptural shapes with arousing accents. Described as "exceptionally knowledgeable, accommodating and practical," Scott takes great care to understand the client's viewpoint and develop long-term relationships. About a quarter of his constituency is in Westchester, where homeowners applaud Scott's availability and involvement.

Clients tell us Scott is a "design psychologist" who understands their physical and spiritual design thoughts better than they do and in turn delivers a highly customized product. Scott has been known to wade through a client's closet to better understand their stylistic interests. Scott teaches residential design at the New York School of Interior Design and previously was in the business end of real estate.

The firm charges Standard hourly fees for design plans and oversight, and Reasonable markups on products with a sliding scale for more expensive antiques. Scott reportedly is flexible about offering a variety of economic alternatives and meets timing deadlines. Most living rooms are in the $100,000 to $200,000 plus range. Patrons comment that Scott is very professional, with a laid-back office of four. The vast majority of clients return for additional projects.

"David truly believes that the best client is a happy client." "I enjoy my home as much today as I did three years ago when it was finished." "I never wanted to go into my living room before, and now it is my favorite room." "It was not only fun but very exciting to transform our house." "David always returns phone calls the same day." "He became like a member of the family." "He maintained a wonderful sense of humor throughout." "We reap the benefit of his wonderful relationships with vendors." "As a businessman, he relies on his contract." "David listened to our dreams and wishes and turned them into a wonderful reality." "He is as nice as he is talented, with real star potential."

	Quality +	Cost $	Value ◆	Recommend? ★

Deborah Quintal Wick

	Quality	Cost	Value	Recommend?
	4	4	4	4.5

49 Church Lane, Scarsdale, NY 10583
(914) 723 - 1080   deborahwick@verizon.net

Evocative, characteristic, comfortable interior design

Ranging form from old-world traditional to clean 20th-century modern, Deborah Wick designs rooms with warmth that speak to the clients' time, travel and intentions. Recent compositions include floral chintz from top to bottom (including a pleated fabric ceiling) and, diametrically, a sleek Palm Beach pied-a-terre in black leather, Lucite and mirrors. But, throughout, high quality is maintained and a consistency of concept is achieved.

Graduating with a BFA from NYSID, Wick trained in the interior design department of Bloomingdale's and was a principal in a NYC design firm for more than ten years. Moving to Scarsdale, she formed her own business in 1981. There are about three large projects active concurrently, ranging from Westport to New York to Florida. Wick is said to really think about the client's use of the rooms, making sure that they are appropriate for the circumstances. For instance, that there is a reading light where you would need one. A one-woman show that escapes to the Hamptons for the summer, references are very satisfied with the progress and professionalism.

Clients commend Quintal Wick for putting the money into the right things. The upholstery may be top end, and then the rest may be filled in with "great looking, inexpensive" wicker. Repro is used most often with good antique accents. Wick's fees are purely hourly, at a Standard rate, no fees are taken on product. This encourages the designer to find the best-priced product to serve the customer's needs. Recommended by architects and neighbors, Wick has an excellent following. ASID.

"Deborah has exquisite flair and is wonderful to work with." "A specific mood is set in each room." "Deborah is very conscious of the budget." "Deborah is practical and caring. She makes the most of what you have and will work in stages according to a master plan." "So smart and clear, Deborah made it easy." "Every dime you pay is worth it."

Deborah T. Lipner Ltd.

	Quality	Cost	Value	Recommend?
	4.5	4	4.5	4.5

310 Round Hill Road, Greenwich, CT 06831
(203) 629 - 2626

Sophisticated, refined, interior design with ease

Transcending a specific nomenclature, Deborah Lipner builds upon a traditional foundation but embellishes with calm comfort and distinct detail. The result is a luxurious cohesiveness, filled with quality and undeniable appeal. She is also applauded for her "softer side of modern." Classic and developed millwork sets the mood with restrained patterns adding a graceful note.

Lipner was a studio art and business major from the University of Toledo. She taught "color and light theory" for many years and has been in her own practice since 1993. There are two "excellent" associates, with Lipner as the primary client contact. Lipner takes on just a few projects at a time, mostly large situations and referrals from past clients.

	Quality	Cost	Value	Recommend?
	✚	$	◆	★

Fees are Reasonable with hourly design time as the project progresses. Lipner is said to be "easy and flexible" in terms of process and economics. Clients and team architects have become advocates, referring many friends.

"The rooms take on a whole new, complex personality at night." "Debbie was really good about using all of our existing furniture." "The rooms are interesting and exciting without being overdone—just what we were looking for." "Color is an incredible strength—there were four variations of crème on the recessed millwork and another three on the ceiling." "I would hire her again tomorrow."

Diamond Baratta Design   4.5   5   4   4.5

270 Lafayette Street, Suite 1501, New York, NY 10012
(212) 966 - 8892   dbd11@diamondbarattadesign.com

Exuberant, colorful, American interior design

Principals William Diamond and Anthony Baratta have conceived a distinct, energetic and playful take on the Americana aesthetic with oversized patterns, vibrant colors and an unconventional twist on the expected. While the indelible signature of the firm is based on this new-wave American vernacular (bright, larger-than-life houndstooth, bold stripes, classic-shaped furniture updated with exuberant color, contrasting millwork, plaid rugs), they have also designed the interiors of stately Westchester homes and refined Upper East Side townhouses with dignity and flair. Clients praise their "extraordinarily innate sense of the appropriate" and their leanings toward the highest quality materials.

Diamond Baratta Design was established 28 years ago. References praise the firm's sources for collectable furnishings, ranging from 18th-century English to 1930s vintage. They are also known for their "unbelievable craftsman" who can match any historically interesting sample to create the perfect pair.

The firm charges High fees, but clients are very satisfied with the total outcome. Achieving great acclaim for their successful and original Lee Jofa fabric line, the firm's projects now range from $1 million to $10 million. Westchester projects account for about one third of their work, where they have received accolades for their architectural contributions and their breadth of scope—just don't ask for beige. HB Top Designers, 1999, 2000, 2001, 2002.

"They restored and dignified our house with fine interior architectural details. Then they added charm with fresh colors and bold chintzes." "They do traditional with merriment, really adding joy to our lives." "The pair was very willing and very able to adapt to my desire for a classic house with understated decoration. They are first-rate designers." "They have an extraordinary eye for architectural concepts, but let someone else draw the blueprints." "It was amazing how they could come up with a solution right then and there. Then they would draw it freehand on the wall for the contractor to implement." "They are not great about babysitting the subs." "They pretty much lost interest at the end of the job." "We could not be happier with the result."

Diana Sawicki Interior Design Inc. 🛍   4   3.5   4.5   5

14 Warnock Drive, Westport, CT 06880
(203) 454 - 5890   dsawigor@aol.com

Conscientious, traditional-based interior design with panache

With care, focus and attention, Diana Sawicki crafts homes that are modern representations of a traditional embrace. Free-flowing luminous silk jabots, transparent embroidered voiles, Louis XVI gilt-edged chairs and mirrored furnishings weave an integrated story of balance and restraint. While each object is declared "a marvel" by clients, the richness of form is counterbalanced by a spareness of line. Patrons, many of whom have used other decorators for years, consider Sawicki to be a "real find."

With a background in couturier clothing in her homeland of Argentina, clients say Sawicki designs curtains "as graceful as ballgowns." The designer studied at Parsons and started in interior design in 1984 in Westport. With an office manager and an assistant, she develops about three large and another six smaller homes concurrently. Sawicki is considered a real professional with a very strong back office.

Reportedly Sawicki "sticks to a budget, but does so creatively." A flat up-front fee is taken, with Reasonable hourlies on architectural consulting and Low product markups. Starting as small as one room with new clients, most will continue on. ASID.

"All the window treatments were incredibly creative, and each one different." "We were tricky—my husband is a traditionalist and has strong opinions, and to this day I still can not predict what he will like. Diana figured it out and made it hip." "When Diana was not happy with the paint samples, she took a paintbrush and hairdryer and worked with the painter to develop the perfect hue." "It is coordinated without being matchy-matchy." "I am a highly organized person, and I was amazed that they kept one step ahead of me." "The project started smaller and snowballed as the older parts of the house paled in comparison to what Diana was doing." "I absolutely love her style. Now if she would only tell me what to wear!"

Diane Peters Interiors   3.5   3.5   4   4.5
14 Pennoyer Street, Rowayton, CT 06853
(203) 866 - 1024
Comfortable, familial, traditional interior design

Respectful of old-world traditions, Diane Peters creates warm, inviting interiors filled with well-worn Aubussons, soft-hued chintzes and layers of pleated and trimmed curtains. Mahogany antique case goods topped with personal treasures usually add to the flow balancing classical and practical millwork. Depending on the client's preferences, this classically traditional framework can be more detailed or toned down. Peters is applauded by clients for her discretion and interest in fulfilling individual dreams.

Passionate and focused in all that she does, Peters grew up in New York City and trained to be a ballerina. The designer always gravitated towards the arts, doing ad styling for Helena Rubinstein and then photo editing for Newsweek, after graduating McGill in European literature and art history. Moving to London, Peters took courses at the V&A, and thus began a lifelong affair with the decorative arts. Settling in Connecticut and decorating her own home, friends implored her to do theirs beginning in 1987.

A one-woman operation, Peters takes joy in working intimately with the client. About five projects are ongoing with a Low hourly fee and Low markups. Projects are often done in a phased evolution, developing long-term relationships with the client. A devoted mother herself, Peters considers family living the highest priority. Meeting a range of budgets, the designer is said to go to The Barn for fabrics as readily as Bennison. But supporters assure us "it will always look elegant."

"I am on my third decorator and Diane is a keeper." "Classy and unobtrusive." "I have seen many of her homes and she never uses the same material twice." "She only has the nicest clients." "For me, Diane did English Country and for my sister, Art Deco." "I feel that Diane actually charges too little for her focus and her time." "Diane's greatest strength is really listening and developing a plan that works for the lifestyle of the client." "She is an artist, not an organizational machine." "Diane does this because she loves it, and that makes it a pleasure."

Dujardin Design Associates   4.5   5   4   4
PO Box 5202, 25 Imperial Avenue, Westport, CT 06881
(203) 227 - 7828 www.dujardin.com
Elegant, comfortable, environmentally conscious interior design

While most clients hire the firm for their evocative, high-quality, classic lines of yesteryear, many are also attracted to the firm's philosophic predilection for "green" and allergy-sensitive materials. Supporters say Dujardin is like a scientist, with an amazing knowledge of materials. Designs will often feature strong, traditional, handsome millwork that juxtaposes comfortable, clean, neutral seating with a touch of country chic.

Dujardin began her firm over twenty years ago, after graduating from Southern Connecticut State University and taking courses at NYU and Parsons. Most the of the firm's work is in Manhattan, Connecticut, and Nantucket, where Dujardin has a home and spends about half her time. Responsive to the clients' interests, Dujardin leads the design decisions and the project managers implement them. The firm also provides a turnkey service including linens, cookware and houseplants.

Clients say that Ms. Dujardin is quite expensive, but well worth it if you are particular. The firm charges a flat design fee and Classic retail, and also offers hourly environmental consulting. She is generally regarded by clients and experts as a leader in her field, having won numerous accolades from the environmental industry. ASID.

"The things she knows would blow your mind." "Everyone in the office is very nice and helpful." "The office support is better now that she has thinned the ranks." "Every piece of hardware and plumbing is an exact reproduction—no detail is too small for Trudy to have custom made." "We did not do the environmental thing with her and found her attention to detail to be excellent." "Trudy can be hard to reach given her multiple locations and multiple commitments." "She is the first decorator that we will use again."

Elouise Spelbrink, ASID   4   4   4   4.5
191 Main Street, New Canaan, CT 06840
(203) 966 - 8498

Tailored, classic, personalized interior design

Known as a "true designer" by her peers, Elouise Spelbrink works in a restrained traditional framework and then introduces flair and fun with a personal touch. Depending upon the interests of the client, this can take the form of American folk art antiques, handsome woodwork or sleeker, retro-tinged accessories. Spelbrink is often brought into projects from gestation, and is said to be quite helpful offering suggestions on the architecture that later enhances furniture placement.

A one-woman design firm, Spelbrink has worked out of the offices of architect, Laurent "Rink" Dupont for the past twenty years. She takes on only two to three major projects at a time to maintain a strong hands-on presence. Most of her clients are strongly family oriented, many with younger children. Spelbrink is happy to do a few rooms to start, offering less expensive alternatives for the children's quarters.

The firm works on a highly Reasonable hourly basis for the upfront design work and then Classic retail on purchases. Budgets tend to evolve as the project progresses. Spelbrink knows and works with many fine workmen in New York and the regional area, but is good about finding a whiter shade of pale. ASID.

"Elouise's taste is so exquisite that it does not look decorated." "We totally trusted her judgment, and she helped a lot with the architectural details." "We were able to buy most of the furniture during construction, and it worked just beautifully." "An easy, lovely person to work with." "Elouise really picks up on what you would like, not what she would like." "We did not have a clue what to allot for a budget, but Elouise never picked anything over our choke point." "Many of our friends have used Elouise once they saw our home."

Eric Cohler Incorporated   4   3.5   4.5   5

872 Madison Avenue, Suite 2B, New York, NY 10021
(212) 737 - 8600   www.ericcohler.com

Updated, traditional, ingenious interior design

Mixing the classically enduring and beautifully erudite with excessive fun is Eric Cohler's modus operandi. Known for realizing his client's visions with a dedicated interest and an edge toward the future, Cohler is said to have his client's view at heart. With a confident countenance, the designer deftly composes the fine and the found, the traditional and the postmodern. Appreciated for his architectural inventiveness as well as his design skills, Cohler effectively works with the client's architect from a project inception, adding significant architectural enhancements.

Clients laud Eric Cohler for his helpful, reliable and diplomatic nature, saying that he quickly understands their intentions. He received a BA in art history and an MS in historic preservation and design from Columbia University. On his own since 1990, he comes recommended by more established designers and the trade as a rising star in the industry. He currently has a staff of six, including two senior designers, but clients feel that Cohler is very accessible. Scarsdale, Purchase, Westport and northwest Connecticut are all familiar territories.

Cohler gravitates to the best quality the budget will allow, but he is perfectly willing to mix this aesthetic with the client's existing furniture and Crate & Barrel items. Known as "Mr. Answerman," his resources are wide and can accommodate many budget levels.

The firm works with a Low up-front design fee and a Reasonable markup over net for products. Alternatively, they can work on an hourly fee basis when shopping for products. Standard oversight fees are charged on a percentage basis. Cohler is noted by clients as being very professional, businesslike and generous. HB Top Designers, 1999, 2000, 2001, 2002. KB 1994, 1999, 2001.

"Eric is so easy, quick and has so much range. He is as good with his left brain as his right—creative and yet so practical." "When my architect and I were perplexed as to how to treat the walls adjoining the three floors in our apartment, Eric envisioned the solution with just one look." "Eric willingly and lovingly helped design our Christmas decorations last year and never asked for a fee. He did the same for my friend's Rosh Hashanah dinner." "His compositions mixing centuries and continents are unifying and uplifting." "He could even make items purchased at Ethan Allen sing on Park Avenue." "I am so glad that Eric is pursing a career in design. It is in his DNA—this is what he was meant to do in life. It is a joy to see." "I would recommend Eric for anything in design and for nonstructural architectural elements." "Eric is my insurance policy because I know everything he suggests will be correct." "There is no question that Eric's decoration was the reason I was able to sell my house so quickly and profitably."

Gleicher Design Group   4   3   4.5   4.5

135 Fifth Avenue, 2nd Floor, New York, NY 10010
(212) 462 - 2789   www.gleicherdesign.com

Comprehensive high-end residential architecture

See Gleicher Design Group's full report under the heading Architects

Greg Jordan Inc.

| 5 | 5 | 4 | 5 |

504 East 74th Street, Suite 4W, New York, NY 10021
(212) 570 - 4470   www.gregjordan.com

Lavish, traditional, heartfelt interior design

Firmly established as one of New York's most esteemed designers, Greg Jordan has won the allegiance of clients with his ability to fulfill their most elaborate design aspirations. Jordan intricately combines historic backgrounds with super luxurious, eclectic ingredients to create texture and movement. This melange creates a relaxed yet stylish environment steeped in historical reference. Clients report that the firm can also develop more traditional interiors and produce sumptuous chintz-laden environments that do not look overdone or fussy. Architecture is now integrated into the mix, creating coherent visions. Connecticut and Westchester historically constitute about a fifth of the mix. Here, family considerations are para-mount with more durable patterns and decorous chintzes taking a role.

Raised in Louisiana, clients describe Jordan as a true "Southern gentleman" with a clear mission. The business was established in 1984 and has cultivated a very impressive roster of clients including Ashley Judd, Blaine Trump, Libbet Johnson and various banking moguls. There are generally ten to twelve substantial projects active at any one time, with a staff of sixteen and Jordan's time now divided between New York and his new LA office. The firm operates like a family, which the clients feel like they join. Recently, the family has gotten somewhat bigger with the senior asso-ciates taking a larger role, especially on the smaller projects. While supporters extol that "a few hours of Greg's time are worth thousands of anyone else's," projects can get mired given Jordan's near-celebrity status.

The designer's own line of furniture is available at Scalamandre, with acces-sories and antiques available in his retail shop. Almost all fabrics, furnishings and trims are custom, according to Jordan's grateful, but well-heeled patrons. Most jobs are between $750,000 and $2 million. Clients roundly acknowledge Jordan for his verve, flourish and commitment to the very best. AD 100, 2000, 2002. HB Top Designers, 1999, 2000, 2001, 2002. KB 1992, 2000.

"Greg absolutely wants to please, and the rest of his office follows up." "Greg is a wonderful listener who not only hears what I am saying but also what I am not say-ing." "He envisions how our family works, making sure all of us are comfortable, and that each room is used." "He has the ability to make any complication or issue disappear, by either fixing it or underplaying it." "He is a master with design details, color and timeless design." "Greg is filled with energy—he hammers nails in a wall or moves furniture himself." "I have worked with many decorators and Greg is a breath of fresh air." "While clearly a creative artist, he is also highly practical with budgets once they are set." "We have complete faith in him." "American Express called to ask why I have not been using my card lately. The real answer is that I just love to be at home after what Greg magically composed."

H. Parkin Saunders Inc.

| 4.5 | 4.5 | 4 | 4.5 |

38 East 57th Street, Fifth Floor, New York, NY 10022
(212) 421 - 5000   www.hparkinsaunders.com

Gracious, edited, luxurious traditional interior design

With a Southern touch harkening back to his Little Rock, Arkansas roots, Parkin Saunders has built his business on relaxed, well-chosen sophisticated designs and discretion. Beginning with the background, including stately architecture, Saunders works in detailed layers to build a home uniquely suited to a client's lifestyle. Concept discussions include a talk with the housekeeper to properly understand what kind of soap will be placed in the soap trays and the client's favorite food for presentation on the night they move in. Generally following a solidly traditional framework, as preferred by his clientele, Saunders enjoys leading his patrons to an edited and luxurious version of traditional. Outstanding English and French antiques are sparingly placed and often clothed in neutral tones, creating a more dramatic and peaceful venue than they may have anticipated.

After attending the University of Arkansas and the NYSID, Saunders apprenticed with a prominent New York designer and then established Saunders and Walsh with the late Christopher Walsh in 1984. The firm's clients are renown, with projects encompassing the decoration of David Koch's oceanfront Hamptons estate, "Aspen East" (in less than six months including monogrammed note pads and monogrammed hangers in each room). Other notables include the Southampton homes of Anne Ford and Teddy Forstmann, the Grosse Pointe Farms lakeside compound of Edsel Ford, II and Nelson Doubleday. Locally, they have completed projects in Greenwich, Bedford and Stamford.

Currently, there are three on staff including an interior architect. Three to four major projects are undertaken at time. The practice will take on a few rooms, if the budget is "realistic." Generally, living rooms are well over $100,000 with one over $4,000,000 including fine art and the best Georgian furniture. There is no upfront fee, but an hourly design retainer and Classic retail on products.

"Parkin was wonderful about opening my eyes to a more refined, less cluttered approach." "We really had fun all the way through the project." "Parkin cares very much about the client's viewpoint and their preferences." "He takes the time to also make sure you have great sheets, beautiful flatware and all the other comforts of gracious living." "Parkin shops nationally and internationally for the most unique items." "I have done two homes with Parkin: one traditional and one contemporary. Both are extremely livable and stylish." "Mr. Saunders and his staff are thoughtful, talented and unfailingly courteous." "While it may take longer than you like and be quite expensive, every detail is perfect and never has to be changed."

Hampton Court Interiors   3   3.5   4   4.5
390 Main Street, Ridgefield, CT 06877
(203) 438 - 6300   lmaine@aol.com

With a realistic perspective and rational expectations, Hampton Court serves its market very well with designs that gently lift the client's style and perspective. Buffalo checks, monochromatic toiles, scalloped pique, repro marquetry and streamlined white cabinetry fill the homes of its customers, who have the highest regard for lead designer Linda Maine. Maine is said to be excellent about working collaboratively with her clients or, at their suggestion, "taking the ball and running with it."

In interior design in Connecticut since 1970, Maine keeps busy with her old clients, assigns new clients to her staff of four, and oversees most jobs. There is a retail showroom of 3,000 square feet that was opened in 1997 and houses countless fabrics, samples and accessories. Projects tend to evolve one piece at a time. No up-front design fees are charged but Historic retail is placed on product. ASID.

"I have known Linda for 25 years, and think she is the best designer around." "She will find things from your house and redevelop them to make it come alive." "Linda totally has a sense of what is appropriate. The very first fabric of the twenty she will show me is invariably the one we use." "She is so much fun. There is lots of give and take. She will challenge you in a very good way." "She will usually call you back the same day." "She pleases me and I am very hard to please." "I absolutely trust her and recommend her to my friends."

	Quality	Cost	Value	Recommend?
	✚	$	◆	★

Hilary Heminway

	4.5	4.5	4	4.5

140 Briarpatch Road, Stonington, CT 06378
(860) 535 - 3110   hahbriarpatch@att.net

Streamlined, indigenous, upscale country interior design

Known for her sophisticated distillations of highbrow rustic, Hilary Heminway is often invited to Montana to supervise the interiors of substantial ranch retreats. Sometimes, riding horseback is the only way to the job site. But based out of Stonington, Heminway has also been called up to serve the local market with projects such as restrained versions of formal English country in Greenwich, casual American country in Old Lyme and country-club chic in Watch Hill. Very little is period pure but noted as "high quality melange with a sense of pastoral humor." After studying art at Boston University, Heminway worked in design for family and friends. In 1985 she established her practice and now undertakes about eight substantial projects at a time with her New York City-based niece Tobin Heminway. The firm does hourly consulting at Standard rates, bills monthly for project management and charges roughly Classic retail on product. Budgets tend to evolve with many supporters offering carte blanche.

"Hilary never over-decorates." "She was our first call when we bought the place in Wyoming." "On her first trip out West to visit us, she brought hundreds of swatches in a suitcase. There were only three that I did not like." "When the outdoor furniture seemed way too expensive, Hilary volunteered to search the earth for a better solution. We ended up with the first option, but really appreciated the legwork." "Twig furniture and Stickley is clearly favored over Louis XVI, but she can mix it up expertly." "She is very strong-minded, but you can work with her." "Hilary is always organized and pleasant."

Horton Design Associates Ltd.

	4.5	4	4.5	5

14 Sherwood Farm Lane, Greenwich, CT 06831
(203) 869 - 0707   Hortondes@aol.com

Delightful, characteristic, traditional interior design

Roundly acknowledged as one of the finest designers in the region, Mimi Horton delights clients with rooms of personality, balance and polish. Though the palette, fabrics, moldings and accessories speak a traditional language, references say she takes it one step further, reaching unexpected sophistication with more than a dash of whimsy. Neutral backgrounds allow the artwork to shine and the depth of character to hearten. Simultaneously more creative and more distilled than the classic "Greenwich look," Horton's clients say it is a compilation of Nantucket preppy meets California urbane.

After college, Horton worked at Vogue and then received a certificate from NYSID. She has been in interior design since 1970, currently working with an established clientele. Horton does work on her own and in cooperation with fellow Greenwich designer Linda Douglas. Projects may start with just a few rooms and tend to evolve. Greenwich, Seal Harbor, Jupiter Island, Sun Valley and East Hampton are all familiar territories, with clients often asking her to do their second home.

With a very low overhead of one, rates are quite Reasonable, with pride taken in the discovery of a fabulous find. Strong, long-term relationships with vendors assure excellent craftsmanship.

"Mimi is so engaged, knowledgeable, clear and smart." "A serious professional with seriously good taste." "She absolutely maintained the character of the house but upgraded it for our lifestyle." "While the fees are reasonable, the overall project cost was substantial given the quality of the goods." "She respected my art by keeping the furniture quiet." "Mimi saved us tons of time and directed the flow." "It was a complete pleasure."

Ingrao Inc.

5   5   4   4.5

17 East 64th Street, New York, NY 10021
(212) 472 - 5400   ingrao@ingrao.com

Luminous, extraordinary, near-epic interior design

Tony Ingrao's projects range from baronial splendor to tempered grandeur. Considered among the most indefatigable of designers, Ingrao's first project over twenty years ago was a spectacular seven-year transformation of a 1920s Norman chateau in Greenwich into an extravagant Louis XIV fantasia "that rivals Versailles. Even Ingrao's "comfortable family homes" are filled with important 16th- century consoles, paired George II mahogany chairs, and floor refinishers that were imported from France for the ultimate layered glow. Unabashed in his manner and design essence, Ingrao is not for the faint of heart.

Projects reportedly average more than $5 million each. Past clients have included numerous money managers, Goldie Hawn and the Broadway producer Marty Richards.

In October 2002, Ingrao and partner Randy Kemper opened a dramatic three-story antiques gallery with gleaming white marble floors and sinuous walls primarily showcasing extraordinary 18th- to 20th-century Continental furniture and cutting-edge contemporary art at 17 East 64th Street in Manhattan. After attending RISD, Ingrao opened his firm, which now includes seven designers, five architectural specialists (non-licensed) and several in administration. About six major projects are taken on at a time.

Over the years, a number of projects have been done for clients in Greenwich, Bedford, Rye, Armonk and Scarsdale, many of whom have done second homes with Ingrao. Most projects are entire home renovations. The firm charges Standard architecture fees, project management fees, millwork and painting fees and Classic retail on product (except antiques, which are purchased on a scaled fee schedule). Clients looking to experience the design dream of a lifetime are drawn to Ingrao.

"Tony delivers flawless, singular creations that are clearly over the top, but never gauche." "Only for families that live comfortably with museum quality art and antiques." "Tony makes your design fantasies into a reality—it may take a while, but it will be amazing." "The journey is just as much fun as the end result."

Insolia Designs

4   3   4.5   4.5

590 Guard Hill Road, Bedford, NY 10506
(914) 234 - 3034   sinsolia@yahoo.com

Fresh, streamlined, traditional interior design

Stephanie Insolia wins accolades from clients for her understated take on modern-hued traditional, her attention to the lifestyle of the client and her fastidious professionalism. With a light touch and an integrated view, it is said that Insolia develops plans that work and are consistent throughout, offering a harmonious flow. Working collaboratively with the client, Insolia enjoys making each project an amalgamation of period, textures and pastiche.

After studying and working in the field of neuroscience for eight years, Insolia took a course in design as a creative outlet. Soon Insolia quit her day job, enrolled at Parsons and is now professionally pursuing her passion for design and the decorative arts. In 2000, Insolia Designs was formed as a sole proprietorship, doing a limited number of homes each year in the Westchester area. Clients tend to be young with families, looking for an easy, comfortable environment.

Just spreading her wings, Insolia charges no design fee, a Low markup on product and Reasonable hourly non-commission rates. A wide variety of product choices are considered with a proclivity toward excellent antiques but an eye to meet budget. Clients feel very lucky to have found Insolia before her "inevitable rise."

"Stephanie has amazing capabilities, both with the left and right side of her brain." "She is a great team player, always making people feel good." "Stephanie follows up without asking—better than anyone I have ever met." "She is able to focus on the big picture and the smallest detail simultaneously." "I have already recommended her to my friends."

Jacqueline D. Cutler Inc.   4   3.5   4.5   4

5 Burgess Road, Scarsdale, NY 10583
(914) 723 - 2820 jackiecutler28@aol.com

Cohesive, expressive, updated, old-world interior design

Offering a rich melange of the elegantly traditional and the unexpected, Jackie Cutler understands her community. Raised in Scarsdale with a loyal following there, New York City and beyond, Cutler deftly composes rooms that are both luxuriously formal and lively comfortable. Leopard-print velvet on Louis XVI chairs and a red toile kitchen are beguiling amongst the more neutral counterpoints in form. And she gets it all done on time according to delighted references.

Cutler graduated from Syracuse with a dual major in architecture and design. Working at a commercial architecture firm for several years, friends and peers began to ask for help on their residences and a career was born. Formerly opening shop in 1988, Cutler works with two staff members on about ten projects at a time, which can start as small as one room. Cutler starts with the architecture and takes it from there.

With a practical sense of the budget and family life, the expensive fabrics are always recommended for the chairs and pillows, not the larger furnishings. But the best upholsters are used for the important pieces. Standard hourlies are charged for architectural consultations and a Low markup on product.

"Jackie did it all. I didn't need an architect." "These were the only people I have ever worked with who actually finished exactly when they said they would." "Jackie always wants the client to be happy." "I never felt intimidated." "Jackie knows how to get something done. When the painters said it was impossible to do the layered lacquer walls due to the humidity of the summer, Jackie found fabulous paint from Holland that was developed to dry below sea level." "Jackie opened my mind to the possibility of color." "She is so organized—everything is in a Ziploc bag." "Jackie is so realistic—she will find another equally good fabric if that one is not in stock." "As an active mother herself, Jackie understands life with kids."

Jean Callan King Interior Design LLC   4.5   4.5   4   4

39 Hopyard Road, East Haddam, CT 06423
(860) 434 - 8816 www.jckinteriordesign.com

Inviting, functional, comprehensive interior design

Serious about her business and highly engaged in the process, Jean Callan King has built a strong following in Connecticut. King often seems to take the role of project manager, which speaks to her organizational skills, technical capabilities and professionalism. Sensitive to her clients' proclivities, King ranges from traditional period pure with depth to contemporary distillations with historic reference. All are said to be thoughtful, comfortable and well conceived.

King is the master of many realms. With a BFA in graphic design from RISD, King has done graphic design and illustration and authored/illustrated several books. She is also an expert in 19th-century ceramics and lectured at the Cooper Hewitt and at other institutions on this subject. In 1988, she opened her interior design firm, which is a full-service firm also offering construction management, lighting plans, plumbing spec and art selection. Many clients are New York-based executives with country homes in Connecticut, who appreciate King's full range.

Whether taking on just one chair or new construction, King is commended for giving a comprehensive budgetary view and determining the level of quality appropriate for the situation. A Reasonable hourly supervision and shopping fee is charged and Classic retail on product. ASID, NCIDQ.

"We are incredibly impressed with Jean. She is one of the few artists we know who can also run a business." "Jean not only did the design but also helped us solve a dilemma with the builder and the stonemason." "Her work ethic is terrific. She is up and available at 7:00 AM each day and lets us know on a daily basis where she is." "She is good about presenting items that are within your cost range once you make that clear, but I suspect not everyone can afford her." "We never felt pushed off to the staff. But when she was away, the staff could keep us on track."

Jeff Lincoln Interiors Inc.   4.5   3.5   5   4.5

675 Madison Avenue, New York, NY 10021
(212) 588 - 9500   lincoln8@ix.netcom.com
Classical, comfortable interior design

With an innate ability to synthesize the best of the classical past that with the allure of edited chic, Jeff Lincoln has built a loyal clientele. He is a favorite of many Darien and Park Avenue families who would not consider a minimalist look. Warm and resonant colors, refined fringes, old-world craftsmanship and creative details are revisited with a modern eye, creating a sophisticated presence. References also praise Lincoln for his knowledge of fine antiques, European and Scandinavian historical details, and unusual custom sources. With restraint and practicality, the serious is set against the comfortable, the economic against the outstanding.

Clients include many young sophisticates, who relate to Lincoln's easy manner, genteel sensibility and businesslike approach. Supporters also appreciate his artistic vision, saying that each project is unique to the setting and taste of the homeowner. While some express concern that he starts slowly, he always wins the clients' hearts with an outstanding end result.

The firm charges a Standard upfront design fee and Classic retail on product. Lincoln is capable of going as high as a client would like in the quality spectrum but is equally open to less costly alternatives. Living rooms are generally in the $200,000 realm. He is highly recommended by many of the most discerning shoppers in New York for timeless comfort. HB Top Designers, 1999, 2000, 2001. KB 1995, 1998, 2001.

"More recently, there is this cleaner, more contemporary thread that is weaving its way through Jeff's work. Holly Hunt visits Darien but is sidetracked by silk taffeta." "His rooms are full of happy luxury without being over the top. And he can add a bit of whimsy, which we really appreciate." "The rooms are never pretentious, but beautiful." "An emerging talent who is just coming of age. While prone to a few bumps, the outcome was fabulous." "Five of my friends in town have used Jeff. All the homes look different, and all are fabulous." "Its all about lighting and patina." "If you do not like it, he will take it right back in his truck." "I have only positive things to say about Jeff. He has great taste and is a great guy." "His balance of the comfortable and the formal exactly matches our lifestyle." "He really listens and responds appropriately."

Jones Footer Margeotes & Partners   5   5   4   5
245 Mill Street, Greenwich, CT 06830
(203) 531 - 1588   www.jfmp.com

Classic, bold, clean high-end interior design

See Jones Footer Margeotes & Partners's full report under the heading Architects

Julia Durney Interiors Ltd.   4   3   4.5   4.5
79 Putnam Park Road, Bethel, CT 06801
(203) 798 - 7110   juliadurney@snet.net

Engaging, timeless, traditional interior design

Hailed for her generosity of spirit and a breezy elegance, Julia Durney has delighted a cadre of loyal clients in the area. Many applaud her easygoing manner, great listening skills and attention to detail. All say that Durney takes pleasure in developing their design visions into refined outcomes. They also applaud Durney's understanding and accommodation to family living and realistic budgets. While most of her rooms are filled with warm colors, classic lines and multigenerational ingredients, they are also said to be "bombproof," and impervious to the whims of children.

Durney began her career as a bond trader, attended Parsons and then started her design business in 1990. About two thirds of her time is spent in Fairfield, where she recently relocated and the balance in New York City's Upper East Side. The Nightingale-Bamford School recently commissioned Durney to redesign their boardroom. While Durney is essentially the firm, clients note that she is very accessible and a "real professional due to that banker training."

The firm charges no design fee and Low markups on product. Hourly consultations are also reasonably priced and fully reimbursable against product fees if Durney is subsequently hired on retainer. Many of her clients are repeat customers, including one family who has completed six projects with Durney, each in a different genre.

"Julia's ideas are well-formed, bright and imaginative." "She was so good about doing our apartment on a project-by-project basis, over time, as the budget allowed." "Julia's patience was a godsend. She dealt with everything from the countertops to the lighting to the bedding. And not one item was wrong." "She will work around your grandmother's sofa and make it work beautifully." "Her ideas are unique and gorgeous, and she also minds the budget through creative thinking." "A true pleasure, she makes it easy."

Karen Houghton Interiors   3.5   3.5   4   4.5
41 North Broadway, Nyack, NY 10960
(845) 358 - 0133

Updated, traditional, characteristic interior design

Starting with a traditional English framework, Karen Houghton works diligently and collaboratively to develop a portrait of the client. Welcoming, unpretentious, grounded environments are abundant with fine mementos and treasured finds that speak to a life well lived. For Martin Scorsese that means vintage movie posters adorn almost every wall, and for others, memories of worldwide expeditions and family photos warm the space. Houghton takes pleasure in finding the clients' "design personality" and in diplomatically working with the team to get the job done.

The child of two antiques dealers in Nyack, Houghton has a passion for antiques and the process of building collections. After receiving a BFA in fine arts from Bennington and developing a restaurant in Seattle for several years, Houghton naturally settled into the design businesses in Nyack in 1986. Here she is lauded for her long-time contacts with local craftsmen and her reasonable approach. Notably, the firm runs its own 2,000-square-foot proprietary workroom, offering strong quality, excellent pricing and infinite flexibility and service to the client. A design fee is taken up front and product is purchased with Reasonable markups.

References report that Houghton does her homework, taking clients to a range of showrooms to gauge style and quality interests. From there, a budget is set forth and every purchase is compared to the original plan to keep the project on track. If the client falls in love with an object that is higher than the estimate, alternatives are suggested for the remaining pieces. Architects and clients are roundly impressed with Houghton's project management skills.

"Karen worked with us from the ground up. She had lots of influence over the architectural structure as well as the interiors." "She listens so well and was a great team player." "Karen was our advocate when we wanted to move in earlier than we really should have." "Karen had fabulous local sources. The sofa cost about half the price of our NY decorator, and her guys will come immediately to fix anything." "She stays ahead of the process. There were no surprises." "Karen dug up some really interesting pieces in London that we could not find anywhere." "The rooms are completely livable and comfortable. She is not your typical decorator, but adds layers of warmth."

Katherine Cowdin Inc.   4   4   4   4.5

33 East Elm Street, Greenwich, CT 06830
(203) 661 - 4844

Classic, well-bred, unpretentious interior design

Applauded for their designs of "inherited ease," Katherine Cowdin had been decorating in the mode of "Greenwich chic" for years before the term was defined. Established in 1928 by her great-aunt Katherine Cowdin, Dotsie Doran has led the firm for the past 27 years. Consistent in purpose and intent, Doran delivers a "pedigreed look" that will be comfortable for children and dogs. Known for their highly traditional focus, even the contemporary homes are filled with antiques or good facsimiles thereof.

Drawn to interior design from the start, Doran graduated from Bennett College majoring in interiors and worked for a New York interior designer, Paul Krauss, for five years before joining her mom and aunt at the firm. The practice now has six senior designers each with their own client base and six in support staff, making it one of the largest firms in the regional area. Impressively, Doran's clients say she will hop over "in a jiffy for a towel consultation," confirming her excellent client service and strong relationship management skills. Randi Filoon, a senior designer with the firm for over fifteen years, also wins accolades from clients for a more tailored and updated approach with the same old-world service.

The firm will start with a Standard retainer and just one room. On product, the company charges a Classic markup and on nonproduct hours, a Standard rate. Many clients continue on with the firm, for the life of their house, continually updating one sofa at a time.

"Unquestionably the timeless standard. I never want my house to be in fashion and never want it to be out of fashion—and it never will be." "Dotsie is fabulous about using all the pieces we have collected over the years, recovering them and creating a coherent look." "These are the decorators to choose to guarantee that you will not embarrass yourself with the country club board." "With children herself that have been through the 'Greenwich system,' Dotsie just gets it." "Riskless design." "I have used Dotsie for over 25 years, and she is the only decorator I would ever trust to understand my lifestyle."

Kathy Abbott Interiors   4   4   4   4.5

398 Cross River Road, Katonah, NY 10536
(914) 232 - 1934

Fresh, elegant, livable, traditional-based interior design

Dexterously blending inherited and found antiques, fine streamlined forms and handsome counterpoints of provenance, Kathy Abbott impresses clients with her creative thinking and professionalism. Juxtapositions are a trademark, adding flair, freshness and interest to the predictable. Fortuny in sherbet hues can cover traditional profiles and contemporary art renderings may be placed in an otherwise traditional setting. All is done with a light hand and a livable view.

With a BA in studio art and art history from Claremont College in California, Abbott has always focused on the aesthetic. When friends asked for interiors advice fifteen years ago, one thing led to another and a business was formed. Pursuing the trade with a clear focus, Abbott is a sole proprietor appreciated for her client attention and ability to "speak the language of the painters." References also credit Abbott for guiding a unique group of "incredible sources, especially craftsmen." While many clients do not have a specific budget and Abbott is known for preferring excellent quality, she is said to mix it up—allocating enough for a fabulous sofa frame and saving somewhere else. A minimal contract fee is charged and Classic retail on product.

"It was amazing. Kathy got much of the house done while I was in Japan for a few years. She is so organized and would send me packages of samples." "She did it all, including monogrammed towels and sheets." "Kathy is an absolute perfectionist. She sent the sofa pillows back three times to the workroom to get the quality of the down just right." "If a lampshade is not quite correct, it will really bother her until it is replaced." "She is available seven days a week, always right back to you." "It is a pleasure working with Kathy."

Kenneth Alpert Associates   4   4   4   4

30 East 76th Street, New York, NY 10021
(212) 535 - 0922   www.kennethalpert.com

Abundant, detailed, traditional interior design

With outstanding client service as his fundamental axiom, Kenneth Alpert takes a sincere, focused and personalized approach to each project. While best known for his traditional-to-the-max style, bedecked with chintzes, toile and elegant trims, Alpert is also fluent in Art Deco, minimalist and formal French. Regardless of the style, the firm delivers comfortable, full-sized, family-oriented designs and brings attention to detail to a new level. About a quarter of the projects are in the Westchester area, particularly Scarsdale, Purchase, Mamaroneck and Rye, with one neighbor recommending him to the next.

Alpert holds a BS from Wharton and an MBA from NYU. While attending classes at the NYSID, he founded the firm almost 30 years ago. Currently with fourteen members on the team, about forty projects are undertaken annually, ten of which are of substantial size and scope. While there are four senior designers, all significant design decisions are made with Alpert. Clients say they do not doubt Alpert more than once "because his ideas are always better."

References appreciate Alpert's formal presentations, and also comment on his excellent budget layouts and refined professionalism. Clients express equal confidence in the back office. The firm charges a Standard design fee and Classic retail on product, with a typical living room baselining at about $150,000. Clients say Alpert "is not a budget designer" but is practical. Also if there is ever an issue, they are known to fix it "faster than you can blink." KB 2003.

"Ken is the most organized person I have ever met." "He interprets what I like and makes sure it is in good taste." "He understands family living, making sure that the floors in the rec room near the pool were not slippery." "He gets the job done bing, bang, boom." "He's a real straight-shooter." "They were very receptive to using the furniture that I already owned." "He is in his office from 7 AM to 7 PM every day." "The project managers did a really efficient job day-to-day." "If we did not get it the first time, he is really patient, going at it until we find something we both like." "I know we were not a huge client for Ken, but he always treated us as if we had twenty two rooms." "I turn to Ken for so many design situations well beyond the decoration of my home—from what to wear to vacation choices to dinner party options." "It was definitely a collaboration." "Excels in every aspect."

LCR

| | 4 | 4 | 4 | 4.5 |

981B Farmington Avenue, West Hartford, CT 06107
(860) 231 - 7712   www.lcrcollection.com

Transitional traditional to comfortable modern interior design

Ranging along the continuum from highly traditional to starkly modern, clients appreciate Peter Robbin of LCR for his ability to sensitively transform their space. A quick study, Robbin develops designs that "look fabulous and always work," such as a particularly soft and comfortable upholstered headboard for a client who loves to read in bed. Similarly, during any construction, Robbin is said to make constructive lifestyle suggestions that the architect never considered. Supporters totally trust his judgment and consult him well after the project is complete.

After majoring in fine arts at Boston University and interior architecture at RISD, Robbin did hospitality design for several years and then worked with three notable New York interior designers—Angelo Donghia, McMillen and Noel Jeffrey. In 1987, Robbin moved to Hartford and partnered with the established John LaFalce, creating LCR. Robbin is currently the sole owner and works with four associates who, clients report, are highly professional. There are also two retail stores specializing in tabletop, one in West Hartford and one in Westport, run by Robbin's sister, Dana Robbin.

Beginning with a small minimum and just one room, Robbin works at Classic retail. References note that Robbin intuitively understands their "reasonablility standard" making economic decisions easy, generally with fine repro quality. Clients seem to stick with Robbin for many years, freshening up with him along the way and recommending him to friends.

"Peter made it all so easy. He would bring a few choices and I would always love at least two." "We went through the process slowly. I never felt rushed." "Peter's facility with high-tech gadgets is excellent. We were just published on the cover of an A/V magazine." "Peter totally adopts to the clients concept." "He is the first one to say that an item is not exactly right and replace it." "After doing my traditional home, he then did my father's quite contemporary apartment with style." "The office makes it so easy, supervising the flooring crew so we did not have to deal." "Peter is broad-brush and Jill makes it happen." "The best part is that the house immediately looked like we had lived here for years." "His work just gets better with age."

Leta Austin Foster

	Quality	Cost	Value	Recommend?
Leta Austin Foster	4	3.5	4	4.5

424 East 52nd Street, New York, NY 10022
(212) 421 - 5918

Historically minded, traditional interior design with panache

Sallie Giordano heads up the New York office of this Palm Beach firm began by her mom more than a quarter of a century ago. Guided by their young something, soiree-set, 90 percent of the work is traditional with a kick. Greenwich meets Lilly Pulitzer by way of a chance meeting with Ray and Charles Eames. Supporters speak to Giordano's creativity, sighting a range of styles that can be expertly executed, including 1930s Art Deco and more modern. Still, most rooms are anchored by traditional American casegoods and custom linen textiles. Supporters also mention that the firm is very well organized, fun to work with and committed to building on the client's thematic cues.

Giordano graduated from Georgetown with a degree in American studies and was a journalist for several years before joining the family practice about ten years ago. The practice has recently completed several first apartments for young New Yorkers, a range of Greenwich and Long Island homes and several vacation homes across the country. A few rooms are often the starting point.

Working with no design fee, a Classic retail is charged on products with Standard oversight fees. Clients mention that Giordano will offer a variety of quality product choices, allowing the client broad economic and stylistic latitude. It has been mentioned, however, that she can be quite adamant that her clients make sound design choices, and that she would rather go back to the proverbial drawing board than settle for anything less.

"They have traditional down pat, with sparkle." "They are practical, helpful decorators who just get it." "In the country, they know where to stop. It is not all glammed up with silks and trims." "Sallie is phenomenal. She will bring twenty to thirty fabric samples and will have an elaborate discussion about them. But if we do not agree, 30 more will be here the following week." "Helped to guide me in the right direction despite my initial reluctance. Now, I'm so glad she was persistent." "Sally is perfect for the client with strong ideas and wants a very active relationship with their designer." "We spent more than I thought we would and I am so glad that we did." "Growing up in an exquisite interior design family really makes a difference. Sallie will custom color the Bennison in a imperceptibly different shade, which makes all the difference." "They are incredibly well organized and implement quickly."

Libby Cameron, LLC

	Quality	Cost	Value	Recommend?
Libby Cameron, LLC	4	4	4	4

24 Ervilla Drive, Larchmont, NY 10538
(914) 833 - 1414   cameronllc@aol.com

Lively, friendly, preppy American interior design

Supporters depend on Libby Cameron for colorful, comfortable, breezy elegance reminiscent of the days of summer family retreats. While Cameron is better known for easy, natural fabrics geared toward the children and the dogs, clients also recount her abilities with more formal English traditions. Cameron has a loyal group of clients up and down the East Coast, many of whom consider her to be a "secret source." About 30 percent of her clientele is in Connecticut and Westchester, where she usually revitalizes entire homes.

Cameron went out on her own about eight years ago after working closely with her mentor, Sister Parish, for fifteen years at Parish-Hadley. Because she has a broad base of operations and an interest in attending each client meeting, patrons say she has certain time limitations but works hard to please. Clients range widely in age, some of which date to Cameron's years at Parish-Hadley, but are consistent in their high-quality focus. More recently, Cameron has partnered with Sister Parish's granddaughter to develop a line of colorful and playful fabrics based on Mrs. Parish's favorite designs (sold through Hinson or at www.sisterparishdesign.com).

The firm charges a relatively small design fee and Classic retail for products. While project cost and budgets are considered, this is not the focus of the work (but clients say they were informed and felt comfortable with charges). Sources range from the top-quality Alessandro mantels to Pottery Barn to whimsical secret sources in the South. Reportedly the D&D building is hardly ever visited. Living rooms can be as low as $30,000, going to about $100,000, not including major antique rugs. Supporters have often completed numerous projects with Cameron and look forward to doing more. HB Top Designers, 1999, 2000, 2001.

"Libby understood that we wanted a comfortable home, not a showpiece." "While she will not sit around and watch the painter, she goes out of her way to give me peace of mind." "She is very easy to deal with. No pretentious ego." "Her schemes tend to lack a detailed master plan or meticulous measurements but turn out beautifully." "She is the only decorator in New York who understands that pedigreed threadbare or chintz-on-chintz look." "Waspy with flair." "People come into the house and purr with delight. I still pinch myself when I wake up—I can't believe how gorgeous it all is."

Lichten Craig Architects, LLP   4   3   5   5
6 West 18th Street, 9th Floor, New York, NY 10011
(212) 229 - 0200 www.lichtencraig.com
High-end residential architecture and interior design

See Lichten Craig Architects, LLP's full report under the heading Architects

Linda Douglass 🛍   4.5   4   4.5   5
85 Pecksland Road, Greenwich, CT 06831
(203) 661 - 0355
Pedigreed, refined, traditional interior design

With impeccable taste, flexibility and integrity of design, Linda Douglass has been inspiring homeowners for over 25 years. Taking on only a select few clients a year, Douglass begins with historic, traditional nomenclature and introduces verve. Unlined, flowing silk curtains, custom hooked rugs and noble antiques are interwoven with pieces from another time or place, heightening the composition.

Douglass is also lauded for her inherent understanding of contextual appropriateness be it a center hall Colonial on Round Hill Road or a family compound on Mt. Dessert. Working alone or in conjunction with Greenwich designer Mimi Horton, the entire house is usually renovated. With the principals doing all the shopping and design personally, patrons extol the process. Detail is another forte; trims and dressmaker folds are always well mastered. While the quality of the product can "shoot the moon," the firm's fees are Reasonable. Douglass takes on a select few number of clients at a time.

"Linda travels in rarified circles, completely knowledgeable of the genteel look." "On everyone's top-five list." "Linda not only knows exactly what she is doing but is very easy to work with." "The look is traditional, only better." "It is very helpful that Linda and Mimi can cover for one another." "I always recommend Linda to friends."

	Quality	Cost	Value	Recommend?
	✚	$	◆	★

Lisa Pak Design 🛍

	4	3.5	4.5	4.5

4 Saddle Ridge Road, Pound Ridge, NY 10576
(914) 764 - 4788   lisa@lisapakdesign.com

Serene, cohesive, enticing interior design

Lisa Pak is creating a following with her reflective classical modernism, educated perspective and balance of form. Using a more neutral palette, clean lines, a depth of textured wovens and a consistency of plan, spaces are both soothing and beguiling. A traditional oak farm table may stand contentedly beside chrome fixtures, an ebonized sideboard, and gauzed linen curtains. Clients are delighted with the mix, which they proclaim is fresh, young and uplifting.

After twelve years as a graphic artist for New York City advertising firms, Pak decided to direct her creative talents to the home. While working toward a degree at Parsons, Pak secured prestigious internships with some of the best names in interior design, including Laura Bohn, Victoria Hagan and Bruce Bierman. Soon thereafter, Pak went out on her own, first with lofts in TriBeCa and apartments on the Upper West Side. Retaining her stylish viewpoint and younger clientele, Pak now does about half of her projects in the Westchester area.

A one-woman operation, Pak keeps the clients happy and is able to keep the fee structure quite modest. Standard design fees are taken upfront, with Low product commissions and no hourly fees. References are impressed with her organization and resourcefulness, with shopping haunts in SoHo, upstate and on the Internet.

"She makes it work." "While I know she would rather do fine antiques, Lisa is very accommodating and creative with custom and repro." "Everyone asks who helped me, and I am always pleased to refer Lisa." "Her inherent sense of proportion and restraint leads to a sophistication well beyond my capability." "Not only are the designs fabulous but Lisa is so professional and good natured. She makes it a pleasure."

Lulu DK

	4.5	4	4	5

136 East 64th Street, Suite 2E, New York, NY 10021
(212) 223 - 4234   www.luludk.com

Decorative painting, hand-painted fabric and interior design

See Lulu DK's full report under the heading Painters & Wallpaperers

Lynn Morgan Design

	4	4	4	4.5

118 Goodwives River, Darien, CT 06820
(203) 655 - 0573

Refined, unpretentious, uplifting country interior design

With a stroke of grace and an allure of form, Lynn Morgan's rooms, be they clothed in cotton stripe, linen check or unlined silk, are unassuming yet sophisticated. Described as home sanctuaries by their owners, the spaces sparkle in the voluminous light and also speak to their purpose. Kitchens are opened with enamel white, stainless and workable marble counters and living rooms are warmed with simple lines and welcoming textures to encourage family play. Morgan is also hailed for her practical nature and client focus.

Morgan has been in and around decorating for 25 years. A decorating editor at *House Beautiful* for many years, Morgan moved to Connecticut and started her own business in 1985. Along with a business/project manager, Morgan has about five major projects and a good number of smaller ones going at a time, mostly close by. Budgets can range from tiny to larger, but are all thoughtfully composed.

A smaller up-front fee is taken along with Classic retail, but a wide variety of product choices are considered. With very few tassels and trims, and less yardage on the tailored curtains, the costs are further mitigated.

"Everything is clean and crisp and pretty." "Roman shades replaced the more elaborate flounces, making the room more inviting and livable." "Lynn is very available, although she has gotten quite busy." "She encouraged us to have fun with the process. I really appreciated her calm and intelligent approach." "Many of Lynn's design's have a Swedish country feel, that is easy and comfortable." "No trims, no tassels." "Now, I am incapable of hanging a picture without her."

Margot Pyne Marston Inc.   3.5   3.5   4   4

PO Box 856, Southport, CT 06430
(203) 255 - 5587   margotmarston@aol.com
Traditional, timeless, reliable interior design

Known for creating classically English decors, using saturated colors and appropriate antiques, Margot Marston has built a local following. Supporters comment that she is clear, knowledgeable and receptive. Projects may occur in several smaller phases, often starting with a few rooms. Most clients come to the party with family heirlooms and personal treasures, which are coherently incorporated into the new arrangement.

Marston was raised in Southport and has been in the design profession for 30 years. After earning a degree from NYSID, Marston was in sales at Dunbar Furniture and then McGuire Furniture, enabling her to understand the bottom line. After working with esteemed New York designer Pamela Banker for a few years, she established her own firm in 1978. A sole proprietor, about a dozen projects are undertaken concurrently, usually about two of them larger. Her experience allows for efficient design work, with clients stating that she can always find a good choice—usually on the first try. There is now a second office in Stonington at (860) 535 - 0814, where Marston tends to spend a few days a week.

No design fee is charged, with a Reasonable markup on product and Standard hourlies for nonproduct consultations. Customers say that she encourages the purchase of the best antiques that the budget will allow but is a constructive realist.

"We have become friends through the decorating process." "Margot guided my taste." "She can now identify better what I will like than I can myself." "She has a gift of understanding color before it goes on the wall or the furniture." "Margot talked me into a much stronger color in the living room than I would have chosen and it is great." "She will bring out the furniture from New York two or three times until we get it just right." "Available all the time." "Everyone in the area knows Margot. She also breeds the most adorable labs." "I recommend her all the time."

Mark Hampton Inc.   4.5   4.5   4   4.5

654 Madison Avenue, 21st Floor, New York, NY 10021
(212) 753 - 4110   info@markhamptoninc.com
Sumptuous, classically inspired, detailed interior design

Clients are consistently impressed with Alexa Hampton's innate design sensitivity, commitment to quality and range of scope. There is always a classical underpinning with a wealth of historical reference. In the country, there is a nod to contextual suitability, but "it is very much a catered affair" with the same ultimate resources being trucked in. Hampton is also credited for her attention to detail, professional demeanor and charming personality. Hampton assumed the reins of Mark Hampton Inc. after the death of her father in 1998. Hampton has ably gained the confidence of past clients and has built a base of her own, reflecting her spirited approach with a pastiche of the finest Chippendale antiques intermingled with the likes of Jean-Michel Frank.

Hampton graduated from Brown and studied at the Institute of Fine Arts at NYU. At age thirteen, she began working in her father's office, developing what clients say are her well-honed design instincts. Hampton's versatile capabilities are reflected in her recent projects. These include a new Louis XIV-style home in Atlanta, a Balinese-style Florida retreat, a formal Anglo-French home, a traditional boat with modern backgrounds and several New York apartments, ranging from modern eclectic to streamlined traditional. Clients say that the common thread is a desire to steer the project to the absolute highest standards, given the budget. Of the five large and twenty smaller ongoing projects, about three are in the regional area. To the delight of clients and the detriment of the schedule, design delegation is not Hampton's forte.

The firm works with a fairly High design fee (but this includes oversight services and auction consultations) and Classic retail on products. Hampton is known to mix it up to meet budgets—De Angelis for the living room and Classic Sofa for the playroom (with some unique tweaks). While most projects are large, the firm is happy to work on smaller assignments. AD 100, 2002. HB Top Designers, 1999, 2000, 2001, 2002. ID Hall of Fame. KB 1997, 1999.

"The ballast is firmly in the keel, the sails are on course." "There is a new focus." "I have been in the real estate development business for over 30 years, and I have not seen anyone with the project management skills Alexa has brought to the table." "Walking through the D&D with Alexa is like being with royalty, everyone rushes to her side." "Architectural details have fallen between the cracks, but the interior design is fabulous." "Alexa has a unique eye. We will go through 200 samples at the D&D and she will know exactly which blue will work. It is amazing." "I am pleased to report that Alexa is quite busy. But this can mean less of her time for the smaller clients." "While not cheap, Alexa is quite fair. Getting it right is a matter of pride and family tradition." "Once you have seen the exemplary quality 'Down the Rabbit-Hole' and experienced the joy of Alexa's dry wit, it is hard to turn back."

Markham Roberts Inc.   4.5   4.5   4   4.5

1020 Lexington Avenue, 2nd Floor, New York, NY 10021
(212) 288 - 6090   markhamrobertsinc@nyc.rr.com
Eloquent, alluring, classic interior design

With a strong knowledge of the most sublime traditions in interior design, Markham Robert creates homes of timeless and gracious appeal with a modicum of the delightfully unexpected. A sumptuous neutral background may be a foil for a blood-red felt table edged in parchment white, brandishing delicate ostrich eggs. Classical architectural bones are a necessity with radiant wit adding appeal. Clients may come to the party with family heirlooms or seeking a fresh start. Roberts will insist upon a minimum of one or two fine antiques and an exquisite paint finish, with the rest dictated by budget. Supporters consistently say the result is the very definition of chic.

An art history and architecture major at Brown, Roberts embarked upon his design career after working for Mark Hampton for five years. In 1997, Roberts began an independent firm, now with six others including two project managers and a licensed architect. Two or three major projects are taken on at a time, with many smaller undertakings completed for past clients. About half the work is Upper East Side and suburban based (Greenwich, Rye, Katonah), with the rest across the United States. The entire team is consistently complimented for its well-honed organizational skills, with Roberts as the primary client contact.

The firm takes a good-sized design fee to start and Classic retail on product, but it charges no hourlies and low workroom markups. An array of amazing-to-outstanding sources is used depending on budgets, with Roberts coaching the lesser vendors to deliver fine goods. He is particularly applauded for his creative abilities with younger family clients, designing pieces which are simultaneously functional and fanciful, and rugged enough to hold up to the PB&J set. Original pieces of his furniture may be purchased at the office/showroom Roberts shares with James Sansum at the address above. Budgets tend to be incremental, with the sky as the limit. Clients believe they are receiving excellent value and have fun in the process. HB Top Designers, 2002.

"Markham is fastidious. My husband is an organization fanatic, and even he was impressed." *"I appreciated his businesslike approach including excellent communication."* *"Mark was there for us on Saturday mornings when that was best for us."* *"Sensitive to our family needs, Markham put a indestructible paisley covered table in the foyer to hide the stroller."* *"My son's Louis XVI daybed is truly unique but is functional and does not look overdone."* *"He does not take on too much, does not give you too many options and never makes a mistake."* *"By reframing all my old artwork he took the merely good and made it monumental."* *"You get him, not an assistant."* *"There was give and take in the budget—when we got sticker shock, he would find another. But when he said it was important, we would bend."* *"There is huge respect for Markham when he walks into a store. He can get it done."* *"I have been in my apartment for 36 years and have redecorated three times before, but this is the first time I was completely happy."*

Matthew Patrick Smyth Inc.   4   3.5   5   5

12 West 57th Street, Suite 704, New York, NY 10019
(212) 333 - 5353   www.matthewsmyth.com

Uplifting, refined, tranquil interior design

Appropriate scale, harmony of light and crystalline placement are the trademarks of Mathew Smyth. Remixing the historically relevant with modern elan, rooms are streamlined with fine antiques and original thought. Clients, peers and the trade speak with great affection for the designer, his general good judgment and accommodating nature. Architecturally, his design plans are said to be very clear and helpful giving the client a visual for informed decision making. The firm is small with clients receiving Smyth's full attention. Many projects have been completed in the regional area in the last few years including homes in Greenwich, Westport, Rye, Bedford, Westport and New Canaan.

After studying at FIT and spending five years with David Easton, Smyth started his own firm in 1987. He often decorates second or third residences, and many of his new customers are family referrals. He is willing to do small projects for interesting new clients but usually undertakes complete renovations. Smyth charges a Standard design fee and a Reasonable markup on product. All bills include the net costs. He can work within a budget and offers a wide range of product possibilities. While he personally tends toward the modern, clients report that he is successful with any style including highly traditional. His own line of furniture can be found at Hinson. HB Top Designers, 2000, 2001, 2002. KB 1995, 1998, 2001.

"I cannot fully describe his respect and concern for his clients." *"I completely admire and trust Matthew's design sensibility. He is involved in everything right down to the last trim selection."* *"Matthew understood the house much better than I did and would come out to visit whenever necessary."* *"His demeanor and his billing is so straightforward."* *"Dealers are always surprised that he speaks of the net price in front of the client."* *"His architectural talents are better than any architect I have ever known."* *"He is unique within the industry. He always makes it right."* *"His friendly countenance belies his determination."* *"I just love being with Matthew. He is tons of fun and has a wide range of interests."* *"He not only understands peoples' design interests but also their values."* *"He can deal with any circumstance. I had to move in a week, and Matthew made it happen."* *"Matthew kept us so calm. I would recommend him to anyone."*

McMillen Inc.   4.5   4.5   4   4.5
155 East 56th Street, 5th Floor, New York, NY 10022
(212) 753 - 5600   flipsey@mcmilleninc.com

Classical, staid, proper interior design

McMillen is regarded as one of the tried-and-true in the business, as genera-tion after generation of discreet old-money clients continue to utilize the firm's timeless design. Founded in 1924 by Eleanor McMillen Brown, the firm's guiding lights are now Betty Sherrill (joined in 1951) and Louis Rey (1972), who lead a strong team of experienced senior designers. Ann Pyne, Sherrill's daughter, joined the firm last fall as an associate. McMillen can deliver a surprising range of styles (way beyond just chintz) and undertakes most of the related architectural work. They focus on the highest quality product available, avoid any and all trendiness and often cultivate unique sources. At a client's request, they will even provide the books on your shelves.

McMillen's list of highly satisfied customers is enormous. Many have a habit of owning several homes over time, all decorated by McMillen. The firm takes great pride in retrofitting clients' old curtains and upholstery to new venues. The company is open to new clients, especially ones that will grow with the firm. The very pro-fessional office of 22 is said to deliver the ultimate in customer service, exchanging items until the client is satisfied. Dozens of projects are taken on annually, each headed by a senior designer. Recent clients are residents of Greenwich, New Canaan, Darien, Pound Ridge, Rye, Bedford, Larchmont and Bronxville.

The firm charges a Standard design fee (for an average-sized project), Standard oversight fees and Classic retail on products. Most projects are full-scale reno-vations. Patrons say that the net product pricing is unknown to them, but that perfection is worth any price. AD 100, 2000. HB Top Designers, 1999, 2000. KB 1993, 1997.

"McMillen functions seamlessly. A senior designer was always on-site, and they faxed my office with any decisions I had to make." "So gorgeous, yet so liv-able." "Managing to a budget is not really their thing past the major pieces." "We had to choose between a new car and the McMillen curtains. Thirteen years later, the curtains still look fresh, and the car would have been dead." "It is a well-oiled machine." "They are embarking on a new phase of the McMillen story." "Everyone of the senior designers is a reliable, accomplished professional." "McMillen rep-resents a system which works, but they are not the most innovative designers." "These are schooled professionals that are not worried about invitations to the south of France." "They are never condescending or haughty. These are practical people who get the job done without an attitude." "The firm operates in the old school of design where you would not dare ask about cost." "It would never occur to me or my family to think about using anyone else."

Michael Whaley Interiors Inc.   4.5   4   4.5   4.5
235 Scofieldtown Road, Stamford, CT 06903
(203) 595 - 9845

Engaging, sophisticated, traditionally-inspired interior design

Michael Whaley is recognized for his classically understated rooms, rich in detail and gracefully suited for family living. Educated by the legendary Albert Hadley early in his career, Whaley builds rooms of character and quality based on a mix of the fine and the found. His clear goal is to make it easy and fun for the customer and to create beautiful and notable results in the process. Clients laud Whaley for offering serious design, rationally modified with a regional sensibility.

Receiving a BA in French from Columbia, Whaley did his graduate thesis in 18th-century French decoration by way of Versailles. After training at Parish-Hadley during the height of the 80s design superfluity, Whaley learned to appreciate the finest. In 1987, Whaley formed his own firm in New York City where he stayed until 2001 when he moved the business to Connecticut. There are currently four on staff including "the best business manager in the business." Married for ten years and the father of two young daughters, Whaley has developed a new appreciation of suitable design investment. Whaley does aim high, with a network of exceptionally skilled artisans including some of the top workrooms in New York.

Usually undertaking entire house redesigns, Whaley will do about three large and three smaller projects at a time. A Standard design fee is taken up front covering most hourly consultations and Classic retail is taken on product.

"Each house that he does for us is extraordinarily beautiful and special. From English formal in Darian to beach elegance in Watch Hill to bay country in Alabama, it just gets better and better." "Michael will not do a white sofa knowing that it will not stand up to the kids over time." "He is a total perfectionist but without an ego." "Michael will send it back even if I do not notice the small scratch." "There are unique and creative solutions that amaze us." "Michael is so diplomatic and makes everyone on the team feel important." "He is a true professional and runs the firm as a solid business venture." "It took us a few tries, but we finally got the perfect decorator." "He taught me all about the world of decorating and upgraded our lifestyle."

Miles Redd, LLC 💼   4.5   3.5   4.5   5
77 Bleecker Street, Suite C111, New York, NY 10012
(212) 674 - 0902   mredd@nyc.rr.com
Dashing, elegant, traditional interior design with sparkle

Miles Redd is hailed as gifted for developing glamorous rooms full of bountiful color and alluring forms while still maintaining a decorous balance. With an original sense of design wit and flair applied to things once traditional, Redd has reconfigured the concept of updated neoclassical. Monogrammed pillows lay atop a rock star's festooned bed, sequins edge Brunschwig chintz swags, Kentshire antiques banter with burlap walls. Clients say Redd's signature style is layered and full, with intricate detail and perfect placement, resulting in a balanced and open feel. In the country, it reflects a dialogue of the ages resulting in a playful yet quiet sophistication. There, twelve-inch heart pine floors ground embroidered linen and unlined taffeta in the main rooms with tartan on the walls of the husband's dressing room.

Redd created the firm in 1999 after he spent five years with Bunny Williams. The designer takes on a wide scope of projects, from small downtown apartments to large homes in Millbrook. Redd has pleased a diverse clientele that includes empty nesters, young professionals and families with his flexibility and excellent collaborative abilities. Running a very small office, Redd is highly accessible with about a third of his time in the regional area.

The firm charges a flat design fee and Low markup on product. There is as much appreciation for flea market finds and forgotten closet items as for exquisite Louis XV antiques. While more modest projects are artfully arranged thrift-store stunners, others are more Fendi meets F. Scott Fitzgerald. Minimum budgets are in the $40,000 ballpark. HB Top Designers, 2000, 2001, 2002.

"Preppy version of new millennium glamour." "It is the very definition of a collaborative effort. Miles is so enthusiastic about all of your ideas, but at the same time he reins you in to make sure that you have a polished result." "He can take others' throwaways and make them grand in the right setting with the right fabric." "Miles has a wonderful foundation of knowledge that he builds upon and runs with." "He took the 18th-century-style curtains that I refused to get rid of and bordered them with Indian gossamer fabric, adding spice to a tired concept." "The designs are filled with spunk but are also completely genteel." "He is such a gentleman—suave and sweet." "Miles is 100 percent responsible, great at returning phone calls and would always keep us in the loop." "Not only a great designer, but Miles is also so practical." "He has exquisite taste, imagination and wit as well as a beautiful sense of color."

	Quality	Cost	Value	Recommend?
	✚	$	◆	★

Milly de Cabrol Ltd.

4   3   4   4

150 East 72nd Street, Suite 2C, New York, NY 10021
(212) 717 - 9317   millyltd@yahoo.com

Unabashed, continental, bonhomie interior design

Milly de Cabrol is praised by her mostly young and chic clientele as being masterful in combining styles and ideas to fulfill their imaginative visions. While ably using a diverse palette of textiles and colors, her editing skills are said to be as strong as her versatility, which often centers on a theme. In the region, de Cabrol favors a Provence-meets-Tuscany feel that is like "taking a vacation and checking into a five-star hotel." Clients appreciate the fact that Milly is the sole contact and inspiration for projects and works highly collaboratively with the client.

Born into an aristocratic and artistic Italian family, de Cabrol lived in London for ten years and traveled extensively in the Far East. In 1984 the designer moved to the States, and started her career in interior design. We're told she most enjoys unusual design projects for which she "pours her heart and soul into them." Recent projects have included a chateau-like house in Westport, an Indian-Swedish apartment on Fifth Avenue, a grand English duplex on the West Side of Manhattan and a NY pied-a-terre filled with modern art. She is said to possess a particularly good touch with collections.

The firm charges a Standard design fee and Low product markups. She is lauded by supporters for her hardworking attitude and helpful nature. HB Top Designers, 2000, 2001, 2002.

"In Connecticut, she does formal that is also so comfortable with panache." "I am so impressed by Milly's skill at combining so many styles into the livable, tasteful composite I call my home." "Milly found these amazing crystal chandeliers from a private collection that were not even available to the public." "She is the complete opposite of stuffy, but at the same time classy—just what we were looking for." "She has a very strong ability to choose just the right amount of 'ethnic style' to give a room verve without it looking overdone." "I love Milly and would absolutely use her again, but she really could use a bit more support." "Her clients are the young nobs and swells of New York."

Nancy Mullan/
NDM Kitchens Inc., ASID, CKD

5   3.5   5   5

By appointment only, New York, NY 10021
(212) 628 - 4629   www.nancymullan.com

Gourmet kitchen design, interior design and space planning

See Nancy Mullan/NDM Kitchens Inc., ASID, CKD's full report under the heading Kitchen & Bath Designers.

Palladio Interior Design

4   4   4   4

108 Campfire Road, Chappaqua, NY 10514
(914) 238 - 1408

Welcoming comfortable interior design

Pamela Banker

4.5   4   4   4.5

136 East 57th Street, New York, NY 10022
(212) 308 - 5030   psb@pamelabanker.com

Formal, traditional, old-school interior design

Pamela Banker is well respected by clients and the trade for her efficient, capable professionalism and her strong, clean designs in the Parish-Hadley tradition. With a calm hand, she will remix classic traditional concepts yielding comfortable, crisp, handsome results. Clients say that she makes a particular effort to save and restore the architectural bones and then trims away any unnecessary embellishments. Room identities are then created through a structured process based upon color preferences, design themes and functionality. She wins accolades from clients for her clear approach, although some say she could be a bit less focused. Patrons remark favorably upon her excellent commitment to budgets and schedule, which has led to a number of recent high-profile country club commissions including the distinguished makeovers of the Round Hill Club and the Cosmopolitan Club.

In the late 60s Banker started her own firm. After twenty years in the business, she joined McMillen at a senior level, and then went with Parish-Hadley after Sister Parish retired. With the quasi-retirement of Albert Hadley, Banker reestablished her namesake firm. Currently, there are six on staff including two strong senior associates. Customers are appreciative that they get Banker as the design leader, with a good amount of delegation. About two large projects a year are in the Connecticut/Westchester area, with a few main rooms as the minimum. Many clients and families have followed Banker wherever she goes. Now younger generations have followed suit.

Classic retail is charged on all products, with a Standard design fee covering hourly costs. While her many clients appreciate her timeless approach, others say that much of her inspiration dates back to her days at Parish-Hadley. But the work is said to always be completed accurately and meticulously. Many devoted clients would not consider using anyone else.

"After 30+ years, she has seen it all. She is the consummate professional." "Sister Parish without the ruffles." "Bold, contemporary jungle prints at the beach and more rarified, traditional silks on Park Avenue. She has a very broad range and really meets the client's objectives." "She totally understands the look that is appropriate for Rye. Impeccable, but you can also put your feet up." "Pam is an excellent listener up-front, but once you are in the implementation phase— watch out! She gets on a roll." "There is no nonsense with Pam." "She will inspect the upholsterer's work on her hands and knees to make sure he has it right." "She is one of the few designers out there that understands what 'classy' means. Trendy is not in her vocabulary." "She would come out to the country for all the meetings in the beginning and was personally there for installations." "I interviewed a handful of other decorators, and she was reasonably priced." "She was on budget to the dime." "I have nothing but admiration for Pam." "Our family has depended on her for years."

Pamela Olsey Interiors Inc.   3.5   3.5   4   4
370 Greenwich Avenue, Greenwich, CT 06830
(203) 869 - 4414
Cheerful, traditional interior design with interest

With a flair for color and a penchant towards the traditional, Pam Olsey has been in interior design since 1972. Based out of her shop on Greenwich Avenue, Olsey enjoys mixing the homeowner's inventory with fun flea market finds and lots of plaid, chintz and silk taffeta. With a practical approach, the old is freshened with interesting trims and a wash of paint. Blue-and-white schemes are a favorite, but all is based on the clients' preferences.

Working in the area for over 30 years, Olsey has seen many trends come and go, none that seem to have affected her focus. About three large projects are generally going on at one time, with a handful of others in progress. Building developers are particularly fond of Olsey's ability to make the new look more situated. Olsey can handle it all with her long-time assistant, from picture moldings on the walls to hangers in the closet.

Charging a Low markup on product and Reasonable hourly rates for non-product time, Olsey keeps clients happy. Many choices are offered and Olsey makes a point of making it work for the client.

"We have used Pam since the early 80s. She moved us several times and always reused the furnishings." "Even with just one room to decorate, Pam treated us like the best customers in the world." "She could work with the devil and design his den beautifully." "Pam worked with our boat manufacturer and redid every square inch of the interiors of our 75-foot cruiser. It is phenomenal." "We have become lifelong friends through the process."

Patricia Hill Designs   4.5   4   4.5   5
13 Meadow Wood Drive, Greenwich, CT 06830
(203) 869 - 1719   phill97236@aol.com

Classical, inviting, comely interior design

Appearing as if the rooms evolved over generations, Patti Hill guides clients with focus, thoughtful reflection and a soft hand. Offering a richness in form, designs are saturated in scope and provenance, commingling the fine and the personally meaningful. Whether starting with a new construction or an historic home, detailed painted millwork, unusual fabrics and textiles and Sheraton mahogany often make a statement. Contributing to both the architectural construct and the building implementation, Hill is appreciated for her skill and practical nature all the way.

Hill learned both the design and the business aspects from the best. She began her career on a trading floor at DLJ, went on to work with Ron Perlman at Revlon and then delved into the design trade with a master, Thomas Jayne. On her own since 1992, there are now four people in the firm, with Hill as the designer, doing all the shopping and client meetings. She also has a varied and professional group of specialty painters and craftsman. Many of Hill's clients are using a designer for the first time and say they "could not imagine ever doing it without her."

Using Fortuny to Pottery Barn, Hill is excellent about starting with just a few rooms and going in phases. There is a Standard design fee and Reasonable markups.

"She professes to love 'ugly' colors, but they look wonderful to me." "Patty took our 1916 house back to the way it was supposed to be." "Classic top-notch Greenwich with family comfort." "My husband was highly predisposed to not get along with any decorator, but Patty completely wowed him." "While she is busy, you never felt rushed." "She will always make time for us, even if it has to be late at night." "Patty understood what we wanted from the moment she walked in."

Patrick Gallagher Decoratives   4.5   4   4   4.5
& Design Inc. 🖼
65 Water Street, Stonington, CT 06378
(860) 535 - 1330   www.patrickgallagherdesign.com

Crisp, timeless, balanced traditional interior design

With clarity of purpose, honesty of design intent and refined simplicity, Patrick Gallagher has been impressing clients in the Stonington area and beyond. While usually bent toward a classic English Regency that reflects his established clientele, Gallagher pares it down, highlighting sleek lines, symmetrical proportion and a modern palette. Noted as highly responsive, the firm develops plans within context and budget, be it a Watch Hill mansion, a rambling Pound Ridge estate, a sleek New York City pied-a-terre or the traditional Inn at Stonington.

With Midwest roots and FIT training, Gallagher ventured into many design endeavors including retail merchandising and buying, showroom design and photographic styling. After several years as the director of Visual Merchandising at

F. Schumacher, Gallagher started his own interior design firm in 1992. With three on staff, the firm is said to be highly professional and proficient, employing the latest CAD techniques. For new clients, the group will take on a few rooms, which usually evolves into many more.

Budgets range considerably based on the situation. The firm works with Standard hourly fees on the up-front design, and takes Classic retail on product with oversight fees. There is much repeat business, with at least one client on their fourth project with the firm.

"Patrick is thinking 24/7 about his clients." "Balance is his watch word, which applies to both the designs, the comfort factor and the economics." "Patrick just gets it. He is as professional as he is nice." "He can take the quality to the highest level but is sensitive to the client." "He makes himself happy by making the client happy."

Paula Perlini Inc.   4   4   4   4

165 East 35th Street, New York, NY 10016
(212) 889 - 6551
Warm, richly-toned, traditional interior design

Perlini wins the respect and loyalty of clients with excellent resources and strong creativity-for example, when one client wanted to wait to find the ultimate Oriental rug, Perlini had a facsimile of a Sultanbad Persian painted on sisal. Now the client considers the sisal one of her favorite processions and would never give it up for the real thing. The designer is also known for her intermingling of the fine and the found, creating friendly environments, comfortable for the adults, children and the pets to share. Rooms tend to be quite traditional, with prevalence of distinct colors for depth and character.

Perlini spent her student years in Italy and Switzerland, studying at the Academia di Belle Arti in Rome and absorbing the artistic wonders at hand. Returning to the US, she moved to Cincinnati, worked in interior design locally and then headed to New York to work for brother-in-law, Mark Hampton, for almost a decade, becoming the head of design. Perlini then formed a design partnership with Alan Tanksley for six years, and went out on her own in 1993. Currently, there are about five large projects going on at any one time, generally in Manhattan and the surrounding areas.

While Perlini usually encourages the client to invest in some excellent upholstery and some interesting antique accents, she is good about designing custom repo casegoods to help meet the budget. On top of the process and the economics, Perlini has a NY-type design fee and charges Classic retail on product. Clients say they would not hesitate to recommend Perlini to a friend.

"Paula is confident yet always gracious." "We have learned to totally trust her judgment." "Paula is way beyond just color and proportion. She always gets it right. My husband used to think he had perfect design sensibilities. But now he fully admits that Paula is way better." "She is always very prepared." "Paula can find a treasure among random things in the garage. She has such an eye." "We always have either a small project or a large project going on with Paula." "She absolutely understands the industry and the profession." "We have never had to ask her to take back a thing." "Paula is so much fun. It is a gift to be around her."

Pegue Associates, LLC   3.5   4   4   4.5

59 Grove Street, Suite 2D, New Canaan, CT 06840
(203) 972 - 2941   pegueassoc@aol.com
Updated traditional with charm

With clean lines highlighted by touches of chintz and the patina of a well-loved antique, Robin Shinnick has brought warmth and character to her clients' homes.

Spare but distinct accessories soften the composite, with many hours devoted to the hunt. Collaboration with the client is a fundamental tenet, making the process fun and rewarding.

With a master's in international management from Thunderbird and years in advertising management, Shinnick takes a practical and businesslike approach. Known to have the highest integrity, outstanding professionalism, and a very gracious manner, clients feel fortunate to have Shinnick on their team. The firm was founded in 1994, after Shinnick returned from a few years in London with studies at the V&A. With two at her side, over ten projects are done at a time, keeping the firm on its toes.

Designs are done at a Reasonable hourly rate with Classic retail taken on product. Shinnick is sensitive to budgets and helps clients manage tradeoffs. Homes are often done in phases, with homeowners wanting more after the initial rooms are complete.

"Very talented and rising in reputation." "Robin is a joy to work with and is so well spoken." "A wealth of information and resources." "The paint colors are so complex and golden—they glow." "I am kicking myself for not hiring Robin sooner. I thought I could do it myself, but I was wrong." "She is so nice and works at our pace." "There is a warmth and translucence of light that emanates from Robin's rooms."

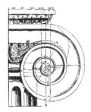

Peter F. Carlson & Associates, LLC   4.5   4.5   4   4.5
162 Joshuatown Road, Lyme, CT 06371
(860) 434 - 3744   pcarlsonassoc@aol.com
Progressive, structured, sophisticated interior design

A master of the sleek, yet soothing, Peter Carlson is a creative force pushing toward the future of interior design. With a love of furniture design, Carlson's forms are elegant and streamlined, sinuous and sensual. Proportion and line take a leading role over the palette that is often monochromatically interwoven into the architecture, but functionality and quality is always a major consideration. Curved wall units full of custom storage may stand near Fortuny-covered chairs and an 18th-century Italian reeded settee. For his Connecticut clients, Carlson can do a toned-down version of chic.

After studying theatre in college and briefly working as an actor, Carlson established his design firm in Stonington in 1980. With four assistants, about four major and several smaller projects evolve at a time. Generally, a quarter of the work is done in the local area. Client service is a very high priority, with Carlson reportedly being highly available and even buying the linens and stocking the fridge upon request. It is not unusual for Carlson to complete three or four projects with a longstanding client.

A Standard hourly fee for all hours and Reasonable product markups are taken. Carlson is also well known for his lighting products company, CL Sterling & Son, launched in 1991. HB Top Designers, 1999, 2000, 2001. KB 1985, 1990.

"It is very hard to make the design look this elegantly simple." "Peter can do understated glamour, which makes sense even in this motherland of center hall Colonials." "I can only say nice things about Peter. He will get on a plane and come visit me whenever necessary." "Peter is a total diplomat." "His rooms are a breath of fresh air." "He always wins any discussions, and that is because he is always right." "He did traditional for me and only beige and gray for my friend. Both were beautiful." "Twenty years later the design held, he just had to reupholster a few pieces."

Reger Designs Inc.   4   4   4   5

45 Tudor City Place, New York, NY 10017
(212) 557 - 6262

Layered, patterned, unabashed traditional interior design

Without missing an inch of possible design expression, clients report that Trish Reger delivers comfortable elegance with "baronial wonder." Beginning most rooms with a luxurious and intricate rug, many patterned fabrics add to the textural composure with damasks, tapestries, plaids and wovens each playing a role. Window treatment designs are another area of detailed craftsmanship, with elaborate layers, trims and fringes. Clients are completely enamored of Reger's diligence and intricate specifications.

After graduating from Mt. Holyoke in English and studio art, Reger did a brief stint as a set designer. She attended The New York School of Interior Design and then worked at Donghia for several years, forming her own interior design firm in 1989. Currently there are five on staff, with "excellent teamwork." Reger has an office in New York City as well as Connecticut, where about 60 percent of the work is done. Building long-term relationships is a priority—four projects have been completed for Steven and Candice Stark of Stark Carpet and others have done three projects with Reger over the last twenty years.

Reger works with a substantial up-front design fee and Reasonable markups on product, which can go from value to the max. She is very involved in the structural issues and often takes a turnkey approach—everything from the china to the toothbrushes may be supplied. Working at a highly deliberate pace, it is said that the designer "gets everything right." ASID. NCIDQ.

"Trish did everything from the exterior color of the house to the hardware inside." "The architect said to me, 'I thought that I was good, but she is better,' when Trish located the perfect wood beams." "I just told Trish that I liked earth tones and not to make it too formal and she took it from there." "We have worked with other decorators before, but Trish was the only one who totally followed through." "She thinks before she acts." "Trish is a perfectionist herself and demands a lot of the subs." "As an architect, I can report that clients don't just like Trish, they love her."

Rinfret Ltd.   4.5   4   4   4.5

165 West Putnam Avenue, Greenwich, CT 06830
(203) 622 - 0000   www.rinfretltd.com

Bespoke, traditional interior design within reason

Completing over a dozen projects a year with a staff of fourteen, Cindy Rinfret has clearly won the Greenwich community's confidence. Handsome antiques stand by traditional forms outfitted in black leather and substantial, well-priced reproductions offering a consolidated and timeless appeal. Sensitive to family lifestyles and fluent with the regional finesse, Rinfret knows where to draw the line between done and overdone while still meeting the budget.

Rinfret established her firm in 1988, after graduating from RISD and apprenticing under a number of prestigious New York decorators including Noel Jeffrey and Ann Eisenhower. There she mastered the updated traditional genre, which is ably applied. Rinfret attends all design meetings and her associates follow up.

Ranging from one sofa to three projects for Tommy Hilfiger, the firm is said to be full-service and "wholly professional." The firm charges hourlies for design work and supervision and Classic retail on product. Rinfret also works well on a consultation basis with those who go at it more independently. Clients report that Rinfret is good about incorporating their existing furnishings, finding good repro alternatives, and effective about "getting it on the first pass with panache."

For a quick view of the company's design aesthetic, visit the large and fully outfitted new showroom at the bottom of Greenwich Avenue. Clients say that the retail product is "good for a quick fix" but the personalized service is the main appeal.

"She came over, looked at our family and knew immediately how we lived and what we wanted." "The colors she chose are the colors I wear." "As an architect I have seen it all. Cindy is steps ahead of the rest of the group." "There is a heavy disposition to Stark carpeting and plaids." "As a real estate agent, I can clearly state that everything Cindy does sells very quickly." "She also came up with great architectural suggestions—the mirrors in the entryway completely upgraded space with an illusion of light." "Cindy understands family living and does not push the envelope." "She kept us in mind even after the project was done."

Robin McGarry & Associates   3.5   4   4   4
11 Riverfield Drive, Weston, CT 06883
(203) 454 - 1825

Updated, streamlined traditional interior design

Pleasing her classically traditional clientele with a comfortable mix of clean lines, reproduction favorites and composed accessories, Robin McGarry serves the region well. Open spaces are left uncluttered and upholstered pieces remain unadorned, allowing the light and architecture to speak for itself. Glass and chrome can juxtapose straight-edged sofas with classic oriental rugs grounding the space or more historic lines can be favored, given the client's interests.

Drawing on her 25 years as a designer, McGarry is known to be highly professional. After working for several years at Ferry-Hayes in Atlanta on contract and residential projects, McGarry established her own shop in Weston in 1995. Lots of work is done on a room-by-room, evolving process. Process is said to be a strength with a specific four-phase design approach. She also receives kudos for a "well-run office and consistently strong subs."

McGarry has a clear and precise contract in which a Reasonable hourly fee is charged for all designer hours and a Lower percentage product commission. There is an up-front applicable retainer and oversight fees. ASID. NCIDQ.

"In New York she did soft contemporary and in Southport traditional." "Robin is really on top of all the costs and is open to a range of choices." "She has a great way about her. She is so nice and keeps the job moving along." "Robin is really excellent and involved with lighting plans." "She is very reflective, paying attention to the realistic needs of a family." "Robin delivers exactly what she says she will when promised it."

Roch & Chase    3.5   3   4.5   5
99 Myrtle Avenue, Westport, CT 06880
(203) 226 - 3927

Refreshing, honest, mostly traditional interior design

With a gentility of design expression and a desire to please, John Roch and Gary Chase are quickly establishing an appreciative audience. The pair, with their thoughtful and restrained placement of objects and a limited use of fringe, is able to maximize the look and simultaneously maximize the budget. Creative with flea market finds and inherited treasures, there is a sense of period authenticity and "correctness" achieved with a $500 settee and the best fabric available. They are said to be excellent listeners and to attentively prevent the clients from making mistakes.

Established in 1996 after Roch successfully attracted potential clients' attention at a Southport showhouse, the two constitute the firm. About six to eight major and several smaller homes are developed at a time. Comfortable in a broad range of historically based styles, from Neoclassical Georgian to Tudor to Moderne, the team works to achieve the client's vision.

Confirmed Luddites, there is not a computer in the office. All the paperwork is lovingly written by hand on engraved stationery, bespeaking a bygone era. Equal care is taken with their client relationships, which are said to be 80 percent repeat. Working incrementally, with a Low product commission and a Reasonable hourly rate, customers feel they are well worth the cost.

"They are frick and frak. You get two opinions and a balance of thought for the price of one." "When we go shopping, we have so much fun that the clients of other decorators secretly ask me for their phone number." "They assume the client is smart." "John and Gary have gotten so popular that they are now able to be quite selective about whom they work with." "They do not want to be the biggest decorators in town or to make a fortune. They are just happy to improve their customers' lifestyles."

Sandra Morgan Interiors Inc. 🛍   3.5   4   4   4.5
70 Arch Street, Greenwich, CT 06830
(203) 629 - 8121   www.sandramorganinteriors.com
Ebullient, colorful, friendly, traditional interior design

With her vivacious take on classic design, strong service orientation and meticulous follow-through, Sandy Morgan has built a loyal following in Greenwich and the surrounding areas. With a traditional, rolled-arm Lawson sofa in beige or chintz typically setting the stage, rooms are enlivened with rolls of trims, hand-printed curtains and leopard woven chairs. American and English pieces sit comfortably with their European cousins and contemporary touches add flow and energy. All is done in a very collaborative manner with the client.

Living in Greenwich for over 30 years, Morgan has been involved in many different realms of interior design. Beginning on the editorial decorating staff after college with *House & Garden* and *Mademoiselle* magazines, Morgan then established an art consulting business based out of the converted barn in her backyard. Later she began Morgan & Co., an art, repro and accessories shop, which segued into interior design full-time. Currently she undertakes about two or three large jobs at a time and a handful of ongoing ones with an assistant.

After a conservative budget discussion, a Standard design fee is taken and product is purchased at Classic retail with oversight. Clients report that Morgan is particularly good about doing "the high-low thing," stretching the budget by having a few good antiques with decent vintage combined with quality reproductions. ASID.

"Sandra is amazingly professional." "She is always available—you never feel as if a question was too small to ask." "Sandy is very realistic, especially when it comes to finances. When the rug was too much, she found great alternatives." "She is an artist but does not act like one." "Sandy is passionate about color." "There are organized written estimates for everything." "It was so much fun to do the house with Sandy that I was sad when it was over. Makes me want to buy a new house."

Sandra Oster Interiors Ltd.   4   4   4   4.5

24 Sawmill Lane, Greenwich, CT 06830
(203) 661 - 2356   sloster@aol.com

Original, characteristic, dramatic takes on traditional interior design

With a predisposition for fulfilling clients' visions, Sandra Oster creates individualistic spaces full of personality, creativity and ease. Described as "romantic cocoons," elaborate draperies, hand-blocked velvets, unique lighting and distinct metal accents highlight the otherwise traditional ensembles. Oster most often is involved at the commencement of a project, working hand-in-hand with the architect and contractor—a role that she prefers and in which she is reportedly highly effective.

A graduate of RISD, Oster worked as Art Director at *Mademoiselle* magazine and then as an art director for Henri Bendel and Revlon. Oster began her foray into interior design in 1983, ramping up in 1998 with three assistants. About fourteen projects are in progress at a time, including four to five larger ones. Known as a mainstay in Scarsdale, many clients have happily referred her to their friends.

Oster is not only respectful of the client's intentions but also of their budget and "leaves a stupendous" paper trail with Excel spreadsheets. With the structural work, there is an hourly architectural fee and a design fee based on hours for the decorative work. Products are purchased with a Reasonable markup and oversight fees for certain service providers.

"Sandy is full of integrity and heart." "I know that she is very busy, but she makes time for everyone." "Sandy was there from the get-go, contributing a lot to the architecture and landscaping. There is nothing she will not pursue." "At one point, I was worried that we were heading down the wrong path. I told her, and she graciously redid three months of work over the weekend." "Everyone in the D&D knows Sandy." "When my husband had sticker shock over the price of the family room sofa, Sandy suggested a Crate & Barrel alternative with a custom piping, and it was perfect." "She cares so much that I get what I want."

Sara Bengur Associates   4   3   5   5

525 Broadway, Suite 701, New York, NY 10012
(212) 226 - 8796   www.sarabengur.com

Exotic, cohesive, classical interior design

Dexterously blending enticing old-world objects and chic cosmopolitan furniture, Sara Bengur and her clients are shaking up the suburbs. Drawing upon her Turkish heritage, Bengur creates a highly customized look that is fresh and original, yet comfortably appropriate for family living. Instead of the expected roman shades, there are goblet pleats in ocher linen. Queen Anne and Kittinger chairs live beside a Jean-Michel Frank in natural duck with antique textile pillows. Sources report that Bengur initially invests a great deal of time to understanding clients' interests and takes deep pride in creating something special and unique.

After working on Wall Street for a few years, Bengur studied at Parsons, then managed large projects for Stephen Sills. She went off on her own about ten years ago. Recent projects include homes in New Canaan, Westport, Rye, Greenwich, Rowayton, Boston and Mt. Desert Island, Maine. There are four in the firm, all with a "highly collaborative and fun attitude."

Clients praise Bengur's close attention to "every little detail" and her strong sensitivity to family traffic. Entire homes are usually undertaken, sometimes in stages with a minimum budget of about $50,000. The firm generally charges a Standard design fee, a Reasonable percentage over net on products (same on antiques) and hourly fees for oversight. HB Top Designers, 2000, 2001, 2002.

"You get to the point where you just trust her reflective designs. I never would have picked these colors, but I love them more each day." "Sara will never do the same thing for any two clients, right down to the last lampshade." "You get the highest possible quality without the headaches and at half the cost." "She

tirelessly searches up and down the eastern seaboard to find unique antiques and objects." "While she does not push, she will encourage us to go for the highest quality we can afford without spending a fortune." "Sara would never purchase mass market, preferring small shop treasures at the same cost." "She has a wonderful sense of human scale and a delicate understanding of propriety, especially for someone so young." "Sara insisted on going to my attic to see if we could reuse any of my family pieces. That meant so much to me." "She designs comfortable, serene rooms of unassuming beauty."

Scott Salvator   4.5   4.5   4   4.5

308 East 79th Street, New York, NY 10021
(212) 861 - 5355   www.scottsalvator.com

Comely, fastidious, traditional interior design

Scott Salvator and Michael Zabriskie win customers' accolades for their businesslike manner, elegant-yet-updated formal, classical style and personable nature. Clients also praise the firm for its refined use of color and intricate layering of fabrics and coordinated trims, saying that it constructs the ultimate "traditional-but-not-stuffy" home. In the country, there are more printed linens, hooked rugs and fewer tassels and trims generally in a relaxed but refined American or English framework. Salvator is noted to be "accommodating, detail-oriented, deeply tied to his work, intense, smart, practical and fun." While some say that his "micromanagement" and legal background can, at times, slow progress, all are effusive about the end results.

Salvator received a BS in accounting and a JD in law, and then studied interior design at FIT and Parsons. Before starting his firm in 1992, Salvatore worked for Mario Buatta, Gary Crain and Robert Metzger. Zabriskie, an associate at the firm, graduated from Parsons and worked with Mario Buatta, McMillen and Parish-Hadley. Their technical competence is often mentioned as a key differentiating strength. About a fifth of the firm's client base is in the regional area and northwest Connecticut, often the second home done with the firm after their apartment on Park or Fifth. Homeowners interface directly with Salvator or Zabriskie, who do all the shopping themselves, and remain quite busy. The back office of four is known for their strong follow-up.

The firm asks for a Standard design fee that is deductible against future purchases. Products are purchased at Classic retail. It is mentioned that the firm enjoys high-end product, but "was not a snob about it when we purchased some items at Home Expo." Clients have strong opinions about the firm, with most life-long devotees and a few that just don't click. HB Top Designers, 1999, 2000, 2001, 2002. KB 1994, 1999, 2002.

"From city house to country house and back again. All were lovely and appropriate." "Everything is analyzed to perfection—they spent more time on the sofa's seat depth and pitch than I did discussing my wedding vows with my husband." "For that kind of money I did not want to talk to an assistant, and I never had to." "I know they are busy, but Scott spent three hours with me at E. Braun picking out linens." "While Scott can talk up a storm, the end product is just right." "I would not use him for my country house, but love his urban vision." "They are traditional without being frumpy." "Everyone is so attracted to the rosy colors and the oversized pieces that are even comfortable for large men." "Scott's glamorous couture product stands out in a sea of neutral sameness." "It was rare when I said no, but if I did, he was good about finding an alternative." "We went through several possible schemes with Scott, but we never really connected." "I did not have to interfere because he totally understood. He is great for people with limited time." "A well-organized system of estimates and billing." "Great sense of dry humor." "I recommended him to a friend but they just couldn't participate in this price range." "Scott has a real flair for living and livability. We continue to go to the movies together."

	Quality	Cost	Value	Recommend?
	+	$	◆	★

Scott Sanders, LLC 🛍

| | 4 | 3 | 4.5 | 4.5 |

524 Broadway, Suite 400A, New York, NY 10012
(212) 343 - 8298   www.scottsandersllc.com

Jaunty, engaging, classic American

With sparkle, wit and focus, Scott Sanders' imaginative use of traditional forms find a whole new meaning in his hands. Grand master portraits juxtapose crème lacquer walls, beadboards are painted fire engine red, navy ticking stripes cover nail-headed antiques. Sanders brings a classically based, comfortably nostalgic yet fresh sensibility to his interiors. Clients turn to Sanders for his original vision and highly personalized interiors from the metamorphosis of an elegant Fifth Avenue apartment with limestone, camel hair and tattersall to a 15,000-square-foot new Harrison home done in new-wave English Country.

After graduating Parsons and spending nine years at Polo/Ralph Lauren, where he established the company's Interior Design Department, Sanders opened his eponymous firm in 2000. A design boutique, clients get Sander's full attention. They tell us he is amazing at follow-up, both during and after the project. Projects have included residences in New York, Palm Beach, Greenwich, Bedford, Palm Springs, Paris and London, which range from New England understated genteel to hot Art Deco beachside. Sander's redesign of The Beach House Bal Harbour in Miami received a stir of attention. Sanders is comfortable working on large or small projects in the region and well beyond.

Clients welcome the firm's unusual methodology of pricing. Sanders charges a flat fee, based on a reasonable mark-up of estimated project costs. Living rooms can be as low at $15,000, demonstrating Sanders's strong creativity and insider resources. Sanders is said to be equally adept at redecorating a few rooms as working with architects on new construction. Clients highly recommend Sanders for addressing clients' practical needs while simultaneously creating manifest design moods.

"I really am grateful for Scott's inherent understanding of my traditional view." "It is like living in a Polo fantasy, with patina." "I use Scott as an example to my staff as to what good customer service means." "He finds a solution even under tight budget situations." "Scott takes flea market finds to an automotive spray shop, and voila, they are amazing." "Scott has a distinct 'well-groomed' style that is organized, but unpretentious." "Scott first develops the overriding concept with the client and the rest flows naturally. It is like going to a world-class theme party strategy session." "Scott really loves what he does and is an absolute pleasure to work with."

Sharon Simonaire Design

| | 4.5 | 4.5 | 4 | 4.5 |

216 West 18th Street, Suite 1102, New York, NY 10011
(212) 242 - 1824

Alluring, reflective, elegant modern interior design

With a worldwide jetsetter clientele and a love of the bucolic Hudson, Sharon Simonaire has brought a tactile warmth to the mid-century mindset. Taking the oft-presented modern mold to an unpretentious, almost camp level, Simonaire installs Tibetan yak wool around the McMakin daybed and a Chinese alter table under the geometric artwork. Instead of botanical prints, there are pressed botanical specimens found in Paris. Wood paneling, flooring and furnishing are also a favorite, polished in the "most extraordinary matte finish available." Each room is a disciplined presentation of the life and times of its inhabitants, who exclaim that each piece she finds is like a "long, lost friend."

Simonaire's joy of the evocative, is well founded in her varied training in the arts. Beginning as an accessories designer, she soon gravitated to photo styling and then cinema costume and set design. A dedicated traveler, Simonaire would discover the exotic before its time and began an eclectic retail operation in LA. After moving back to New York with her husband (*Saturday Night Live* producer Jim

Signorelli), Simonaire's interior design interest took a serious turn when clients such as Meg Ryan and Dennis Quaid, Robert De Niro and daughter Drena, and Richard Gere and Carey Lowell (who Simonaire introduced) prevailed. About three large and another seven smaller projects are pursued at a time, with about a third in the Katonah, Pound Ridge, Bedford areas.

Simonaire will start with a few rooms and a practical budget, aiming for a characteristic look that evolves, not a showpiece. A substantial design fee is taken up front and reasonable markup taken on product. While many clients report that they "fell in love with many pieces that were way over budget," Simonaire was then able to compensate by locating great flea market items with finesse.

"Sharon absorbs what she sees in Paris and with appropriate grace applies incredible chic to Westchester." "Sharon creates a better version of what you thought you wanted." "She not only found the perfect mid-century pieces but she also located the historical references in books for us, educating us along the way." "We did go way over budget as we started a serious furniture collection along the way." "Sharon will override the architect to get a better look and save you money in the process." "Despite her own full family life, Sharon always gets back to you right away." "There was no angst whatsoever solely due to Sharon's professionalism and inherent understanding of a reasonability factor." "She is so dedicated to the final product."

Susan Lifton Interiors Inc.   3.5   4   4   4

Box 686, Village Green, Bedford, NY 10506
(914) 234 - 9043

Proudly traditional, colorful, interior design with charm

A mainstay on the Bedford green for over a decade, Susan Lifton offers unabashed classical, layered warmth full of multipatterned materials and tailored silhouettes. Clients appreciate Lifton's multigenerational mix, which looks as comfortable today as it did twenty years ago. Lifton is also known for her patience, fine detailing and practical budgetary considerations.

A French major in college, Lifton ran the ad department at Cartier and then did PR at *Vanity Fair* before moving to Bedford and starting her own business in 1982. Lifton has thousands of fabrics and samples stacked on shelves. Beginning with just a few chairs, clients say Lifton is good about taking it one step at a time, eventually creating a master plan that is designed to work as "long as we own the house."

About three large projects are done at a time with an experienced assistant, mostly in the local area with additional projects in Fairfield and New York City. Detailed trims and welts finish off most pieces, with Lifton often suggesting ways to extend the look without extending the budget. Products are purchased at Classic retail after a minimal home design consultation fee.

"We valued Susan's opinions so much that we had her look at the house before we purchased it." "Susan is very responsive. She never hesitates when I want to change something—she will either take it back or will get the tradesman to alter it." "While she has a formal air, Susan is highly service-oriented." "We went to New York four times together before I purchased anything." "I have to plead with her to let me choose the more expensive fabric—and then she suggests using it on a pillow or dust ruffle to stretch the budget and get the same look." "When I wanted to do scallops on both the sofa and the chairs, Susan restrained me—rightfully so."

Susan Thorn Interiors Inc.   4.5   4   4.5   4.5

88 North Salem Road, Box 187, Cross River, NY 10518
(914) 763 - 5265   thorninteriors@earthlink.net

Uplifting, judicious, country and traditional interior design

Speaking the language and understanding the dreams of her clients, Susan Thorn builds rooms of gentle beauty, strength of character and depth of detail.

Chintz, checks, tassels and tortoiseshell are offset with a quality of restraint and an interwoven esprit, such as a fine Chippendale armchair in an unexpected ivory leather cover. The result is comfortable, familial warmth, which is both calm and stylish. On the cover of Classic American Home a few years ago, the work was highlighted for its polish and ease.

Thorn, in business for herself for over 40 years, has clearly figured out how to keep a number of active projects on target with a sound back office, including in-house CAD capability. With a propensity for finding period hardware at costs far less than the contractors, it is no wonder clients are impressed and appreciative. Thorn is also known for keeping the workmen in line, consistent with her high expectations.

Upfront design schemes are charged at a Reasonable rate by the hour, and a Reasonable commission is charged on product. A wide range of economic choices are considered, with a living room at anywhere from $25,000 (very low) to more typical costs. Young, new homeowners are attracted to Thorn's open views and those more established return for work on their second and third homes. ASID.

"Susan is amazing in her detailed involvement. She helped me spec all the hardware and even found antique beams for the living room when the contractor couldn't." "She is so good about retrofitting all of your current furnishings to fit into the improved space." "It was so much fun, a great example of teamwork." "Susan has phenomenal resources." "It totally looks like us, only way better than we ever could have done." "It could have been here for generations."

T. Keller Donovan Inc.   4   3.5   5   5

325 West 38th Street, Suite 1101, New York, NY 10018
(212) 760 - 0537   tkellerdonovan@aol.com

Heartwarming, colorful, traditional interior design

Clients are enchanted with T. Keller Donovan for his good humor, livable interiors and traditional design sensibility infused with flashes of contemporary whimsy. He favors crisp lines, comfortable furniture and geometric shapes. Mixing all-American traditional silhouettes in dashing colors with sleek and beguiling counterpoints is a favorite, but he can also do classic traditional with fresh appeal.

Donovan studied at Parsons and then held apprenticeships with Barbara D'Arcy, Tom O'Toole and David Easton. Starting his own firm in 1977, consistently a large part of his clientele has been based in the suburbs. He is known to be resourceful, with an eye toward economical solutions, successfully mixing Hyde Park or Pottery Barn with clients' existing furnishings. He also enjoys finding wonderful objects in Europe. Donovan does everything himself and would, according to his many supporters, have it no other way, focusing intensely on client service. He can start with just a few rooms or coordinate an extensive renovation.

The firm works with a design fee and a Reasonable markup over net on products. Living rooms can be in the $70,000 arena. References say Donovan is very professional in his business dealings and is a good listener. Even other decorators say they would happily hire him. HB Top Designers, 1999, 2000, 2001, 2002. KB 1993, 1998, 2002.

"Keller is such a sweetheart. I love his use of color and bold patterns." "I appreciate the way he mixes high style with comfortable living. He had very appropriate ideas, given the way we live." "He never guilds the lily." "The key to his decorating success is that our house does not look decorated." "He taught us everything, including how to arrange the books on the shelves." "Keller can make a cheap basket look like an exquisite ottoman, but then he loves a few rich details for balance such as hand-painted lamp shades." "He works 24/7. When he is not working, he is dreaming about improvements." "Any questions will be answered or fixed immediately." "He honored our economic priorities." "From the storyboards on, he knew exactly where we were headed." "Every room now has a purpose." "We call him 'our Keller,' taking great pride in his success."

The Interior Edge 　　　4　3.5　4　4.5
56 Arbor Street, Hartford, CT 06106
(860) 233 - 4244　www.interioredge.com

Comfortable, thoughtful, classical interior design

Joanne Riley quickly sets her clients at ease, as they know that she will make the right choices for their lifestyle and interest. Whether it be restrained opulence, subtle classicism or sleek sophistication, Riley finds the tone and depth that is appropriate. Lending a hand in the architectural details and the lighting plans and going right through to the accessories and fresh flowers, Riley works with the client to obtain a polished finished product.

Professionalism and thoroughness come naturally to Riley, who competed internationally in equestrian events after college. She soon gravitated to the family business, Simmons Furniture Company, where she learned much about marketing and management. After studying interior design at Paier College of Art, Riley was the very first employee of John LaFalce's, becoming a Senior Designer. Riley opened her own firm in 1990, where there are now five on staff, including a full time draftsman. About six projects are undertaken at a time, usually on a soup-to-nuts basis, ranging from large central Connecticut homes to New York City studios.

The firm will start with one room and has great flexibility. Budgets tend to evolve, but clients report that Riley quickly understands the scope of their economics. On the edge of a trend, The Interior Edge charges by the hour regardless of the cost of the products and passes along the net pricing to the client. Riley's easy manner and cooperative attitude result in numerous recommendations. ASID.

"Joanne always made it enjoyable." "Never felt she had an agenda, she just wanted it to work for us." "We started with a house without any character at all. Joanne made it come alive with beautiful solutions that made sense in real life." "Joanne has a gift for finding and managing excellent craftsmen. We never found anyone on our own anywhere close to Joanne's recommendations." "I never would have thought of the colors and ideas that Joanne came up with." "Her brother is an amazing theatre set designer who did the decorative painting. What a find." "I was so comfortable that Joanne would understand what we could live with in the long term. And she became a great friend in the process."

Thomas Jayne Studio Inc.　　　4.5　4.5　4　4.5
136 East 57th Street, Suite 1704, New York, NY 10022
(212) 838 - 9080　www.thomasjaynestudio.com

Historically-based, individual, spirited interior design

Heralded for his preservationist expertise in fine antiques and appreciated for his design integrity, Thomas Jayne has won the respect of his clients and peers. While retaining a historic mood, he adds whimsy with high-spirited colors and modern accents offering a heightened reality. Best known for his compositions of fine American heritage, his work broadly runs from fun to serious, from Colonial Revival to Continental, but references say it is always gorgeous. Most clients note that Jayne is also captivating company, highly focused and charmingly intent.

Jayne received a master's degree in American architecture and decorative arts from the Winterthur Museum. He then trained at Cooper Hewitt, Christie's and Parish-Hadley. Clients say he takes his training seriously and believes in "period-pure" rooms without "gimmicks" or reproductions, though he will mix styles to give these rooms a comfortable, sophisticated touch. Thomas also has creative takes on classic favorites: stenciled floor cloths in unexpected tones, hand-painted Greek key shades, framed antique scarves for color. But the architecture must be "correct before the fun can begin."

His clients are often well-funded art and antique collectors, many from the South. Projects include uptown Manhattan townhouses and apartments, as well as a variety of homes in Connecticut and Westchester ranging from a small Saltbox to a 30,000-square-foot Greenwich estate. Given the size and perspective of many of the regional commissions, these projects are often less saturated with antiques and more filled with color. Many clients are repeat customers with one or two who own five residences all decorated by Jayne. They tell us with delight that by the time the fifth house is completed, it's time to do the first over again. Jayne reportedly has a hard time saying "no" to a client, sometimes accepting more jobs than he can handle. All, however, remark that he meets the important deadlines and is "very conscientious."

The firm charges Classic retail on products and a Standard markup on antiques. Customers say Jayne has a strong preference for high-end fabrics (some quite over the top) and serious rugs. Living rooms can start low for "guerrilla decorating," and can go as high as the imagination with fine antiques. All believe that Jayne is quite earnest and honest. He is highly recommended by major collectors of American antiques and others who are looking for intelligent quality with a modern twist. HB Top Designers, 1999, 2000, 2001, 2002. KB 1996.

"No one knows how to make formal Americana sing more joyfully than Thomas." "If you give him free rein, you will get full attention." "Working with Thomas is like a really good addiction, it is hard to stop once you get going." "He knows when he is right, but patiently waits for you to come around." "Timing used to be an issue, but now he has a hyper-efficient back office." "Tom is a one-of-a kind gem. He has done eight projects for us, designing close to 100,000 square feet in total, including the family mausoleum." "He lets it slide for the kids rooms, but otherwise all the period antiques were upholstered in period-appropriate fabrics." "We actually had a very specific and reasonable budget, and Thomas did not go over." "He has a passion for doing things the right way starting with the architectural bones." "When the rectory of his church was in disrepair, he took it upon himself to refurbish." "He has amazing common sense, great judgment and an original dry wit." "He is so calm, yet so specific and clearly a genius."

Todd Alexander Romano Interior Design   4   3.5   4   4.5

1015 Lexington Avenue, New York, NY 10021
(212) 879 - 7722   toddaromano@earthlink.net

Classical, high-end, residential interior design

Todd Romano has a loyal set of clients who relate to his easy design elegance and helpful nature. Much of Romano's settings are founded on classical American motifs highlighted with unexpected colors, inherited furnishings and rich details. He is known to interweave fine antiques with quality reproductions, creating a finished product at a reasonable price. Romano often works with architect Patrick Carmody, and clients say the two make a terrific team.

The firm works with Standard design fees, Standard percentages over net and Reasonable hourly oversight fees. Romano is also available for hourly consultations. Most clients are the young carriage trade of Park Avenue or those in the suburbs referred by friends to their first real decorator. Other clients include more established homeowners who appreciate Romano's breadth of product choices. References report that Romano is willing and able to take the quality to the highest level, but that he never pushes and has many interesting sources. Project costs average in the $250,000 to $500,000 neighborhood.

He recently opened a shop at the above address with furniture ranging from eighteenth-century English to 1970s Lucite. He is highly recommended by clients for the "right look" created with good humor, thoughtfulness and high-quality workmanship. HB Top Designers, 2002.

"He took my inherited English and funky Victorian and created something beautiful." "He has great Texas warmth." "He was able to do a great job with our first apartment, and then he created a whole new, more sophisticated and polished look for our Park Avenue apartment. I can't wait to see what he will do with the country house." "The cost of the children's beds were more that I expected, but they looked great." "He is a real gentleman. While my project was not very large, I got lots of attention." "Todd even considered what colors I look best in, and flooded the house with those tones." "If I didn't like it, he would take it back." "Todd oversaw the entire operation really well." "He has a great group of custom vendors. The light fixtures were particularly fabulous and changed the whole construct of the apartment." "Timely, likable, straight down the fairway."

Todd Klein Inc.   4   4   4   4.5
27 West 24th Street, Suite 802, New York, NY 10010
(212) 414 - 0001   todd@toddklein.com
Modern interior design with traditional grounding

Color, candor and confidence draw clients time and time again to Todd Klein. Known to the upper echelons of New York society as well as appreciative newlyweds, Klein focuses on comfortable, classic designs highlighted with modern accents and punches of color. Spectacular window treatments are a signature often featuring fashion couture lines and contrast trims. This spirited give and take between the modern and the historic is what makes his designs come alive, according to loyal clients.

Klein developed his soft spot for the traditional growing up in Louisville, Kentucky. After majoring in art history at Denison, Klein returned to his hometown, first working as a retail banker, then settling into interior design, where he received a historic preservation award for his work. On moving to New York, he trained with master Albert Hadley for several years. In 1999, he formed his own firm and has been jetting around the country every since. A staff of four assists Klein, always the primary client contact, with three major projects a year. Budgets start at about $50,000 and easily fall into the million-dollar range, evolving with the process. The firm will work with new clients on just one room if the chemistry is right.

Taking its cue from architects, the practice will work on an hourly consultation basis at Standard levels (especially for clients with lots of existing antiques) or on a Standard up-front design fee, a commission on product and hourlies for non-product consultations. Clients enjoy Klein's intelligent choices and his practical, long-term approach. HB Top Designers, 2000, 2001, 2002.

"Todd introduced me to colors I never even knew existed. Now I love them." "While ABC remnants are not his normal stomping ground, he was very amenable for the kids' rooms." "Todd has the most amazing ability to see how things will come together. I could never have imagined it would have been so great from the swatches." "He really knows his antiques, incorporated mine and has unique economically viable Southern sources." "Todd stuck to the budget and encouraged us to finish over time." "Todd just gets it, which really takes the pressure off." "He is Southern-charmed and New York-edged."

	Quality	Cost	Value	Recommend?
	✚	$	◆	★

Toni Gallagher Interiors

4.5 4.5 4.5 4

10 Thistle Lane, Rye, NY 10580
(914) 967 - 3594   toniginteriors@aol.com

Gracious, polished, felicitous, traditional interior design

Transforming the client's concepts into a magical oasis of original thought, Toni Gallagher has won the admiration of many. With a palette of soft greens, crèmes and golden yellows anchoring the work, tailored furnishings are harmoniously balanced against the fine antiques collected by Gallagher on her frequent trips to England. Thus, a level of finesse is achieved that is well priced and "does not look decorator-done." Clients say she can "do it all"—from large-scale preppy to high sophistication and everything in between.

After working in investment management for several years for big banks, Gallagher started with a few smaller interior design jobs, and the clients response was so positive that she "just kept going." Eighteen years later, Gallagher keeps the touch personal with one "outstanding" assistant and only about three major jobs at a time, mostly in Rye. All clients say they feel like her top priority.

Younger people with limited budgets may work with Gallagher on an incremental basis or more frequently, whole houses are redone. Product is bought at Classic retail and workroom costs at Reasonable markups. Repeat work is the norm.

"She is the picture of patience." "It is never cookie-cutter, but polished elegance." "As the architect I found the clients to be very difficult, but Toni got along with them splendidly." "Toni has impeccable taste." "We became great friends in the process." "It is so stressful when I go about it alone, but a blast with Toni— we laughed our way through it." "Toni has a treasure trove of incredible antiques that are priced so reasonably, only available to clients." "I feel guilty and am constantly telling Toni that she should charge more." "She is the best."

V.W. Interiors, LLC

4 3 4.5 4

25 Halsey Drive, Old Greenwich, CT 06870
(203) 637 - 3348   www.vwinterior.com

Thoughtful, original interior design

With a bold palette, traditional underpinnings and a strong desire to please, Veronica Whitlock launched her design career in 1994 and is building a clientele. Rooms are carefully crafted with fine, creative manifestations of traditional form and an appreciation for historic reference. With a studied eye and excellent organizational skills, the firm reportedly works well with the most discriminating clients.

Whitlock has distinguished academic credentials in the interior design field. She graduated from the New York School of Interior Design (NYSID) with honors and from Duke University, cum laude, with a double major in studio art and art history. Whitlock has been teaching drafting and kitchen and bath design at NYSID for several years. Between academic experiences she trained at William Doyle. A sole practitioner, Whitlock has won homeowners' respect with substantial projects both regionally and in Palm Beach.

There is excellent flexibility in Whitlock's scope. She will start with a limited budget and minimal design fee. Product markups are Low. Taking the lead from the client, very fine antiques, repro or retail product may be used, but it all comes together in a coherent, genteel manner with a dash of panache. ASID. NCIDQ.

"A great listener with an academic bend." "Veronica is so incredibly responsive. Ten minutes after I call her, the vendor has already called me to answer my question." "Veronica grew up in Greenwich, did Foxcroft and just gets the whole preppy thing." "While she prefers great quality, she understands budgets." "Due to her strong industry contact, she had really original ideas. The hand-painted wallpaper is extraordinary." "Regardless of her laid-back manner, she really puts in a major effort." "A real professional."

	Quality ✚	Cost $	Value ◆	Recommend? ★

Vanderpoel Schneider Interiors

| | 4.5 | 4 | 4 | 5 |

81 Pondfield Road, Bronxville, NY 10708
(914) 663 - 8525

Warm, welcoming, English interior design

After twenty years as a Park Avenue mainstay, Sandra Schneider has taken her office to Bronxville, where she and many of her clients reside. Bringing an "authentic English traditional look," supporters applaud the classical richness and bountiful color that is "layered to perfection but never overdone." Schneider also is noted for her gracious style and efficient and dependable project management skills.

Schneider joined cousin Barrie Vanderpoel in 1984 developing an understated, yet eloquent style that pleased the most discriminating. Both principals continue to pursue design, with Schneider's clients mostly in the suburban areas. Schneider is an expert in executing complete renovations, including the purchase of antiques, and is also willing to take on one room at a time. While accommodating a wide range of budgetary choices, the designer advises clients to wait to purchase higher-quality products. A particular strength is Schneider's highly organized up-front assessment, which takes into full account the client's traffic patterns and lifestyle.

A Standard up-front design fee is charged and products are purchased at a Reasonable markup. Living rooms can range from $30,000 to $150,000, depending on the client's preferences. Patrons report that the firm's expense is clearly worth the investment and that the timeless designs remain fresh. KB 1996, 2002.

"Sandy delivers the perfect English country manor house reinterpreted—not the scary chintz look. This is the real thing." "Elegant, but completely livable for the children and the dogs." "She was incredibly accommodating about using lots of curtains and furniture from our old house." "When we could not afford the real thing, Sandy found fabulous substitutes that look the part." "It was a joy to work with Sandy, I had certain specific ideas and she took it from there." "As the mayor of a town, I have seen a lot of service providers come and go. Sandy pulls a room together like no other, and I recommend her all the time."

Victoria Hagan Interiors

| | 4.5 | 5 | 4 | 4.5 |

654 Madison Avenue, Suite 2201, New York, NY 10021
(212) 888 - 1178   www.victoriahagan.com

Elegant, eclectic, edited interior design

Noted for her sculptural, harmonious, monochromatic designs and her professionalism, Victoria Hagan stands out among the new set of contemporary designers. Clients praise the quality of her workmanship, her handsome and spare forms and her incorporation of every modern comfort. Warm velvets and cashmeres enhance clean, cerebral lines. Hagan's work is further distinguished by a generous use of fine antiques, strong architectural details, natural materials and eclectic embellishments. Designs are thoughtfully integrated into the settings. While references say that she is firm in her design opinions, they also acknowledge that she is determined to make clients happy. Hagan reportedly presents several options and works with the clients to lead them through the process.

A graduate and moard member of Parsons, Hagan founded her firm in 1991. She accepts only a few projects per year and devotes significant attention to each one. Clients include Jack Welsh in Fairfield, Revlon head Ronald Perelman, movie director Barry Sonnenfeld and the Bronfmans. While lesser knowns are taken on, project scopes remain large and serious, and none are undertaken without a specific commitment. Recent projects include a Greenwich manor house, a Westchester country home, a bucolic South Carolina retreat, and several Manhattan apartments. An exclusive architectural consultant often works on projects with Hagan.

Clients are often repeat customers. It is said that the cost of her work is quite high (with budgets usually in the generous six figures), but well worth the expense and on budget. AD 100, 2000, 2002. HB Top Designers, 1999, 2000, 2001, 2002. KB 1990.

"Victoria is thoughtful, smart and interesting to work with, but she is no pussy-cat. She gets it done." *"Her ego does not get in the way. She does what is best for the client."* *"There is a peacefulness to the finished product."* *"While a model of restraint, her designs have energy, with the unexpected in scale or form."* *"Her office does all the shopping for you. She presents three choices and does not overload you."* *"We asked Victoria to come look at the historic restoration of an important building, but she would not even talk to us without a consulting contract."* *"She makes a conscious effort to have a small, select clientele so as to not spread herself too thin."* *"To her credit she is at my girlfriend's house almost everyday. But it is a 30,000 square foot house—there is a lot to do."* *"Her designs are so livable, full of sunshine with room to breathe."*

Wadia Associates, LLC   5 4.5 4.5 5
112 Main Street, New Canaan, CT 06840
(203) 966 - 0048 www.wadiaassociates.com
Highly detailed elegant large-scale traditional architecture

 See Wadia Associates's full report under the heading Architects

Westport Interiors   3.5 3.5 4 4.5
1 Kings Highway North, Westport, CT 06880
(203) 227 - 7090 wsptint@aol.com
Interior design

 Paige Hammond is said to be able to do it all—from transitional contemporary in a historic saltbox to updated traditional in a modern-framed townhouse. While there may be leanings toward a more restrained look, many a center hall colonial have been done in the "Connecticut Classic style." Reportedly, Hammond's biggest distinguishing factor is "her ability to be creative and also businesslike." Strong communication skills and good command of the budget are also cited.

 As a Junior Leaguer volunteering in the local consignment shop, Hammond was often asked by friends for her design advice. One thing led to another, and Hammond matriculated to the University of Connecticut, received a degree in interior design and established her firm in 1976. Growing up in Bedford Hills, Hammond has strong ties to the local region and continues to give back. The designer helped redesign the Saugatuck Congregational and Christ and Holy Trinity Episcopal churches over the years. Hammond has two on staff and an extensive library of fabrics, wallpapers and trims at her design studio, which makes for an effective process.

 The firm works with Reasonable up-front design on all hours and Classic retail on product. Many clients return—one having completed seven projects with Hammond. ASID.

 "Paige has been in this market so long, I really trust her judgment." *"She did everything including the linens."* *"Paige really looked after us, especially with the architect and the contractor."* *"Paige was so good about building on what we already had."* *"She will work in phases, which has to be less efficient for her."* *"It was phenomenal what Paige did with our son's 5-foot-by-8-foot room. He has everything he needs and it looks great."* *"If she says it will work, it will get done. She totally stays on top of the tradespeople."* *"My husband and I were on the go with work during the renovation, and Paige coordinated everything. She is so practical."* *"We have recommended her to many."*

William Green & Associates   4 3.5 4 4
6 West 18th Street, 7th Floor, New York, NY 10011
(212) 924 - 2828 www.wgaarchitects.net
Residential and commercial architecture and interiors

 See William Green & Associates's full report under the heading Architects

Hiring a Kitchen & Bath Designer

The perfect kitchen won't make you a great cook, and an all-marble bathroom will still need cleaning. But the fact remains that a kitchen or bath remodel can make your life at home enormously more pleasurable on a daily basis. They are often the two rooms that see the most use, and so their planning and construction deserve careful thought. A good kitchen and bath designer will listen attentively to a client's desires and incorporate them into rooms that are as functional as they are beautiful.

Finding a Designer

Some architects, interior designers, space planners and certified remodelers dabble in kitchen and bath design. There are even "designers" who work for manufacturers and home improvements stores. But if your sights are set on a specialist, you'll want to look for a Certified Kitchen Designer/Certified Bath Designer (CKD/CBD). To get certified, the designer needs at least seven years of hands-on experience in addition to coursework, and must pass a series of tests administered by the National Kitchen and Bath Association (www.NKBA.org), the field's main professional organization. Remember, it's not a bad idea to inquire about your designer's involvement in trade organizations or whether he or she frequents trade shows. Even after certification, continuing education will enable a designer to stay abreast of current styles and the latest advances in equipment.

Most designers have either a showroom or portfolio to give you a sense of their particular style. You may think that you are on the same page when you talk on the phone, but when you see the ideas embodied in a room you may find that you have very different ideas of what a word like "contemporary" or "traditional" means. You'll be a giant step closer to getting what you want if you can find a designer whose style is similar to your own. Take a look at your prospective designer's recent work history while you're at it. At the very least, a designer should be able to produce three current references, and a history of two or more projects per month shows a healthy demand for the professional's work.

Finding someone you feel compatible with will make the whole process more pleasant and productive—especially if you see eye-to-eye on budgetary considerations. It will also help alleviate some of the inevitable stress. With the right designer, you'll be able to openly discuss such issues as project cost, time frame for completion, product information and warranty issues. You should feel comfortable asking for advice on the logical and functional placement of appliances, how to make cabinets childproof, lighting alternatives, your storage needs, personal preference for gas or electric stoves, the upkeep involved in tile kitchens vs. stainless steel and other design considerations. Also, do you want to work with the appliances you have or completely replace them? If you want new appliances, the designer may or may not coordinate their purchase. Don't assume that a designer can read your mind and know that you will not—under any circumstances—part with your matching canary yellow refrigerator and stove.

On Cost

There are generally two ways in which designers can charge for their services. The first type of pricing structure is a percentage—about ten percent—of the project's total cost. This type of fee schedule is common when the designer coordinates the entire project as well as supplies the artistic template. Coordinating the project includes ordering all materials and finding and managing the workers to install everything. This approach is often a good value. It also relieves you of having to find someone else to carry out the project, or of immersing yourself in the hassles of ordering and overseeing.

The second method of pricing is an initial fee called a retainer or pure design fee. If your designer charges a pure design fee, this means that your money buys only the designer's ideas and plans for creating the kitchen or bath of your dreams. The price will depend upon the designer's experience, education and general reputation and generally ranges from $65 to $200 or more per hour. The other possibility is a retainer fee. This usually includes the project design, and often covers the cabinetry deposit and any initial paper work necessary to get the ball rolling. In either case, most designers will deduct the initial fees from the total cost of the project as indicated on the contract.

It is imperative to discuss total cost prior to starting the job, of course, so you know what to expect. If you have your heart set on a new kitchen layout that requires new plumbing and electrical work, for example, know that this will be a more expensive renovation than one that involves existing systems. If the cost of such a renovation is more than you'd like to spend, work with the designer to match your dreams with your budget.

Once you've chosen a designer, you'll need a contract to protect both parties. No professional will be offended if you request one. The contract should spell out the services you are expecting and include a timetable for payment. Expect to part with a down payment of 40 to 50 percent to secure a good designer.

Many designers are sole proprietors, which means that the designer may be the only employee of the company. Others are part of a large firm with designers representing a range of specialty areas. Deciding whether or not to use an individual or a firm is a choice that depends upon your own style and the scope of your project: a firm's diverse collection of talent may come in handy if your project is especially complex. Some clients prefer dealing with one person, while others may feel more confident having a number of designers available. If, after speaking to a few of the vendors in this book, designers from both large and small firms interest you, make some comparisons such as their availability to begin work and how long they anticipate it will take to complete it. Their answers may help you narrow your search.

As with any major home project, you'll go through a period of upheaval when everything—including the kitchen sink—gets overhauled. But the result will be worth the trouble, whether your fantasy is to cook dinner for twenty with ease or to sink into a tiled Roman bath.

TREND IDEAS

- ✧ **In the bathroom:** When space is at a premium, installing a bathtub may not always be possible. If you can't go without soaking yourself in relaxation, give your stand-up shower the capacity to be a "steam room." All it requires is the plumbing of the steam device, a tiled seat and sealed glass door. Hint: a frameless glass shower enclosure lends a spacious and seamless look to smaller bathrooms.
- ✧ **In the kitchen:** Use an open cabinet for storing all your everyday dishes and glassware. This will break up the monotony of all-doored cabinets and comes in handy when washing dishes—you'll duck beneath open doors less frequently. Placing your everyday dishes in open cabinets may also motivate you to clear out any mismatched pieces and to better organize your frequently used tableware.

Kitchen & Bath Designers

Ann Sacks   5   5   4   5
23 East Putnam Avenue, Greenwich, CT 06830
(203) 622 - 8884   www.annsacks.com
Handcrafted tiles and luxury bathroom fixtures
　　See Ann Sacks's full report under the heading Tile, Marble & Stone

Beverly Ellsley Design Inc.   3.5   3.5   4   4
175 Post Road West, Westport, CT 06880
(203) 454 - 0503   www.beverlyellsley.com
Kitchen design and interior design, custom handmade cabinetry
　　Clients applaud the "rustic elegance" and exquisite custom cabinetry that this mother-daughter interior design duo brings to their high-end kitchen projects. Beverly Ellsley teams with daughter Rebecca to design, build and decorate entire kitchens from scratch for clients in Westchester and Fairfield counties and Manhattan. We hear the handmade cabinets are the hallmark of a Beverly Ellsley kitchen, work that has appeared in publications such as *House Beautiful.*

　　Ellsley has helmed the firm for over three decades, and we hear her staff "leaves little room for mistakes." The design professionals interact closely with clients from the beginning stages of wish lists and floor plans all the way through project completion. The firm offers a lifetime guarantee on all of its work. KB 1992, 1996, 1998, 2000.

Bilotta Home Center   4   3   5   5
564 Mamaroneck Avenue, Mamaroneck, NY 10543
(914) 381 - 7734   www.bilotta.com
Kitchen and bath design and installation
　　Responsive customer service and high-end product at a reasonable cost has boosted this firm's popularity. Known to have the best designers, and products in Westchester and Fairfield counties and favored amongst architects, designers and retail clients, Bilotta Home Center takes kitchen and bath renovations from initial designs to installation. Showrooms carry products such as Rutt, SieMatic and Wood-Mode and Clive Christian's cabinetry, along with a wide selection of natural stone and ceramic tile for countertops.

　　Jim Bilotta, Sr. established the business now run by his three children, Regina, Maria and Jim, Jr. in 1985. The company's main home center is located in Mamaroneck, with two additional showrooms in Westchester, one in Greenwich, CT and one in New York City.

　　"The Bilotta's have been such wonderful people to work with. They always returned my phone calls." "An honest company that offers quality service."

Chappaqua Kitchens, Baths & Design   4   4   4   4
39 South Greeley Avenue, Chappaqua, NY 10514
(914) 861 - 9180
Kitchen design and installation
　　Be it sleek contemporary or cozy traditional, this kitchen and bath expert is up for the design and installation challenge. Sources say owners John Vassallo and

Tom Dziena handhold clients throughout the process. We're told all work is in-house—Chappaqua custom manufactures its own cabinets and offers a wide range of door style and wood selections. Project budgets typically fall anywhere between $55,000 and $75,000.

"They are professional and knowledgeable the entire way through a project—from offering design and layout ideas to helping select the light fixtures." "They were willing to answer all of my questions without getting frustrated." "Outstanding craftsmanship. Exacting attention to detail. Stands by all commitments. Responds to problems immediately. Quality design, work and people."

Christian's of Greenwich   4   4   4   4
40 East Putnam Avenue, Greenwich, CT 06830
(203) 629 - 9417   www.clivechristian.com
Luxury kitchen and bath design and custom cabinetry

Internationally esteemed by clients and members of the industry, Clive Christian has a reputation for delivering top-quality design and installation of kitchens, bathrooms, bedrooms and dens reminiscent of the English Country tradition. Clients include many high-profile media and entertainment figures, top designers and architects. Sources say Christian's professional and knowledgeable staff will introduce clients to a variety of stock designs, that are of custom-made quality and detailing, at a lower price than most custom work. References praise the entire process of working with Christian, calling the overall experience "luxurious."

"The perfect English look with excellent quality." "A Christian kitchen is an exquisite kitchen—I recommend them for my best clients." "The staff works with you to perfection—a surprisingly good resource for issues outside of cabinetry design.

Christopher Peacock Cabinetry   4.5   4   4.5   4.5
34 East Putnam Avenue, Greenwich, CT 06830
(203) 862 - 9333   www.peacockcabinetry.com
Highly detailed custom cabinetry

Customers can't wait to show off their cabinets from Peacock. Based in Greenwich, Christopher Peacock Cabinetry opened over twenty years ago and has established a reputation for some of the finest cabinetry manufactured in the United States. We're told each piece is carefully constructed with strict attention to the smallest detail. Cabinets are primarily patterned on fine traditional English style and craftsmanship.

Once a customer's cabinets have been commissioned and completed, the company's professional installers make sure that each piece fits perfectly and that moldings and cornices are scribed on-site. Peacock offers a wide selection of stains and finishes, and its artists work to achieve the exact shade, including the various painterly effects, that each client wants.

"Extraordinary." "Quality work." "I am so happy with my beautiful kitchen cabinets." "I don't believe people can be perfect all the time, but always accountable. That is Christopher Peacock."

Culin & Colella Inc.   4   3   4.5   4.5
632 Center Avenue, Mamaroneck, NY 10543
(914) 698 - 7727   rculin@hotmail.com

Custom millwork and furniture

See Culin & Colella Inc.'s full report under the heading Millworkers & Cabinetmakers

Edelmann Kitchen, Bath & Interior Design   3.5   3.5   4   4

128 Greenwood Avenue, Bethel, CT 06801
(203) 730 - 1144

Kitchen and bath design and interior design services

After twelve successful years tailoring kitchens and baths to a Fairfield and Westchester clientele, Joseph Edelmann teams up with Chris Rowan, who contributes his interior design outlook to the outfit. Their firm designs and coordinates the construction of interior remodels, and also provides decorating services. We're told Edelmann and Rowan stay with their customers every step of the way, from choosing colors to buying knobs. The small firm takes on a significant number of jobs a year, with kitchens pricing out between $38,000 and $62,000.

Euro Concepts Ltd.   4   4   4   4

1100 Second Avenue, New York, NY 10022
(212) 688 - 9300   www.euroconceptsltd.com

High-end kitchen cabinetry design and installation

Insiders scoop that this top-tier and budget-friendly firm creates kitchens for the "decorator's decorator." Euro Concepts offers innovative designs and professional installation services, and has so for more than 30 years. Two showrooms, each in Manhattan and Huntington, carry a broad selection of high-end appliances and cabinetry ranging from the mod to the positively old-world.

"Their design team is ingenious, they were actually able to harmonize my husband's and my wacky tastes with something simpler." "They were able to create a classic yet modern space that is timeless and elegant."

Form Ltd.   3.5   4.5   3.5   4

32 West Putnam Avenue, Greenwich, CT 06830
(203) 869 - 6880   www.formlimited.com

Kitchen and bath design and installation

Form and function go hand in hand with this one-stop shop. Clients retain this firm for creative design and complete installation of kitchens and baths. Form's craftsmen also custom create libraries and dens. Working for the most part in Fairfield and Westchester counties, the company coordinates kitchen and bath projects as far away as Bermuda and Puerto Rico. We're told the displays and selections at Form's two showrooms really get clients' creative juices flowing.

Co-owners John Leontiou and John Waters founded the firm in 1987. With a staff and crew of fifteen, all work remains in-house on the firm's roughly forty to fifty projects per year. The cost of a mid to high-end Form kitchen can range between $125,000 and $200,000. A $1,000 design fee per room is applied toward the contract.

"Nothing but 'oohs' and 'aahs' from visitors. No detail is overlooked." "John Waters was always on-site making sure that everything went according as planned."

French Country Living/Provence Kitchens

34 East Putnam Avenue, Greenwich, CT 06830
(203) 869 - 9559

High-end kitchen design

	Quality	Cost	Value	Recommend?
	✚	$	◆	★

Front Row Kitchens

3.5 4 3.5 4

117 New Canaan Avenue, Norwalk, CT 06851
(203) 849 - 0302   www.frontrowkitchens.com

Kitchen design and installation

Design professionals tell us Front Row Kitchens never settles for backseat quality. The firm takes on the design and installation of kitchens small and large, traditional and contemporary. Family owned and operated since 1985, the firm has accumulated an impressed clientele from around the New Canaan vicinity.

Brother and sister team Matt Giardina and Barbara Laughton are the faces of Front Row. In addition to specializing in kitchen design, the firm also designs and supplies cabinetry for other rooms and areas of the homes such as libraries and entertainment centers.

Garth Custom Kitchens Inc.

4 4 4 4

24 Garth Road, Scarsdale, NY 10583
(914) 723 - 1223   www.garthcustomkitchens.com

Kitchen and bath design and installation

Contractors commend Garth Custom Kitchens for its splendid showroom and service-savvy staff. Principal Sam Owen, along with his team of qualified designers, is reputed to conjure up and install "amazing" and "practical" kitchens and bathrooms. We also hear Garth designs home offices, dressing rooms and closets for the firm's Connecticut and Westchester County clientele. The showroom features the finest products on the market, from Wood-Mode and Brookhaven cabinetry to Viking and Sub-Zero appliances.

"A company that clearly knows its stuff."

Godwin Inc.

4.5 3.5 5 5

215 East 58th Street, Suite 503, New York, NY 10022
(212) 308 - 0558   www.godwin-inc.com

Residential general contracting, kitchen and bath design, gut renovations

See Godwin Inc.'s full report under the heading Contractors & Builders

Kitchen Design Studio

4.5 4 4.5 4

21 South Avenue, New Canaan, CT 06840
(203) 966 - 0355   www.kitchendesignstudios.com

Kitchen design and installation

The KDS two-story showroom contains a plethora of styles, finishes and design options for customers at a relatively reasonable cost for their kitchen remodel needs. In addition to the KDS signature collection, the company also carries Imperia, Honey Brook and Rutt Handcrafted Cabinetry.

Kitchen Design Studio was established in 1990 by architect Alex Kaali-Nagy and his wife, Karen, who oversees day-to-day operations. Their team of fourteen includes award-winning kitchen designers whose work has been published in *Metropolitan Home and Garden Design* magazines. Clients say the firm's energetic staff answers any questions thrown their way.

"What is so unbelievable about Kitchen Design Studio is that their kitchens are beautiful at every price level." "The designers are detailed, service-oriented and at the top of their game."

Kitchens By Deane

5 4 4.5 5

1267 East Main Street, Stamford, CT 06902
(203) 327 - 7008   www.kitchensbydeane.com

Kitchen design and installation

Those in the know swear by this third-generation kitchen and bath design/build guru, roundly regarded as the best in the biz since 1961. Kitchen

by Deane's superb service is complemented by a diversity of products. In addition to Deane's own collection of cabinets, it sells appliances, fixtures and countertops. Sources say that whenever a problem arises, the firm's in-house service department is prompt and efficient.

Carrie Deane and her brother, Peter, now run the Stamford showroom, which boasts twenty kitchen displays, two full working kitchens and periodic cooking demonstrations. Word is the New Canaan location is equally as impressive. An in-home consultation fee and 10 percent design deposit apply to the total cost of the project. ASID.

"Kitchens by Deane was very comfortable with making decisions without being overbearing." "Carrie has been a pleasure to work with and she and her staff have been very professional." "Their attention to detail is remarkable. Whenever site conditions warranted, they were able to adopt the project to suit the altered conditions."

Kitchens Etc.   3   3   4   4

149-42 Cross Island Parkway, Whitestone, NY 11375
(718) 352 - 8818   joel@culbertsonbc.com
Kitchen remodeling, architectural detailing

In business since 1959, Kitchens Etc. designs and installs kitchens and baths for clients in Manhattan, the outer boroughs and Nassau and Westchester counties. The firm also does custom architectural work, and we hear these professionals can accommodate all styles of cabinetry. For most projects, the shop design and some of the installation work is done in-house, with the remainder of the job assigned to a team of outside subcontractors. The staff at Kitchens Etc. encourages clients to visit the company's showroom in Whitestone, which features cabinet lines such as Wood-Mode and Brookhaven, as well as a selection of kitchen appliances.

Klaff's   4.5   4.5   4   4

28 Washington Street, South Norwalk, CT 06854
(203) 866 - 1603   www.klaffs.com
Kitchen and bath design and tile and stone sales

What began in 1921 by the Klaff family as a small plumbing supply business is now a designer destination for distinctive, premium kitchen and bath products as well as design services. With three retail showrooms and two plumbing supply houses, the company offers a wide selection of lighting, kitchens, baths, accessories, decorative hardware and tile and stone.

Klaff's kitchen showroom, displaying over fifteen custom-designed kitchens, features Mark Wilkinson "fitted" furniture line from England along with Klaff's own brand of custom cabinetry. Additionally, the firm's corps of kitchen and bath designers utilize state-of-the-art computer software to conjure their cooking or bathing creations.

"All of the products sold at Klaff's are high-end and their selection is absolutely phenomenal." "I was impressed with their door hardware."

Mr. Shower Door Inc.   3.5   3.5   4   3

651 Connecticut Avenue, Norwalk, CT 06854
(203) 838 - 3667   www.mrshowerdoor.com
Frameless shower door manufacturing and installation

With a name like Mr. Shower Door, it should come as no surprise that this firm furnishes and installs custom shower doors. Clients certainly admire the appearance of the finished product, but some show less confidence in long-term follow-up and service. Still sources say that with nineteen years in the trade, Mr. Shower Door must be doing a lot right.

"Mr. Shower Door does the job." "I was very pleased with the actual shower door. However, I tried to call them years later when I had a leak and it was impossible to get them to come look at the problem."

	Quality	Cost	Value	Recommend?
	✚	$	◆	★

Nancy Mullan/ NDM Kitchens Inc., ASID, CKD

| | 5 | 3.5 | 5 | 5 |

By appointment only, New York, NY 10021
(212) 628 - 4629   www.nancymullan.com

Gourmet kitchen design, interior design and space planning

Clients call designer Nancy D. Mullan a "traditional New York Lady." Mullan's services span from full-service design to space-planning consultation for any room in the house, with kitchens and home offices her forte. From the culinary novice to the professional chef, Mullan begins each project by interviewing her clients and having them complete a ten-page questionnaire. By doing so, this expert gets an accurate idea of her clients' lifestyles and can proceed accordingly with her "inventive" designs. One customer, a caterer, used Mullan to transform her family kitchen into a professional one and told us she could not have been more pleased. References say that Mullan oversees all aspects of a job, and her subcontractors and craftsmen receive stellar reports, as well. We are told she manages the project with strict attention to detail. Clients laud her ability to finish on time and on budget, and say that during the project she's flexible, easily accessible and fun to work with.

Mullan studied at Parsons School of Design and has been practicing for twenty years. The bulk of her clientele is in New York City, New Jersey, Connecticut and Long Island and is quite high-end. In addition to designing, Mullan also consults on an hourly basis. She handles projects across the USA and as well, has done some as far afield as the Bahamas. Sources say she "designs rooms that people are drawn to." ASID. KB 1992, 1995. NCIDQ.

"She took care of everything, from soup to nuts." "Nancy and I worked as a team. Planning with her made me feel as though I had my best friend's opinion on everything!" "She is very eclectic in her abilities. I was most impressed with her hat-changing from designer/decorator to general contractor extraordinaire."

Poggenpohl Westport

| | 4 | 4 | 4 | 4 |

6 Wilton Road, Westport, CT 06880
(203) 227 - 1723   www.poggenpohl-usa.com

Innovative German kitchen design

Industry leaders laud Poggenpohl for its slick, durable German designs. The firm has something for everyone and offers a wide selection of styles, from contemporary to traditional. In order to design kitchens that not only suit their clients' needs, but also their budgets, Poggenpohl separates its selection into eight different price groups. At the forefront of high-end kitchen design and cabinetry for more than 100 years, Poggenpohl has a worldwide network of showrooms, including one in Westport. This showroom offers wood veneers and high-gloss lacquers along with stainless steel and glass accents. Poggenpohl also sells countertops available in teak and exotic granite and limestone.

"The process of choosing finishes, concept and design and development was exciting and the result is a dream kitchen. My wife calls it her stress reliever." "It's not a perfect world and creating and installing a kitchen is no exception— however, the Poggenpohl kitchen experience was first rate by comparison." "I was very impressed not only with how the Poggenpohl kitchens looked, but they were also incredibly functional."

SBD Kitchens, LLC   4.5   4.5   4   5

215 Cross Ridge Road, New Canaan, CT 06840
(203) 972 - 8341   www.sbdkitchens.com
Kitchen sales, design and installation

This talented, generous firm makes the experience a treat, while delivering a product clients savor. Able to design and install kitchens for the most complicated spaces, the SBD design team insures each project reflects the lifestyle of the client. Industry leaders and homeowners alike rave that the folks at this firm "get along with everybody" and always seem to go above and beyond the call of duty.

"I have used SBD for numerous projects and I absolutely love their personali- ties." "I have never had them not be nice and pleasant to my clients." "Fine attention to detail." "Not only do I now have a beautiful country kitchen, but they threw in a spice rack and compost bucket."

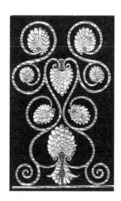

Smallbone of Devizes   4.5   4   4   4

105/109 Fulham Road, London, UK SW3 6RL
(011 - 44 - 20) 7838 - 3636   www.smallbone.co.uk
Fine hand-painted English cabinetry, custom design and installation

High-quality painted cabinetry is Smallbone of Devizes' hallmark. The London- based firm has an elite following in New York and other high-design hubs worldwide. This firm claims to allow clients to choose "any color from the twenty or so the human eye can detect" and will paint each piece by hand, according to client-specified painting techniques. Smallbone uses a variety of woods for its cabinet construction, the most popular choices being oak, olive ash, sycamore, pine, teak, maple and chestnut. Smallbone also designs custom fur- niture and wall paneling.

The firm operates from overseas, so choosing its services can be a big com- mitment. To insure optimum client relations, the firm assigns a personal design team consisting of designers, a draftsperson and a professional installation man- ager to each project. Some clients report that the quality is not quite up to the price, while others are completely satisfied, praising the designs as "free-flowing, stately and elegant." KB, 2001.

Springline Inc./Michael R. Golden   5   3.5   5   5

205 West 89th Street, New York, NY 10024
(917) 446 - 0278   springline@mac.com
Tile mosaics, hand-carved stone, terrazzo and scagliola treatments

See Springline Inc./Michael R. Golden's full report under the heading Tile, Marble & Stone

Waterworks

	4.5	4.5	4.5	5

23 West Putnam Avenue, Greenwich, CT 06830
(203) 869 - 7766   www.waterworks.com

High-end bathroom design, sales and installation referral

Clients know Waterworks as a high-end bathroom outfitter offering top-quality project support and service for its luxurious products. Both the trade and private clients tell us this is the place for someone who is serious about creating a sophisticated, elegant, albeit pricey, bathroom.   While qualified Waterworks sales associates guide you through the design and spec phase, we hear they do advocate bringing an interior designer or architect on board for any involved project. Tips on the process and commentary by featured designers can be found at the company's handsome, helpful website.

Waterworks works closely with contractors, providing tile and stone samples, facilitating quotes and bidding packages and providing tech support. Products include fittings, fixtures and tubs, bath accessories, lighting, furniture, kitchen and bar, textiles and personal care and apothecary. Waterworks does not install, but will refer clients to a stable of trusted professionals. Its service associates coordinate and track delivery of materials and will even visit a site to troubleshoot for proper installation. The company maintains a complete parts department and offers a lifetime warranty.

The very top decorators and architects depend on Waterworks for its unique and "ultimate quality-products that last a lifetime." Homeowners often believe that by using Waterworks lines, they can get that "high-class, decorator look," while avoiding the cost of the decorator. Waterworks has additional showroom locations in Danbury and Westport.

"Their lighting is inexpensive, quick ship and well made. It's so good-looking that it might just find it's way into other rooms in your home." "The word 'no' is seldom in their vocabulary." "They sell one of the narrowest tubs available and it will fit in most situations—it is also nice and deep." "It is one-source shopping— even down to accessories and bath linens."

White Birch Builders, LLC

	3.5	3	4	4

18 Beech Street, Greenwich, CT 06830
(203) 531 - 0300   www.whitebirchbuilders.com

Remodels, renovations and additions

See White Birch Builders, LLC's full report under the heading Contractors, & Builders

Hiring a Landscape Architect/Designer

Signing up someone who understands your exterior space is an extension of the design intent of the interior is key in choosing a landscaping professional. The ultimate refuge is your very own green space where sunlight, plants, flowers, walkways, trellises—or simply a colorful flower box in the window—creating a delightful escape. The artisans who turn these dreams into reality are garden designers, horticulturists and landscape architects. Experts in both art and science, these professionals create natural havens in any type of space. Garden and landscape designers use plants and masonry to plan, design and construct exterior spaces—in the city, the suburbs or the countryside.

More Than Planting

Planning a garden paradise for your surroundings is a job for professionals, as many technical elements are involved. Garden designers create water and soil systems that are unique to city landscapes, and their craft requires a complex blend of botanical knowledge, construction expertise and creativity. Suburban or country projects can be more or less involved, incorporating large trees and bushes, masonry and rock formations, ponds and streams.

Service providers included in *The Franklin Report* reveal a common thread—artistry combined with a passion for creating the ultimate natural space to suit each client's unique habitat.

Where Do I Start?

The most general decision to make about your garden or country landscape is what type of purpose it will serve. Are you a cook who loves using fresh ingredients and would like to build an herb, vegetable or cutting garden? Have you discovered the joy of exotic plants and wish to install a greenhouse for your orchids? Or are you dreaming of a superbly designed terrace with benches and several layers of growth? With your overall purpose in mind, take stock of the space available in and around your home. Is privacy—building a hedge to separate your yard from your neighbor's—an important issue? Do you prefer the informal charm of an English cottage garden or the elegance of a neoclassical French one? Keep in mind that the more complicated the design, the more maintenance there is involved. Nurture your ideas by looking through home, garden and architecture magazines before you contact a garden designer.

Foremost in a landscape designer's mind is building a setting that can be enjoyed year round. The designer will have many ideas for you, but if you have done some research and fallen in love with specific plants and flowers, you will be a step ahead in designing your perfect oasis.

On Cost

The pricing system for landscape design varies from firm to firm. Some designers charge an hourly rate—others determine a flat fee after analyzing the job. The average hourly rate in Fairfield and Westchester counties is between $50 and $75, translating into a baseline of 3 for Cost in our book. Like other professional services, garden design companies will produce a written agreement for the client that lists what will be done and at what cost. It is not unusual for these agreements to leave room for flexibility in scheduling and pricing, should unforeseen circumstances, such as bad weather delaying the work, affect the job.

WILL A DESIGNER ALSO MAINTAIN MY GARDEN?

Services provided by garden designers vary from firm to firm and depend on the scope of your project. Many companies provide a complete package of design, installation and maintenance, and thus establish a long-term relationship with the client. Other professionals are limited to design and consulting, and subcontract for installation and maintenance. Landscape projects can vary drastically in size and detail and therefore in degrees of maintenance. Discuss these aspects with your designer and make sure you're aware of the amount of attention your yard or garden will require. Like interior designers, garden designers, horticulturists and landscape architects work closely with clients on a one-to-one basis to bring their creative ideas to fruition.

PERMITS AND PROFESSIONAL CONSIDERATIONS

A garden-design project that includes structural hardscape may require permits. Designers are well-schooled in this process. No license is required to be a garden or landscape designer, and these green specialists come from a variety of educational backgrounds, including degrees in horticulture, study programs affiliated with arboretums and botanical gardens, degrees in sculpture and other studio arts and lifetime experiences with plants and nurseries. Landscape architects, many of whom focus primarily on the hardscape aspects of garden design rather than on horticulture and maintenance, have degrees in the field and are licensed.

There are organizations such as the Association of Professional Landscape Designers (APLD) that continually educate the landscaping field by offering classes and conferences. Although it is not necessary for the landscape architect or designer to be a member of such an organization, it certainly enhances their qualifications. All the those drawn to the garden design profession, especially those devoted to the challenges of city landscapes, undoubtedly share the view of Thoreau, who wrote, "In wildness is the preservation of the world."

HERBACEOUS PLANTS FOR ALL SEASON INTEREST

- ✧ **Asarum europaeum "European Wild Ginger"** An excellent ground cover for the woodland garden. The heart shaped leaves are glossy, dark green and it is evergreen in most places. This is a very hardy and lovely woodland plant.
- ✧ **Helleborus orientalis "Lenten Rose"** One of the finest early flowering plants in cultivation. The flowers begin in March and go through May. It also has semi-evergreen foliage and so it stays attractive during much of the winter. It needs to be cut back in early spring.
- ✧ **Liriope muscari 'Silvery Sunproof' "Lily Turf"** A sturdy member of the Lily family, the Liriope also bears very attractive lavender flowers in the fall. It can grow almost anywhere and is very easy to get established.
- ✧ **Pennisetum alopecuroides "Fountain Grass"** Great all season grass. Has attractive lowers during the summer and fall. This grass has great winter interest. Very handy, but can be slow to get established.
- ✧ **Sasa veitchii "Low Bamboo"** Summer foliage is a solid green and in the fall the leaf margins develop a tan to white border. The characteristic marginal stripe gives an attractive variegated appearance for outstanding winter foliage. It spreads slowly and grows well in the shade.
- ✧ **Vinca minor 'Ralph Shugert' "Myrtle"** Very pretty low variegated ground cover that is covered with purple flowers in the spring.

LANDSCAPE ARCHITECTS/DESIGNERS

Ann Catchpole-Howell — 4 4 4 4
448 Long Ridge Road, Bedford, NY 10506
(914) 764 - 4317   gardnergb@aol.com
Personalized garden consultation and maintenance

Interior designers and pleased clients say that Ann Catchpole-Howell is the lady to call if your gardens are in desperate need of some TLC. Catchpole-Howell specializes in taking gardens that have been overlooked and returning them to a pristine state. She calls herself "gardener for a day." Catchpole-Howell and two subcontractors visit clients and take care of anything outside that needs attention and transform gardens by adding special touches such as correctly placed plants. She will do anything from designing, pruning and weeding to transplantation. Clients rave that Catchpole-Howell is amazing at advising her clients in regards to the proper placement and maintenance of their plants. She also stays mindful and respectful of their budgets.

Formerly a fashion designer in England, Catchpole-Howell became interested in gardening from her mother, who had a true love of gardens and the outdoors. After taking courses at the New York Botanical Gardens, Catchpole-Howell furthered her understanding of the "classical bones" of the garden. Whether she visits your home once a week or once a month, rest assured she will have your estate in tip-top shape in no time. The company charges $950 for an eight-hour day, and that includes three workers.

"*I absolutely fell in love with Ann because she was completely approachable and I trusted her advice.*"

Anne Homer Polk & Associates — 3.5 4.5 3.5 4
PO Box 456, Bedford, NY 10506
(914) 234 - 3261   annepolk@aol.com
Residential landscape and swimming pool design

Anne Homer Polk has been designing residential landscapes and swimming pools for more than 25 years. Polk specializes in rare and unusual plant material. Her designs are not overly complicated and exhibit a strong architectural theme, creating a connection between the house and the landscape. Polk can design gardens that range from formal to naturalistic. Along with her two associates and two crews, she takes on projects throughout Westchester County, New York City and Nantucket.

Polk has a strong background in art history and sources say she has "an artistic and creative eye for designing the phenomenal." She also travels all over the world, attending various landscape seminars. Clients say that Polk is a master at educating her clients about plant care and maintenance and that she follows up on a regular basis. She is also commended for her flexibility and for forming long-lasting relationships with her customers. An average project is in the $100,000 range.

Anne Penniman Associates, LLC — 4 4 4 4
PO Box 181 2 South Main Street, Essex, CT 06426
(860) 767 - 7540   ap@annepenniman.com
Landscape architecture and site planning

Architects and interior designers roundly praise Anne Penniman for her ability to combine amazing landscape designs with a strong sensitivity to ecology and the environment. Penniman's landscapes range from naturalistic to formal in style and she is a pro at taking the historical and cultural influences of the home into consideration when creating her landscapes. Because she works closely with architects on a project, she has become well-versed in the architecture arena. Clients also report that Penniman has proven to be a "master at mediating" between the client and the contractor—a talent that is often hard to find.

Sources say that Penniman's formal education and training in landscape architecture has given her not only a plethora of knowledge, but that she understands and has high standards when it comes to taking care of the land. Penniman graduated from the University of Virginia in 1986 with a master's in landscape architecture. In 1990, she started her firm that now consists of another in-house landscape architect and one administrative assistant. Together with her small team, they have completed projects from Connecticut to Rhode Island, with many repeat clients. Penniman charges either hourly or for the total cost of a project and has an average of twenty to twenty-five clients per year.

"A charming lady with an incredible wealth of knowledge."

Armand Benedek & Glenn Ticehurst Ltd.   4.5   4   4.5   4
448H Old Post Road, Bedford, NY 10506
(914) 234 - 9666   www.abgtla.com
Landscape architecture and swimming pool design

Past clients and industry leaders praise partners Armand Benedek and Glenn Ticehurst for being well versed in a wide range of landscape design styles. This firm can design everything from Japanese Gardens to natural pools to traditional perennial gardens.

Leading his pack of stellar landscape architects and designers, Benedek has over 40 years of landscape design and architecture experience. He studied Environmental Design at the University of Georgia and continued his education at the University of Massachusetts and Cornell. His partner, Ticehurst, has an equally impressive background with over twenty years of experience and is a graduate of the State University of New York's College of Environmental Science and Forestry at Syracuse. The company's projects have been featured in *Architectural Digest* and *House & Garden*.

"As I began the renovation of the grounds surrounding our 1740s farmhouse and barn, I wanted to work with a landscape architect that could create a visually interesting enclosure while remaining sensitive to the unique history of the area. Armand has notable experience in the Bedford area—his plans enhance and yet respect the original landscape." "I was impressed by his conscious attempt to design a natural looking property hedge. It is filled with varied elements of interest, giving onlookers the impression that the plantings have always been here." "Armand's sensitivity to scale and knowledge of the traditional plantings native to our region were key in our project."

Better Lawns & Gardens   ▱   ▱   ▱   ▱
10 Thornhill Road, Riverside, CT 06878
(203) 637 - 4062
Landscape maintenance

Connecticut Arborists Inc.   4   3   4.5   5
501 Pepper Street, Monroe, CT 06468
(203) 459 - 0737   ctarborist@aol.com
Tree care service and maintenance

Customers say that when it comes to tree care, Connecticut Arborists has climbed to new heights of providing superb service and quality. Owner, Don Parrott, established the company eight years ago. Along with his crew of eight, Parrott prunes, fertilizes and cares for thousands of trees in and around the Fairfield area. In addition to taking on new clients, Connecticut Arborists also offers routine annual tree care that we hear is "amazing." They even send out notices to clients when it is time for a tree check-up.

The firm charges per hour and per man. Parrott oversees every project, making sure to leave no leaf unturned. All of their clients come via word of mouth, a true testament to their high-quality service.

"I really appreciated Don's straightforward and honest work ethic." "Not only is the work they do for me amazing and consistent, but I love Don's Boston accent." "They are a company that really knows how to care for and maintain trees." "Don knows his trees and will personally climb 30 feet to get to a dead branch before it falls on you or your pet." "As a landscape architect, I continually recommend Connecticut Arborists to my clients—they are friendly, honest and dependable while being professionally capable as well."

Cornerstone Contracting Group   5   4.5   4.5   5
23 Benedict Place, 2nd Floor, Greenwich, CT 06830
(203) 861 - 4200   www.cornerstone-builders.com
High-end custom residential construction and landscaping

See Cornerstone Contracting Group's full report under the heading Contractors & Builders

Cummin Associates   5   5   4   5
114 Water Street, Stonington, CT 06378
(860) 535 - 4224
Landscape design

Clients from the Hamptons to Chicago tell us that Peter Cummin's charming personality and jaw-dropping landscapes instantly win them over. Hardly a Yankee, Peter Cummin is a Connecticut-based, English-born landscape architect, known around the world for his talent as a horticulturist. Although his architect and interior design clients nominated Cummin Associates for inclusion in history's all-time "Who's Who" of landscape architecture, Cummin himself still describes the company he founded in 1985 as a "boutique."

Cummin's interest in horticulture began during childhood, and his dedication to the company's projects prompts him to visit them often, even after the plans are completed. Clients have high praise for the firm's professionalism and for Cummin's own skills and character. Various projects have been featured in *Architectural Digest* and *House & Garden*.

"Peter is a walking plant encyclopedia." "Fabulous landscape design."

Deborah Nevins   5   4.5   4.5   5
270 Lafayette Street, Suite 903, New York, NY 10012
(212) 925 - 1125
Landscape design, installation and maintenance

Interior designers and clients from all over the United States rank this firm at the top of the compost heap, which, in the world of horticulture, is a high honor. This small company of six designs and installs gardens in New York and has worked as far afield as Chicago, Texas and California.

According to clients, Nevins creates gardens that are not only spectacular in the spring but in the winter as well. Paying close attention to the structural elements of rooftop terraces and gardens is one reason why sources say Nevin's company is one of the best in the industry. Nevin's interest in gardens and horticulture began during childhood and prompted her to found the company in 1983. She personally visits the company's gardens, regardless of location, to oversee maintenance plans and procedures.

Delalla & Von Ohlson, LLC   ◻   ◻   ◻   ◻
30 Old Quarry Road, Suite 203, Ridgefield, CT 06877
(203) 438 - 6643
Landscape architecture

	Quality +	Cost $	Value ◆	Recommend? ★

Devore Associates
2557 Burr Street, Fairfield, CT 06430
(203) 256 - 8950
Landscape architecture

	Quality	Cost	Value	Recommend?
Devore Associates	4	4	4	5

Edmund Hollander Landscape Architect Design PC
153 Waverly Place, 3rd Floor, New York, NY 10014
(212) 473 - 0620   www.hollanderdesign.com
Landscape architecture, swimming pool design and environmental planning

	Quality	Cost	Value	Recommend?
Edmund Hollander Landscape	5	5	4	4.5

Edmund Hollander and partner, Maryanne Connelly, have established one of the most prestigious landscape architecture firms in New York City and its surrounding areas. Started in 1990, the company has offices in New York City and Sag Harbor with a staff that includes twelve landscape architects. Taking on around 40 projects at a time, Hollander works in Greenwich, Bedford, the Hamptons, Virginia and has even worked as far as the Caribbean and the United Kingdom. The company specializes in residential and estate landscapes, historic landscapes, vineyard properties, swimming pool design and horse farms. We hear that Hollander and Connelly have an outstanding knowledge of architectural elements and are capable of taking care of the smallest details in addition to the big picture.

Hollander received a history degree from Vassar and holds a Master of Landscape Architecture from the University of Pennsylvania. Some of the finest architects in the business say that Hollander's work is unparalleled when it comes to both master planning and choosing sophisticated plant material. His impressive projects have been published in *Architectural Digest, The New York Times* and *House Beautiful*, to name a few. Although the company's work comes with a price tag that starts at around $250,000, architects rave that you will get a design that far exceeds your expectations.

"Ed is a great guy to work with."   *"They can design anything and everything."*

Ellen Hines
115 Plumtrees Road, Bethel, CT 06802
(203) 744 - 1478
Residential landscape architecture

	Quality	Cost	Value	Recommend?
Ellen Hines	3.5	3.5	4	4

Ellen Hines has been creating landscapes in all areas of Fairfield and Westchester counties since 1989. Sources say that Hines is a true professional when it comes to establishing strong relationships with her clients. She does not have a particular style, but rather blends her client's vision with the architectural style of the home and the site. Contractors tell us that the result of her recipe yields an outdoor masterpiece. Hines does not do landscape maintenance, but she takes on about two dozen projects per year that vary in size and style. Her fees and prices also vary accordingly. She received a BS in landscape architecture from Cornell and fans say that her hard work has definitely paid off.

Florence Boogaerts Garden Design
316 Valley Road, Cos Cob, CT 06807
(203) 629 - 1297   www.boogaerts.com
Landscape design and installation

	Quality	Cost	Value	Recommend?
Florence Boogaerts Garden Design	4.5	4.5	4	4.5

Since 1988, Florence Boogaerts was the landscape designer at Sprainbrook Nursery in Scarsdale, New York, where she designed and supervised the installation of gardens and landscapes. In the spring of 2003 Boogaerts started her own

business working for clients, primarily in Westchester and Connecticut, though she does some work in Manhattan. According to clients, Boogaerts strives to create maintainable and beautiful landscapes. "I like it when clients have something specific in mind. Then, I can give it to them in a tasteful, practical manner," Boogaerts says. While she does not offer long-term maintenance, clients have been thrilled with her creations.

Boogaerts received her certificate in landscape design from the New York Botanical Garden, where she has lectured since 1994. In addition to a flat design fee, Boogaerts charges an hourly fee that ranges from $85 per hour to $150 per hour. Sources comment on her warmth, dry wit and intelligence, and call her designs and installations "appropriate" and "exactly what I hoped for."

"Florence is a very talented designer. She is always prompt with meetings and does good work." "She was lovely to do business with and is honest and creative." "Florence's design work is both imaginative and sensible." "I have used Florence several times over the years—both alone and with a landscape architect. She is practical and has great ideas."

Focal Point Outdoors, LLC   4   4   4.5   4.5
151 Sound Beach Avenue, Old Greenwich, CT 06870
(203) 698 - 3260
Outdoor and landscape lighting design and installation

Light and landscapes intersect at Focal Point. Steve Lancia's firm designs, installs and maintains landscape and outdoor lighting systems with what clients call "imaginative ideas and excellent implementation." They will also assemble any wooden garden structure, such as gazebos and trellises. Focal Point works mostly with homeowners and landscapers, "painting pictures with light" in the gardens of its Westchester, Fairfield and NYC clients.

No other lighting guru is as landscape-friendly as Lancia, who holds a degree in forest biology and is both a certified landscaper and lighting designer. Plying his unique combination of talent since 1983, Lancia formed Focal Point in 1999. The firm consists of two electricians and two technicians, with Lancia on top of design. Projects are run casually, with everything, including contract documents, kept simple. Jobs range from the $120 minimum to your wildest (and most expensive) dreams.

"Exceeded our expectations! Focal Point succeeded in completing the project ahead of schedule. Steve's designs were creative yet functional." "Reliable, fun and easy to work with." "Steve approached the project with the earnest desire to satisfy the outcome my wife and I had expected and promptly corrected anything that was not done to our satisfaction."

Fulton Landscape Design Inc.
27 Tait Road, Greenwich, CT 06830
(203) 637 - 1637
Landscape design

Garden Designs by Jody Staunton   4   4   4   4.5
38 Wilson Avenue, Rowayton, CT 06853
(203) 838 - 4010   www.jodysgardendesigns.com
Landscape design and perennial gardening services

We hear that Jody Staunton is a master at combining her clients' visions with their lifestyle in order to create original, timeless works of art. Staunton's love for landscape design blossomed while watching and helping her father maintain his vegetable garden. Since 1993, Staunton has taken her love of the natural world and plants and made it her profession. While she designs all projects herself, she uses subcontractors to complete the installations. Sources say that her crews are polite and pleasant to deal with. She also uses one other person to help her with maintaining her gardens since she is a firm believer that "a garden is never complete." Staunton's style depends on the actual site of the project, blending the home with nature.

Staunton received her undergraduate degree from the University of Vermont and studied in the Landscape Design program at Radcliff College. She completed her studies by receiving a professional certificate in landscape design from the New York Botanical Garden in 1992. While Staunton has been known to take on projects for as little as a few thousand dollars, her completed projects range from $5,000 to $300,000. She charges $125 per hour for her design services. Staunton has been featured in *The New York Times* and *House Beautiful*, true testimonials of her talent.

"Good sense of design and space. Great listener." "Jody does not cut corners." "Friendly and reliable crews." "Jody presents comprehensive design with in-depth knowledge of plant material. She has an impressive list of references." "We will definitely use her services again." "Our garden gets rave reviews from all who pass by." "She is careful to watch costs and respects clients' budgetary parameters."

Glen Gate Company   4   4   4   4

644 Danbury Road, Box 724, Wilton, CT 06897
(203) 762 - 2000   www.glengatecompany.com
Swimming pool design, installation maintenance and landscape design

See Glen Gate Company's full report under the heading Swimming Pools–Construction & Maintenance

Green Earth Gardens   4   4   4   4.5

7005 Shore Road, Suite 2F, Brooklyn, NY 11209
(718) 836 - 1754   plantsmen@aol.com
Landscape design, installation and maintenance

We hear the Green Earth Gardens' client list includes the most demanding elite and upscale boutiques for projects large and small. The company, owned and operated by James Johnson, is a small landscape design firm that can handle very big projects. Creating gardens in every style, clients tell us Johnson and his crew design, install and maintain landscapes throughout New York City, Connecticut and beyond. In his effort to realize his clients' dreams, Johnson has, since the firm's inception in 1994, reportedly designed and installed everything from a rain forest (which actually rains) to a dry Zen landscape. Sources say he also oversees the Narrows Botanical Gardens in Brooklyn. There he has installed a variety of gardens, including a sandbox that he converted into a water garden and a native plant garden. At 4.5 acres, it is the largest community garden in New York City and is visited by thousands each year.

Johnson finds designing for ten acres or a terrace equally challenging, saying, "I can create just as much surprise and intrigue in both spaces." Sources completely support his assertions, calling his designs "truly exciting."

"Very skilled." "Adaptable."

Greg Yale Landscape Illumination   4.5   4   4.5   4

27 Henry Road, Southampton, NY 11968
(631) 287 - 2132
Landscape lighting design, installation and maintenance

Sources praise Greg Yale's careful planning and the balanced, subtle effects and glare-free lighting schemes. A nationally recognized expert in the landscape lighting field, it is said Yale has been working to inform and reshape the landscape architecture and design world through lighting. Landscape lighting has been steadily growing as a significant niche within the lighting design world and an important part of landscape architecture and design. Sources say customers are discovering that carefully planned illumination of the natural environment can beautify their properties, extend hours of garden use and contribute to home security.

"A master." "His lighting reshaped our property. At night, looking out, we can still enjoy our garden. It's just beautiful."

| | Quality | Cost | Value | Recommend? |

Gro Pro Landscape Company — 3.5 4 4 4

151 Sound Beach Avenue, Old Greenwich, CT 06870
(203) 637 - 2004   www.groprogardens.com

Landscape design and installation, swimming pool design

Gro Pro landscaping is a full-service design/build company capable of designing and installing projects ranging from small specialty gardens to full master plans which details the layout for a properties masonry, plantings, pool and driveway. Offering free consultations, Gro Pro charges a minimal design fee depending on the scope of the work. One-third of the fee is applied towards installation costs.

Serving the areas of Westchester and Fairfield counties, Gro Pro currently employs over 30 people including an in-house landscape architect. Established in 1986 by Peter Grunow, the company's steady growth can be attributed to its strong foundation of good design sense and an unyielding commitment to integrity.

Peter developed his passion for landscaping from his mother, an accomplished garden designer. Upon earning a degree in business, Peter continued to refine his horticulture skills studying at the New York Botanical Garden.

"Peter is a fabulous landscape designer." "His work can transform how a house looks."

Halsted Welles Associates Inc. — 4 3.5 4.5 4.5

287 East Houston Street, New York, NY 10002
(212) 777 - 5440

Landscape design, installation, maintenance

Halsted Welles is commended by customers for his ability to do it all when it comes to landscaping. The firm brings engineering, architecture, horticulture, construction and maintenance together under one roof. Welles, the owner and main designer, came to landscape design through a background in sculpture. Involved in "a little of everything," the firm does fireplace planning, masonry and metalwork from ornamental iron to elaborate aluminum gazebos. The company has over 30 years of experience and includes a multi-talented crew of architects, horticulture designers and artisans.

Clients appreciate the way Halsted Welles Associates handles every aspect of garden design, including hardscape features like arbors and pergolas, garden lighting, irrigation systems, pools and fountains and all plant design and installation. According to Welles, the firm's current passion is "the design of gardens and garden processes that are ecologically sensitive, including water nutrient recycling, water tables to limit the need for irrigation and nontoxic pest control."

"Amazing maintenance team." "Totally in-depth service—one stop shopping." "I have great respect for Halsted and his company. They are extremely talented, reliable and thorough."

Hamady Architects — 4.5 4 4.5 5

656 Broad Axe Road, Charlottesville, VA 22903
(434) 977 - 5592

Services and specialities

See Hamady Architects's full report under the heading Architects

	Quality +	Cost $	Value ◆	Recommend? ★

Highland Design · 4.5 · 4 · 4.5 · 4.5

30 Westchester Avenue, Pound Ridge, NY 10576
(914) 764 - 5480   mosscott@optononline.net

Landscape design and planting

Insiders describe Tim Paterson as, "exquisitely Scottish, very sensitive, talented, and a craftsman who can handle large projects." Paterson established Highland Design twelve years ago after studying landscape architecture at the University of Edinburgh. According to architects and contractors, he is gifted at garden design and specialty maintenance. We also hear that he "knows what it takes" to keep your garden growing and evolving. Paterson and his crew of five do the design and installation, while he subcontracts any hardscape work. Projects range from $25,000 to $300,000. Clients rave that Paterson has an amazing eye for design and is a dream to work with.

"Tim has exceptional taste and a complete understanding of understated elegance. He will forever persuade me to put a smaller plant to assure its success in the future." "He embraces the environment he is working in first, and then begins the formulation of a plan, unlike most landscape designers who always have the same formula for every client." "Tim has the wonderful ability to create country in the suburbs."

IQ Landscapes · 4 · 4 · 4 · 4

326 Bedford Road, Bedford Hills, NY 10507
(914) 666 - 6024

Landscape architecture and design

J.P. Franzen Associates Architects · 4.5 · 3.5 · 5 · 4.5

95 Harbor Road, Southport, CT 06890
(203) 259 - 0529

Adaptive, high-end custom residential, commercial and institutional architecture

See J.P. Franzen Associates Architects's full report under the heading Architects

Jane Gil Horticulture · 4.5 · 3 · 5 · 5

290 Riverside Drive, New York, NY 10024
(212) 316 - 6789   janeagil@aol.com

Landscape design, installation and maintenance

Sources praise Gil's talents as a horticulturist and designer and say that her client care and attention to detail are "top-notch." We hear Gil designs, creates and maintains many gardens, including those of several illustrious clients in Greenwich and Riverdale. Overseeing all aspects of garden creation and care, clients say Gil and her three-man crew install all plants, supervise tree maintenance and take care of all irrigation and grounds issues. She tells us, "When I take on a new client I first determine their particular needs and preferences. Then, using my suggestions, we work together to create a garden that is unique to them."

After leaving her position as the plant buyer at Surroundings, an established New York City plant supplier, Jane Gil embarked on extensive horticulture training at the New York Botanical Garden. Sources say Gil does not limit herself to a single garden style, but rather uses her wide knowledge of plant material to create gardens specifically tailored to each individual client's taste. She strives to create variety for her clients to enjoy throughout the four seasons. According to clients, Gil has done just that.

"Jane's work is outstanding." "Her gardens are very unique and cause passers by to stop and comment on their natural beauty." "My experience with Jane has been fabulous in every way. She has worked for us responsibly, creatively, intelligently and energetically for twenty years." "The most wonderful aspect of her work is the full, unending palette that's always changing." "Jane is great to work with and has incredible taste."

	Quality	Cost	Value	Recommend?

Janice Parker Landscape Design

| | 4 | 3.5 | 5 | 5 |

52 Wakeman Hill Road, Sherman, CT 06784
(860) 350 - 4497 www.janiceparker.com
Landscape architecture and design, swimming pool design

Janice Parker is roundly praised for being able to "read clients and deliver a project which always exceeds their expectations." Parker has been in the landscape business for over eighteen years. Her oldest memories are of peonies and ever since she has been pursuing her love of plants and flowers. Parker has three employees, including an in-house landscape architect. Always devoted to her customers, Parker chooses her clientele carefully, establishing relationships that are able to evolve with her designs. We also hear that every project she does "reflects the client and is unique, timeless and utterly beautiful.

Educated at Parson's in New York City and having studied abroad in England, Parker also teaches classes at the New York Botanical Gardens. Working primarily in Connecticut and Westchester, she has also completed projects in New York City and as far as Florida. The firm charges a design fee that ranges from $3,000 to $15,000 depending on the size of the project. The firm is also commended for donating their design services to charities such as the New York Restoration Project.

"*Janice is very knowledgeable of plant material and has a keen eye for detail in assembling trees, shrubs and flowers. Definitely a unique designer in the industry.*" "*She provided constant supervision and ensured that the plans were complete. She made constant improvements as the project progressed and managed the subcontractors well.*" "*We've worked together twice and each time, I came out with a truly enviable project. She would always be my first choice.*"

Jean Brooks

875 Main Street, 1st Floor, Cambridge, MA 02139
(617) 354 - 0643 www.jeanbrookslandscapes.com
Landscape design

Katie Brown

| | 4 | 3.5 | 5 | 4.5 |

399 Riversville Road, Greenwich, CT 06831
(203) 622 - 0250
Landscape design and swimming pool design

Gardens designed by Katie Brown are described by her clients as "elegant and charming without being pretentious." For over twenty years, Brown has been creating gorgeous landscapes throughout Fairfield and Westchester counties. Although Brown considers herself to be an independent landscape designer (with Cheryl Bailey), she still takes on between twenty to thirty projects per year. Brown can design anything from simple flower beds to swimming pools. Once the design process is completed, we hear that Brown is a "phenomenal mediator" between the client and the contractor, insuring that her designs are implemented correctly.

Brown's background in art history, along with a certificate in landscape design from The New York Botanical Gardens, has given her a strong foundation for designing backyards using a wide array of colors and textures. Brown charges an hourly rate of $125 for design.

"*Katie has vision, imagination, drive and is a total pleasure in partnership with all of her colleagues on any project.*" "*She is a dynamo. The gardens she designs are spectacular without being overdone and each keeps with the individual setting.*" "*Impeccable taste.*" "*Creative, reassuring, responsible and down-to-earth.*"

Keith Simpson Associates

3 Forest Street, New Canaan, CT 06840
(203) 966 - 7071
Landscape architecture

	Quality +	Cost $	Value ◆	Recommend? ★

KokoBo Plantscapes, Ltd.

	3.5	3	4.5	4

4 Fourth Avenue, Garden City Park, NY 11040
(516) 294 - 7308   www.kokobo.com

Residential and commercial landscape contracting

According to clients, Michael Madarash, owner of KokoBo Plantscapes can do anything and everything with interior and exterior plants. From full-size lawns in the country to small city rooftop terraces and patios, we hear that this firm is great for everyday landscape services. In addition to Connecticut and Fairfield, Madarash and his team also work in New York City and Long Island.

Madarash began his love for horticulture while working with both his grandfather and father in the landscape industry. After receiving a bachelor's degree in horticulture and turfgrass management from the University of Massachusetts, Madarash founded his firm in 2000. The firm includes nine employees, one of whom is a landscape architect. For good, consistent work that doesn't cost a year's salary clients say that KokoBo is the firm to call.

"*KokoBo has excellent, professional, dependable workers. The design and execution was amazing.*" "*The landscaping transformed the patio and the surrounding area from a bare, flat area into a lovely wonderland.*" "*I am very happy and satisfied with the work.*" "*Very professional and outstanding landscaping firm.*"

Laurel Hill Farms

	4.5	4	4.5	5

2 Laurel Hill Drive, Valley Stream, NY 11581
(516) 791 - 5676   hortdiva@aol.com

Landscape design, installation and maintenance

We hear that Sherry Santifer is consistently ahead of trends when it comes to landscape design. For example, she has been incorporating tropicals into her work for the past six years, while others are just beginning to add them to their plant palette. With 21 years experience, Santifer of Laurel Hill Farms has a very impressive track record of designing, creating and maintaining a wide variety of gardens in, around and above the urban landscape. Her considerable talents have not gone unnoticed, as her client list includes an international elite, whom Santifer is too discrete to confirm.

Santifer also specializes in forcing bulbs. She draws on this talent to create designs with a wide variety of texture, color and interest, references report. Her work has been extensively recognized at the Philadelphia Flower Show.

Sources report that Santifer and her staff of five provide the same impressive level of excellence in customer care as they do in garden design. If clients wish to be involved in light garden maintenance, Santifer is more than happy to train them. If, however, clients want the garden oasis without the work, the Laurel Hill Farms crew will take care of absolutely everything. Clients could not be more pleased with Santifer and highly recommend her.

"*Meticulous.*" "*Great client coddling.*" "*Very knowledgeable horticulturist and a very impressive person.*"

	Quality 	Cost $	Value ◆	Recommend? ★

Madelyn Simon & Associates Inc.

3.5 3.5 4 3.5

510 West 34th Street, New York, NY 10001
(212) 629 - 7000   msaplants@aol.com

Landscape and plantscape design, installation and maintenance

References claim that this firm stays on top of everything. With a staff of 80-plus employees, Madelyn Simon & Associates (MS&A) provides a dizzying variety of "green services" to commercial and residential clients throughout Manhattan and beyond. MS&A offers fresh and silk flower arrangements, outdoor furniture and accessories, seasonal displays, irrigation systems, as well as complete landscape and interiorscape design, installation and maintenance. Uniformed, experienced field personnel go to clients' homes for regularly scheduled maintenance and pride themselves on offering top-quality, on-going garden care.

While references caution that they "do not have the same attachment to MS&A servicemen as close friends have with their personal landscape designers," they insist that they receive variety and interest in design, great plant and garden care and extremely good value for the money. Clients also comment on MS&A's initiative, reporting that the staff "calls ahead to confirm regular appointments," "arrives on time" and leaves sites "neat and well-tended.

"They really take the initiative and call ahead to make appointments to come service my garden." "Madelyn Simon & Associates have made sure I've received a great deal of enjoyment from my garden over the years." "Really, really great."

Mary Riley Smith Landscape & Garden Design

4 4 4 5

2211 Broadway, New York, NY 10024
(212) 496 - 2535   gardensmith@aol.com

Landscape design

References are all "just thrilled" with Mary Riley Smith and her work. In New York City and Connecticut circles and beyond, Smith is considered "among the best of the best" in landscape design. Smith renovated and now oversees the prestigious Cooper Hewitt Museum garden, which is generally recognized as the best gallery garden space on Museum Mile. Smith is known for designing gardens with four seasons of interest, incorporating a wide variety of plants, from shrubs and evergreens to exotic annuals.

Smith also includes pots, urns and trellises in her designs. While she does work throughout Greenwich, Bedford and the Hamptons, approximately half her clients are in Manhattan. Smith contracts out and then oversees all garden installation and is happy to train her clients or their gardeners in maintenance techniques. Concerned by the number of poorly planned and underused front properties, Smith wrote *The Front Garden: New Approaches to Landscape Design,* in which she provides creative ways and detailed plans for making front yard gardens both decorative and functional.

"We have a beautiful house on a difficult piece of property. We are very pleased with the way in which problems were tackled." "An absolute pleasure to work with."

Memrie M. Lewis Landscape Design, LLC

5 4 4.5 5

15 Pecksland Road, Greenwich, CT 06831
(203) 869 - 7740

Landscape design

Insiders say that Memrie Lewis, considered one of the most amazing landscape designers in the Connecticut/Westchester area, has definitely found her calling. Part of what sets Lewis apart from her competitors is that she chooses properties and projects where she feels "empathy for the land." Lewis began her career in 1991 at the suggestion of interior designer David Easton, who had observed her renovation of the 1911 azalea garden on her own property over many years.

Sources say that she is the the one to call if you want your house to look like it belongs to the land. Lewis also makes sure that the plants she uses will make her designs glow and bloom year-round.

Lewis takes on around five projects a year and depending on the size of the job, a landscape can cost anywhere from $50,000 to $850,000. Clients say that in addition to her vast knowledge of plant material and softscape, she is also good with hardscape and swimming pool design. Lewis has worked with a number of acclaimed architects and interior designers and her clientele includes many celebrities and socialites.

"My terrace was ripe, lush and incredibly beautiful in less than a year. There was a stunning rose arbor, Japanese yews, flowering crabapples with red berries in the winter." "When I sold my place, the new buyers really bought the garden." "I have one word that best describes Memrie—talented!"

MetroScapes   4.5   2.5   5   4.5
16 Burnett Terrace, West Orange, NJ 07052
(973) 243 - 5585

Landscape design, installation and maintenance

Clients agree that Bill Mitchell not only has great artistic sensibilities, but he's also a pleasure to work with. We hear MetroScapes is a small, up-and-coming landscape design firm owned and operated by Mitchell. Since 1996, Mitchell has been designing, installing and maintaining gardens around New York City and Connecticut, although the firm is not equipted to do large jobs outside its core area. He also serves as a contractor, helping other landscape designers actualize their garden plans. We're told Mitchell's history of interest in plants and plant design dates back to early childhood—"In the third grade I was the one they looked to to take care of the class plants because they knew I wouldn't kill the African Violet." Years later, after leaving a career in computer design, Mitchell went back to school to study horticulture at the New York Botanical Garden.

New to the field, Mitchell is not yet associated with a particular style of garden design and he is open to client suggestions. His current projects include penthouse, sculpture and terrace gardens. Owners report that they could not be more pleased with Mitchell's reasonable pricing. Additionally, references comment on his "lush and beautiful design," the pride and enjoyment he takes in his work and his "true artistic sensibilities.

"Bill takes great pride in his work...he brought his parents around to see the garden." "He is a delightful young man, and our garden is just beautiful." "He's the nicest guy, and he does great work."

Michael Trapp   🗁   🗁   🗁   🗁
7 River Road, West Cornwall, CT 06796
(860) 672 - 6098

Landscape architecture

Mingo Design, LLC 💼   4   4   4   5
470 West End Avenue, Suite 7D, New York, NY 10024
(212) 580 - 8773   MingoDes@aol.com

Landscape design, installation and maintenance

Kari and Andrew Katzander and their small team at the landscaping firm Mingo Design have a reputation for offering brilliance on a budget. The firm designs, installs and maintains a variety of gardens and grounds throughout Fairfield/ Westchester and New York City. Kari Katzander brings a strong family background in contracting, having gained experience with her father's company restoring farms and farmhouses. After a confident fifteen-year run owning landscape maintenance and design company on Fishers Island, she brings considerable practical construction and installation knowledge to her position as the creative director of Mingo Design. Andrew Katzander contributes a design and contracting resume that includes nods from The New York Botanical Garden to the Pratt Institute.

The Katzander couple strives to "bring the outside in and the inside out" in their designs. Sources mention their commitment to designing for all four seasons, their use of color and the trust they instill in clients. The firm's commitment to finding the best craftsmen to implement its designs has led to its evolution to include contracting work, bringing the Katzanders full circle. In addition, a request that Kari Katzander use her eye for color to coordinate her clients' interior decor with their newly installed Mingo Design garden has led them to expand the firm's repertoire. Having recently established the firm in the contracting and interior design worlds, they have arrived with their latest venture in designing the rooftop terrace for MTV's *The Real World*.

"Mingo Design walked the land as well as viewed photos and videos of the property, along with evaluating each room of the house to get ideas." "Kari was exceptional in 'hearing out' my ideas and incorporated them into the final design." "I have a wonderful honeysuckle fence for privacy, which bloomed very quickly." "Our landscaping at a seaside house along the Connecticut shore two hours from New York City was masterfully conceived and executed by Mingo."

Perennial Gardens Inc.   3.5   4   3.5   4
Route 22, Bedford, NY 10506
(914) 234 - 6311   www.perennialgardensny.com
Landscape design/build and pool construction

Owner of Perennial Gardens, Augustine Alvarez (Augie) has created one of the largest landscape contracting firms in the Connecticut/Westchester area. With more than 90 employees, Perennial specializes in high-end landscaping, site work and masonry. However, they are also pros at spa and pool construction, creating waterfalls and decorative ponds. Alvarez and his staff oversee every aspect of projects, including sales, design, contracting and project management. They also have a retail garden center and nursery. We hear that this company has established long-lasting relationships with not only their residential customers, but also with some of the best contractors and architects in the business.

Clients say that despite the large size of Perennial, they always promptly return phone calls and respond to clients' needs. The firm covers a wide range of projects that can be as little as $5,000 and as much as $1,000,000.

"Perennial Gardens is a staple for garden plants in the tiny village of Bedford." "It is more convenient and less pricey than its Greenwich competitors." "The quality of garden plants offered at Perrenial Gardens is consistently very high." "The staff is courteous and this is the destination for Christmas trees and wreaths." "A Bedford gardening landmark."

Roberto Fernandez   4   3.5   4.5   5
23 Porchuck Road, Greenwich, CT 06831
(203) 869 - 3171   lospiches@aol.com
Landscape and estate management

Roberto Fernandez has been managing some of the most posh estates in Connecticut and Westchester since 1990. Originally from Argentina, Fernandez

	Quality	Cost	Value	Recommend?
		$	◆	★

moved to Connecticut to manage horses for a polo team. He developed such a following that he decided to manage estates full time and now has a staff of fifteen. Although the company manages a wide variety of styles, Fernandez is partial to English- and French-style gardens.

Clients say that Fernandez is a pleasure to work with and that his strength is his "incredible" creativity. He charges hourly plus the cost of materials. The hourly fee depends on the job.

"Roberto will do it all, including snow plowing for me in the winter." "Promptly returns my calls and is such a charming and pleasant man."

Rocco Pennella Landscaping Contractor Ltd.

107 Dixon Road, Carmel, NY 10512
(845) 225 - 9212

Landscape construction

Rosedale Nurseries Inc.

| 4.5 | 4 | 4.5 | 4 |

51 Saw Mill River Road, Hawthorne, NY 10532
(914) 769 - 1300   rosepow@aol.com

Nursery and garden center, landscape design and installation

Clients rave that Rosedale is the "quintessential" nursery and design center. Well known among its peers, Rosedale Nurseries has a sizable client base in the Fairfield/Westchester area as well as in Manhattan. Rosedale offers a full range of landscape design and contracting services. References verify that the firm carries a considerable selection of high-quality, unusual plants and that the staff is comprised of helpful, knowledgeable horticulturists. From street tree service to terrace garden installation, sources report that Rosedale Nurseries is a reliable choice.

"I work with Rosedale on my projects in Fairfield/Westchester and would never consider using anyone else." "Rosedale is as good as it gets."

Rutherford Associates

| 4 | 4 | 4 | 4 |

199 Sound Beach Avenue, Old Greenwich, CT 06870
(203) 637 - 2718

Landscape design

Sam Bridge Nurseries

| 4 | 4 | 4 | 4 |

437 North Street, Greenwich, CT 06830
(203) 869 - 3418   www.sambridge.com

Full service gardening center

Landscape architects and designers recommend Sam Bridge Nursery for providing top quality plants and superior plant material to Connecticut and Westchester and say it's always their first stop when choosing plants. If you can grow it, chances are Sam Bridge has it. They are the largest perennial growers in Fairfield County. We also hear that their well-trained and knowledgeable staff can answer any questions regarding horticulture, plant care and the company even offers gardening classes.

"Sam Bridge provides the highest quality possible for garden plants and landscape design." "The nursery has been around since 1930 and sits on twenty pristine acres." "Although somewhat pricey, the superior cultivation practices are worth every penny if you are looking for only the best in landscape design." "Purchasing garden plants at Sam Bridge is not only an education, but a very wise investment."

	Quality	Cost	Value	Recommend?

Sanctuary Garden Design, LLC
3 Glendale Road, Cos Cob, CT 06807
(203) 869 - 0011
Garden design and perennial maintenance

Silvia F. Erskine Associates, LLC
525 Danbury Road, Wilton, CT 06897
(203) 762 - 9017   www.erskineassoc.com
Landscape architecture

Studer Design Associates
27 Governor Street, Ridgefield, CT 06877
(203) 894 - 1428   studerdes@aol.com
Landscape design

Summer Rain Sprinkler Systems, Inc.   3.5   3.5   4   4
288 Valley Road, Cos Cob, CT 06807
(203) 629 - 8050   www.summerrainsprinklers.com
High-end irrigation specialists

Established in 1980 by William H. Gallagher, Summer Rain custom designs, installs, and services turf and shrub irrigation systems for residential and commercial clients. The bulk of their business is in Fairfield, Westchester, Long Island and Manhattan. This firm is commended for its fast response time and same day service. We also hear the staff is customer-service oriented and goes above and beyond the call of duty for its clients. During the irrigation installation process there is always a senior management team member present to assure that everything runs smoothly. Should problems arise after the installation, Summer Rain's service department promises not to leave you high and dry.

"William and his team always come on a moment's notice." "When you need irrigation work, Summer Rain is the place to call."

Susan Cohen   5   4   4.5   4.5
7 Perkely Lane, Riverside, CT 06878
(203) 637 - 0113   scohenla@aol.com
Landscape architecture and design

The Care of Trees Inc.   3.5   4   3.5   4
44 Slocum Street, Ridgefield, CT 06877
(203) 847 - 1855   www.thecareoftrees.com
Tree Care and preservation

A love of trees and the preservation of them is what has kept this firm growing in popularity in Connecticut and New York since 1919. The firm has over 60 trained arborists with 25 offices located throughout the US. The Care of Trees works with both residential and commercial clients in order to properly care for trees and shrubs. The firm offers a wide range of services, from simple tree and shrub pruning to tree risk assessment and insect and disease management.

Tree Care Consultancy of New York Inc.   4   3   5   5
310 Park Place, Brooklyn, NY 11238
(718) 638 - 8733   treedocnyc@aol.com
Master arborist

Sources call Bruce McInnes of the Tree Care Consultancy of New York "The King of Trees." After working for a tree maintenance company in the 1970s, McInnes started his firm in the 1980s when it became impossible to "get advice that wasn't tied to a buzzsaw." McInnes offers consultations on "trees and tree issues." He is also a member of the American Society of Consulting Arborists (ASCA).

Though much of his work involves overseeing tree rescue, McInnes works with landscape architects or retail clients, advising on overall design or the installation of attractive site-appropriate trees. He also performs site analysis and sets up proper tree maintenance programs for his clients. McInnes will visit a site in Manhattan for $160 to $200. He then charges an hourly rate of $75 to $80. "I try to be available for any tree situation," McInnes says. References verify that he more than meets that objective. However, if a tree falls in the forest and nobody hears, we wonder: Where's Bruce McInnes?

"Reasonable rates, very reasonable, but don't tell him." "Bruce McInnes is incredibly knowledgeable. He works very hard to do the best work possible, be helpful and act as a resource to his clients." "Goes out of his way to be excellent to people. I always recommend him." "Thumbs up. He's a fine man and certainly a qualified arborist." "Bruce is a pleasure to work with, a very easy-going man." "Nice guy. Fun to work with. Knows his stuff. Well-regarded in the business."

Worcester & Worcester Inc.   4.5   4   4.5   5
PO Box 177, Old Lyme, CT 06371
(860) 434 - 4669
Landscape architecture

Industry leaders say that Rick Worcester is in a league of his own when it comes to landscape architecture and call his work "simply fabulous." Sources laud Worcester for both his ability to create strong outdoor spaces as well as his overall comprehension of architecture. Worcester works on his own and takes on a staggering 30 projects—from small to large—per year.

Worcester studied landscape architecture and graduated from the University of Virginia in 1992. He also worked under some of the top names in the landscape architecture field before starting his own firm. Although most of Worcester's projects are in Westchester and eastern Connecticut, he has taken on challenging landscapes from Vermont to Florida. Depending on the size and the scope of the project, most of his work is in the $100,000 to $500,000 range. Aside from clients praising Worcester for his talent as a landscape architect, we also hear that he "is a pleasure to work with" and that he is always willing to roll with the initial uncertainty of a difficult project, ready to tackle any challenges.

"Rick knows the Bedford way." "Really nice, laid-back guy." "Fabulous landscape designs." "He is not at all ostentatious and he always gets it right." "Rick not only understood what I wanted, but he also understood my budget."

Yolac & Lloyd Landscape Design   📁   📁   📁   📁
1201 Oldfield Road, Fairfield, CT 06430
(203) 259 - 9361
Landscape design

Zeller's Design   📁   📁   📁   📁
54 Van Rensselaer Avenue, Stamford, CT 06902
(203) 363 - 0688
Landscape design

Hiring a Millworker or Cabinetmaker

In any renovation, millwork buttons up the newly pressed suit of your home. The integrity and artistry of old-world craftsmanship hasn't been lost on today's generation of woodworking professionals, who create cabinets, moldings, doors, mantels, staircases and furniture. These service providers can tuck a plasma TV into architectural detail of a custom design/built library or reproduce antique furniture.

Choosing a Millwork Firm

Not all millworkers are cut from the same piece of lumber. The right service provider must fit plumb with your project and personality. Some firms relish working directly with homeowners, taking an idea from concept to completion. Others are more comfortable realizing the defined plans of a designer or architect. In either case a millworker will produce detailed shops, or working drawings for you to sign off on. Significant projects that involve the coordination of other trades (like electrical and plumbing for a serious kitchen remodel) or that involve complex structural elements (stairways) should always have a designer or contractor involved. In this case, finding a millwork firm that collaborates well with other design and construction professionals is essential.

Service providers range from a single talented craftsman with a few helpers to a large full-service woodworking firm with retail showrooms. Where you may get a more businesslike approach and greater capacity, you may lose that artisan appeal and personal touch. Visit the shops of those firms you are considering. You'll not only get a good idea about the vibe of the place, but see the product being produced, whether by highly precise, computer-controlled (C&C) machines or by skillful hand and eye. Last but not least, check out the finished result and talk to references. You should be as concerned with the quality of the work—tight joints, pristine finishes and plum doors and drawers—as with the style. Don't go with Mr. Euro-style sleek who's a wizard incorporating laminates and stainless steel into his kitchen cabinets when you're looking for someone to hand-carve a built-in window seat at your English library.

Three Levels of Quality

Once you've determined the scope of your project, it is wise to determine the caliber of workmanship and quality of wood that is most appropriate for your needs. There are essentially three tiers of woodworking quality to choose from, each with its own standards for materials and craftsmanship.

Economy is the lowest grade of woodwork and may be chosen for projects that will not put a lot of demand on the structure or materials. For example, a built-in desk and shelving unit in a guest room that gets very little use could be constructed at the economy level. Although the work must be attractive, it need not be made from exotic wood or constructed with intricate joinery.

The next grade is custom woodwork, the level of craftsmanship most frequently requested. Custom woodwork ensures good quality wood and workmanship and is suitable for such popular projects as household cabinetry and moldings. A beautiful kitchen makeover with glass-paneled cabinet doors and a new butcher-block island could be constructed using custom woodwork.

The highest grade is premium woodwork, top-of-the-line millwork that delivers the highest quality of craftsmanship, wood and finishing. Premium jobs include outfitting an entire room with elaborately carved wall and ceiling panels made of top-grade wood, or building a grand staircase using imported wood and marble.

ON COST

Due to the specialized, diverse nature of the millwork business, there is no standard pricing structure. Most firms determine their fees based on the materials that are being used and the complexity and scope of the project, which is why it is important to collect several bids for your job. When requesting bids, it is also important to note whether or not the cost of installation is included. Some firms subcontract the installation process. Before you sign a contract, be sure that you know exactly who will install the work you ordered in its intended place in your home.

WHAT TO EXPECT FROM YOUR MILLWORK COMPANY

Your millworker should be as familiar with the actual installation space as he is with his client's lifestyle needs. A good millworker, like any service provider, should prove meticulous in the planning stages: asking questions, massaging the design and triple-checking measurements—from the opening width for appliances in kitchen cabinets to the knee-height of a custom built desk for a taller client. You must also plan ahead, as lead times for fabrication and delivery are usually six to sixteen weeks.

The quality of any end product is only as good as the installation, however, not every firm installs or finishes what it fabricates. If the shop milling the pieces isn't the one assembling the puzzle, know who will be before you spill any ink on the contract, and qualify them as well. The same goes with finishing, a messy process that can effectively shut down the job site. A great deal of product comes pre-finished, however, so the dirty work is completed in a controlled environment off site.

If the structure of your home will not be altered by your millwork project (as with replacement kitchen cabinets, for example), the job will not require a permit and can probably be done without a contractor or architect (if the millwork shop does detailed drawings.) This work is very much a craft in the old-world sense, where skills are often passed down from master to apprentice. As such, there are no license or permit requirements for millwork firms, nor are there any trade associations through which millworkers are generally certified. Before you sign a work agreement, request proof of the company's insurance and warranty policies, which vary from firm to firm. If craftsmen will be working in your home, you'll want to be sure they are covered by the company's workman's comp policy. You don't want to be held responsible for a misguided nail or toppled ladder.

MILLWORK MASTERY TIPS

✧ It's your millworker's duty to measure! If you do it yourself and give him the dimensions, you're only asking for trouble.

✧ Plan the electrical and plumbing layout meticulously or you may have to rip up fine work, send it to the scrap heap and pay to have it redone.

✧ Don't install millwork too early in a renovation project. Your millworker should be the last person in so that other workers won't scratch your beautiful new wood finish.

✧ Hire excellent professionals for the entire renovation. Millworkers must have a level surface on which to work, and shoddy workmanship from carpenters, drywall or plastic contractors will haunt the millwork.

✧ Remember to design backing structures where necessary. You don't want a cabinet that will store heavy cookware fastened to a mere half-inch of drywall.

✧ Don't be afraid to reject a panel or piece of molding that doesn't match the quality of its brothers and sisters.

MILLWORKERS & CABINETMAKERS

AJ Duggan Contracting Inc.   3.5   3   4   4
140 East Lewis Avenue, Pearl River, NY 10965
(845) 735 - 5651
Interior remodels and custom millwork
   See AJ Contracting's full report under the heading Contractors & Builders

Anglo-Inscape Inc.   4.5   3   5   5
2472 Broadway, Suite 368, New York, NY 10025
(212) 924 - 2883   www.angloinscape.com
Custom furniture and high-end finishes

Clients are so taken with principal Andrew Rouse's good-looking, British charm that they invite him to houses all over the country to do his exquisite work. Rouse studied in the UK and has been in business for fifteen years. In addition to designing a furniture line, he also specializes in antique furniture restoration and refinishing and decorative wall finishes. Rouse's French Polish is reportedly magnificent, and we are told he works in oil- and water-based glazes, graining, marbling and specialty plaster treatments.

We also hear Rouse values the integrity of old-world methods and uses only traditional techniques, hand applying rubs and finishes. Clients praise Rouse's enormous body of knowledge and recommend him for projects that call for preserving the character of a valuable piece. Insiders say that in an industry of divas, Rouse stands out for his reliability and absence of ego.

"Work is of the highest quality and is completed within the time specified." "Andrew's work is outstanding and his commitment is unfailing." "Some high-end finishers are difficult to work with. Andrew is not one of these. His pricing is fair, he's there when he says he will be and goes the extra mile to make sure the job is done right."

Breakfast Woodworks   4   4   4   4
135 Leetes Island Road, Guilford, CT 06437
(203) 458 - 8888   www.breakfastwoodworks.com
High-end custom millwork

This firm combines age-old skills with high technology to deliver top-drawer quality. Breakfast Woodworks creates custom woodwork for high-end home and commercial interiors and exteriors, from the cutting-edge to historic preservation. Sources say the firm recently completed new benches for the Great Hall in the Metropolitan Museum of Art. While many clients insist they "would choose no other," they also report that firm doesn't always have the manpower or carving skills to satisfy everyone and at times may refer prospects to other shops.

Principal Louis Mackall, a Yale-educated architect, cofounded Breakfast Woodworks with master craftsman Kenneth Field. Clients describe the principals as forthright and dependable.

"Extraordinary attention to detail and design intention. Willingness to work with experimental design and construction technologies as well as traditional forms." "Beyond our wildest dreams."

	Quality	Cost	Value	Recommend?
	✚	$	◆	★

Budd Woodwork Inc.

4   4   4   4

54 Franklin Street, Brooklyn, NY 11222
(718) 389 - 1110

Historic restoration and preservation of millwork

Clients tell us they wish they could work with Budd Woodwork "365 days a year." A high-end mill shop with a talent for historic restoration, replication and preservation work, the firm specializes in a classic French style, especially Louis XV and Louis XVI. Budd works exclusively with architects and decorators, catering to a sophisticated and exclusive clientele.

Founded in 1952, the company employs eighteen. We hear Budd's staff is humble and polite and that the firm takes on a limited number of jobs each year so they won't have to shy away from doing a simple bookcase.

"They are impeccable, courteous, quiet and punctual. No detail is overlooked." "Experts all the way." "Very thoughtful about how to achieve the best quality. Very principled about maintaining the highest level of consistent quality."

Catskill Fine Woodworking/Robert Allen

4   3   4.5   4.5

11 Field Court, Kingston, NY 12401
(845) 339 - 8029   www.catskillfurniture.com

Custom millwork and furniture

The "Cat-skills" of this custom millwork shop have customers purring. Principal Robert Allen's eye for detail, responsible management and pleasant personality gain high praise. Working with trade professionals in New York City and Westchester and Fairfield counties, the firm offers high-end product at a very good price.

Allen also runs Catskill Furniture Makers, which combines historic reproduction work with contemporary design ideas. The firm's Web site features an online gallery, and its Kingston showroom shows off the real thing.

"Not every millworker is ready to throw himself into the job when the contractor is ready. Bob is always ready with the ultimate solution." "Excellent people, excellent work."

Century Woodworking

3.5   3   4   4.5

PO Box 164, 40 River Road, Pleasant Valley, CT 06063
(860) 379 - 7538   www.centurywoodworking.com

Full-service custom architectural millwork, windows and doors

Clients restoring a residence from bygone centuries or building one for the next rely on this fine custom woodworker. Principal Brad Hammil established Century Woodworking in 1983. Connecticut's design and construction gurus call on the firm as a technical and artistic resource for their interior millwork and window and door needs.

We're told Century Woodwork also helps homeowners by providing full design and engineering services, handholding the client from concept to completion. References recommend the Century experience, whether for a window replacement or full architectural millwork in a new home.

"Nice people and exceptional work."

	Quality	Cost	Value	Recommend?
	✚	$	◆	★

Chanler Lewis Inc.

4.5   4   4.5   5

1495 Thomaston Avenue, Waterbury, CT 06704
(203) 755 - 3005

High-end custom millwork

Elite contractors and world-class architects trust Chanler Lewis to deliver. This firm outfits flagship corporate offices, historic municipal buildings, universities and high-end residences. Commissions range from $5,000 to $3 million. Clients tout the company as unmatched in meeting tight schedules on big-ticket jobs without sacrificing its standout quality.   While pleased to accommodate homeowner projects, we're told Chanler-Lewis does not assist in the actual design.

A Dartmouth grad, Tom Officer brings 25 years of high-end woodworking experience to his firm, which he established in 1996.   His two key officers—Joe Bennan, head of estimating and sales, and Bruce Wyatt, head of operations—each bring twenty years of their own experience to the business.   The Chandler-Lewis 70,000-square-foot shop features CNC equipment and a full-finishing facility.   A skilled staff of 60, including cabinetmakers, project managers and draftsmen, round out this all-inclusive company.

Christopher Peacock Cabinetry

4.5   4   4.5   4.5

34 East Putnam Avenue, Greenwich, CT 06830
(203) 862 - 9333   www.peacockcabinetry.com

Highly detailed custom cabinetry

See Christopher Peacock Cabinetry's full report under the heading Kitchen & Bath Designers

CJS Millwork Inc.

4.5   4   5   5

425 Fairfield Avenue, Suite 3A, Stamford, CT 06902
(203) 708 - 0080

High-end cabinetry, architectural millwork, carving and custom furniture

Word is there's absolutely nothing this well-rounded shop can't do with wood. CJS produces and installs "incredible product" for high-end interiors, new construction or renovation.   The company also does carving and custom furniture, although design is not this firm's forte.   With the lion's share of projects ballparking between $100,000 and $200,000 for the trade, CJS is still available for your little cub's vanity, working mostly in Westchester and Fairfield counties, and occasionally in New York City.

Owner Chris Sculti has steered CJS from its start as a builder into a high-caliber cabinet and mill shop.   Assisted by twenty employees, Sculti personally supervises field installations and oversees the development of drawings, which we are told are subbed out.   Customers tell us CJS shows consideration to the work of other trades as well as to the demands of the overall project schedule.   In addition, they say the firm keeps at it until everyone is satisfied.

"All the woodwork was fantastic. They made Kathie Lee Gifford happy." "Good custom shop." "Hid the wires for the home office." "The product is beautiful."

Colonial Housewrights, LLC

3   3   4   4

371 Hammertown Road, Monroe, CT 06468
(203) 452 - 9119   colhousewright@aol.com

Interior build-out and renovations

See Colonial Housewrights, LLC's full report under the heading Contractors, & Builders

	Quality	Cost	Value	Recommend?
	+	$	◆	★

Crane Woodworking   5   4   5   5
15 Rockland Road, South Norwalk, CT 06854
(203) 852 - 9229   craneww@snet.net

High-end architectural millwork and cabinetry

Garnering kudos as "great communicators," the workers at this firm are known to produce perhaps the most comprehensive shop drawings in the entire Fairfield/ Westchester area. The result, say contractors and architects, is a refined finished product. Crane Woodworking fabricates and installs high-end architectural millwork, from a wet bar to a pool house, working with exotic woods and seamlessly integrating sound systems and lighting.

Owner Doug Crane began as a hobbyist furnituremaker. He turned his talents to high-end architectural millwork in 1984 and now oversees a staff of 25 and a 20,000-square-foot state-of-the-art shop. We're told Crane works alongside his draftsmen to ensure the best blueprint for the job. Crane continues to create furniture, inspired by Mission, Arts and Crafts and Prairie styles. Clients say the firm's stellar reputation makes the upper-end prices a "very good value."

"Doug Crane is great with clients." "Can change on the fly without tons of paperwork." "Knowledgeable installers. Helpful in resolving problems." "Every project completed has been done with the highest of quality standards. Entire staff is a pleasure to deal with. Only woodworker we would use." "Best shop drawings. Good service. Always a pleasure to do business with them."

Craz Woodworking Associates Inc.   4.5   4   4.5   5
86 Horseblock Road, Unit A, Yaphank, NY 11980
(631) 205 - 1890

High-end woodworking and casework

Clients go Craz-y for this Long Island-based woodworker's "great ideas and great eye." A favorite resource among top-tier trade professionals, Craz's projects range from a $2,000 side-table to $400,000 casework packages. Sources say the company is involved from materials selection to finish. We hear this small firm showers its clients with attention. In turn, its Manhattan, Hamptons and lower Westchester/Fairfield clientele shower the inspired end products with praise.

Owner Peter Craz gained a degree in economics and studio art before teaching industrial arts in the Peace Corps in Korea. Upon his return, he embarked on his woodworking career and opened shop in 1983. Craz plays a hand in every project, assisted by a select in-house team and longstanding network of relationships with the area's best finishers and installers.

"Pete takes the extra step and engineers it." "He did a kitchen for a difficult client of mine and kept everyone happy. Working in pear wood and mahogany, he matched veneers perfectly." "Realizes it takes extra time. Knowledgeable and expensive but worth it."

Culin and Colella Inc.   4   3   4.5   4.5
632 Center Avenue, Mamaroneck, NY 10543
(914) 698 - 7727   rculin@hotmail.com

Custom millwork and furniture

Sources say husband-and-wife team Ray Culin and Janis Colella promise an excellent experience. Their shop creates custom woodwork and one-of-a-kind furniture designs, with finish work a highlight. Clients find the folks at Culin and Colella "nice, decent people," as well as "patient and imaginative craftsmen." The firm works closely with both designers and homeowners in New York City and Westchester and Fairfield counties, remaining small to keep the collaboration with the principals personal.

"Janis Colella is an artist with her finishes." "The work they did is the highlight of our house." "They really want to do a good job." "Outstanding quality, workers and execution."

Curtis Terzis
211 Strawberry Hill Avenue, Stamford, CT 06902
(203) 961 - 1775

Quality	Cost	Value	Recommend?
4	3.5	5	5

Custom cabinets and built-ins

With an eye for design and an ear for the customer, this custom cabinetmaker comes highly recommended. Built-ins such as libraries, entertainment centers, home offices and vanities are the firm's bread and butter. Curtis Terzis can execute for both decorators and architects, and personally designs over 80 percent of the cabinets he builds. Serving middle-class to world-class clients, he is known to work well with budgets and steer clients from excess.

Terzis holds a BA in finance and worked as a property master, building sets for TV commercial production before evolving into a woodworking craftsman. A sole proprietor with a shop in Stamford, Terzis tackles multiple or larger projects in collaboration with a trusted network of outside mill shops.

"Completes on schedule. Very easy and pleasant to work with and stays within budget or within original quote. He has a great sense of scale and proportion. He delivers on time and works very hard to please both designers as well as clients."

Custom Cabinets Plus
34 Bergen Street, Paterson, NJ 07522
(973) 790 - 9960

Quality	Cost	Value	Recommend?
3.5	3	4.5	4.5

Custom millwork and cabinets

Clients say this "very easy to work with" New Jersey-based mill shop delivers concept to completion due to devotion by owner Matthew Di Gioia. Custom Cabinets Plus crafts, installs and finishes woodwork and cabinet projects of all sizes, working in high-end and exotic materials and reproducing old-fashioned finishes. Catering primarily to homeowners in Westchester, Fairfield, Manhattan and all of New Jersey, the firm can assist with design.

Di Gioia, who hails from a civil engineering background, established the firm in 1993. He oversees eight employees and plays point man for every job. It's this personal attention as much as the well-crafted product that puts the plus in this custom cabinet shop.

"Outstanding service, personal attention to problems or concerns." *"Matt is very accessible, even after the project is completed."*

DCI Design + Millwork
76 Finch Street, Milford, CT 06460
(203) 877 - 2992 dcimrl@aol.com

Quality	Cost	Value	Recommend?
4	4	4	4.5

Fine-tuned millwork and cabinetry

Industry insiders tell us this firm "continues to go above and beyond expectations." With its 13,000-square-foot shop, expert installers and on/off-site finishing capabilities, DCI is equipped to handle anything from a single vanity piece to the floor-to-ceiling casework of a new residence. The exclusive millwork source for high-end builder, Davenport Contracting, DCI collaborates closely with the trade and is also willing to work directly with homeowners. The company's fine reputation in Westchester and Fairfield counties has earned it projects farther afield in New York, New Jersey and Rhode Island.

Principals Larry Silks and Rick Kovacs bring a combined 44 years of cabinet-making, millwork and construction experience to the firm. References are especially impressed with their willingness to walk job sites in the rough framing phase and communicate with other trades to realize a better design, such as the location of a light switch in relation to the millwork. While this extra effort translates into extra dollars, clients say they wouldn't want it any other way.

"*Good client relations.*" "*They willingly returned a number of times until we were completely satisfied.*" "*The intangible aspect of working with DCI is their ability to communicate and coordinate with designers and clients.*" "*The quality of the firm's shop drawings are unsurpassed.*"

East End Woodstrippers Inc. 3.5 3.5 4 4.5
27 Glenmere Way, Holbrook, NY 11741
(516) 472 - 5206   www.eastendwoodstrippers.com
Refinish and restoration of woodwork, window casing and doors

This long-standing firm specializes in the stripping, refinishing and refurbishment of old woodwork, doors, stairways, window casings, shutters, cabinets and furniture. It also finishes new installations. Most of East End's work is performed on-site in New York City and the surrounding Tri-State area. The company teams with architects, decorators and contractors as well as with homeowners on projects ranging from a fireplace mantel to larger jobs, with budgets from $20,000 to $50,000.

Owner Dean Camenares brings over twenty years of experience to this family business, established in 1959 by his father-in-law. Camenares with a staff of seven, oversees every detail. Basic refinishing is $400 to $500 per door and $200 and up for basic window, shutter, casing and sash refinishing.

"*Dean is thoughtful about details, carefully recording them all.*" "*They definitely knew what they were doing. It wasn't cheap but when I saw the effort and the result, I felt that the price was reasonable.*" "*They were on time, respectful of my belongings, of the house.*" "*Very cooperative.*" "*Dean is very good at what he does. A very patient man.*"

Elements of Architecture 4 3.5 4 4.5
PO Box 186, 9 Turney Road, Redding, CT 06876
(203) 938 - 0840
Custom cabinets and built-ins

European Woodworking 4.5 3 5 5
167 Sawmill River Road, Yonkers, NY 10701
(914) 969 - 5724
Architectural millwork

Clients rain kudos down on fourth-generation millworker Joe Lo Nigro, who heads European Woodworking's small shop of three. Sources compliment Lo Nigro's delightful personality, humility and strong sense of responsibility. We hear European Woodworking executes custom millwork with exactitude and abundant detail. The inside scoop is Lo Nigro typically completes assignments early and his firm delivers great value.

"*He's dependable, he comes through and is a real artist. I couldn't recommend anyone more than this young man.*" "*No one is perfect in this world, but Joe is certainly striving for it.*" "*Whenever I need work, I go to him, because I know I'll get the best job at the best price.*"

Fairfield County Millwork 3.5 3 4 4
955 Connecticut Ave, Bridgeport, CT 06607
(203) 367 - 9755
Custom cabinets and built-ins

	Quality	Cost	Value	Recommend?
	+	$	◆	★

Fairfield Woodworks
7 Lexington Avenue, South Norwalk, CT 06854
(203) 380 - 9842

Custom millwork and cabinetry

Fanuka Custom Cabinets
59-49 56th Avenue, Maspeth, NY 11378
(718) 353 - 4518

Interior millwork and cabinetry

	4.5	4	4.5	5

A second-generation master cabinetmaker, the enthusiastic and young Steve Fanuka has some serious fans. The firm designs, builds and installs interior millwork in New York, Fairfield and Westchester and performs general contracting duties on interior renovations in and around Manhattan. While the firm has even done work for the White House, its services are available to John Q. Public.

Principal Steve Fanuka apprenticed with the same craftsman in Croatia who taught his father, spending summers pulling nails out of cabinets, straightening them and re-setting them in order to learn how to respect the wood. Steve and project managers oversee installations, while his father, Rod, still at it, keeps the mill shop running masterfully. Clients find this firm "friendly, busy, but reliable."

"Actually returns phone calls, albeit at night. Has a project manager, which makes life easier for all." "Will come back for any complaint, any time in the future and will throw in extras on the job." "Fanuka makes some of the most beautiful cabinetry around."

Greenwich Millwork Co.
99 Indian Field Road, Greenwich, CT 06830
(203) 869 - 1693

Custom millwork and cabinets

	3	3	4	4

H&B Woodworking Co.
105 East Main Street, Plainville, CT 06062
(860) 793 - 6991

Custom furniture and built-ins

	4	3.5	4	4

H&B satisfies a unique woodworking niche with its artisan-inspired design/ build approach. Alois Hager, who hails from a long line of Austrian woodworkers, established the firm in 1970. After eighteen years at the shop herself, Hager's daughter, Lydia Senick, now runs H&B operations along with business partner Matthew Malley. We hear Senick contributes her design expertise— honed early on with interior designer John Lafalce—in working closely with clients to nail their desired aesthetic. H&B focuses on fabricating, installing and finishing smaller, detail-laden built-ins such as entertainment centers and dressing rooms. The firm will also create freestanding furniture and, if the design requires something special and particularly refined, full kitchen casework.

Senick works well with other designers and is assisted by five full-time employees. We're told that since she both conceptualizes with clients and coordinates installations, Senick will not design something that can't be built. Centered in the Avon-West Hartford area, the firm also works in southern Connecticut, Massachusetts and NYC. The pricing is noted as fair.

Hallmark Woodworkers
11 Precision Road, Danbury, CT 06810
(203) 743 - 3223

Custom millwork and cabinets

	4.5	3.5	4.5	4.5

	Quality ✚	Cost $	Value ◆	Recommend? ★

Jacob Froehlich Cabinet Works   5   4   5   5

550-560 Barry Street, Bronx, NY 10474
(718) 893 - 1300   jfcwi@aol.com

High-end millwork, varnishing

In the woodworking business since 1865, insiders say Jacob Froehlich Cabinet Works represents the "Rolls-Royce of millworking." The firm fields a standout architectural department and follows through with flawless execution and installation. Its skills in using stains and varnishes are reputed to be a class apart from others in the field. The firm works in New York City and Westchester County.

Jacob Froehlich draws accolades for its flexible, skilled and extremely organized staff. We hear a distinguished trade and celebrity clientele find the firm as thorough as it is accommodating. We're also told that Froehlich meets on the mark target dates and budgets, but this "top-of-the-line" quality and service translates into top-dollar total tickets.

"*They're so communicative and articulate that there are never any problems.*" "*We have worked with Froehlich for twenty years and have tremendous respect for the workers' ability to prioritize and coordinate.*" "*Very sophisticated and familiar with the top-end work of architects and designers.*" "*They can handle anything—totally unflappable.*"

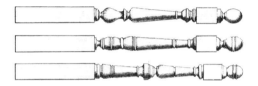

James Schriber   4.5   4   4.5   5

PO Box 1145, 57 West Street, New Milford, CT 06776
(860) 354 - 6452

Contemporary woodworking

This studio furniture maker has run his own small shop since the 1970s and is regarded as "outstanding in every respect." James Schriber builds for designers and designs for clients in a contemporary aesthetic. Inspired by forward-looking French and Scandinavian designs of the 30s, 40s and 50s, Schriber leaves the country woodworking to others. Instead, he focuses on freestanding pieces and large-scale architectural millwork. Schriber works most often in New York City and Westchester and Fairfield counties. There is no minimum cost, and no maximum to the understanding Schriber has with his clients.

Sources describe Schriber as a "meticulous craftsman" and a "good business man." We hear his small three-man shop is "patient and committed." The firm out sources its finish work. While word is "the quality of Schriber's work goes unmatched," costs are consistent with those of his high-end peers.

"*Artist's sensibility and core. A dear to work with.*" "*It is extraordinary to have a furniture-maker with a full design vocabulary, brilliant command of materials and details, and willing to apply himself to millwork and architectural installation. He is a pleasure to work with in every way.*" "*My family and I have worked with him for years—and we would only recommend him with the highest praise and enthusiasm. His clients are fortunate indeed.*"

Jonathan Podmore Cabinetry, LLC   4   4   4   4

375 Fairfield Avenue, Building 3, Stamford, CT 06902
(203) 359 - 4630   www.jpodmorecabinetry.com

Custom millwork and cabinets

	Quality +	Cost $	Value ◆	Recommend? ★

Jorgensen-Carr

111 First Street, Jersey City, NJ 07302
(201) 792 - 2278   jorgcarr@msn.com

Custom interior millwork

Quality **4** Cost **4** Value **5** Recommend **5**

We hear Jorgensen-Carr finds the ultimate solutions to tricky problems. Working across the Tri-State area, the firm earns client praise for feats in stainless steel, wood and leather. Insiders say Jorgensen-Carr distinguishes itself with intricate designs, moldings, finishes and veneers.

Partners Mike Jorgensen and Ken Carr have been working together since 1987. Clients say they admire the good-natured team, describing the two as "creative and resourceful at solving problems." This popular firm isn't always easy to pin down, but once a date is committed, projects fly with "super quality."

"Mike and Ken are just the greatest guys on the face of the Earth. Working with them was such a pleasant experience." "I can't wait to do another project with them." "They were the one bright spot in my renovation."

Joshua Fischer

Route 121, Cross River, NY 10518
(914) 763 - 9613

Handcrafted millwork and cabinetry

Quality **4.5** Cost **4** Value **4.5** Recommend **5**

Joshua Fischer designs, measures, fabricates, installs and finishes every job with his own two hands, and clients say he handles the schedule and the service with care. His high-end millwork commissions run the gamut from minimalist to traditional, furniture to kitchens. Trades trust Fischer to interpret design intent and deliver finely detailed shop drawings, while homeowners can work with Fischer to sketch out smaller jobs.

Fischer has been woodworking since his college days, when he earned a degree in fine arts. After a stint at a high-end New York City mill shop, Fischer opened his own business out of his garage in 1992. Today from his 1,000-square-foot shop, he serves a devoted client base in Manhattan and Fairfield and Westchester counties.

"He's the easiest person to work with. Great craftsmanship and quality."

Keats & Waugh

15-19 Pollock Avenue, Jersey City, NJ 07305
(201) 451 - 3911   KeatsWaugh@aol.com

Custom cabinetry, architectural millwork and furniture

Quality **4** Cost **3** Value **4.5** Recommend **5**

Any classic library starts with Keats & Waugh—the millworkers that is! This small firm builds custom armoires, cabinets, bookcases, entertainment units and furniture of a complicated nature. It works only off drawings facilitated by architects and interior designers, and does not do kitchens. Clients come from Manhattan, the Hamptons, and the affluent New Jersey, Westchester County and Connecticut suburbs.

Owner Bill Keats, who studied oceanography and served as an officer in the merchant marine, is self-taught in the trade. Clients find the "nice, chatty" Keats keeps communication easy and open. The small firm takes on a select number of projects at a time and is reasonably priced.

"Bill is meticulous and reviews each detail so there are no surprises." "If he's available, we use him." "He doesn't take on more work than he can do, which means he isn't always available, but he is always true to his deadline." "Returns calls, calls with questions and suggestions, discusses detail." "Price base is excellent. He doesn't do shop drawings, which keeps costs low."

	Quality	Cost $	Value	Recommend? ★

M&R Woodworking

	3.5	3	4.5	4

49 Withers Street, Brooklyn, NY 11211
(718) 486 - 5480

Custom cabinetry, architectural millwork and furniture

M&R Woodworking wins accolades for precision craftsmanship and customer savvy. Tri-State architects and homeowners have looked to this firm for high-end cabinetry and furniture since 1983. This woodworker's skill for integrating stone and metal into its product also gains notice.

Master woodworker Robert Wieczorkowski studies each project with a desire for perfection. His can-do attitude and sense of humor elevates the experience, while prices stay grounded.

"Great value. Good work."

Mead & Josipovich Inc.

	4.5	4.5	4.5	5

140 58th Street, Brooklyn, NY 11220
(718) 492 - 7373

High-end millwork and custom furniture

Clients rely on this firm for top-quality specialty jobs on an unlimited budget. Mead & Josipovich differentiate their firm with a creativity and attention to detail that clients laud as "truly special." Industry insiders praise this millworker's meticulously rendered shop drawings and ability to meet tight deadlines. The fashion industry has called upon the firm, which is said to be a purveyor of unparalleled finishes and veneers.

Principals Boris Josipovich and Larry Mead have a reputation for being reliable, honest and communicative. We hear the duo dares to deliver exactly what the client wants, as opposed to many other millworkers who impose their ideas on the client.

"What differentiates Boris is that perfection is his standard." "Boris is a mensch." "I can't always afford them on my jobs. Would my life be a lot easier in terms of getting the right work at the right time if I could? The answer is yes."

Michael Gordon Inc.

	4.5	4	5	5

252-C Lake Avenue, Yonkers, NY 10701
(914) 965 - 3800

Custom millwork and furniture

Clients openly adore this family-run firm. Michael Gordon Inc. produces built-in units and stand-alone furniture for a diverse slate that includes sophisticated offices and fanciful children's rooms with technical virtuosity and imaginative flair. While the firm is willing to transform private clients' conceptual designs into reality, most of its commissions come from the best in the trade.

Owner Michael Gordon has more than 30 years of experience in millwork. Clients find him and his son Eric charming, cooperative and "thoughtful." Backed up by a skilled staff of 28 and the most up-to-date technology, the company leaves behind a truly "amazing" product.

"He never just runs with the architect's plans, but always makes them better." "A pleasure. One of the best. Really fun to work with."

Nordic Custom Builders Inc.

	4	3.5	4.5	5

125 Greenwich Avenue, 3rd floor, Greenwich, CT 06830
(203) 629 - 0430

High-end general contracting and construction management

See Nordic Custom Builders Inc.'s full report under the heading Contractors & Builders

	Quality	Cost	Value	Recommend?

Richard Anthony Custom Millwork   4   3   4.5   4
54 Orchard Hill Road, Katonah, NY 10536
(914) 767 - 9014

Custom cabinetry and architectural millwork

Clients call on this firm for everything from a single custom fireplace mantel to the complete architectural millwork and cabinetry for a dream kitchen, and they tell us "the workmanship is superb." The shop boasts its own spray booth and has been known to create custom hardware for its milled product. Richard Anthony Custom Millwork caters to both homeowners and contractors in southern Connecticut and Westchester, and is willing to sit down with clients to help develop a design.

Operated by partners Richard Scavelli and fourth-generation builder Anthony DeVito (see Contractors & Builders), the firm is described as "versatile" and "reliable." We hear the shop's staff of draftsmen, shop men and installers are "hard-working, excellent craftsmen" who share the "same values as Mr. DeVito." While no level of quality is too high for the firm, Richard Anthony can design within a budget.

"This organization is a delight to work with overall." "Workers are considerate, neat and tidy."

S. Donadic Woodworking Inc.   5   4   5   5
36-34 35th Street, Long Island City, NY 11106
(718) 361 - 9888

High-end architectural millwork and cabinetry

This European-trained wood craftsman has been at it for over 30 years. Owner Steve Donadic's portfolio of high-end residential commissions includes TriBeCa lofts, Pound Ridge libraries and Greenwich kitchens. He has even been beckoned for work as far off as Bermuda. Often working in specialty veneers and exotic materials, his shop will start with a single room or do a whole house.

Area architects consider Donadic a "must-have" and tell us his large staff communicates and coordinates extremely well. The firm is noted to nail the proportions and details on the most refined of designs. S. Donadic Woodworking can also facilitate full-fledged design/build jobs. The firm installs its own work with a 45-man crew and all the finish-work is done in their in-house shop.

"Great guys." "Amazing work."

Smallbone of Devizes   4.5   4   4   4
105/109 Fulham Road, London, UK SW3 6RL,
011 44 (207) 838 - 3636   www.smallbone.co.uk

Fine hand-painted English cabinetry, custom design and installation

See Smallbone of Devizes's full report under the heading Kitchen & Bath Designers

	Quality ✚	Cost $	Value ◆	Recommend? ★

Sonrise Woodcarving Studio

| | 4 | 3.5 | 4.5 | 4.5 |

PO Box 12419, Cottekill, NY 12419
(845) 687 - 9139   www.sonrisewoodcarving.com

Millwork replication, repair, restoration and carving

Insiders tell us Stephan Toman's elaborately detailed carvings are truly special. Toman's talents in interior and exterior millwork and ornament run from replication to repair and restoration. Whether he's working with architects, contractors or directly with homeowners, he always displays "a knack for working with his customers over a long distance."

Self-taught, Toman has been carving since 1985. Clients call him a man of "great humor" who "never gets frazzled" and is "very dedicated to his work." Insiders tell us Toman's respect for the craft and disregard for the bottom line means he won't rush a job if it will compromise the quality, even if that means turning down work.

"*Stephan's work is totally unique, all hand-done—he is truly an artist.*" "*A guy like Stephan is one in a million—it took me forever to find someone who can do that kind of work.*" "*There are very few people in the country who can do the intricacy or fine carving of Stephan.*"

St. John's Bridge

| | 3.5 | 2.5 | 4.5 | 5 |

25 Railroad Street, Kent, CT 06757
(860) 927 - 3315

Custom decorative millwork

We hear Greg St. John does divine things to bookcases, cabinets and moldings. He adds decorative inlays, veneers and professional paintings to put a spin on his custom millwork. With a fine arts education and a love for creative expression, St. John creates many of his own designs. He will also work from those of a client or period reproduction. Insiders say he is highly skilled with mixing metals and exotic woods into his work.

"*He's talented, conscientious and plans ahead.*" "*If you explain what you want, he can come up with the design. He's very thorough and a very nice person.*" "*He uses the best materials and the cost is never a surprise.*"

Statham Woodwork

| | 4.5 | 4 | 4.5 | 5 |

38 Hemlock Place, 1st Floor, Norwalk, CT 06854
(203) 831 - 0629

High-end woodworking and casework

We hear this firm "will do whatever is required to get it right." It has stayed small to maintain owner Gary Statham's signature precision and pride in each job. Caring for both homeowners and the trade in Westchester and Fairfield counties, Statham Woodwork's service extends from doing a single paneled room to a half-million dollars' worth of architectural woodwork for an entire estate. Clients tell us the firm's consideration of its work in relation to other parts of construction and up-front care in its drawings set it apart.

Gary Statham's knowledge of woodworking dates back 40 years, when he helped his father make plaques and candle boxes. After a period crafting Shaker style furniture, Statham opened his mill shop in 1985. We're told the "intelligent" and "friendly" Statham designs everything himself on AutoCAD. His wife, Emily, accompanies him in the office and a crew of four installs in the field.

"*People you want to invite to dinner and maintain lasting relationships with.*" "*Every piece of molding and paneling fits together like a well-made glove even after the home has settled for several years.*" "*Very high end. Very proud of their work.*" "*Gary's work exceeded our expectations. He listened to our thoughts about the room and incorporated our desires wonderfully.*"

	Quality	Cost	Value	Recommend?
	✚	$	◆	★

Walston Stairbuilders, LLC

131 Nut Plains Road, Guilford, CT 06437
(203) 453 - 5929

Custom stair fabrication

| 4 | 4 | 4 | 4 |

Windsor Woodworking

3402 Fairfield Avenue, Bridgeport, CT 06605
(203) 335 - 0495

Custom casework and cabinetry

The good word on Windsor says this "great resource" listens to clients and avoids shortcuts, delivering exactly what was conceived. The firm's skilled artisans provide full woodworking capabilities for builders and designers and are available to the design whimsy of homeowners. Working in lower Fairfield County, the small firm takes on projects of varying scopes, with more difficult, detailed jobs others won't execute being the norm.

After a traditional apprenticeship in a shop in Vermont reproducing furniture, Jim McNolty established Windsor in 1983. As the shop has grown, McNolty has evolved from a master furniture-maker to a millwork and casework specialist. He supervises three employees and is personally involved from the first meeting to the last nail. Clients find McNolty and company "very creative, knowledgeable and helpful on any project, large or small."

"Jim McNolty is an excellent person to work with on any project." "Very creative, professional and fair. His work is the highest quality!" "Windsor was proactive and responsive."

HIRING A MOVER

Whether moving the family and pets to the suburbs, or temporarily relocating to "the summer house," just the thought of moving can bring the most poised individual to tears. Even more worrisome than organizing the process is the thought of placing all of one's worldly goods into the hands of a truckload of burly strangers. The less-than-sterling reputation of the moving industry doesn't help either. According to the Better Business Bureau, moving companies consistently make the list of the top-ten industries consumers complain about. Even moving companies themselves admit that three in ten moves result in a complaint against the mover. While those odds don't sound promising, there are several precautions you can take to ensure that you are one of the satisfied customers who end up providing glowing references about your moving company to your friends—and to *The Franklin Report*.

WHERE DO I START?

Hundreds of moving companies are listed in the Yellow Pages. Consider four main factors in making your choice: reputation, reliability, cost and availability. Begin with an assessment of your needs. According to most movers, a family of two adults and two children will require approximately 120 to 200 boxes. Most companies will provide an informal verbal estimate based on your description of items, number of rooms, the on both ends of the move, etc. If you're looking for a binding estimate, some movers will provide one after surveying your property and assessing your needs for themselves. Be forewarned that in this industry, a binding estimate is an elusive thing. Be prepared to consider any estimate a rough calculation rather than a binding agreement. In any event, be prepared with the requisite information before you call movers for estimates. Keep in mind that some movers only perform in-town moves while others are licensed to do countrywide and international moves as well.

Most movers provide packing services in addition to transportation. Packing, of course, incurs additional cost. If you choose to have your items packed by movers, you'll need to schedule packing days. Be sure to take inventory of what gets packed into each box, making sure to make a note of any existing damage. Keep a copy of the inventory list handy as you unpack to ensure that all your items have arrived safely. While movers assume liability for damage incurred by any items they packed themselves—they will not accept responsibility for items packed by you. Be sure to get estimates both with and without packing services in order to ensure that you opt for the services best suited to your needs and budget.

ON COST

Local moves are generally billed at an hourly rate, ranging anywhere from $85 per hour (a 1 on our Cost scale) to $225 per hour (a 5 on our Cost scale). This rate generally includes a truck and the labor of three men. Usually, moving companies will stipulate a minimum number of hours of moving time, and sometimes also a minimum amount of travel time. You should plan to factor in a gratuity of at least $5 per man per hour. Most movers will supply blankets and other padding material at no extra cost, but anything additional—rope, boxes, packing material, tape, bubble wrap, Styrofoam—will be supplied at a significant markup over retail. So you're better off buying your own packing materials ahead of time.

Weight-rated fees are usually used for long-distance moves. The charges are based on the weight of the goods and the distance they are moved. The truck is weighed before it is loaded with your household items and furniture, and then again after. The difference between the two weights will determine how you are charged. Again, get the best estimate you can before the move, but realize that the actual cost will be calculated after all the goods are loaded on the truck and weighed.

To keep the cost down, budget-minded consumers should consider packing their own books and clothes, but leave the packing of breakable items to the movers. That way the cost of moving can be contained and yet the cost of breakage and any other kind of damage can be absorbed by the moving company.

Summer is the most popular moving season. Not surprisingly, movers are generally over-extended during the summer months. The busiest time of year is generally also the most expensive. Many movers will offer up to a 30-percent discount on moves after Labor Day. Some will also charge less for weekday moves. However, these are options that movers don't readily mention, so make sure to ask about them when you're getting an estimate.

CONTRACTS, INSURANCE AND LICENSES

As with most business relationships, make sure that you negotiate a written contract before you move. Most moving companies have a standard contract form. If it doesn't include every foreseeable detail of the move, insist on adding these details. As with any contract, scrutinize it carefully before signing it. Ensure that any agreed-upon terms such as mileage, packing, standard charges, additional costs and insurance are all included in the contract. The contract should state that the men will stay after 5:00 PM to finish the move if it takes longer than expected. If possible, attach a copy of the inventory to the contract as well. Retain a copy of the signed contract well after delivery has been completed to ensure that all of your possessions are delivered in the manner that the contract dictates. Be aware that most standard contracts require that the movers be paid before they unload their truck at your new home.

For interstate moves, basic insurance usually provides $.60 of coverage for each pound of goods transported ($.30 for local moves). While there is usually no additional cost associated with this kind of coverage, you do need to sign an additional contract to activate it. Unfortunately, the coverage itself is less than adequate: for instance, if your $500 television weighs ten pounds, you can collect only $3. Several other insurance plans are provided at additional cost, and protecting the value of the $500 television might require purchasing one of these supplemental plans. Optional plans come at varying costs and provide different degrees of coverage. The American Moving and Storage Association (www.moving.org) can provide you with greater insights about moving insurance—they also supply guidelines to follow when planning a move.

COST-SAVING MOVING TIPS

✧ Packing items yourself will save you a bundle. However, movers are only liable for damage resulting from *their* packing, so limit the do-it-yourself items to unbreakables such as books and clothes.

✧ Packing materials cost significantly more when purchased from the moving company. If you're doing your own packing, buy the materials at an office products or packing products store.

✧ Insurance may seem like an expensive frill, but it can save you a lot of money and headaches in the event of damage. There are many types of coverage, so check out all your options before choosing one.

✧ The time of year and/or week during which you move will affect the cost. Since movers are typically busiest on weekends and in the summer, many companies offer discounts on moves that take place during the week and between Labor Day and Memorial Day.

| Quality | Cost | Value | Recommend? |

MOVERS

AirSea Packing Group Ltd.   4   3.5   4.5   4
40-35 22nd Street, Long Island City, NY 11101
(718) 937 - 6800   www.airseapacking.com
Packing and shipping of delicate and valuable items

A family-owned company in business for more than 30 years, AirSea Packing Group specializes in the packing and shipping of art and special items worldwide. With a client list that includes private collectors, commercial customers and museums, this firm has operations in London, Paris and Los Angeles, in addition to its New York location, which serves the Tri-State area. Consulting services include on-site advice on packing, installation, transportation and security. The firm also assists in purchasing and project management and boasts a storage facility offering the "ultimate in protection and security." In addition, computerized temperature-controlled facilities, custom-designed storage vaults, a viewing gallery and restoration and appraisal services make AirSea Packing a "one-stop-shopping" experience for your fine art needs.

We hear the 80-person staff is well trained and works with integrity and discretion for the well-heeled and high-profile clients it serves. References say the services AirSea Packing offers are expensive, but that "door-to-door" estimates given include everything, and are typically "right on the money."

"*The level of experience and professionalism is high, and worth the price for my piece of mind.*" "*Thorough and detail oriented.*" "*Perfect for high-end jobs.*"

All-Star Moving & Storage   4.5   2.5   4.5   4.5
88 Sanford Street, Brooklyn, NY 11205
(212) 254 - 2638   www.allstarmoveandstore.com
Residential moving and storage

Describing him as "honest, hardworking and compassionate," clients say owner Rich Barrale sets the tone from the top for the team at All-Star, a full-service moving and storage company in business for over a quarter century. While primarily serving the Tri-state area, we hear the firm has moved customers as far away as Chicago. All-Star also offers storage services. References report they were treated fairly, and that the move went smoothly and as planned. Free estimates are done on-site and sources tell us that the prices are reasonable given the extraordinary treatment they received. Barrale's commitment to outstanding quality service sets this company apart— making it truly an All-Star in the industry.

"*All-Star came on time, they were far and away above the rest and everything worked out to our expectations.*" "*There were no surprises, everything went smoothly.*" "*Unbelievably accommodating crew, they were outstanding!*" "*The workmen took pride in their work, and there was a great team effort.*" "*A great experience.*" "*Professional, thorough and accurate estimate.*"

Barr Brothers Moving Co. Inc.
86 Millwood Road, Millwood, NY 10546
(914) 762 - 8542
Residential moving

We hear this company sets the Barr for household moves. References are quick to note the company charges half the price of its competitors, yet maintains the same quality of service.

"Great job all around." "I am happy to say that moving day went—dare I say it—smoothly."

Big John's Moving   4   4   4   4.5
1602 First Avenue, New York, NY 10028
(212) 734 - 3300   www.bigjohnsmoving.com
Residential and commercial moving

Big John's responsive staff shoulder household moves on a local and national scale. Appreciative that moving is a stressful experience, the crews are patient, compassionate and come equipped with a sense of humor to usher customers through moving day "jitters." We hear the firm delivers supplies before the scheduled move and guarantees pick-up and delivery times for long-distance moves. While Big John's service comes at a premium, clients tell us they feel good paying for peace of mind.

"They could not have been nicer." "I just asked for boxes, and they delivered them quickly and at a reasonable price." "From start to finish, an excellent experience." "Everything was handled with care and arrived in good condition."

Brownstone Brothers   4.5   4   4   4.5
426 East 91st Street, New York, NY 10128
(212) 289 - 1511   www.brownstonebros.com
Residential and commercial moving and storage

Whether the move is large or small, we hear this streamlined company is "responsive, accommodating and capable." Serving the Tri-State metropolitan area since 1977, many decorators and the carriage trade have been long-time customers of Brownstone Brothers. The firm also offers packing, moving and storage services as well as a retail store that sells everything you could possibly need to move. References tell us the job quality is particularly good, and the prices, while not inexpensive, are worth it for the level of service provided.

"Efficient and effective. They had a quick response time, and have never broken anything!" "Very reliable." "I was dreading moving day, but in the end everything was just fine."

Buck's Transport   4.5   3.5   5   5
525 Fan Hill Road, Monroe, CT 06468
(203) 452 - 0910   www.buckstransport.com
Trade only—Receiving and delivering for interior designers

This exclusive "to-the-trade" operation has been serving top interior designers for the past twenty years. The firm handles jobs ranging from one piece to an entire household. Clients say Bucks Transport thoroughly inspects each item, even fielding an on-site repair shop to handle that rare, but inevitable damaged arrival.

Bucks Transport is made up of a small team led by owners Patty and Kevin Buckley. The definition of hands-on, Kevin is on the truck every day. Industry supporters tell us this top-rate outfit is worth the top rates it charges.

	Quality	Cost	Value	Recommend?
	+	$	◆	★

"Buck's makes me look good!" "They repair freight damage, are flexible when we need them to be and clients love them." "They have prevented many possible disasters for us because of their efficiency." "Business is all about contacts and relationships with quality companies. We are a better company because of Buck's excellence in all areas of deliveries."

Callahan Brothers   4.5   3   4.5   4.5

133 East Putnam Avenue, Cos Cob, CT 06807
(203) 869 - 2239
Residential moving and storage

Callahan Brothers, a family-owned business, has been a favorite of local decorators and homeowners for years. We hear the team is organized, easy to work with and can be counted on for personalized service with no hassles, hidden charges or other "moving day nightmares." An affiliate of North American, Callahan can handle local and long-distance moves, and can also help with storage needs.

Sources say the crews are very helpful and accommodating. Prices prove reasonable considering the high level of service and care.

"We have used Callahan for years and have nothing but great things to say about them." "Dependable and professional." "The guys were so nice—made my stressful moving day a little calmer." "From the time I called to inquire about their services until their spotless truck pulled out of the driveway of my new home, I knew I chose the right company."

Celebrity Moving   4.5   3.5   5   5

4-40 44th Drive, Long Island City, NY 11101
(212) 936 - 7171   www.celebritymoving.com
Residential and commercial moving and storage

Specializing in local, high-end moving, this firm receives rave reviews from private clients as well as the trade, who say the crew at Celebrity is one of the best in the industry. Working almost exclusively through referrals from top-tier decorators, Celebrity Moving, led by Jim Gomiela, ushers merchandise through many phases of shipping for its clients. In addition to the sophisticated controlling of inventory, services include the crating of art and pianos, as well as storage. We hear Celebrity is famous for their work ethic and high level of customer care.

"Jimmy and his crew are the best!" "After working with Celebrity for over twenty years, I have learned to disregard the claims of others." "They are there for you when you are in a bind." "Celebrity provides the highest quality of service—this company is outstanding." "We are an interior design firm and our clients are very demanding. Celebrity is extremely professional and always bends over backward for our requests."

Collins Brothers Moving Corporation   4   3.5   4   4

620 Fifth Avenue, Larchmont, NY 10538
(914) 646 - 6316   www.collinsbros.com
Residential and commercial moving and storage

In business for over 90 years, the heart of this large, full-service moving and storage company is its staff. Three hundred strong, Collins Brothers performs local and long-distance residential moves as well as international and commercial relocations. We hear the rigorous training the team at Collins Brothers goes through pays off in the professionalism demonstrated on the job. All estimates are done on-site, eliminating surprises. Clients say a field supervisor monitors each move, assuring the best possible outcome.

"Collins Brothers ensured that everything was done correctly." "What a wonderful job." "Not only are they skilled packers, but gentlemen you will be happy to have in your home." "The crew was very reliable, polite and helpful." "They got the job done with no pain."

	Quality	Cost	Value	Recommend?

Dahill Moving & Storage 3.5 2.5 4.5 4.5
5620 1st Avenue, Brooklyn, NY 11220
(800) 765 - 0905   www.dahillmoving.com
Residential and commercial moving

A leading moving company in business since 1928, Dahill is an agent for Mayflower International and can move you locally, across the country or across the globe. With a sizable staff, this firm handles all phases of relocation, from packing and moving to long- and short-term storage for jobs big or small. Despite their large size, we hear that the service is personal and attentive. Clients praise the crew for their care and flexibility and the fact that they "go the extra mile" to make sure things are done correctly. Local rates, which we are told are competitive, are charged by the hour. Outside a 60-mile radius of New York City, fees are calculated based on weight.

"They provided me with more information about moving and my rights as a consumer than any company has ever given." "Dahill handled everything with great care—they even sent packing specialists along with different staff to move the boxes and furniture." "Very flexible." "Great service for a fair price."

Designer Moving & Storage, Ltd. 4.5 3 5 5
35-15 11th Street, Long Island City, NY 11106
(718) 726 - 6777   www.designermoving.com
Residential and commercial moving and storage

Whether it's a move to the country house or a temporary relocation during a major renovation, the firm's diverse client base of high-end decorators, celebs and regular Joes are glowing about their treatment. The team at Designer Moving & Storage has made quite a reputation for itself as a detail-oriented mover in a short four years. Their storage is reportedly "amazing," with every piece logged and digitally photographed. Clients tell us, "I never need to visit the warehouse" because they "know exactly where everything is." From the initial meeting with owner Tom Farruggio to the actual moving day, professionalism is the word du jour, while the prices won't leave you speechless.

"Great with last minute pick-ups and deliveries." "Completely and totally trustworthy." "We made some strange requests and they were always honored." "The guys will stay on the job until it is completed—often late into the evening." "The crew is so polite and so careful. You definitely get what you pay for."

Gander & White 4.5 4.5 5 4.5
21-44 44th Road, Long Island City, NY 11101
(718) 784 - 8444
Residential moving, art and antiques

Providing climate-controlled storage, Gander & White is a high-end residential mover, packer and shipper of fine art and antiques both domestically and abroad. With offices in New York, London and Paris, this firm is truly an international operation. Clients are quick to note the personalized attention they receive from the professional and reliable staff. Many report that they are meticulous and accommodating, and while they're not the cheapest on our list, all agree that a stress-free move is well worth the price.

"A truly professional job." "They are used to the most discriminating clientele, and have foremen that can relate to the clients." "While quite expensive, they stayed until the job was done. It was worth the cost." "They didn't even bat an eyelash when my husband and I had them move a large armoire four times back and forth across the room." "They will even hang pictures on the wall!" "When the platform they promised didn't come on the right day, they sent it later and moved our entire garage onto it at no extra charge."

	Quality ✚	Cost $	Value ◆	Recommend? ★

HTR Moving & Delivery Services

	4	3.5	4.5	4.5

737 Canal Street, Stamford, CT 06902
(203) 323 - 8600 htrmover@aol.com

Residential moving and delivery

This ten-year-old firm is a favorite amongst area designers and decorators. The small team at HTR Moving & Delivery Services is known in the industry for their "white glove" handling of jobs, from a single exquisite antique to an entire household in need of relocation.

HTR offers services as varied as hand-packing your worldly goods to "engineered" loading of items into trucks, eliminating damage during transit. Upon arrival, the crew stays until everything is perfect. While wallets must open a little wider for this treatment, clients wave goodbye to HTR movers with ear-to-ear grins.

"Incredibly responsible." "I love these guys—I do not worry for one single second that things will go smoothly and efficiently." "When I moved, I did not want to be involved at all—they did it all and did it perfectly." "HTR is expensive, but peace of mind does not have a price tag."

MHO Movers/Antique Delivery Service

	4.5	3	5	5

737 Canal Street, Stamford, CT 06902
(203) 229 - 0102 www.mhomovers.com

Residential and commercial moving and storage

Led by former teacher and coach Michael Ornato, the MHO team gets their game on for high-end residential moves in Connecticut and Westchester. Fans of the firm admire its dedication and professionalism. We hear MHO's fair billing makes this mover a winner.

"They have an excellent attitude and are timely and trustworthy." "Our possessions are very expensive. The MHO employees handled them with care and expertise." "This is a truly exceptional company—fair, ethical and service oriented."

Morgan Manhattan Moving & Storage

	4.5	5	4.5	5

16 Bruce Park Avenue, Greenwich, CT 06830
(203) 869 - 8700 www.morganmanhattan.com

Residential moving, fine art and antiques, wine storage

Catering to discriminating, high-end clients as well as celebrities, Morgan Manhattan performs residential moves locally and nationally. The firm is literally the oldest moving company in the USA, having been in business since 1851. While typically shying away from smaller jobs, Morgan Manhattan will handle single, priceless pieces.

In addition, the company cares for the storage and inventory control of fine wine collections, housing them in their refrigerated and humidity-controlled facility. Since Morgan has a sophisticated, interactive computer system, clients tell us they can view their wine collections right online and make notations as to vintage, price and "best drinking date," making the service not only highly professional, but extremely high-tech. While many say this fifth-generation firm charges a generous sum, they also say you get generous service back in return.

Quality	Cost	Value	Recommend?

"Very careful, very seamless, very professional." "The service was impecca-ble." "I wouldn't trust my valuables to anyone else." "Very personal attention." "I demand the best, and I got white-glove treatment from this company." "I was amazed at the technology used to track my wine collection. My husband is in the computer industry, and even he was completely impressed."

Moving Ahead   4.5   3   4.5   5
101 5th Avenue, Garden City, NY 11040
(212) 262 - 0600   www.movingahead.com
Residential and commercial moving and storage, truck rental services

Sporting an exemplary record up and down the East Coast, Moving Ahead comes highly recommended by both private and commercial clients. Led by John Tarko, the team is described as knowledgeable and professional as well as cour-teous and flexible. This firm is designated as the only official mover of Manhattan Mini Storage. From their spotless trucks to the work ethic of their employees, ref-erences tell us that Moving Ahead is the only company they will use for both personal and business relocations. Moving Ahead charges by the hour and gives estimates upon request.

"We had relationships with other movers and always had issues with customer service. Five years ago we gave Moving Ahead a shot and we've never looked back!" "They're extremely professional and helpful—our relationship is based on trust." "What sets them apart is that they work with the customers to resolve the few issues that ever arise, instead of simply turning their backs and walking off, as most movers tend to do." "We would never use another moving company."

MZ Movers Systems   3   3.5   3.5   4
543 Tarrytown Road, White Plains, NY 10607
(914) 421 - 9095
Residential and commercial moving

This firm comes recommended by private clients as well as the trade who tell us MZ Moving Systems has proven to be a company dedicated to total customer service. The firm handles each customer uniquely, customizing each job based on their needs. Visual inspections are done to determine cost, which we hear is rea-sonable given the high quality of service.

"Honest, fair." "Did a very good job—we had no problems at all."

Personal Touch   5   4.5   5   5
70-04 67th Street, Glendale, NY 11385
(718) 417 - 6740
Residential moving

Working exclusively through referrals, Personal Touch has developed a reputa-tion for being one of the finest moving companies in the Tri-State area. Owner Sal DiPiazza takes the name Personal Touch to new levels by meeting with each client to estimate the individual needs of the job and establish a flat fee to cover the entire move. Clients remark that there are no hidden costs—the price estimated is the price paid. Personal Touch is expensive, but sources say the bill is worth every cent for the level of service and a "job extremely well done."

Customers report that DiPiazza outdoes expectations with the number of men he brings to each job. All involved seem to benefit from this unique "high manpower policy"—the customer gets a speedy move and the crew gets in and out in a rea-sonable time. We hear clients couldn't be happier with DiPiazza and his "amazing" staff and they add that the value and service at Personal Touch is truly exemplary.

"Best mover I have ever used!" "There is no reason to consider another com-pany." "The entire experience was pleasant from the time they arrived until the time they left." "Efficient, courteous, careful and anxious to please." "Not only is Sal one of the hardest working men I have ever met, his staff is equally moti-vated and enthusiastic." "Unbelievably organized, pleasant, and fast."

	Quality ✚	Cost $	Value ◆	Recommend? ★

The Packing Shop — 4.5 · 4 · 4.5 · 4.5

89 Leuning Street, South Hackensack, NJ 07606
(201) 342 - 9097   www.thepackingshop.co.uk
Packing, storage and transportation of fine art and antiques

The Packing Shop, founded in London in 1987, is one of Europe's leaders in the specialized field of the packing, storage and transportation of fine art and antiques. Clients throughout the United States can enjoy all of the benefits of those in Europe, as this company now has a US operation headquartered in northern New Jersey. The firm serves trade clients including decorators, art dealers, galleries and auction houses, as well an impressive list of private collectors and art investors who laud the efficiency, reliability and professionalism of the 50-strong team.

Capable of dealing with large volumes of extremely valuable shipments by land, air and sea, The Packing Shop boasts high-tech security and tracking systems and state of the art, climate-controlled and secure warehouses in London and New Jersey. We hear the staff is well trained, and that they constantly strive to remain leaders in the field. References tell us that the peace of mind they get from knowing their precious cargo is in safe hands is well worth the cost.

"Incredibly reliable and efficient." "Packing is exceptional." "A joy to deal with."

The Velvet Touch — 4 · 3.5 · 4 · 4

145-21 23rd Avenue, Whitestone, NY 11357
(718) 742 - 5320
Residential and commercial moving and storage, art and antiques

This relatively young company has taken the Tri-State moving industry by storm, developing a client list of top decorators and antique dealers who praise The Velvet Touch for being professional, trustworthy and most importantly, careful. With a team in the moving business for sixteen years, the firm handles residential and commercial jobs, specializing in art and antiques.

Clients tell us that the crews at The Velvet Touch handle their delicate and expensive items with the utmost care, as if they were their own possessions. Others nod to the personalized service, citing owner Kimon Thermos' personal involvement in each move.

"They are always willing to work with clients to agree on fair pricing." "I have confidence in them." "They are very reliable and very careful." "Working with The Velvet Touch was a pleasure. They have moved millions of dollars worth of antiques for us and I can confidently say they are one of the best truckers in New York."

William B. Meyer Inc.   📁 📁 📁 📁

255 Long Beach Boulevard, Stratford, CT 06615
(800) 873 - 6393   www.williambmeyer.com
Residential and commercial moving and storage

Combining the efficiency of a well-oiled machine with the old-fashioned honesty and integrity of a family business, William B. Meyer Inc. impresses both residential and commercial clients. Whether moving from the Tri-State area to anywhere in the country or anywhere in the world, we hear that this 85-year-old company has both the manpower, facilities and experience to get the job done right. In addition, the firm accommodates commercial moving services, rigging, courier services and off-site data protection services for businesses. The added muscle, however, comes at extra expense.

"We moved from Connecticut to Florida, and needless to say we were very anxious. The crew made us feel that we were in good hands." "They suggested ways we could save money on our move by packing ourselves—they even showed us how to do it!"

Hiring Painters & Wallpaperers

Walk into a room painted a beautiful celadon green and immediately your mood changes—you become calmer, more relaxed. By merely changing the color of a space, you can produce a feeling of drama or tranquility. Designers know that painting is one of the quickest, most versatile and cost-effective things you can do to transform a room. But painting can be a messy and hazardous proposition for the novice, so many homeowners opt to hire a professional contractor.

Paint contractors with a wide range of abilities and services abound. Choices range from small start-ups to large established firms, and from straight painters to custom muralists. Depending upon the size of the job and the quality and complexity of the work, there is a paint contractor out there for you.

Where to Look for a Professional

Finding the right paint contractor for your job involves some research. It is important to check references and ask to see a certificate of insurance. Each contractor should have worker's compensation and general liability insurance which protects you from job site-related liabilities. Several trade organizations, such as the Painting and Decorating Contractors of America (www.pdca.org), list paint contractors in your area. And of course, *The Franklin Report* offers a range of client-tested choices.

Contracts

Reputable contractors will encourage using a written contract. Your contract should clearly explain the scope of the work to be performed and include a list of the surfaces to be painted, a time schedule for the project, payment procedures and any warranty or guarantee the contractor might offer.

Pricing Systems

When considering the price for painting it is important to know that the cost structure for straight painting is much different than that of decorative work. While some firms do both types of work your bill will be determined using different factors.

The cost for straight painting in residential homes varies based on such factors as the cost of the materials and the company's overhead costs. You should invite at least three paint contractors to bid on your paint job, and ask each to submit a detailed written proposal. Painting contractors charge on a per person per day basis, which generally runs in the $425 to $475 range for nonunion jobs (this equates to approximately a 2.5 to 3 on our Cost scale). Union jobs start at about $500 per-person per-day. The contractor should provide you with an overall cost estimate for the job that is broken down by room. Also ask for a step-by-step plan outlining how the job will be spackled, skimmed and painted. If colors are being matched, ask the painter to apply 24-inch-square samples on the walls.

Decorative painting, and which in the case of murals or decorative finishes, is often considered "art" and is much more subjective price wise. This process is usually more involved—there are meetings with the homeowner, decorator and painter to determine a style or theme and to incorporate the decorative work into the overall design plan. Time frames for completing a job are usually longer compared to straight painting. All of these factors contribute to the cost of decorative painting.

When considering the "bottom line" for any painting job, ask for client references. They can provide valuable insight into not only the quality of work and timing, but cost as well.

HOW MANY PAINTERS WILL BE IN MY HOUSE?

The size of the crew largely depends upon the scope of the job involved. Some painters listed in this guide are sole proprietors who work on small jobs themselves and subcontract larger jobs—others are larger companies with complete crews. Ask how many men will be working on your job and whether there will there be a supervisor or principal on-site.

THE ELEMENTS OF A PROFESSIONAL PAINT JOB

Flat painting a room involves preparing the walls, trim and ceiling surfaces for the paint as well as the paint job itself. To prepare walls, paint crews will do all the taping, plastering, plaster restoration, if needed, and skim coating. This prep work is considered one of the most important elements of a paint job as it provides the foundation for the paint. A primer coat, which prepares the walls for the paint, should be applied to dry walls. Two coats of high-quality paint should be applied to the wall surfaces.

WHICH PAINT?

The quality of the paint is crucial in determining its longevity. Fine quality paint, properly applied, should last for six to seven years. If you or your contractor skimp on the quality of the paint, you may be facing a new paint job a lot sooner than you would like. The two most common types of paints are latex and oil-based paints. Latex paint is water-based and dries quickly, which allows for more than one coat to be applied in a day. Latex paint is better at resisting mildew, easier to clean and lasts longer than alkyd paints, which are oil-based. Alkyd paints are preferred by many painters because they are durable and long lived, but they take longer to dry, have a significant odor and can yellow over time. Most experts agree that oil-based paints are best suited for the doors and trim, and latex paint for the walls and ceilings.

LEAD PAINT HAZARDS

The presence of lead paint presents health hazards in many homes. The federal government banned the use of lead paints in 1978 therefore, if you live in an older home or apartment building, it may contain a layer of lead paint if it was painted prior to that year. When sanding is done in advance of painting, the sanding may cause lead dust to enter the air in your home. Your contractor should provide you with a pamphlet that discusses lead issues in your home. Ask your contractor what measures he takes to ensure that lead particles are eliminated. If you need to have your home inspected or have lead removed, the Environmental Protection Agency (www.epa.gov) issues licenses for companies and professionals who work with lead control, including removal, inspection and risk assessment. Other good resources for more information about lead and asbestos include the American Lung Association (www.lungusa.org), the US Consumer Product Safety Commission (www.cpsc.gov), the American Industrial Hygiene Association (www.aiha.org), the Department of Housing and Urban Development (www.hud.gov) and the Occupational Safety and Health Administration (www.osha.gov).

WALLPAPER

Wallpaper can add depth, texture and visual interest to a room. Floral or striped wallpaper can make even small windowless rooms cheerful. It can also be a costly investment, so it is important to find a qualified, competent professional to install your paper. Finding a wallpaper hanger can be as easy as talking to your paint contractor, as most also provide this service. Depending upon the complexity of the job, it may be appropriate to contact a professional who specializes in wallpaper hanging. One source is the National Guild of Professional Paperhangers (NGPP). For their local chapter local, call (800) 254-6477 or visit www.ngpp.org.

Cost for wallpapering is based on a per roll basis with rates averaging about $50 per roll. Most wallpaper is sold in double-roll units, which measure approximately 60 square feet. The price quoted should include trimming the sides of the paper if necessary. Professionals will strip your walls of existing paper and prep it for the new paper for an additional fee. Your wallpaper hanger should calculate the quantity of paper you will need for the room based on the room size as well as the "repeat" pattern on your paper. The larger the repeat, the more paper you will need. The newer vinyl wallpaper comes pre-pasted, while traditional and costlier papers need to be trimmed and pasted with wheat paste.

DECORATIVE FINISHES: THE ART OF IMITATION

Decorative finishes, often called "faux finishes," are used by painters to add depth or to imitate materials such as marble, wood, paper, stone, metal and fabric. These finishes can be elegant, whimsical or dramatic, depending upon the artist and the paint technique utilized. Current trends today include fake wood ("faux bois") paneled libraries, limestone facades and "washed" finishes. When done by a gifted artist, a faux finish can cost more than the material being imitated. Decorative finishes can customize a space with color and texture and dramatically reflect the owner's style.

DECORATIVE PAINTING: A MASTER TRADITION

A wall-sized mural that recreates a Pompeian gallery . . . majestic Greek columns beside the swimming pool . . . famous storybook characters dancing along the walls of a child's room . . . these enchanting effects are the work of decorative painters.

Decorative painting is an art form that uses techniques that have been passed down by artisans throughout the centuries. Today, decorative painters can come from a variety of backgrounds—some have fine art degrees, many have studied the techniques of the Old Masters in Europe and others have been schooled specifically in decorative painting. These professionals carry the legacy of a tradition that was once passed from master to apprentice. Both artists and craftsmen, many decorative painters have a thorough knowledge of specific historical and decorative styles and have the ability to translate this knowledge in a historically accurate artistic rendering. Others, however, are clearly unqualified to be attempting this work.

There are many forms of decorative painting. Some of the most popular include fresco, murals and trompe l'oeil. Over time, techniques and materials have been enhanced and improved, allowing artists and artisans to produce works that have lasted—and will last—for centuries.

When you are considering any decorative painting style, ask to see a portfolio of the artist's work and, if possible, visit a home that has work of a similar nature. Decorative showhouses are also an excellent venue in which to witness the artistry of decorative painting. Many decorative painters use these showcases to demonstrate their talents. If working with an interior designer, consult with him or her on the project and how it will enhance your overall room design. If the designer finds the artist for you, ask how that affects fees. Artists should also provide you with renderings of the work being produced.

Fees vary widely for decorative painting and are based on many factors, including the scope and scale of the project, degree of difficulty and expertise of the painter. Ask your contractor to provide you with a sample board of the paint technique you desire. Some charge for this service while others include it in the total cost of the project. Decorative finishes can be charged on a per person or on a per day basis, and sometimes a square foot basis, but are usually priced per job.

Decorative painting can be a major investment, but certainly one with exquisite results.

PAINT-CHOOSING TIPS

✧ Use oil-based paint for metals and trim; latex for wood and drywall.

✧ High-traffic areas need a durable, easy-to-clean paint job. Use delicate paint applications in light-traffic areas only.

✧ Use flat paint for base coats; gloss to set off trim and doors.

✧ Be alert to the number of coats required. Eggshell paints, for example, take at least one extra coat.

PAINTERS & WALLPAPERERS

Alatis Interiors Co. Ltd.   4.5   3.5   4.5   5
40-22 College Point Boulevard, Flushing, NY 11354
(718) 358 - 9051   alatisinc@aol.com
Decorative and straight painting and wallpapering

Alatis, in business since 1933, is a family-run painting company that comes highly recommended by some of the areas' top contractors and decorators. The timely and professional Alatis team does everything from straight residential painting and wallpapering to specialty painting and decorative finishes, including glazing and stucco. In addition to being really nice to work with, owners Tom and Jimmy Alatis are known to be involved in every project and sources tell us they execute a great finished product.

"We couldn't ask for more." "The crew showed up on time and was extremely conscientious and professional." "I am very picky, and these guys really made me happy, which says a lot for the company." "I was truly impressed with their care and concern." "A high-quality painter with even higher quality service." "He is a marvelous, thorough and reliable contractor." "There are very few companies we would recommend this highly."

Alton Inc.   4   3.5   4.5   5
40-19 35th Avenue, Long Island City, NY 11101
(718) 784 - 4230   altonpainting@aol.com
Decorative and straight painting and wallpapering

The painter of choice for a number of high-end building professionals, Alton offers straight residential painting, wallpapering and decorative painting. We hear they excel in faux finishes, trompe l'oeil, graining, gilding, Venetian plaster and stucco. Unlike many other practitioners of decorative work, this firm does all of its own prep work, which we're told is exemplary. Alton's clients keep coming back for value, service and outstanding work.

"I was so impressed with Tom's workmanship and incredible reliability that I have continued to use him for every project." "Very responsive." "Great prep work." "They did a fantastic job—well worth the money." "Their Venetian stucco is extremely beautiful."

Ambiance Interiors   🗀   🗀   🗀   🗀
67 Murray Street, Norwalk, CT 06851
(203) 943 - 4234
Painting and wallpapering

Andrea & Timothy Biggs Painting   4.5   4   5   5
279 Sterling Place, Brooklyn, NY 11238
(718) 857 - 9034   amtgbiggs@aol.com
Faux finishes and murals

We're told "there isn't anything these two better halves can't do." Andrea and Tim Biggs collaborate to produce a wide variety of decorative paintings and finishes for both residential and commercial clients. Together they have developed an expansive portfolio that includes trompe l'oeil murals combined with landscape painting to create architectural illusions, large-scale murals with a focus on floral, organic or fantasy imagery and faux finishes that include glazing and marbleizing for ornamental pieces, walls and ceilings. Clients remark that the Bigg's work is consistently completed with "beautiful quality." The duo often produces their own creations, but they also reproduce traditional artworks and create pieces that bring their clients' visions to fruition. Sources say they work closely with designers and architects to integrate their work into the overall design.

"Their faux-marble work has held up beautifully for ten years and counting." "They always do what they commit to—flexible and client oriented." "Such a delight—they even played lovely classical music while working." "Head and shoulders above the rest." "I love working with them—they're honest, businesslike and reliable."

Andrew Tedesco   5   4   4.5   5
122 West 26th Street, New York, NY 10001
(212) 924 - 8438   www.andrewtedesco.com

Decorative painting and murals

From the high-end glazing and gold-leaf ceilings to murals, trompe l'oeil and fine art customers are very impressed with the quality and creativity of Andrew Tedesco's painting. For over ten years, Tedesco has done residential and commercial work, both on-site and in his studio. Clients have been particularly impressed with his ability to take their ideas to another level, adapting the work to fit the space while balancing their taste with his style of painting. He is known to work with top decorators and in addition to New York and its surrounding areas, Tedesco's work has also taken him around the country on projects in Miami, Chicago and Boston.

Educated at the Parsons School of Design, Tedesco spent some time working with Broadway scenic artists and has drawn on these experiences to create a unique personal style, often using the palettes of old masters. We hear his impressive results may come at quite a price, but are well worth it.

"His work is just exquisite." "An extremely high quality painter." "Very good at what he does and really great to work with." "Andrew's talent is complemented by his charming and engaging personality—a delight to work with." "Andrew has always kept up with the latest techniques and presentation methods." "His imagination and creativity along with his artistic skills are superb."

Anton Sattler   5   4.5   4.5   5
466 Main Street, New Rochelle, NY 10801
(914) 636 - 2916

Decorative and straight painting and wallpapering

In business since 1891, Anton Sattler has developed a premier, international reputation for the very finest high-end residential painting. Clients include some of the most prominent businesspeople and most exclusive decorators worldwide. Sattler does straight painting as well as a range of decorative custom work. The firm's team of 50 craftsmen is said to be professional, tidy and courteous. References uniformly judged the quality of Anton Sattler's work to be the very best and, while costly, worth the price.

"Very beautiful work—this is as good as it gets." "A painter's painter." "They do the highest quality work."

	Quality	Cost	Value	Recommend?

Applied Aesthetics

Quality	Cost	Value	Recommend?
4	3	5	5

90 Valentine Avenue, Glen Cove, NY 11542
(516) 759 - 2188   aapaintstudio@netscape.net
Decorative painting, gilding and plaster finishes

Sought after by some of the areas' most reputable decorators and architects, Jennifer Hakker and the team at Applied Aesthetics perform all kinds of decorative and specialty painting. Specializing in plaster finishes, gilding and wood graining, Hakker also handles trompe l'oeil, painted furniture and fabrics. References tell us that she is a marked creative talent who shows a real interest in the ideas her clients bring to the table. Many comment on the firm's professionalism, reliability and noteworthy attention to detail. Loyal customers appreciate the "consistently superior results," so much so that they often call upon Applied Aesthetics to work in their second residences and vacation homes.

"A magician with paint!" "Applied Aesthetics are modern-day masters." "The final project is always more brilliant than I imagined." "Jennifer and her crew are the most reliable, focused and talented decorative painters I have ever worked with." "Her work is consistently superior and she is extremely professional." "I would never have anyone else touch my walls." "Wide range of skills that she executes remarkably well."

Arturo Moreno

538 Pelham Road, New Rochelle, NY 10805
(914) 632 - 4532
Residential painting

Barcello Painting

737 Canal Street, Stamford, CT 06902
(203) 329 - 8699
Residential painting

Barnes Wallpapering

PO Box 705, Bethel, CT 06801
(203) 798 - 0092
Wallpapering

We hear that Gary Barnes is so good that decorators not only recommend him to their clients, they also use him on their own homes. Known to be both easy to work with and extremely skilled at his craft, Barnes Wallpapering gets rave reviews from adoring fans. Prices are said to be quite reasonable given the superior service.

"Gary Barnes is a perfectionist and a delightful person." "He is my first choice to work on my own home which is the highest recommendation I can give."

Bill Gibbons Studio

Quality	Cost	Value	Recommend?
4	4	4	4

368 Broadway, Suite 203, New York, NY 10013
(212) 227 - 0039   www.billgibbons.com
Murals on canvas and tiles

Bill Gibbons designs and creates traditional murals on canvas in his New York City studio and, once painted, he installs them like wallpaper in the client's residence. His work includes classical pieces, architectural renderings, landscapes, trompe l'oeil paintings and decorative ceiling tiles. Clients say Gibbons' murals can be removed and relocated if needed. In business for over thirteen years, he works frequently with top interior designers and with private clients. We understand his prices are slightly bolder than most, but then again, so, they say, is his art.

	Quality +	Cost $	Value ◆	Recommend? ★

BK Wallcovering
4.5 3.5 4.5 4.5

500 West 42nd Street, Suite 6B, New York, NY 10036
(212) 629 - 3040   www.bfkinc.com

Wallpapering

Strictly a wallcovering specialist, BK Wallcovering led by Brian Kehoe, has been serving area residents and businesses for seventeen years. The firm handles both large and small projects with care and has been entrusted with the hanging of a mural at the Guggenheim and the wallpapering of designer showrooms. But don't be intimidated—we hear the adorable print you pick out for the bathroom, or the exquisite formal paper you chose for your living room will be hung with this same skill and craftsmanship.

References tell us the team is a pleasure to work with, and praise their reliable, accommodating and professional service. While the firm's expert services are pricey, we hear they are competitive with similarly tiered professionals.

"Their work is outstanding." "Willing to be flexible and accommodate our schedule." "Brian has always provided the highest level of professional, reliable service." "I find his prices competitive and his work excellent." "I would recommend Mr. Kehoe and his staff with complete confidence."

Bonnie Buggee
4.5 3.5 5 4.5

2 Champlin Square, Essex, CT 06426
(860) 767 - 3926   bbinessex@aol.com

Decorative painting

Sources tell us that if you are looking for a realistic look and old-world craftsmanship, Bonnie Buggee fits the bill. From intense floors painted to look like they are inlaid to faux bois, woodgraining, Venetian plaster and any other decorative finish you can think of, Bonnie's straightforward approach makes clients stand up and take notice.

Working primarily with decorators, Buggee is best at executing the clients end goal rather than "hand-holding" throughout the entire process. If you know what you want, sources tell us Buggee is the "no-nonsense" contractor for you. Prices are high-end, but clients appreciate the fact that Buggee uses only the finest materials and that she puts time and care into each project.

"Bonnie is the best." "She is creative, has a "right on" color sense and is a dream to work with." "Clients always like her." "A wealth of information and ideas." "Generous with her time and talent."

Branko Mrdelja Painting & Decorating
4.5 4 4.5 5

18 Schubert Lane, Cos Cob, CT 06807
(203) 561 - 5135

Interior and exterior painting, wallpapering

Described as "all around great guys" the team at Branko Mrdelja Painting & Decorating have been beautifying the walls of area residences for upwards of 32 years. Inheriting the painting business from his father, Branko and his crew do interior and exterior painting, hang wallpaper, strip and refinish wood surfaces such as panels, doors etc. An added bonus is that they are known to be quite handy at any household task you request of them. Homeowners rave about the fact that they did not have to call someone else in for a minor repair, Branko's team was more than capable and happy to do the job for them. Prices are not cheap but "worth the extra" for the outstanding work.

"Truly an amazing paint job." "I love Branko—nothing is ever a problem." "The crew is always there for last minute fixes." "When I saw the final result, I couldn't believe it."

	Quality	Cost	Value	Recommend?
	✚	$	◆	★

Broken Colour   4.5   3   4.5   5
1889 Palmer Avenue, Lower Level, Larchmont, NY 10538
(914) 833 - 9519   brkncolour@aol.com

Decorative painting

Peggy Taylor of Broken Colour has been been painting for over 25 years. She began in California and then five years ago started her own business in this area. With a menu of decorative finishes to choose from, clients are impressed with Taylor's skill, attention to detail and most of all, her wonderful personality, which is said to shine through on each job. When you hire Taylor, you get Taylor who works with one assistant. We hear that her glazes and faux stone work are outstanding, and happy customers say her prices are right on the money.

"I love the fact that she can do anything—ceilings, furniture, floors—not afraid to tackle any assignment with class and flair." "Really good and really nice to work with." "Professional—she is not someone who is 'doing this on the side.'" "Peggy is easy-going, hardworking and flexible. Willing to work with you and understands there is always another way."

Bruce Lawner   4.5   4   5   4.5
By Appointment Only, (203) 708 - 2057

Wallpapering and interior straight painting

Called a wallpaper master, Bruce Lawner "has paste in his blood." Lawner has been in business for over 25 years and in addition to being a graduate of the US School of Professional Paperhanging in Vermont, Lawner passed on his experience and knowledge of the craft by teaching there. He now treats area residents to his skill, which has been described as "superb" and "impeccable." Able to work with any kind of paper or textile imaginable, there is probably nothing Lawner has not seen.

In addition to wallpapering, Bruce Lawner handles interior straight painting jobs. We hear that price wise he is on the higher end, but the quality is "so incredible" that customers write the check with pleasure. Add the one-year guarantee to the mix and sources say Bruce Lawner is a great deal.

"He is neat, timely and very pleasant to work with." "We hope to have the good fortune of dealing with someone like Bruce Lawner when we have other home improvement projects."

C&H Plastering & Drywall   📁   📁   📁   📁
29 West Devonia, Mt. Vernon, NY 10552
(914) 906 - 5984

Plastering

C&S Wallpaper   📁   📁   📁   📁
10 Wild Oaks Road, Suite 212, Goldens Bridge, NY 10526
(914) 767 - 0094

Wallpapering and painting

Clients rave at the painstaking time and care Carlos Ribeiro gives to his wallpapering projects. They love the fact that he takes such pride in his work, and is always there to help. C&S Wallpaper also does painting, which we hear is equally fantastic."

"Fastidious—clients love him."

	Quality	Cost	Value	Recommend?
	✚	$	◆	★

Campbell's Painting Inc.

12 Long Hill Road, Bethel, CT 06801
(203) 431 - 3797 dcampb1783@aol.com

Interior and exterior painting and wallpapering

A favorite among the area's best contractors, Dan Campbell and the crew at Campbell's Painting are known in the industry to do excellent work on projects large and small. Whether it's new construction or a renovation job, sources tell us that the eighteen-year-old company is consistently "high-quality," and is also easy to work with and efficient. Campbell strives to make scheduling easy for the client and when the team is on the job, we hear that they are equally as cooperative. Customers tell us that they are never inconvenienced—when Campbell's comes at night, the work-space is so clean you would never know anyone had been there.

In addition to offering both interior and exterior painting, Campbell's can handle decorative work and wallpapering projects. We're told prices are on the higher side, but fair and competitive for the level of care and attention to detail.

"Dan and his crew are great on large projects." "Very ethical and professional." "The crew is genuinely concerned about making the customer happy." "Dan's motto is 'forget not,' and that says it all—no stone is ever left unturned."

Carol Cannon

4	3	4.5	5

32-45 37th Street, Astoria, NY 11103
(718) 956 - 9334 www.carolcannon.com

Decorative painting and murals

Clients are equally impressed with Carol Cannon's decorative painting, which includes all types of special effect treatments for walls and ceilings, murals in both classical and abstract motifs, and dedication to the craft. We hear the "charming Cannon" is unsatisfied until she can capture exactly the right color. References describe her as reliable, fair and very honest. Cannon works throughout New York City, Connecticut, Westchester and the Hamptons and has been known to travel the world to handle projects in the vacation homes of her clients.

"Delivers that dreamy look." "Can get you exactly the right texture, color and mood." "Very accommodating—works hard to get it right." "Very consistent and very professional."

Charles R. Keoshgerian
Woodfinishing & Painting

4.5	4.5	4.5	5

93 Richards Avenue, Suite 801, Norwalk, CT 06854
(203) 981 - 5339 ckwoodfinishing@earthlink.net

Wood finishes, gold leaf, lacquers and plasterwork

If your library, den or kitchen has wood that is screaming for attention, high-end contractors will undoubtedly mention Charles Keoshgerian. With 33 years of experience in painting and wood finishing, we hear he runs a business based on being sensitive to the customer. Catering to the area's most discerning clientele, Keoshgerian is described as "a real find," and a true star in the business. While not inexpensive, the high level of service and quality leave happy patrons saying "you get what you pay for."

Chuck Hettinger

4.5	3.5	4.5	4.5

208 East 13th Street, New York, NY 10003
(212) 614 - 9848

Decorative painting, color consultations

Clients say Chuck Hettinger merges the skills and sensibilities of mixed media and decorative painting with great success. For the past 23 years, Hettinger has focused on decorative surface work, including special glazes, stripes, faux bois and marbling. A notable specialty is his stenciling, which is often custom designed, site specific and has been described as "modern and

| | Quality | Cost | Value | Recommend? |

practical." In addition to his other work, he will also do color consultations. A number of distinguished clients and top decorators recommended Hettinger, labeling him "a true artist" who also has "a sense of humor." They say working with the witty, friendly and easygoing artisan is a treat.

"Really great to work with." "Knows what to do and how to do it beautifully." "The stencil work is really fantastic."

Coastal Painting   4.5   4.5   4   4.5
6B Barry Avenue, Ridgefield, CT 06877
(203) 438 - 2592
Interior and exterior painting, decorative finishes and wallpapering

Top contractors in the area highly recommend Coastal Painting. Headed by Alex Scavone, the firm handles projects ranging from a simple paint job to luxurious custom finishes including kitchen cabinet finishing, Venetian plaster and antiquing. Coastal also handles restorations and wallpapering projects with finesse and craftsmanship.

Known in the industry for being service-oriented, the crew of perfectionists at Coastal make sure that no matter what it takes, the homeowner is completely satisfied. Prices are described as high, however all are quick to note that the quality speaks for itself.

"Excellent painters." "Gets it done fast and well." "Exceptional quality—prices are high, but worth every dime."

Creative Wall Decor & Decorating Inc.   5   4.5   5   5
4 Mallard Drive, West Nyack, NY 10994
(203) 509 - 8256
Wallpapering

Not only does Peter Milmore and the team at Creative Wall Decor & Decorating work with the best decorators in the area, he is often called upon to consult for some of the most prestigious wallpaper manufacturers in the industry. Milmore, who represents the third generation in a family of craftsmen, was taught by his father and grandfather. We hear he learned well—customers say when he does a job, the results are flawless. Fans quickly note that they keep coming back for Milmore's attention to detail and endless experience. Prices are said to be high, but the perfect seams are said to be worth every penny.

"He is a genius—an absolute perfectionist."

Custom Painting & Decorating by Val
76B Peck Avenue, Rye, NY 10580
(914) 967 - 5126
Custom painting

Decorative Art & Design   5   3.5   5   5
418 Lakeside Drive, Stamford, CT 06903
(203) 968 - 8445   www.decartdesign.com
Plaster and decorative painting

Milé Djuric of Decorative Art & Design has created a virtual who's who fan base in his twelve years in business—yet we hear he is down to earth and wonderful to work with. Often collaborating with designers and architects, Djuric works in their own homes in addition to those of their clients. In the design community, this is the highest compliment.

Largely self-taught, Djuric constantly strives for excellence—contemplating common problems in the industry and making sure they do not happen on his projects. He focuses his small business on the artful application of decorative plasters in every imaginable form. We hear he uses rare techniques, is constantly experimenting to come up with new ideas and is a master of color. From Venetian plasters to satin, flat, mica and glossy finishes, clients are thrilled with the results and the prices. While not the cheapest guy on the block, Djuric's work leaves customers in awe.

"He is my favorite craftsman to work with—insightful, professional and above all—talented." "Milé is a true gem." "A wonderful artist and businessman." "Djuric is such an interesting person—he is so talented, and when you get to know him as a person, you immediately have a friend." "Not only is Milé wonderful, he assembled a staff of artisans who are equally as nice to have on any project." "I wish all of my contractors were just like Milé"

DeersTooth Hand Painted	4.5	3	4.5	5

Murals & Furniture
10 Cedar Street, Dobbs Ferry, NY 10522
(914) 674 - 6413   www.deerstooth.com

Murals, decorative painting and hand-painted furniture

From their first visit to this small company's "storefront headquarters," a living, breathing portfolio of their work complete with painted rugs, windows and shelves, clients are hooked. Founded in 1998 by artist Lisa Samalin, DeersTooth specializes in murals, decorative painting and hand-painted furniture, and is known to paint on almost any surface. Samalin, who studied fine art at the School of Visual Arts, corrals her small stable of artists to create projects that are described as thoughtful, inspired and magical. Whether she's transforming a local restaurant into "Portofino, Italy" or turning a residential dining room into a 1920s speakeasy, clients tell us Samalin really "connects" with them, using her taste and talent to reflect their vision.

Sources tell us Samalin thoroughly researches each project and spends many hours consulting with the customer prior to actually putting brush to wall (or anything else they let her paint). Throughout the process the DeersTooth team is said to be detail-oriented and to show a genuine concern for the client's needs, all at a reasonable price.

"The only way to describe the magnificence of Lisa's work is to say that she is divinely inspired." "She is generous with her time, her creativity is boundless, and she is really nice." "Lisa is no ordinary painter. She is an enchantress." "This is by far the best work I have ever had done for me." "I was pregnant and knew I was having a girl. We found Lisa to paint a garden theme in the nursery, but I was scheduled to have the baby delivered before I could see the finished room. When I came home from the hospital, I was greeted by the most magical nursery I could have ever imagined."

Donald Kaufman Color	5	3.5	5	5

336 West 37th Street, Suite 801, New York, NY 10018
(212) 594 - 2608   www.donaldkaufmancolor.com

Paint color designers and color consultants

Donald Kaufman and his partner and wife, Taffy Dahl, are recognized as America's foremost architectural color consultants. Using their own proprietary pigment-saturated paint, the duo mixes custom paint colors to uniquely suit the site location, the intensity of the light, the interior fabrics and trim hues and the personality of the client. Both trained in the fine arts, they have created a devoted clientele of color aficionados including Richard Meier, Mariette Himes Gomez and Philip Johnson who gave them "color carte blanche" for his New York apartment. They do about half of their work for architects and decorators and the other half directly for homeowners.

Kaufman and Dahl arrive with a large rolling suitcase of thousands of brushed samples and go to work considering each room like a doctor approaching a patient. They bring to this specialized craft a wealth of experience and specific, discrete analysis. While clearly masters, there is a "yin-yang" to their views with Kaufman more focused on the technical and Dahl more sensitive to the ambiance. Between them they get it exactly right, and are never miffed if the client asks for a "whiter shade of pale."

The firm has created custom color palettes for innumerable residences across the country and also for galleries and museums including the Frick, the Metropolitan Museum of Art and the J. Paul Getty Fine Arts Center. Commercial endeavors include the Delano Hotel in Miami and the Calvin Klein flagship store in New York. The pair has also written two books on color, which display and out-lines their philosophy. Sixty-six shades of their specialty-mixed paint may be purchased directly by calling (800) 977-9198 with gallons at $55 to $70. There is a minimum consultation cost of $5,000.

"I was a skeptic that their paint colors could make a difference, but the depth and luminosity of the paint is magical." "All of the finest decorators and painters know and respect Don and Taffy." "The millwork glows as it never did before." "I would highly recommend them to anyone. While not cheap, they clearly can make more of an impact than a decorator if you are on a tight budget." "They make an otherwise agonizing process fun with a glorious result."

Douglas Painting   4   3.5   5   4.5
535 Main Street, New Canaan, CT 06840
(203) 972 - 7908   shaund67@aol.com
Straight and decorative painting

Sources say Shaun Douglas is one of those people that you immediately trust when you meet him. Combine this with the fact that he is a highly skilled and cre-ative painter, and you've got yourself a real gem. Trained by an old-world painter who taught Douglas how to mix paints from scratch, sources say he runs his small firm, Douglas Painting, with the pride and professionalism of days passed.

Clients love his style—both creatively and personally, and are quick to note that he can handle any kind of decorative finish imaginable. Douglas is also known to give one of the best straight paint jobs in the area. Like his art, Douglas's prices are executed with integrity and honesty. Happy customers are thrilled to get what they pay for and then some.

"Having Shaun work in my home is always a pleasure. He treats a jobsite the way he would treat his own home—everything is cleaned up at night so I can actu-ally come home from work and live in my own house even though it is being renovated." "I never felt 'put out' at all during my long project." "Shaun is a real artist—when it comes to executing a beautiful finish, he hits the mark with flying colors." "His gold-leafing has gotten me so many compliments."

Drew The Painter   5   3.5   5   4.5
198 Park Lane, Trumbull, CT 06611
(203) 527 - 5278
Wallpapering and decorative painting

Clients absolutely adore Drew the Painter, both for his skills in the art of wall-paper and decorative painting, and for his fanatical attention to detail. Taking tremendous pride in his work, sources tell us that Drew Ciambriello is a perfectionist, yet works efficiently to get the job done on time. We also hear that this craftsman's easygoing manner makes him a delight to work with.

Ciambriello has over 30 years of experience and is often called upon to work for some high profile clients But whether you're president of a major corporation, or president of the PTA, Drew The Painter is said to be professional and reasonably priced.

"Drew has been doing work for me for twenty years. I wouldn't dream of using anyone else." "In this industry of divas and prima donnas, you would be hard pressed to find a more down to earth wallpaper maven."

Dygert Brothers

📁   📁   📁   📁

Brewster, NY 10509
(845) 278 - 0286
Custom plasterwork

Edward Micca Decorative Painting

4.5   3   5   5

312 Bayport Avenue, Bayport, NY 11705
(631) 472 - 3559   edmicca@yahoo.com
Decorative painting, cabinet glazing and special finishing

A one-man operation, Edward Micca keeps tight control of his projects from start to finish and makes it a priority to do all of his own prep work. Micca will do any paintable surface, creating interesting "leather" walls, tinted and colored plasters, wood graining and glazes, as well as pearlized finishes. He has also been known to tackle trompe l'oeil projects with finesse. A favorite among professionals, the charming and low-key Micca has been creating his decorative finishes in New York, Connecticut, Westchester and farther afield in the United States and Europe for more than 23 years. Clients tell us his work, primarily his cabinet glazes, rivals some of the best in the field. They also say his expertise comes at a moderate cost given the high-quality work he produces.

"His glazing is absolutely amazing!"

Eric Johnson

4.5   4   4.5   4.5

348 Delavan Avenue, Greenwich, CT 06830
(203) 531 - 7865
Interior and exterior painting, woodstaining and finishing

Eric Johnson and his namesake company have been beautifying the homes of area residents for twenty years. Clients describe Johnson as neat, clean and reliable, and repeat customers (of whom there are many) will attest to the fact that Johnson is easy to work with and great to have on a project.

Specializing in "old school" paint jobs and woodstaining and finishing work, we hear prices are on the higher end, but since the results are so wonderful, customers pay the bill with delight.

"Eric is truly special—talented, organized and a real funny guy." "He makes the whole process tolerable." "He kept the work area so spotless, I did not even know he had been there." "Not only is he a great painter, he is a professional businessman. All bills are detailed so I knew where every penny was going."

EverGreene Painting Studios

4   4   4   4

450 West 31st Street, 7th Floor, New York, NY 10001
(212) 244 - 2800   www.evergreene.com
Trade only—Decorative painting, murals, plaster, restoration and conservation

A large decorative arts studio with a national presence, EverGreene has both the manpower and the experience to handle a large commercial project or finely finished residence. Working exclusively through decorators and architects, the 25-year-old business employs experts who are fluent in every aspect of decorative painting, murals, plaster and restoration work. While EverGreene fields over

100 employees on projects nationwide and provides literally thousands of samples to peruse and inspire, the firm's dedicated and diverse staff still gives personalized service. Prices have been described as upper-end, but worth it for the body of knowledge the EverGreene team brings to a project.

In 2001, EverGreene added a hand-painted wallpaper division to its repertoire, named Studio E Inc. Located at the EverGreene office, Studio E creates luxury wallpapers for sale through Niermann Weeks Inc. in New York.

"Huge capabilities—they can do just about anything." "I call on them regularly for their talent, professionalism and creativity."

Executive Craftsman   4.5   4   4.5   5
PO Box 4787, Stamford, CT 06907
(203) 324 - 6383   slanef4003@yahoo.com   *called 3/16*
Interior and exterior painting

Clients love Steve Lanefski and the team at Executive Craftsman because they say they are reasonable, responsive and always there when they say they will be to provide true "executive" treatment from start to finish. In addition to his painting crew, Lanefski has three carpenters on board, saving his customers the need to call in another contractor. We hear his work is outstanding and that although the cost is high, it is worth the price-tag for a job well done.

"Steve is the tops—I only use him and for good reason, he does it right all the way."

Expert Painting & Decorating   4.5   4   4.5   4.5
49 Greenwich Avenue, Greenwich, CT 06830
(203) 629 - 2985
Straight and decorative painting and wallpapering

Sources tell us that the experts at Expert Enterprises truly live up to their name in everything they tackle. We also hear that the crew can handle assignments ranging from wonderful paint jobs and wallpaper projects to "outstanding decorative work." They are known to please even the most difficult clients, and will not leave a job unless it is "just right." Prices are said to be on the higher end—but long-time customers say it is worth it for the level of service and attention to every detail.

"Amazing—these guys really know how to do a great job." "I am pretty finicky, but I couldn't find anything to pick on—every part of the project was perfect." "Excellent work—not cheap, but worth the extra money."

Faust + Shields Decorative Arts, LLC   🗁   🗁   🗁   🗁
PO Box 212, Pottersville, NJ 07979
(908) 439 - 0124   www.f2sda.com
Decorative painting and murals

Two Fausts and one Shields represent this small decorative painting company, and the fact that the Fausts are twins makes working with them double the fun. Chris and David Faust are the creative branch of the company and partner Noel Shields represents the business side (although we hear she paints as well.) Clients love that getting the Fausts is like getting two times the talent since both were similarly educated and both have similar experiences. We hear the combination leads to great working relationships with both decorators and homeowners.

Able to handle projects both large and small, clients say the Fausts excel at faux bois and glazing, but have an extensive repertoire of decorative painting techniques. In addition to decorative finishes, the firm also offers plaster work and murals.

Gotham Painting
4.5   3   4.5   5

123 East 90th Street, New York, NY 10128
(212) 427 - 5752

Straight painting, plastering and wallpapering

For top-quality workmanship and exceptional service, notable designers, contractors and private clients all highly recommend this large, full-service firm. Crews are said to be attentive and neat. Gotham also impresses clients with their skill in straight painting, including skim coating, restorative plastering and wallpapering. In addition, the company handles period restorations as well as some decorative work. We are told that for the service, you can't beat the price.

"Gotham painting is perfection." "Very responsive and professional."

Grand Illusion Decorative Painting Inc.
5   4   5   5

20 West 20th Street, Suite 1009, New York, NY 10011
(212) 352 - 2037

Decorative painting and special finishing, murals

We hear that through the use of original 18th- and 19th-century techniques, Pierre Finkelstein of Grand Illusion produces finishes that are extraordinarily realistic. His small firm focuses on very high-end residential and museum work and also creates murals. Finkelstein comes to the decorative painting world with an impressive background, including training at the Van Der Kellen Painting Institute in Brussels. He has authored two books on the subject of decorative painting and finishes and teaches classes in his studio. Clients say that Finkelstein is charming and an absolute delight to work with. Finkelstein will hire freelancers if needed to round out his work force.

Grand Illusion works with some of the top decorators and designers and the firm's private client list has its share of instantly recognizable names. They consider Finkelstein's work outstanding, and while we hear it can cost a pretty penny, there's no doubt about its remarkable quality.

"The best painter of faux bois in the world!" "Best of the best." "For that quality, I was surprised that it was not insanely priced." "The only issue is how to get on his dance card."

Guy Demasi Decorative Painting
📁   📁   📁   📁

83 Mohawk Trail, Stamford, CT 06903
(203) 322 - 7853

Residential painting

Ivan Lozina Painting & Decorating
4.5   3.5   5   4.5

27 Washington Avenue, Hastings-on-Hudson, NY 10706
(914) 478 - 5969   iadmi@aol.com

Decorative painting

Contractors, decorators and homeowners use Lozina and praise him for his attention to detail and work that is described as "nothing short of perfection." Lozina, described as an "old-world craftsman," excels in a variety of techniques, from glazing to Venetian plaster. Sources say his crew can handle all types of projects, both small and large with professionalism and creativity. The cost for a job is not inexpensive, but we hear the results defy penny-pinching.

"He does not know how to do a middle-of-the-road job—just the best job." "Lozina takes so much pride in his work." "Every project is a part of him and he does not let go until it is just right." "Truly museum quality."

	Quality +	Cost $	Value ◆	Recommend? ★

James Alan Smith

| | 5 | 4 | 4.5 | 5 |

174 Red Creek Road, Hampton Bays, NY 11946
(631) 728 - 1340

Decorative painting and murals

James Alan Smith brings superior skills, focus and a wide range of abilities to the diverse artistry of his decorative painting. Trained in dance at Ohio State University, Smith is known for the lyrical style of his work, which includes complex trompe l'oeil and murals on both canvas and walls. His education in the decorative arts came from his mentor, the late master Richard Lowell Neas, and from time spent learning and teaching at the Isabel O'Neil studio in New York. Clients tell us Smith's work is phenomenal, and his personable and trustworthy disposition make the entire process a pleasant experience. Smith's parquet patterned floors, hand-painted in Japan oils, round out his skills in all areas of a room. He is "the anointed one" in the world of high-end interior design and clients say deservedly so.

"Fabulous. A real gentleman." "James gets the picture and then paints it flawlessly!" "The top and only choice for those who can afford him in the trade."

John A. Weidl Inc.

| | 5 | 4 | 4.5 | 5 |

379 Huguenot Street, New Rochelle, NY 10801
(914) 636 - 5067

Straight and decorative painting

Working primarily through decorators, John A. Weidl Inc. is considered by many to be one of the best painting outfits in the area. Sources say they are "as professional as it gets," noting the fact that crews work hard to build a relationship with the homeowner. John A. Weidl Inc. is known for its extraordinary attention to detail, and clients concur, raving that every single brushstroke is handled with care.

This large firm, established in 1975, performs decorative painting in the form of glazing, faux finishing and trompe l'oeil in addition to straight residential painting, which we hear is exquisite. Freelancers are brought in for mural work. Some references have told us the firm's pricing is reasonable, while others feel it is quite high. But all agree on the quality of the work and say it is worth the price.

"You have to go a long way to find a better painter." "Just terrific—from start to finish they did a really wonderful job." "The only painter I can trust who will go to a client without upsetting a household." "They strike a balance between high quality and price—not inexpensive at all, but when you see the results, you know why you wrote such a large check." "They know every decorator in town on a first-name basis." "Their in-house colorist was there to consult with us at the drop of a hat."

John Gregoras Paper Hanging & Painting, LLC ■

| | 4.5 | 3 | 5 | 5 |

18 Londonderry Lane, Somers, NY 10589
(914) 248 - 8893   www.johngregoras.com

Interior and exterior painting and wallpapering

Described by clients as extremely professional and easy to work with, John Gregoras and his crew handle wallpaper projects as well as interior and exterior painting projects with finesse and skill. Whether working for a high profile client or "your average Joe," sources tell us that Gregoras treats each project with personalized care and genuine interest in every aspect. We also hear he is a detail fanatic, yet is a "no-nonsense and easy-going guy" who is not only knowledgeable and experienced, but "a real sweetheart" as well. Whatever a client needs, insiders say Gregoras is there every step of the way at a price that won't break the bank.

"Reasonably priced for his exemplary caliber of work." "Super job on all counts—high quality, fast and pleasant." "John and his crew are great—they are respectful, talented, neat as a pin. They left the place cleaner than when they got here." "I heard that John works for some celebrity types so I was a little intimidated—when I met him that feeling immediately vanished. He was so down to earth—he took as much care and interest in my project as I did."

	Quality +	Cost $	Value ◆	Recommend? ★

John Licata
4 3 4 4

12 Linwick Place, Yonkers, NY 10704
(917) 566 - 6457

Residential painting

Decorators recommend John Licata who is known for understanding both home-owners' and designers' needs and translating them into a beautifully finished product. His prices are said to be quite reasonable given his high-end work.

"John knows what to do and does it." "Easy to work with—a really good painter!"

John Sponza Painting
🗁 🗁 🗁 🗁

46 Grumman Hill Road, Wilton, CT 06897
(203) 762 - 3676

Interior and exterior painting

Lauren J. Chisholm
4 3 5 5

669 East Olive Street, Long Beach, NY 11561
(917) 538 - 7684

Decorative painting, murals and tiles

Lauren Chisholm approaches each project with a positive attitude and sincere interest in pleasing clients with her decorative painting, murals and glazing in New York City and its surrounding areas We are told that she does extensive research and planning for her trompe l'oeil and mural projects which makes the end result all the more spectacular. Chisholm also hand paints silk pillows as well as kitchen tiles, bath tiles and sinks with botanical designs.

Impressed with the quality of the work she turns out, Chisholm's customers often comment on her masterful trompe l'oeil and lovely stroke work. All are pleased with the pricing.

"A very talented woman who can design and paint almost anything." "Her work is outstanding and her imagination and ideas are endless." "Lauren is an extremely talented trompe l'oeil artist with original and unique ideas." "She is a delight to work with and deserves only the highest praise." "Magnificent painting skills."

Lillian Heard Studio
3.5 3.5 4 4.5

790 President Street, Suite 3R, Brooklyn, NY 11215
(718) 230 - 8693

Murals and Venetian plastering

Lillian Heard specializes in decorative plaster techniques, including Venetian plastering and traditional lime putty plaster, producing walls that resemble polished marble, stone or fresco. Trained at the Art Institute of Chicago, she works throughout New York City, Westchester, Connecticut and does work internationally. In addition to her skills in specialty plasters, Heard is also known for the spare style of her "atmospheric landscape" murals. She and her team of two also do painted floors, stencils and glazes.

"Everyone that walks into my home comments on the beautiful walls and ceilings she executed." "Her work is elegant yet durable." "Heard is a sensitive and dedicated artist, but expensive."

Lulu DK
4.5 4 4 5

136 East 64th Street, Suite 2E, New York, NY 10021
(212) 223 - 4234   www.luludk.com

Decorative painting, hand-painted fabric and interior design

Lulu Kwiatkowski's contrasting styles of geometric and floral designs result from an amalgamation of her studies, travels and ability to embrace both chaos and control. After graduating from Parson's School of Design with a degree in interior design, Kwiatkowski studied trompe l'oeil at IPEDEC in Paris and then traveled

throughout Europe under the apprenticeship of Italian trompe l'oeil artist Francesco Gurnari. Kwiatkowski began her own business seven years ago and since then has expanded it to include a line of hand-painted fabrics of her own design. Whether she's designing a refined pattern of shaded squares that evokes the feeling of light penetrating through the wall or a chaotic mix of colorful flowers, paisleys and squiggles, we hear that Kwiatkowski's use of color, light and style can enliven almost any surface. HB Top Designers, 2000

"She can always be counted on to produce." "Lulu is among the most talented people I have worked with." "She has her finger on the pulse of 'what's now,' but also an eye on the classic." "Fresh and certainly hip, but not at all trendy." "A great sense of color and an appreciation of the value of simplicity." "A pleasure to do business with."

Marcia Simha   4.5   3.5   4.5   4.5
PO Box 8, Ridgefield, CT 06877
(203) 438 - 5204
Murals, trompe l'oeil and painting on furniture

Loyal clients keep coming back to Marcia Simha for her ability to incorporate their ideas into creating something special for that particular family. She is described as a true artist—this fact speaks for itself. With a BFA in fine art from Cooper Union, we hear that Simha's strong suit is her ability to work in a multitude of styles. She always approaches a project with a myriad of ideas and information and once "on assignment," Simha can be found in the library researching the concept to bring even more depth to the job.

Sources tell us her trompe l'oeil is fabulous, and prices, while not cheap, are reasonable for the outstanding results.

"Unbelievable work—Marcia is a true artist."

Martin Moreno Painting, Inc.   5   4.5   5   4.5
377 Oxford Road, New Rochelle, NY 10804
(914) 632 - 0141
Interior and exterior painting and wallpapering

We hear that this large firm is often hard to get a hold of, but once you do, the results are fabulous. Decorators and contractors alike rave about the quality and level of skill this team incorporates into their projects. Clients are quick to note the outstanding preparation Moreno does to get walls in shape for the "final coat."

"Martin Moreno is wonderful and very professional." "Lots of manpower." "Their timing is flawless—when they say they will be done, they are done."

Mary Lou Schempf   4.5   4   4.5   4
60 Clifton Terrace, Weehawken, NJ 07086
(201) 865 - 9116
Decorative finishes, trompe l'oeil and murals

Decorators and homeowners alike turn to Mary Lou Schempf to turn their dreams into reality—at least on their walls and floors. Schempf has had a paintbrush in her hand since she was a child, and her years of experience and education (she was trained at both RISD and the Kansas City Art Institute) are evident in her projects. From murals to decorative finishes of all kinds, Schempf delights her clients with a talented hand and an intuitive heart. Sources tell us that she brings a wealth of ideas to a project and has a way of knowing exactly what a client is aiming to do and executes it beautifully.

"Her stencilled floors are phenomenal." "Mary Lou has such a wonderful way about her—I hated for the project to end." "My friends are so jealous of the work she did for me." "Considering the amazing work she did for me, the price is not out of this world—but the painting is."

Michael Tyson Murphy Studio   4.5   3.5   4.5   4.5
135 West 20th Street, Suite 400, New York, NY 10011
(212) 989 - 0180

Decorative painting and murals

A multidimensional, multitalented artist, Michael Tyson Murphy extends his painting projects into the fields of architecture and interior design. His clients note that he approaches the many surfaces of a room the way a fine artist composes a painting. His stated goal is to create a space that works with the architecture of the room, often incorporating custom-designed or custom-painted furniture, or playing off the colors and patterns of existing pieces of art. Rooms are frequently completed by pieces of his own original fine art on canvas.

Murphy began with trompe l'oeil painting as a teenager, then expanded his repertoire through his education at the San Francisco Art Institute and his assistantship with the artist Helen Frankenthaler. His extensive worldwide travels have influenced the effects he creates, from Russian-inspired faux bois floors featuring mahogany, ebony and walnut to mosaics drawing on Portuguese themes.

Milan Painting & Wallpaper   5   3   5   5
35 Bullard Court, Stratford, CT 06614
(203) 377 - 7978

Interior and exterior painting, decorative painting and wallpapering

Decorators have called Milan to work on their own homes—a truly high recommendation in itself. Milan Fanclik started his painting and wallpapering business eight years ago, and has been winning fans ever since. Able to handle all kinds of jobs including decorative work and wallpapering, Milan's list of repeat clients will make you take notice. We hear that he is a joy to work with, takes great pride in his craft, and given the level of skill and attention to detail he gives each job, the prices are "quite reasonable."

"He is my first choice for every project—large or small." "He is so good—he is usually booked for a few months ahead of time, but he is definitely worth waiting for." "My project was a historical building and was a challenge with its high ceilings, crown moldings, plaster and irregular walls. There was much detail to be considered and Milan has won my highest praise." "He is charming, reasonably priced, totally dependable and his crew is excellent."

Miro-Art Interiors   5   4   5   5
20 Bronxville Glen Drive, Bronxville, NY 10708
(914) 237 - 6306

Decorative painting and frescoes

The quality is breathtaking and the projects very high-end (for example, the Blue Room in the White House) when clients mention Roman Kujawa and Miro-Art Interiors. The team of five is in high demand by some of the most prestigious decorators and architects in the New York metropolitan area and throughout the country, specializing in decorative painting finishes like gilding and imitation limestone. These artists are also well known for their frescoes and trompe l'oeil work. Miro-Art does not do its own prep work, preferring to have a few select firms perform that task.

"Not just good but great. A real master." "Their work is exquisite."

	Quality	Cost $	Value ◆	Recommend? ★

My Decorator Inc.
10 Garfield Place, East Northport, NY 11731
(631) 266 - 1808   www.mycountryusa.com

Wallpapering, plastering and painting

4.5   3   4.5   4

Clients love John "Jack" Fallon for his strong work ethic, his willingness to go above and beyond, and for his creative skill and talent. In business for over twenty years, Fallon apprenticed with a European paperhanger before venturing out on his own. Known for his ability and willingness to get the job done flawlessly and time-lessly, decorators, contractors and homeowners depend on My Decorator Inc. not just for painting, plastering and wallpapering, but for any renovation project they might have. Sources tell us Fallon is a "one-stop-shop" for home projects. And best of all, they say his prices are reasonable.

"So great to work with." "Really down to earth and professional in every way." "Honest and careful."

Natasha Bergreen & Liza Cousins
40 East 94th Street, New York, NY 10128
(212) 427 - 2928   ncbnyc@aol.com

Decorative painting and finishing, color consulting

4   3.5   4   4

In business for fifteen years, the sisters Bergreen and Cousins's partnership has benefited from a lifetime of complementing each other's talents. With two assistants, they provide an abundance of services, including painting stripes, gilding, glazing, marbleizing and other classic and contemporary finishes. Although their specialties are decorative painting and finishes, the firm has begun to accept some design projects as well. Both professionals have a background in the arts. After attending art school, Bergreen studied with Leonard Pardon and Cousins studied decorative painting in London. We hear their talents are in demand by many top designers.

"Not your average decorative painter—creative, original and a pleasure to work with." "My clients are always impressed with their work and the style they inject into a project." "They have been my primary decorative painters for the last nine years and I think they are wonderful."

Old Vienna Painting
24316 Thornhill Avenue, Douglaston, NY 11362
(718) 428 - 5457

Decorative and straight painting, wallpapering

4.5   3   5   5

Led by Hans Pavlacka, who has been painting all of his life, Old Vienna Painting specializes in straight and decorative painting as well as wallpapering. Trained by apprenticeships throughout Europe, Pavlacka handles glazing, faux finishes, plastering and restoration of moldings. Clients tell us that the small team at Old Vienna restores old residences back to their original glory through meticulous prep work and a great sense of color. They say Pavlacka is the only person allowed near their walls with a paintbrush. Pavlacka always maintains excellent relationships with his clients, which explains why he has sustained a business for 36 years, largely on referrals.

"Reliable, consistent and top quality." "The only painter I would use." "Consider yourself fortunate if Hans paints your home." "His painting is beautiful, his prep work is first rate." "Great eye for color." "Old Vienna is the absolute top end of what a great painter should be."

P.J. McGoldrick Co. Inc.
Called 3/16
34 Young Avenue, Pelham, NY 10803
(914) 712 - 1280   pjmcgoldrick@earthlink.net

Interior and residential painting and wallpapering

4.5   4   5   5

Clients and peers describe Paul McGoldrick as upfront, easily accessible, and extremely good at what he does. His painting company, P.J. McGoldrick Co. Inc., has a reputation for superior quality and is said to have a team of painters that are both skilled and talented. We hear the crews always do their best to make the client comfortable and that each member of the staff is more courteous than the next. The firm has done work for some "notable names" who appreciate the professional demeanor and dignified approach to each project. Prices are reported on the high-end, but worth it for the results.

"Expensive but worth it." "I did not even know they were there—so respectful of my home and my time." "Paul returns calls immediately and all issues are resolved without delay." "His crew is extremely good, well trained and knowledgeable." "My clients expect the best and Paul delivers—and then some."

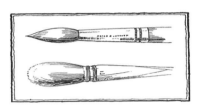

Paulin Paris   5   4.5   5   5
409 East 64th Street, Suite 6H, New York, NY 10021
(212) 472 - 2485 www.paulin-paris.com
Decorative painting, sculptures and murals

For over seventeen years, Paulin Paris has catered to an A-list clientele that has brought him from his homeland of France to countries around the world. With a PhD in philosophy and a degree from the Ecole des Beaux Arts, Paris has been able to take his inspiration from the past, but treat it in a modern way. Paris's versatility can be seen in the broad range of his clientele—from the fashion houses of Dior and Valentino to commissions for private residences and interior designers and the Alsatian fabric and wallpaper studio, Zuber, Paris works hard to incorporate his vision with the owners' vision, with spectacular results. Clients praise Paris's work alongside the architect and designer. This painter divides his time between his studios in New York, Los Angeles and Paris, where he works on murals, paintings and sculptures.

"A modest man, generous with his clients." "His work is exquisite—he has the ability to take an idea and bring it to life." "Our experience with Paulin was the most delightful and rewarding of all the trades involved in our project." "A true artist with all of the creativity and charm one would hope for—and none of the attitude and condescension." "Genuine, lovely and brilliant."

Penna, Inc.   4   3.5   4.5   4
405 East 51st Street, Suite 6F, New York, NY 10022
(212) 935 - 5747 www.pennainc.com
Straight painting, custom designed glazes, wallcovering and leather installations

Clients describe owner Dean Penna as a professional, hardworking perfectionist. His team of 25 also has a reputation for being polite, friendly and an "absolute pleasure" to deal with. Whether a straight painting job or an elaborate decorative project, we hear the firm's finished product is marvelous and that throughout the process crews are known for being meticulously neat.

In business since 1989 and often working with decorators, Penna's talents go beyond the paintbrush. The company handles more complicated tasks such as fabric wallcovering and leather installations that have been called "masterful." Sources say the firm is on the higher side price-wise, but from its clear and upfront job descriptions, proper staffing and immaculate upkeep during the project to its timely execution and completion of the work, those "in the know" say Penna Inc. is well worth the cost. Expect exceptional results.

"Dean has a 'can do' personality that actually delivers." "A no-fuss painting contractor. They understand the service business." "I've known Dean for years, and he keeps getting better with each job." "Dean's mantra is 'no sweat.'" "All of Penna's tradespeople are highly skilled, efficient and a pleasure to work with." "I wish all my experiences with contractors could be this rewarding. They may be a bit pricey, but it is worth it."

Pennington Painting & Restoration, LLC   5   4   5   5
800 Hoydens Hill Road, Fairfield, CT 06824
(203) 319 - 1800
Interior and exterior painting, decorative finishing, cabinet glazing, and wallpapering

Judging by the list of clients and decorators on Penninngton's "to-do" list, you would think you were reading a who's who in construction and interior design. Industry leaders and homeowners alike praise Frank Ball and his multi-talented staff for their skill at their craft and their business practices. Equally comfortable with a designer, on a construction site or in the home of a well-to-do area resident, the team at Pennington could never be called "prima donnas." In fact, quite the opposite is true, the crew has been described as "flexible, accommodating and professional—real team players."

Truly a full-service firm, Pennington, in business for over sixteen years, handles interior and exterior painting, an endless list of decorative finishes and wallpaper installation.

"A higher class of painting contractor." "Their personal touch along with the highest level of detail that I have seen in the industry, without question separates the men from the boys." "The decorative finishes are so good that people often think it is wallpaper." "Frank encourages the homeowner to learn more about the process— I felt a great sense of ownership with respect to our project—I even joined the crew in sanding the edges of knot holes in antique floor boards before they were stained."

Piotr Sernicki   📁   📁   📁   📁
24 East Avenue, New Canaan, CT 06840
(203) 866 - 9155
Residential painting

Plateau Painting   📁   📁   📁   📁
37 Elwood Avenue, Hawthorne, NY 10532
(914) 747 - 5525
Residential painting

Poltime Interiors   4.5   3.5   5   5
99 Newel Street, Brooklyn, NY 11222
(718) 383 - 9402
Decorative and straight painting

Poltime Interiors address a range of jobs, from basic residential painting to complex, decorative finishes. Working for private clients as well as some of the city's most respected decorators, principal John Stephanski keeps up with the most recent trends in painting. Many laud Stephanski's ability to duplicate any existing color or find its perfect complement. In addition to his masterful eye, his glazes and faux finishes get great reviews—we hear the mahogany is incredible. References say he produces excellent cloud ceilings, but is not a general muralist.

Stephanski is described as meticulous, dependable and businesslike, arriving with full crews and finishing in record time. While some clients may quibble about how wide they have to open their wallet, they all agree that they get what they pay for.

"An artist who is amazing with color." "Love them. Amazing work, high quality, great value." "European craftsman." "An absolute joy to deal with." "So talented, I couldn't have imagined more beautiful results." "John will work with you until it is right."

	Quality ✚	Cost $	Value ◆	Recommend? ★

Reardon Restoration Inc.

| | 4 | 4 | 4.5 | 5 |

180 Yonkers Avenue, Yonkers, NY 10701
(914) 965 - 2179   www.reardonrestoration.com

Old-world furniture repair, antique restoration, decorative painting and Venetian plaster

See Reardon Restoration Inc.'s full report under the heading Furniture Repair & Refinishing

Renaissance Decorative Artistry

| | 4 | 2.5 | 5 | 5 |

111 East 14th Street, Suite 202, New York, NY 10003
(212) 252 - 2273   deanbarger@earthlink.net

Murals, custom stencils and faux finishes

Serving a clientele of celebrities and top designers, some of whom are reluctant to share him with the public, Dean Barger and the small team at Renaissance Decorative Artistry create murals, multilayered stenciling and high-end faux finishes that have earned them quite a following. Dividing his time between the New York City area and Maine, Barger, who has a background in fine art and studied in Europe, is described as pleasant, low key, and an absolute delight to work with. We hear his work is inspired and his rates are moderate.

"Extraordinary work." "I don't want to give him up." "Dean is wonderful and his work is outstanding."

Richard Pellicci Decorative Painting

| | 5 | 3 | 5 | 5 |

65 Radnor Avenue, Croton-on-Hudson, NY 10520
(914) 271 - 6710   yofaux@earthlink.net

Decorative painting and murals

Low-key, charming and talented are just three of the words clients have used to describe Richard Pellicci. The former book illustrator, who studied at The New York Phoenix School of Design (now the Manhattan outpost of Pratt,) was inspired by the decorative finishes he saw on trips to Europe—and a business was born.

Customers rave about Pellicci as their secret source. They say his work is quite beautiful and love the fact that he comes up with original ideas, matches fabrics and can contribute to the entire design process. Pellicci's repertoire includes wall glazing, faux bois, strié, marbleizing and murals. His work has been featured in major design publications.

"I only allow great artisans' to work on my home, and Richard is at the top of my list." "Richard is talented, warm, funny, considerate—and when he leaves, his work is a lovely reminder of him." "His color choices literally make the project." "The grape leaves he did in my powder room are so good that people think it is wallpaper." "Richard has painted a variety of finishes—his plaid is our favorite, but his traditional work is also wonderful." "Impeccable design sense."

Rigby & Hamilton

| | 4.5 | 2.5 | 5 | 5 |

28 Old Conklin Hill Road, Stanfordville, NY 12581
(518) 398 - 1453   www.rigbyandhamilton.com

Decorative painting, plaster and murals

Rigby & Hamilton—actually Leora Armstrong and her trusty pooch Rigby (Armstrong's maiden name is Hamilton)—have clients falling in love with her work the moment they see it. Maybe it is her art background, or that she gives a fresh eye on the scene (she has been in the US for two years—she's originally from England) that keeps her customers enamored. Or maybe it is the fact that her prices have not quite caught up to New York (City and State—she works in both). Decorators and homeowners tell us that considering the level of skill and taste Armstrong brings to her projects, whether it be a mural, a decorative finish or plaster of all types, "she really needs to raise her prices." Catch her before she "catches up."

"She can do anything and does it with a positive attitude and a smile." *"After our project was completed, there was a burst pipe in the building. The Venetian plaster Leora did was the only material that did not sustain any damage."* *"A really talented artist."* *"My dining room has to be seen to be believed."* *"Leora is not only a great artist, but truly exciting to work with."*

Robert Hoven Inc.   4.5   4   4.5   4
260 Main Street, Catskill, NY 12414
(917) 597 - 6663
Decorative painting, plaster and murals

Drawing on his appreciation and knowledge of all things beautiful (including art, antiques and music) and by keeping his hand on the pulse of the design world, Robert Hoven delights his clients with his decorative painting skills. From inlaid floors made to look like flowers, to specialty finishes that make you ask "is it real or is it painted?" Hoven and his small team handle any conceivable finish with what we hear is brilliance and professionalism.

"Robert's floors are amazing." *"Such a treat to work with—so talented and fun to be around."* *"He knows how to make things beautiful."* *"Not only is he talented, but you are just drawn to his personality, style and flair."* *"I was tickled pink with the results."*

Robert J. Braun   4.5   3.5   5   5
104 West 87th Street, New York, NY 10024
(212) 799 - 6282
Decorative painting and murals

Working primarily through the referral of designers and decorators, Robert Braun flexes his decorative painting muscles for both residential and commercial clients on both coasts of the United States and abroad. Working for many years doing theater set design, Braun brings a wealth of creative input to his projects. He works on canvas for future on-site installation, and focuses on historic period styles, including architectural trompe l'oeil which we hear is outstanding.

"Artistic, qualified and professional." *"One of the best trompe l'oeil artists!"* *"Robert is extremely talented."* *"He collaborates with designers for a fabulous product."* *"He will always be at the top of my list."*

Robert Roth   4   4   4.5   5
305 East 46th Street, 10th Floor, New York, NY 10017
(212) 758 - 2170   rothpainting@yahoo.com
Decorative and straight painting, architectural trompe l'oeil

Popular with the trade and private clients alike, the father and son team at Robert Roth receives high marks for their decorative and straight painting. The two have been praised for very successful trompe l'oeil work and their dedication to meticulous preparation which leads to flawless painting. We hear they are detail-oriented and clean up thoroughly every night. One client happily left them the keys to her home when she was out of town, saying she would never do that for anyone else. Sources say that with its wide range of skills, this firm is best for larger jobs and can be quite expensive, but is wonderful to work with.

"Brilliant." *"I have never written such a large check with such pleasure!"* *"True European artists."* *"Impeccable."* *"The end result is perfection."*

	Quality	Cost	Value	Recommend?

Signature Paint & Paper, LLC

4.5   4   5   5

46 Cliffdale Road, Greenwich, CT 06831
(203) 622 - 3111 www.signaturepaintandpaper.com

Custom interior and exterior painting, decorative finishes and wallpapering

The painter of choice for some of the area's best architects and decorators, the team at Signature Paint & Paper is said to deliver exceptional quality and skill. Anthony Ruberti leads the fairly large crew capable of handling jobs large and small, or basic to intricate with equal care and attention. We hear that every detail is agonized over and that the results truly show the painstaking effort. While not cheap, sources tell us that the workmanship far outweighs the pricetag.

"The work this firm does is fantastic—each molding, seam and knothole is as smooth as polished glass." "I am thrilled with their work." "Anthony runs a tight ship and it shows in the incredible work his team does." "Very considerate crew."

Simonson & Baric

5   4   4.5   5

847 Lexington Avenue, New York, NY 10021
(212) 570 - 1996

Straight residential painting and wallpapering

Knowing that you are only as good as your last job, the team of Simonson and Baric put customer service at the head of the table when serving up residential painting and wallpapering. We hear they can handle anything, and the "over-the-top" attention exhibited on each job translates into exceptional quality. Of course, this comes at a premium, but sources tell us it is well worth it.

"Simonson is the best of the best." "Expensive, but you get what you pay for." "Their work is superb."

Skinner Interiors

4.5   3.5   5   5

71 First Place, Brooklyn, NY 11231
(718) 243 - 1378

Straight and decorative painting, plaster and wallpapering

Skinner Interiors is a favorite of both hot young designers looking for exceptional craftsmanship at decent prices and old-guard designers who have been pleased with this firm's work for years. When not working for a demanding New York City clientele, Skinner and Co. can be found attending to clients at their weekend homes in Connecticut or the Hamptons. Known for their attention to detail and professionalism, Skinner Interiors is frequently referred by showrooms in the D&D building for its expertise in wallpapering as well as for decorative projects including faux bois, faux stone, glazing and plaster finishes. Skinner and his team offer their "unending skill" using traditional paints and wallpapers. But their talent really shines when dealing with fine European paints (such as Schreuder Hascolac or Farrow & Ball) and high-end wallpapers (such as foils or paperback silks).

In business for twelve years, principal Mark Skinner carries a "hands-on" reputation. In addition to supervising all the painstaking prep-work required to achieve a fine finish, he is said to nurture close relationships with clients during the process, keeping them updated on progress and staying sensitive to their needs and budgets.

"From the first day of preparation to the completion of the job, we knew we had made the right choice." "They understand quality and were sensitive to our needs." "Great employees with a great attitude." "Skinner Interiors is highly creative and professional." "A true artist." "Truly worth every penny for the most meticulous work."

Stephen & Lisa Longworth

4   3.5   4.5   4

432 Valley Road, Upper Montclair, NJ 07043
(973) 886 - 2858 pupcity@aol.com

Decorative painting, murals and color consulting

Known for their "incredible murals" and exquisite decorative techniques, this husband-and-wife team has been beautifying Connecticut and the surrounding areas for eighteen years. In addition to the wide array of looks this duo can handle, we hear that they are extremely adept at assisting homeowners with color choices. Clients tell us that the Longworth's go to extremes to make a job perfect, from supervising the prep work to tirelessly attending to the final details of a project. We hear the results are fabulous.

"So easygoing and fun to work with." "They are a wealth of ideas and visions." "Very caring—they take the time to get it just right." "Steve once met my kindergartner at the bus stop when I couldn't get home in time—that's how much I trust them." "A total find—I am reluctant to share them with the world, but I wish them the best, so I am."

Steve Zeisler's Painting Inc.   4.5   3   5   5
316 Hoydens Lane, Fairfield, CT 06824
(203) 359 - 3414   www.szpainting.net
Exterior and interior painting, powerwashing

Steve Zeisler's motto is "no regrets" and apparently his long list of happy clients do not have any. In business for over twenty years, Steve Zeisler's Painting Inc. specializes in exterior and interior painting, powerwashing and sealants for roofs and decks. We hear the quality is exceptional and the crews are professional, neat and truly care about a job well done. Able to handle projects large and small, the company boasts a touch-up crew, which clients say is not only efficient, but cost effective.

Sources say Zeisler's pricing is very fair, and quite a bargain given the exemplary quality. In addition, customers say the company has special pricing on interior painting during the winter months making the deal even sweeter.

"Everyone who sees the work Steve and his crew did remark that it looks like a brand new house." "They always kept their equipment and supplies neatly tucked away—they left their work areas virtually spotless." "The workmanship is the highest caliber and the conduct of the crew is exceptional." "I was particularly impressed by the care the team took in protecting my antiques." "Steve is notorious for superior service—from the estimate to the final touch ups."

Teles & Adams   4.5   3.5   5   5
PO Box 682, Palisades, NY 10964
(845) 365 - 2917
Decorative painting

Clients absolutely adore this duo for both their "professional approach and incredible talent." Coming from unique backgrounds (James Adams went to Yale and studied forestry, biology and art history and Brazilian-born Rubens Teles is on the faculties of The American Folk Art Museum and Marymount College in New York City) they bring a wealth of ideas and inspiration to their twelve-year-old decorative painting business.

Teles & Adams work frequently with decorators and are praised for their ability to handle a wide array of finishes and techniques—but industry insiders say their American- and English-inspired designs really put them on the map. They have such a passion for this genre that in 1994, the two wrote a book on the subject entitled *Folk Finishes*. In addition to painting walls and floors, Teles & Adams are involved in customizing a line of accessories for the home—clients love the fact that they can take a swatch of fabric or carpet, and have their trays, waste baskets and other items painted to match.

"I love working with Rubens and James—they are polite, professional and fun to work with." "Sometimes hard to get on their schedule, but worth the wait." "They have such a complete range of skills in addition to their folk art specialty." "You have to see their work to know how happy I was to write the check." "My clients love having them in their homes—so respectful and so talented." "Their strength is Americana faux painting and stencilling." "They came in and came up with the perfect color within minutes." "The price was completely appropriate for the work."

	Quality	Cost	Value	Recommend?
	✚	$	◆	★

The Finished Wall

4 3 4.5 4.5

880 West 181st Street, Suite 2A, New York, NY 10033
(212) 740 - 8118   angelacaban@aol.com

Gilding and fine decorative wall finishes

Described by clients as energetic, creative and professional, Angela Caban of The Finished Wall combines her background as a Broadway actress with an education in fine art and restoration to create a unique perspective on decorating the home or business with paint and plaster. We hear that she really knows how to connect with her customer and can create something special and magical for each individual project.

Sources say she is an expert at wall finishes and in addition to working in clients' homes, she can be found in her studio creating pieces for future installations, such as gilded panels or murals. Prices are described as surprisingly moderate for the level of skill, quality and customer service Caban and her small staff provide.

"Her work has exceeded our expectations." "Angela's enthusiasm, knowledge and professionalism are what truly set her apart from her competition." "Really fun to work with." "It is a treat to find a fine craftsman who is also bright, personable, witty and willing to make that extra effort."

Tomo

4 3.5 4.5 5

4235 64th Street, Woodside, NY 11377
(718) 426 - 4316

Decorative and straight painting and wallpapering

Prestigious real estate agencies and top-tier general contractors call upon this high-end painter, who has operated in Manhattan and Connecticut for over 32 years. Tomo and his sizable staff of 45 do both straight and decorative work, wallpapering, and in-house prep work. Clients that include celebrities say this well-run and organized company produces a superb finished product, and that Tomo himself is a gem to work with.

"Amazing, flawless work." "Tomo is an excellent painter, very high-end, great quality."

Trayner & Company

🗁   🗁   🗁   🗁

66 Bowman Avenue, Rye Brook, NY 10573
(914) 934 - 5151

Residential painting

Twins Painting, LLC

4.5 3.5 5 4.5

PO Box 5193, Greenwich, CT 06830
(203) 978 - 1878   kasuc@sbcglobal.net

Interior and exterior painting

Decorators swear by Twins Painting for straight painting projects in the Connecticut area. Owner Chris Suchocki and his small crew earn praise for their professionalism, integrity and skill—Twins (named after Suchocki's twin children) is a local favorite. We hear that Suchocki does what he says he will do—a trait that is sometimes hard to come by. If he says "two coats" you will get two coats. Prices are said to be reasonable given the level of care and attention given to each project.

"Chris is committed to excellence, and it shows in his work." "I wouldn't dream of doing a paint project without him." "Chris and his crew are great to work with—nothing is ever too much to ask." "I always feel completely confident recommending Twins to my friends and family—he never disappoints." "I am crazy about him."

UK Fabric & Wallcovering

	Quality	Cost	Value	Recommend?
UK Fabric & Wallcovering	4.5	3.5	5	4.5

28 Greystone, Huntington, CT 06484
(914) 490 - 3293

Fabric and English wallpaper installation, decorative painting

Clients say they thank their lucky stars when they discover David Haith and his twenty-year-old company, UK Fabric & Wallcovering. Specializing in fabric and English wallpaper, the charming and personable Haith began training at the tender age of sixteen in his native England. There he learned the old-world techniques and graduated from Her Majesty's School of Professional Paperhanging. Working primarily through decorators, Haith has developed a reputation of excellence in the industry—so much so that he has been called upon to do instructional seminars for the likes of Osbourne & Little and other high-end paper houses.

Haith handles all of the wallpapering himself, but has a wonderful and caring crew that takes care of all the prep work. In addition, Haith also has a decorative painter on staff to round out the company's offerings. UK's prices are not inexpensive, but sources tell us that it costs money to get a master.

"Beautiful work—the only one I'd trust to hang English "paper" paper."

Village Murals

	Quality	Cost	Value	Recommend?
Village Murals	4.5	3.5	5	4.5

PO Box 32, Old Town Hall, Falls Village, CT 06031
(860) 824 - 5474   www.villagemurals.com

Murals and handpainted wallcoverings

Muralist Clifton Jaeger delivers old-world style creations rich with texture and glazes painted on linen or canvas. He and the small team at Village Murals do all of the painting in their studio, then transport and install the work—which is convenient for the client. Whether it is working with decorators and architects or directly with homeowners, Jaeger can create a one-wall mural or many feet of exquisite, hand-painted wall covering. The murals can be fitted to the wall or hung like a tapestry—either way, when the client moves, so does the mural.

Inspired by old masters in his grad school days in Venice, (he did his undergraduate work at the Rhode Island School of Design,) Jaeger makes his own paints with medieval and renaissance recipes using natural earth and organic pigments. The result is non-toxic, with a handcrafted appearance. We hear that Jaeger's results are so fabulous they often get compared to the icons who influenced him.

Vivid Painting

35 Watermelon Hill Road, Mahopac, NY 10541
(845) 628 - 2041

Residential painting

Wayne Johnston Painting & Paperhanging

	Quality	Cost	Value	Recommend?
Wayne Johnston Painting & Paperhanging	4	3	4.5	4

67 Broad Street, Norwalk, CT 06850
(203) 847 - 0243   wrj53@optonline.net

Interior and exterior painting, wallpapering

Clients swear by Wayne Johnston and his small crew for both interior and exterior paint jobs at reasonable prices. Used by decorators and homeowners, Johnston, who has been in the business for over 30 years, is noted for his outstanding wallpapering skills. Sources say he always stays on top of every aspect of the job and can handle any paper, from basic to luxurious, with both care and expertise.

"Nothing is ever too much to ask." "They do things that I could never get another painter to do—truly full-service which includes everything from repairing plaster to fixing my damaged ceiling. I could not have asked for more." "So pleasant to deal with—no fuss, no mess!"

Yona Verwer Studio   4   3   4.5   5

103 East 97th Street, Suite 4W, New York, NY 10029
(212) 674 - 5015   www.yvstudio.com

Decorative painting and murals

Lauded as a true artist, Yona Verwer has been doing decorative painting and murals for seventeen years. While the firm does all kinds of specialty finishes including glazes, gilding, stencilling, plaster effects and faux finishes, it's the murals that particularly charm clients. These pieces, described as whimsical, fanciful and inspiring, are applied on canvas and on walls. We hear Verwer will create contemporary pieces of her own design or will execute any style a client prefers, including classical and trompe l'oeil. References report she has created an extensive planning process designed to keep the customer involved at every stage of the project.

Verwer, who holds an MFA from the Royal Academy of Fine Art at the Hague, is described by many as patient, understanding and a pleasurable collaborator. Sources tell us that she is extremely ethical, citing the fair prices and exceptional quality that this company delivers.

"Yona is an excellent artist—her work is truly valuable." "Yona is patient, understanding and will work through anything to make sure the designer and end user are happy." "It's a pleasure to work with her." "Not only do I feel I got more than I paid for, but visitors have uniformly remarked that the piece 'makes the room' and upgrades the overall value of the apartment."

York & Company Decorating   3.5   3.5   4   4.5
Contractors Inc.

1076 East Putnam Avenue, 1st Floor, Greenwich, CT 06870
(203) 698 - 3460   nick@yorkinc.net

Designer-oriented interior renovations

See York & Company Decorating Contractors Inc.'s full report under the heading Contractors & Builders

Zeccodec Painting   4   3.5   4   5

42 Stuyvesant Street, New York, NY 10003
(212) 254 - 1500

Decorative and straight painting and wallpapering

Repeat business and referrals make up the majority of Zeccodec's client list, which includes both private clients and the trade. Maybe they just like saying the name—more likely, as clients report, it's the high-quality straight and decorative painting and wallpapering services this small firm has been offering area residents for seventeen years. We hear principal Glenn Zecco is a straightforward professional who offers good work for the price. References say his staff of twelve, many of whom were trained in Europe, are conscientious, efficient and do a good job.

"Easy to talk to." "Very professional." "I am very happy with the results."

Hiring a Plumber

Whether it's trimming out a kitchen and bath remodel, installing an entire system for a new home, a routine repair or maintenance call or an absolute emergency, you need a plumber you can count on.

Although most plumbers are available for a simple service call, some high-end service providers prefer to limit such calls, especially 24-hour emergency service, to existing customers. This practice ensures that you will receive the highest level of service and quality with a prompt response.

Where Do I Start?

Hold on to that plumbing contractor who has proven himself over the course of a major project. Handpicked by your trusty general contractor (GC), he knows the guts of your home better than anyone. Even if you aren't planning a renovation and just need someone to handle more mundane problems like leaky faucets, it's worth putting in the effort to build a relationship with a plumber who can offer quality and service, so he'll be there before you're sunk.

If you are starting from scratch, remember some plumbers focus only on larger-scale contract installations and remodels, while others devote their efforts entirely to service and repair. Marry your job to the right plumber. The best first sign is someone answering the phone—not just an answering service—but a live company employee in an actual office. If you can't get hold of someone during business hours, the chances you'll get a response on a Saturday night when your bath looks like Niagara Falls are slim.

A decent high-end plumber shouldn't be spooked by foreign or custom fixtures, nor should he force his standard ones down your throat. With product he is unfamiliar with he should do his homework, consulting with the manufacturer to insure proper installation. While plumbing basics haven't changed much in 100 years, the firm should also be up to the latest technology like energy-efficient tankless water heaters and sound suppression systems and be able to deliver options at different price points.

Calling references is your last line of defense. For larger jobs like kitchen remodels that require coordination between trades, contractors are the best assessors of a firm's performance. For smaller service and maintenance jobs, clients are your best bet. To both you'll want to ask the usual questions about quality of work and whether the project was finished on schedule and on budget. However, because plumbing can be a messy business, respect for surroundings and cleanliness are equally important.

A Job for Professionals

You should only consider a full-time licensed professional for your plumbing needs. He can't file for permits without one. As always, ask about insurance, including worker's compensation and liability insurance. Your plumbing professional should always be responsible for obtaining all permits necessary for your job.

On Cost

For larger projects, each plumbing contractor will submit its bid to the GC, who will then incorporate it into the overall bid submitted to the client. Often the GC for your project will bring in a trusted plumber for the job, but you are free to ask your GC to include another plumber in the bidding process, which ensures that bids are competitive. If your renovation is relatively small and a GC is not involved, get several estimates for the proposed work.

For smaller jobs and service calls, which include repair and maintenance, most companies charge an hourly rate, typically $80 for a single plumber, $115 for a dispatched two-man team. A 3 Cost rating in *The Franklin Report* approximately reflects these standards. However, please remember, a company's standards in relation to product and safety, the depth of its resources and the demand of its customer base can all affect cost on top of hourly rates, and are factored into the rating.

Some companies charge a set one-time diagnostic fee to produce an estimate even for smaller jobs, while others will send troubleshooters or technicians to assess the work and come up with a price free of charge. All will work up fixed estimates for larger jobs to be executed in a contract. Fees for contract renovation work are typically higher than fees for new construction per hour and per square foot. In the end, it should come down to the company with the best reputation for quality and service, not just the low bidder.

GUARANTEES AND SERVICE AGREEMENTS

When your equipment is installed, it should come with both a warranty from the manufacturer and a guarantee from the service provider. Be sure to ask about service agreements. Many plumbing professionals will provide regular "checkups" and inspections. It may seem like wasted money at first, but over time these measures can prevent an emergency.

SAVE MONEY BY SAVING TIME

If you inventory the state of your plumbing and think ahead about work that will need to be done, your plumber will be able to work more effectively. Check faucets, drains, radiators and fixtures throughout the house and compile a list. Present this list to the plumber upon arrival so he can prioritize the various tasks and work simultaneously if possible. This way, you won't have to call him in again for another minor repair in a few weeks.

If the plumber will need access to the pipes under your kitchen sink, clear out the area to save billable time. Also put away or protect anything vulnerable to damage. Your plumber will appreciate being able to get to work without having to wade through piles of children's toys or rummage around in a cabinet full of cleaning supplies.

Don't wait until your bathroom is flooded with four inches of water. Develop a good relationship with a plumber now, and you'll never have to page frantically through a phone book and throw yourself at the mercy of whatever plumber happens to be free.

MORE THAN PIPES

YOUR PLUMBER IS TRAINED TO DO MUCH MORE THAN FIX CLOGGED DRAINS. A FULL-SERVICE PLUMBER CAN:

✧ Provide condensation drains for air-conditioning units.
✧ Install the boiler, lines and radiators necessary for household heat.
✧ Install hot water recirculation and water pressure booster pumps.
✧ Hook up major appliances (gas stoves, washing machines).
✧ Make a gas-meter connection, install gas lines and provide gas shutoff valves.
✧ Install storm/slop drains for the kitchen, patio, garage, laundry rooms greenhouse and roof.

	Quality	Cost	Value	Recommend?
	+	**$**	**◆**	**★**

PLUMBERS

Anthony Pici Plumbing & Heating

	Quality	Cost	Value	Recommend?
	4	4	4	4

370 Ashburton Avenue, Yonkers, NY 10701
(914) 376 - 7300

Plumbing and heating service and installation

Demanding designers and well-heeled residential clients turn to Pici Plumbing for keen attention to detail and great care in the maintenance and installation of premium plumbing systems and fixtures. A charter member of the Radiant Heating Association, Pici lends its meticulous standards to boilers and radiant heat applications. The firm has worked solely on referral in Connecticut and Westchester County for more than eight years.

As a small firm, owner Anthony Pici remains actively involved in each job. Clients appreciate access to his two decades worth of industry knowledge. Pici keeps himself educated on the latest and greatest in the plumbing field and will not shy away from new or challenging assignments.

Botticeli Plumbing

	Quality	Cost	Value	Recommend?
	3.5	3	4	4

48 Padanaram Road, Danbury, CT 06810
(203) 794 - 9297

Full-service residential plumbing and heating

This insider-recommended firm accommodates typical plumbing duties in a workmanlike manner at a "very good price."

Forger-Kunkel Plumbing & Heating Co.

	Quality	Cost	Value	Recommend?
	4.5	4	4.5	4.5

PO Box 1035, Fairfield, CT 06825
(203) 255 - 0383

High-end plumbing and heating systems

This company's knowledge of upper Fairfield's towns and historic homes is unrivaled. Clients are smitten over Forger-Kunkel, who they deem the county's "society plumber." In business for nearly 60 years, the firm services and remodels high-end plumbing systems and fixtures. Owner Peter Kunkel directs eight skilled employees. We hear they produce "great" work and "call you back immediately."

Gateway Plumbing

	Quality	Cost	Value	Recommend?
	3	3	4	4

152 Mead Avenue, Greenwich, CT 06830
(203) 531 - 5201

Plumbing service and installation

J. Mulvaney Plumbing & Heating Inc.

	Quality	Cost	Value	Recommend?
	3	3	4	4

32 Bailey Avenue, Ridgefield, CT 06877
(203) 438 - 1354

Plumbing and heating service and repair, well water and sewage pump service

Ridgefield resident Joe Mulvany has provided plumbing and heating help to his hometown and surrounding Connecticut environs for 24 years, even on a 24-hour emergency basis. What he is best known for is his skill with well water and sewage pumps, which he can repair, and if necessary, replace.

	Quality	Cost	Value	Recommend?
	✚	$	◆	★

Jack Dilger Plumbing & Heating Contractors

4   3.5   4.5   4.5

605 Bedrod Road, Greenwich, CT 06830
(203) 629 - 0131   www.dilgerplumbing.com
Plumbing and heating service and installation

Jack Dilger Plumbing approaches plumbing as an art form, and patrons are lining up for a look. We're told every one of the company projects is a detailed creation meant to provide both form and function. The firm's plumbing division does everything from piping to fixture and fitting installation, often on the most complex of projects. Dilger's heat options include in-floor radiant heat, cast-iron radiators, and installations of everything from boilers to oil tanks. The firm accommodates the greater New York area, including Connecticut and the surrounding region through a Fairfield and Dutchess counties office (845) 677- 8818.

Committed to craft, the Dilger company name goes back about 30 years. President Wally Sroka coaches a team of service-oriented project managers and highly-trained technicians. Clients cite the Dilger double check—a rigorous point-by-point inspection at the rough and punch phases—as a reason for the flawless end product.

John Tulipani & Sons Inc.

3.5   3   4.5   4

77 Ivy Hill Road, Ridgefield, CT 06877
(203) 438 - 2986
Plumbing and heating design and installation

Established in 1962 by John Tulipani, the firm comes recommended "on all counts" for plumbing, heating service and installation in Connecticut.

Joseph S. Wilcox Plumbing & Heating

4   3   5   5

21 Ward Street, Norwalk, CT 06851
(203) 846 - 2699   jswph@msn.com
Plumbing and heating installation and service

With great precision this firm tackles everything from service calls and small jobs to complex and professionally engineered residential projects in the five-figure square-foot range. Working in Fairfield and Lichtfield counties for contractors, designers and homeowners, Wilcox Plumbing and Heating also takes on multifaceted heating and cooling systems.

The eponymous Joseph Wilcox established the firm in 1985. He runs a team of five plumbers who are as knowledgeable about high-end plumbing products as they are conscientious of the fine finishes they work around. Clients say Wilcox is a "nice plumber at a nice price."

Lee Seward Plumbing & Heating

3.5   3.5   4   4.5

27 South End Plaza, New Milford, CT 06776
(860) 350 - 4400
Plumbing and heating service and installation

Homeowners find Lee Seward an "excellent" choice for all their plumbing needs. They say this "practical" and "quick" working firm is both responsive and crewed up with great guys.

Neves Plumbing Service

4   3.5   4.5   5

5 South Avenue, Danbury, CT 06810
(203) 790 - 8018
Plumbing and heating installation and repair

Connecticut customers "have complete confidence" in Neves Plumbing. The "well-organized" firm furnishes first-class service, whether installing new plumbing systems, retrofitting for a restoration or simply doing repairs. We're told that the company responds in a flash and sticks to schedule.

	Quality	Cost	Value	Recommend?
	✚	$	◆	★

A plumbing professional since 1985, Mark Neves broke out on his own in 1994. His wife Karen keeps the office in order along with Joyce Seaman, while he leads a platoon of ten plumbers, including masterful Jim Morrisettte, who has worked with Neves since day one. We hear the moderately priced firm offers 24-hour emergency service.

"When it's a crunch, he's there." "Responsive, honest, polite and knowledge-able." "Work done in a timely and quality manner." "Excellent work. Always responds to issues."

Paretti Plumbing & Heating   3.5   3   4.5   4.5
587 Broadway, Hastings on Hudson, NY 13076
(914) 478 - 1006
Plumbing and heating service

This "nice and honest" plumber has served the Westchester area for over half a century. In addition to plumbing work for bath and kitchen remodels, whole-house alterations and new additions, Paretti also installs new heating systems that include radiant, gas and oil boilers and water heaters. Clients respond positively to the family-owned-and-operated feel.

Paul The Plumber Inc.   5   4   5   5
PO Box 33, Seymour, CT 06483
(800) 201 - 7285
Plumbing service, installation and repair, radiant heat

Paul the Plumber might as well be Paul McCartney considering the number of fans he has. Esteemed for his "thorough," "prompt" and "neat" service, Paul Konwerski handles small repairs, high-end, fit-out or replacement and larger remodels. He also specializes in radiant heat. We're told the firm pairs an easy-going personality with ambitious workmanship.

Paul, who opened his small shop in 1992, has nearly twenty years of experience in the trade. His firm focuses on servicing residents in Fairfield and western New Haven counties. Clients report that Paul and his two helpers are "polite, considerate and kind" and that Paul himself explains "everything without being condescending." Sources say this rock star performance comes in at a pedestrian price.

"Absolutely, hands down, the most reliable, professional plumber we have ever hired." "The main reason that he impressed us was when at 10:30 PM on a stormy, icy winter night, Paul came to melt a frozen pipe. If it had waited until morning, the damage might have been very expensive." "Paul is the only work-man we have employed who covers his feet. He is extremely neat." "He is clean, courteous, prompt and always explains problems clearly."

Pickwick Plumbing & Heating   4.5   4.5   4   5
98 Riverdale Avenue, Greenwich, CT 06831
(203) 531 - 6100
Full-service, high-end plumbing and heating

Pickwick is the perfect antidote for plumbers who scare the dickens out of their clients. Available for everything from bath and kitchen renovations to higher-end faucet repairs and installations, the often-recommended company services and installs plumbing systems in alterations, additions and new construction in southern Fairfield and western Westchester counties. We're told it also takes on boilers and hot work heat applications.

	Quality	Cost	Value	Recommend?
	+	$	◆	★

Pickwick Pluming & Heating was established in 1979. Sources say the outfit of plumbers and technicians parry every detail on route to a superior-quality end result. Pickwick doesn't pinch pennies, however, and comes at a price.

Plumb-Rite

4   3   4.5   5

107 Wood Avenue, Ardsley, NY 10502
(914) 779 - 7900

Plumbing service and remodels

Clients tell us Plumb-Rite has been the favored plumber of their families for over 25 years. The firm provides "first-rate" plumbing service and full installations. The work is "excellent," crews are professional and the firm is very responsive to customer's needs.

Owner and the firm's high-end fixture and finish guru, Gil Porcelli, receives the most praise. He delights contractors and private customers alike, all of whom vow to use Plumb-Rite into the future.

"Ask for the owner, Gil, and you will get an amazing job!" "Plumb-Rite staff is very professional and responds to all calls with the utmost speed." "I do not get other quotes. The rough work is excellent."

Putnam Plumbing & Heating Inc.

5   4.5   4.5   5

77 North Water Street, Greenwich, CT 06830
(203) 661 - 6806

High-end plumbing and heating systems

Those in the know crown Putnam tops in its trade, highly recommending the firm for its "fantastic quality and service." We're told owner Dick Edinas is "more knowledgeable of plumbing than anyone who ever lived." However, expect to pay a princely sum for his work.

Richard Bell Plumbing

4   4   4   4

84 Millwood Road, Millwood, NY 10546
(914) 941 - 8792

Plumbing and heating installation and service

RLJ Plumbing & Heating

4   3.5   4   4.5

25 Sand Street, Port Chester, NY 10573
(914) 934 - 9025

Plumbing and heating installation and service

Clients enjoy working with this classy family-run plumbing and heating shop. From outfitting a five-story brownstone in Manhattan to a bathroom repair in Wilton, the firm excels in all areas of high-end plumbing and heating work, especially fancy Waterworks fixtures and radiant heat. Sources say RLJ distinguishes itself by being as keyed into the clients' experience as they are to the plans and specs.

Principal Bobby Jones and his helper established the firm out of high school a dozen years ago. He keeps a hands-on presence while supervising sixteen employees. It's a good thing his wife Theresa watches the office because we hear this small shop can get overly busy.

"Great plumber, great guy."

Romeo Morelli & Sons Plumbing & Heating

📁   📁   📁   📁

1 Silver Hill Drive, New Fairfield, CT 06812
(203) 746 - 9427

Plumbing and heating service

	Quality	Cost	Value	Recommend?
	+	$	◆	★

Rudolph Biagi & Sons Plumbing & Heating   4.5   4.5   4   4.5
74 Hamilton Avenue, Greenwich, CT 06830
(203) 869 - 3220

Full-service, high-end plumbing and heating

This choice firm has customers cooing, "I love my plumber!" Rudolph Biagi & Sons is a must for high-end plumbing and heating projects. Sources say Biagi technicians show a keen eye and make the extra effort. We also hear that after installations contractors don't have to make the company come back for punch lists because the work "was so perfect."

Sabino Plumbing   4.5   4   4.5   4.5
96 Knapp Street, Stamford, CT 06907
(203) 325 - 1622

Plumbing and heating installation and service

Area architects who rely on this boutique family plumbing operation for their own residences, highly tout it. Clients remark that founder, Joseph Sabino and his son, Greg, are quick to respond to any call, and even quicker in an emergency. Fielding a staff of five, Sabino Plumbing and Heating both services and installs for the most savvy of clients.

Stephen D. Rozmus Plumbing and Heating Inc.   4.5   3   5   5
11 Connecticut Avenue, Greenwich, CT 06830
(203) 552 - 1658

Plumbing and heating installation and service

This "creative" and "effective" small plumbing shop does "fabulous work" for its lower-Fairfield clientele. "SDR" specializes in residential renovation and service, switching out high-end plumbing fixtures or new installations for multiple bathrooms. Heating expertise runs from radiant to boiler systems. Sources say the firm delivers a tidy and expedient effort and stands behind its good work.

Third-generation plumbing pro, Stephen D. Rozmus, learned his trade from his father after college and opened SDR five years ago. With three employees and his wife working the office, Rozmus keeps it personal and fairly priced. Clients compliment the "well-planned out" jobs and tell us they are "very pleased with every aspect of service provided."

"Very intelligent, responsible men who you trust implicitly." "We are thrilled with the end result." "Very prompt in returning calls." "Flexible about scheduling. Works to complete job in a timely and effective manner."

Stephen Miller Plumbing & Heating Inc.   📁   📁   📁   📁
20 Perry Avenue, Norwalk, CT 06850
(203) 847 - 1547

Plumbing and heating service

Waterworks   4.5   4.5   4.5   5
23 West Putnam Avenue, Greenwich, CT 06830
(203) 869 - 7766   www.waterworks.com

High-end bathroom design, sales and installation referral

See Waterworks's full report under the heading Kitchen & Bath Designers

Hiring a Rug Cleaning, Installation & Repair Service Provider

Does your heirloom Oriental display a record of your adorable yet hard-to-house-train puppy? Did Uncle Mike spill a Bloody Mary on your Persian? Did your cat sharpen his claws on that hidden corner of your needlepoint? Or is your rug just overdue for its regular cleaning (every two to four years, according to The Oriental Rug Importers of America)? Not to worry: rug cleaners and restorers can address every kind of need on every type of rug, from museum-quality handmade rugs to inexpensive carpeting.

Gathering Information

When choosing cleaners or restorers, there are many factors to consider. Ask if they perform free, written estimates. If they make house calls, do they charge a travel fee, and do they have free pickup, delivery and reinstallation? Before they quote you a price, you may wish to inquire how they set their rate—is it by the job, the hour or the size of the rug? Do they require a deposit? Will they arrange a payment plan if you need one? Do they offer discounts for multiple rugs or rooms? It's a good sign if they honor their estimate, even if the job overwhelms their expectations. It's an even better sign if they guarantee perfection, and don't consider the job finished until you are satisfied. Such an assurance (especially in writing) may be more valuable than letters of reference or membership in one of the professional associations, though both of these would add further reassurance of competence.

If your rug is handmade and you think it may be valuable, you may want to get it appraised by a rug-care service before having it cleaned or repaired. If it is valuable, you'll need to consider more expert (and expensive) services. On the other hand, you may also discover that the rug isn't worth nearly as much as you believed, and hence may not warrant lavish attention. Either way, a professional appraisal certifies the value of your belonging in case of mishaps—you may want to inquire beforehand whether liability falls in your court or whether the cleaner/restorer's insurance covers any mishaps. Many rug cleaning and reweaving establishments appraise rugs for insurance, estate sale, tax and charitable donation. Watching appraisers evaluate your rug also allows you to preview their professionalism. If their work instills confidence, hire them for the whole job—if not, you can still use their appraisal (and estimate, if they perform one simultaneously) as a first opinion in approaching another establishment. For complicated (expensive) repair or restoration jobs, ask how long it will take. Often, the expert restorers have other jobs they must finish before they can get to yours. If your rug is valuable, it is worth waiting for the best.

If the rug needs repair before cleaning, confirm that the restorer knows the techniques of the tradition in which the rug was made: Navajo yarn-dying and rug-weaving methods differ vastly from those of Iran. Ask to see a portfolio of their previous repair work, which often displays side-by-side "before" and "after" pictures. Inspect how well they match colors, recreate designs, and blend repairs into existing weaves. If your rug is valuable, inquire whether an expert or an apprentice will perform the repair work. Also, see to it that all repair work is included in the estimate, from reweaving holes to remapping worn areas; restoring moth damage to rewrapping seams and re-fringing to re-blocking your rug to its original shape. Particularly thorough rug conservationists will even unravel strands and overcast weaving in order to blend repairs into the rug's existing texture and design.

Cleaning and Drying Techniques

There are many different cleaning methods, each of which addresses different situations with varying degrees of efficacy and expense. Carpet cleaners typically have mobile operations, and will clean rugs in your home with hot "carbonating" systems, steam-cleaning or dry-cleaning. Will they move the furniture to clean under it or do they expect it ready when they arrive? Rug cleaners, on the other hand, usually perform the cleaning at their site. They may expect the rug to be rolled up and waiting for their pick up. Silk rugs, fragile tapestries and textiles with "fugitive" (short-lived) dyes, or bright colors that might "bleed" (run), should be hand-washed—the most delicate and expensive method. Luster cleaning immerses the entire rug in cleaning solutions, and thus achieves a deep clean while minimizing wear on the fabric. Soap washing involves running a vacuum-like machine over the rug; this vigorous method is only for particularly rugged or less-valuable rugs. Discuss in advance what problems the cleaner can and can't fix. For example, excessive wear on a hallway rug will still be there after a cleaning, though it will be much less noticeable. If you are health or environmentally conscious, ask whether the company offers nontoxic cleaners.

Any rug that's washed must also be dried properly to avoid mildew and dry rot. Be sure to ask about the time and drying technique for in-home jobs—you should know beforehand if you need to reroute traffic through the patio for three days. For in-plant jobs, bigger outfits have dry-rooms where they control temperature and humidity levels. In the home, drying basically involves not walking on the rug until it is dry, which depends on humidity and other factors. Some businesses also offer stain protectants, which they apply directly to the rug to shield it from future accidents (should the tipsy uncle return). Other companies may take a purist approach, preferring periodic cleaning to chemical protestants.

Carpet and Rug Installation

Before the carpet or rug is put down, padding should always be laid first. Padding gives more cushioning for your feet and keeps the rug from sliding, which helps prevent slips, falls and spills. Ask what kind of padding the installer will use, as there are generally different quality and price options.

For wall-to-wall carpeting installation, the most common method is to lay wooden tack strips around the perimeter of the room. The tack strips have pins sticking up that grab the carpet and hold it in place. The tack strips are attached to the floor using small nails, which leave holes in the floor when the carpet is removed. The padding also is usually either nailed or stapled to the floor. If you must cover your nice wood floors (for the kids, maybe), you should discuss with the installer how to minimize the floor damage. Unfortunately, there is not that much that can be done if you want wall-to-wall. Some installers may suggest attaching the carpet with double-faced tape, but most say that this doesn't hold well and the carpet shifts and buckles. If your floor contributes to the value of your apartment, it is simply better to stick with area rugs. Remember to ask if there are any potential extra charges, such as for ripping up existing wall-to-wall carpeting before installing the new one or for disposing of the old carpeting and pads if you don't want to keep them.

Some rug cleaners focus on just stain and odor removal services to meet the needs of pet owners, smokers and families with small children (or just klutzes). Many providers offer stain protection for future spills, which, depending on your lifestyle, may be a sound investment. Other companies specialize in emergency services in case of fire, smoke or water damage, and may even be available round-the-clock. If you're moving, remodeling or otherwise in need of storage, look to the larger outfits for mothproofing and storage services. After storage or in-plant services, many companies will reinstall your rug over appropriate padding.

Rug cleaners and restorers also offer many other services for rugs and other furnishings. Many rug cleaners also clean curtains and upholstered furniture. Some businesses prefer to remove the draperies from the home and wash them at their facilities. In-home carpet cleaners are more likely to clean curtains in the house.

Since curtains, upholstered furniture and rugs dominate most of the space (not to mention the attention) in a room, rug cleaners and restorers emphasize the importance of maintaining these items. Their colors will be clearer, they'll last longer, you'll be inhaling less dust—and your home will look more beautiful.

ON COST

Prices among rug companies vary immensely because each has its own specialties and services. Some rug firms work on standard cleaning and focus on wall-to-wall broadlooms, upholstery and drapery. For this type of cleaning, some charge by the square foot, which could start at $.25 per square foot and could go up to $1 to $1.25 per square foot. Most companies charge $.30 to $.60 per square foot. Then again, some give a flat rate after inspecting the carpet and seeing how much cleaning needs to be done. This usually conforms to their minimum rate, which most companies have. Minimum rates start at $50 and go up to $150 for standard wall-to-wall broadloom cleaning.

Area rugs are a different terrain altogether. The Tri-State area has numerous experts and "specialized" firms that only deal with area rug cleaning, repair and restoration—those that work mostly with the rare, the old, the valuable and in most cases, only the handmade ones. Most companies who do standard wall-to-wall cleaning also clean area rugs, but the older and rarer the rug is, the more specialized the cleaning, repair and attention it needs. Pricing for area rug cleaning starts as low as $1 per square foot and could go as high as $3 to $5 per square foot, depending on the amount of cleaning needed and the value of the rug. These firms also have minimum rates, and fees start at $100 minimum up to $700. Then again, if your area rug is not 100 years old and requires only regular cleaning or minimal repairs, you could end up paying a standard $50 to $100 per job or $1.25 to $2 per square foot.

DON'T LET THE RUG BE PULLED OUT FROM UNDER YOU!

✧ Get several bids. Prices among competent cleaners can vary quite a bit.
✧ When you have an estimate, ask if it's binding. Ask what factors might cause it to become higher (or lower) when the job is actually done.
✧ Is there a minimum charge for a house call? If the cost of cleaning your rug is below the minimum you might want to have them perform another service (such as clean or stain-proof another rug, piece of furniture or curtains) at the same time.
✧ Once they are in your house, the rug cleaner wll often do another rug for much less money, especially if paid in cash.
✧ Some of the larger more commercial cleaners have regular "sales." Get on their mailing list to receive updates. If you're not in a hurry, wait for a sale.

RUGS — CLEANING INSTALLATION & REPAIR

800 Rug Wash   4   2   5   5

20 Enterprise Avenue, Secaucus, NJ 07094
(800) 784 - 9274   rugwash@aol.com

Rug and upholstery cleaning and repair, flooring installation and maintenance

800 Rug Wash's specialty is cleaning, repairing and selling rugs but the company also cleans upholstery, fabric walls, draperies and fabric blinds. Recently, the company began doing general cleaning for commercial establishments. The company also has a flooring division which handles installation, sanding and finishing of all types of floors. We are told that even before establishing the company in 1980, owner Benjamin Hatooka, a chemist by trade, had a number of rug dealers come to him to change the colors of rugs and make them look old. Today, one of the firm's specialties is still antiquing.

The firm cleans residential and commercial interiors in Manhattan, New Rochelle, Greenwich, Stamford, New Canaan and Woodbury. Rug dealers from as far away as Los Angeles, Florida, Boston, Virginia and Canada send 800 Rug Wash rugs to be cleaned on a regular basis. 800 Rug Wash is a member of the Oriental Rug Importers Association and The National Wood Flooring Association. Pricing is generally per square foot, and sources say that the firm's prices are moderate. Clients have expressed satisfaction with this firm's reliability, promptness and good work ethic.

"Gets the job done." "Knows his business." "Prompt. Very good work." "Fair prices for efficient service." "A professional, persistent, precise and committed organization."

A.T. Proudian Inc.   4   2.5   4.5   4.5

120 East Putnam Avenue, Greenwich, CT 06830
(203) 622 - 1200   www.atproudian.com

Area rug, carpet and tapestry cleaning, rug retail, installation and repair

This family business has inspired trust and delight among its growing number of loyal patrons since opening its doors in 1923. Established by its namesake, Aram Thomas Proudian, the company is now managed by his son, Armen and his grandson, Gregory. A.T. Proudian cleans, repairs, installs and sells carpets and area rugs, kilims and tapestries.

The company has commercial and residential clients in most states in the US and has done projects in far away places such as London, Paris, Moscow and Curacao. The firm has showrooms in New Rochelle and Greenwich. Cleaning is generally priced by the square foot, installation by the yard and repairs by the job.

"Good selection of rugs in their showroom." "Can take out even the most stubborn stains."

Alix Unlimited   5   3   5   5

45 Mayhew Avenue, Larchmont, NY 10538
(914) 834 - 2478   alixperrachon@hotmail.com

Area rug consultant, appraisal and sales

"I couldn't live without her," one designer told us. "Her" refers to Alix Perrachon, the woman behind Alix Unlimited. While living in Turkey, Perrachon learned about rugs and immersed herself in "rug culture." She started writing about kilims and antique Orientals and continued to do so in the States for prominent publications like *Hali* and *Oriental Rug* magazine. Gradually, she became one of the few "authorities" on rugs and established Alix Unlimited, a consulting firm. Clients call Alix a "navigator" in the "cliquish world of rugs," a liason between the client and the source. Decorators swear she has saved their clients thousands of dollars because Alix can get the rug directly from the manufacturer or a dealer for an "insider's price." Dealers, manufacturers, art collectors and auction houses are some of Perrachon's sources.

Perrachon also does appraisals (and will even send a certificate) for clients thinking about buying a rug as an investment or after flood or water damage. Customers rely on the firm to find, shop and appraise any kind, size, or color rug for any type of budget. Pricing is a case-by-case basis—either a retainer fee or a 25 percent handling fee (after all purchases) will be billed to the client. References across the board agree Perrachon is "one-of-a-kind," professional and knowledgeable about her craft.

"An unbelievable source." "I was starting to think the rug my client wanted did not exist, but Alix managed to find it at such short notice and at a cheaper price too." "Prior to Alix, I had to take a dealer's word on the value of a rug, crossing my fingers that they were telling me the truth." "The rug industry people know her and we get preferential treatment from showrooms, dealers or auction houses." "When in doubt, I call Alix."

All Clean Carpet & Upholstery Cleaning   4.5   2.5   5   5
10 Hilltop Place, Albertson, NY 11507
(516) 621 - 0524

Carpet, area rug, furniture & upholstery cleaning, water damage restoration

Since its establishment twenty years ago, All Clean Carpet has been a favorite choice among notable carpet retailers, celebrities and high-end residential clients. This company cleans rugs, furniture, upholstery, drapery and wall fabrics. The firm also specializes in protection systems which they apply to newly cleaned or purchased carpets and upholstery.

Capable of cleaning fine Orientals, the firm does only on-site residential work. Clients tell us they are "thrilled" with the skill and knowledge John Mauser and his team bring to the job. They commend the firm for its willingness to make emergency visits for regular customers. Patrons also appreciate that the crew moves furniture and puts it back, rather than just cleaning around it.

"Fabulous, very high standards." "Does an outstanding job." "On time, efficient, courteous. Very nice in every regard." "Quick and thorough. Spends extra time and effort to address problem areas."

Anita deCarlo Inc.   4.5   3.5   4.5   5
605 Madison Avenue, New York, NY 10022
(212) 759 - 1145   rugsbyanita@aol.com

Antique rug restoration, brokerage, cleaning and maintenance

This "one-woman band" has more than 30 years experience in the high-end rug business. Anita deCarlo is known by clients as a rug broker who does accurate appraisals and can locate the finest and rarest pieces for the discriminating tastes of her sophisticated clientele. She also offers cleaning and restoration services for rugs, needlework and textiles. We hear most of the work is done in-house, but very large pieces are done on-site. She usually works in Manhattan but takes on projects in the Hamptons and Fairfield and Westchester counties. Clients rave about her work quality and entrust her with their most valuable rugs. References also compliment her professional demeanor and charm.

"Honest, delightful, efficient." "Marvelous." "Extremely competent and a pleasure to work with." "Her credentials and knowledge are very impressive." "Complete professional in the sometimes shady world of carpet dealing."

	Quality	Cost	Value	Recommend?
	✚	$	◆	★

Beauvais Carpets
4.5 3 5 5

201 East 57th Street, 2nd Floor, New York, NY 10022
(212) 688 - 2265 www.beauvaiscarpets.com

Dealer—fine rug and tapestry cleaning and restoration

Located in midtown Manhattan, Beauvais Carpets is primarily a dealer with a "pre-eminent collection of fine antique rugs and tapestries." The firm also provides high-quality restoration, appraisal and cleaning services for fine antique, semi-antique and contemporary rugs. Beauvais also sells and installs wall-to-wall carpets. Insiders tell us that the firm's gallery is a haven for rug collectors since it features an outstanding selection of rugs and tapestries from sixteenth- through nineteenth-century Europe and Asia. Beauvais also offers custom broadloom carpets.

Pricing is generally by the job and there is a charge for pick-up and delivery. Though the firm deals mostly with designers and architects, it also serves an impressive list of distinguished residential clients. With regard to spot cleaning, we hear that Beauvais pretests stains and informs the client of the predictable result. Repair and cleaning is done in the company's workshops located in Brooklyn and Manhattan. Sources say the workmen are thorough, polite and knowledgeable. The firm's work has been featured in *Kips Bay Showhouse* and in *Town & Country* magazine.

"The definitive source for fine antique rugs." "Exceeded my expectations." "Amazing eye for color and meticulous attention to detail."

Beyond the Bosphorus
5 3 5 5

79 Sullivan Street, New York, NY 10012
(212) 219 - 8257

Antique rug cleaning, retail and restoration

Aside from the eye-catching name, its impressive credentials and vast resources of Turkish and Oriental flatwoven rugs make Beyond the Bosphorous stand out among its peers. The company is owned and managed by Istanbul native Ismail Basbag, who boasts ten years of training and experience working in the Grand Bazaar of Istanbul before founding Beyond the Bosphorous in 1985.

This firm cleans, repairs, sells and restores antique and semi-antique Turkish flatwoven rugs called kilims, Turkish cylindrical pillows (bolster pillows), trunks upholstered with kilims and other types of Oriental area rugs. Work is done in or out of Basbag's workshop, depending on the type of project. We're told Basbag's sophisticated clients appreciate his fine taste and ability to share his knowledge of antique rugs. The firm has clients at some of New York's most elite addresses as well as in California, New Jersey, Connecticut and Texas. Beyond the Bosphorous was also mentioned in a recent *New York* magazine issue of "Manhattan's 1,000 Best Shops."

Sources describe Basbag as a nice, quiet and polite man who "does a splendid job" with a pleasant demeanor and excellent work philosophy. Though prices are a bit high-end, clients say the service is worth every penny.

"Reliable & excellent at following up." "Excellent work ethic." "Knowledgeable about his work." "One of the few remaining old-world craftsmen." "Entering his shop is like entering another time and place."

	Quality	Cost	Value	Recommend?
	✚	$	◆	★

Cleantex Process Co.

	Quality	Cost	Value	Recommend?
	3.5	2.5	4.5	4.5

2335 Twelfth Avenue, New York, NY 10027
(212) 283 - 1200   cleantex@lycos.com

Cleaning and repair of rugs, upholstery and draperies

Cleantex has been handling the rug, wall-to-wall carpets and drapery cleaning needs of its devoted clientele for nearly 75 years. This firm also cleans and repairs upholstery and furniture. References, many of whom have used the company for years, find Cleantex reliable, professional and cooperative. We hear that several dealers of fine Oriental rugs refer their clients to Cleantex. Should clients need it, flameproofing is one of this firm's specialties. The firm also has convenient pickup and delivery services for fine and standard carpets. Cleantex serves most of Manhattan as well as some areas in Connecticut, New Jersey, Long Island, Westchester County and the Hamptons.

"Wonderful, cooperative, no-nonsense people." "We know it will be done professionally." "Everything always goes smoothly." "They are getting up there with some of the best in the area."

Cohen Carpet, Upholstery & Drapery Cleaning

	Quality	Cost	Value	Recommend?
	3.5	3	4	4.5

2565 Broadway, New York, NY 10025
(212) 663 - 6902

Rug and upholstery cleaning

Clients across the region say David Cohen does most of the work personally for this firm, and has maintained a high level of customer service since he established the company in 1983. Cohen cleans area rugs, wall-to-wall carpets, upholstery, fabric blinds, fabric walls and draperies both on- and off-site, mostly for residential customers. He doesn't do restoration but will do minor repairs. Clients tell us that Cohen comes recommended by furniture firms and designers alike, who are pleased with the quality of his work and confident in his professional conduct. They say he is always pleasant, prompt and straightforward about pricing.

"Easy to work with." "Really great with tough stains—nail polish, cranberry juice, etc." "The rugs look like new." "Not cheap, but very fair." "Great at troubleshooting." "We were ready to get new carpeting, but he somehow managed to repair our old one." "Performed miracles on our carpet."

Costikyan Carpets Inc.

	Quality	Cost	Value	Recommend?
	4	3.5	4	5

28-13 14th Street, Astoria, NY 11102
(718) 726 - 1090   www.costikyan.com

Dealer—Fine rug and fabric upholstery cleaning and restoration

Known for its exceptional cleaning and restoration work, we hear Costikyan Carpets has been satisfying discriminating clients since its founding in 1886 by Kent Costikyan. The company is now managed by his great-grandson Philip. Costikyan buys, sells, cleans, repairs, restores, manufactures and imports fine antique, semi-antique and modern rugs. The firm also cleans fabric upholstery and fabric walls. Costikyan also patented a rug protectant called Costikyan Bond, which is a stain repellent and soil release system that binds to the rug fibers for longer protection. Prices are high-end, but for valuable pieces, clients say they will trust no other. The firm works on- and off-site, and in most cases gives free pickup and delivery. Costikyan works in Manhattan, the Hamptons and Westchester. This mostly residential company also works with designers, dealers, private collectors and museums.

A number of the area's top designers and homeowners go to Costikyan for repairing their most expensive and rare rugs. The "highly skilled" workmen at Costikyan are professional, reliable and trustworthy.

"Easy to work with—will go the extra mile." "One of the best in the business. Impeccable standards." "My carpets were beautifully cleaned." "Courteous, conscientious, efficient and on time."

Delmont Carpet & Upholstery Cleaning 3.5 2.5 4 4
217 East 86th Street, New York, NY 10028
(212) 513 - 7500 www.delmontcleanny.com

Rug, drapery, window treatment and upholstery cleaning, application of protective sealant

For cleaning carpets, upholstery and draperies, Delmont Carpet is the top choice for numerous references in and around New York City. The company has served residential and commercial clients around Manhattan, Brooklyn, Long Island, the Hamptons and Westchester County since 1973. Sources describe this company's workmen as prompt, courteous and efficient. The firm is also known for its attentive and personalized service. Pricing is usually "by the rug" and we hear the workmen will move furniture, at no extra cost, as long as it is non-breakable and not too heavy. Appreciative clients applaud the firm's reasonable rates.

"Fastidious job." "The only company in the city I will use." "I personally couldn't have imagined a better job. On time and so reliable."

Exclusive Home Care Specialists 3.5 2.5 4 4
217 East 86th Street, Suite 177, New York, NY 10028
(212) 795 - 7727 www.sealtexstainprotection.com

Rug and upholstery cleaning

Exclusive Home Care Specialists offers professional cleaning services for fine upholstery, wall-to-wall carpeting, oriental and fine rugs, draperies, custom shades and fabric walls. Sources tell us the firm's staff combines friendliness with professionalism and has earned the trust of its clientele. Exclusive Home Care offers emergency stain removal and can provide Seal-Tex lifetime stain protection (its version of Scotchgard) for upholstery, carpeting and rugs. Exclusive Home Care is also experienced in wood floor waxing and polishing.

The firm, established in 1990 by Tony Athas, serves mostly residential clients in Manhattan, the Hamptons, Westchester County, Connecticut and Long Island. Prices are generally by the square foot and most of the cleaning is done on the site.

"Honest, friendly and reliable." "They sometimes are hard to reach, but will call back eventually." "Top-notch stainproofing." "Courteous staff."

F.J. Hakimian 4.5 4 4 4.5
136 East 57th Street, 2nd Floor, New York, NY 10022
(212) 371 - 6900 www.fjhakimian.com

Dealer of fine rugs, tapestry cleaning, restoration and conservation

F.J. Hakimian has earned a reputation of being "one of the best" in the rug business. Primarily a dealer, retailer and appraiser of fine antique handmade rugs, this firm also offers cleaning, restoration and conservation of rare tapestries, needlepoint and area rugs. Owned and managed by Joseph Hakimian, the firm has been in business for 30 years and serves dealers, decorators, homeowners and private collectors.

The firm's clients say its craftsmen do excellent work and consider Hakimian the natural choice for specialized jobs. However, hiring this firm wouldn't make sense for those who are looking for an inexpensive company to clean an average rug. In fact, insiders tell us the relatively high cost and high-end focus would make it less suitable for anything but valuable, top-quality antique rugs and tapestries. Although some insiders say Hakimian's busy schedule makes him almost impossible to reach, most say it is worth the wait. Sources tell us that top decorators and collectors will trust only F.J. Hakimian with their valuable treasures.

"A gentleman and honest businessman." "Excellent work." "Very good, but expensive." "A true craftsman."

	Quality ✚	Cost $	Value ◆	Recommend? ★

Fabra Cleen Carpet & Fabric Specialists Inc.

	4	2.5	5	4.5

PO Box 280471, Queens Village, NY 11428
(212) 777 - 4040

Carpet, upholstery and fabric cleaning and repair

"Some of the nicest people around," is how many clients describe the staff at Fabra Cleen. This company cleans and repairs area rugs, carpets, upholstery, leather furniture, fabric headboards, fabric walls and drapery. The company also sells and installs wall-to-wall carpets, does post-construction cleanup and has been known to handle some minor repairs on carpets and rugs. Established in 1949 by Samuel Kornet, the firm is now managed by his son Brian, and Brian's wife, Wendy. Fabra Cleen serves both residential and commercial clients in Manhattan, the Hamptons and Westchester County. Cleaning is done on location or at the company's facilities, in which case, pick-up and delivery is free. Sources tell us Fabra Cleen prides itself on meticulous attention to detail and will move furniture for free in order to clean under it.

Honest, trustworthy, reliable, responsive and punctual are some of the superlatives used to describe this company. Sources say they appreciate the efficient service and the moderate prices that come with it.

"Excellent." "When I need them they are here at the drop of a hat." "They have my keys and my security codes—they are completely trustworthy." "Courteous." "With a baby and two dogs, I would have had to replace my carpets if not for Fabra Cleen." "Pleasant and fantastically effective at carpet and upholstery cleaning."

Fairfield County Cleaning Service, LLC

	4.5	3	5	5

647 California Street, Stratford, CT 06614
(203) 386 - 1688

Residential window cleaning, post-construction, gutter, carpet and upholstery cleaning

See Fairfield County Cleaning Service, LLC's full report under the heading Window Washers

Fiber-Seal of Western Connecticut, Inc.

	4.5	3	4.5	5

500B Howe Avenue, Suite 205B, Shelton, CT 06484
(203) 924 - 4998

Application of protective sealant and cleaning for carpets, drapery and upholstery

Fiber-Seal is a popular protective sealant that is applied to new and freshly cleaned carpets, upholstery and fabrics. The professionals at Fiber-Seal spray an invisible, odor-free stain-repellent coating on any home fabric. They are also proficient in cleaning area rugs, wall-to-wall broadlooms and upholstery. Pricing is generally by the piece or by square foot. The company even gives clients a "Fabric Care Kit" for everyday accidental spills. Fiber-Seal serves residential and commercial clients across Connecticut. The firm is an industry member of ASID.

"An invaluable service." "Not cheap, but worth it." "Consistently organized." "Thorough and terrific follow-ups."

	Quality ✚	Cost $	Value ◆	Recommend? ★

Hayko Restoration & Conservation   4.5   3   5   5

857 Lexington Avenue, Second Floor, New York, NY 10021
(212) 717 - 5400   www.hayko.com

Antique carpet, tapestry and needlepoint cleaning, retail and restoration

The buzz among Hayko Oltaci's loyal clientele is that he is a man who understands that rugs are "not only decorative and functional pieces but trademarks of history." Hayko Restoration & Conservation restores, conserves and cleans fine antique, semi-antique and contemporary area rugs, tapestries and needlepoint. He also buys and sells rugs, and even gives consultation for his valued clients. Mr. Oltaci established his business in New York in 1992 but worked in the rug business for ten years prior in France. Originally from Istanbul, Turkey, Oltaci also worked and trained at the Grand Bazaar. Insiders tell us his industry knowledge and industrious nature makes him a favorite of top designers, upscale private collectors, homeowners, museums, dealers and auction houses.

High-end clients rave about Mr. Oltaci's warmth and charm as well as his exceptional skill and knowledge of rugs. Christie's considers him "quite a find" and recommends him to its clients. Sources appreciate his efficiency, reliability, and the fact that he will go out of his way to serve his loyal clientele. Prices may be top of the line, but clients agree that quality doesn't come cheap.

"The most honest man I know." "There's nobody else as good as Hayko." "A wonderful craftsman. I've been using him for at least ten years now." "He goes out of his way for his clients. He came to my aid in an emergency and came to my home in the evening and repaired my rug right there." "Major museums know his work is nothing short of perfect."

Health First Cleaning Specialists   4.5   2.5   5   5

20 Palace Place, Portchester, NY 10573
(914) 690 - 9294   cleanairtech1@msn.com

Rug, drapery, upholstery, fabric and leather cleaning

References tell us that for quick and efficient cleaning of fabric, carpets, drapery and upholstery, Health First is the company to call. Founded by George Boticelli in 1979, the firm serves residential and commercial clients in Fairfield, Westchester and New Jersey. The company provides mobile cleaning units for on-site cleaning, but also does a substantial amount of work at its Portchester plant. A certified member of the Institute of Inspection, Cleaning and Restoration Certification, Health First can also address emergency situations like water, smoke, fire and mold damage.

"Their protective sealant saved my upholstery." "Responsive to inquiries." "Polite and courteous."

Irwin Cohen   4.5   2.5   5   5

16-10 212th Street, Bayside, NY 11360
(718) 224 - 9885

Carpet, area rug and upholstery spot cleaning and repair

When others give up on a stain, sources tell us they call on Irwin Cohen. We hear that he has yet to be truly stumped by a stain despite being faced with some very stubborn ones. Clients say he will personally come out and tend to stains on short notice and always does so with a smile, using little potions from his briefcase. Irwin, a third-generation Cohen in the business, has been serving clients around Manhattan, New Jersey, Long Island, Connecticut, Westchester County and the Hamptons for 36 years. This firm is a specialist in spot cleaning only (he doesn't clean whole rugs) and will work on area rugs, wall-to-wall broadlooms, fabric walls and upholstery. The company also demonstrates a talent for reweaving and minor repairs. Pricing is by the job and all work is done on-site.

"Couldn't live without him." "Excellent! Takes out spots that baffle other carpet cleaners." "Pleasant and easy to work with." "The man with the golden hands."

	Quality ✚	Cost $	Value ◆	Recommend? ★

John M. Evans Window & Carpet Cleaning Service

| | 4 | 2.5 | 5 | 5 |

10 Windward Road, Norwalk, CT 06854
(203) 866 - 3799

Residential window cleaning and wall-to-wall carpet cleaning

See John M. Evans Window & Carpet Cleaning Service's full report under the heading Window Washers

Kalust Barin

| | 4.5 | 3 | 4.5 | 4.5 |

1334 York Avenue, New York, NY 10021
(212) 606 - 7896

Antique rug and tapestry restoration and repair

"A man of many talents," is how people describe Kalust Barin. Clearly, Sotheby's thinks so too, since he holds fort in their building on the Upper East Side. There, Barin does a number of jobs for some of the auction house's distinguished clients. Barin has been in the rug business his entire life, starting with his family's business in Turkey where he worked in the Grand Bazaar. This soft-spoken man serves mostly residential clients in Manhattan, New Jersey, Westchester and Fairfield. The firm repairs, restores and cleans antique rugs, with a specialty in American, European and Middle Eastern pieces. Barin also conserves tapestries and needle-point. While most of his work is done at Sotheby's, he occasionally works on-site and has several clients whose rugs he checks on a regular basis. Barin's show-room in Sotheby's is open to the public and the trade.

Sources tell us that this gentleman is a hard worker who is dedicated to his craft. We hear he is reliable and honest, and though his prices are upper-end, references say the service is worth the price tag.

"Has done quality work for us for fifteen years now." "Extremely skilled." "Best man for the job." "Has such a discriminating eye for repairing and restoring fine pieces."

Kenny Rug & Upholstery Cleaning

| | 4 | 2 | 5 | 5 |

PO Box 2297, Stamford, CT 06906
(203) 329 - 0606

Area rug, carpet and upholstery cleaning

One of the old-timers in the business, Kenny Rug & Upholstery Cleaning continues to satisfy its loyal patrons since opening its doors in 1967. Established by John Kenny, the firm is now managed by his son Mark. The firm cleans all types of area rugs, wall-to-wall carpets and upholstery. Ninety percent of their work is done on-site.

Kenny works all over Connecticut and Fairfield. Pricing for rugs and carpets are by the square foot and by the piece for upholstery cleaning. The company also offers deodorizing and application of protective sealants. Estimates are free and Kenny and his team work with both decorators and directly with homeowners.

"No hidden costs. Very fair prices." "Gets the job done quickly." "I trust Mark completely. I give him my keys and security codes." "Been dealing with the family for 30 years."

Majestic Rug Cleaners

| | 3 | 2 | 4 | 4 |

644 Whittier Street, Bronx, NY 10474
(212) 922 - 0909

Rug and upholstery cleaning

This large company cleans wall-to-wall carpets, area rugs, drapes and fabric upholstery. Majestic was established in the 1930s and has been satisfying res-idential and commercial clients in the greater New York area ever since. Through the years, Majestic acquired some other rug cleaning companies as part of its expansion process. Some of its sister companies are J&J Williams Rug, Metropolitan, AAA Radiant, Master Craft, Prince, Perfect Carpet and Upholstery, Fibre Guard and Capital Atlantic.

"Fabulous work done on my Orientals."

	Quality	Cost	Value	Recommend?
	+	$	◆	★

Ronnee Barnett Textile Restoration — 5 3 5 5

182 Cherry Hill Road, Accord, NY 12404
(212) 966 - 3520   ronneebarnett@hvc.rr.com

Fine antique rug, tapestry, needlepoint and textile restoration, repair and cleaning

References agree that Ronnee Barnett is a woman dedicated to her craft and passionate about her work. Barnett started her own textile restoration business in 1978 after deciding to give up psychology because she "had an intense desire to weave." She restores, conserves, cleans, reweaves and repairs rare antique area rugs, needlepoint, tapestries and textiles. She also works part-time for the Metropolitan Museum of Art where she restores and mounts medieval textiles.

The firm does business mostly in Manhattan, but has clients from all over the US. This one-woman company works with museums, decorators, dealers, private collectors and homeowners. We are told Barnett believes in in-depth client interviews to discuss the project in advance to determine the specifications of her customers. We're told Barnett also educates clients in the proper way to care for their priceless treasures. Sources consider her work museum-quality and find her incredibly professional and communicative. Clients say she takes her time, does the job right and treats each piece like a work of art.

"She is the best—such a find." "Artistic, capable and businesslike." "Can't tell it was repaired. Great workmanship." "A joy to work with." "She examines the problem with intelligence and insight."

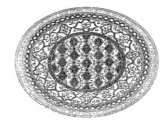

Ronny Reliable's Cleaning — 4 2 5 5

11 American Legion Drive, Ardsley, NY 10502
(914) 674 - 9000   www.ronnyreliable.com

Window washing, carpet, blinds & furniture cleaning, post-construction cleanup

See Ronny Reliable's Cleaning's full report under the heading Window Washers

Safavieh Carpets — 4 3.5 4.5 4

902 Broadway, New York, NY 10010
(212) 477 - 1234   www.safavieh.com

Dealer and restorer of antique and contemporary rugs, needlepoint and tapestries

One of New York's prominent retailers, appraisers and restorers of fine antique, semi-antique and contemporary rugs, Safavieh Carpets has been serving affluent clients since its establishment by Hamil Yaraghi in 1914. Now managed by his grandson Arash, the firm continues to provide the same top-notch service to its discriminating clientele. The firm also does some restoration and conservation for museums.   Safavieh's wide selection of rugs includes Oriental, Aubusson, Persian, Pakistani, Indian and Tibetan. The company also works with tapestries and needlepoint. Safavieh takes pride in its restoration department, where workmen meticulously do all the work by hand and in the same method that the orginal weaver used. All cleaning and repair is done in-house and is heavily supervised.

With three showrooms located in Manhattan—one of them exclusively open to the trade—Safavieh also maintains seven more locations around Long Island, Connecticut, Westchester and New Jersey.

"Fabulous. Wouldn't think of going to anyone else."

	Quality +	Cost $	Value ◆	Recommend? ★

The Durotone Company Inc.   3.5   2.5   4.5   5
510 Ogden Avenue, Mamaroneck, NY 10543
(914) 381 - 1167

Carpet, rug, upholstery, drapery cleaning and repair

A favorite among homeowners, interior decorators and rug dealers, we hear that The Durotone Company "gets the job done without the fuss." A specialist in cleaning wall-to-wall carpets, area rugs, fabric walls and upholstery, Durotone can also clean sisal, jute, hemp and seagrass rugs. The firm can clean in house (it has a 6,000-square-foot workshop) or on-site. Durotone was founded in 1944 by Irving Mermer and is now managed by his great-grandson, Howard Sklar. Price is usually by the square foot for rugs and carpets, by the piece for upholstery and by the size for draperies. The company is a member of The World Floor Coverings Association and Sklar is a certified Master Cleaner and Senior Practicing Carpet Inspector by the Institute of Inspection, Cleaning and Restoration Certification (IICRC).

Sources tell us they are delighted with Durotone's quick and efficient workmen who always "clean underneath the furniture" and check "every inch" to make sure the job is perfect.

"I take them to my clients' homes to put protective seal on every piece of furniture they own." "A pleasure to work with. Reasonable turnaround time." "Hard to reach sometimes, but will always call back."

Triple S Carpet & Drapery Cleaners   4.5   3   5   5
337 Westport Avenue, Norwalk, CT 06851
(203) 847 - 8000   www.triplesclean.com

Carpet, upholstery and drapery cleaning and repair and window treatment production

From standard wall-to-wall broadlooms to Oriental area rugs to draperies and upholstery, Triple S "can clean them all." A popular choice among well-known designers, rug galleries and homeowners, the firm cleans and repairs all types of area rugs, upholstery, wall-to-wall carpets and draperies. With three locations in Connecticut (Norwalk, Stamford and Stratford), Triple S sends out mobile crews for on-site cleaning and can also accommodate drop-offs or pickups to be cleaned in its plant. The firm is also proficient in cleaning natural-fibered rugs like jute, hemp, seagrass and sisal. The business also specializes in applying Pro-Seal, a fabric protective sealant. Established in 1963 by Steve De Marco Sr., the company, with more than 80 employees, still involves the main family members making it "an old-fashioned family business" that clients say "makes us feel at ease." Price is per square foot and Triple S works mostly in Greenwich, Stratford, Stamford, Darien, New Canaan and some parts of Westchester.

The firm takes pride in the fact that almost everyone in the company is certified by the Institute of Inspection, Cleaning and Restoration Certification. The firm is also a member of The Association of Specialists In Cleaning & Restoration. Their sister company, Triple S Reupholstery Center is well-known for producing beautiful custom upholstery and drapery. References say they appreciate the "moderate-to-upper-end" prices as well as the thorough, courteous and professional service that goes along with it.

"Very knowledgeable crew. I'd trust them with anything." "The upholstery workroom is great for the basics. Reliable and well-priced." "They are thorough and have handled work for me for years." "I like the way I can turn to them for so many different services."

HIRING A SECURITY SYSTEM
SERVICE PROVIDER

There are those of us for whom turning on the TV when leaving the house is considered a security measure. Of course, with an American home burglarized once every eleven seconds, it could also be considered hospitality. In fact, security systems, the first centrally controlled integrated system to make it into most homes, are branching out into fire/life-safety and the convenience/lifestyle sectors that are now becoming the backbone of home automation. So, if you don't really think "*Three's Company*" re-runs will scare away potential burglars, you can program your TV's routine, along with the rest of your security system, over your cell phone or the Internet while vacationing halfway around the world. Now if only you could get the vacuum cleaner to pick up your mail.

Like their A/V brethren, security system service providers are marketing themselves as the one-stop shop for your home's central nervous system. No one company may be best at everything yet, but security is a natural place to start to smarten up your home.

A HOST OF HIGH-TECH OPTIONS

Options once reserved for technophiles, supervillains, museums or celebrities have become available to anyone. Closed circuit television (CCTV) can now be fed through your television or computer to eyeball for trouble and can be monitored online from virtually anywhere. Sensors can be installed that detect motion, change in temperature, smoke and carbon monoxide, fluctuation of sound waves, broken glass or breached barriers. When tripped, they transmit the offended sensor's serial number to a central control panel, which in turn relays the home location and the point of alarm to the monitoring company. The monitoring company will immediately attempt to contact the homeowner to verify that a break-in has occurred. If there is no response, or the respondent fails to give the proper secret password, the police or fire department is notified. In addition, some monitoring companies will dispatch their own personnel to check out the situation, either from the street or, if keys are provided, from inside the home itself.

The explosion of cellular and wireless technology promises further protection and convenience to homeowners. Teamed with battery packs in the event of power failure, communication is fully safeguarded. Wireless modular components (touch pads) can be placed in convenient locations by homeowners themselves, as no cords or wires are needed. This is great for renters, too, who can take the wireless system with them when they move. Alarm devices range from the sounding of a voice wistfully repeating "fire" to the crazed bark of a pack of 100-pound Rotweillers, to the snapping on the lights in your home as if it were Yankee Stadium.

All of these functions are managed through a central control panel, traditionally a keypad and display. But as this industry charges toward the home automation front, touch screens, or a platform on your PC, are increasingly becoming the way to go. This makes it much easier to program and manage your systems. You can keep tabs on the alarm history and security status, play back the sequences of which lights you turn on and off or kick on the air-conditioning while driving home from work—and do it all remotely via computer or cell phone.

Choosing the right system for is as much about the logistical characteristics of your location (i.e., apartment vs. house, rural vs. urban) and budget as it is about the degree of system integration you want in your home. The options range from an "I'm Protected" warning sticker on a window to a virtual HAL 5000. How sophisticated do you want to get? How intrusive? A homeowner's personal circumstances and susceptibility must also be considered.

ON COST

The cost of any security system depends upon the number of devices, the sophistication of the control unit, the degree of integration, the term and service of the monitoring and whether it's wireless or hardwired technology. Basically, the cost reflects the time and material for installation plus the monitoring agreement, which can range from month-to-month to five years. Shorter terms are aimed at renters, but these agreements may include higher-than-average installation costs. At the end of the term, the monitoring agreement should be automatically renewable, with a ceiling for rate hikes spelled out in the contract. Payment can be made on a monthly, quarterly or annual basis. If you break your contract, don't be surprised if you're held responsible for as much as 90 percent of the unexpired term as liquidated damages. If you sell your home, however, you should be able to transfer your monitoring agreement over to the new homeowners.

It is important to know the parameters of your monitoring agreement, before you sign it. Many people are involved in your security, and awkward mistakes will cost you. Security providers allow a familiarization period in which no signal will be acted upon. Use this time wisely. Once you're up and running, you may be charged for false alarms by both the monitoring company and the city for wasting their time. They will also charge you to reprogram controls. Be absolutely sure you're comfortable with the system setup and its use before signing the agreement. Warranties should cover parts and labor for one year and you can opt for a maintenance agreement that covers such extras as emergency service.

After you invest in a security system, check with your homeowner's insurance company. You may be able to get a reduction in your insurance rate.

GETTING PLUGGED IN

Finally, your security system provider may need a permit and certain components and installation methods may need to comply with local regulations. It's the municipality's call. As the homeowner, you must provide permanent electrical access and a permanent telephone connection.

WHAT TO CONSIDER WHEN CHOOSING A SECURITY SYSTEM

- ❖ Do you own or rent?
- ❖ Is it a house or apartment?
- ❖ How many entrances and windows?
- ❖ Are there children or pets in the home?
- ❖ How often are you around?
- ❖ Who has access while you're away (housekeeper, etc.)?
- ❖ Is the neighborhood crowded or isolated?

SECURITY SYSTEMS DESIGN & INSTALLATION

ADT Security Services Inc.   3.5   3   4.5   3

10 Research Parkway, Wallingford, CT 06492
(203) 741 - 4000   www.adt.com

Security systems with central monitoring

ADT has been helping homeowners across New York and Connecticut secure and monitor their homes and businesses for over 125 years. A well-known national security firm, ADT installs and maintains systems encompassing burglary, fire, flood and carbon monoxide detection. Clients describe ADT as "serious security" and praise the efficiency and quality of the service. Sources tell us the systems are reasonably priced but caution that clients shouldn't forget the ongoing monthly fees.

"*If the baby sets off the alarm, there will be two fire trucks at your door, even if you call ADT.*" "*Even though they're a large national company, I still felt like I got personalized, attentive service.*"

All-Time Detection Inc.   5   4   5   5

28 Willett Avenue, Port Chester, NY 10573
(914) 937 - 2600   www.alltimedetection.com

High-end security systems with in-house monitoring

This local security design and installation firm is said to be "one of the last of the local guys that compete with the big national companies." With 200 employees and a reputation across New York and Connecticut for providing some of the best service around, All-Time Detection is a popular choice. Michael Backer is the principal of this firm, which was established in 1960 by his now-retired business partner. Most of the company's work comes by way of trade referrals from architects, but All-Time welcomes inquiries from the homeowners as well.

The firm has 24-hour service, its own monitoring facility and handles all forms of security issues from home CCTV surveillance and fire detection to electronic parking control systems for commercial establishments. All-Time boasts a service fleet of 40 trucks and scores of certified installers. And when it comes to on-site training, Backer has a staff (seriously) whose sole job is to make sure clients know how to use their system. Monitoring rates are competitive and service costs are on the high end.

American Security Systems Inc.   4   3.5   4.5   4

18 West 23rd Street, New York, NY 10010
(212) 633 - 8080   www.americansecuritysys.com

Security systems with central monitoring, video intercoms

Since 1979, American Security Systems has been protecting homes and businesses in and around New York City in a variety of ways. In addition to its specialty alarm systems such as burglary and fire, American also provides video intercoms, locks, card access systems, telephone entry systems and closed-circuit televisions.

Clients give the firm high marks for the quality systems it installs and praise American's staff as reliable, skilled with specialty systems and detail-oriented. Numerous clients were impressed that American has its own central monitoring station for its alarm systems, noting that it made a huge difference in service. Some clients, however, did note that the technicians can be a bit slow at times because they are often working on several jobs at once.

"The manager of my building researched security firms and recommended American to me as the most responsive. I've been extremely pleased with the results—both with the system they installed and the monitoring service." "They did an excellent job on a system that had both hard-wired and wireless parts." "Good, consistent and reliable." "They installed a security system with video so I can watch my kids play while I'm traveling."

Brink's Home Security   4   3.5   4   4

1132 Route 23, Catskill, NY 12414
(800) 334 - 9750   www.brinkshomesecurity.com
Broad-based home security systems and monitoring

Whether you want a standard burglar alarm or a more advanced 24-hour monitoring system with heat and carbon monoxide detectors, Brink's can provide it. All of the company's installers are certified by the National Burglar and Fire Alarm Association. One of the largest home security companies in the US, Brink's Home Security was founded in 1983 as an offshoot of the 140-year-old armored car delivery service. Today Brink's Home Security monitors home security systems for more than 700,000 customers in more than 98 cities across North America. But keep in mind, Brinks only provides coverage for some areas of Westchester County.

Although some say Brink's huge organization can befuddle clients, making them feel lost in the crowd, others say the 24-hour phone support and other customer services make dealing with the company a joy. Brink's offers a number of services for the average small household, but it is not well known for designing highly-customized state-of-the-art security systems. However, we are told the firm has very competitive pricing and boasts its own monitoring facilities.

Design Associates Inc.   5   5   5   5

60 Connolly Parkway, Hamden, CT 06514
(203) 407 - 8913   autogates@att.net
Custom high-end security gates

This isn't your typical security company. And although the company doesn't exactly design motion detecting home alarms, their highly customized (and expensive) hydroelectric gates bring peace of mind to well-off clients across New York, Connecticut and beyond. These gates are often made of hand-forged steel or mahogany and have custom lighting systems. Some can even withstand a direct hit from a truck traveling at 30 mph. Design Associates often collaborates with traditional security companies to integrate the gates into the overall security system. The firm's clientele is made up of corporate tycoons, athletes, rock stars and the Hollywood set.

Touting their one-year warranty on parts as well as its "mom-and-pop shop" feel, Design Associates has enjoyed a solid client base across southern Connecticut. This small company only has three employees, two of whom handle installation and service. Clients appreciate the personalized service and the neighborly approach, but these gates are not for everyone, as they start at $25,000.

Mastrojohn Security Systems Corp.   3.5   2.5   4.5   4.5

45 Alpha Street, Tuckahoe, NY 10707
(914) 779 - 7332   www.mastrojohnsecurity.com
Family-owned home security systems installation

This family-owned company has served Westchester County and suburban New York since 1968. A small company of four, they handle all kinds of security systems from closed-circuit television systems to fire alarms to card-access control and even locksmith services. The firm works with architects and builders, but most of its work comes directly from homeowners. The bulk of the company's work deals with mid-market systems.

John Mastrojohn, who is said to have a very loyal and reliable staff of certified installers, leads the company. All equipment is sold directly to the client and comes with yearly third-party monitoring services. Service calls are said to be "quick" and Mastrojohn himself is involved in every project. Each system comes with a one-year warranty on parts and labor, and hourly service rates are relatively low.

Meenan Security Systems
3.5 3 4 4

475 Commerce Street, Hawthorne, NY 10532
(888) 633 - 6265   www.meenanoil.com
Basic home security systems

Meenan Security Services is your safe bet for basic home protection and alarm systems. The company provides 24-hour service, CCTV surveillance systems and fire and security alarms. Meenan Security is an offshoot from the larger Meenan Oil company, and has a number of satellite offices, including Hawthorne, Long Island, New Jersey and Pennsylvania. The Hawthorne location, established in 1995, staffs a team of six with three installers.

Service calls are said to be quick—usually the same day—and we're told the staff makes sure to explain each system thoroughly to the client before leaving the job. Monitoring is done a by a third-party company and contracts run quarterly. All equipment is sold to the customer and backed up with a one-year parts and labor warranty. Rates are reported as reasonable for labor and monitoring fees.

New Canaan Alarm Co.
4.5 4.5 4 4.5

102 Main Street, New Canaan, CT 06840
(203) 966 - 8713
Custom residential alarm and security systems

Northeast Signal
4 4 4 4

PO Box 5153, Hamden, CT 06514
(203) 623 - 1257   nesignal@cttel.net
High-end residential and commercial security systems

George Bildstein has been securing the homes of clients from Rhode Island to Westchester for more than twenty years. It is this experience and his personalized service that has clients singing the praises of the company. They also point to the fact that Bildstein takes great pride in designing and installing systems that require "little if any maintenance" and are easy to use. The company takes on equal numbers of residential and high-end commercial projects.

We're told Northeast Signal deals mostly with high-end security systems that can include 24-hour service, CCTV systems, fire alarms and card-access control. The company has a small staff of three—two of whom handle installations. All work comes with a one-year parts and labor guarantee. Clients love the quick service calls—most happen within 24 hours and are billed at standard industry rates.

	Quality	Cost	Value	Recommend?
	✚	$	◆	★

Protection One Inc.   3.5   3   4   4
2066 Thomaston Avenue, Waterbury, CT 06704
(800) 438 - 4357   www.protectionone.com

Standard home burglar alarms and home monitoring systems

One of the largest monitored security companies in the country, Protection One serves more than 1.3 million people across North America. With more than 60 offices, numerous call centers and a staff of 2,300, it's easy to see why some sources say personalized service is not the company's strong suit. For those who are seeking solid security systems without all of the bells and whistles (literally), Protection One is a safe bet. The company has a branch office in Waterbury, Connecticut and potential clients are invited to stop in for a consultation about its modestly priced services.

Scarsdale Security Systems   4.5   3.5   5   5
132 Montgomery Avenue, Scardale, NY 10583
(914) 722 - 2222   www.scarsdalesecurity.com

Security systems

Since 1982, residential, commercial and industrial clients across Connecticut, New York and New Jersey have put their trust in Scarsdale Security Systems to keep them safe and secure. From monitored burglar and fire systems to closed-circuit TV and access control system installations, this firm has proven "exceptional," particularly in high-end residential work. Clients concur that Scarsdale stacks up to some of the best out there and reserve particular praise for the pleasant and accommodating technicians. Some customers will trust only Scarsdale for their larger projects.

"They are exceptional and do incredible work. I use them for all my large, high-end jobs." "They go out of their way to do extra things."

Scott Security Systems Inc.   3.5   4   3.5   3
236 West 30th Street, 10th Floor, New York, NY 10001
(212) 594 - 2121

Security systems with central monitoring

For those serious about security, Scott Security offers high-tech solutions, as well as some unique services. The firm specializes in sophisticated alarm systems that include CCTV and access control, which can be integrated into any home system by an on-hand computer specialist. Central monitoring and comprehensive service round out the menu. But what really makes the company unique, according to its clients, are its escorts for the movement of valuables and a stable of private investigators and polygraph experts. Started in 1984 and serving metropolitan and suburban New York, Long Island and New Jersey, this firm deals in commercial and strictly high-end residential security.

HIRING A SWIMMING POOL
SERVICE PROVIDER

There's nothing like a cool dip on a hot summer day. So why should building a swimming pool be stressful? Here's a primer on how to find a pool professional who won't leave you high and dry.

DIPPING YOUR TOE IN

Most swimming pools today are made of concrete and finished with a material called gunite. Those constructed of fiberglass present an alternative of lesser quality. The classic rectangular, aqua-blue swimming pool still exists, but the options today are as varied as your imagination. For example, the texture and color of the gunite finish can affect the hue of the water, and consequently the character of the pool. Grays create a deep blue quarry feel, while whites speckled with flakes of color create a sparkling effect, not unlike that of crushed sea shells in beach sand. A popular contemporary design is the "natural look." Free-formed and employing rock or faux rock, these pools blend into the landscaped surroundings. Another popular swimming pool is the "vanishing edge" pool which has an edge that appears to drop off into the surrounding area.

After choosing a style, another consideration should be how you intend to use the pool. If you're a swimmer, a pool long enough for legitimate laps is a must. However, if there are going to be a lot of young children using the pool, depth can become an issue. Do you like to float aimlessly into little nooks or pull half-gainers off the diving board? "Power Pools" with their slides and other waterpark amenities are an increasingly popular form of entertainment.

MAKING THE PLUNGE

Swimming pools are certainly not cheap, but if you are savvy about materials and design, your pool professional can help you get the most for your money. In-ground concrete and gunite pools range anywhere from $35,000 to over $1 million. Cost is determined by the complexity of the design and quality of the materials. Significant amounts of engineering often required for hillside or beachside construction, will increase costs considerably. Although fiberglass swimming pools, which range from $25,000 to $50,000, represent a less-expensive alternative, in-ground concrete pools wear better, and last longer, and are, quite simply, more attractive. Other costs to consider are the pool deck (which can consist of concrete pavers, poured concrete, tile, stone or even sod), housing or camouflage of the mechanical equipment and fencing with a self-closing gate (often a code requirement).

Pool contractors typically perform all the work themselves. This work includes site excavation, concrete work, irrigation plumbing, mechanical and electrical work, tile and stone work and putting in the gunite overlay. Because much of the most complicated work is encased in concrete and buried under a deck (we are talking water here), an incompetent installation can be a disaster—and expensive and dirty to fix. Landscaping firms, which often coordinate with pool professionals are a good source for recommendations. Your pool should complement its environment, so it's always important to have a landscape architect, architect, general contractor and pool professional who can talk to one another.

CERTIFICATIONS ASSOCIATIONS & SAFETY

It is essential that the company you choose to build your pool be a member of the National Spa and Pool Institute (NSPI). Members of this organization are kept well informed of not only the technical side of pool construction, but also the current state and national safety requirements for pool construction. Warranties should be long term. The NSPI has a comprehensive website (www.nspi.org) that is targeted to both consumers and retailers. Masters Pool Guild, which is comprised of 90 reputable swimming pool building companies from all over the world, also has a website (www.masterpoolsguild.com).

While swimming pools can be an incredible form of entertainment, they are also an enormous responsibility and potential safety hazard if used improperly. A dependable, respected swimming pool company can not only inform you of your aesthetic options, but also can talk to you about safety options, such as fences to surround your pool area and pool alarms.

WHAT ABOUT SAFETY?

✧   Aesthetics are no excuse for leaving your pool unprotected. There are many types of pool fences on the market that will detract very little from the overall appearance of your pool and backyard.

✧   Ask your pool builder about pool alarms. Alarms can alert you if someone or something unexpectedly enters the water.

✧   There is no substitute for adequate supervision. Be aware of who is near your pool at all times. If a child is in the water, always have a "spotter" near by.

	Quality	Cost	Value	Recommend?

SWIMMING POOL
CONSTRUCTION & MAINTENANCE

All American Custom Pools & Spas Inc.   3.5   3.5   4   4
225 Main Avenue, Norwalk, CT 06851
(203) 847 - 2704   www.allamericanpools.com
Swimming pool design and installation

Insiders say from start to finish All American does it all. Established by John Romano over 27 years ago, the firm guides clients through the conceptual phase with trained design consultants, performs most of the installation without sub-contracting and fields a service department to keep your pool looking and working great. There is an extended three-year warranty on major equipment, while the shell is covered for a lifetime.

Anne Homer Polk & Associates   3.5   4.5   3.5   4
PO Box 456, Bedford, NY 10506
(914) 234 - 3261   annepolk@aol.com
Residential landscape and swimming pool design

See Anne Homer Polk & Associates's full report under the heading Landscape Architects/Designers

Anthony & Sylvan Pools   3.5   3.5   4   4
528 Post Road, Darien, CT 06820
(203) 655 - 4040   www.anthonysylvan.com
Swimming pool design and construction

Clients who appreciate everything that larger, national pool companies have to offer go "where America swims." Anthony & Sylvan Pools boasts over fifty years in the business and has established more than forty company-owned sales and design centers in sixteen states, including Connecticut and New York. The company's growth can be attributed to years of referrals from pleased customers, who compliment the consistent quality service.

Armand Benedek & Glenn Ticehurst Ltd.   4.5   4   4.5   4
448H Old Post Road, Bedford, NY 10506
(914) 234 - 9666   www.abgtla.com
Landscape architecture and swimming pool design

See Armand Benedek & Glenn Ticehurst Ltd.'s full report under the heading Landscape Architects/Designers

Bedford Pool Scapes   📁   📁   📁   📁
PO Box 793, Bedford, NY 10506
(914) 234 - 3732   www.bedfordpoolscapes.com
Swimming pool design and construction

Edmund Hollander Landscape   5   5   4   4.5
Architect Design PC
153 Waverly Place, 3rd Floor, New York, NY 10014
(212) 473 - 0620   www.hollanderdesign.com
Landscape architecture, swimming pool design and environmental planning

See Edmund Hollander Landscape Architect Design PC's full report under the heading Landscape Architects/Designers

	Quality +	Cost $	Value ◆	Recommend? ★

Glen Gate Company

| | 4 | 4 | 4 | 4 |

644 Danbury Road, Box 724, Wilton, CT 06897
(203) 762 - 2000   www.glengatecompany.com

Swimming pool design, installation maintenance and landscape design

Contractors recommend this solid pool and landscape company for its excellent customer service and quality workmanship. Glen Gate "knows no bounds" when it comes to your backyard, performing landscape design and installation as well as masonry. The firm works primarily in Fairfield and Westchester counties but will venture to Long Island and all over New England.

In business for over 30 years, brothers Jeffrey and Jordan Scott operate the company. Among the 90 people on staff, there are two in-house landscape architects and eight landscape designers. Clients say this firm gets ahead of the game because they service everything they build.

"A lot of my clients have used Glen Gate for their pools and have always been pleased." "I recommend Glen Gate time after time."

Gro Pro Landscape Company

| | 3.5 | 4 | 4 | 4 |

151 Sound Beach Avenue, Old Greenwich, CT 06870
(203) 637 - 2004   www.groprogardens.com

Landscape design and installation, swimming pool design

See Gro Pro Landscape Company's full report under the heading Landscape Architects/Designers

Janice Parker Landscape Design

| | 4 | 3.5 | 5 | 5 |

52 Wakeman Hill Road, Sherman, CT 06784
(860) 350 - 4497   www.janiceparker.com

Landscape architecture and design, swimming pool design

See Janice Parker Landscape Design's full report under the heading Landscape Architects/Designers

Katie Brown

| | 4 | 3.5 | 5 | 4.5 |

399 Riversville Road, Greenwich, CT 06831
(203) 622 - 0250

Landscape design and swimming pool design

See Katie Brown's full report under the heading Landscape Architects/Designers

Meehan & Ramos Pools, LLC

| | 📁 | 📁 | 📁 | 📁 |

160 Carter Henry Drive, Fairfield, CT 06430
(203) 256 - 8900

Swimming pool design and construction

Perennial Gardens Inc.

| | 3.5 | 4 | 3.5 | 4 |

Route 22, Bedford, NY 10506
(914) 234 - 6311   www.perennialgardensny.com

Landscape design/build and pool construction

See Perennial Gardens Inc.'s full report under the heading Landscape Architects/Designers

Pools By Al

| | 4 | 3.5 | 4.5 | 4 |

484 West Mayflower Place, Milford, CT 06460
(203) 556 - 5913

Swimming pool design, construction and maintenance

With perfect scores in customer service, Pools By Al has made a real splash in the industry. The firm provides swimming pool design and installation, poolside masonry as well as weekly pool maintenance. Pools By Al completes an average of fifteen pools per year, budgeted anywhere from $40,000 to $100,000.

Owner Al Rodrigues has been designing and installing gunite pools for over eighteen years. A staff of eight supports Rodrigues, who oversees every project. Clients rave that they receive the utmost attention from the firm. Pools By Al guarantees the shell for ten years and the equipment comes with a standard manufacturer's warranty.

"Al is responsive and helpful." "I was very price sensitive and the company always took that into consideration."

Scott Swimming Pools Inc.   4   4.5   3.5   4
75 Washington Road, Woodbury, CT 06798
(203) 263 - 2108   www.scottpools.com
Swimming pool design and construction

Recognized among landscape design professionals as the creator of some of the most lavish pools in Fairfield and Westchester counties, Scott Pools has been at it for 50 years. Family owned and operated, the company constructs and maintains both residential and commercial pool projects in Pound Ridge, Rye, all over Connecticut and as far as the Virgin Islands. While sources say Scott Pools come at a pretty penny, the firm unearths a true treasure.

"I was impressed with Scott's presentation—it was really quite lovely."

Shoreline Pools Inc.   5   4.5   4.5   5
393 West Avenue, Stamford, CT 06902
(203) 967 - 1203   www.shorelinepools.com
Swimming pool design, construction and maintenance

Shoreline has been a leader and a well-regarded name in the pool trade since 1968. The company does everything from implementing simple, yet elegant pool designs to engineering more complicated projects complete with exotic water features, masonry and decks. For clients who want to give their old pool a new sparkle, the firm even performs pool restoration.

Principal Dave Linonetti's father, Lou, started the Shoreline Pool legacy. With over 175 employees, the firm serves Fairfield and Westchester counties, and has been beckoned from as far as Martha's Vineyard. A pool from Shoreline can cost anywhere from $75,000 to $135,000, an investment, clients say, as good as the experience.

"Whether we're entertaining guests or just relaxing with the family, Shoreline has added a wonderful new dimension to our lives." "Shoreline executed our pool designs exactly as envisioned and stand behind their work." "Shoreline constructs the finest pools using the best materials and most talented craftsmen. There is no better company to work with for efficiency and quality, especially on the most complex projects."

	Quality	Cost	Value	Recommend?
	✚	$	◆	★

Signature Pools — 4.5 4 4.5 5

#2 Reynolds Street, Norwalk, CT 06855
(203) 866 - 7665

Swimming pool design, construction and maintenance

Landscape architects and designers ascribe Signature Pools as "one of the best in the business." Not only does the company design and build superior pools, according to clients, but it also provides phenomenal customer service. The firm constructs around 50 pools a year, with budgets running from $40,000 up to $200,000. Weekly maintenance and service is available on all Signature installations.

Co-owners Bruno Iacono and Joesph and Christopher Autouri have devoted the past nine years to designing the highest-quality swimming pools. They supervise a staff of 35, including in-house masons. All pool shells are supported by lifetime warranties from Signature, while manufacturers cover equipment.

"Bruno is absolutely amazing and the actual construction of the pool is far better than others in the industry."

Wagner Swimming Pools — 4 3.5 4.5 4

750 Wordin Avenue, Bridgeport, CT 06605
(203) 335 - 3960   www.wagnerswimmingpools.com

Swimming pool design and construction

The finest contractors in Connecticut and Westchester roundly praise Wagner Swimming Pools for designing and creating solid, high-quality pools. Edward Wagner established the firm in 1919. Sources say that the long history of the company is a true testimonial of the craftsmanship of a Wagner Pool. As far as pool companies are concerned, sources say Wagner has established itself as one of the industry leaders in the area. Whether you want to design a new pool for your backyard or update your existing pool, this firm is described time and time again as "dependable and reasonably priced."

"Wagner is definitely on my list of recommendations." "I have found Wagner to be a more reasonable pool company, always meeting deadlines." "They know how to build a fine pool."

HIRING A TILE, MARBLE & STONE SERVICE PROVIDER

Tile, marble and stone can transform a room. Granite kitchen counters make beautiful surfaces on which to work. Marble brings a dramatic flair to the bathroom, and what could be more elegant than a travertine fireplace in the hearth of your home? Colorful, artistic tiles can brightly define the style of a kitchen—Spanish, French, Scandinavian. These materials come in a staggering range of types, qualities, shapes and colors. Tiles, for example, range in size from five-eighths of an inch square to one square-foot and up. Marble can come in tile form or in slabs that can be as small or as large as you need. Slabs—pieces of stone larger than 24 inches square—can be cut in various sizes and shapes to fit the area.

WHERE DO I START?

The kind of tile that you choose will depend on your specific needs. For example, if you are selecting tiles for a high-traffic area like an entryway or kitchen, you'll want durable tiles that will not show wear and tear. If you are tiling your kitchen, you might consider a durable stone such as granite or a ceramic tile that is easy to clean and maintain. Smaller tiles tend to be used for decorative purposes because they are more laborious to install and harder to clean, while the larger tiles are used for more practical purposes such as covering a floor. Remember, each kind of tile has its advantages and drawbacks. The installer that you choose should be able to help you explore what kind of tile will work best for you.

Tiles, either man-made or natural, can be as plain as classic bathroom-white ceramic or as intricate as hand-painted/embossed pieces from Portugal. Man-made tiles are generally porcelain or ceramic and are durable and resistant to stains. Some manufacturers rate ceramic tile on a scale from 1 to 4+, from least to most durable. Porcelain is considered more durable than ceramic because porcelain is not glazed. Note that porcelain is actually a form of ceramic, but is fired at such high temperatures that it is denser than the material labeled ceramic. Porcelain is vitreous, or glass-like—water cannot penetrate it—and this is one reason why porcelain is stronger than ceramic. Because of the firing process that ceramic tile undergoes, the color as well as the shape of the tile is permanent.

NATURAL TILE AND STONE

Most natural tiles—such as marble, granite, limestone and slate—will last forever. That doesn't mean it will look like new forever. Marble is one of the most classic, desired and expensive stones, and because it scratches and stains easily it must be sealed after installation. Even after the marble is sealed, it will still be more vulnerable to scratching than other stone, such as granite, so be prepared to care for and maintain a marble installation. There are many types of seals to choose from: a matte seal preserves the stone's natural color or texture, a glossy seal makes the stone appear shiny and smooth and gives it a more formal appearance, and a color enhancement sealer brings out the stone's colors and beauty.

Like marble, granite is a natural stone that comes in both tiles and slabs. Granite is one of the strongest stones, but it also needs to be sealed after professional installation. Granite is more impervious to stains than marble, and also less expensive.

In general, marble and granite slabs are more expensive than tile because the slabs are customized and take more of the installer's time. Slabs are commonly used for areas such as countertops and around fireplaces. Installing slabs requires different skills than installing tile; therefore, you should ask a potential installer if he normally installs tile or slab.

ON COST

With the exception of hand-painted tiles, tile is generally priced per square foot. This simplifies price comparisons of tiles that differ greatly in size or shape: once you know how many square feet you need for your area, it's easy to calculate the difference in total cost between tile choices. Basic ceramic and porcelain tiles range from $2 to $20 per square foot. Hand-painted tiles can cost anywhere from $8 to $150 each.

On the whole, stone tiles like marble and granite are more expensive than their ceramic counterparts. The price of marble and granite depends on color and type. Natural stone is quarried all over the world, and a particularly desirable origin can make it more expensive. Some stone is easier to find and is not considered as rare as other types of stone. Like ceramic tiles, natural stone tiles are priced per square foot. Marble and granite slab, however, is priced per project because there are so many variables in slab work. The price depends on the edges, customization and amount of work that goes into the actual installation. Slabs also have to be cut to fit the area precisely. The pricing of slab work depends on how difficult the stone was to get and how large the slab is. The larger the slab, the more expensive it is going to be to transport.

Tile and stone installers generally charge per project. The more custom work they have to do, such as edges and corners, the more expensive the project. Also, note that more artistic tile installation, such as creating mosaics, is much more expensive. Hiring a larger company can be cheaper because much work can be done in house, and the company can buy in bulk to save on materials. Also, installers will not have to be subcontracted and the materials will often be in stock. If you order from a smaller company and they do not keep a particular, expensive tile in stock, the price could be higher than from a larger company. With any installer, tile or marble that has to be ordered can significantly delay your project.

WHO INSTALLS THE TILE, MARBLE AND STONE?

Some of the service providers in this guide use their own installers and some subcontract the work out. If you choose a company that uses installers that are not in house, make sure that the company has used them before and ask for references. Some companies also keep a list of installers that they use on a regular basis.

Qualifications

No professional certification is required to install tile, marble and stone, but there are other ways of screening potential installers. For example, they should have a business license and, ideally, a general contractor's license. An excellent way to evaluate a potential installer is to ask for references, speak to them, and look at photographs of previous installations. Membership in professional organizations may also confer credibility to this service provider. These associations can offer general information as well as answer some of your simple questions about tile and marble installation.

The main professional associations to contact for information are:

The Marble Institute of America (440) 250-9222 www.marble-institute.com
Ceramic Tiles Distributors Association (800) 938-2832 www.ctdahome.org
The Tile Council of America (864) 646-8453 www.tileusa.com
The Ceramic Tile Institute of America (805) 371-TILE www.ctioa.com

Whether you decide to install simple ceramic tile in your shower or rare marble in your living room, the entire process will go more smoothly with a basic understanding of these special materials as provided above.

Decorative Ideas

- ✧ For tile in the kitchen or high-traffic areas, consider a darker grout for easier up-keep and a more formal appearance.
- ✧ Install tile mosaics around kitchen windows and, add a tile inlay to your floors and walls or scatter tiles with a thematic print (herbs for a kitchen or shells for the shower).
- ✧ Use a stone or tile molding to crown your master bathroom or mix marble countertops with a ceramic tile backsplash.
- ✧ For the children's bathroom, use hand-painted tiles in favorite colors to make washing more fun or give the playroom some pizzazz with a bright tile chair-rail or "homemade" mosaic.
- ✧ Too traditional? Exotic stones such as quartzite, slates and alabaster can offer a unique alternative to other natural surfaces and are just as functional!
- ✧ Don't overlook the nouveau! Some of the latest metallic and glass tiles are made to refract light, giving a glimmer to the dullest spaces.

	Quality	Cost	Value	Recommend?
	+	$	◆	★

TILE, MARBLE & STONE

A&G Marble Inc.   3.5   3   4.5   4.5
132-19 34th Avenue, Flushing, NY 11354
(718) 353 - 9415

Marble and granite installation and fabrication

The efficient and affordable old-world artisans at A&G Marble have been fabricating and distributing natural stone throughout the United States since 1968. Family owned and operated, we hear A&G provides individualized customer service to both residential and commercial clients. The firm takes on projects ranging from exterior tiles to vanity and kitchen countertops, and offers clients a broad selection of stone imported from around the world.

"I have worked with A&G Marble for fifteen years and find them to be the finest marble workers. They are pleasant to work with and have always handled the jobs with responsibility and professionalism." "Work is always completed without a problem." "I am always confident in recommending them to friends and family."

Amarko Marble & Granite   3.5   3   4   4
60-14 60th Place, Maspeth, NY 11378
(718) 821 - 0323 amarkomarble@aol.com

Marble flooring installation and maintenance

See Amarko Marble & Granite's full report under the heading Flooring

Ann Sacks   5   5   4   5
23 East Putnam Avenue, Greenwich, CT 06830
(203) 622 - 8884 www.annsacks.com

Handcrafted tiles and luxury bathroom fixtures

Clients and industry insiders alike consider Ann Sacks a leader in "creative and adventurous" tile and stone. Ann Sacks stores can be found in prime locations across the continental United States—including Manhattan, Chicago, Los Angeles, San Francisco, Denver, Dallas, Portland and Seattle—with plans for further expansion. Specializing in handcrafted tile, limestone slab, antiquated stone and terra-cotta custom mosaics, Ann Sacks brings an ever-changing palette of products to its showroom floors. In fact, we hear that Sacks' unique offering now extends to luxury plumbing products, bathroom fixtures and exclusive tile collections by Barbara Barry and Rebecca Gore.

"Every time I set foot in the showroom I'm like a kid in a candy store because there is just so much to marvel at." "My clients are always pleased with their tile selection."

C.A. Sanzaro Inc./TriBeCa Stoneworks   4.5   4.5   4   5
718 South Fulton Avenue, Mount Vernon, NY 10550
(914) 699 - 2030

Marble and stone installation

Over the course of three decades an impressive roster of retail and trade clients has recruited this skilled tile and stoneworker for projects as close to home as Connecticut and Rhode Island and as far as Florida and Bermuda. Owner Caesar Sanzaro handles the installation process while his son Chris runs the showroom, Tribeca Stoneworks, the latest addition to the company. Among this amply staffed firm's 100 craftsmen are carvers who work on commission. References tell us customer service and quality control is top-notch.

Residential projects run anywhere from $10,000 to $5 million. Estimates are based on square footage or time plus materials. In both expense and finished product, clients find Sanzaro a cut above the rest.

"Someone finally put together a winning formula, great initial response to clients, physical templates, client review and approval, and the best installation teams we've ever experienced." "It is always a pleasure dealing with Caesar." "Their scheduling is always on time, and their workmanship is amazing." "Excellent attention to detail."

Ceramica Arnon Tile Setting 4.5 3 4.5 4.5
134 West 20th Street, New York, NY 10011
(212) 807 - 0876 www.ceramicaarnonus.com
Specialty tiles, custom tile murals, fabrication and installation

A third-generation artisan, Arnon Zadok of Ceramica Arnon fabricates and installs handcrafted tile murals for private clients and design pros in Connecticut, Westchester and New York City. Ceramica Arnon's showroom features an array of products on display from ceramic and glass tiles to metallic tile mosaics. The company also carries newer lines, including a series of French-Gothic and rustic Moroccan tiles.

Ceramica's contract division installs both custom creations and stock products. We hear the company prides itself on its old-world installations and clients appreciate the reliable service, guaranteed work and appropriate pricing.

"Arnon takes great pride in his work." "The first project he did for us was to replace our kitchen floor followed a year later with redoing our outdoor deck. In both instances, he helped us find the perfect tile and as an artisan, his installation is unsurpassed."

Certified Marble & Ceramic 3.5 2 4.5 4
24 Demerest Avenue, West Haverstraw, NY 10993
(845) 429 - 1868 certifiedtile@aol.com
Tile and marble installation

Fifteen years of client referrals certify Joe Del Biondo's skill. He provides installation, maintenance and repair services to homeowners and to the trade. Be it setting a simple backsplash or the highly detailed installation of century-old tile, customers trust Del Biondo to deliver. Primarily working in Westchester and Fairfield, we hear he's "willing to travel anywhere for a job" when given the opportunity and the proper accommodations.

"Joe is pleasant to work with and did not cause any extra headaches." "I always recommend him and I'll continue to do so." "Joe is honest and explains all of my options to me, taking into consideration certain aspects of my lifestyle." "I'm comfortable working with him because he's so down-to-earth."

Classic Tile Installation Inc. 3.5 3.5 4 4
4 Sodom Lane South, Brewster, NY 10509
(845) 279 - 7027 classictile@rcn.com
Ceramic tile and stone installation

Those in the know swear by principal Martin McCaffrey, who they dub "nothing short of dependable and superb." In the trade since 1974, he established Classic Tile over fifteen years ago. Today, McCaffrey oversees a staff of fourteen, accommodating both retail and trade clients in Fairfield and Westchester counties. The firm installs ceramic tile along with slate, marble and limestone.

Installations begin at $2,000 and all work is guaranteed for one year. Clients find Classic Tile a classic tale of reasonable prices and reliable customer service and are quick to refer the firm to friends and family.

	Quality ✚	Cost $	Value ◆	Recommend? ★

Classical Country Floors   3   3   4   4
7 Windsor Brook Lane, Tappan, NY 10983
(845) 359 - 7413

Installation and repair of clay terra-cotta floors

See Classical Country Floors's full report under the heading Flooring

Connecticut Stone Supplies Inc.   4   4   4   4
138 Woodmont Road, Milford, CT 06460
(203) 882 - 1000   www.connecticutstone.com

Tile, marble and stone sales, fabrication and installation

What began in 1953 as a small mom-and-pop-shop by Leo Dellacroce has since grown into one of the largest stone sales and fabrication companies in the Fairfield/Westchester area. The firm fields over 85 employees who spearhead sales and fabrication. The 10,000-square-foot showroom offers a selection of natural stones and tiles from around the world.

Interior designers and architects tell us the firm's phenomenal product selection and helpful staff pit Connecticut Stone as a perennial top pick. In addition to its showroom, Connecticut Stone boasts a contractor's yard in Stamford to accommodate the trades.

"I keep going back to Connecticut Stone for their amazing selection and their friendly, knowledgeable staff." "Although the company is quite large, I have always had excellent customer service."

Country Floors, Inc.   4   4   4   4
12 East Putnam Avenue, Greenwich, CT 06830
(203) 862 - 9900   www.countryfloors.com

Handmade and imported tile sales and installation

A notably great place for rare tiles, some swear it's "the source for any flooring need." The company carries a wide variety of handmade and imported tiles, from rustic to sleek, as well as those it manufactures. We hear County Floors' Mediterranean and French floral tiles are client favorites. The showroom staff is said to be reliable and efficient, and the overall experience of working with the company is a pleasurable one. While in-house Country Floors crews do not install its product, we're told its outsourced installers are dedicated and exacting.

"Great source for hard-to-find tiles." "The installers were excellent and they were right on the ball with everything from start to finish." "Surprisingly, there were no time issues or delays."

D.M.S. Studios   4   3.5   4.5   4
5-50 51st Avenue, Long Island City, NY 11101
(718) 937 - 5648   www.dms-studios.com

Traditional marble and stone fabrication, carving and sculpting

Known best for its custom fireplaces, D.M.S. has been creating and carving custom stonework for more than twenty years. Owner Daniel Sinclair has earned a reputation by his clients as the "beautifier of stone." We are told Sinclair creates

unique fireplaces and mantels by combining traditional methods of handcrafts-manship with genuine marble and limestone from its quarries in Europe and America. We hear that the firm specializes in all areas of stone carving, fabricat-ing and sculpting, and insiders say D.M.S. is taking on more complicated and elaborate jobs such as artistic and architectural detailing. Because fireplaces and mantels are handmade, it may be longer for a project to be completed, but accord-ing to clients, "that's the price for a true work of art."

"Great attention to detail and extremely talented." "He copied a fireplace per-fectly from a magazine for our country home in Greenwich—a real sculptor." "Daniel is an old-world technician—all he uses is a hammer and chisel."

Dennis Cofrancesco   4   4   4   5
100 Brooklawn Drive, Milford, CT 06460
(203) 494 - 0068   marmac9@aol.com
Ceramic tile and stone installation

The best contractors in Fairfield and Westchester counties recommend Dennis Cofrancesco and his small staff of five without hesitation. In addition to working with contractors, designers and architects, we hear that the firm is exceptional at taking on projects for retail clients as well. Cofrancesco installs anything from the simplest ceramic tiles to the more ornate mosaics and marble. In the installation arena for over 34 years, clients rave that Cofrancesco, "knows his stuff."

Depending on the size and scope of the project, installations range anywhere from $30,000 to $250,000, a price that insiders say is well worth it. The firm guarantees its installations for one year, and we hear that Cofrancesco has also been known to extend its guarantee should any problems arise. In addition to the company's high marks for customer service, insiders say that you will never have a problem reaching Cofrancesco and that calls are always promptly returned.

"Cofrancesco is capable of extremely detailed, flawless work." "In particular, our kitchen is extremely impressive." "Very good work and solid pricing."

Dionysus Inc.   3   3   4   4
1189 Lexington Avenue, New York, NY 10028
(212) 861 - 5616   dionysusmarble@aol.com
Marble and tile sales, installation, maintenance, repair, plumbing and electrical work

"Rome might have been built in a day if Dionysus had opened its doors before 1989," sources say. Working in ceramic, marble, limestone and mosaic, the firm can handle everything from design to installation. It will even perform the plumb-ing and electrical work. Additional services include creating cast-iron bases for consoles and tables, restoration of marble and ceramic vases and fabrication of custom fireplaces. Clients tell us the firm's service-oriented staff is exemplified by the "infinite patience" shown by principals Mike Giordas and wife Joanna.

Fairfield County Tile   4.5   4   4.5   5
563 Elm Street, Monroe, CT 06468
(203) 268 - 9473   ffldcountytile@aol.com
Tile and natural stone installation

Owner of Fairfield County Tile, Armando Gallucci, receives glowing reports from clients who say that they refuse to use anyone else when it comes to tile and stone installation. In addition to general tile and stone installation, this company also installs mosaics. Gallucci established his company over twenty years ago after inheriting a talent in the trade from his father and five uncles. He has a total of four employees who are divided into two teams, consisting of one installer and one assistant. However, Gallucci makes sure to personally oversee every project. The firm charges by the square foot and although its work is guaranteed for a year, insiders say that Gallucci is always more than happy to return to a project should any problems arise.

"Armando came back to my house with a smile on his face and regrouted all the tile in the bathroom." "He is as honest as they come, a real class act." "Fairfield County Tile works with speed and still manages to do an amazing job." "Armando is a true old-world artisan."

Felix Lorenzoni Studio Inc.   4   3.5   4.5   4
25 Bowman Drive, Greenwich, CT 06831
(203) 531 - 6050   lorenzonimarble@aol.com
Tile, marble and stone sales and installation

This third-generation marble company sells and installs marble, natural stone, ceramic and porcelain tiles. No project is too small or too large for Lorenzoni, ranging anywhere from $3,000 to $500,000. The firm's work has been in demand as far off as Nantucket and Atlanta. The company showroom displays over 375 samples of marble and granite and up to 50 samples of ceramic and porcelain.

Brothers Ron and Raymond Lorenzoni continue the 50-year family tradition of providing unbelievable customer service and quality to their clients. We're told they will even take the customer directly to the stone yard in order to hand pick slabs. Pricing is based either on time or square footage.

Fordham Marble 💼   4.5   3.5   5   4.5
421 Fairfield Avenue, Stamford, CT 06902
(203) 348 - 5088   www.fordhammarble.com
Marble sales and installation, kitchen countertops and flooring

Since 1905, Fordham has forged a reputation on outstanding work and upstanding customer service. The firm closely guides architects, designers and homeowners through the material selection process and installs its product. While it guarantees its work for one-year, the firm does not do maintenance or repair on that which it does not install. Based out of its original Bronx-based show-room and a second location in Stamford, CT, the firm cares for clients from Manhattan to Fairfield County and everywhere in between.

"Very accommodating when we need to change gears, which is unusual in this business!" "Fordham Marble is a unique resource for me and my clients. They are extremely helpful, guiding the client through the maze of materials and in the construction phase. The work is installed accurately and on time." "They are absolutely top-notch." "They have one of the best showrooms in the Fairfield County area, not to mention a professional team that understands quality and good design."

Greenwich Tile & Marble Co.   🗁   🗁   🗁   🗁
388 West Putnam Avenue, Greenwich, CT 06830
(203) 869 - 1709
Tile and natural stone sales and installation

HartzStone, LLC   4   3   4.5   5
PO Box 631, Bedford, NY 10506
(866) 710 - 6688   HartzStone@earthlink.net
Stone maintenance, cleaning and restoration

Sources maintain this stone and tile restorer is one of the "best in the business." HartzStone can revive the beauty of any natural stone, working its wonders with such surfaces as limestone, slate, marble and even Mexican saltillo tiles. Services include removing scratches and stains on kitchen countertops to stone fireplace restoration. Clients particularly appreciate owner Ed Hartz's patient tutorial on the technical aspects of the process.

HartzStone charges $80 to $125 for an estimate and prices restoration work on a per day basis. A half day comes in between $500 to $800, a full day $800 to $1,700. The company satisfies the needs of both homeowners and the trade, primarily in Westchester and Fairfield counties—however, its Manhattan customer-base continues to increase.

"Ed is personable, intelligent and a pleasure to work with. Best of all he really knows his tile." "I would trust him with any tile work in the future and have already recommended him to my friends." "Ed was willing to work with our badly stained limestone to restore it and bring it back to an acceptable, improved level. He was happy to be of service."

Klaff's   4.5   4.5   4   4
28 Washington Street, South Norwalk, CT 06854
(203) 866 - 1603   www.klaffs.com
Kitchen and bath design and tile and stone sales

See Klaff's's full report under the heading Kitchen & Bath Designers

Lucchese Marble   4.5   4   5   5
100 Columbus Avenue, Tuckahoe, NY 10707
(914) 779 - 9446   lucca.marble@verizon.net
Natural stone fabrication and installation

Top-tier contractors and architects enlist Larry Lucchese for his talent in tackling the most challenging of projects. Lucchese and a helper fabricate and install granite, marble, limestone and other natural stones on a very select number of projects each year. They occasionally do restoration work. Lucchese took over the reins of the shop from his father in 1965 and has ridden it to high praise. Working with professionals and homeowners, Lucchese is known to accompany his clients to the stone yard to hunt for the best materials for the job. We hear they love his "old-world" charm.

Consultations are free of charge, with installations running anywhere from $60 to $100 per square foot. Lucchese guarantees his work for one year.

"Larry is the best around, hands down." "He insists on selecting the slabs with the architect and client."

Marble America   4   4   4   4
517 Fifth Avenue, New Rochelle, NY 10801
(914) 632 - 3110   www.marbleamerica.net
Custom stone fabrication and installation

With twenty years in business, Marble America fabricates and installs vanities, countertops and fireplace facades throughout the Westchester and Fairfield region. A Mount Kisco showroom (located at 309 North Bedford Road) displays custom mosaics, tumbled stone and a wide selection of tiles and styles. Al Hanna operates Marble America with his daughter Nicole, their efforts oft-praised by interior designers for fine craftsmanship at a fair price. Priced per square foot, totals run from a few hundred bucks to $350,000. No matter the scope, insiders insist this company will do an "incredible job."

"I'm always amazed at the fabulous service." "Unbelievable, beautiful execution."

MFA
920 Knollwood Road, White Plains, NY 10603
(914) 592 - 3844
High-end stonework and masonry

N. Pietrangelo Inc.   4.5   4   4.5   4
55 Roberts Lane, Yonkers, NY 10701
(914) 969 - 1234
Tile, marble and stone installation

Paul Pietrangelo's family has thrived in the tile, marble and stone business since 1915. His grandfather founded the firm in 1915 and was incorporated by Paul's father in 1954. Pietrangelo's modest five-man crew takes on big-ticket installations in Westchester and Fairfield counties, coming in around $300,000. Pietrangelo provides free consultations and guarantees labor for one year.

"Paul and his team are excellent and are always accommodating."

	Quality	Cost	Value	Recommend?
	✚	$	◆	★

Natural Stone Refinishing Corp./ Dimensional Stone & Tile Design

| 4.5 | 3 | 5 | 4.5 |

192 Drake Avenue, New Rochelle, NY 10805
(914) 654 - 1407

Natural stone installation and restoration

Insiders tell us, be it the installation of antique, carved fireplaces or restoration of historical sites such as churches and synagogues, this is one of the premier stone specialists in Westchester and Fairfield counties. Brian Cordone established the company in 1977 and has since been joined by partner Mike Merole. We're told Cardone personally looks at every job and that during a project there is minimal disruption to the home. The firm's stellar reputation has taken it to Boston and Bermuda for projects.

Clients commend Cardone for his in-depth proposals. The firm charges by the job, with a restoration typically falling anywhere between $1,500 and $4,500. Installations may go up to $300,000, yet no job is too small for this dedicated duo.

Paris Ceramics

| 4 | 4 | 4 | 4 |

37 East Elm Street, Greenwich, CT 06830
(203) 862 - 9538   www.parisceramics.com

Antique stone, mosaics and decorative tile sales

We hear that Paris Ceramics is the place to go if you are a client in search of the rare and unusual. Since 1982, this firm has established a reputation for supplying high quality limestone, antique stone and hand-cut mosaics from around the world. Sources say that the sales people at the Greenwich showroom work closely with customers, staying involved from the design through the completion of a project. In addition to its Greenwich shop, Paris Ceramics also has design studios in London, New York, Chicago, Los Angeles, Palm Beach, San Francisco, Boston and Atlanta.

"Paris Ceramics is an amazing place for more specialized tile and stone products."

Springline Inc./Michael R. Golden

| 5 | 3.5 | 5 | 5 |

205 West 89th Street, New York, NY 10024
(917) 446 - 0278   springline@mac.com

Tile mosaics, hand-carved stone, terrazzo and scagliola treatments

Michael R. Golden is revered by clients who claim he will fly out to install tile anywhere in the country. Those who have worked with him rave about his superior service and high-quality work, calling both "amazing." Golden's company provides installation of tile and tile mosaics, decorative and hand-carved stone, and even incorporates treatments such as scagliola and terrazzo into his work. Golden's work ranges from bathroom tile shopping with clients to planning and producing elaborate reproductions. After nine years in the business, we hear that he has paved his way into some impressive residences, working with everyone from well-known athletes to top interior designers.

Terra Tile & Marble

| 3.5 | 3 | 4.5 | 4 |

525 North State Road, Briarcliff Manor, NY 10510
(914) 923 - 4295   www.terratileandmarble.com

Tile marble and stone fabrication

In business for well over twenty years, Terra Tile & Marble is a trusted resource for marble and stone fabrication. Owned and operated by the Gasch family, Terra has showrooms in Briarcliff Manor and Fishkill, NY. Clients say an array of granite, ceramic tile and hand-painted tile is on display. With the exception of countertops, the firm does not usually install its product.

"Terra was a great resource when I needed some initial ideas about what kind of materials I wanted to use in my home."

	Quality +	Cost $	Value ◆	Recommend? ★

Valley Marble & Slate Corp. 4.5 4 4.5 5
15 Valmar Drive, New Milford, CT 06776
(860) 354 - 3955 valmar9@aol.com

Custom stone fabrication

Since the firm's inception over 35 years ago sources say that "time and again, projects large and small have been completed at the highest possible level." We hear nothing leaves the shop floor until it is flawless, whether it is a fabrication of marble, limestone, soapstone or slate. While Valley Marble works on projects all over the United States and abroad, the firm concentrates its efforts in Fairfield and Westchester counties and occasionally in New York City. The firm works with both retail and trade clients, assuming hundreds of projects a year.

Valley Marble owners Mark and Michael Wiston supervise a staff of seven. We're told the Wistons guarantee the highest quality materials and craftsmanship and that "their word is as good as their work."

"Blow-your-mind marble." "The teamwork of Michael and Mark Wiston in solving problems and providing guidance for their customers is the key to their success and the consistency and quality of their product." "They are able to take rough quarried marble and stone blocks and slice them into any shape or form." "The Wistons understand their product and do excellent work of the highest quality."

Vladimir Obrevko Stoneworks Inc. 4.5 2 5 5
79 Putnam Park Road, Bethel, CT 06801
(203) 798 - 7713

Custom stone fabrication and installation, fireplace and sculpture restoration

Amiable is not a word heard everyday to describe craftsmen, but it is one used time and again by clients describing Vladimir Obrevko of Stoneworks. For several years before coming to the US, Obrevko worked restoring cathedrals in Old St. Petersburg, Russia, a trade he learned from his father. Now Obrevko's architectural stonework can be seen in elaborate homes and commercial locations throughout New York City, Long Island and Westchester and Fairfield counties. Obrevko's latest specialty is hand carving sink and vanity tops out of marble and limestone. Clients laud his pleasant demeanor and dedicated work ethic, calling him "personable and true to his craft."

Stoneworks offers fabrication and installation services in marble, granite, limestone and slate. The company also does specialty work such as fireplace and sculpture restoration.

"Vladimir is extremely professional and courteous. His stonework and attention to detail are exceptional." "He carved the most beautiful mantel that is the focus of my living room." "He conceived, designed and carved a limestone sink for our wine cellar based on a 17th-century Italian Bacchus image. I can't recommend him enough."

Walker Zanger 4 4 4 4
31 Warren Place, Mount Vernon, NY 10550
(914) 667 - 1600 www.walkerzanger.com

Ceramic and natural stone tiles and project management

For 50 years, Walker Zanger has enjoyed a solid reputation coast-to-coast for exceptional ceramic and natural stone tiles. On the firm's impressive client roster, high-end residences join such prestigious commercial projects as the Bellagio Hotel & Casino in Las Vegas and the Kimbell Art Museum in Fort Worth, Texas. References report Walker Zanger's attractive showrooms and well-versed sales staff are nicely complemented by project managers who oversee the installation process.

"Despite the mammoth size of the company, I always feel like I am their only client."

Waterworks 4.5 4.5 4.5 5
23 West Putnam Avenue, Greenwich, CT 06830
(203) 869 - 7766 www.waterworks.com

High-end bathroom design, sales and installation referral

See Waterworks's full report under the heading Kitchen & Bath Designers

HIRING AN UPHOLSTERY & WINDOW TREATMENT SERVICE PROVIDER

Did you find a gorgeous set of Chippendale chairs at a local antique store that need reupholstering? Would you like to transform your aging—yet amazingly comfortable—armchair into a spectacular piece that matches your sofa and decor? Or are you ready to buy a complete set of custom-upholstered furniture for your living room? Whether you are thinking about the design and construction of your piece or which fabric to choose, upholstery and window treatment experts are the professionals to call.

Many high-end upholsterers and drapers who do specialized work deal exclusively with the trade (decorators and architects), and not the public at large, which is noted in our reviews. Also, many of these service providers focus on custom work—creating a piece from scratch rather than from a line of showroom choices. Usually the decorators provide sketches or pictures to point the artisans in the right direction, and fabrics are provided by the customer.

WHAT TYPE OF UPHOLSTERY SERVICE DO I NEED?

Your three basic choices are custom upholstery fabrication, reupholstery and custom slipcovers. You may not need a completely new piece of furniture. Depending on the condition of your frame and webbing, you may choose to reupholster or have custom-made slipcovers as a less-expensive alternative. A favorite decorator trick is to use a Crate & Barrel frame and upgrade the fillings to create a well-priced custom piece.

To help narrow down the service you need, determine how the furniture will be used. Is it a piece that is frequently used by the family and guests (and pets), or a more stylized piece that is used in a less frequently? If it will receive heavy use, you'll choose springs and cushioning that will stand up to this treatment as well as a fabric that is durable and easy to clean.

KNOW YOUR UPHOLSTERY CONSTRUCTION

FRAMES: The frame is the skeleton of your piece, determining the sturdiness as well as overall appearance of the object. The best frames are made of kiln-dried hardwood, preferably premium alder maple. Oak and ash are less expensive, but decent options. Pine will fall apart very quickly. Kiln drying removes moisture and sap from the wood, which could cause the frame to warp or bend. When assembling the frame, the ideal method involves using dowels and cornerblocks. This is more costly than using nails and glue but will greatly increase the quality and add years to the life of your piece. Tacks are the preferred method for attaching fabric to the frame, although staple guns are sometimes used. Staple guns should never be used in constructing a quality frame, however.

SPRINGS: The main function of springs is to support the furniture's cushioning. The two basic spring systems for upholstered furniture are round coil springs (like a slinky) and flat, continuous s-shaped, "no-sag" coils. Most fine, traditional pieces use round steel spring coils, in which these coils are tied by hand in eight places around the diameter of the spring ("8-way, hand-tied").

S-shaped continuous or zigzag coils are sometimes used in contemporary pieces for a flatter look, but do not provide the same support as spring coils. Also, S-shaped springs can become lumpy or uneven over time and put much more pressure on the frame since they are attached directly to it. Therefore, if you are using s-coils, the frame must be built much sturdier so it won't break apart over time.

In very high-quality cushion construction, the springs are then individually wrapped, encased in foam, and covered in a down and feather mixture (see below for details). This is all encased in a muslin bag in order to contain the fluff before being covered with fabric. This combination provides firmness and helps the cushion to hold its shape. The ultimate upholstery houses also put down in the arms and backs of their pieces, but this generally adds about 30 percent to the price.

CUSHIONS: These come in two types—attached and loose. In attached construction, fiber or down and feather are wrapped around a foam core and placed over the spring system, which is then covered with fabric. Loose cushions resemble big pillows that are easily fluffed, moved or turned over to prevent signs of wear. Both types of cushions can be stuffed with a wide variety of fillings, from luxurious pure goose down and down blends to synthetic foam.

Down is the ultimate cushion filling and comes at a premium price. The typical down-feather blend consists of 50 percent goose down and 50 percent duck feathers, and is used for very high-end custom upholstery. The ultimate puff look is 100 percent goose down, which offers almost no support and must be fluffed by the housekeeper once a day to look right and remain comfortable. Because of the high level of maintenance and much higher cost required for goose down, many consumers prefer to go with a combination of 50/50 down and feather over a foam core. Upon request, however, most of the houses reviewed below can deliver whatever the customer prefers. A lesser-quality cushion is 25 percent goose down and 75 percent duck feathers, which is harder and should cost less. All Dacron foam is the least costly alternative, and is not generally found in high-quality work.

FABRICS: The possibilities are endless when choosing upholstery fabric. With so many options, you can narrow your search by exploring a few basic issues. Prices vary widely, from $10 to well over $250 per yard. The most important issue is how the piece will be used. Do you need a super durable fabric that can withstand daily use? Or is it a not-to-be-touched showpiece or curtains that can use in a delicate silk? Some fabrics are simply stronger than others. Ease of cleaning should also be considered. Pieces in the family room or children's bedroom may attract more dirt. Darker, patterned or more durable fabric that withstands frequent cleaning would be appropriate for this situation. Upholsterers handle the issue of fabric in a variety of ways. Some have catalogs and swatches from which you can choose—but most ask you to bring in your own fabric, better known as COM (customer's own material).

Keep in mind that the ease or difficulty of working with a particular fabric will affect the price of the job. Thicker fabrics, velvets and horsehairs can be more difficult to edge properly. Also, you will need more yards of fabric with a large repeat or pattern, so the upholsterer can match the design perfectly at the seams—a key factor in separating fine quality from hoi polloi work.

WHAT TO LOOK FOR IN QUALITY WORK

When viewing the work of an upholstery professional in the workroom or at someone's home, keep the following points in mind:

❖ Check all the seams for pattern matching and a perfectly centered and balanced design on any cushions or surfaces. This can be particularly important with more intricate patterns.

❖ Are the sofa skirts lined? Is the cushion of the slipper chair invisibly secured with clips, as it should be? Is the welt or trim tightly stitched?

❖ Ask what percentage of the seams are hand sewn. In the finest workrooms, all the curtain trims, leading edges and hems are completely hand done. Some even do the curtain basting and sofa seams entirely by hand.

✧ Check to see if any of the seams pucker, such as those along the arm of a sofa or on the back of a club chair. Seams and welts should be perfectly smooth, unless you are looking for that old-world, slightly delapidated, hand-sewn look. Slight needle marks on the edges are fine if the pieces are actually done by hand (and the ultimate look for the sofa connoisseur), but wavy edges are unacceptable.

On Cost

As with any specialized custom work, upholstery prices vary significantly based upon the quality aspects discussed above. To choose the appropriate expense level, you should assess the application. Most decorators separate the "public" (living room, dining room) vs. "private" (bedrooms, playrooms) with two different price points.

For the high-quality work reviewed above, sofas are generally $350 to $450 per foot for attached cushion, and an additional $25 per foot for loose cushions. This means a high-quality, eight-foot sofa is $3,000 to $4,000 before the cost of the fabric, and receives a 4 or "standard" rating in the reviews of *The Franklin Report*. Of course, you can get a $1,000 sofa at a retail store including fabric, and this may be very appropriate for many circumstances, but is not of the same genus.

Window Treatments

From a simple minimalist panel to a layer-upon-layer, elaborate design, many elements come together to make a window treatment. Carefully selected shades, sheers, curtains and valances may be held together with various trims, chords, brackets and hardware—and possibly finished off with decorative finials. Some upholstery and window treatment professionals also do hard window treatments, which include all types of shades, laminated shades (roller shades, covered in your choice of fabric) and blinds, custom made in your choice of materials to coordinate with your curtains.

Where Do I Start?

To help you decide on the perfect window treatment for your room, many shops can do miracles with photos and magazine clippings. Once you've settled on a basic design (perhaps with the help of your decorator or examples from your upholsterer), measurements are taken. Most high-quality service providers will come to your home and measure as part of the cost. Less expensive workrooms or retail stores will charge a fee to take measurements, which may or may not be applied to the order. Ask about the costs before asking for a home visit.

It is highly recommended that you do not take the measurements—then you will not be responsible when they are twelve inches too short. Most treatments, for example, take up wall space as well as cover your window—which is not obvious. Will you have finials that may add extra yardage on each side of the window? Will your draperies actually open and close or just be decorative? All of these factors will need to be considered when measuring and drawing up the plans.

Window Treatment Fabric and Construction

As with custom-furniture upholstery, fabric choices for window treatments are endless. As with upholsterers, retail window treatment shops will provide you with a choice of fabrics and custom workrooms will require you to provide your own (COM). Some retail stores will charge you extra if you provide your own fabric. In addition to selecting a fabric for color, texture and print, consider how easy it will be to clean. Curtains and windowsills in the city are vulnerable to dust, dirt, grime and soot, whereas the elements are a bit more forgiving in the suburbs.

Most window treatments require more than one layer of fabric. For the most luxurious look, with excellent volume, curtains have a three-layer construction: fabric, a lining of silk or Dacron and interlining. The interlining is commonly made of flannel, which not only provides heft and a bit of structure but also a measure of soundproofing. The ultimate interlining is bump—a special, hard to get super-thick flannel from England. If you are looking for a lighter, airy look, a thinner lining may be sufficient, or no lining at all for the new breezy look.

ON COST

High-quality, mostly hand-sewn curtains are expensive. A three-layer construction, with lining and interlining, will be significantly more expensive to produce than a single or two-layer construction. For an eight-foot-wide by nine-foot-tall window with a double fabric panel trimmed on each side, and a box-pleat valance, the fabrication can cost about $1,000 to $1,400, before fabric and trim costs. This is considered a 4 or "standard" in *The Franklin Report*, including lining and interlining provided by the workroom, home measuring and installation.

TIPS ON CARING FOR UPHOLSTERED FURNITURE

GENERAL CARE

✧ Ask your upholsterer or fabric supplier exactly how to care for your new fabric.

✧ Vacuum often to get rid of dirt particles that cause abrasion and wear.

✧ Don't allow pets on fine fabrics—their body oils rub off onto the fabric and are tough to remove.

✧ Protect fabric-covered pieces from the sun—if not in use—to avoid fading and deterioration.

✧ Turn over loose cushions every week for even wear.

✧ Beware of sitting on upholstered furniture while wearing blue jeans or other fabric-dyed clothing—the color may "bleed" onto the fabric.

✧ Do not set newspapers or magazines onto upholstered furniture, as the ink may also bleed onto the fabric.

✧ Regular professional cleaning is ideal.

SPILLS

✧ Immediately after the spill, blot (don't rub) the area with a clean cloth. Dried spills are more difficult to remove.

✧ Carefully follow the instructions on the cleaning product (don't wing it). Most professional Upholstery cleaners just say to use club soda.

✧ If you use water for cleaning, be sure it is distilled.

✧ Choose a hidden area on the fabric to pretest the cleaner for color fastness before applying to the spill.

✧ Avoid making a small spill larger by working lightly, blotting out from the center. To avoid rings, 'feather' the edges by dampening the edge of the spill irregularly and blotting quickly.

✧ Using a small fan or blow-dryer (on low setting), quickly dry the cleaned area.

Upholstery & Window Treatments
Service Providers

Accent On Interiors   3.5   2.5   4.5   4
742 North Bedford Road, Bedford Hills, NY 10507
(914) 666 - 8036

Retail and Trade—Window treatments and upholstery

"Their window treatments are as good as anyone in New York, but the upholstery is not quite up to snuff." "I was stunned at the quality of the curtains, given this small operation." "Excellent quality at a very reasonable cost."

Angelo Bordonaro Upholstery   4   4.5   4   4
18 Liberty Street, Stamford, CT 06902
(203) 356 - 9390   kiddos@optonline.net

Trade only—Custom upholstery

A one-man show with some part-time help, Angelo Bordonaro does things the correct way, but it can take some time. After working in Italy and on several cruise ships—upholstering while afloat, Bordonaro came to the States in 1983 where he worked on projects for five star restaurants in NYC and Long Island, and then with one of the areas most prominent upholsterers. In 1987, Bordonaro set up his own shop in a 2,000-square-foot workspace. Several big-name Greenwich and New York decorators recommend the firm, but only for smaller jobs. Prices speak to the outstanding quality of the work, which generally takes about three to four weeks for re-upholstery and eight weeks for custom work. ASID.

"He does it to perfection, but cannot handle much volume." "We use Angelo for the showcase pieces in our projects." "He is a very detailed craftsman."

Anthony Lawrence-Belfair   4.5   4.5   4   4.5
53 West 23rd Street, 5th Floor, New York, NY 10010
(212) 206 - 8820   www.anthonylawrence.com

Trade only—Very high-end custom window treatments and upholstery

Anthony Lawrence's roots are in Connecticut, and many local decorators continue to believe that there is no one better. Moving to New York about five years ago, Lawrence recently joined forces with Belfair Draperies to deliver a full range of upholstery and window treatments from one workroom. Some of the greatest New York names in decorating have depended on these two companies separately for generations and consider this consolidation a godsend.

Extraordinary work quality and outstanding showroom selection (with over 70 floor models) are the strengths Belfair brings to the table, even though some found the firm "a bit disorganized," especially to the unfamiliar customer. Anthony Lawrence received outstanding reviews for its high-quality custom furniture, professionalism and reliability. Since the merger, we understand that the company still offers some of the highest quality available. Workers are in Connecticut and Westchester regularly measuring and making deliveries.

"Phenomenal quality at not completely insane prices." "Most of my local clientele will not step up to the plate and go for this quality. But when they do, they are happy." "We tend to use these guys only for the important, public pieces." "They work hard to build long-term relationships, and have done a good job of holding on to the Connecticut base."

	Quality +	Cost $	Value ◆	Recommend? ★

Anthony Totilo Custom Upholstery   4   3.5   4   4
219 Belltown Road, Stamford, CT 06905
(203) 323 - 4490

Trade only—Reupholstery

Tony Totilo may be a one-man operation and semi-retired but Martha Stewart continues to rely on him. In the business for almost 50 years, Totilo does everything the proper way and is reasonably priced. There is an eight-week delivery time with strong reliability, but limited throughout.

BB Shades   4.5   4.5   4   4.5
501 Westport Avenue, Suite 332, Norwalk, CT 06851
(203) 849 - 9345   bbshades@earthlink.net

Trade only—Custom lampshades

Going where no lampshade company has gone before, Cynthia Beebe used her executive marketing skills and savvy to develop excellent client service. For large projects, decorators and architects can send pictures or can arrange for BB Shades to go to the job site, take digital pictures and measurements, and produce the ultimate shade. The company develops new, innovative concepts as it has done with its star-shaped shade and its woven card lampshade in two tones. A variety of silks, trims, ribbons and stringing, as well as more standard fare are available.

Beebe graduated from Finch College and Parsons and previously worked in advertising at Avon Products and in new products at Revlon. She has lectured at the Cooper Hewitt Museum, Scalamandre and the Royal Oak Society. Many top New York decorators engage BB on a regular basis, and say the pricing is about the same as the best New York firms, but the client service is "clearly better." Shades can range from $115 for a pleated silk chandelier shade to $400+ for a twenty-foot masterpiece. ASID.

Ben Baena & Son   4   3.5   4.5   4.5
218 Charles Street, Bridgeport, CT 06606
(203) 334 - 8568

Trade only—Window treatments

Established in 1945 by Ben Baena, now Irene and Matthew Baena have joined this well-regarded and well-organized family firm. A team of ten work in a 2,000-square-foot workroom doing all soft and hard window and related works including cornices, lambrequins and headboards, but not vertical shades.

The two are known for their high-quality and operate one of the first workrooms in the US to use bump—in fact, they still supply bump to the trade. Production time is usually six to eight weeks. Many decorators accustomed to the best in New York are loyal customers.

"Just one step down from the finest in New York at a much more reasonable price." "These are intelligent, reasonable people—the kind of people you enjoy working with." "They understand the details, but are not tied to a particular way of doing anything."

Bill Watson   3.5   3   4   4
610 Quaker Lane South, West Hartford, CT 06110
(860) 232 - 3728

Trade only—Window treatments

On his own since 1970, Bill Watson picked up the trade as a stage designer. Using ingenuity, he is said to have developed ways to make the process more efficient, yielding good quality and excellent pricing throughout. With a range of local designers, Watson has become a mainstay in the region.

"Bill has his own way of doing things." "We trust it will be on target." "He knows how to get it done."

	Quality +	Cost $	Value ◆	Recommend? ★

Blind Vision
3.5   3   4.5   4.5

648 Central Park Avenue, Scarsdale, NY 10583
(914) 284 - 4212   www.blind-vision.com

Retail and Trade—Hard window treatments

A sole proprietor working in the industry since he was seventeen, Mark Tuckman is a reliable and helpful source for some of the best contractors and designers. Tuckman is a "specialist with that extra warmth," who supplies brand name manual and motorized shutters, blinds, shades. Training at Handy Andy for thirteen years, Tuckman knows the goods and can deliver without the overhead. Product is usually available in two to six weeks.

"Bill is the best. He put in temporary shades for the dinner party until the real ones got here." "Very customer-oriented and effective." "Does a great job and is such a nice guy to boot." "Comes and measures in a blink."

C&D Upholstery
4   4   4   4.5

234 East Avenue, Norwalk, CT 06855
(203) 838 - 2200

Trade only—Custom upholstery

Chris Simoulidis has been in Norwalk doing "beautiful European work" for over twenty years. Learning the trade in Greece beginning when he was thirteen, Simoulidis now has sons Nick and Peter in the business. With five additional in staff, the firm can "copy any picture" with good attention to detail. They go as far as making their own frames and can double stuff with horsehair, sewing all by hand.

Coming soon will be a line of 32 sofas, chairs and ottomans under the Christopher London line showcased in their 10,000-square-foot building. Many fine Connecticut designers are long-time customers.

"A bit of a tight operation, but very good results." "They take pride in their work."

Charlene's Interiors
4   3.5   4.5   4.5

24 Johns Street, Clinton, CT 06413
(860) 669 - 7167

Retail and Trade—Window treatments and soft goods

Charlene Denhardt has been working in the design and production of draperies for over 35 years. Now daughter Cheryl is at hand, adding to the overall craftsmanship. Known to be extremely flexible and accommodating, they will do one pillow or the most elaborate European designs. The leading edges may be sewn by hand with the interlining hand sewn into the hems. Fabric books are in the shop featuring such manufacturers as Greff, Schumacher, Waverly and Duralee. Excellent Connecticut designers are loyal customers.

"These are incredibly nice, reasonable professionals." "Meticulousness is their watch word." "They take the time to do it right." "A complete bargain." "Their curtains took my breath away."

Classic Sofa
3   3   4   4

79 East Putnam Avenue, Greenwich, CT 06830
(203) 863 - 0005   www.classicsofa.com

Retail and trade—Two-week custom upholstery

The Greenwich location of this New York City-based upholsterer seems to receive higher marks for client service and flexibility. Managed by Carl Del'Spina, who is said to "want to make every experience a success." Del'Spina has been with this 23-year-old firm since 1997, when the Greenwich outpost was opened. Previously he was an account exec at the advertising firm of Young & Rubicam, and worked in a his family business in New York City.

Offering about a dozen sofa styles, chairs and ottomans that can be somewhat modified, the real upside here is the timing—two weeks once the fabric is in. Clients appreciate the speed with which you can choose a piece from the floor and get it in your home, but are less impressed with the "uniqueness of the choices." We are told that Classic Sofa produces "decent quality at lower prices." The firm sells both to the trade and retail, with a client list that includes celebrities and top decorators.

"Expedient and responsive to quote requests." "Pleasant about changes to the standard fare. Great product." "While the drape of the skirt may not be perfect, it is the perfect choice for a playroom or a kids room." "Carl could not be nicer and really makes it happen for you."

Classic Upholstery   4   3.5   4   4.5
20 North Avenue, Norwalk, CT 06851
(203) 845 - 8776

Trade only—Custom upholstery

Many top regional decorators and a few top-notch New York decorators rely on Lefty Petridis at Classic Upholstery. Noted for its excellent client service and workmanship, Custom does everything by hand, the old-fashioned way. Items usually take six to eight weeks.

Management goes to all customer sites for measurements to assure correct fittings. After receiving a degree in marketing from Central Connecticut University, Lefty and his Ecuadorian partner who trained at Anthony Lawrence opened Classic in 1994. After five years, Lefty's partner returned home and Lefty further developed the reputation of Classic. There is a 9,000-square-foot workroom/showroom where ten to twenty pieces are generally on display.

"Lefty is really good about getting me out of any jams with my clients. If there was a misunderstanding, Lefty will make it right." "There is a friendly attitude and open access." "The work is always checked thoroughly before it leaves the shop." "Excellent work at two-thirds the cost of Brunshwig." "Lefty works hard at making his clients satisfied and builds good relationships."

Custom Decorator Service   4.5   4   4.5   5
415 East Main Street, Denville, NJ 07834
(973) 625 - 0516

Trade only—Window treatments and reupholstery

Established over 50 years ago, Custom Decorator was first based in New York City and then moved to New Jersey. Walter Kunzel learned the trade from his uncle, who trained in Europe. Kunzel's son has now been in the family business for thirty years and his daughter for fifteen. Mostly doing window treatments and associated soft goods, some reupholstery is also done. Anything can be created from the most exquisite draperies with fine details to the simple.

Seven people work out of a 4,000-square-foot workroom creating all hand finished goods. Most of the customers are serious New York designers, and other notables in the trade. Several regional decorators are also fans, and the staff visits the Connecticut/Westchester area on a regular basis.

"They are as good as the well-known New York guys at lesser cost." "The timing is always perfect." "Not only amazing work, but delightful and intelligent people."

Custom Upholstery Workshop, LLC

Quality	Cost	Value	Recommend?
3.5	2.5	4.5	4.5

10 Greenfield Street, Fairfield, CT 06432
(203) 367 - 4231

Trade only—Custom upholstery and window treatments

Running a tight family operation, John Hayes has built a strong business offering excellent value. A group of eight in business for thirty years, Hayes and wife Sharon along with sons Keith and John are said to stay on top of all details. There is a 5,000-square-foot workspace, where most of the product is competed in the most efficient and effective way possible. While knowledgeable of the older ways of the trade, more modern methodologies are used.

Some very strong regional decorators use Custom regularly (especially on the upholstery side) with great success. Upholstery is usually completed in three to four weeks and draperies in four to five weeks.

De Angelis Inc.

Quality	Cost	Value	Recommend?
5	5	3.5	5

312 East 95th Street, New York, NY 10128
(212) 348 - 8225

Trade only—High-end custom upholstery

Clients rhapsodize about the fabulous work of De Angelis while critics are left speechless by the even more fabulous prices. The craftsmen at De Angelis specialize in serious old-world, hand-done work, and clients say their pieces last forever. The service level also receives very high marks, as does the selection of fabrics and trim. Additionally, there is an impressive showroom with a vast number of pieces to help in your selection—all completely adjustable.

While several references suggest that comparable quality could be found elsewhere for less, many decorators think De Angelis is in a class by itself. Many of the very top New York decorators doing work in Connecticut/Westchester urge their clients to use De Angelis for the public rooms for a world-class look and polish.

"Truly extraordinary furniture at outrageous prices." "Nothing else will do for your, top-of-the-line client." "If you have the money, do it. The quality of the product and the service is amazing." "It takes forever and a day." "They can do it with no direction. Timing can be an issue though."

Delon Freres Inc.

Quality	Cost	Value	Recommend?
4.5	4.5	4	4

601 West 26th Street, Suite M223, New York, NY 10001
(212) 206 - 8396

Trade only—Window treatments and wall upholstery

Working all over the country, Alby Delon has about ten on staff in NY and another ten in LA working with brother Maurice. Doing the Miami Delano with Philip Stark and The Hudson with Ian Schrager, the firm has built a reputation for quality. The firm also has a strong following in Connecticut and Westchester.

The Delons learned the wall upholstery business with the famed La Tenture Murale in Paris, and began doing window treatments at the request of its clients. In the States for eighteen years, many of the fabric houses in the D&D in New York also are clients. Implementing all hand sewing, the draperies usually take about four to six weeks for completion out of the 4,000-square-foot workroom.

"Not a bargain, but amazing work." "Very professional people that work with the most demanding clients, so they can deliver."

Design Upholstery

Quality	Cost	Value	Recommend?
3	3	4	4

22 Westport Avenue, Westport, CT 06880
(203) 221 - 0088

Retail and Trade—Upholstery and window treatments

"They did a perfect job with my cushions, which were a difficult fabric design to line up." "They really try to please the customer." "A reliable new business in the area." "They have the necessary knowledge, but could do a bit better in the communication department." "A total range of quality, as you like—but you'd better be specific."

	Quality +	Cost $	Value ◆	Recommend? ★

Draperies Inc.
226 Main Street, Norwalk, CT 06851
(203) 847 - 4553

| | 3.5 | 3.5 | 4 | 4 |

Retail, Trade and Commercial—Window treatments and blinds

With an operation that is mostly commercial, Larry LeClerc can deliver good quality with excellent speed and pricing. In two weeks, most curtains can be measured, made and installed. Highest-end contractors especially appreciate the efficiency delivered with twenty-eight on staff including four commercial sales people working out of the 12,000-square-foot workroom with a 1,800-square-foot showroom. Several-high end regional decorators also use the firm.

They are known to be able to "beat any price" under negotiation, particularly for large jobs. The quality can range considerably, depending on the requirements of the job. Most clients return for the reliable and expedient service.

Ernest Studios Inc.
207 East 84th Street, New York, NY 10028
(212) 988 - 4900   erneststudios@aol.com

| | 4.5 | 4.5 | 4 | 5 |

Trade only—Window treatments and custom upholstery

Learning the trade in the family business in Hungary, Ernest Mandel does work for decorators around the country. About fifty percent of his work is in the regional Connecticut/Westchester area. In a 7,500-square-foot workroom with 30 pieces on display, Mandel meets the highest demands of perfection. Many well-known New York decorators use their services and a few of the highest quality regional firms as well. Sixteen workmen and a business manager make sure all goes smoothly.

"Client service and detail is their focus." "Ernest Studios is earnest about their work." "They keep some of the most difficult decorators in the business happy— a true testament to their ability to get it done." "Working with Marc on the business side is a real pleasure."

Ewald's Furniture & Upholstery Co.
443 Main Street, Torrington, CT 06790
(860) 489 - 8901   www.ewalds.net

| | 3.5 | 3.5 | 4 | 4 |

Retail and Trade—Upholstery

Ewald's was founded in 1959, and sold to its present owner, Zygmunt Michna, in 2000. Four people work in the shop, which serves both the trade and retail clientele. All foam or feather-down are used in the pieces, depending upon the circumstances. They specialize in reupholstering antiques.

"It is all hand-tied, with European skills." "Not the friendliest to deal with at first." "If you show them what to do, they can do anything."

Expresiones Inc.
113 Webster Avenue, Harrison, NY 10528
(914) 835 - 4041

| | 3.5 | 4 | 4 | 4.5 |

Trade only—Mostly window treatments

As a couture dressmaker in Colombia, Amparo Bahamon learned to get the seams just right. Taking her talent to the US in 1995, Bahamon now has her son, daughter and brother working with her to create "whatever you want." This small shop does most everything by hand and is lauded for its practical and engaging attitude.

"A secret source that will create something special for you." "What they do not have in experience they make up for in focus, hard work and smarts." "I hate to give her name up, but she so deserves it."

Frederick W. Karl

4.5	4.5	4	4.5

5 North Street, Roxbury, CT 06783
(800) 261 - 1281

Retail and Trade—Custom upholstery

Known by others in the trade as "the master," Fred Karl has taught 54 apprentices how to create upholstery the "correct way." Karl learned from his father, who was trained in Germany and started the family business in 1926 in Greenwich Village. After studying architecture at Pratt, Karl started working with his father in 1968.

Remarkably, Karl has over 300 clients a year with only about two on staff. Karl is said to be obsessive about overseeing every detail in his 1,200-square-foot workshop. Many fine dealers and Sotheby's count on Karl's fastidiousness. Everything is done by hand with tools that fit into a little overnight bag.

"This is the top of the class in Connecticut." "Karl is the ultimate in personalized and knowledgeable service." "You not only receive a piece of incredible furniture but also an education working with Karl." "I would trust him with the finest antique."

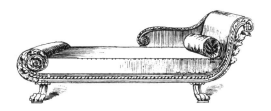

Giorgio's Upholstery & Interior Decorating Inc.

3.5	3	4	4.5

363 Main Avenue, Norwalk, CT 06851
(203) 846 - 1112

Retail and Trade—Upholstery and window treatments

With strong family roots in the upholstery business, Giorgio and Debbie Taiyanides have built a reliable firm used by designers and the public. Giorgio learned the trade in Greece and Debbie under the tutelage of his father Leonard, of Leonard's Upholstery. There is a 2,500-square-foot workroom where Giorgio and Debbie attend to every detail personally. Offering a good value, flexible concepts and always meeting their deadlines, Giorgio's has forged a solid reputation.

"We can count on Giorgio and Debbie. They know what they are doing and they do not charge a fortune." "They promised delivery for an important client party, and made it happen."

Hemming Birds Ltd.

4	4	4.5	5

343 Adams Street, Bedford Hills, NY 10507
(914) 666 - 5812

Trade only—Window treatments and bedding

Roger Faynor, who established Hemming Birds in 1968, has developed a strong, upper-end following in the regional area. Creating soft goods of all kinds, the curtains are of excellent quality with hand sewing on all the leading edges and the interlining into the hem. Clients are loyal to Faynor not only for the excellent product but also for the initiative and pride he takes in his work.

"When the job is finished and Roger installs at the client's home, I do not have to be there because I know it will be done right." "He just gets it. Not only smart but also highly aware of the interests of his upscale market." "A great guy who will suggest the perfect trim." "My clients adore him."

Interiors by Royale Inc.   3   2.5   3   3
964 Third Avenue, New York, NY 10022
(212) 753 - 4600   intbyroyale@aol.com
Trade only—Curtains and bedding

   Housed in a shop near the D&D building, clients have discovered a good selection of fabrics and a helpful staff at this firm. Interiors by Royale does upholstery work at its Long Island workshop, and specializes in custom window treatments and bedding. Many of the top designers drop by this shop exclusively for draperies. We hear the product is excellent and the timing is good, with a typical turnaround of six weeks.

Interiors Haberdashery   4.5   4   4   4.5
533 Pacific Street, Stamford, CT 06902
(203) 969 - 7227
Trade only—Upholstery and window treatments

   With urbane sophistication, Philip Shortt and Paul Guzzetta know their market and their trade. Shortt graduated from the Royal College of Arts in London, majoring in fashion and then worked at Valentino. Guzzetta graduated from Parsons in fashion and then worked at Yves St. Laurent. Taking his fashion verve to the home, these partners formed Interiors Haberdashery in 1993.

   Hand-sewn draperies are modeled after the English craft. The store is also a great resource for designers with a range of muslin slipcovered showpieces and curtain hardware. Many of Connecticut and Westchester's best designers are grateful these two are in the neighborhood.

   "Excellent craftsmanship—but expensive." "Philip and Paul are totally on the ball. They are smart and creative." "As good as the NY crowd and more fun."

J. Paul Inc.   4.5   4.5   4   4.5
404 Irvington Street, Pleasantville, NY 10570
(914) 747 - 8917
Trade only—Window treatments and upholstery

   Jeffrey Mandelbaum differentiates J. Paul with a superior level of service. Mandelbaum established the firm in 1997 after receiving a degree in mechanical engineering from City College, working for GE for a year, and then working with a Polish old-world craftsman for seven years. With 22 on staff and 10,000 square feet of work space, J. Paul impresses all his clients with excellent service and effective process. Many on the team can create CAD drawings and if they cannot find the perfect wrought iron fitting, they will have it produced.

   Several of NY's biggest names work with J. Paul and the firm works in the regional area regularly. Upholstery takes about eight to ten weeks and drapery work about four to six weeks.

   "While I know I am not a very big client, I feel like they do their very best for me." "They are really good a holding your hand through the process, which is soup-to-nuts." "When they go to our clients' homes they are sure to pick up the last staple." "While expensive, they will work with you to find the right solution."

J&M Upholstery   3   3   4   4
1717 Barnum Avenue, Bridgeport, CT 06610
(203) 367 - 0667
Trade only—Upholstery

   "My reliable buddies." "Old-world in Bridgeport—who would have guessed?" "Reasonable cost and fast service." "Perfect for the basics."

	Quality +	Cost $	Value ◆	Recommend? ★

Johansen Interiors

	5	5	4	5

706 North Division Street, Peekskill, NY 10566
(914) 739 - 6293

Trade only—Window treatments and bedding

Joan Johansen wins accolades from clients for her stunning draperies and accommodating nature. Working with some of New York's most notable designers (who work for some big-time, household-name clients), Johansen stops at nothing short of perfection. If it is "too long," it will be brought back and fixed immediately. All is done by hand with great care.

Johansen was a remedial reading teacher who taught herself the craft as a hobby. With "the patience of a saint," Johansen is said to create a heavenly product, paying attention to the smallest details. Four on staff help Johansen is in a small but efficient 1,600-square-foot workshop.

"It may take a while, but it is always worth the wait." "A gem that can deal with any personality and any situation." "She makes it right."

John Paul Schriever Upholstery

	4	4	4	4

92 Old Ridgefield Road, Suite A, Wilton, CT 06897
(203) 834 - 1266

Trade only—Custom upholstery

Jonas Upholstery

	5	5	4	4

44 West 18th Street, New York, NY 10011
(212) 691 - 2777

Trade only—High-end upholstery and curtains

Unquestionably recognized as one of the very top upholstery and curtain workrooms in New York City (many say the best), this year, the astronomical pricing seems to be diminishing the appeal. While top decorators agree this high-end practitioner is definitely one of their favorites, more clients are balking at the cost, suggesting the decorators go elsewhere. Others continue to find the sophisticated approach, good timing and phenomenal quality "worth any price," knowing that each piece was made with the highest-quality materials and crafted with care.

Many decorators enjoy bringing their clients to Jonas's workroom to see their pieces being made. One decorator described it as being like a trip to Santa's workshop—a real treat—adding that everyone is always friendly and informative and "even the naked frames are beautiful." The firm's attention to detail is "superior" and decorators tell us that its professionals are honest and reliable. However, since the workroom just services the trade, the ultimate end users have had trouble communicating with the firm.

"The most comfortable piece of furniture I have ever sat in." "While we used to use Jonas all the time, now my clients demand lower cost alternatives." "I continue to come back because they inherently know what I want with little guidance." "We find them less flexible than others." "When I called a few years later for the reupholstery of my living room sofa, and it came back with the innards ripping the expensive fabric, they refused to deal with the situation." "My big issue is that they send a technician to measure on-site, and you can not really discuss any design details with him." "Not worth the timing drama." "If one does very high-end design and quality, this is the only place to go." "They will customize to the millimeter and really put your clients at ease."

Lanera Decorating

	3.5	3.5	4	4

801 East Boston Post Road, Mamaroneck, NY 10543
(914) 381 - 0908   www.laneradecorating.hdwfg.com

Retail, Trade and Commercial—Upholstery and window treatment

Taking over their parent's firm that was begun in 1969, Sally (on the residential and trade end) and James (on commercial) Lanera run a large and effective

	Quality	Cost	Value	Recommend?
	✚	$	◆	★

operation. With twenty on staff and 10,000 square feet of workshop, the company services all markets and a variety of price points. We understand that they have thousands of sample books and are very willing to work with the client to meet his or her needs.

"Nice people with a good operation." "They will do zig-zag or eight-way hand-tied. Whatever the situation demands." "Reliable and helpful."

Leon's Upholstery   3   3   4   4
601 Broad Street, New London, CT 06320
(860) 444 - 7679

Retail and Trade—Upholstery and window treatments

Doing mostly reupholstery in the regional area, Leon's was established in 1964. The current owner bought the business in 1997 and has carried on the traditions and kept the predominantly retail clientele pleased. In a 3,000-square-foot workroom with six on staff, Leon's pays keen attention to detail and has strong client service. Product is generally released within four to six weeks.

"The staff is very nice and very practical." "More sophisticated than your average retail operation because they also cater to excellent decorators in the area." "Reliable and clear."

Marshall Randolph Ltd.   4.5   4.5   4   4
360 Fairfield Avenue, Stamford, CT 06902
(203) 348 - 9990 www.marshallrandolph.com

Trade only—Window treatments and upholstery

Owners Randy Hampson and Casey Chiaraluce have combined their skills, building an excellent reputation for full-service Marshall Randolph in a relatively short time. Hampson has been a showroom owner and interior designer for many years. Chiaraluce was previously a couture fashion designer. In 1999, the pair opened Marshall Randolph. A multifaceted operation, the firm has a burgeoning custom upholstery line and is an agent showroom for Lee Jofa and Kravet fabric lines. The staff measures, installs and fabricates all soft goods, upholstery and wall upholstery.

Many of the region's best decorators use Marshall Randolph, saying that the staff is unique in its creative approach and can deliver outstanding product.

"They really get it. The biggest challenge is to get my client to understand the quality they are producing and be happy to pay for it." "Putting up their curtains is like putting on a good suit. It just looks better." "They roll the edge of their sheers like a chiffon gown." "Not for everyone, but really interesting work."

Marvel Home Decorating   3.5   3   4   4.5
351 North Frontage Road, New London, CT 06320
(860) 443 - 8437 marvel@cttel.net

Retail—Window treatments, hardware and fabrics

With strong experience, excellent client service and more than a 1,000 fabric samples in books, Marvel Home Decorating serves the Eastern Connecticut and Rhode Island market very well. Established over 73 years ago, Gail Grillo prides herself on creating anything the client needs, especially finding solutions for unusually shaped windows. Grillo studied at RISD and is always learning about the latest technologies. With good pricing and expedient delivery times of two to three weeks, Marvel is a market favorite.

"Northern Connecticut's Manhattan Shade and Glass." "They are really expert in this field, often suggesting a better methodology."

Munrod Interior Upholstery   4   3.5   4.5   4.5
111 East Sandford Boulevard, Mount Vernon, NY 10550
(914) 668 - 2200   munrod111@aol.com
Trade only—Mostly upholstery

Munrod is a large operation with excellent customer service. While catering also to the commercial market with clients such as The Grand Floridian at Disneyland, the firm's roots are in residential. The home market is still about half the volume, and all the work maintains residential standards. All clients receive the benefit of economies of scale, and thus good pricing.

Started in 1978, the firm now has a 34,000-square-foot shop and thirty five people, including five sales representatives. On the residential side, Maurie Cyms is the design director and "is excellent understanding the nuances of the interior designers and homeowners." Cyms is an industrial design grad from Pratt. Owner Manny Munoz is a third-generation furniture maker, learning the trade in Honduras. Making everything "except for the trees" including their own frames, Munrod controls the process and therefore can meet deadlines. Workers are used to doing prototypes and have a large showroom in which about 50 pieces are displayed.

"They pay attention to every detail down to the level of a loose thread." "They can meet all quality levels with good pricing at each." "They will fix your sofa ten years later at no charge." "They get the old-school concept without bankrupting your clients."

Norton Upholstery Company Inc.   4.5   4   4.5   5
1012 Orange Avenue, West Haven, CT 06516
(203) 934 - 5747   bennyb1025@aol.com
Retail and Trade—Upholstery and reupholstery

Benny Becker takes great care to understand his client's perspective. He even took courses in interior design for several years to get it just right. Designers believe that he has achieved his goal, saying that he can create sofas comparable to the great English brands at about two-thirds of the price. Becker's father started the business in 1960, coming from Poland after WWII. Benny received a degree in sales and marketing from the University of New Haven and jumped right in.

Now there is a team of five, all reported to be very "reasonable and on top of it all." Becker prides himself on client satisfaction, insisting that the customer tries out a new piece of upholstery in muslin first to check the pitch. There is even a motorized chair at the shop for the customer to test various angles before committing to production.

"Benny can do almost anything. He created an amazing curved sofa for us that looked like it melted perfectly into the corner." "He is so fastidious, it can make you crazy—but he will always come through." "Cutting edge design at prices that do not hurt." "Benny will work day and night for you to get it just right. As good as the finest in New York."

	Quality	Cost	Value	Recommend?

Norwalk Upholstery Co.   3.5   3   4   4
141 Main Street, Norwalk, CT 06851
(203) 847 - 5724

Retail and Trade—Upholstery and window treatments

After training with his family for ten years in Greece, and then working for an American upholstery company for another ten, Leonard was well prepared when he opened his firm in 1979. Through years of experience in the regional area, Leonard has developed a strong following. Working in a 4,000-square-foot space with a team of four, many excellent decorators use the firm. They can make upholstery the old fashioned way with eight-way hand-tied springs or accommodate for smaller budgets. Leonard is known to be especially helpful about restyling old furniture to make it look more up-to-date.

"Even the guy that picks up and delivers is nice." "You must keep them focused on direction and timing." "They always fix it, if there are any issues." "He is really from the old country, but knows his business and has a range of options." "I adore Leonard—he will work with you to find the right price and solution."

Pamela Hatfield Studio   3.5   3   4.5   4.5
118 Woodland Avenue, Bridgeport, CT 06605
(203) 330 - 1149

Trade only—Draperies and soft goods

Pam Hatfield established this boutique business in 1997. After working in institutional sales on Wall Street, in fashion at *Ingenue* magazine and then as a sales assistant in the garment district, Hatfield is making excellent use of her diverse skills. There are two FIT graduates that assist Hatfield in their 1,700-square-foot workspace. Clients include fine regional decorators that come to the firm for its intelligent perspective and well-priced products.

"They quickly understand the objectives and are so easy to work with." "Focused and reliable."

Peter Germain Interiors, LLC   4   4   4   4
931 Bantam Road, Bantam, CT 06750
(860) 567 - 1442   petergrmn@aol.com

Retail and Trade—Upholstery and window treatments

Working in the "archaic methods" of fine European craftsmanship, Peter Germain carries on old-world traditions. Using horsehair for the upholstery work and all hand sewing for the curtains, several New York decorators and New Yorkers with second homes in the Northwest corner of Connecticut frequent his shop. At this location, there is a showroom studio that displays about fifteen custom upholstered pieces and other furnishings. Germain and three others create in a 1,500-square-foot workroom with timing at about eight to ten weeks for this very detailed work.

"Stands out as one of the very finest in Litchfield County." "Peter is also good about offering interesting suggestions that really upgrade the look." "He enjoys a tailored fit—he is beyond the English overstuffed genre."

Ralph Dominguez Interiors   4   3.5   4   4
25 Lewis Avenue, Poughkeepsie, NY 12603
(845) 485 - 5248

Trade only—Upholstery and window treatments

Robert McCoy   4   4   4.5   4.5
14 Bridge Street, Westport, CT 06880
(203) 222 - 1473   cat3208ta@aol.com

Retail and Trade—Reupholstery and upholstery

In the business for twenty five years, Bob McCoy opened his own shop in 1995 after working with his father for seventeen years. Working with only a seamstress, clients appreciate the personalized and innovative approach. McCoy is said to know the business "inside and out" and is good about offering alternate methodologies to fit the situation or meet a budget. Boats and upholstered panels have been outfitted seamlessly. Most of the work is in reupholstery, but new, custom pieces are also done.

"He is really on top of the details." "Excellent quality for the price."

SH Davidson Interiors	4	4	4	4

350 Lexington Avenue, Mount Kisco, NY 10549
(914) 241 - 4345

Retail and trade—Upholstery, window treatments and antique restoration

Shades From the Midnight Sun	5	5	4	5

66 Boulder Trail, Bronxville, NY 10708
(914) 779 - 7237   swellott@msn.com

Trade only—Lampshades

Considered a "prized secret source" by many of New York's ultimate decorators, Sue Wellott has been creating classic and over-the-top shades since 1991. Winning accolades for her excellent client service and broad range of pricing choices, Midnight Sun will make it work for the customer. Wellott, trained in the fashion and textile industry, previously heading the merchandising for Eagle's Pierre Cardin men's shirt line. Offering trims and silks at the shop where a team of six constructs the shades, production time is usually around four to seven weeks.

"Sue gives it her all to find the perfect solution." "A well-known resources for the top end of the trade." "Priced less than the big New York options."

Stylish Decorators	3.5	3.5	4	4

3314 White Plains Road, Bronx, NY 10467
(718) 881 - 7691

Retail and Trade—Upholstery and reupholstery

Doing eight-way hand tying since he was eight years old, John Peloso focuses primarily on reupholstery and slipcovers. With three on staff, Peloso took over the firm that his father established in 1955. Doing everything from Madison Square Garden suite seating in poly/Dacron to high-end residential in 80 percent down, the firm offers all options. Several top regional decorators use Stylish.

"He can do sixteen-way hand tied if you like, but is good about keeping the labor and the costs down." "John always tries to do the right thing by his customers."

	Quality	Cost	Value	Recommend?

SUMA, LLC   4   4   4.5   4.5

10 Cooley Avenue, Middletown, CT 06457
(860) 346 - 4843   markbijleveld@cs.com

Trade only—Upholstery and window treatments

Mark and Susan Bijleveld came to the United States from native Holland bringing the fine old-world ways with them. Mark was a master apprentice at Pander, the most prestigious upholstery firm in Holland and then worked for his uncle in the Hague for several years. SUMA was opened in 2001 as an extension of the Dutch business. There is a massive, three-story building of 35,000 square feet that serves as the workroom. As of now, there are four on the team with Mark heading up the upholstery side and Susan in charge of the drapery work.

Several renowned New York and Connecticut decorators have already found there way to SUMA, where all the work is done with traditional methodologies. Suma is looking to expand—with their excellent craftsmanship and very good pricing, this American dream should become a reality.

"Superb work with fine European detailing." "Young people on the up-and-up."

Triple S Reupholstery Center Inc.   3   2.5   4.5   4

337 Westport Avenue, Norwalk, CT 06851
(203) 849 - 1089   www.duc-interiors.com

Retail and trade—Custom upholstery and window treatments

Offering full service at excellent pricing, DUC has carved out a firm market niche. Used by top-drawer decorators and upscale homeowners, the firm does everything from new custom furniture and draperies to upholstered walls to all forms of motorized treatments. Working in the commercial arena as well, the company knows how to efficiently and effectively price, produce and deliver. While most is machine stitched, they reportedly "fill a market need with aplomb."

Under the direction of Steve DeMarco, DUC is associated with Triple S Carpet & Drapery Cleaners, and clients enjoy building upon that relationship. There are twelve employees working in a 5,000-square-foot work area and 1,800-square-foot showroom. Products are usually produced within four weeks.

"Excellent for straightforward jobs." "Ed is very thorough, handling most of my upholstery for years." "There is never an issue." "Outstanding service for wooden and roller shades." "Highly competent at digestible prices."

Tudor House Furniture Co. Inc.   4   3.5   4.5   4.5

929 Sherman Avenue, Hamden, CT 06514
(203) 288 - 8451   hemargo@aol.com

Trade only—Custom upholstery

Harold Margolies is maintaining the traditions his in-laws began in 1963. Using only double kiln-dried hardwood made into frames which are glued and double-dowelled for strength and hairpads on all "normal" seating, Margolies knows all the trades ins and outs and delivers at a reasonable price. In a 20,000-square-foot space with twenty employees, there is a lot going on at Tudor House. Some of the strongest regional decorators use the firm who say that Tudor House can do anything from a sketch and produce on schedule. Margolies is also known for his outstanding client service and perspective, applying the lessons learned as a sociology major at University of Connecticut.

"They are heroes on price compared to the best of New York, at a quality that compares." "Excellent about encouraging the client to see the piece in muslin first, and happily adjusting as requested."

	Quality +	Cost $	Value ◆	Recommend? ★

Vitanza Finishing & Upholstery   4   3   5   5
728 East 136th Street, New York, NY 10454
(718) 401 - 1022 www.vitanzafurniture.com

Furniture restoration, particularly Art Deco, upholstery

See Vitanza Finishing & Upholstery's full report under the heading Furniture Repair & Refinishing

White Workroom   4.5   4   4   5
62 White Street, fifth floor, New York, NY 10013
(212) 941 - 5910

Retail and Trade—Custom window treatments

Top-flight designers say it "doesn't get any better than this" when it comes to curtains, White Workroom's specialty. The firm "inherently understands the drape and flow of fabric," and is also said to offer the ultimate in service. Connecticut and Westchester designers go the extra distance to use White for their most creative projects.

"They are extraordinary. If you think you can cut corners and expense by going somewhere else, you're wrong." "White creates works of art that please clients forever. While a true capital investment, the annual depreciated value is a bargain."

Yorkville Caning   4   2   5   5
31-04 60th Street, Woodside, NY 11377
(212) 432 - 6464 yorkvillecaning@aol.com

Furniture refinishing, caning and wicker repair

See Yorkville Caning's full report under the heading Furniture Repair & Refinishing

Hiring a Window Washer

There are too many beautiful views in Westchester and Fairfield counties to accept a grimy window. Window washing may seem like a straightforward project, but because residences and commercial establishments come in a variety of shapes, sizes and conditions, there are many variables for your service provider to deal with. You'll want to review your situation with the cleaning service before it shows up to do the actual cleaning.

Do Your Homework

Before contacting any window washers, you should note some facts about your windows. How many do you have? Are they storm windows, French windows or just regular ones? Do they have window guards? How many have grates? Are there panes? How many? Do the windows open in, slide up and down, tip out? Are they old or new? Are they dirty enough that they'll need to be power-washed or scraped? If you live in a building, does it have hooks outside the window to which the washer can connect himself and his equipment? If so, are they all intact? Taking these factors into consideration, the service provider should give you a rough "guesstimate" over the phone. If you omit any information, the work may end up costing more than the original quote once they come for the formal estimate.

It's customary for window washers to provide a free estimate, but you may want to confirm this on the phone with the service provider, too. Once they inspect the job to be done, they should be able to provide you with a written estimate. Getting the estimate in writing will help prevent unexpected charges later. For example, the service provider could claim that the job was more involved than expected, and try to charge a higher fee after the work is done.

What Should I Expect?

You'll also want to ask the service provider a few questions before signing any contracts. Inquire about the length of time they have been in business (the longer, the better), where most of their customers are located and whether they can provide references. The references will help you get an idea of how reliable they are: how long it takes to schedule an appointment, whether they get the work done on time and thoroughly, whether they clean up after themselves. Be sure that your service provider is fully insured and can show proof of worker's compensation and liability insurance. If they do not have this coverage, you may be responsible for any accidents that happen on your property. There is no specific license or certification for window cleaning companies other than filing to operate as a business with the Department of Labor.

On Cost

There are three general methods of pricing: per window, per job or per hour with an estimate of the time necessary to complete the job. In addition, some companies have minimums and/or charge for estimates. The most common method of pricing is a basic rate per window that is usually based on window size. It is a good idea to inquire about a discount if you have a larger job (20 or more windows), as many vendors will negotiate a better price if there is a substantial amount of work to be done. For a basic 6-over-6 window (a window that has two frames that slide up or down, each with six separate panes) with no window guards, paint or unusual amounts of dirt, you can expect a price range from $4 to $15 per window, with the majority of vendors charging $8 to $10. However, factors like location (Are you in town or on an estate?), type of window (Do you have thermal panes, storm windows, French, etc.?), type of residence or building, accessibility (Are the windows hard to reach? Do you have hooks or crevices for the window washer to attach himself to?) and amount of dirt should be considered and discussed as these might affect the final estimate.

PREPARING FOR WINDOW-WASHING DAY

Once you have set up an appointment, clear a path to the windows to prevent mishaps. Move that antique table with the priceless lamp. Clear objects that may obstruct access from sills and benches. Draw back your curtains and window treatments. Most service providers will show the utmost respect for your home and will protect your carpets and walls from drips and spills. If it makes you more comfortable, schedule free time for yourself on window-washing day so you can keep an eye on the process.

CLEANING CALENDAR

A professional window cleaning twice a year is usually sufficient, but if your residence is particularly exposed to the elements, you may need cleaning more often. Spring and fall are generally the busiest times of the year for this industry. An early spring cleaning will remove any dirt and grime left by winter rains, snow and frost, and a scrub in the fall will wash away spring and summer's pollen, bugs and dirt. Be sure to call well in advance if you want your windows cleaned at peak times.

SOMETHING EXTRA

Window cleaners often offer a variety of other services, from cleaning screens and blinds to waxing and sanding floors. They might pressure-wash canopies, awnings, sidewalks, garages and greenhouses; do heavy-duty cleaning of gutters, carpets, upholstery and appliances; some do basic handyman services, house painting and clean-up after renovations. If you are pleased with the company, you may have another project for them to do. Now that you can see through your windows again, you might notice all kinds of things.

TIPS FOR WASHING WINDOWS
BETWEEN PROFESSIONAL SERVICE CALLS

✧ Never wash windows in the bright sunlight. They'll dry too fast and carry a streaky residue.
✧ Use a squeegee instead of paper towels.
✧ For best results, skip the store-bought spray cleaner and use a mixture of one cup white vinegar diluted in a gallon of warm water.
✧ Sponge the cleaning solution onto the window then drag the squeegee across the glass. Wipe the squeegee blade with a damp cloth fter each swipe.
✧ For extra shine, rub window glass with a clean blackboard eraser after cleaning.
✧ If you absolutely *don't* do windows, share these tips with your housekeeper.

Window Washers

Ace Maintenance Company   3.5   2   4.5   4
606 Post Road East, Suite 521, Westport, CT 06880
(203) 227 - 7435   enrcap79@aol.com
Residential and commercial window washing

A fixture in the window washing industry since 1980, the bulk of Ace Maintenance Company's jobs is residential. Founder Richard Capozzi and his wife, who are described as "punctual, reliable and fair," manage the family business. Capozzi's loyal clients include A-list celebrities, and corporate clients Kinko's, Linens n' Things and others. Though Capozzi does most of the work himself, he will hire extra help during the company's busy times—particularly the spring.

Free estimates are done on-site in person. In-and-out cleaning for standard windows starts at $5 per window. Ace Maintenance serves New Canaan, Darien, Westport, Greenwich and the surrounding area. The company also does some post-construction cleaning.

"Great husband-and-wife team." "Responsive and reliable."

Alpha Window Cleaning   4   2   5   5
4 Anchor Street, Danbury, CT 06811
(203) 730 - 2025
Residential, commercial window washing; gutter cleaning

"Fabulous," "professional" and "personable" are the words most commonly used to describe Alpha Window Cleaning. Founded in 1986 by owner Kevin Laroche, the company's prices start at $4 per window with considerations on type, size and location. Laroche gives free estimates in person after looking at the home, rather than over the phone. Customers are mostly residential, with a few commercial clients. The firm will provide post-construction cleaning services for buildings up to six-stories high. Laroche, known for establishing good vendor-client relationships with his longtime customers, works alone on most projects. Most of the company's work takes place in Ridgefield, Weston, Fairfield and Westport. Alpha also does chandelier-cleaning and gutter cleaning.

"The whole neighborhood loves him!" "Friendly and professional." "Extremely neat and thorough."

County Window Cleaning, LLC   4   3   4   5
PO Box 282, Westport, CT 06881
(203) 226 - 5888   countywindow@spcglobal.net
Residential and commercial window washing

One of the oldest window washing companies in town, County Window Cleaning was established in the 1960s and is managed by Rich Johnson. The firm's prices start at $6 per window (inside and out). Johnson generally works in the field, while his wife handles all administrative aspects of the business. The company has an equal number of residential and commercial clients, but generally steers clear of high-rise buildings. County Window specializes in bay windows and storefronts (Talbot's, Tavern on Main) and an average residential project is in the 65-to-95-window range.

"Pleasant." "On time and responsive to calls."

	Quality +	Cost $	Value ◆	Recommend? ★

David's Window Cleaning   4   2   5   5
52 Temple Street, Stratford, CT 06615
(203) 378 - 6947   dcamarero@aol.com

Residential window washing

"It runs in the family," a client says of the high-quality service David's Window Cleaning provides. A former chef, owner David Camarero followed in his brother John's footsteps and got into the window cleaning business. David established his company in 1989 and has since enjoyed a steady increase in business (and satisfied customers). Camarero works by himself and cleans only residential windows in and around Westport, Weston, Stamford, upper Westchester County and parts of Rhode Island. The company's projects are usually in the 30-to-50-window range. Camarero happily gives on-site estimates. Most references agree this "conscientious" man "delivers when he says" and is "totally trustworthy."

"Have been using him for years." "Reliable and organized." "Doesn't nickel and dime people to death."

Fairfield County Cleaning Service, LLC   4.5   3   5   5
647 California Street, Stratford, CT 06614
(203) 386 - 1688

Residential window cleaning, post-construction, gutter, carpet and upholstery cleaning

Established twenty years ago, Fairfield County Cleaning Service serves mostly residential clients, with a few commercial customers. Founded by Tom Baker (window washer by day, saxophone player extraordinaire by night), the company serves most areas in Fairfield County as well as Port Chester and White Plains. Pricing is per window, with projects typically in the 28-to-35-window range. This small company also provides services like post-construction cleanup, gutter, carpet and upholstery cleaning and power washing.

Clients tell us this "hands-on" businessman is very thorough and "a man of his word." We hear that the moderate to upper-end prices are a good value for the excellent service.

"I completely trust him with the keys to my house." "Never leaves a mess." "An excellent window cleaner and an amazing jazz musician."

John M. Evans Window   4   2.5   5   5
& Carpet Cleaning Service
10 Windward Road, Norwalk, CT 06854
(203) 866 - 3799

Residential window cleaning, wall-to-wall carpet cleaning

Clients can't say enough good things about the husband-and-wife team behind John M. Evans Window & Carpet Cleaning Service. Established in 1978 by John Evans, the company is now managed by John and his wife Mary Ann, and serves mostly residential and some commercial clients in Westport, Greenwich, Weston, Ridgefield and some parts of Westchester County.

Sources tell us they appreciate the "neat" and "efficient" service that this firm provides and the "moderate" prices that go along with it. Projects are in the 60-to-70-window range and there is a modest minimum for Evans to do a project.

"Been using them for many years and have recommended them to all my friends." "Courteous, polite, extremely professional." "Quick, neat and efficient." "Gets the job done without the fuss." "Excellent."

John's Window Cleaning   4.5   2.5   5   4.5
273 Derby Avenue, Suite 410, Derby, CT 06418
(203) 734 - 9083

Residential and commercial window washing

This Derby-based firm has served residential and commercial clients since opening its doors in 1998. John Camarero is the sole owner of the firm, which also cleans buildings up to three-stories high. Camarero usually works by himself, but hires part-time workers during the busy spring and fall seasons. Estimates are free and are usually given over the phone. The firm serves neighborhoods in Greenwich, Stamford, Darien, Westport, Glastonbury and parts of Rhode Island.

References tell us that Camarero is a "pleasure to work with" and is "reliable and diligent." Prices are described as moderate and "have not gone up in years."

"A man who genuinely loves his work." "Professional with a pleasant demeanor."

Magic Touch Window Cleaning   4.5   3.5   5   5
PO Box 497, Milford, CT 06460
(203) 783 - 1247
Residential and commercial window washing

Brazil-native Fabian Lima was a window washer with another company for sixteen years before he decided to branch out and start his own business in 1998. Now a favorite among many well-heeled residential clients and store owners, Lima and his team work around Weston, Westport, Wilton and Greenwich. Pricing starts at $8 per window, in and out. An average project is in the 35-to-40-window range. The firm also does gutter cleaning and power washing. With three full-time employees, sources tell us Lima and his crew are a pleasure to work with. Though prices are upper end, sources tell us the quality is worth every penny.

"Very thorough. Will not just clean around the screen, but will take out the screen, clean it and put it back again." "Always calls the next day to check up on his job."

Mr. Beez Windows & Cleaning, LLC   3   3.5   3   4
PO Box 651, Stamford, CT 06902
(866) 247 - 9177
Residential and commercial window washing

Billy Thompson established the company in 1986 after working for many years as a window washer for other companies. Mr. Beez has a strong residential following, mostly in Greenwich, Fairfield and Weston. Though serving largely residential clients, Mr. Beez has several storefronts and commercial accounts. Pricing is generally per window (average prices are in the $8-to-$10 range) and there is no minimum number of windows required.

Ronny Reliable's Cleaning   4   2   5   5
11 American Legion Drive, Ardsley, NY 10502
(914) 674 - 9000   www.ronnyreliable.com
Window washing, carpet, blinds and furniture cleaning, post-construction cleanup

Relied on by its loyal patrons, Ronny Reliable's Cleaning serves all of Westchester and some parts of Connecticut. Founded in 1973 by owner Ronny Ymbras, this full-service cleaning company cleans windows, furniture, rugs and carpets and blinds. The firm also specializes in deodorizing (especially pet odors), gutter cleaning, jewelry and ceramics cleaning, water damage restoration and post-construction cleanup. Rates depend on each job and there is a modest minimum fee. With ten full-time employees, Ymbras and his men are considered by clients to be polite, efficient workers who "get the job done with a pleasant demeanor."

"Very responsive. Can rely on them during emergencies."

Steven Windows Co.   4.5   3.5   4.5   5

342 West 71st Street, New York, NY 10023
(212) 595 - 6620

Commercial and residential window cleaning

Steven Windows Co. has accumulated some very devoted celebrity clients, including one who flies the principal out to Beverly Hills periodically to take care of his West Coast panes. We hear Steven Windows will cheerfully clean windows for all clients near and far, from Manhattan to Queens to New Jersey to Fairfield to the West Coast. Available for service seven days a week, insiders advise potential clients to call Steven Windows about two weeks in advance to set a date. The firm is owned and run by Steven Troubich who has nine years of experience behind him. Installing and removing air conditioners, repairing glassworks, and doing general housecleaning are some of the additional services that this company provides.

"Dependable, trustworthy and hardworking." "Simply charming." "Very professional." "Good people." "Used him for several years. Would not consider using anyone else."

Young & White Company   🗁   🗁   🗁   🗁

145 Old Stone Hill Road, Pound Ridge, NY 10576
(914) 764 - 4854

Residential and commercial window washing

THE FRANKLIN
REPORT®

INSTRUCTIONS: To contribute to a service provider's review, fill out the form below and **fax** it back to us at **212-744-3546** or mail to 506 East 74th Street, Suite 1E, New York, NY 10021. Or you may complete a reference on our website, www.franklinreport.com. Please make sure that you give us a contact e-mail address and a phone number. While all information will remain anonymous, our editorial staff may need to reach you to confirm the information.

Thank you.

FILL-IN REFERENCE REPORT FORM

Client Name:

Client E-mail: _____ Client Phone:

Service Provider Company Name:

Company Contact: _____ Company Phone:

Service (i.e. plumbing):

Company Address:

PLEASE RATE THE PROVIDER ON EACH OF THE FOLLOWING:

QUALITY: ❏ Highest Imaginable ❏ Outstanding ❏ High-end ❏ Good
❏ Adequate ❏ Poor

COST: ❏ Over the Top ❏ Very Expensive ❏ High-End ❏ Moderate
❏ Inexpensive ❏ Bargain

VALUE: ❏ Worth Every Penny ❏ Good Value ❏ Fair Deal ❏ Not Great
❏ Poor Value ❏ Unconscionable

RECOMMEND?: ❏ My First and Only Choice ❏ On My Short List/Would Recommend
❏ Very Satisfied/Might Hire Again ❏ Have Reservations
❏ Not Pleased/Would Not Hire Again ❏ Will Never Talk to Again

COMMENTS:

_____

_____

_____

_____

_____

_____

_____

_____

_____

_____

_____

THE FRANKLIN
REPORT®

FILL-IN REFERENCE REPORT FORM

Client Name: _____

Client E-mail: _____ Client Phone: _____

Service Provider Company Name: _____

Company Contact: _____ Company Phone: _____

Service (i.e. plumbing): _____

Company Address: _____

PLEASE RATE THE PROVIDER ON EACH OF THE FOLLOWING:

QUALITY: ❏ Highest Imaginable ❏ Outstanding ❏ High-end ❏ Good
❏ Adequate ❏ Poor

COST: ❏ Over the Top ❏ Very Expensive ❏ High-End ❏ Moderate
❏ Inexpensive ❏ Bargain

VALUE: ❏ Worth Every Penny ❏ Good Value ❏ Fair Deal ❏ Not Great
❏ Poor Value ❏ Unconscionable

RECOMMEND?: ❏ My First and Only Choice ❏ On My Short List/Would Recommend
❏ Very Satisfied/Might Hire Again ❏ Have Reservations
❏ Not Pleased/Would Not Hire Again ❏ Will Never Talk to Again

COMMENTS:

_____

_____

_____

_____

_____

_____

_____

_____

_____

_____

_____

Notes

NOTES